Re-allocated to DIUS (Legal)
SP 03/03/09

OXFORD COMMENTARIES ON INTERNATIONAL LAW

General Editors: *Professor Philip Alston*, Professor of International Law at New York University, and *Professor Vaughan Lowe*, Chichele Professor of Public International Law in the University of Oxford and Fellow of All Souls College, Oxford.

Sub-Series:

OXFORD COMMENTARIES ON THE GATT/WTO AGREEMENTS

General Editor: *Professor Robert Howse*, Professor of International Law at the University of Michigan.

Trade Related Aspects of Intellectual Property Rights

Trade Related Aspects of Intellectual Property Rights

A Commentary on the TRIPS Agreement

CARLOS M. CORREA

OXFORD
UNIVERSITY PRESS

OXFORD

UNIVERSITY PRESS

Great Clarendon Street, Oxford OX2 6DP

Oxford University Press is a department of the University of Oxford.
It furthers the University's objective of excellence in research, scholarship,
and education by publishing worldwide in

Oxford New York

Auckland Cape Town Dar es Salaam Hong Kong Karachi
Kuala Lumpur Madrid Melbourne Mexico City Nairobi
New Delhi Shanghai Taipei Toronto

With offices in

Argentina Austria Brazil Chile Czech Republic France Greece
Guatemala Hungary Italy Japan Poland Portugal Singapore
South Korea Switzerland Thailand Turkey Ukraine Vietnam

Oxford is a registered trade mark of Oxford University Press
in the UK and in certain other countries

Published in the United States
by Oxford University Press Inc., New York

British Library Cataloguing in Publication Data

Data available

Library of Congress Cataloging in Publication Data

Correa, Carlos.
Trade related aspects of intellectual property rights : a commentary on the TRIPS
agreement / Carlos Correa.
p. cm. — (Oxford commentaries on international law)
Includes bibliographical references and index.
ISBN 978–0–19–927128–3 (hardback : alk. paper)   1. Agreement on Trade–Related
Aspects of Intellectual Property Rights (1994)   2. Intellectual property (International
law)   3. Foreign trade regulation.   I. Title.
K1401.A41994C68   2007
346.7304'8—dc22

2007008575

Typeset by Newgen Imaging Systems (P) Ltd., Chennai, India
Printed in Great Britain
on acid-free paper by
Antony Rowe Ltd., Chippenham, Wiltshire

ISBN   978–0–19–927128–3

1 3 5 7 9 10 8 6 4 2

To Liliana, for her permanent support and tolerance of my intense travel and long working hours, and to my children Julia, Carlos, Laura, Juan, Elisa and Carolina.

Preface

The Agreement on Trade Related Aspects of Intellectual Property Rights ('the TRIPS Agreement') sets out a number of obligations that the Members of the World Trade Organization (WTO) need to comply with when designing their intellectual property regimes. Unlike the other components of the system, the TRIPS Agreement does not aim at liberalizing trade, but at establishing rules for the appropriation of intellectual assets and the control over the production and trade of the products derived therefrom.

The TRIPS Agreement stipulates (except with regard to transitional periods and technical assistance) the same rules for developed and developing countries. Given the profound asymmetries existing amongst WTO members in their levels of development, particularly as regards their scientific and technological base, it is not surprising that this Agreement became one of the most controversial pieces of the multilateral trade system. An appropriate interpretation of its provisions is essential, therefore, to ensure a balance between the public interests and those of right holders.

This book provides elements for the interpretation and application of the TRIPS Agreement, having in view the implications of different provisions in various sectors of the economy. The analysis is based on the rules of interpretation codified in the Vienna Convention on the Law of the Treaties. It aims at clarifying the content and scope of the obligations created by the Agreement, as well as the room available to governments to adapt their legal regimes to different circumstances and policy objectives.

A basic notion underlying this book is that the TRIPS Agreement does not set forth a uniform law on intellectual property; rather it stipulates a set of minimum standards that may be differently implemented in Member countries, while it leaves many aspects to the discretion of national laws. As result, there are different legal options that may be chosen, within certain limits, in implementing the Agreement to develop national intellectual property systems that promote a competitive environment for innovation and the diffusion of new products and technologies.

The book provides commentaries on each of the provisions of the Agreement taking into account, where available, the rulings of WTO panels and the Appellate Body. Inevitably, the analysis builds on my previous work on the subject.[1] I am thankful to all who have contributed to the analysis of the Agreement from different

---

[1] See, eg 'Review of the TRIPS Agreement and transfer of technology to developing countries', in K Gallagher (editor), *Putting Development First. The Importance of Policy Space in the WTO and IFIs*, (2005: London and New York, ZED Books); 'The TRIPS Agreement from the perspective of developing countries', in P Macrory, A Appleton, and M Plummer (editors), *The World Trade Organization: Legal, Economic and Political Analysis*, (2005: New York, Springer); 'Managing the

positions and perspectives, and to the various organizations that have allowed me to be closely related to the inception and implementation of the TRIPS Agreement.

Carlos M. Correa
Buenos Aires
November, 2006

Provision of Knowledge: The Design of Intellectual Property Laws', in I Kaul, P Conceicao, K Le Goulven, and R Mendoza (editors), *Providing Global Public Goods–Managing Globalization*, (2003: New York, Oxford University Press); 'Pro-competitive measures under the TRIPS Agreement to promote technology diffusion in developing countries', in P Drahos and R Mayne (editors), *Global Intellectual Property Rights: Knowledge Access and Development*, (2002: New York, Palgrave and Oxfam GB); 'TRIPS and access to drugs: toward a solution for developing countries without manufacturing capacity?', Emory International Review, vol 17, No. 2, Summer, 2003; *Protection of data submitted for the registration of pharmaceuticals. Implementing the standards of the TRIPS Agreement*, (2002: Geneva, South Centre/WHO); 'Internationalization of the patent system and new technologies', Wisconsin International Law Journal, vol. 20. No. 3, 2002; 'Fair use in the digital era', International Review of Industrial Property and Copyright Law, vol. 33, No. 5/2002; Implementation of the WHO General Council Decision on paragraph 6 of the Doha declaration on the TRIPS Agreement and Public Health, (2004: Geneva, WHO); 'Protection of geographical indications in the CARICOM countries' Caribbean Regional Negotiating Machinery, 2002, available at <www.crnm.org/documents/studies/Geographical%20 Indications%20-%20Correa.pdf>; Implications of the Doha Declaration on the TRIPS Agreement and public health, (2002: Geneva, WHO); Implementation of the WHO General Council Decision on paragraph 6 of the Doha declaration on the TRIPS Agreement and Public Health, (2004: Geneva, WHO); author's contributions to UNCTAD–ICTSD, *Resource Book on TRIPS and Development* (2005: New York, Cambridge University Press); *Integrating public health concerns into patent legislation in developing countries*, (2000: south centre, Geneva); 'Intellectual property in the field of integrated circuits: implications for developing countries', World Competition, Vol.14, N1 2, December 1990.

Contents

List of Abbreviations

AB	Appellate Body
BIT	Bilateral Investment Treaty
CAFTA-DR	Dominican Republic–Central America Free Trade Agreement
DSU	Dispute Settlement Understanding
ECJ	European Court of Justice
EMRs	Exclusive marketing rights
FDI	foreign direct investment
FTAA	Free Trade Area of the Americas
FTAs	free trade agreements
GATT	General Agreement on Tarriffs and Trade
IP	intellectual property
IPR/IPRs	intellectual property rights
ITC	International Trade Commission
LDCs	least-developed countries
MAI	Multilateral Agreement on Investment
MFN	most-favoured nation
NAFTA	North American Free Trade Agreement
OEM	original equipment manufacturer
R&D	research and development
TK	traditional knowledge
TOT	transfer of technology
TRIPS	Trade-related Aspects of Intellectual Property Rights
UPOV	International Union for the Protection of New Varieties of Plants
VCLT	Vienna Convention on the Law of Treaties
WCT	WIPO Copyright Treaty
WIPO	World Intellectual Property Organization
WPPT	WIPO Performances and Phonograms Treaty
WTO	World Trade Organization

Table of Cases

TABLE OF PANEL AND APPELLATE BODY REPORTS

Table of International Instruments and National Laws

WTO AGREEMENTS

FREE TRADE AGREEMENTS

TREATIES

LEGISLATION BY COUNTRY

EC DIRECTIVES

EC REGULATIONS

OTHER

Chapter 1

PREAMBLE

The purpose of the TRIPS Agreement

As in other WTO agreements and the WTO Agreement itself, the TRIPS Agreement contains a detailed Preamble where the negotiating parties expressed the objectives that they sought in adopting this component of the WTO system. While the provisions of the Preamble reflect, to some extent, the different positions that the negotiating parties brought to the negotiating table, they substantially respond to the protectionist paradigm advocated by the United States and other developed countries with regard to intellectual property. As examined below,[1] some of developing countries' concerns about the implications of stronger IPRs for their economies and, in particular, for transfer of technology, received limited attention.

> *Members,*
>
> *Desiring* to reduce distortions and impediments to international trade, and taking into account the need to promote effective and adequate protection of intellectual property rights, and to ensure that measures and procedures to enforce intellectual property rights do not themselves become barriers to legitimate trade;

This paragraph encapsulates the basic assumption for the negotiation of the TRIPS Agreement, one of the more difficult of the Uruguay Round, both politically and technically.[2] The wording was entirely drawn from the paragraph in the Punta del Este Ministerial Declaration that launched the Uruguay Round.[3]

What is 'effective' and 'adequate' protection may be subject to different interpretations. For the purposes of implementing the TRIPS Agreement, however, national standards of protection consistent with the Agreement's obligations

---

[1] See p 13 below.

[2] B Hoekman and M Kostecki, *The Political Economy of the World Trading System: The WTO and Beyond* (1st publ. 2001: Oxford, 2nd edn), p 283.

[3] The relevant paragraph stated: 'In order to reduce the distortions and impediments to international trade, and taking into account the need to promote effective and adequate protection of intellectual property rights, and to ensure that measures and procedures to enforce intellectual property rights do not themselves become barriers to legitimate trade, the negotiations shall aim to clarify GATT provisions and elaborate as appropriate new rules and disciplines. Negotiations shall aim to develop a multilateral framework of principles, rules and disciplines dealing with international trade in counterfeit goods, taking into account work already undertaken in the GATT.'

are to be considered 'effective' and 'adequate'. There is no room, hence, for an argument of non-effectiveness or non-adequateness to justify demands of 'TRIPS-plus' protection (that is, beyond the TRIPS standards) as required in some bilateral agreements and FTAs entered into by a number of developed and developing countries (eg Australia, Bahrein, Chile, Jordan, Morocco) with US and the EC European Communities and their Member States.

The Preamble's chapeau highlights the reduction 'of distortions and impediments to international trade' as the main target of the Agreement. This statement suggests that improving the protection of IPRs could contribute to such reduction, in line with the overall objective of the WTO.[4] This idea, however, contradicts the conventional notion of IPRs as a *barrier* to trade as contained in Article XX(d) of GATT 1947,[5] which permitted GATT Contracting Parties to justify trade restrictions imposed by IPRs.[6] Since IPRs may allow the title-holder to prevent the importation of the protected subject matter, they can in fact be used to segment markets and erect obstacles to trade. Likewise, exports of products protected by IPRs may also be prevented by the title-holder. For instance, the possible exercise of patent rights to prevent exports of patented medicines to countries without manufacturing capacity in pharmaceuticals triggered the adoption by the Council for TRIPS of a special waiver with regard to Article 31(f) of the TRIPS Agreement.[7]

Developed countries, notably the US, argued during the negotiations about the absence or lack of adequate protection of IPRs, as well as about the lack of appropriate enforcement measures.

As regards inadequacies in the scope and availability of rights, reference was made to the absence in certain countries of patent or copyright laws or of the protection of designs, computer programs, or geographical indications; exclusions of categories of products or of works from protection; insufficient duration of protection; misuse

---

[4] The third paragraph of the Preamble to the Agreement Establishing the World Trade Organization states the Members' desire 'of contributing to these objectives by entering into reciprocal and mutually advantageous arrangements directed to the substantial reduction of tariffs and other barriers to trade and to the elimination of discriminatory treatment in international trade relations'.

[5] 'Article XX. General Exceptions. Subject to the requirement that such measures are not applied in a manner which would constitute a means of arbitrary or unjustifiable discrimination between countries where the same conditions prevail, or a disguised restriction on international trade, nothing in this Agreement shall be construed to prevent the adoption or enforcement by any contracting party of measures:
. . .
(*d*) necessary to secure compliance with laws or regulations which are not inconsistent with the provisions of this Agreement, including those relating to . . . the protection of patents, trade marks and copyrights . . .'.

[6] The application of this article was considered, with different outcomes, in two GATT disputes (*United States—Import of Certain Automotive Spring Assemblies*, L/533-30S/107, 26 May 1983, and *United States—Section 337 of the Tariff Act* of 1930, L/6439-36S/345, 7 November 1989).

[7] See WTO Decision on the Implementation of Paragraph 6 of the Doha Declaration on the TRIPS Agreement and Public Health of 30 August 2003 available at <http://www.wto.org> (last accessed on 24 May 2005).

of compulsory licensing; and procedural obstacles or de facto discrimination that makes it difficult for foreign firms to obtain protection for their intellectual property. With regard to difficulties facing intellectual property right owners in the enforcement of their rights, mention was made of: lack of police enforcement or access to border enforcement measures in appropriate circumstances; difficulties of gaining access to competent judicial or administrative bodies; procedural problems with the burden of proof and assembly of evidence; unavailability of preliminary relief; insufficient penalties; the relationship between local and federal jurisdictions; and in general the duration and cost of legal proceedings.[8]

Moreover, it was argued that shortcomings in availability and enforcement of IPRs may constitute a barrier to trade, as potential exports by inventors or creators may be prevented or diminished by infringing copies of their products in foreign markets. It was stated that

trade distortions and impediments were resulting from, among other things: the displacement of exports of legitimate goods by unauthorized copies, or of domestic sales by imports of unauthorized copies; the disincentive effect that inadequate protection of intellectual property rights had on inventors and creators to engage in research and development and in trade and investment; the deliberate use in some instances of intellectual property right protection to discourage imports and encourage local production, often of an inefficient and small-scale nature; and the inhibiting effect on international trade of disparities in the protection accorded under different legislations.[9]

It is of note that the last sentence in the chapeau does not refer to IPRs as such as possible barriers to trade, but only to 'measures and procedures to enforce intellectual property rights'. This wording seems to overlook the concerns expressed during the negotiations, and after their conclusion, about the trade implications of the recognition of IPRs, not just about the ways in which they may be enforced.

The trade distortion that the recognition of IPRs may create can be mitigated by the adoption of the principle on international exhaustion, as incorporated into Article 6 of the TRIPS Agreement.[10] However, the adoption of this principle is not mandatory to WTO Members. By their very conception, IPRs are not intended to promote free trade, but can instead be used to restrict it. For this reason, some trade analysts have argued that, 'in contrast to the rest of the Uruguay Round, the TRIPS negotiations were not about freeing trade, but about changing domestic regulatory and legal regimes',[11] and that the TRIPS Agreement is misplaced in the multilateral trade system and should have never been part of the Uruguay Round negotiations.[12]

---

[8] MTN.GNG/NG11/1, 10 April 1987, para 3.   [9] Idem, para 4.
[10] See Chapter 3 below.   [11] Hoekman and Kostecki, op. cit. (2001), p 284.
[12] J Bhagwat and A Panagariya, 'Bilateral Trade Treaties Are a Sham' (2003), *Financial Times*, 13 July available at <http://www.globalpolicy.org/globaliz/econ/2003/0714rta.htm>, last accessed on 21 February 2004 ('[D]uring the Uruguay round of trade liberalisation, the US was able to insert the trade-related intellectual property regime (TRIPs) into the WTO, even though no intellectual case had ever been made that TRIPs, which is about royalty collection and not trade, should be included').

The first paragraph of the Preamble was invoked by Canada in *Canada—Patent Protection of Pharmaceutical Products*,[13] but the Panel only incidentally mentioned it as one of 'other provisions of the TRIPS Agreement which indicate its object and purposes'.[14] Canada called attention to a number of other provisions of the TRIPS Agreement as relevant to the purpose and objective of Article 30. Primary attention was given to Articles 7 and 8.1. Attention was also called to the text of the first recital in the Preamble to the TRIPS Agreement and to part of the text of Article 1.1.[15]

> *Recognizing*, to this end, the need for new rules and disciplines concerning:
>
> (a) the applicability of the basic principles of GATT 1994 and of relevant international intellectual property agreements or conventions;
>
> (b) the provision of adequate standards and principles concerning the availability, scope and use of trade-related intellectual property rights;
>
> (c) the provision of effective and appropriate means for the enforcement of trade-related intellectual property rights, taking into account differences in national legal systems;
>
> (d) the provision of effective and expeditious procedures for the multilateral prevention and settlement of disputes between governments; and
>
> (e) transitional arrangements aiming at the fullest participation in the results of the negotiations...

The second paragraph of the Preamble states 'the need' to introduce 'new rules and disciplines' in relation to a number of matters:

> (a) The applicability of the basic principles of GATT 1994 and of relevant international intellectual property agreements or conventions...

GATT 1947 contained a few provisions that specifically referred to intellectual property, such as Article IX.6 on marks of origin, and Articles XII.3 and XVIII.10, which require that balance of payment safeguards and measures restricting imports do not 'prevent compliance with patent, trade mark, copyright, or similar procedure'. Perhaps the most important reference to intellectual property rights (IPRs) was in Article XX(d), wihch allowed, among other general exceptions, those 'necessary to secure compliance with laws or regulations which are not inconsistent with the provisions of this Agreement, including those relating to...the protection of patents, trade marks and copyrights, and the prevention of deceptive practices'.[16]

---

[13] WT/DS114/R, Report of the Panel, 17 March 2000, para 7.23.   [14] Idem, para 7.26.
[15] Idem, para 7.23.
[16] Other GATT provisions were also identified at the initial stages of the TRIPS negotiations as being relevant to IPRs: 'In regard to the identification of relevant GATT provisions, it was suggested that, in addition to the provisions referred to in the secretariat compilation, Articles X, XXII and XXIII had a relevance to enforcement issues in connection with intellectual property rights .... As regards the other issues raised, reference was made to the relevance of Articles I, III and IX.6, and it was said that the General Agreement recognised both the legitimacy of measures to protect intellectual property rights and that these could affect trade.... However, the point was widely made that the General

An important implication of the inclusion of the TRIPS Agreement as one of the covered agreements in the WTO is the application to IPRs of the three 'basic principles of GATT'. Those principles are:

(1) National treatment;
(2) Most-favoured-nation (MFN);
(3) Transparency.

The national treatment principle was not unknown in the IPR field. It was one of the pillars of the Paris Convention for the Protection of Industrial Property (adopted in 1883), and of other conventions entered into in the pre-TRIPS era. In GATT, such a principle was applied to goods, while in the case of IPR it directly benefits title-holders.

The TRIPS Agreement extended the application to IPR of the two other basic principles of GATT (MFN and transparency), which were absent in the pre-TRIPS conventions on IPRs. As examined below,[17] the MFN principle has important implications, as the enhanced levels of IPR protection granted to one WTO member (for instance, in the context of a free trade agreement) unconditionally and automatically benefit all other WTO members.

It may be argued that the TRIPS Agreement is not only subject to the GATT 'principles' but to the whole system of rules and disciplines incorporated into GATT 1994.[18] The panel in *India–Patent Protection for Pharmaceutical and Agricultural Chemical Products* held that the TRIPS Agreement has a 'relatively self-contained, *sui generis* status within the WTO'.[19] However, it also held that the Agreement is 'an integral part of the WTO system, which itself builds upon the experience of over nearly half a century under the GATT 1947'.[20] In *United States–Section 110(5) of the US Copyright Act*, the panel noted that

given that the agreements covered by the WTO form a single, integrated legal system, we deem it appropriate to develop interpretations of the legal protection conferred on intellectual property right holders under the TRIPS Agreement which are not incompatible with the treatment conferred to products under the GATT, or in respect of services and service suppliers under the GATS, in the light of pertinent dispute settlement practice.[21]

The panel also affirmed that the

consideration of both actual and potential effects when assessing the permissibility of the exemptions would be consistent with similar concepts and interpretation standards as

Agreement contained little apart from Article IX.6 to address the issues raised in connection with the inadequate enforcement of intellectual property rights or inadequacies and excesses in the scope and availability of intellectual property rights (MTN.GNG/NG11/3, 8 October 1987, para 8).

[17] See Chapter 2 below.
[18] See, eg F Weiss, 'International public law aspects of TRIPS' in J Cohen Jehoram *et al*, *Trade Related Aspects of Copyright* (1996: Deventer, Kluwer), p 82.
[19] *India–Patent Protection for Pharmaceutical and Agricultural Chemical Products*, WT/DS50/R (1998), para 7.19.　　　　　　　　　　　　　　　　　　　　　　　　　　[20] Ibidem.
[21] *United States—Section 110(5) of the US Copyright Act*, WT/DS160/R, 15 June 2000, para 6.185.

developed in the past GATT/WTO dispute settlement practice. For example, proof of actual trade effects has not been considered an indispensable prerequisite for a finding of inconsistency with the national treatment clause of Article III of GATT where there was a potentiality of adverse effects on competitive opportunities and equal competitive conditions for foreign products (in comparison to like domestic products) (*footnote omitted)'*.[22]

However, the panel cautioned against the use of GATT concepts in the TRIPS context:

We wish to express our caution in interpreting provisions of the TRIPS Agreement in the light of concepts that have been developed in GATT dispute settlement practice.[23]

This hesitation is probably explained by the fact that, while affirming the integration of the TRIPS Agreement into the GATT/WTO framework, the panel in the *United States–Section 110(5) of the US Copyright Act* also made clear that the Agreement should be firmly integrated into the framework of the Berne Convention.[24]

Panels and the Appellate Body have, in fact, applied previous GATT and WTO jurisprudence extensively in cases involving the TRIPS Agreement. They have used the same method of interpretation applied to cases involving other WTO Agreements, ie, the customary rules of treaty interpretation contained in Article 31 and Article 32 of the Vienna Convention on the Law of Treaties. Sufficient consideration has not been given to the fact that while IPRs constitute private rights,[25] the other components of the WTO system deal with restrictions imposed on governments.

The clarification of the relationship between the TRIPS Agreement and the GATT/WTO may be crucial for the interpretation of several aspects of the Agreement, such as the permissibility of banning parallel imports,[26] the extent to which exceptions can be established under Article 8.1, and, more generally, the criteria to be applied to the interpretation of exceptions provided under the TRIPS Agreement. Under GATT/WTO jurisprudence the exceptions to Members' obligations have been generally construed narrowly.[27] This also applies to the case of TRIPS as illustrated by the panel's opinion in *Canada–Patent Protection for Pharmaceutical Products* on the exceptions to exclusive patent rights conferred by Article 30 of the TRIPS Agreement.[28] However, IPRs themselves

---

[22] Ibidem.   [23] Ibidem.

[24] See, eg, J Oliver, 'Copyright in the WTO: The Panel Decision on the Three-Step Test' (2002) 25 Colum JL & Arts 119,163.

[25] See the Preamble to the TRIPS Agreement, fourth paragraph.

[26] As discussed below, the prohibition of parallel imports may be deemed inconsistent with one of the basic GATT principles regarding the elimination of quantitative restrictions (Article XI of GATT).

[27] See Carlos Correa, 'Implementing National Public Health Policies in the Framework of the WTO Agreements', (2000) 34 (5) Journal of World Trade, p 92.

[28] 'As long as the exception is confined to conduct needed to comply with the requirements of the regulatory approval process, the extent of the acts unauthorized by the right holder that are permitted

constitute exceptions in terms of the GATT—authorized by GATT Article XX(d)—since by their very nature such rights restrict trade.[29] Article XX(d) is fully in force, and cannot be dismissed as a simple 'mistake'.[30] In applying the exceptions under TRIPS, therefore, panels and the Appellate Body should carefully consider the trade *restrictive* effects of IPRs and the need to ensure as much competition as possible. The purpose and effects of IPRs should be appraised in the light of the general principles and objectives of the WTO system and, in particular, the objectives of the TRIPS Agreement as stated in Article 7.[31]

(b) **The provision of adequate standards and principles concerning the availability, scope and use of trade-related intellectual property rights:**

The TRIPS Agreement sets forth the principles and standards in order to ensure the availability of a minimum level of protection for IPRs. It also determines the scope of such rights by defining the set of rights conferred to title-holders (eg Article 28 of the Agreement). Since IPRs confer negative rights (that is, the right to exclude others from exploiting protected subject matter), essentially the 'use' of such rights aims to ensure their enforcement, but may include other acts, such as licensing and assignment.

While the Preamble and the title of the Agreement itself refer to 'trade-related' aspects of IPRs, the negotiating parties did not make too much effort to conceptually distinguish those rights from non trade-related aspects of such rights. In fact, with the exception of 'moral' authors' rights, virtually all dimensions of IPRs are caught by the Agreement's provisions.

What 'adequate' standards and principles are is a matter of opinion. What is adequate at certain point in time may not be so when circumstances have changed. Likewise, what is adequate for a developed country may not be so for a developing country. In fact, the history of intellectual property strongly suggests that developed countries have adapted the IPRs systems to the conditions prevailing at different stages of their development process, a possibility allowed under the pre-TRIPS intellectual property system. As noted by the UK Commission on Intellectual Property Rights (CIPR),

historically IP regimes have been used by countries to further what they perceive as their own economic interests. Countries have changed their regimes at different stages of economic development as that perception (and their economic status) has changed. For instance between 1790 and 1836, as a net importer of technology, the US restricted the issue of patents to its own citizens and residents. Even in 1836, patents fees for foreigners

by it will be small and narrowly bounded. Even though regulatory approval processes may require substantial amounts of test production to demonstrate reliable manufacturing, the patent owner's rights themselves are not impaired any further by the size of such production runs, as long as they are solely for regulatory purposes and no commercial use is made of resulting final products.' *Canada—Patent Protection for Pharmaceutical Products,* WT/para 7.45.

[29] See also the Preamble of the TRIPS Agreement, first paragraph.
[30] See N Pires de Carvalho, *The TRIPS Regime of Patent Rights* (2002: The Hague, Kluwer Law International), p 43. [31] See Chapter 4 below.

were fixed at ten times the rate for US citizens (and two thirds as much again if one was British!). Only in 1861 were foreigners treated on an (almost wholly) non-discriminatory basis ... Until 1891, US copyright protection was restricted to US citizens but various restrictions on foreign copyrights remained in force (for example, printing had to be on US typesets) which delayed US entry to the Berne Copyright Convention until as late as 1989, over 100 years after the UK. It is for this reason that some readers may remember purchasing books which had on the cover the words: '*For copyright reasons this edition is not for sale in the USA*'.[32]

Although the TRIPS Agreement sets forth minimum standards of IPRs protection and does not constitute a harmonized system, it obliges all WTO Members, independently of their level of development, to apply the same standards. No special and differential treatment for developing countries and Least Developed Countries (LDCs) was allowed by the Agreement, except for the possibility of applying transitional periods, all of which have expired so far except for LDCs. This has been one of the most criticized aspects of the TRIPS Agreement. As put by the World Bank, in the field of IPRs 'one size does not fit all'.[33] This is true not only at the national level, but also in relation to different sectors (eg the semiconductors industry is much less sensitive to IPRs than pharmaceuticals) and types of enterprises (some forms of IPRs, such as patents, are largely applied for and benefit big, rather than small, companies).

Whatever the reasons that led developing countries to finally accept the TRIPS Agreement were, the fact is that the Agreement established what the negotiating parties deemed 'adequate' standards and principles in this area. There are, hence, justified reasons to question why, almost immediately after the adoption of the Agreement, the US and the EC sought, through various ways, to obtain TRIPS-plus standards of protection.

(c) **The provision of effective and appropriate means for the enforcement of trade-related intellectual property rights, taking into account differences in national legal systems**

Unlike the pre-existing conventions on IPRs, the TRIPS Agreement included a detailed set of provision on the enforcement of such rights. This reflected the view of the US and other developed countries, which consistently argued during the negotiations that ensuring the availability of rights was not sufficient; the opportunity for right-holders to effectively exercise them should also be secured.

This paragraph makes clear that 'differences in national legal systems' are to be taken into account with regard to enforcement measures. As examined below,[34] should the negotiating parties have attempted to draft more precise standards, the development of disciplines on this matter would have been impossible. It is also to

---

[32] CIPR, Integrating Intellectual Property Rights and Development Policy. Report of the Commission on Intellectual Property Rights (London, 2002) 20, available at <www.iprcommission.org>.
[33] *World Bank, Global Economic Prospects and the Developing Countries 2002* (2001: Washington DC), p 129.   [34] See Chapter 4 below.

be noticed that the Agreement is more rigid with regard to the availability of rights than to enforcement measures, as the differences in national legal systems are only taken into account with regard to the latter. However, as examined in these commentaries, Members were left with some leeway to determine how to implement the substantive obligations imposed by the Agreement. This is confirmed by this provision of the Preamble, as well as by Article 1.1 of the Agreement.

(d) **The provision of effective and expeditious procedures for the multilateral prevention and settlement of disputes between governments**

At the time of the adoption of the TRIPS Agreement, the US government actively used Special Section 301 to pursue increased levels of protection for IPRs. The adoption of the TRIPS Agreement as a component of the WTO system[35] means that any controversy relating to compliance with the minimum standards established by the Agreement should be resolved under the multilateral procedures of the WTO. The adoption by another Member of unilateral trade sanctions would be incompatible with the multilateral rules. Any complaint should be brought to and settled according to the rules of the Dispute Settlement Understanding (DSU).

(e) **Transitional arrangements aiming at the fullest participation in the results of the negotiations**

The TRIPS Agreement allowed Members which are developing countries, economies in transition, or LDCs to delay, without any prior approval,[36] the implementation of the obligations contained in the Agreement (with the exception of Articles 3, 4, and 5). This possibility (permitted also in other WTO agreements) was regarded as one of the means to curb developing countries' reluctance to accept new standards on IPRs, and to provide them time to introduce the massive legislative reforms needed for compliance therewith. As examined below,[37] however, many countries that could have benefited from the transitional periods did not apply them, and adopted TRIPS-consistent legislation before the expiry of such periods. In some cases (eg Mexico, Brazil) protection was even retroactively recognized. Most notably, the transitional period allowed by Article 65.4, of particular importance for pharmaceutical products, was only used by a handful of countries.

> *Recognizing* the need for a multilateral framework of principles, rules and disciplines dealing with international trade in counterfeit goods;

The need to adopt multilateral rules to fight counterfeiting was articulated by the US, with the support of the EC, in the Tokyo Round of GATT. The US tabled a draft code on counterfeiting goods that never found consensus among the

---

[35] The TRIPS Agreement is contained in Annex 1C to the Marrakesh Agreement Establishing the WTO. [36] See, however, Article 66.2 of the TRIPS Agreement.
[37] See pp 493–4 below.

Contracting Parties. The issue of counterfeiting was formally introduced into the GATT agenda in November 1982. A Group of Experts established to advise the General Council recommended, in 1985, that multilateral action be taken on the matter.[38]

In fact, while accepting to initiate negotiations on IPRs at the Punta del Este Conference, developing countries essentially relied on a literal interpretation of the last sentence of the Ministerial Declaration that launched the Round: 'Negotiations shall aim to develop a multilateral framework of principles, rules and disciplines dealing with international trade in counterfeit goods, taking into account work already undertaken in the GATT.'

Although developing countries maintained for some time that the Punta del Este commitment did not go beyond counterfeiting, developed countries actively engaged in the preparation of proposals that covered a whole spectrum of IPR issues, as finally reflected in the adopted TRIPS Agreement.

Recognizing **that intellectual property rights are private rights;**

As noted by many commentators, the TRIPS Agreement has a very special status in the WTO system. It does not impose constraints on measures that States can take at the border, but deeply interferes with national discretion in establishing rights that can be claimed by private parties in national jurisdictions. As noted by two commentators, the Agreement is

a prominent illustration of the trend to extend disciplines on 'behind the border' regulatory regimes . . . The agreement is unique in the WTO context in that it imposes obligation upon governments to adopt a set of substantive rules in an area that traditionally has been regarded to be in the purview of domestic regulation. It is an example of what Tinbergen (1954) has called positive integration. This contrasts with the negative integration found in the GATT, which involves agreements not to use certain policies that directly affect (distort) trade flows . . . '.[39]

It is unclear why the negotiating parties included in the Preamble a statement about the 'private' nature of covered IPRs. One possible reason is that the TRIPS Agreement uncomfortably fits within the WTO framework, as it is the only multilateral agreement that deals directly with rights of private parties rather than with governmental measures. Another possible reason is the desire to make clear that Members were not obliged to take action *ex officio*, and that title-holders should bear the burden of exercising and defending their rights.[40] This may be particularly relevant with regard to criminal offences.[41]

---

[38] Hoekman and Kostecki op. cit. (2001), p 282.   [39] Idem, p 274.

[40] In many countries, however, *ex officio* action is provided for, particularly in the area of copyright.

[41] See eg D Gervais, *The TRIPS Agreement. Drafting History and Analysis* (2003: London, Sweet & Maxwell, 2nd edn), p 80.

Another area in which that statement may be relevant is in relation to regulated products, in view of the condition established in US-promoted FTAs requiring a drug regulatory agency to refuse third parties the marketing approval of a patented product, except with the authorization and acquiescence of the patent owner.[42] Such condition seems to ignore the private nature of patents, as it imposes on a State agency a direct obligation to protect patent owners' interests.

It has also been held that the reference in the Preamble to 'private rights' aims at characterizing IPRs as an 'investment in intangible assets' and at clearly prohibiting the expropriation of IPRs without compensation.[43] This interpretation, however, goes beyond the literal text of the Preamble and, most probably, the drafters' intent. As elaborated below,[44] knowledge is, by its very nature, a public good. IPRs provide for a temporary exclusion in order to attain certain policy objectives (such as encouraging the disclosure of inventions and investments in research and development). In many countries inventions are deemed the State's eminent property; this concept has justified the extensive exploitation of inventions by the US government (and its subcontractors) under non-commercial government use.[45]

It is also to be noted that the protection of investment is not part of the WTO disciplines. An attempt was made (notably by the EU) to incorporate, as one of the 'Singapore issues', investment rules in the already burdened agenda of the WTO. The outcome of the WTO Ministerial Conference in Cancun, however, showed a strong resistance by developing countries to accept new disciplines on that matter as a component of the WTO system. IPRs have been, however, characterized as 'investment'. The USA started to include provisions on intellectual property in its bilateral investment treaty programme during the 1980s. OECD countries attempted to develop a Multilateral Agreement on Investment (MAI) in the 1990s, which would have included specific provisions on IPRs as a covered investment. This initiative, however, collapsed as a result of significant divergences among OECD countries and opposition from civil society.[46]

BITs and the investment chapters of recent FTAs generally refer to IPRs as a covered investment. Some explicitly indicate the types of IPR covered. For

---

[42] See, eg, C Correa, 'Bilateralism in intellectual property: defeating the WTO system for access to medicines' [2005] 36:1 Case W Res J Int'l L, pp 10–12.

[43] Pires de Carvalho op. cit. (2002), pp 33–5.   [44] See p 95 below.

[45] See, eg, J Reichman and C Hasenzahl, *Non-Voluntary Licensing of Patented Inventions: Historical Perspective, Legal Framework under TRIPS, and an Overview of the Practice in Canada and the United States of America* (2002: Intellectual Property Rights & Sustainable at <http://www.ictsd.org/pubs/ictsd_series/iprs/CS_reichmann_hasenzahl.pdf> (last accessed on 24 May 2005).

[46] See, eg, C Correa and N Kumar, *International Rules for Foreign Investment. Trade-Related Investment Measures (TRIMS) and Developing Countries* (2003: London & New Delhi, ZED Books /Academic Foundation).

instance, the BIT between the USA and El Salvador (1999) specifies that 'investment' includes:

- copyrights and related rights,
- patents,
- rights in plant varieties,
- industrial designs,
- rights in semiconductor layout designs,
- trade secrets, including know-how and confidential business information,
- trade and service marks, and
- trade names.

In some BITs[47] and FTAs[48] reference is also made to 'technical process' or 'know how' and 'goodwill'.[49]

Whatever BITs and the investment chapters of FTAs provide for, the TRIPS Agreement does not create investors' rights. In the absence of WTO rules on the matter, Members are free (subject to other international obligations they may assume) to define whether IPRs will benefit from investment protection and, if so, under what terms.[50]

> *Recognizing* the underlying public policy objectives of national systems for the protection of intellectual property, including developmental and technological objectives

Intellectual property cannot be regarded in isolation from broader national policies, such as competition and development policies. In order to contribute to national objectives, the intellectual property system must be integrated into such policies.[51] The recognition in this paragraph of the Preamble of 'underlying public policy objectives' including 'developmental and technological objectives' would

---

[47] See, eg, the United Kingdom 1991 model BIT, Article I(a)(iv).

[48] See, eg, the EFTA–Singapore agreement (2002).

[49] See, eg, the (still bracketed) US proposal for Article 1.1 of the investment chapter of the FTAA. According to current IPR law, secret 'technical process' or 'know how' may be protected as *undisclosed information* (see Article 39 of the TRIPS Agreement). 'Goodwill' is the benefit and advantage of the good name, reputation and connection of a business. It may be protected under unfair competition law (which condemns dishonest commercial practices) or, in common law countries, under the doctrine of 'passing-off' (the wrong of misrepresenting one's business goods or services as another's, to the latter's injury, generally by using a confusing trademark or trade name). Protection often encompasses not only the use of trademarks, but also of a particular packaging, 'get up' or 'trade dress' and advertising styles (L Bently and B Sherman, *Intellectual Property Law* (2001: New York, Oxford University Press), pp 673–8.

[50] For instance, NAFTA's provision on expropriation and compensation (Article 11.10.7) includes an exception with regard to compulsory licences. Similarly, the FTA between Chile and USA stipulates that the provision on expropriation and compensation '... does not apply to the issuance of compulsory licenses granted in relation to intellectual property rights in accordance with the TRIPS Agreement' (Article 10.9.5).

[51] See, eg, CIPR (n 32 above); J Barton 'Integrating IPR policies in development strategies' [2003], *ICTSD-UNCTAD Dialogue, The Rockefeller Foundation's Bellagio Conference Center, 30 Oct–2 Nov 02*, available at <http://www.iprsonline.org/unctadictsd/bellagio/docs/j_Barton.pdf> (last accessed on 24 May 2005).

seem to address this need. However, such recognition is made in a somewhat restrictive manner, as the stated 'underlying public policy objectives' can be read to relate only to 'the national systems for the protection of intellectual property' and not to more general national policies. This approach is more restrictive than the practice followed in many countries. For instance, although recent developments in the US are clearly biased in favour of IPR holders, the tradition in that country has been to incorporate users' rights, and the appropriate level of competition into the calculus of 'underlying policy objectives' of the national IP system, by a balancing of public and private interests.

This paragraph, hence, could be of little value for those seeking an interpretation of the provisions of the TRIPS Agreement favourable to balancing its protectionist goals against the pro-competitive goals of GATT and to consider the critical role of public goods in the so called 'information economy'. It is noticeable, in this regard, that the Preamble does not contain any reference to issues of particular concern to developing countries, such as transfer of technology. The negotiating parties expressed 'the need to promote effective and adequate protection of intellectual property rights' but not to promote its transfer.

> *Recognizing* also the special needs of the least-developed country Members in respect of maximum flexibility in the domestic implementation of laws and regulations in order to enable them to create a sound and viable technological base;

This paragraph of the Preamble seems to recognize the particular situation of LDCs. On a careful reading, however, it is apparent that such recognition is significantly limited.

On the one hand, 'maximum flexibility' is only predicated with regard to the 'domestic *implementation* of laws and regulations' (emphasis added), thus suggesting that such flexibility does not extend to the obligations themselves. As examined elsewhere in this volume, the TRIPS Agreement has left a number of flexibilities (derived from gaps, ambiguities and options available to Members) that LDCs can exploit. But they are not conferred a differential treatment altogether. This deficit forced the WTO Members to extend the transitional period for the recognition and enforcement of pharmaceutical patents, in order to allow them to address the public health problems identified in the 'Doha Declaration on the TRIPS Agreement and Public Health'.[52] This concession, however, falls short of considering the significant burden (and limited benefits) that the implementation of the TRIPS Agreement generate in those countries.

On the other hand, the room for 'maximum flexibility' is restricted to one particular objective: 'to enable them to create a sound and viable technological base'. A literal reading of this paragraph would suggest that the flexibility that LDCs need in implementing the TRIPS obligations to protect public health, improve nutrition, alleviate poverty, or achieve other essential objectives was largely

---

[52] WT/MIN(01)/DEC/W/2, 14 November 2001.

ignored during the TRIPS negotiations. And it is precisely in these areas where an effective recognition of 'maximum flexibility' is called for.

> *Emphasizing* the importance of reducing tensions by reaching strengthened commitments to resolve disputes on trade-related intellectual property issues through multilateral procedures;

As indicated above, the second paragraph of the Preamble refers to the provision of procedures for the multilateral prevention and settlement of disputes. The seventh paragraph alludes to the same procedures, but adds the concept that 'tensions' may be reduced by 'strengthened commitments' to use the multilateral system for resolving disputes. This paragraph looks rather odd in the light of the developments that took place after the adoption of the TRIPS Agreement. Despite the commitment to multilateral solutions, many developing countries have continued to be subject to unilateral demands by some developed countries, notably the US and the EU, in the area of IPRs, aiming not only at the implementation of the TRIPS Agreement standards, but often asking for 'TRIPS-plus' protection; that is, levels of protection beyond the minimum standards required by the TRIPS Agreement. A telling case that received considerable public attention was the attempt by the US government and pharmaceutical industry to block the use of parallel imports and compulsory licences by the South African government to obtain access to cheaper HIV/AIDS drugs.[53] In other cases, developing countries were persuaded to adopt 'TRIPS-plus' standards in order to benefit from trade concessions under bilateral agreements.[54]

President Clinton's submission to the US Congress of the Uruguay Round Agreements Act stated that '[I]f Members of the Dispute Settlement Understanding (DSU) do not comply with their obligations at the end of the dispute settlement process, trade action under section 301 of the Trade Act of 1974 will be legitimized and there will be no risk of counter-retaliation'. Although this may have been interpreted as an expression of the desire to abandon the application of unilateral sanctions under the 'Special 301 Section' of the US Trade Act, this Section has continued to be invoked by the US government in a large number of cases. In November 1998, the European Communities requested a panel alleging the inconsistency with WTO rules of Sections 301–310 of the said Act.

---

[53] See, eg, B Byström and P Einarsson, *TRIPS–Consequences for Developing Countries: Implications for Swedish Development Cooperation* 38 (2000), Consultancy Report to the Swedish International Development Cooperation Agency, available at <http://www.grain.org/docs/sida-trips-2001-en.pdf> (last accessed on 24 May 2005).

[54] For example, the bilateral agreements entered into between the EC and their Member States and South Africa (1999), Tunisia (1998), and the Palestinian Authority (1997) require the latter to ensure adequate and effective protection of intellectual property rights 'in conformity with the highest international standards'. See, eg, P Drahos, *Developing Countries and International Intellectual Property Standard-Setting* (2002), study prepared for the UK Commission on Intellectual Property Rights, available at <www.iprcommission.org>, pp 14–18.

The panel, however, did not find such inconsistency, based on an undertaking by the US government not to apply sanctions before WTO procedures have been completed.[55]

The US not only kept the possibility to apply trade sanctions under its Trade Act in IPR-related cases, but reformed the Trade Act in a way that empowers the US Administration to do so even in cases where the targeted country does comply with the TRIPS Agreement.[56]

Acceptance by developing countries of the TRIPS Agreement was due in part to the expectation of increased market access for agricultural products and textiles,[57] and to the fear that if they did not agree they would be increasingly vulnerable to unilateral arm-twisting by the major powers.

Desiring to establish a mutually supportive relationship between the WTO and the World Intellectual Property Organization (referred to in this Agreement as 'WIPO') as well as other relevant international organizations;

Developing countries resisted negotiations on TRIPS until they realized, by mid-1989, that they would not be able to prevent a new set of rules on IPRs being adopted. One of the reasons for such resistance was that the World Intellectual Property Organization (WIPO) was the specialized United Nations (UN) organization in the area of IPRs, and that GATT or its successor was not the appropriate place for norm-setting on IPRs.[58] Thus,

[S]ome of these participants [in TRIPS negotiations] were of the view that the mandate did not provide for an exercise to set standards of protection of intellectual property rights or to attempt to raise the levels of such protection through the strengthening of enforcement procedures. These tasks, in their view, should be undertaken in other negotiating fora, such as the World Intellectual Property Organization. The task of the Group was not to deal with the intellectual property rights themselves but with the effects on trade in goods of action to protect such rights, particularly so as to ensure that such action does not cause barriers to legitimate trade.[59]

The proponents of the TRIPS Agreement, however, claimed that WIPO lacked 'teeth' to ensure the enforceability of the obligations administered by that organization. They strategically moved to a forum that would ensure greater capacity to

---

[55] United States–sections 301–310 of the Trade Act of 1974, WS/DT152R, 22 December 1999. The DSB adopted the report in January 2000. See <www.wto.org> (last accessed on 16 May 2005).
See, eg, C Arup, 'TRIPS: across the global field of intellectual property' (2004) 26 EIPR 1, p 9.
[56] Section 301 of the Trade Act of 1974, as amended (19 USC § 2411) stipulates that practices considered 'unreasonable' include 'denial of adequate and effective protection of intellectual property rights, even if the foreign country is in compliance with the WTO Agreement on Trade-Related Aspects of Intellectual Property (TRIPS)'.
[57] Concessions by developed countries in these two areas would have been unlikely if developing countries had refused disciplines on IPRs. See Hoekman and Kostecki op. cit. (2001), pp 280, 285.
[58] Idem, p 283.   [59] MTN.GNG/NG11/1, 10 April 1987, para 8.

force changes in legislation and enforcement of rights. This move was the result of an effective lobbying by a group of industries in the US, which convinced the government about the linkage between IPRs and trade. In fact, '[w]ith the TRIPS Agreement, US pharmaceutical, entertainment, and information industries, obtained much of what they sought when negotiations were launched'.[60]

The role of WIPO during the negotiation of the TRIPS Agreement was limited. Despite WIPO's Director General's request for the organization to 'be fully associated in all activities that GATT will undertake in the field of intellectual property',[61] it was only admitted as an observer to formal meetings, while the real negotiations took place in the informal ones. WIPO provided technical inputs to the negotiating parties.[62] After the TRIPS Agreement was adopted, WIPO came back into the norm-setting scene with the adoption of treaties on copyright and performers' rights in 1996[63] and on patent law.[64] Since then, however, their efforts to further harmonize patent law have become increasingly controversial and raised growing opposition from developing countries, as illustrated by the proposal, submitted by Argentina and Brazil, and supported by other developing countries, on the Establishment of a Development Agenda for WIPO.[65]

The possible cooperation between the Council for TRIPS and WIPO with regard to the establishment of a common registry for notified laws and regulations was contemplated in Article 63.2 of the TRIPS Agreement.[66] WIPO and WTO signed an Agreement in 1995 to cooperate in different areas relevant to the implementation of the TRIPS Agreement. Among other things, it ensures WTO Members access to the WIPO collection of laws and regulations, provides that the communication of emblems and transmittal of objections under the TRIPS Agreement shall be administered by the International Bureau in accordance with the procedures applicable under Article 6ter of the Paris Convention (1967), and requires the International Bureau and the WTO Secretariat to enhance their cooperation on assistance for developing countries relating to TRIPS.

---

[60] Hoekman and Kostecki, op. cit. (2001), p 297.

[61] See MTN.GNG/NG11/W/1, 25 February 1987, Communication from the Director General of the World Intellectual Property Organization.

[62] See, eg, the document Existence, Scope and Form of Generally Internationally Accepted and Applied Standards/Norms of the Protection of Intellectual Property, MTN.GNG/NG11/W/24.

[63] WIPO Copyright Treaty (1996) and WIPO Performances and Phonograms Treaty (1996).

[64] Patent Law Treaty (2000).

[65] See WIPO document WO/GA/31/11, 27 August 2004. The document states, inter alia, that 'WIPO is currently engaged in norm-setting activities in various technical Committees. Some of these activities would have developing countries and LDCs agree to IP protection standards that largely exceed existing obligations under the WTO's TRIPS Agreement, while these countries are still struggling with the costly process of implementing TRIPS itself. The current discussions on a draft Substantive Patent Law Treaty (SPLT) in the Standing Committee on the Law of Patents (SCP) are of particular concern. The proposed Treaty would considerably raise patent protection standards, creating new obligations that developing countries will hardly be able to implement. In the course of discussions, developing countries have proposed amendments to improve the draft SPLT by making it more responsive to public interest concerns and the specific development needs of developing countries.'   [66] See pp 476–7 below.

The reference to WIPO in this provision of the Preamble should not lead us to disregard the role that other international organizations, such as UNESCO,[67] may have in the area of IPRs.

Despite the expressed desire to establish a mutually supportive relationship between the WTO and WIPO, there is no coordination in the work of these organizations and, in some cases, the same issues are dealt with in both of them. An illustration is the developing countries' demand to establish an obligation to disclose the origin of biological materials claimed in patent applications, which has led to debates and proposals both in WIPO and the Council for TRIPS.[68]

Preambular provisions are important for the interpretation of treaty obligations. They do not create by themselves any rights or obligations enforceable through dispute resolution. In accordance with Article 31 of the Vienna Convention on the Law of Treaties (VCLT), the preamble provides part of the 'context' of the treaty for purposes of interpretation. The text of the preamble is an important source of interpretation to clarify the meaning of treaty provisions. In fact, owing to the controversial nature of the issues covered by the TRIPS Agreement, many of its provisions are ambiguous or deliberately leave Members room for interpretation. The 'context' provided by the preamble becomes, hence, particularly relevant in this case.

Article 2.3 of the Dispute Settlement Understanding (DSU) calls upon the use of public international law rules for interpretation of WTO disciplines.[69] Treaty interpretation in international law is dealt with by Articles 31 and 32 of the Vienna Convention on the Law of Treaties. According to Article 31(2) of the Convention, the context to be taken into account for the purposes of interpretation includes the Preamble and the annexes of the treaty, and any other agreement or text concluded by the parties in connection with that treaty.

Parties in WTO cases, as well as panels and the Appellate Body, often rely on the preamble of the WTO agreements for the interpretation of their provisions, particularly their object and purpose. Thus, in *Korea–Dairy*, the Appellate Body referred to the Preamble of the *Agreement on Safeguards* as additional support

---

[67] For instance, the Universal Copyright Convention (signed at Geneva on 6 September 1952, revised at Paris in 1971, available at <http://portal.unesco.org/en/ev.php-URL_ID= 15241&URL_DO=DO_Topic&URL_SECTION=201.html>) was developed in the framework of UNESCO.

[68] See, eg, C Correa, 'The politics and practicalities of a disclosure of origin obligation' (2005, Geneva: QUNO Occasional Paper 16), available at <www.quno.org> (last accessed on 16 May 2005).

[69] DSU, Article. 2.3.: 'The dispute settlement system of the WTO is a central element in providing security and predictability to the multilateral trading system. The Members recognize that it serves to preserve the rights and obligations of Members under the covered agreements, and to clarify the existing provisions of those agreements *in accordance with customary rules of interpretation of public international law*. Recommendations and rulings of the DSB cannot add to or diminish the rights and obligations provided in the covered agreements' (emphasis added). See, eg, R Howse, 'The jurisprudential achievement of the WTO Appellate body: a preliminary appreciation', <http://www.law.nyu.edu/kingsburyb/spring03/globalization/robhowsepaper.pdf> (last accessed on 18 February 2005).

for its finding that all provisions of both Article XIX of *GATT 1994* and the *Agreement on Safeguards* apply cumulatively and must be given their full meaning and legal effect.[70] In a finding in *US–Lamb* the panel referred to the object and purpose of the *Agreement on Safeguards*, as evidenced in the Preamble, as relevant context for its more restrictive approach to the concept of 'domestic industry'.[71] In the 1998 *Shrimp–Turtle Case* the panel noted that 'the first paragraph of the Preamble of the WTO Agreement acknowledges that the optimal use of the world's resources must be pursued in accordance with the objective of sustainable development', and the the Appellate Body (AB) stated that sustainable development 'must add colour, texture and shading to our interpretation of the agreements annexed to the WTO Agreement'. In the GMO dispute before the WTO, the US relied on the next to last introductory sentence of the Cartagena Protocol Preamble to argue that the Protocol would not be applicable to the dispute because it would not 'change the rights and obligations under any existing international agreements'.[72]

In the specific context of the TRIPS Agreement, and in line with Article 31(2) of the Vienna Convention, the panel in *Canada–Patent* referred to the legal value of the Preamble as part of the context for interpretation of the Agreement's provisions. It stated:

In the framework of the TRIPS Agreement, which incorporates certain provisions of the major pre-existing international instruments on intellectual property, the context to which the Panel may have recourse for the purposes of interpretation of specific TRIPS provisions [. . .] is not restricted to the text, Preamble and Annexes to the TRIPS Agreement itself, but also includes the provisions of the other international instruments on intellectual property incorporated into the TRIPS Agreement, as well as any agreement between the parties relating to these Agreements within the meaning of Article 31.2 of the Vienna Convention on the Law of Treaties.[73]

---

[70] 'Our reading . . . is consistent with the desire expressed by the Uruguay Round negotiators in the Preamble to the *Agreement on Safeguards* 'to clarify and reinforce the disciplines of GATT 1994, and specifically those of its Article XIX . . . , to re-establish multilateral control over safeguards and eliminate measures that escape such control . . . ' (Appellate Body Report *on Korea–Dairy*, para 88. See also Appellate Body Report on *Argentina–Footwear*, para 95.

[71] Panel Report on *US–Lamb*, paras 7.76 and 7.77. The Appellate Body also referred in this case to the object and purpose of the *Agreement on Safeguards* in distinguishing between the concepts of 'serious injury' under the *Agreement on Safeguards* and 'material injury' under the Anti-Dumping Agreement and the Agreement on Subsidies and Countervailing Duties (Appellate Body Report on *US–Lamb*, para 124).

[72] See *Executive Summary of the US Rebuttal Position – 07/29/2004 . . . op cit*, § 18. See also F Sindico, 'The GMO Dispute before the WTO: Legal Implications for the Trade and Environment Debate' (Natural Resources Management, The Fondazione Eni Enrico Mattei, Note di Lavoro Series, 2005), available at <http://www.feem.it/Feem/Pub/Publications/WPapers/default.htm>, last accessed on 23 February 2005.

[73] *Canada–Patent Protection of Pharmaceutical Products*, WT/DS114/R, Report of the Panel, 17 March 2000, para 7.14.

Annex

Negotiating history[74]

In his 23 July 1990 report on the status of work in the TRIPS Negotiating Group, the Chairman (Lars E R Anell) presented two sets of proposals. In an Annex to the report, he presented a composite text that was taken from various proposals by delegations to the Negotiating Group, indicating the source of each proposal by numerical reference to the source document.

Composite text of July 23 1990[75]

'PART I: PREAMBULAR PROVISIONS; OBJECTIVES[76]

1. *Preamble* (71); *Objectives* (73)

1.1 *Recalling* the Ministerial Declaration of Punta del Este of 20 September 1986; (73)

1.2 *Desiring* to strengthen the role of GATT and its basic principles and to bring about a wider coverage of world trade under agreed, effective and enforceable multilateral disciplines; (73)

1.3 *Recognizing* that the lack of protection, or insufficient or excessive protection, of intellectual property rights causes nullification and impairment of advantages and benefits of the General Agreement on Tariffs and Trade and distortions detrimental to international trade, and that such nullification and impairment may be caused both by substantive and procedural deficiencies, including ineffective enforcement of existing laws, as well as by unjustifiable discrimination of foreign persons, legal entities, goods and services; (73)

1.4 *Recognizing* that adequate protection of intellectual property rights is an essential condition to foster international investment and transfer of technology; (73)

1.5 *Recognizing* the importance of protection of intellectual property rights for promoting innovation and creativity; (71)

1.6 *Recognizing* that adequate protection of intellectual property rights both internally and at the border is necessary to deter and persecute piracy and counterfeiting; (73)

---

[74] For an analysis of the negotiating history, see *UNCTAD-ICTSD, Resource Book on TRIPS and Development* (2005: New York, Cambridge University Press), pp 1–17.

[75] Chairman's Report to the GNG, Status of Work in the Negotiating Group, Negotiating Group on Trade-Related Aspects of Intellectual Property Rights, including Trade in Counterfeit Goods, MTN.GNG/NG11/W/76, 23 July 1990, presented by the Chairman of the TRIPS Negotiating Group (Lars E R Anell). Alternatives 'A' correspond to texts from developed countries and 'B' from developing countries.

[76] The numbers in brackets refer to the draft texts submitted by the European Communities (NG11/W/68), the United States (NG11/W/70), Argentina, Brazil, Chile, China, Colombia, Cuba, Egypt, India, Nigeria, Peru, Tanzania, and Uruguay, and subsequently also sponsored by Pakistan and Zimbabwe (NG11/W/71), Switzerland (NG11/W/73), Japan (NG11/W/74), and Australia (NG11/W/75).

1.7 *Taking into account* development, technological and public interest objectives of developing countries; (71)

1.8 *Recognizing* also the special needs of the least developed countries in respect of maximum flexibility in the application of this Agreement in order to enable them to create a sound and viable technological base; (71)

1.9 *Recognizing* the need for appropriate transitional arrangements for developing countries and least developed countries with a view to achieve successfully strengthened protection and enforcement of intellectual property rights; (73)

1.10 *Recognizing* the need to prevent disputes by providing adequate means of transparency of national laws, regulations and requirements regarding protection and enforcement of intellectual property rights; (73)

1.11 *Recognizing* the need to settle disputes on matters related to the protection of intellectual property rights on the basis of effective multilateral mechanisms and procedures, and to refrain from applying unilateral measures inconsistent with such procedures to PARTIES to this PART of the General Agreement; (73)

1.12 *Recognizing* the efforts to harmonize and promote intellectual property laws by international organizations specialized in the field of intellectual property law and that this PART of the General Agreement aims at further encouragement of such efforts; (73)

2. *Objective of the Agreement* (74)

2A The PARTIES agree to provide effective and adequate protection of intellectual property rights in order to ensure the reduction of distortions and impediments to [international (68)] [legitimate (70)] trade. The protection of intellectual property rights shall not itself create barriers to legitimate trade. (68, 70)

2B The objective of the present Agreement is to establish adequate standards for the protection of, and effective and appropriate means for the enforcement of intellectual property rights; thereby eliminating distortions and impediments to international trade related to intellectual property rights and foster its sound development. (74)

2C With respect to standards and principles concerning the availability, scope and use of intellectual property rights, PARTIES agree on the following objectives:
  (i) To give full recognition to the needs for economic, social and technological development of all countries and the sovereign right of all States, when enacting national legislation, to ensure a proper balance between these needs and the rights granted to IPR holders and thus to determine the scope and level of protection of such rights, particularly in sectors of special public concern, such as health, nutrition, agriculture and national security. (71)

  (ii) To set forth the principal rights and obligations of IP owners, taking into account the important inter-relationships between the scope of such rights and obligations and the promotion of social welfare and economic development. (71)

  (iii) To facilitate the diffusion of technological knowledge and to enhance international transfer of technology, and thus contribute to a more active participation of all countries in world production and trade. (71)

(iv) To encourage technological innovation and promote inventiveness in all countries. (71)

(v) To enable participants to take all appropriate measures to prevent the abuses which might result from the exercise of IPRs and to ensure intergovernmental co-operation in this regard. (71)'

Draft text transmitted to the Brussels Ministerial Conference (December 1990)

The PARTIES to this agreement (hereinafter referred to as 'PARTIES'),

i. *Desiring* to reduce distortions and impediments to international trade, and taking into account the need to promote effective and adequate protection of intellectual property rights, and to ensure that measures and procedures to enforce intellectual property rights do not themselves become barriers to legitimate trade;

ii. *Recognising*, to this end, the need for new rules and disciplines concerning:

(a) the applicability of the basic principles of the GATT and of relevant international intellectual property agreements or conventions;

(b) the provision of adequate standards and principles concerning the availability, scope and use of trade related intellectual property rights;

(c) the provision of effective and appropriate means for the enforcement of trade related intellectual property rights, taking into account differences in national legal systems;

(d) the provision of effective and expeditious procedures for the multilateral prevention and settlement of disputes between governments;

and

(e) transitional arrangements aiming at the fullest participation in the results of the negotiations;

iii. *Recognising* the need for a multilateral framework of principles, rules and disciplines dealing with international trade in counterfeit goods;

iv. *Recognising* that intellectual property rights are private rights;

vi. *Recognising* the underlying public policy objectives of national systems for the protection of intellectual property, including developmental and technological objectives;

vi. *Recognising* also the special needs of the least developed countries in respect of maximum flexibility in the domestic implementation of laws and regulations in order to enable them to create a sound and viable technological base;

vii. *Emphasising* the importance of reducing tensions by reaching strengthened commitments to resolve disputes on trade related intellectual property issues through multilateral procedures;

viii. *Desiring* to establish a mutually supportive relationship between GATT and WIPO as well as other relevant international organisations;

Hereby agree as follows:

Chapter 2

NATURE AND SCOPE OF OBLIGATIONS

Coverage of the Agreement

Nature and Scope of Obligations

1.1. Members shall give effect to the provisions of this Agreement. Members may, but shall not be obliged to, implement in their law more extensive protection than is required by this Agreement, provided that such protection does not contravene the provisions of this Agreement. Members shall be free to determine the appropriate method of implementing the provisions of this Agreement within their own legal system and practice.

The first sentence of Article 1.1 of the TRIPS Agreement re-states a basic principle of international law: *pacta sunt servanda*.[1] It makes clear that the obligations imposed by the Agreement are to be given effect by Members within their respective jurisdictions.

Neither this article nor any other provision of the Agreement specifies how such obligations are to be implemented. In countries that follow a 'dualist' approach to international law, implementing regulations would be needed, as the Agreement would not be recognized as self-executing. In those adopting a 'monist' approach, the Agreement may be directly applied by judicial and administrative authorities, at least to the extent that the provisions are clear enough and self-contained.[2] This would be the case, for instance, in many Latin American countries, where international treaties are deemed self-executing and can be directly invoked by private parties.[3] There are also jurisdictions in which the direct application of the TRIPS Agreement (as well as other WTO agreements and treaties) has been denied by

---

[1] Vienna Convention on the Law of Treaties, Article 26: *'Pacta sunt servanda*: Every treaty in force is binding upon the parties to it and must be performed by them in good faith.' The Preamble of the Convention also notes that this principle is 'universally recognized'.

[2] There is also a middle ground approach (eg, in the United States) between monism and dualism, in which treaties may be given direct effect, but they may also be modified by the legislature. See, eg, UNCTAD–ICTSD, *Resource Book on Trips and Development*, (2005: New York, Cambridge University Press), p 26.

[3] In the case of Argentina, for instance, the Supreme Court categorically held the self-executing character of certain provisions of the TRIPS Agreement, including some dealing with enforcement. See, eg, the decisions of the Argentine Supreme Court of Justice in *Unilever NV c/Instituto Nacional de la propiedad Industrial s/denegatoria de patente* of 24 October 2000, and *Dr. Karl Thomae Gesellschaft mit Beschränker Haftung c/Instituto Nacional de la propiedad Industrial s/denegatoria de patente* of 13 February 2001.

law or the courts. In the case of the US, for instance, Section 102(a)(1) of the Uruguay Round Agreement Act (URAA) provides that '[N]o provision of any of the Uruguay Round Agreements, nor the application of any such provisions to any person or circumstance, that is inconsistent with any law of the United States shall have effect'. In addition, Section 102 (c) (1) of the URAA stipulates that:

[N]o person other than the United States—

(A) shall have any cause of action or defense under any of the Uruguay Round Agreements or by virtue of congressional approval of such an agreement, or (B) may challenge, in any action brought under any provision of law, any action or inaction by any department, agency, or other instrumentality of the United States, any State, or any political subdivision of a State on the ground that such action or inaction is inconsistent with such agreement.

The TRIPS Agreement has also been deemed not self-executing in the EU. The European Court of Justice (ECJ) denied its direct applicability under the EC law in *Parfums Christian Dior v Tuk Consultancy* (2000),[4] with the caveat that, since the TRIPS Agreement imposed international obligations on the EC States, the courts should endeavour to interpret EC law consistently with the TRIPS Agreement. This decision was in line with the ECJ's previous rulings, particularly in *Portugal v Council*,[5] where it had held that that the WTO Agreements were not directly effective under EU law. In Germany, the direct applicability of the enforcement provisions of the TRIPS Agreement has been denied.[6]

The implementation of the TRIPS Agreement has been problematic, particularly in developing countries. The expansion and strengthening of IPRs required by the Agreement was bound to take place in a scenario of deep North–South scientific and technological asymmetry. Only around 4 per cent of world research and development (R&D) expenditures is made in developing countries, who are overwhelmingly dependent for their development upon innovations made in the industrialized world.

The way in which the Agreement is implemented may have important implications on the conditions for the access to and use of technology, particularly in developing countries and on their economic and social development. It is crucial, therefore, to clearly identify the options left by the Agreement to implement its provisions in a manner that is consistent with Members' interests and strategies. As noted by one commentator, 'perhaps the negotiators in the Uruguay Round may have gone too far in extracting intellectual property-related concessions from developing countries'.[7]

---

[4] *Parfums Christian Dior SA and Tuk Consultancy BV,* joined cases C-300/98 and C-392/98, 14 December 2000, p 44.   [5] Case C-149/96 *Portugal v Council* [1999] ECR I-8395, p 47.

[6] See the legal memorandum of the German Federal Government, BT-Drucks. 12/7655(neu), pp 335, 347, quoted in P Katzenberger, 'TRIPS and copyright law', F Beier and G Schricker (eds) in *From GATT to TRIPS—The Agreement on Trade-Related Aspects of Intellectual Property Rights,* (1996: Munich, IIC Studies Max Planck Institute for Foreign and International Patent, Copyright and Competition Law), p 73.

[7] N Pires de Carvalho, *The TRIPS Regime of Patent Rights* (2002: The Hague, Kluwer Law International), p 61.

The implementation of the TRIPS Agreement has proven to be a very complex task, due to coverage of the Agreement and the need to reform most, if not all, national statutes on the matter in the short periods mentioned above. While the TRIPS Agreement left room for manoeuvre in different areas, this flexibility was not used by many countries. They thus renounced the possibility of tailoring the implementation legislation, to the extent possible, to their own needs and conditions. The reasons why developing countries failed to use such flexibility need more exploration. But the pressures exerted by some developed countries were critical in that respect.[8] The technical assistance that they received probably failed to alert them with regard to available legislative options that could mitigate the possible negative impact of implementing the Agreement's obligations.

Although the TRIPS Agreement has contributed to the harmonization of intellectual property law, it does not give rise to a uniform supranational law, but to an IPR system with a large number of common elements, based on domestic legislation firmly grounded on the principle of territoriality.[9]

The second sentence of Article 1.1 clarifies that the provisions contained in the Agreement constitute *minimum* standards of protection,[10] and the extent of the Members' basic obligation to give effect to the provisions of the Agreement. While the US and the EC proposals on Article 1 were drafted in a negative form,[11] the adopted text clearly indicates that the granting of TRIPS-plus standards of protection is facultative. Moreover, in language that seems to address developing countries' concerns, it explicitly states that no Member can be 'obliged' to implement in its national law 'more extensive protection than is required by this Agreement'.[12]

It has been argued that the possibility of granting a 'more extensive' protection does not apply with regard to the enforcement provisions in Part III of the TRIPS Agreement, since such provisions would provide 'mandatory standards' and leave 'WTO Members no alternative to the measures thereby established'.[13] In fact, enforcement measures must be fair and equitable for *both* parties in an IPR controversy; in this sense, the TRIPS Agreement may be considered as creating maximum standards.[14]

---

[8] See, eg, S Sell, *Private Power, Public Law: The Globalization of Intellectual Property Rights* (2003: Cambridge University Press), pp 151–2.

[9] See, eg, Katzenberger op. cit. (1996), pp 72–3.

[10] Although the reference to 'minimum' standards does not appear in the text of the Agreement, it had been suggested in some of the negotiating drafts. See, eg, Gervais, *The TRIPS Agreement. Drafting History and Analysis* (2003: London, Sweet & Maxwell, 2nd edn), p 86.

[11] 'Nothing shall prevent PARTIES from . . .'. See the EC document MTN.GNG/NG11/W/68 and US document MTN.GNG/NG11/W/70.

[12] The wording 'more extensive protection' is probably based on Article 20 of the Berne Convention.   [13] Pires de Carvalho op. cit. (2002), p 32.

[14] See, eg J Drexel, 'La evolución del Acuerdo TRIPS: hacia un multilateralismo flexible', paper submitted to the Seminar 'El Acuerdo ADPIC 10 años después: visiones cruzadas Europa y Latinoamérica', AIDE/CEIDIE, Buenos Aires, 31 October–1 November 2005.

'More extensive' protection may mean, in the context of Article 1.1, for instance, longer terms of protection or the patenting of matters that Members may exclude from patents in accordance with Article 27.3(b). These and other TRIPS-plus requirements, including with regard to enforcement measures, have become a standard feature in US FTAs, such as those signed by the US with Chile, the Central American countries, Singapore, Australia, and Morocco, among others.[15]

A 'more extensive' protection may also result from the weakening of requirements for the acquisition of rights, or from the stipulation or conditions that are not present in the TRIPS Agreement. An example of the first situation is the establishment of a ceiling to the disclosure requirement for patent applications.[16] The second is illustrated by the initiative for the harmonization of patent law under the auspices of WIPO, which would erode, if successful, much of the flexibility that Members have to decide on key aspects of their patent regimes.[17]

The TRIPS Agreement, unlike pre-existing conventions on IPRs, was negotiated and adopted as a component of the multilateral trading system. Despite the Preamble's opening provision indicating that IPRs should not 'become barriers to legitimate trade', the proponents of the Agreement focused on the trade distortion created by the lack of effective protection (eg, as a result of counterfeiting). But they overlooked the extent to which higher levels of IPR protection may create barriers to legitimate trade. For instance, if parallel imports are restrained, international trade in legitimate products may be prevented. When low standards of patentability are allowed, barriers against imports of products that should otherwise freely circulate may be created. In view of these possible effects, governments negotiating the TRIPS Agreement should have considered establishing upper, and not only lower limits on the level of IPRs protection.

Such upper limit may arguably be incorporated in the last part of the examined sentence in Article 1.1, as it states that a 'more extensive' protection may be granted 'provided that such protection does not contravene the provisions of this Agreement'.

Situations in which a TRIPS-plus protection may 'contravene' the provisions of the Agreement may arise if such protection is conferred on a discriminatory basis, for instance, only in favour of the nationals of the country or of the nationals of some countries with the exclusion of other Members. A contravention of Articles 3 or 4, respectively, of the TRIPS Agreement would be found in these cases.

---

[15] See, eg, C Fink and P Reichenmiller, 'Tightening TRIPS: The Intellectual Property Provisions of Recent US Free Trade Agreements' (World Bank, 2005), available at <http://siteresources. worldbank.org/INTRANETTRADE/Resources/Pubs/TradeNote20.pdf>, contentMDK:20115046~ pagePK:148956~piPK:216618~theSitePK:239071,00.html, last accessed on 15 February, 2005; P Roffe, 'Bilateral agreements and a TRIPS-plus world: the Chile-USA Free Trade Agreement' (Quaker International Affairs Programme, 2004), available at <www.qiap.ca>.

[16] See, eg, J F Morin, 'The Future of Patentability in International Law According to CAFTA' (2004) Bridges 8(3), p 15.

[17] See, eg, C Correa and S Musungu, 'The WIPO Patent Agenda: the Risks for Developing Countries' (Working Paper No 12, Geneva: South Centre 2002).

A more extensive patent protection that discriminates according to the field of technology, the place of invention or whether the infringing products are locally produced or imported may also be deemed a violation of Article 27.1 and, hence, of Article 1.1. For instance, in the US, biotechnological inventions were subject in practice to patentability criteria more favourable than in other sectors.[18] In the US, Europe and other developed countries, an extension of the patent term is allowed for pharmaceutical inventions in order to compensate for the delays in procedures for marketing approval. The consistency of this special treatment with Article 27.1 is at least controversial. Canada filed a complaint against the EC before the WTO arguing that Regulations EEC No 1768/92 and EEC No 1610/96, which allow for the extension (via a 'certificate') of the term of pharmaceutical and agro-chemical product patents, were inconsistent with Article 27.1 of the TRIPS Agreement.[19]

Whether the discrimination is positive or negative is, in fact, irrelevant in the light of Article 27.1. An additional period of patent protection for specific categories of products may well be deemed not TRIPS-compliant.[20] Members that provide more extensive protection of this nature are likely to argue, in line with the ruling in the *Canada–Patent Protection for Pharmaceutical Products*, that the TRIPS Agreement does not prevent *differentiation*, for instance, of the situation of regulated products. Owing to lengthy regulatory procedures, inventors of those products may enjoy a more limited period of effective protection than those of other products. This could prevent the inventor from fully recouping his R&D investment. While there is very little concrete evidence to support this argument, in many other areas the implementation of innovations also requires significant time for engineering, design, testing, etc before putting the product on the market.

Another situation of a 'more extensive' protection that contravenes the TRIPS Agreement can arise in the case of 'revalidation', 'confirmation', or 'importation' patents; that is, patents that are granted on the basis of foreign patent grants, without consideration of the novelty requirement. This kind of patent was introduced as a means to facilitate the importation of technologies in some patent laws and treaties[21] of the nineteenth century, and survived in some countries (eg Argentina, Chile) until recently. The more extensive protection conferred by these patents conflicts with Article 4*bis* of the Paris Convention for the Protection of Industrial Property,[22] as interpreted more than half a century ago in relation to Article 29 of the French law of 1844.[23] The inconsistency of revalidation patents with the

---

[18] See, eg, D Burk and M Lemley, 'Is Patent Law Technology-Specific?', (2002), Berkeley Technology Law Journal, Fall.   [19] Document WT/DS153/1 of 7 December,1998.

[20] See, eg, N Pires de Carvalho, *The TRIPS Regime of Patent Rights* (2002: The Hague, Kluwer Law International), p 57.

[21] See eg The Montevideo Treaty on Patents, signed on 16 January 1889.

[22] As discussed below, this Convention was incorporated into the TRIPS Agreement.

[23] See A Casalonga, *Traité Technique et pratique des brevets d'invention* (1949: Paris), pp 273, 296.

TRIPS Agreement was also found by the Argentine Supreme Court,[24] which declared that they were incompatible with the Paris Convention and the principles of the TRIPS Agreement.[25]

An important implication of the approach adopted in Article 1.1 is that the TRIPS Agreement cannot be seen as a *uniform* law, but rather as a set of elements that IPR national laws must observe, thereby leaving Members total discretion to deal with matters not specifically addressed in the Agreement, as well as significant room for interpreting and implementing its provisions in accordance with the Members' policy objectives and legal systems. The extent of this room will be examined in detail in this volume.

The 'method of implementing' the TRIPS Agreement provisions can be freely determined within the 'own legal system and practice' of each Member country. There are considerable differences between legal systems, particularly those based on Anglo-American and continental European law. These differences are noticeable, for instance, in the field of copyright and neighbouring rights, trademarks, and trade secrets protection. Other differences may arise from various levels of economic and technological development and, particularly, from the institutional capacity and resources available to grant IPRs (for instance, through the examination of patent and trademark applications) and to ensure their enforcement.

Article 1.1 allows diversity in the *methods of implementing* the provisions of the Agreement. Some countries may adopt specific legislation and regulations; others, as discussed below in this section, may consider some of the obligations imposed by the TRIPS Agreement as self-executing. In some jurisdictions, notably in common-law countries, the Agreement's standards may be implemented through court decisions, which could be subject to the scrutiny of panels and the Appellate Body in case of dispute. For instance, in *United States–Section 110(5) of the US Copyright Act*,[26] the panel examined court decisions in the US and judicial trends, and made a ruling on the basis of what could be drawn from the 'vast majority of cases'. It held that

since 1976 US courts have in the vast majority of cases applied the homestyle exemption in a sufficiently consistent and clearly delineated manner.[27]

The leeway given to Members under Article 1.1 of the Agreement seems to be limited in two ways. First, Members are not authorized to decide what they consider

[24] See *Unilever NV v Instituto Nacional de Propiedad Industrial s/denegtoria de patente*, reproduced in El Derecho, 2 August 2001.

[25] Bodenhausen argued that the principle of independence of the Paris Convention did not apply with regard to special patents like 'revalidation' patents. This argument, however, is unconvincing as the principle is to be applied, according to the Convention, in an 'unrestricted sense' (G Bodenhausen, *Guide to the Application of the Paris Convention of Industrial Property as revised at Stockholm in 1967* (1991: Geneva, WIPO) pp 208–9). [26] WT/DS160/R, 15 June 2000.

[27] Idem, para 6.144. The panel rejected the EC argument alleging a judicial trend towards broadening the homestyle exemption of 1976 in recent years: 'We cannot exclude the possibility that in the future US courts could establish precedents that would lead to the expansion of the scope of the currently applicable homestyle exemption as regards covered establishments' (ibidem).

the appropriate level of protection, but only to decide *how* to implement the levels set forth by the Agreement. A reading of Article 1.1 expanding Members' room for manoeuvre beyond implementation would provide more flexibility to Members, but is unlikely to pass the scrutiny of a panel or the AB.

Second, the chosen method of implementation should be 'appropriate . . . within their own legal system and practice'. A question arises as to the extent to which a panel or the AB could question the appropriateness of a particular method of implementation chosen by a Member. It does not seem within their authority to second guess national governments and decide what is appropriate within a particular legal 'system and practice'. However, they may consider the extent to which the adopted method of implementation permits a Member to comply with its obligations.

In *India–Patent Protection for Pharmaceutical and Agricultural Chemical Products*, India held that Article 1.1 legitimized the way it had decided to implement—through administrative regulations—the 'mailbox' provisions of Article 70.8(a) of the TRIPS Agreement. The AB confirmed that Members

. . . are free to determine how best to meet their obligations under the TRIPS Agreement within the context of their own legal systems. And, as a Member, India is 'free to determine the appropriate method of implementing' its obligations under the TRIPS Agreement within the context of its own legal system.[28]

However, the AB refused to give India the right to determine by itself whether the implementation means were appropriate to put in practice the 'mailbox' provisions. The AB found that, in that particular case, the administrative rules established by India were insufficient for that purpose.

The freedom preserved by Article 1.1 cannot be seen, hence, as a blank cheque for Members to decide by themselves whether they have complied or not with their obligations. Their legislation is subject to investigation under the DSU, for the purpose of determining such compliance, and there is room for a panel or the AB to disagree with the Member about what is 'appropriate' for implementing particular obligations. But they cannot ignore the Member's right to choose any method that is adequate (although it may not be the best available) to implement its obligations.

In the case referred to, the panel and the Appellate Body were confronted with the issue of the extent to which they could interpret national law in order to determine whether or not it was consistent with the TRIPS Agreement. The Appellate Body stated that there was simply no way for the panel to make a determination without engaging in an examination of Indian law, and that the panel was not interpreting Indian law 'as such', but only for the purpose of determining whether India had met its obligations under the TRIPS Agreement:

In this case, the Panel was simply performing its task in determining whether India's 'administrative instructions' for receiving mailbox applications were in conformity with

---

[28] Appellate Body Report, WT/DS50/AB/R, 19 December 1997, para 59.

India's obligations under Article 70.8(a) of the TRIPS Agreement. It is clear that an examination of the relevant aspects of Indian municipal law and, in particular, the relevant provisions of the Patents Act as they relate to the 'administrative instructions', is essential to determining whether India has complied with its obligations under Article 70.8(a). There was simply no way for the Panel to make this determination without engaging in an examination of Indian law. But, as in the case cited above before the Permanent Court of International Justice, in this case, the Panel was not interpreting Indian law 'as such'; rather, the Panel was examining Indian law solely for the purpose of determining whether India had met its obligations under the TRIPS Agreement. To say that the Panel should have done otherwise would be to say that only India can assess whether Indian law is consistent with India's obligations under the WTO Agreement. This, clearly, cannot be so.[29]

An interesting situation would arise if the domestic law were silent with regard to an obligation imposed by the TRIPS Agreement, in a Member that follows a 'monist' approach towards international law.[30] For assessing a situation like this the panel or AB should not only look at the particular provision or set of provisions of the domestic law pertinent to a particular case, but should systematically examine the relevant provision/s in the context of the overall national legal system. In jurisdictions where, according to constitutional law, treaties are deemed to be self-executing and binding on domestic courts, the failure of the domestic implementing legislation to adequately incorporate certain standards of the Agreement should not lead to a determination of inconsistency, unless a positive action by the Member were required.[31] Since under Article 1 of the TRIPS Agreement, Members can determine the means of implementing their obligations, any inconsistency with the Agreement in such a situation would be *de jure* cured by the direct application of the Agreement. Therefore, the panel or Appellate Body should decide in this case on the basis of how the legal system effectively operates, and not only rely on isolated provisions. This is also what the doctrine of 'consistent interpretation' suggests.[32]

The degree of freedom preserved under Article 1.1 of the Agreement was invoked in *Canada–Patent Protection of Pharmaceutical Products*.[33] Canada argued that said Article 1.1 gave it sufficient leeway to determine the scope of exceptions to patent rights. It argued that

The provision of this discretion, in the interests of achieving an appropriate balance in each of the national legal systems, reflected Members' desire to ensure that the limitations on the scope of patent rights that existed within—or were contemplated for—their own

[29] Idem, para 66. See also Chapter 14.

[30] This was not certainly the situation in the Indian case, since a dualist approach is applied in India in line with the Commonwealth tradition on the matter.

[31] See below, eg, Article 50 of the TRIPS Agreement, requiring that courts be given certain authority to issue provisional measures.

[32] According to this doctrine, where national law permits different interpretations, the one in accordance with the treaty obligations is to be applied. See, eg, T Cottier, 'The Impact of the TRIPS Agreement on Private Practice and Litigation', in J Cameron and K Campbell (eds), *Dispute Resolution in the World Trade Organization* (1998: London, Cameron May Ltd., International Law Publishers) p 124.

[33] WT/DS114/R, 17 March 2000.

intellectual property laws at the time the Agreement was being negotiated would be taken into account.[34]

In response, the EC held that the flexibility allowed by said Article 'related to the means by which this minimum level of protection was secured in each Member's legal system'.[35] The panel did not gave an opinion on the interpretation of Article 1.1. It stated that Articles 7 and 8.1 and 'other provisions of the TRIPS Agreement which indicate its object and purposes' must 'obviously be borne in mind' for interpretation of the Agreement.[36]

Finally, the 'flexibility' provided by Article 1.1 was invoked by the US to sustain its position on the interpretation of the exception allowed under Article 13 of the TRIPS Agreement, in *United States–Section 110(5) of the US Copyright Act*.[37] The panel alluded to this argument.[38] The flexibility of the TRIPS Agreement was also articulated by the US but in relation to a substantive standard, in responding to a questioning about the standard applied under 35 USC Section 102(a), which provides for a relative requirement of novelty regarding inventions disclosed outside the US in a non-written form. The US held that in the TRIPS Agreement there was 'no prescription as to how WTO Members define what inventions are to be considered "new" within their domestic systems' and, hence, that its legislation was 'perfectly consistent with the provisions of the TRIPS Agreement'.[39]

It has been argued that 'the appropriate method of implementing the provisions' of the TRIPS Agreement must be based on *effective* legal practices applied in the Member concerned, thereby excluding implementing measures without a tradition in the country.[40] This interpretation is clearly beyond the meaning of Article 1.1, which empowers Members to implement the Agreement's provisions within their 'own legal system and practice'; that is, to determine how such provisions will be put into practice. A legal system is not static, and many Members (especially the developing countries) had no prior practices in many areas in which the Agreement imposed standards of protection. There is no textual or contextual basis to interpret that Members' capacity to adopt implementing measures is historically determined or that once a certain method of implementation has been adopted, the Member loses the ability to modify it or implement a new

---

[34] Panel Report, *Canada–Patent Protection of Pharmaceutical Products*, WT/DS114/R, 17 March 2000, para 4.13.   [35] Idem, para 4.29.

[36] Idem, para 7.26.

[37] It stated: 'Article 1.1 of TRIPS also emphasizes flexibility, and provides that "Members shall be free to determine the appropriate method of implementing the provisions of this Agreement within their own legal system and practice".' Panel Report, WT/DS160/R, 15 June 2000. Annex 2.1, First Written Submission of the United States, 26 October. 1999, p 21.

[38] Idem, para 6.189, note 167.   [39] See document IP/Q3/USA/1, 1 May 1998.

[40] N Pires de Carvalho op. cit. (2002), p 59. The example given as not based on effective legal practice is the intervention in the examination of pharmaceutical patent applications of the Agencia Nacional de Vigilancia Sanitaria (ANVISA) of Brazil, established by law 10.196 of 14 February 2001.

method. Members, in sum, are free to design (and redesign) the legal instruments they deem fit to implement their obligations under the Agreement.

1.2. For the purposes of this Agreement, the term 'intellectual property' refers to all categories of intellectual property that are the subject of Sections 1 through 7 of Part II.

'Intellectual property' is used in the Preamble and in the initial provisions of Part I of the Agreement, while in Articles 5, 6, 7, 8, 40, and in several provisions of Part III reference is made to 'intellectual property rights'.

The areas that, for the purposes of the TRIPS Agreement, constitute 'intellectual property' include copyright and related rights, trademarks, geographical indications, industrial designs, patents, layout-designs (topographies) of integrated circuits, and undisclosed information. The Agreement does not provide a notion of 'intellectual property',[41] but rather specifies which are the covered rights, as dealt with in sections 1–7 of Part II of the Agreement. A definition of 'intellectual property' may be found in the Convention Establishing the World Intellectual Property Organization (1967),[42] but this definition includes subject matter that is in the public domain (scientific discoveries), as well as matters that are not deemed, under many national systems, subject to property rights (rights of performing artists, phonograms, and broadcasts).

The poor wording of Article 1.2 leaves many questions open.

First, the different sections of the Agreement do not contain clear-cut 'categories' of intellectual property. Thus, Section 5 of Part II on patents refers to the protection of plant varieties under an 'effective sui generis regime' but does not elaborate the standards thereto. Should this be considered a 'category' of intellectual property?

---

[41] It does not refer either to 'industrial property', the expression used in the Paris Convention in relation to patents, utility models, industrial designs, trademarks, service marks, trade names, indications of source, or appellations of origin, and the repression of unfair competition (Article 1.2).

[42] Article 2(viii) of the Convention states: 'intellectual property' shall include the rights relating to:
 – literary, artistic and scientific works,
 – performances of performing artists, phonograms, and broadcasts,
 – inventions in all fields of human endeavor,
 – scientific discoveries,
 – industrial designs,
 – trademarks, service marks, and commercial names and designations,
 – protection against unfair competition, and all other rights resulting from intellectual activity in the industrial, scientific, literary or artistic fields.'
A number of developing countries have argued that, given this definition, WIPO should not concentrate on promoting IPRs but intellectual activity more broadly, including by non-IPR measures, such as open source schemes. See, eg, the document submitted at the 31st Session of the WIPO General Assembly (27 September to 5 October 2004) by the delegations of Argentina, Bolivia, Brazil, Cuba, Dominican Republic, Ecuador, Egypt, Iran, Kenya, Peru, Sierra Leone, South Africa, Tanzania, and Venezuela, proposing a 'Development Agenda' for the World Intellectual Property Organization (tabled as Document WO/GA/31/11, available at <http://www.wipo.int>, last accessed on 30 May 2005).

Section 2 of Part II deals with 'Copyright and Related Rights'. In the continental law tradition, however, the so called 'related rights' (attributed to Performers, Producers of Phonograms, and Broadcasting Organizations) are distinguished from authors' rights and do not belong to the same 'category' of rights, despite being 'neighboring rights'.

Moreover, Section 7 of Part II relates to 'undisclosed information' but in the context of unfair competition.[43] Such secrets (covered under Article 39 of the TRIPS Agreement) are protected in the context of the discipline against unfair competition.[44] They do not give rise to exclusive rights, as in the case of patents or trademarks, but possessors of trade secrets can only act against those who have acquired or used the secret information in a manner contrary to dishonest commercial practices. Likewise, the data submitted for the marketing approval of pharmaceutical and agrochemical products—protected under Article 39.3 of the TRIPS Agreement—cannot be deemed a new category of 'intellectual property'.[45]

Second, it is unclear whether the categories refer to subject matter or to the rights conferred. If the former interpretation applied, it would mean that any rights not covered by the TRIPS Agreement that are conferred at the national level would be subject to the provisions of the Agreement. Thus, should a Member adopt, for instance, anti-circumvention measures (which are not provided either under the TRIPS Agreement or the Berne Convention) they would automatically be subject to the general provisions and enforcement rules of the Agreement. This interpretation would permit rights not specifically provided for in the Agreement but pertaining to covered subject matter under the norms and principles established by the Agreement to be embraced.

This is not the case if it is understood that protection of 'intellectual property' only applies to 'the intellectual property rights specifically addressed' under the Agreement, as stated in footnote 3 to Article 3.1.[46] If this is correct, Members would not be bound to respect the general and enforcement[47] provisions of the Agreement in respect of rights not covered by the Agreement, even if relating to subject matter dealt with therein. The latter interpretation is better grounded on the literal text of the Agreement, and preserves in the hands of national governments flexibility to design their IPR systems in line with their own needs and objectives.

The interpretation of Article 1.2 with regard to the coverage of the Agreement was raised in *United States–Section 211 Omnibus Appropriations Act of 1998* in

---

[43] See Article 39.1, Chapter 11 below.

[44] According to Pires de Carvalho op. cit. (2002) p 25, 'the protection of undisclosed information is not designated by the TRIPS Agreement as an intellectual property field per se, but merely as an aspect of protection against unfair competition'.

[45] See, eg, L Arrivillaga, 'An International Standard of Protection for Test Data Submitted to Authorities to Obtain Marketing Authorization for Drugs (2003) vol 6 No 1 The Journal of World Intellectual Property, p 143.   [46] See pp 61–2 below.

[47] Article 42 of the Agreement does not refer in general to categories of IPRs, but to 'any intellectual property right covered by the Agreement'.

relation to trade names, which are not specifically mentioned in the Agreement, but are referred to in the Paris Convention (Article 1(2)). The panel argued as follows:

We interpret the terms 'intellectual property' and 'intellectual property rights' with reference to the definition of 'intellectual property' in Article 1.2 of the TRIPS Agreement. The textual reading of Article 1.2 is that it establishes an inclusive definition and this is confirmed by the words 'all categories'; the word 'all' indicates that this is an exhaustive list. Thus, for example, the national and most-favoured-nation treatment obligations contained in Articles 3 and 4 of the TRIPS Agreement that refer to the 'protection of intellectual property' would be interpreted to mean the categories covered by Article 1.2 of the TRIPS Agreement. We consider the correct interpretation to be that there are no obligations under those Articles in relation to categories of intellectual property not set forth in Article 1.2, eg, trade names, consistent with Article 31 of the Vienna Convention.[48]

The European Communities maintained that the panel erred in its analysis by considering that Article 1.2 of the TRIPS Agreement contains an exhaustive definition of intellectual property. The European Communities considered that Article 1.2 was illustrative and no more than a very general definition of intellectual property rights covered by the Agreement. It argued that the panel's interpretation reduced the express inclusion in Article 2.1 of Article 8 of the Paris Convention (1967) to inutility, and that several matters that are included within the disciplines of the Agreement are not specifically referenced in Article 1.2.[49]

   The AB reversed the panel's ruling with regard to the interpretation of Article 1.2 of the TRIPS Agreement. It reasoned as follows:

The Panel interpreted that the phrase "intellectual property" refers to all categories of intellectual property that are the *subject* of Sections 1 through 7 of Part II' (emphasis added) as if that phrase read 'intellectual property means those categories of intellectual property appearing in the *titles* of Sections 1 through 7 of Part II'. To our mind, the Panel's interpretation ignores the plain words of Article 1.2, for it fails to take into account that the phrase 'the subject of Sections 1 through 7 of Part II' deals not only with the categories of intellectual property indicated in each section *title*, but with other *subjects* as well. For example, in Section 5 of Part II, entitled 'Patents', Article 27(3)(b) provides that Members have the option of protecting inventions of plant varieties by *sui generis* rights (such as breeder's rights) instead of through patents. Under the Panel's theory, such *sui generis* rights would not be covered by the *TRIPS Agreement*. The option provided by Article 27(3)(b) would be read out of the *TRIPS Agreement*.[50]

   Moreover, we do not believe that the Panel's interpretation of Article 1.2 can be reconciled with the plain words of Article 2.1. Article 2.1 explicitly incorporates Article 8 of the Paris Convention (1967) into the *TRIPS Agreement*.[51]

---

[48] WT/DS176/R, 6 August 2001, para 8.26.
[49] WT/DS176/AB/R, 2 January 2002, paras 54–5.   [50] Idem, para 335.
[51] Idem, para 336.

The Panel was of the view that the words 'in respect of' in Article 2.1 have the effect of 'conditioning' Members' obligations under the Articles of the Paris Convention (1967) incorporated into the *TRIPS Agreement*, with the result that trade names are not covered. We disagree.[52]

Article 8 of the Paris Convention (1967) covers only the protection of trade names; Article 8 has no other subject. If the intention of the negotiators had been to exclude trade names from protection, there would have been no purpose whatsoever in including Article 8 in the list of Paris Convention (1967) provisions that were specifically incorporated into the *TRIPS Agreement*. To adopt the Panel's approach would be to deprive Article 8 of the Paris Convention (1967), as incorporated into the *TRIPS Agreement* by virtue of Article 2.1 of that Agreement, of any and all meaning and effect. As we have stated previously:

One of the corollaries of the 'general rule of interpretation' in the *Vienna Convention* is that interpretation must give meaning and effect to all the terms of a treaty. An interpreter is not free to adopt a reading that would result in reducing whole clauses or paragraphs of a treaty to redundancy or inutility.[53]

The AB also dissented with the panel's view about the negotiating history of the Paris Convention:

As for the import of the negotiating history, we do not see it as in any way decisive to the issue before us. The documents on which the Panel relied are not conclusive of whether the *TRIPS Agreement* covers trade names. The passages quoted by the Panel from the negotiating history of Article 1.2 do not even refer to trade names. There is nothing at all in those passages to suggest that Members were either for or against their inclusion. Indeed, the only reference to a debate about the categories for coverage in the *TRIPS Agreement* relates, not to trade names, but to trade secrets. The Panel itself acknowledged that '[t]he records do not contain information on the purpose of the addition' of the words 'in respect of' at the beginning of Article 2.1. Therefore, we do not consider that any conclusions may be drawn from these records about the interpretation of the words 'in respect of' in Article 2.1 as regards trade names.[54]

The AB concluded:

Thus, in our view, the Panel's interpretation of Articles 1.2 and 2.1 of the TRIPS Agreement is contrary to the ordinary meaning of the terms of those provisions and is, therefore, not in accordance with the customary rules of interpretation prescribed in Article 31 of the Vienna Convention. Moreover, we do not believe that the negotiating history confirms, within the meaning of Article 32 of the Vienna Convention, the Panel's interpretation of Articles 1.2 and 2.1.[55]

For all these reasons, we reverse the Panel's finding in paragraph 8.41 of the Panel Report that trade names are not covered under the TRIPS Agreement and find that WTO Members do have an obligation under the TRIPS Agreement to provide protection to trade names [*footnotes omitted*].[56]

---

[52] Idem, para 337.　　[53] Idem, para 338.　　[54] Idem, para 339.
[55] Idem, para 340.　　[56] Idem, para 341.

In sum, the concept contained in Article 1.2 is a definitional tool, not a substantive provision that *creates* modalities of 'intellectual property' not covered in the conventions incorporated in the Agreement. The coverage of the TRIPS Agreement can be circumscribed as follows:

(i) The Agreement only creates obligations with regard to subject matter covered either in Sections 1–7 of Part II of the TRIPS Agreement or in the IPRs conventions that the Members are bound to comply with. This implies that, for instance, non-original databases, web-casters' rights (under discussion in WIPO[57]) are not covered by the Agreement.

(ii) The Agreement only imposes obligations with regard to the rights spelled out in sections 1–7 of Part II of the Agreement or the incorporated conventions pertaining to subject matter indicated in (i).[58] As a result, for instance, the right to prevent anti-circumvention measures, or to prevent third parties from relying on test data submitted to a health authority (often called 'data exclusivity') are not subject to the disciplines set forth in the Agreement.

Members have, hence, some flexibility in determining what types of legal entitlements will be considered 'intellectual property', as well as the scope of rights not specifically addressed in the Agreement or the conventions that it incorporates. One implication of this interpretation is that the MFN clause would not apply in cases Members grant another Member/s advantages relating to subject matter or rights not 'specifically addressed' in the TRIPS Agreement itself or the Paris, Berne, and Rome Conventions, or the Washington Treaty on integrated circuits.

It is appropriate to recall in this regard that the Appellate Body held in the *Havana Club* case that ownership claims were not subject to the TRIPS disciplines, and that a Member only had an obligation under Article 42 of the TRIPS Agreement to permit the assertion of ownership claims under *domestic law*.[59] Such claims—like others relating to substantive rights not covered by the Agreement—are not subject to dispute settlement under WTO rules.

Utility models (petty patents) and breeders' rights are not specifically mentioned as covered by the TRIPS Agreement.[60] *Sui generis* rights in databases, such as those adopted in the European Union, and domain names, are not alluded to in the Agreement either.

---

[57] See WIPO Revised Consolidated Text for a Treaty on the Protection of Broadcasting Organizations, SCCR/12/2, 4 October 2004.

[58] With the exception of the rights of performers, producers of phonograms and broadcasting organizations, which do not include those provided for in the Rome Convention but not in the Agreement.

[59] *United States–Section 211 Omnibus Appropriations Act of 1998*, WT/DS176/AB/R, paras 139–48.

[60] The Agreement does not mention 'invention certificates' either, which have been granted in the past in socialist and other countries.

Utility models or petty patents

The utility models or 'petty patents' protect minor innovations, mainly in the mechanical field.[61] In general, as with a patent, to be protected by a utility model, an invention must be new, involve an inventive step, and be susceptible to industrial application. Novelty, however, is assessed in some countries locally, while the level of required inventive step is less strict than for patents.[62] These titles have been recognized in many developed (Spain, Germany, Japan, etc) as well as developing countries (Argentina, Brazil, Andean Community members, China, etc).

Given the lack of reference in the TRIPS Agreement to utility models, and the inherent flexibility of the Paris Convention, it has been interpreted that there is no obligation on WTO Members to provide protection for utility models or petty patents.[63] Those countries who opt to recognize such models are bound by the national treatment principle and other relevant provisions in the Paris Convention, but not by the disciplines contained in the TRIPS Agreement, the application of which is limited to the rights 'specifically addressed in this Agreement'.[64]

Breeders' rights

The TRIPS Agreement requires in Article 27.3(b) the protection of plant varieties under patents, an effective *sui generis* regime, or a combination of both, but neither 'breeders' rights'[65] nor UPOV, the Convention that regulates them, are referred to in the text.[66] This may indicate that the major actors in the negotiation of TRIPS—particularly the US—privileged a patent approach with regard to issues relating to innovation in the field of plants, and deliberately omitted the breeders' rights regime.[67] In fact, the US biotechnology industry—which seeks global patent protection in the field of plants—was an active proponent of the expansion of patent protection to cover biological materials during the TRIPS

[61] In Germany, the scope of protection was broadened in 1987 to include inventions concerning chemicals and polymers.

[62] In Germany, however, legislation has tried to make utility models and patents as similar as possible. Whereas the Patent Act requires an 'inventive activity', a utility model requires an 'inventive step'. However, it often turns out that this difference is of more academic than practical relevance. This allows applicants to simultaneously file and obtain patents *and* utility models in parallel, since both can co-exist. See, eg, R Schuster and P Hess, 'Enforcing utility models in Germany' (November 1997) Managing Intellectual Property, p 27.

[63] See, eg, U Suthersanen, 'The Economic Efficacy of Utility Model Protection', in C Heath and A Kamperman Sanders (eds), *Industrial Property in the Biomedical Age, Challenges for Asia* (2003: The Hague Kluwer Law International).   [64] See Article 3, fn 3.

[65] Breeders' rights apply with regard to plant varieties that are distinct, uniform and stable.

[66] UPOV sets forth standards, including national treatment, for the granting of 'breeders' rights'. There are four versions of UPOV (1961, 1972, 1978, and 1991). The 1991 version entered into force on 24 April 1998, technically closing the 1978 version to new members.

[67] This conclusion is not contradicted by the fact that, in accordance with Article 1(3) of the Paris Convention, '[I]ndustrial property shall be understood in the broadest sense and shall apply not only

negotiations. The lack of reference to breeders' rights does not mean that they cannot be considered a specific kind of intellectual property right, since they convey all the characteristics of such rights. Moreover, in *United States–Section 211 Omnibus Appropriations Act of 1998*, in reversing the panel's opinion the AB alluded to the case of '*sui generis* rights (such as breeder's rights)' referred to in Article 27.3(b) as an example of subject matter not mentioned in the titles of the Agreement's sections, but which undoubtedly constitutes covered 'intellectual property'.[68]

The AB's reasoning to reverse the panel's ruling with regard to the interpretation of Article 1.2 of the TRIPS Agreement was as follows:

The Panel interpreted the phrase ' "intellectual property" refers to all categories of intellectual property that are the *subject* of Sections 1 through 7 of Part II' (emphasis added) as if that phrase read 'intellectual property means those categories of intellectual property appearing in the *titles* of Sections 1 through 7 of Part II'. To our mind, the Panel's interpretation ignores the plain words of Article 1.2, for it fails to take into account that the phrase 'the subject of Sections 1 through 7 of Part II' deals not only with the categories of intellectual property indicated in each section *title*, but with other *subjects* as well.[69]

Yet, Members are not obliged to apply the UPOV or other substantive standards.[70] *Sui generis* rights for the protection of plant varieties that Members may adopt are only subject to the national treatment and MFN obligations established in the TRIPS Agreement and to the enforcement rules included in Part III thereof. This is the only way in which such rights may be deemed as subject to the TRIPS disciplines. The absence of specific standards in the TRIPS Agreement on breeders' rights leaves the UPOV Convention as the sole existing international instrument providing for minimum standards of protection for plant varieties.[71]

---

to industry and commerce proper, but likewise to agricultural and extractive industries and to all manufactured or natural products, for example, wines, grain, tobacco leaf, fruit, cattle, minerals, mineral waters, beer, flowers, and flour'. This statement only applies to the categories of industrial property rights enumerated in Article 1(1) of the Convention.

[68] See below.

[69] *United States–Section 211 Omnibus Appropriations Act of 1998*, WT/DS176/AB/R, 2 January 2002, para 335.

[70] However, adherence to the UPOV standards has become a typical requirement under FTAs promoted by the US and the EU. The number of UPOV members significantly increased since 1994, reaching 58 as of 9 November 2004 (see <http://www.upov.org/en/about/members/pdf/pub423.pdf>, last accessed on 2 December 2004).

[71] According to the UPOV Convention, as amended in 1991, there are seven acts of exploitation for which the breeder's authorization is required: (1) production or reproduction (multiplication); (2) conditioning for the purpose of propagation; (3) offering for sale; (4) selling or other marketing; (5) exporting; (6) importing; and (7) stocking for any of these purposes. These rights can be exercised in respect of the propagating material, and also in respect of the harvested material (including whole plants and parts of plants), provided that the latter has been obtained through the unauthorized use of propagating material, and that the breeder has had no reasonable opportunity to exercise his or her right in relation to the propagating material. The breeder's right extends, in addition to the protected variety itself, to varieties which are not clearly distinguishable from the protected variety, which are

Databases

Databases are protected under the TRIPS Agreement if they are original (Article 10.2). The protection of non-original databases, as provided in the European Union,[72] cannot be deemed 'intellectual property' in the generally accepted meaning of this expression, as they are protected as an investment, not as a creation.[73] The US Supreme Court, for instance, has refused to recognize copyright protection over factual databases,[74] and the scientific and librarian communities are strongly opposed to the establishment of a European type of database protection in the US.[75]

Unfair competition

Article 1(1) of the Paris Convention lists the 'the repression of unfair competition' as one of the objects of industrial property protected under the Convention. Despite the discussions on the matter during the negotiations, the TRIPS Agreement does not contain general rules on this subject. One reason for this may be the fact that unfair competition is not recognized as a discipline in all countries, particularly the US. Given the power that this country exercised during the negotiations to frame the TRIPS rules consistently with its own legal system,[76] this is a plausible explanation.

However, through the general clause of Article 2.1, the TRIPS Agreement made mandatory compliance with Article 10*bis* of the Paris Convention on unfair competition. In addition, the Agreement incorporated specific rules with regard to undisclosed information in the context of Article 10*bis*, including commercial trade secrets and undisclosed data submitted to obtain marketing approval of pharmaceuticals and agrochemicals.

In this regard, the European Court of Justice (ECJ) examined in *Parfums Christian Dior*[77] whether the right to sue under general provisions of national law concerning wrongful acts, in particular unlawful competition, in order to protect

'essentially derived' from the protected variety, and those whose production requires the repeated use of the protected variety.

[72] Directive 96/9/EC on the legal protection of databases (11 March 1996).

[73] The same observation applies to test data covered in Article 39.3 of the TRIPS Agreement. The difference is, however, that such data are embraced under the broad definition of 'intellectual property' of Article 1.2.

[74] See *Feist Publication Inc v Rural Telephone Services*, III S Ct 1282, 1991.

[75] See, eg, K Maskus and J Reichman, 'The globalization of private knowledge goods and the privatization of global public goods', in K Maskus and J Reichman (eds), *International Public Goods and Transfer of Technology under a Globalized Intellectual Property Regime* (2005: Cambridge University Press), p 23.

[76] As exemplified by the exclusion of moral rights from the obligations under the Agreement. See p 118 below.

[77] *Parfums Christian Dior SA and TUK Consultancy BV* (joined cases C-300/98 and C-392/98), 14 December 2000.

an industrial design against copying was to be classified as an 'intellectual property right' within the meaning of Article 50(1) of the TRIPS Agreement. The Court concluded that

It is apparent from the foregoing provisions as a whole that TRIPs leaves to the Contracting Parties, within the framework of their own legal systems and in particular their rules of private law, the task of specifying in detail the interests which will be protected under TRIPs as 'intellectual property rights' and the method of protection, provided always, first, that the protection is effective, particularly in preventing trade in counterfeit goods and, second, that it does not lead to distortions of or impediments to international trade.
...

It follows that a right to sue under general provisions of national law concerning wrongful acts, in particular unlawful competition, in order to protect an industrial design against copying may qualify as an 'intellectual property right' within the meaning of Article 50(1) of TRIPs.[78]

Domain names

A domain name is 'concerned primarily with facilitating access to a particular website. It is a based on the specific technical characteristics of the domain name system, ie, a unique address for each Internet location. Domain names are functional means of enabling a user to access a desired location on the Internet.'[79] Hence, a domain name is not a trademark.[80] Once allocated, a domain name by definition can only identify a single location on the Internet, and 'there can never be any confusion with respect to the use of a domain name per se'.[81]

Domain names are not covered by the TRIPS Agreement. However, claims related to the use of such names may be dealt with under trademark law, whenever trademarks are improperly used as a domain name, or under unfair competition law which, as mentioned, is covered by the Agreement through the reference to Article 10*bis* of the Paris Convention.[82] This means that enforcement measures

[78] Idem, p 60 and 62.
[79] N Wilkof, 'Trademarks and the public domain: generic marks and domain names', in *International Intellectual Property Law & Policy*, Vol 6, H Hansen (ed.), (2001: Huntington, Juris Publishing), pp 21–9.
[80] Domain names have been conceptualized as equivalents to titles to land. In the US, for instance, the owner of a trademark can file an *in rem* action against a domain name in the judicial district 'in which the domain name registrar, domain name registry, or other domain name authority . . . is located' (Lanham Trade-Mark Act 43(d)(2)(A), 15 USC: 1125(d)(2)(A) (1998 Supp 2001). For a discussion on this subject, see R Dreyfuss and J Ginsburg, 'Draft Convention on Jurisdiction and Recognition of Judgments in Intellectual Property Matters–Commentary', (2002) 77 Chicago-Kent Law Review 3, p 1100.
[81] N Wilkof, 'Trademarks and the public domain: generic marks and domain names', in H Hansen (ed.), op. cit. (2001), pp 21–9.
[82] WIPO has developed 'soft law' in the form of a Joint Recommendation of the Paris Union Assembly and the General Assembly of WIPO on the protection of marks, and other industrial property rights in signs, on the Internet. See <http://www.wipo.int> (last accessed on 21 May 2005).

available under the Agreement would be applicable to domain name cases in appropriate circumstances.

1.3. Members shall accord the treatment provided for in this Agreement to the nationals of other Members.(1) In respect of the relevant intellectual property right, the nationals of other Members shall be understood as those natural or legal persons that would meet the criteria for eligibility for protection provided for in the Paris Convention (1967), the Berne Convention (1971), the Rome Convention and the Treaty on Intellectual Property in Respect of Integrated Circuits, were all Members of the WTO members of those conventions.(2) Any Member availing itself of the possibilities provided in paragraph 3 of Article 5 or paragraph 2 of Article 6 of the Rome Convention shall make a notification as foreseen in those provisions to the Council for Trade-Related Aspects of Intellectual Property Rights (the 'Council for TRIPS').

(1) *When 'nationals' are referred to in this Agreement, they shall be deemed, in the case of a separate customs territory Member of the WTO, to mean persons, natural or legal, who are domiciled or who have a real and effective industrial or commercial establishment in that customs territory.*

(2) *In this Agreement, 'Paris Convention' refers to the Paris Convention for the Protection of Industrial Property; 'Paris Convention (1967)' refers to the Stockholm Act of this Convention of 14 July 1967. 'Berne Convention' refers to the Berne Convention for the Protection of Literary and Artistic Works; 'Berne Convention (1971)' refers to the Paris Act of this Convention of 24 July 1971. 'Rome Convention' refers to the International Convention for the Protection of Performers, Producers of Phonograms and Broadcasting Organizations, adopted at Rome on 26 October 1961. 'Treaty on Intellectual Property in Respect of Integrated Circuits' (IPIC Treaty) refers to the Treaty on Intellectual Property in Respect of Integrated Circuits, adopted at Washington on 26 May 1989. 'WTO Agreement' refers to the Agreement Establishing the WTO.*

Article 1.3 defines who can benefit from the protection established by the Agreement. The beneficiaries are the 'nationals of other Members'. Footnote 1 clarifies the application of this concept to the nationals of 'separate customs territory Member of the WTO', as in the case of the EC. This footnote also clarifies the concept of 'nationals' of a Member, who include the natural and legal persons who are domiciled *or* who have a real and effective industrial or commercial establishment in that Member. This means that domicile in the territory of a Member is sufficient to qualify for protection. Non-profit organizations, who do not have a 'real and effective industrial or commercial establishment' in a Member also qualify as beneficiaries of protection.

The reference to 'other Members' also makes clear that the Agreement does not apply to purely domestic relations.[83] While domestic laws may not differentiate the treatment given to nationals and foreigners, the former cannot claim any right

---

[83] See, eg, P Katzenberger, 'TRIPS and copyright law', in F Beier and G Schricker (eds), *From GATT to TRIPS—The Agreement on Trade-Related Aspects of Intellectual Property Rights*, (1996:

under the TRIPS Agreement, nor are Members obliged to implement the Agreement's provisions in their regard. What rights nationals are accorded is not a matter for the international treaty.[84]

Who is eligible for protection depends, in the last instance, on what is determined by each Convention referred to in Article 2 of the Agreement.[85]

Under the Paris Convention, protection is conferred to 'nationals' of any country of the Paris Union. No requirement as to domicile or establishment in the country where protection is claimed may be imposed upon nationals of countries of the Union for the enjoyment of any industrial property rights (Article 2(1) and (2). In addition, nationals of countries outside the Union who are domiciled or who have real and effective industrial or commercial establishments in the territory of one of the countries of the Union shall be treated in the same manner as nationals of the countries of the Union (Article 3).

In the Berne Convention, the points of attachment of protection are defined in some cases with respect to the authors and, in other cases, with respect to the works concerned. According to Article 3(1), the protection of this Convention shall apply to:

(a) authors who are nationals of one of the countries of the Union,[86] for their works, whether published or not;

(b) authors who are not nationals of one of the countries of the Union, for their works first published in one of those countries, or simultaneously in a country outside the Union and in a country of the Union.

According to Article 5(1) of the IPIC (which never entered into force), the beneficiaries of protection are:

(i) natural persons who are nationals[87] of, or are domiciled in the territory of, any of the other Contracting Parties, and

(ii) legal entities which or natural persons who, in the territory of any of the other Contracting Parties, have a real and effective establishment for the creation of layout-designs (topographies) or the production of integrated circuits,

In the case of the Rome Convention the point of attachment is exclusively related to the performance. The nationality of the performer was rejected by the

---

Munich, IIC Studies Max Planck Institute for Foreign and International Patent, Copyright and Competition Law), p 70.

[84] This issue was raised, for instance, at the Rome Diplomatic Conference (which adopted the Rome Convention). The US, in particular, emphasized that the Convention covered only 'international situations' (Report of the Rapporteur-General, Records of the Diplomatic Conference on the International Protection of Performers, Producers of Phonograms and Broadcasting Organizations (ILO, UNESCO and BIRPI, Geneva, 1968, p 41).   [85] See pp 44–51 below.

[86] Authors who are not nationals of one of the countries of the Union but who have their habitual residence in one of them shall, for the purposes of this Convention, be assimilated to nationals of that country (Article 3(2) of the Convention).

[87] Article 5(3)clarifies that where the Contracting Party is an Intergovernmental Organization, 'nationals' means nationals of any of the States members of that Organization.

majority of the delegates to the Rome Diplomatic Conference as a criterion of eligibility,[88] and the TRIPS Agreement has not modified this approach,[89] as it provides that 'the nationals of other Members shall be understood as those natural or legal persons that would meet the criteria for eligibility for protection provided for in ... the Rome Convention'. The criteria for the application of the national treatment principle are set out in Article 4 of the Convention:

> Each Contracting State shall grant national treatment to performers if any of the following conditions is met:
>
> (a) the performance takes place in another Contracting State;
> (b) the performance is incorporated in a phonogram which is protected under Article 5 of this Convention;
> (c) the performance, not being fixed on a phonogram, is carried by a broadcast which is protected by Article 6 of this Convention.[90]

The main objective of the approach followed in the TRIPS Agreement on this subject was to allow States to implement remuneration rights in respect of analog sound recordings, without imposing on them the obligation to recognize such rights to countries where they are not granted, such as the US (where remuneration rights are limited to copying of digital media).[91]

The concept of 'nationals' is to be interpreted, in accordance with public international law, as encompassing individuals and legal persons to whom the legislation of the State whose nationality is claimed accords that *status*. In *European Communities–Protection of trademarks and geographical indications for agricultural products and foodstuffs*,[92] noting that neither the Paris Convention nor the TRIPS Agreement specifies the meaning of 'nationals', the panel held that, consistently with public international law,

> With respect to the meaning of 'nationals of other Members' for the purposes of the TRIPS Agreement, WTO Members have, through Article 1.3 of the TRIPS Agreement, incorporated the meaning of 'nationals' as it was understood in the Paris Convention (1967) and under public international law. With respect to natural persons, they refer first to the law of the Member of which nationality is claimed (*footnote omitted*). With respect to legal persons, each Member first applies its own criteria to determine nationality.[93]

While—as stated in the Preamble of the TRIPS Agreement—IPRs are 'private rights', the concept of nationals is to be deemed to also include States, as well as any division thereof if they hold IPRs covered by the Agreement. It is unclear,

---

[88] The main reason for this was that in many cases performances are given by groups composed of performers of different nationalities. See, eg, O Morgan, *International Protection of Performers' Rights* (2002: Oxford and Portland, Hart Publishing), p 129.

[89] The same approach was later adopted by the WPPT.

[90] These conditions need to be read in the light of the definitions contained in Article 3 of the Rome Convention.   [91] See O Morgan op. cit. (2002), pp 130, 133.

[92] Panel Report, WT/DS174/R, 15 March 2005.   [93] Idem, para 7.147.

however, whether the rights held by international organizations would also be subject to the rules of the TRIPS Agreement, unless they hold such rights on behalf of its members.

The panel also considered in *European Communities–Protection of trademarks and geographical indications for agricultural products and foodstuffs* the interpretation of footnote 1 to Article 1.3 of the TRIPS Agreement. It held that

> The text of the TRIPS Agreement contains a recognition that discrimination according to residence and establishment will be a close substitute for nationality. The criteria set out in footnote 1 to the TRIPS Agreement are clearly intended to provide close substitute criteria to determine nationality where criteria to determine nationality as such are not available in a Member's domestic law. These criteria are 'domicile' and 'real and effective industrial or commercial establishment'. They are taken from the criteria used for the assimilation of nationals in Article 3 of the Paris Convention (1967). It is clear that, in using these terms, the drafters of footnote 1 of the TRIPS Agreement chose terms that were already understood in this pre-existing intellectual property convention. Under Article 3 of the Paris Convention (1967), 'domicile' is not generally understood to indicate a legal situation, but rather a more or less permanent residence of a natural person, and an actual headquarters of a legal person. A 'real and effective industrial and commercial establishment' is intended to refer to all but a sham or ephemeral establishment *(footnote omitted)*.[94]

> The object and purpose of the TRIPS Agreement depends on the obligation in Article 1.3 to accord the treatment provided for in the Agreement to the nationals of other Members, including national treatment under Article 3.1. That object and purpose would be severely undermined if a Member could avoid its obligations by simply according treatment to its own nationals on the basis of close substitute criteria, such as place of production, or establishment, and denying treatment to the nationals of other WTO Members who produce or are established in their own countries.[95]

As examined below, the TRIPS Agreement was negotiated with a view to supplement international conventions on intellectual property. It follows a 'Convention-plus' approach, although in some cases[96] also 'Convention-minus' solutions may be found. For this reason, it seems logical that Article 1.3 of the Agreement applies the concept of 'nationals' found in each of the conventions referred to.

Article 1.3 also refers to the particular situation in which a Member avails itself of the possibilities provided in paragraph 3 of Article 5 or paragraph 2 of Article 6 of the Rome Convention. The Member shall make in this case a notification, as foreseen in those provisions, to the Council for Trade-Related Aspects of Intellectual Property Rights (the 'Council for TRIPS').

Finally, footnote 2 clarifies that Members are obliged—to the extent provided for by the Agreement—to comply with the conventions spelled out in accordance with their latest revisions. This requirement aims at narrowing the fragmentation that may

---

[94] Idem, para 7.198.   [95] Idem, para 7.199.
[96] As in the case of authors' moral rights provided for under Article 6*bis* of the Berne Convention. See pp 116–19 below.

be found within WIPO-administered conventions, as contracting parties have been able to adhere to and apply different versions of the Paris and Berne Conventions.

Intellectual Property Conventions

2.1. In respect of Parts II, III and IV of this Agreement, Members shall comply with Articles 1 through 12, and Article 19, of the Paris Convention (1967).

The strategy of the proponents of the TRIPS Agreement aimed at ensuring compliance with the main existing international conventions on IPRs,[97] and supplementing them with additional obligations. The TRIPS Agreement is, in fact, built on the three major conventions on intellectual property and to the Treaty on Intellectual Property in Respect of Integrated Circuits (IPIC). The Agreement does not mention specifically other pre-existing IPR conventions. Article 5 makes, however, a general reference to 'multilateral agreements concluded under the auspices of WIPO'.

The TRIPS Agreement distinguishes between the conventions that need to be complied with, even by countries which have not adhered to them, and one convention (Rome Convention for the Protection of Performers, Producers of Phonograms, and Broadcasting Organizations) that will continue to be binding only for countries that have adopted it. Thus, all Members are obliged to comply with the substantive provisions of the Paris Convention, as well as with rules governing 'special agreements', and with the substantive provisions and the Appendix of the Berne Convention (as revised in 1971). Moreover, the TRIPS Agreement requires all Members to apply (with some exceptions) the standards of protection established under the Washington Treaty (1989) on layout-designs of integrated circuits, notwithstanding that this Treaty never entered into force.

The differentiation made between the Paris Convention, referred to in Article 1.1, and the other conventions (Berne Convention, Rome Convention, and the Treaty on Intellectual Property in Respect of Integrated Circuits) mentioned in Article 2.2 is to be noted.[98] Article 2.1 is formulated in the form of a positive mandate ('...Members shall comply...') and alludes to the 'articles' of the Convention, and to Parts II, III, and IV of the Agreement. Article 2.2, for its part, is negatively formulated ('Nothing...shall derogate from existing obligations...'), and only refers to the 'obligations' that Members may have, but applies to Parts I–IV of the Agreement.

---

[97] The European Community, in particular, advocated the incorporation of provisions of existing intellectual property conventions by reference. See MTN.GNG/NG11/W/20, para 9.

[98] This article also refers to the Paris Convention, thereby emphasizing the need to comply with its obligations and making clear that nothing in Part I of the TRIPS Agreement shall derogate from existing obligations under the Convention.

One important implication of Article 2.1 is that it must be complied with even by Members that are not contracting parties.[99] The use of 'articles' rather than obligations, suggests that the full set of rights and obligations provided for by Articles 1–2 and Article 19 of the Paris Convention are applicable in the context of Parts II, III, and IV of the TRIPS Agreement.

The interpretation of Article 2.1 of the Agreement was briefly addressed by the AB in *United States–Section 211 Omnibus Appropriation Act of 1998 ('Havana Club')*:

Article 2.1 of the *TRIPS Agreement* provides that: '[i]n respect of Parts II, III and IV of this Agreement, Members shall comply with Articles 1 through 12, and Article 19, of the Paris Convention (1967)'. Thus, Article 6*quinquies* of the Paris Convention (1967), as well as certain other specified provisions of the Paris Convention (1967), have been incorporated by reference into the *TRIPS Agreement* and, thus, the *WTO Agreement*.

Consequently, WTO Members, whether they are countries of the Paris Union or not, are obliged, under the *WTO Agreement*, to implement those provisions of the Paris Convention (1967) that are incorporated into the *TRIPS Agreement*. As we have already stated, Article 6 *quinquies* of the Paris Convention (1967) is one such provision.[100]

One divergence between the TRIPS Agreement and the Paris Convention can be found in relation to the national treatment principle. Whereas the Paris Convention requires equivalent treatment for nationals and foreigners, the TRIPS Agreement requires treatment 'no less favourable' than that conferred to nationals (Article 3.1). While Article 2.1 of the Agreement does not apply to its Part I, this Part is expressly referred to in Article 2.2 of the Agreement according to which '[n]othing in Parts I to IV of this Agreement shall derogate from existing obligations that Members may have to each other under the Paris Convention . . .'.

Other situations in which a potential conflict between the Paris Convention and the TRIPS Agreement was debated relate to Article 5.A of the Paris Convention and Article 27.1 of the Agreement,[101] and to a conflict with regard to the right to assign a trademark, which is conditional under the Paris Convention upon the 'transfer of the business or goodwill to which it belongs' (Article 6*quater*), while under the TRIPS Agreement assignment can take place 'with or without the transfer of the business to which the trademark belongs' (Article 21). Thus, the TRIPS Agreement broadens the trademark owner's rights in a manner that, under certain circumstances, may affect consumers, as they may be confused about the source of the marked products. The Paris Convention and the TRIPS Agreement also treat differently the border measures with regard to trade names,

---

[99] While in the past ten years, the membership of the Paris Convention has increased significantly (41 new contracting parties adhered since 1995), during the 1970s many developing countries were reluctant to accept what they considered provisions restrictive of their freedom to regulate industrial property.

[100] Appellate Body Report *United States–Section 211 Omnibus Appropriations Act of 1998*, WT/DS176/AB/R, 2 January 2002, paras 124 and 125.

[101] This issue is further developed at p 48 below.

as under Article 51 of the TRIPS Agreement such measures are only mandatory with regard to copyright pirated goods and false trademarks.

The wording of Article 1.2 ('. . . Members shall comply with . . .') suggests that the Articles of the Paris Convention mentioned therein override the TRIPS Agreement in relation to its Parts II–IV. According to Article 30(2) of the VCLT, when 'a treaty specifies that it is subject to, or that it is not to be considered as incompatible with, an earlier or later treaty, the provisions of that other treaty prevail'. This would mean that, in case of inconsistencies between the Paris Convention and the TRIPS Agreement, the former would apply. This conclusion seems to be confirmed by the express reference in Article 1.2 of the TRIPS Agreement to Article 19 of the Paris Convention, which stipulates that any future agreement between the parties cannot contradict the provisions of the Convention.[102]

It has been held that when the TRIPS Agreement provides for a 'Paris minus' standard of protection (eg, with regard to border measures relating to trade names referred to in Article 9(1) of the Convention, but not mentioned in Article 51 of the TRIPS Agreement), the implication is that Members failing to comply with the Convention standard may not be subject to dispute settlement under WTO rules.[103] However, this can only be true with regard to the obligations contained in Part I of the Agreement, since compliance with the Paris Convention is mandatory in respect of Parts II, III, and IV of the Agreement, as established in its Article 2.1. But enforcement under WTO rules might be sought if issues covered in Parts II, III, or IV of the Agreement were involved.

> **2.2 Nothing in Parts I to IV of this Agreement shall derogate from existing obligations that Members may have to each other under the Paris Convention, the Berne Convention, the Rome Convention and the Treaty on Intellectual Property in Respect of Integrated Circuits.**

Article 2.2 preserves the obligations provided for under the Paris, Berne, and Rome Conventions, and the IPIC Treaty. It makes clear that the TRIPS Agreement is not intended to override such conventions. This provision aims at ensuring that Members do not apply the TRIPS Agreement in a manner that leads to a violation of the obligations under the mentioned conventions.[104] In fact, both the Berne Convention (Article 20) and the Paris Convention (Article 19) contain provisions requiring that special agreements entered into between the contracting parties do not contravene the provisions in those conventions. In addition, Article 2.2 would indicate that in areas not covered by the Agreement (eg utility models), the contracting parties continue to be bound by the respective conventions they have adhered to.

---

[102] A similar provision is contained in Article 20 of the Berne Convention.

[103] Pires de Carvalho, op. cit. (2002), p 72.

[104] The Patent Law Treaty contains a similar obligation with regard to the Paris Convention (Article 15(2)(a)): 'Nothing in this Treaty shall derogate from the obligations that Contracting Parties have to each other under the Paris Convention.'

Three differences between Article 2.2 and Articles 2.1 and 9.1 may be noted. First, Article 2.2 is a non-derogation clause; it does not impose any new obligation. Second, unlike those articles, Article 2.2 only applies to Members that are also parties to the Paris Convention, the Berne Convention, the Rome Convention, and the IPIC Treaty. Third, unlike Articles 2.1 and 9.1, Article 2.2 does not refer to specific Acts of the Conventions. Hence, Members that are parties thereto continue to be bound by the Acts they have subscribed to.

A question arises with regard to certain aspects of the Agreement that may be regarded as 'Convention-minus', as is the case of the moral rights covered by Article 6*bis* of the Paris Convention. The arbitration award in *EC–Bananas* provided a clarification on this point. It held that

This provision can be understood to refer to the obligations that the contracting parties of the Paris, Berne and Rome Conventions and the IPIC Treaty, who are also WTO Members, have between themselves under these four treaties. This would mean that, by virtue of the conclusion of the WTO Agreement, eg Berne Union members cannot derogate from existing obligations between each other under the Berne Convention. For example, the fact that Article 9.1 of the TRIPS Agreement incorporates into that Agreement Articles 1–21 of the Berne Convention with the exception of Article 6*bis* does not mean that Berne Union members would henceforth be exonerated from this obligation to guarantee moral rights under the Berne Convention.[105]

It has been argued[106] that the provisions in the Paris Convention and Berne Convention that allow contracting parties either to limit the scope of a right or impose formalities do not create obligations and may, hence, be derogated from the TRIPS Agreement. While Article 2.2 only refers to the non-derogation of 'obligations', one of the basic obligations[107] of the contracting parties is to respect the rights recognized by the Convention to other contracting parties (*pacta sunt servanda*). In addition, that argument ignores that Articles 2.1 and 9.1 incorporate the 'Articles' of the Paris Convention and of the Berne Convention, respectively. The second sentence of Article 9.1, which refers to 'rights or obligations', seems to confirm that the 'Articles' of the Conventions need to be taken integrally into account. If the framers of the Agreement wanted to limit the incorporation of the Conventions to the obligations provided for, they could have opted for the method used for the incorporation of the IPIC in Article 35 of the Agreement, which specifically excludes provisions of the Treaty limiting the scope of rights conferred.[108]

---

[105] See *European Communities–Regime for the Importation, Sale and Distribution of Bananas—Recourse to Arbitration by the European Communities under Article 22.6 of the DSU*—Decision by the Arbitrators, WT/DS27/ARB/ECU, para 149.   [106] See, eg, Gervais op. cit. (2003), p 95.

[107] The equivalent provision in the FTA between the US and Chile (2004) alludes to both *rights* and *obligations* of one Party with respect to the other under all the multilateral treaties concluded or negotiated in the framework of WIPO. The reference to 'rights' does not seem to entail, however, a substantive difference from Article 2.2 of the TRIPS Agreement.   [108] See p 10 below.

Thus, Article 5A of the Paris Convention recognizes the right of a Contracting Party to grant, under certain circumstances, compulsory licences. The other parties cannot challenge such grant, if consistent with the provisions of the Convention. The US filed a complaint against Brazil alleging that the Brazilian compulsory licensing system was in violation of Article 27.1, to the extent that it established a local working obligation for patented inventions, thereby discriminating against imported products. Although the case was not finally subject to dispute resolution, Brazil was likely to invoke in its defence the right recognized by Article 5A(2) of the Paris Convention[109] to grant compulsory licenses to remedy abuses, such as the lack of working.[110] Given the linkage between the TRIPS Agreement and the Paris Convention, as established by Articles 2.1 and 2.2, and in view also of Article 19 of the Paris Convention, such compulsory licences are arguably not challengeable under the TRIPS Agreement.

The incorporation of the provisions of the above-mentioned Conventions has systemic implications for the system set forth by the TRIPS Agreement. Those Conventions have been in force for a long time (more than one century in the case of the Paris and Berne Conventions) and a significant body of State practice has developed around them. The Vienna Convention stipulates how 'subsequent practice in the application of the treaty' (Article 31.3(b)) is to be utilized for interpretive purposes, but is silent about *prior* practice. The jurisprudence already developed around the TRIPS Agreement suggests, however, a tendency of the panels and the AB to rely heavily as an auxiliary source of interpretation, on precedents related to the negotiation of said Conventions and their revision. Therefore, a negotiation that took place more than one hundred years ago, such as in the case of the Paris Convention, may be used as a supplementary means of interpretation of the Agreement.

Thus in *Canada–Patent Protection for Pharmaceutical Products*, the panel noted that in the framework of the TRIPS Agreement, which incorporates certain provisions of the major pre-existing international instruments on intellectual property, the context to which the panel may have recourse for purposes of interpretation of specific TRIPS provisions is not restricted to the text, Preamble and Annexes of the TRIPS Agreement itself, but also includes the provisions of the international instruments on intellectual property incorporated into the TRIPS Agreement,[111]

---

[109] Article 5A(2): 'Each country of the Union shall have the right to take legislative measures providing for the grant of compulsory licenses to prevent the abuses which might result from the exercise of the exclusive rights conferred by the patent, for example, failure to work.'

[110] Both Article 5a(2) of the Paris Convention and Article 8.1 of the TRIPS Agreement refer to 'abuse', strongly suggesting that the 'appropriate measures' referred to in the latter includes compulsory licences consistently with Article 31 if the Agreement. See P Champ and A Attaran, 'Patent rights and local working under the WTO TRIPS Agreement: an analysis of the US–Brazil patent dispute' (2002) 27 Yale J Int'l L, p 365.

[111] In this case, the panel considered the negotiating history of Article 9(2) of the Berne Convention, from which part of the text of Article 30 of the TRIPS Agreement was drawn. See WTO *Canada–Patent Protection for Pharmaceutical Products*, WT/DS114/R, 17 March 2000, paras 7.70–7.72.

as well as any agreement between the parties relating to these agreements within the meaning of Article 31(2) of the Vienna Convention on the Law of Treaties. Also, in *United States–Section 110(5) of the US Copyright Act*, the panel supported its interpretation by reference to the negotiating history of the Berne Convention that has become part of the TRIPS Agreement.[112]

In *United States–Section 211 Omnibus Appropriations Act of 1998*, the panel had used the preparatory work of the Paris Convention (1967). The EC argued that such an invocation was erroneous under Article 32 of the Vienna Convention, since none of the conditions for the application of that rule were present in this case and the history of the Paris Convention failed to provide a clear indication of the intentions of the negotiators. The Appellate Body, however, relied on the negotiating history of the Paris Convention in order to confirm its own interpretation of Article 6*quinquies*B of the Convention.[113]

This jurisprudence indicates a clear inclination by panels and the Appellate Body to firmly consider the obligations emanating from the IPR conventions incorporated in the TRIPS Agreement as forming part of the set of Members' obligations under the Agreement, as well as to have recourse to the negotiating history of the Conventions to confirm their own interpretations. This approach may put an unexpected burden on developing countries, since many of them were not parties to the Conventions at the time of the adoption of the Agreement, or were not familiar with developments with respect to the Conventions. The full integration of the obligations imposed by the Conventions may, however, in some cases support developing country claims, such as in the case of Article 5A of the Paris Convention as a basis for legitimizing the granting of compulsory licences due to the lack or insufficient local working of a patented invention.[114]

An issue open to discussion is whether IPRs international conventions (pre- or post-TRIPS) that are not incorporated by reference to the TRIPS Agreement could play some role in the interpretation of the provisions of the TRIPS Agreement. Two approaches have been articulated on the extent to which WTO panels are entitled to rely on international law to interpret WTO provisions. Howse has argued that 'the substantive normativity of the entire international system should be brought to bear on the interpretation of WTO law, as relevant, and indeed that the adjudicator should seek a fit between her readings of specific provisions of WTO law and her construction or imagination of the entire international legal system'.[115] This

---

[112] See Appellate Body Report, WT/DS160/AB/R, 15 June 2005, para 6.18. The panel held that the 'minor exceptions' doctrine—not formally incorporated either in Berne or in the TRIPS Agreement—was part of the 'Berne *acquis*' (paras 6.60–6.66)

[113] See Appelate Body Report, WT/DS176/AB/R, 2 January 2002, paras 145–6.

[114] See the submission by the African Group, Barbados, Bolivia, Brazil, Cuba, Dominican Republic, Ecuador, Honduras, India, Indonesia, Jamaica, Pakistan, Paraguay, Philippines, Peru, Sri Lanka, Thailand, and Venezuela, TRIPS and Public Health, IP/C/W/296, 29 June 2001, para 31.

[115] R Howse, 'The jurisprudential achievement of the WTO Appellate Body: a preliminary appreciation', available at <http://www.law.nyu.edu/kingsburyb/spring03/globalization/robhowsepaper.pdf> (last accessed on 25 May 2005).

approach would support the interpretation of WTO agreements both in the light of pre-existing and evolving international law. While the AB reasoning in *United States–Import Prohibition of Certain Shrimp and Shrimp Products*[116] can be read as having broad implications in this regard—even beyond a straightforward application of the Vienna Convention[117]—embracing a purely evolutionary approach in the field of IPRs may deepen the unbalances that are already present in the TRIPS Agreement, as intellectual property law continues to evolve towards broader and higher levels of protection, in particular, to capture new technological developments such as digital technology.[118] Should the panels and Appellate Body apply an evolutionary interpretation of TRIPS rules in the light of such developments, higher standards of protection adopted in response to demands from industries from developed countries may become part of the interpretive framework for the TRIPS Agreement.

Article 71 of the TRIPS Agreement specifically provides for the TRIPS Council to review the Agreement 'in the light of any relevant new developments, which might warrant modification or amendment of this Agreement'. This makes clear that amendments or adaptations cannot be made via interpretation. The panels and Appellate Body should confine themselves to the meaning of the terms as understood at the time of their adoption, to the extent that an evolutionary interpretation would lead to imposing obligations not negotiated and accepted during the Uruguay Round.

In *Canada–Patent Protection for Pharmaceutical Products*, the panel examined the status of the legislation *at the time of the negotiation* of the Agreement to determine the concept of 'legitimate interest' as contained in Article 30. In the panel's opinion, on balance:

the interest claimed on behalf of patent owners whose effective period of market exclusivity had been reduced by delays in marketing approval was neither so compelling nor so widely recognized that it could be regarded as a 'legitimate interest' within the meaning of Article 30 of the TRIPS Agreement, notwithstanding the number of governments that had responded positively to that claim. Moreover, the Panel believed that it was significant that concerns about regulatory review exceptions in general, although well known at the time of the TRIPS negotiations, were apparently not clear enough, or compelling enough, to make their way explicitly into the recorded agenda of the TRIPS negotiation. The Panel believed that Article 30's 'legitimate interests' concept should not be used to decide,

---

[116] The AB held that certain terms in the WTO Agreements are not 'static' but evolutionary (in relation to the term 'exhaustible natural resources' as it appears in GATT Article XX(g), adopted more than fifty years ago). Report of the Appellate Body, WT/DS58/AB/R (1998), paras 127, 130.

[117] See Howse op. cit. (2005).

[118] For instance, in 1996, very shortly after the adoption of the TRIPS Agreement, two new treaties were adopted by the World Intellectual Property Organization (WIPO) relating to copyright and related rights: the WIPO Performances and Phonograms Treaty (WPPT), 20 December 1996 and the WIPO Copyright Treaty (WCT), 20 December 1996.

through adjudication, a normative policy issue that is still obviously a matter of unresolved political debate.[119]

However, in the report in the *United States–Section 110(5) of the US Copyright Act* case, the panel stated that the WIPO Copyright Treaty of 1996 should be viewed as 'relevant to seek contextual guidance . . . when developing interpretations that avoid conflicts within the overall multilateral copyright framework . . .'[120] Although the panel cautioned that the statement concerning WCT Article 10 adopted by the signatory parties did not fall under the Vienna Convention rules on a subsequent treaty on the same matter or subsequent practice,[121] the recourse to a post-TRIPS treaty—not even in force—constitutes a troubling precedent[122] as long as it may lead to interpretations of the TRIPS Agreement well beyond its own boundaries.

The GATT negotiating parties reached a delicate balance when adopting the TRIPS Agreement. Reading in it what was not negotiated 'would be equivalent to a renegotiation of the basic balance of the Agreement', as noted by the panel while examining Article 30 thereof in *Canada–Patent Protection for Pharmaceutical Products*.[123] This does not mean that the TRIPS Agreement should be seen as a bargain fixed by the intentions or expectations of the 'contracting parties' at the time it was made, since such intentions and expectations obviously differed significantly among the parties. It simply means that interpreting bodies should respect the basic rule that prevents panels and the Appellate Body from adding rights and obligations when adjudicating disputes (Article 3.2 of the DSU) through a constructionist interpretation of international law.

National treatment

3.1. Each Member shall accord to the nationals of other Members treatment no less favourable than that it accords to its own nationals with regard to the protection[3] of intellectual property, subject to the exceptions already provided in, respectively, the Paris Convention (1967), the Berne Convention (1971), the Rome Convention or the Treaty on Intellectual Property in Respect of

---

[119] WT DS114/R, 17 March 2000, para 7.82. This approach is consistent with the general principle of treaty interpretation requiring that the meaning of the terms of a treaty be considered at the time of its signature. On the importance of the principle of 'contemporaneity' in treaty interpretation, see Ian Brownlie, *Principles of Public International Law 627* (1998: Oxford, Oxford University Press).   [120] Appellate Body Report, WT/DS160/AB/R, 5 June 2005, para 6.70.

[121] Idem, para 6.69.

[122] According to S Williams, this was one of the panel's 'most adventurous remarks' and 'an aberration from the Panel's otherwise constructionist approach' (S Williams, 'Developing TRIPS Jurisprudence—The First Six Years and Beyond', (2001), 4(2) The Journal of World Intellectual Property 191, p 203.

[123] Appellate Body Report, WT/DS176/AB/R, 2 January 2002, para 7.26.

Nature and Scope of Obligations

Integrated Circuits. In respect of performers, producers of phonograms and broadcasting organizations, this obligation only applies in respect of the rights provided under this Agreement. Any Member availing itself of the possibilities provided in Article 6 of the Berne Convention (1971) or paragraph 1(b) of Article 16 of the Rome Convention shall make a notification as foreseen in those provisions to the Council for TRIPS.

2. Members may avail themselves of the exceptions permitted under paragraph 1 in relation to judicial and administrative procedures, including the designation of an address for service or the appointment of an agent within the jurisdiction of a Member, only where such exceptions are necessary to secure compliance with laws and regulations which are not inconsistent with the provisions of this Agreement and where such practices are not applied in a manner which would constitute a disguised restriction on trade.

   3 For the purposes of Articles 3 and 4, 'protection' shall include matters affecting the availability, acquisition, scope, maintenance and enforcement of intellectual property rights as well as those matters affecting the use of intellectual property rights specifically addressed in this Agreement.

Three major principles are established by the TRIPS Agreement: national treatment, most favoured nation, and international exhaustion of rights.

The principle of national treatment has been an outstanding and common feature in the pre-TRIPS international conventions on IPRs. In the opinion of the AB, national treatment has been the 'cornerstone of the Paris Convention and other intellectual property conventions'.[124] At the inception of the IPR international system, countries basically aimed at preventing discrimination against their nationals, rather than ensuring that the same level of protection be granted in foreign countries. This objective has been pursued, in the Paris Convention and subsequent IPR international conventions, by recognizing the principle of national treatment.

The national treatment principle essentially protects against discrimination of foreigners vis-à-vis nationals. It means that each contracting party should accord to the nationals of other parties no less favourable treatment than it accords to its own nationals. While the principle restrains the room for manoeuvre for countries to provide more favourable conditions to their own nationals, it leaves great flexibility to design the IPR national laws and policies, as the principle as such does not commit States to provide certain levels of protection. The protection of industrial property was essentially built up under the Paris Convention on the basis of that principle.[125] Other pre-TRIPS conventions, however, included both that principle and an important set of standards to be complied with. Thus, Article 5(1) of the Berne Convention provides that '[A]uthors shall enjoy, in respect of works for which they are protected under this Convention, in countries of the Union other than the country of origin, the rights which their respective laws do now or may

---

   124 *United States–Section 211 Omnibus Appropriations Act of 1998*, Appellate Body Report, WT/DS176/AB/R, 2 January 2002, para 241.
   125 See, eg, E Penrose, *The Economics of the International Patent System* (1951: Johns Hopkins Press).

hereafter grant to their nationals, *as well as the rights specially granted by this Convention*' (emphasis added). Similarly, the Rome Convention specified that 'national treatment shall be subject to the protection specifically guaranteed, and the limitations specifically provided for, in this Convention' (Article 2(2)).

The national treatment principle has been retained in the TRIPS Agreement, jointly with detailed minimum standards that limit the flexibility inherent thereto. Its incorporation means that that principle will now be applied in the context of the GATT/WTO jurisprudence on the matter,[126] despite the fact that such jurisprudence developed with regard to 'like products' and not persons, as is the case under the TRIPS Agreement.[127] One implication of this development is that compliance with national treatment is to be judged in the light of that jurisprudence, in relation to both *de jure* and *de facto* discrimination.

A key aspect for the interpretation of Article 3.1 is the concept of 'nationals'. This was extensively addressed, as noted above, in *European Communities– Protection of trademarks and geographical indications for agricultural products and foodstuffs*.[128] The panel noted in this case the need to define not only the concept of other Members' nationals but also that of a Member's 'own nationals', as it refers to the treatment that each Member accords to them as the benchmark for its obligation to accord national treatment under Article 3.1, as well as under the other national treatment obligations incorporated by reference, including Article 2 of the Paris Convention (1967). The panel considered that the criteria to determine who the 'own nationals' are appear to be the same as those used in public international law. Therefore, the panel used them to determine which persons are 'nationals' under Article 3.1 of the TRIPS Agreement.[129]

A violation to the principle of national treatment may occur under two different circumstances:[130]

(a) Rules in the national law that formally accord more favourable treatment to nationals vis-à-vis foreigners (*de jure* discrimination):

A violation to the national treatment principle may be found in these situations, but this is not automatically the case. Differential treatment may be provided for, but still be consistent with that treatment. Article 3.1 of the TRIPS Agreement refers, as examined below, to one such case (differentiation with regard to judicial and administrative procedures), albeit in terms more restrictive than in the Paris Convention.

---

[126] See the Appellate Body Report in *United States–Section 211 Omnibus Appropriations Act of 1998*, WT/DS176/AB/R, 2 January 2002, where it is argued that the jurisprudence on Article III.4 of GATT will be instrumental in interpreting Article 3 of the TRIPS Agreement (para 242). See also *European Communities–Protection of trademarks and geographical indications for agricultural products and foodstuffs*, para 7.135.

[127] The same applies in the case of the General Agreement on Services (GATS), though Members have flexibility in this case to determine which sectors are subject or not to that principle (Article XVII).

[128] Panel Report, WT/DS174/R, 15 March 2005.   [129] Idem, para 7.150.

[130] See generally, eg, UNCTAD–ICTSD op. cit. (2005), pp 75–7.

Whether a *de jure* differentiation between nationals and foreigners to the apparent prejudice of the latter would survive the scrutiny under the national treatment principle in a WTO dispute, will depend on the circumstances of each case. Despite that such differentiation is not banned, the complained country is likely to be required to prove that it is not in violation to that principle. In the *United States–Sector 211 Omnibus Appropriations Act of 1998* case, the AB held that the differentiation made in the complained US legislation suggested a *prima facie* case of discrimination.[131] This amounted to a shift in the burden of proof to the complained party.

Another issue is the assessment about the likelihood and importance of the discriminatory effect caused by the legal differentiation. The discriminatory effect may be immediate or remote, significant or small. This issue was raised and examined in the referred to *Havana Club* case, leading to a sharp difference of opinion between the panel and the AB. The panel disregarded the formal legal differences between the way US nationals and foreign nationals were treated and held that the US legislation regulating trademarks that had been confiscated by the Cuban government was not inconsistent with Article 3 of the TRIPS Agreement.[132]

The AB dissented with this opinion, and interpreted Article 3 of the TRIPS Agreement in a way that leaves a narrow margin for a *de jure* differentiation that discriminates against foreign nationals. Relying on prior GATT jurisprudence,[133] the AB articulated a very strict standard, as it concluded that even 'even the *possibility* that non-United States successors-in-interest face two hurdles is *inherently less favourable* than the undisputed fact that United States successors-in-interest face only one'.[134]

(b) Rules that formally treat on an equal footing nationals and foreigners, but the *effect* of which may be deemed discriminatory:

One possible situation of *de facto* discrimination may arise, for instance, when copyright collecting societies distribute revenues to national authors only, as is generally the case when there are no reciprocal arrangements with other countries.[135]

A GATT panel was given the opportunity to scrutinize a situation of *de facto* discrimination in relation to Section 337 of the US Tariff Act. This section was found inconsistent with the GATT in *United States–Section 337 of the Tariff Act of 1930*,[136] since it accorded less favorable treatment to imported products challenged as infringing US patents than the treatment accorded to similarly challenged

---

[131] *United States–Section 110(5) of the US Copyright Act*, Appellate Body Report, WT/DS160/R, 15 June 2000, Appellate Body Report *United States–Section 211 Omnibus Appropriations Act of 1998*, WT/DS176/AB/R, para 281.   [132] UNCTAD–ICTSD op. cit. (2005), p 83.

[133] *United States–Section 337 of the Tariff Act of 1930 Panel Report*, adopted 7 November 1989, BISD 36S/345.

[134] Appellate Body Report, Havana Club WT/DS176/AB/R, para 265.

[135] See, eg, J Watal, *Intellectual Property Rights in the WTO and Developing Countries* (2001: The Hague, Kluwer Law International), pp 213–14. This situation is not subject, however, to the rules contained in the TRIPS Agreement.

[136] *United States–Section 337 of the Tariff Act of 1930 Panel Report*, adopted 7 November 1989, BISD 36S/345.

products of United States origin.[137] In *Canada–Patent Protection for Pharmaceutical Products* the panel considered that claims against both formal and practical discrimination are possible under the TRIPS Agreement.[138] Likewise, in *European Communities–Protection of trademarks and geographical indications for agricultural products and foodstuffs*, the panel observed that 'on its face, the [EC] Regulation contains formally identical provisions vis-à-vis the nationals of different Members, with respect to the availability of GI protection',[139] but it 'is well recognized that the concept of 'no less favourable' treatment under Article III:4 of GATT 1994 is sufficiently broad to include situations where the application of formally identical legal provisions would in practice accord less favourable treatment'.[140] Accordingly, the panel considered that

> even if the provisions of the Regulation are formally identical in the treatment that they accord to the nationals of other Members and to the European Communities' own nationals, this is not sufficient to demonstrate that there is no violation of Article 3.1 of the TRIPS Agreement. Whether or not the Regulation accords less favourable treatment to the nationals of other Members than it accords to the European Communities' own nationals should be examined instead according to the standard we set out at paragraph 7.134, namely, the 'effective equality of opportunities' with regard to the protection of intellectual property rights.[141]

The panel added in this respect that

> the standard of examination is based on 'effective equality of opportunities'. It follows that the nationals that are relevant to an examination under Article 3.1 of the TRIPS Agreement should be those who seek opportunities with respect to the same type of intellectual property in comparable situations (*footnote omitted*). On the one hand, this excludes a comparison of opportunities for nationals with respect to different categories of intellectual property, such as GIs and copyright. On the other hand, no reason has been advanced as to why the equality of opportunities should be limited a priori to rights with a territorial link to a particular Member.[142]

The relationship between the national treatment principle in the pre-TRIPS conventions and in the TRIPS Agreement raises some interesting questions. Since Members are obliged to comply with the obligations contained in the Paris Convention, the Berne Convention, and the IPIC (Articles 2.1, 9.1, and 35 of the TRIPS Agreement), the principle would in any case apply to subject matter

---

[137] (The USA 'hesitantly effected an amendment of Sec. 337 in 1994 in order to improve the position of foreign respondents, but left the substance of the proceedings unchanged'. M Haedicke, 'US Imports, TRIPS and Section 337 of the Tariff Act of 1930', (2000) International Review of Industrial Property and Copyright Law, 31 (7/8), p 774.) Although the express maximum time limits of twelve and eighteen months were abolished, the Section 337 proceedings still needed to be concluded by the International Trade Commission (ITC) 'at the earliest practicable time', and within 45 days after the initiation of the proceedings the ITC had to establish a target date for its final determination. If the complainant requested an exclusion order during the investigation, a determination with regard to that petition had to be made within the relatively short period of ninety days.

[138] *Canada—Pharmaceutical Patents*, WT/DS114/R, 17 March 2000 paras 7.100–7.105.
[139] Panel Report WT/DS174/R, 15 March 2005, para 7.172.   [140] Idem, para 7.173.
[141] Idem, para 7.176.   [142] Idem, para 7.181.

protected under such conventions and could be enforced through WTO dispute settlement mechanisms.

The provision of Article 3 of the TRIPS Agreement, however, ensures that the principle is applicable with regard to subject matter (eg test data) and rights (eg, exclusive rental rights for computer programs) not covered by such conventions but dealt with in the Agreement. It has also been argued that Article 3 is necessary with regard to the Agreement's provisions on enforcement of rights, as procedures for enforcement of IPRs are not covered by said conventions.[143] Since, as examined below,[144] the Rome Convention has not been incorporated into the Agreement in the same manner as the Paris and Berne Conventions and the Washington Treaty, the national treatment principle of the Agreement is clearly necessary with regard to the 'related' rights provided for therein.

The TRIPS Agreement requires the granting to nationals of other Members of 'treatment no less favourable than that it accords to its own nationals'. This formulation implies, as mentioned, that foreigners could be given a treatment more favourable than nationals. It is unclear why the well-established formula of the pre-TRIPS conventions was so amended and why a country might opt to discriminate against its own nationals in this way. The most plausible explanation is the influence of Article III of GATT—which is based on a 'no-less-favourable-standard'—despite the fact that it does not apply to natural and legal persons as such, but to traded goods.

The pre-TRIPS conventions mandated that foreigners be given the same treatment as nationals. Thus, the Paris Convention provides in Article 2(1) that:

Nationals of any country of the Union shall, as regards the protection of industrial property, enjoy in all the other countries of the Union the advantages that their respective laws now grant, or may hereafter grant, to nationals; all without prejudice to the rights specially provided for by this Convention. Consequently, they shall have the same protection as the latter, and the same legal remedy against any infringement of their rights, provided that the conditions and formalities imposed upon nationals are complied with.

The Berne Convention provides in Article 5(1):

Authors shall enjoy, in respect of works for which they are protected under this Convention, in countries of the Union other than the country of origin, *the rights which their respective laws do now or may hereafter grant to their nationals*, as well as the rights specially granted by this Convention.

May a Member that applies the national treatment standard as contained in the Paris Convention or the Berne Convention be deemed in violation of Article 3 of

---

[143] See, with regard to the Berne Convention, Katzenberger op. cit. (1996), pp 73–4. In the case of the Paris Convention, Article 3 provides that 'Nationals of countries outside the Union who are domiciled or who have real and effective industrial or commercial establishments in the territory of one of the countries of the Union shall be treated in the same manner as nationals of the countries of the Union'.

[144] See p 155 below.

the TRIPS Agreement? The reply to this question is rather complex. The TRIPS Agreement does not specifically incorporate the national treatment provision of the Paris Convention, as Article 2.1 applies only '[I]n respect of Parts II, III and IV' of the Agreement, thereby leaving out Part I where the national treatment obligation is provided for. However, Article 9.1 of the Agreement does not make this differentiation in the case of the Berne Convention.

The observed difference in the national treatment principle between the Paris Convention and the TRIPS Agreement was practically unnoticed in the *United States–Section 211 Omnibus Appropriations Act of 1998* case,[145] where the principles of both instruments were deemed applicable. In this case, the AB stressed the fundamental nature of the national treatment principle in the context of the TRIPS Agreement, and stated that the jurisprudence developed with regard to Article III:4 of GATT 'may be useful in interpreting the national treatment obligation in the TRIPS Agreement'.[146] This observation needs to be taken with caution, as in the case of the TRIPS Agreement, as noted, the national treatment applies to right-holders and not to goods. The AB itself was prudent in indicating that such jurisprudence was 'useful' for the interpretation of the Agreement, thereby implying that it can be invoked as a reference but not as a precedent with decisive weight.[147]

In *Indonesia-Cars*,[148] however, the panel refused to interpret the national treatment principle of the TRIPS Agreement in relation to the maintenance of trademarks as preventing the grant of tariff, subsidies, or other measures of support to national companies on the grounds that this would render the maintenance of trademark rights by foreign companies wishing to export to the respective market 'relatively more difficult'.[149]

---

[145] Appellate Body, *United States–Section 211 Omnibus Appropriations Act of 1998*, WT/DS176/AB/R, 2 January 2002, para 240. In *European Communities–Protection of trademarks and geographical indications for agricultural products and foodstuffs*, Panel Report WT/DS174/R, 15 March 2005, the panel refused to consider differences between the TRIPS Agreement and the Paris Convention ('. . . the panel observes that, unlike Article 3.1 of the TRIPS Agreement, Article 2(1) of the Paris Convention (1967) refers to "the advantages that . . . laws now grant, or may hereafter grant" and not to "no less favourable" treatment. Therefore, the Panel has not actually reached a conclusion on this claim. However, further findings on this claim would not provide any additional contribution to a positive solution to this dispute and are therefore unnecessary', para 7.216).

[146] Appellate Body, WT/DS176/AB/R, 2 January 2002, *United-States–Section 211 Omnibus Appropriations Act of 1998*, at 242. Further, in Panel Report, WT/DS174/R, 15 March 2005, the panel noted that 'there is no hierarchy between the TRIPS Agreement and GATT 1994, which appear in separate annexes to the WTO Agreement. The ordinary meaning of the texts of the TRIPS Agreement and GATT 1994, as well as Article II:2 of the WTO Agreement, taken together, indicates that obligations under the TRIPS Agreement and GATT 1994 can co-exist and that one does not override the other. This is analogous to the finding of the Panel in *Canada–Periodicals*, with which the Appellate Body agreed, concerning the respective scopes of GATS and GATT 1994 (*footnote omitted*). Further, a "harmonious interpretation" does not require an interpretation of one that shadows the contours of the other. It is well established that the covered agreements apply cumulatively and that consistency with one does not necessarily imply consistency with them all', para 7.208.

[147] In any case, the panel and AB rulings do not have, in the WTO system, precedential value.

[148] See WT/DS54/R, 2 July 1998.   [149] Idem, para 14.273.

The concept of 'less favourable' was addressed by the panel in *European Communities–Protection of trademarks and geographical indications for agricultural products and foodstuffs*. Relying on WTO case law[150] relating to the examination of whether a measure involves 'less favourable treatment' of imported products within the meaning of Article III:4 of the GATT 1994, the panel opined that such examination must be grounded on close scrutiny of the 'fundamental thrust and effect of the measure itself'.[151] The panel differentiated this assessment from that required under the TRIPS Agreement:

in the present dispute, the Panel considers it appropriate to base its examination under Article 3.1 of the TRIPS Agreement on the fundamental thrust and effect of the Regulation, including an analysis of its terms and its practical implications. However, as far as the TRIPS Agreement is concerned, the relevant practical implications are those on opportunities with regard to the protection of intellectual property. The implications in the marketplace for the agricultural products and foodstuffs in respect of which GIs may be protected are relevant to the examination under Article III:4 of GATT 1994....[152]

The panel found an inconsistency between the national treatment principle as contained in the TRIPS Agreement and the Council Regulation (EEC) No 2081/92 of 14 July 1992 on the protection of geographical indications and designations of origin for agricultural products and foodstuffs, as amended, and its related implementing and enforcement measures. It held that:

Although the parties disagree on whether the equivalence and reciprocity conditions in Article 12(1) of the Regulation discriminate in a manner inconsistent with the covered agreements, it is not disputed that those conditions accord less favourable treatment to persons with interests in the *GIs* to which those conditions apply (*footnote omitted*). The Panel considers that those conditions modify the effective equality of opportunities to obtain protection with respect to intellectual property in two ways. First, GI protection is not available under the Regulation in respect of geographical areas located in third countries which the Commission has not recognized under Article 12(3). The European Communities confirm that the Commission has not recognized any third countries. Second, GI protection under the Regulation may become available if the third country in which the GI is located enters into an international agreement or satisfies the conditions in Article 12(1). Both of those requirements represent a significant 'extra hurdle' in obtaining GI protection that does not apply to geographical areas located in the European Communities (*footnote omitted*). The significance of the hurdle is reflected in the fact that currently no third country has entered into such an agreement or satisfied those conditions.[153]

Accordingly, the Panel finds that the equivalence and reciprocity conditions modify the effective equality of opportunities with respect to the availability of protection to persons who wish to obtain GI protection under the Regulation, to the detriment of those who wish to obtain protection in respect of geographical areas located in third countries, including WTO Members. This is less favourable treatment.[154]

---

150 Appellate Body Report, *US–FSC (Article 21.5–EC)*, para 215.
151 Panel Report, WT/DS174/R, 15 March 2005, para 7.136.
152 Idem, para 7.137.   153 Idem, para 7.139.   154 Idem, para 7.140.

The application of the national treatment principle had been qualified in the pre-TRIPS conventions by a number of exceptions. The TRIPS Agreement incorporates that principle subject to the exceptions specifically provided under the Paris Convention, the Berne Convention, the Rome Convention, and the Washington Treaty on integrated circuits. The preservation of exceptions to the national treatment principle recognizes that reciprocity has often been required under IPRs laws[155] and treaties.[156] In most cases, such exceptions can be directly applied by Members.[157] In two cases, however, they are conditional upon notification to the Council for TRIPS, as indicated.

The exceptions to national treatment provided for under the Conventions and Treaty referred to are the following:[158]

Paris Convention

i) the provisions of the laws of each of the countries party to the Paris Convention relating to judicial or administrative procedure and to jurisdiction, which may be required by the laws on industrial property, are expressly reserved (Article 2(3));

ii) the provisions of the laws of each of the countries party to the Paris Convention relating to the designation of an address for service or the appointment of an agent, which may be required by the laws on industrial property, are expressly reserved (Article 2(3)).

Berne Convention

i) where a work is protected in the country or origin solely as an industrial design—and not (also) as a work of applied art, ie, by copyright law—that work is entitled in another country party to the Berne Convention only to such special protection as is granted in that country to industrial designs—even though copyright protection is available in that country (Article 2(7), second sentence, first part);

ii) where a country not party to the Berne Convention fails to protect in an adequate manner the works of authors who are nationals of one of the countries

---

[155] eg the US Semiconductor Chip Protection Act (1984) provided for substantive reciprocity. See also the European Directive on the Protection of Data Bases (Directive 96/9/EC, 11 March 1996, Article 11).

[156] See, eg, Article 3(3) of the UPOV Convention 1978 ('Notwithstanding the provisions of paragraph (1) and paragraph (2), any member State of the Union applying this Convention to a given genus or species shall be entitled to limit the benefit of the protection to the nationals of those member States of the Union which apply this Convention to that genus or species and to natural and legal persons resident or having their registered office in any of those States').

[157] For example, the possibility of limiting the term of protection to that determined in the country of origin of a copyrighted work, in accordance with Article 7(8) of the Berne Convention.

[158] Based on WIPO, Beneficiaries of and Exceptions to National Treatment under Treaties Administered By WIPO, Communication from the World Intellectual Property Organization, MTN.GNG/NG11/W/66, 28 February 1990.

party to the Berne Convention, the latter country may restrict the protection given—on the basis of their first publication in that country—to the works of authors who are, at the date of the first publication thereof, nationals of the other country and are not habitually resident in one of the countries party to the Berne Convention; if the country of first publication avails itself of this right, the other countries party to the Berne Convention are not required to grant to works thus subjected to special treatment a wider protection than that granted to them in the country of first publication (Article 6(1));

iii) in the country where protection is claimed, the term of protection shall not, unless the legislation of that country otherwise provides, exceed the term fixed in the country of origin of the work (Article 7(8));

iv) the right (*'droit de suite'*), enjoyed by the author, or, after his death, by the persons or institutions authorized by national legislation, to an interest in any sale of the work—which is either an original work of art or an original manu-script of a writer or composer—subsequent to the first transfer by the author of the work may be claimed in a country party to the Berne Convention only if legislation in the country to which the author belongs so permits, and to the extent permitted by the country where this right is claimed (Article 14*ter*(1) and (2));

v) in relation to the right of translation of works whose country of origin is a country—other than certain developing countries—which, having used the limited possibility of reservations available in that respect,[159] has declared its intention to apply the provisions on the right of translation contained in the Berne Convention of 1886 as completed by the Additional Act of Paris of 1896 (concerning the restriction, under certain conditions, of the term of protection of the right of translation to ten years from the first publication of the work), any country has the right to apply a protection which is equivalent to the protection granted by the country of origin (Article 30(2)(b), second sentence).

Rome Convention

i) Article 15 of the Rome Convention allows for certain fair use exceptions to protection.

ii) Article 16(1)(a)(iii) and (iv) allow for limitations on the obligation to pay equitable remuneration for secondary uses of phonograms based, inter alia, on reciprocity.[160]

iii) Article 16(1)(b) allows contracting states to exempt protection of television broadcasts in public places, permitting affected states to withdraw such protection.

---

[159] Only four States have maintained such a reservation.

[160] This exception means that States that have provided for a remuneration right for their domes-tic performers may declare a reservation and exclude foreign performers.

iv) Article 17 allows contracting states which granted protection of producers of phonograms solely on the basis of fixation on October 26, 1961, to maintain that criterion for certain purposes.

IPIC Treaty

i) any Contracting Party is free not to apply national treatment as far as any obligations to appoint an agent or to designate an address for service are concerned (Article 5(2));

ii) any Contracting Party is free not to apply national treatment as far as the special rules applicable to foreigners in court proceedings are concerned (Article 5(2)).

Footnote 3 to Article 3 of the TRIPS Agreement—which also applies to the MFN principle—provides a broad definition of 'protection' with the intention of preventing discrimination not only with regard to the availability and scope of intellectual property rights, their maintenance and enforcement, but also with regard to their acquisition and use.[161] This broad concept may provide a legal platform to claim national treatment (and MFN) before IPRs are acquired in conformity with applicable procedures, thereby excluding the possibility of conditioning the acquisition of IPRs on the fulfilment of certain requirements, including the granting of reciprocity to the Member's own nationals.

The concept of 'protection', although expressly confined to Articles 3 and 4 of the TRIPS Agreement, may also have implications beyond them. For instance, the reference to 'acquisition' may be read under bilateral investment agreements (BITs) and FTAs that apply the national treatment principle to the pre-establishment phase,[162] as providing investors' rights to parties seeking to acquire IPRs. The US–Singapore FTA, for instance, defines 'investor of a Party' as 'a Party or a national or an enterprise of a Party that is *seeking to make, is making*, or has made an investment in the territory of the other Party' (Article 15.1.17).

Footnote 3 adds that protection also includes 'those matters affecting the use of intellectual property rights specifically addressed in this Agreement'. In the absence of full records on the discussions that led to this provision, it is unclear why the 'use' is separately considered[163] in the second part of the sentence 'specifically' with regard to IPRs 'addressed in this Agreement'. This wording raises the question of what is 'use' of IPRs in this context. IPRs confer *negative* rights; that is,

---

[161] The panel in *Canada–Term of patent protection* WT/DS114/R, 17 March 2000, incidentally referred to this footnote. It only indicated that 'it can serve as context in interpreting protection to be provided for intellectual property rights' (WTO/DS170/R, 5 May 2000, fn 33). However, the implications of the footnote, as examined below, may be more substantial.

[162] See, eg the Model US BIT (2004), available at <http://www.ustr.gov/assets/Trade_Sectors/Investment/Model_BIT/asset_upload_file847_6897.pdf> (last accessed on 4 July 2004).

[163] The title of Part II also refers to 'use' ('Standards concerning the availability, scope and *use* of intellectual property rights' (emphasis added).

the right to exclude third parties from the use of protected subject matter. In *Canada–Patent Protection of Pharmaceutical Products*, the panel said:

> The normal practice of exploitation by patent owners, as with owners of any other intellectual property right, is to exclude all forms of competition that could detract significantly from the economic returns anticipated from a patent's grant of market exclusivity.[164]

Hence, the normal way of using IPRs is by enforcing them against third parties to prevent infringement. IPRs do not confer positive rights, for instance, the right to sell a patented invention that may be harmful, or to circulate a copyrighted work that is morally repugnant. However, since 'enforcement' is referred to in the first part of the footnote, 'use' should have a different meaning, such as exploiting the protected subject matter, and licensing or assigning the respective rights.

Another question is whether footnote 3 confines the concept of 'protection' to such rights the 'use' of which is 'specifically addressed' in the Agreement.[165] The plain text of the provision does not seem to justify this interpretation,[166] but rather that Members' obligations are limited to the *rights specifically addressed* in the Agreement (and the incorporated conventions) and not to the *categories* of IPRs referred to in Article 1.2 of the Agreement as such. This means that:

(a) the national treatment principle applies to all rights relating to the subject matter covered in the Paris Convention, the Berne Convention, and the Washington Treaty, as established in these international instruments;

(b) the national treatment principle applies with regard to subject matter not covered by those instruments only in respect of the rights specifically addressed by the Agreement. For instance, only the rights specifically conferred with regard to test data (Article 39.3 of the TRIPS Agreement) are subject to that principle, but not the *sui generis* data exclusivity protection accorded in the USA and other countries;[167]

(c) copyright-related rights are subject to national treatment and MFN only to the extent that such rights are provided for under the Agreement (Articles 3.1 and 4(c) of the Agreement).

A panel applied the footnote to Article 3 in interpreting Article 20 of the Agreement (relating to 'other requirements' for the use of trademarks)[168] in *Indonesia–Cars*.[169] It interpreted that Article 20 was limited 'to matters affecting the use of intellectual property rights specifically addressed in this Agreement'.[170]

---

[164] Report of the Panel, WT/DS114/R, 17 March 2000, para 7.55.

[165] See, eg, Pires de Carvalho op. cit. (2002), p 81.

[166] The footnote makes clear ('...as well as...') that matters relating to 'use' are subject to Articles 3 and 4, but does not necessarily exclude the categories of rights (plant varieties, unfair competition) for which there are no provisions dealing with use.   [167] See p 11 above.

[168] See pp 199–201 below.   [169] See WT/DS54/R, 2 July 1998.

[170] Idem, para 14.275.

The national treatment principle under the TRIPS Agreement only is binding, with respect to the rights of performers, producers of phonograms, and broadcasting organizations, in relation to the 'rights provided under this Agreement'. The reason for this clarification is that performers, producers of phonograms, and broadcasting are treated differently under the continental authors' right tradition and under Anglo-American law, and that the Rome Convention recognizes rights beyond those specifically contemplated under the TRIPS Agreement.

An implication of this provision is the preclusion of the Members (like the US) who are not parties to the Rome Convention from receiving the full Rome Convention protection for their nationals without committing themselves to grant such protection to the nationals of other Members.[171] A specific purpose of this clarification was also to leave outside the TRIPS Agreement what was a highly controversial issue during the Uruguay Round negotiations between US and Europe: the distribution of revenues from levies applied in Europe to blank audio and video cassettes in order to compensate for the unauthorized reproduction of music and films. This issue remained unresolved notwithstanding the strong demands from the US government to obtain national treatment in this field.

While the TRIPS Agreement does not allow for reservations,[172] it respects the reservations that can be made in accordance with Article 6 of the Berne Convention (1971) and with Article 16.1(b) of the Rome Convention.

Article 6 of the Berne Convention (1971) allows for an exception to the 'national treatment' principle with regard to authors from countries outside the Berne Union which fail to protect 'in an adequate manner' works of authors who are nationals of one of the countries of the Union. This exception, however, is generally considered to have fallen into disuse.[173]

Article 16.1(b) of the Rome Convention permits an exception to the national treatment principle with respect to the communication to the public of television broadcasts in places accessible to the public against the payment of a fee, in the case of States that have made a reservation with regard to Article 13(d) of the Rome Convention.

The referred to reservations, after the adoption of the TRIPS Agreement, need to be notified to the Council of TRIPS. The notification requirement does not entail approval by the WTO Members, as they are allowed by the respective conventions.

According to Article 3.2, exceptions to the national treatment principle are acceptable in relation to judicial and administrative procedures, including the designation of an address for service or the appointment of an agent within the

---

[171] See J Dratler Jr, *Intellectual Property Law: Commercial, Creative and Industrial Property* (1996: New York, Law Journal Seminars Press), paras 1A-36.

[172] According to Article 72 of the Agreement, 'reservations may not be entered in respect of any of the provisions of this Agreement without the consent of the other Members'.

[173] See, eg, Gervais, op. cit. (2003), p 100.

jurisdiction of a Member,[174] and where such practices are not applied in a manner which would constitute a disguised restriction on trade' (Article 3.2 of the TRIPS Agreement).[175]

As drafted, this exception is more limited than the exceptions with similar purpose found in the Paris Convention. It is subject to three tests:

(a) The exception must be 'necessary to secure compliance with laws and regulations'. This means that procedures convenient, but not necessary to this purpose may be challenged under the DSU. 'Compliance' in this provision should be understood in a broad sense, as encompassing requirements imposed on title-holders for the acquisition (eg domicile for procedures before the patent office) as well as the enforcement and defence of rights (eg provide a guarantee in cases where the title-holder has no patrimony in the country where he litigates).

(b) In addition, the laws and regulations to be complied with must not be 'inconsistent with the provisions of this Agreement'. This test opens up the door for challenging exceptions to the national treatment not based on the nature of the requirement imposed as such or its necessity, but on the basis of the consistency of the law or regulation to which such requirement is linked. The inconsistency of the latter would entail that of the exception to the national treatment with Article 3.2.

(c) Finally, in order to be admissible under the examined Article 3.2 the exceptions must not be 'applied in a manner which would constitute a disguised restriction on trade'. This text—which borrows wording ('constitute a disguised restriction on trade') from the chapeau of Article XX of GATT—means that the exception may be necessary and justified by its purpose (to secure compliance with laws and regulations), and that the laws and regulations may be consistent with the provisions of the Agreement, but still a Member may challenge—in line with GATT/WTO jurisprudence[176]—the way in which the exception is applied. The last sentence of Article 3.2 refers to 'practices' and not 'exceptions'. There is no clear explanation for the choice of this wording, except possibly the desire of the drafters to emphasize that this third test refers to the *manner* in which an exception is applied and not to the content or extent of the exception as such.

The interpretation given to the chapeau of Article XX of GATT may be useful for elucidating whether an exception to the national treatment principle in the context of the TRIPS Agreement amounts to an inadmissible 'disguised practice'.

---

[174] This is a common requirement for the procedures relating to the acquisition of industrial property rights and for litigation in judicial courts.
[175] This exception may also be applied in relation to the MFN clause. See, eg, Dratler op. cit. (1996), paras 1A-36 and 1A-37.
[176] See *United States–Imports of Certain Automotive Spring Assemblies*, L/5333, BISD 308/107, 26 May 1983.

The chapeau language of Article XX received little consideration before the *Reformulated Gasoline* case,[177] where the AB stated that:

The purpose and object of the introductory clauses of Article XX is generally the prevention of abuse of the exceptions of (what was later to become) Article (XX). This insight drawn from the drafting history of Article XX is a valuable one. The chapeau is animated by the principle that while the exceptions of Article XX may be invoked as a matter of legal right, they should not be so applied as to frustrate or defeat the legal obligations of the holder of the right under the substantive rules of the General Agreement.

The AB added that the burden of demonstrating that a measure within one of the concrete Article XX exceptions does not, in its application, constitute abuse under the chapeau, rests on the party invoking the exception.[178] It is questionable whether the AB has not gone too far with this interpretation, which can make it too difficult for a potential defendant to justify an exception if required to produce the negative proof that the manner in which the exception applies does *not* amount to a disguised restriction.

Most-favoured nation

4. With regard to the protection of intellectual property, any advantage, favour, privilege or immunity granted by a Member to the nationals of any other country shall be accorded immediately and unconditionally to the nationals of all other Members. Exempted from this obligation are any advantage, favour, privilege or immunity accorded by a Member:

(a) deriving from international agreements on judicial assistance or law enforcement of a general nature and not particularly confined to the protection of intellectual property;

(b) granted in accordance with the provisions of the Berne Convention (1971) or the Rome Convention authorizing that the treatment accorded be a function not of national treatment but of the treatment accorded in another country;

(c) in respect of the rights of performers, producers of phonograms and broadcasting organizations not provided under this Agreement;

(d) deriving from international agreements related to the protection of intellectual property which entered into force prior to the entry into force of the WTO Agreement, provided that such agreements are notified to the Council for TRIPS and do not constitute an arbitrary or unjustifiable discrimination against nationals of other Members.

---

[177] WT/DS 52 and WT/DS4. See, eg, M Trebilcock and R Howse, *The Regulation of International Trade* (1999: London and New York, Routledge), p 154.

[178] See, eg, E Vermulst, P Mavroidis, and P Waer, 'The Functioning of the Appellate Body after four years. Towards Rule Integrity' (1999) Journal of World Trade, Vol. 3, No 2, p 22.

The TRIPS Agreement requires Members to apply a principle traditionally reserved to trade in goods:[179] the 'most-favoured-nation treatment' (MFN). Such principle was absent from pre-TRIPS international conventions,[180] and indicates the will of the negotiating parties in GATT to firmly integrate TRIPS disciplines into the multilateral trading system.[181] This intention was unambiguously affirmed by the AB in *United States–Section 211 Omnibus Appropriations Act of 1998* where it held:

Like the national treatment obligation, the obligation to provide most-favoured-nation treatment has long been one of the cornerstones of the world trading system. For more than fifty years, the obligation to provide most-favoured-nation treatment in Article I of the GATT 1994 has been both central and essential to assuring the success of a global rules-based system for trade in goods. Unlike the national treatment principle, there is no provision in the Paris Convention (1967) that establishes a most-favoured-nation obligation with respect to rights in trademarks or other industrial property. However, the framers of the *TRIPS Agreement* decided to extend the most-favoured-nation obligation to the protection of intellectual property rights covered by that Agreement. As a cornerstone of the world trading system, the most-favoured-nation obligation must be accorded the same significance with respect to intellectual property rights under the *TRIPS Agreement* that it has long been accorded with respect to trade in goods under the GATT. It is, in a word, fundamental.[182]

In accordance with the MFN principle, as formulated in the TRIPS Agreement, 'any advantage, favour, privilege or immunity granted by a Member to the nationals of any other country shall be accorded immediately and unconditionally to the nationals of all other Members'.

It is to be noted that the MFN principle applies in relation to benefits accorded to nationals of 'any other country'. Hence Members should be accorded the MFN treatment when benefits were granted to non-WTO Members. As incorporated, the MFN clause aims at ensuring that nationals of Members receive the *best* treatment accorded in a Member to nationals of other countries.[183]

Arguably, the implications of the MFN clause are less significant than the national treatment principle, since, except in rare occasions, intellectual property laws do not discriminate among nationals of different countries.

According to the analysis made above in relation to footnote 3, the MFN principle only applies to the rights specifically addressed in the Agreement and the incorporated conventions. Rights relating to categories of IPRs covered in the Agreement but not specifically addressed therein (e.g. anti-circumvention rights,

[179] Also applicable to trade in services under the General Agreement on Trade in Services (GATS).
[180] However, some European copyright bilateral treaties prior to the Berne Convention were linked to broader trade agreements. See, eg, J Watal, op. cit. (2001), p 209, fn 10.
[181] Owing to unilateral pressures, some countries had given preferential treatment to nationals of the US. See, eg, S Sell, *Power and Ideas. North South Politics of Intellectual Property and Antitrust* (1998: New York, State University of New York Press), p 190.
[182] Appellate Body Report, *US–Havana Club* case WT/DS160/AB/R, 15 June 2005, para 297.
[183] See, eg, Dratler op. cit. (1996), para 1A-37.

data exclusivity, databases' extraction rights) are not subject to MFN. This means, for instance, that TRIPS-extra rights recognized in the context of FTAs promoted by the US need not be extended by the contracting parties to non-contracting parties. The most likely situation is, however, that the parties will enact domestic legislation that will equally benefit nationals from non-contracting parties as well.

The application of this principle, as well as of national treatment, is exempted in connection with procedures for the acquisition of maintenance of intellectual property rights under multilateral agreements concluded under the auspices of WIPO (Article 5). This is the case, in particular, of the Patent Cooperation Treaty (Washington, 1970).

There are, however, a number of exceptions to the MFN principle based on the existing or future international agreements or in connection with certain subject matter:

(a) **international agreements on judicial assistance or law enforcement**

The agreements referred to in the first exception are of a 'general nature and not particularly confined to the protection of intellectual property'. This exception would apply, for instance, in relation to the Inter-American Convention on Mutual Asssistance on Criminal Matters (1992), and to the New York Convention on the Recognition and Enforcement of Foreign Arbitral Awards (1958).

The exception would also apply in cases where a treaty on judicial assistance and law enforcement contains particular provisions on intellectual property, to the extent that the treaty is 'not confined' to intellectual property.[184]

(b) **Rights granted under the Berne Convention (1971) or the Rome Convention based on the treatment accorded in another country;**

This exception will apply, for instance, in the case of Article 7(8) of the Berne Convention, as it permits limitation of the protection to be granted in the country of protection to the extent of protection conferred in the country of origin of the work. It will also be pertinent in relation to Article 14*ter* of the Berne Convention, which provides with respect to original works of art and original manuscripts of writers and composers for an 'inalienable right to an interest in any sale of the work subsequent to the first transfer by the author of the work' (Article 14*ter*(1)). However, this right (known as '*droit de suite*') 'may be claimed in a country of the Union only if legislation in the country to which the author belongs so permits,

---

[184] The Convention on Choice of Court Agreements (concluded 30 June 2005) applies to exclusive choice of court agreements in international cases in civil or commercial matters. Article 2 stipulates that the Convention does not apply to exclusive choice of court agreements relating, inter alia, to the validity of intellectual property rights other than copyright and related rights (Article 2(n)), and to 'infringement of intellectual property rights other than copyright and related rights, except where infringement proceedings are brought for breach of a contract between the parties relating to such rights, or could have been brought for breach of that contract' (Article 2(o)). See also R Dreyfuss and J Ginsburg, 'Draft Convention on Jurisdiction and Recognition of Judgments in Intellectual Property Matters—Commentary', (2002) 77 Chicago-Kent Law Review 3, pp 1090–100.

and to the extent permitted by the country where this protection is claimed'
(Article 14*ter*(2)).

> (c) **rights of performers, producers of phonograms and broadcasting organiza-
> tions not provided under this Agreement;**

As examined below, the TRIPS Agreement deals with certain specific aspects of
copyrights and 'related' rights. While the Berne Convention (with the exception
of Article 6*bis*) is applicable to all Members—whether they have subscribed to it
or not—this is not the case for the Rome Convention, which is only applicable to
Members that are parties to it. This exclusion has the same effect as the second
sentence of Article 3.1. It prevents back-door benefits for Members that have not
adhered to the Rome Convention.

> (d) **rights deriving from pre-TRIPS international agreements**

This is probably the most significant exception, as it grandfathers rights and obligations granted to contracting parties in international conventions. Several conditions of this exception need consideration:

(i) The advantages are conferred by 'international' agreements

The provision refers to 'international' agreements (in contrast with Article 5 of
the TRIPS Agreement, which alludes to 'multilateral' agreements). It may be
interpreted that the concept of 'international' includes any instrument between
States, including bilateral and regional agreements.[185]

(ii) The exception will apply to any international agreement 'related to the protection of intellectual property'.

The determination of the scope of this exception is of particular importance
for the future evolution of IPR protection internationally. First, it is noteworthy
that the exception does not refer to the customs unions and free trade areas that
can be exempted from the MFN obligation under GATT (Article XXIV). It
applies instead to any international agreement 'related to the protection of intellectual property'. '[R]elated to' suggests that such agreements are not limited to
those exclusively dealing with IPRs (such as the European Patent Convention),
but which somehow 'relate' to them. This interpretation seems to be confirmed by
Members' subsequent practice, examined in subsection (iv) below.

(iii) The agreements should have entered into force prior to the entry into force
of the Agreement Establishing the WTO.

The Agreement Establishing the WTO entered into force on 1 January 1995.
This means that the parties to pre-TRIPS IPR conventions, who are also WTO
Members, are exempted from an MFN obligation. In contrast, those which have

---

[185] See the chapeau of Article 4, which refers to the advantages conferred to the 'nationals of any
other country' (in the singular).

adhered to IPRs treaties established after that date (such as the WIPO Copyright Treaty and the WPPT of 1996) are bound by the MFN principle. Nationals of non-parties to those treaties, which are WTO members, would, hence, benefit from the rights and advantages conferred thereunder with regard to intellectual property rights covered under the TRIPS Agreement, without being encumbered, however, by the obligations they impose.

A troublesome implication of this provision would be that the rights and advantages granted in bilateral agreements and FTAs that contain chapters on IPRs should be extended to nationals of non-parties who are WTO Members, without getting any trade concession in return. Thus, if the Free Trade Agreement for the Americas (FTAA) were adopted with IPR provisions, European countries, Japan, etc would have access to the same rights as US nationals who, in theory at least, would have paid a price via trade concessions to obtain such rights and advantages.

However, the impact of the MFN principle is limited by the coverage of the TRIPS Agreement. As elaborated above, the Agreement only creates obligations with regard to subject matter covered either in Sections 1–7 of Part II of the TRIPS Agreement or in the IPR conventions that the Members are bound to comply with. Its scope of application is, in addition, limited to the rights spelled out in Sections 1–7 of Part II of the Agreement or said conventions (with the noted exception with regard to copyright-related or neighbouring rights). For instance, the United States obtained in the Central American Free Trade Agreement (CAFTA-DR[186]) an objective actively pursued by its pharmaceutical industry: a linkage between drug registration and patent status.[187] There is no provision of this kind in the TRIPS Agreement. Patent owners do not have thereunder the right to prevent health authorities from granting a third-party marketing approval with regard to a patented product. This right is clearly beyond the TRIPS Agreement and, hence, excluded from the MFN obligation. Many similar examples can be found in CAFTA and other US FTAs.[188] Members cannot be

---

[186] The Dominican Republic has also signed the Agreement.

[187] Article 15.10.2 of CAFTA-DR provides:

Where a Party permits, as a condition of approving the marketing of a pharmaceutical product, persons, other than the person originally submitting safety or efficacy information, to rely on evidence or information concerning the safety and efficacy of a product that was previously approved, such as evidence of prior marketing approval in the territory of a Party or in another country, that Party:

(a) shall implement measures in its marketing approval process to prevent such other persons from marketing a product covered by a patent claiming the previously approved product or its approved use during the term of that patent, unless by consent or acquiescence of the patent owner; and

(b) shall provide that the patent owner shall be informed of the request and the identity of any such other person who requests approval to enter the market during the term of a patent identified as claiming the approved product or its approved use.

[188] See C Correa, 'Bilateralism in intellectual property: defeating the WTO system for access to medicines', Case Western Reserve Journal of International Law, vol 36, No 1, Winter 2004; P Roffe, 'Bilateral agreements and a TRIPS-plus world: the Chile-USA Free Trade Agreement' (Quaker International Affairs Programme, 2004), available at <http://www.qiap.ca>.

presumed to have extended a blank cheque under the TRIPS Agreement to extend MFN treatment to other Members with regard to any extra concession made in the field of IPRs.[189]

The patent-registration linkage ignores the fact that patents are private rights, as stated in the Preamble of the TRIPS Agreement, and that, whether a given product infringes a patent or not is a legal matter entirely separate from the scientific issues concerning safety and efficacy of drugs.

In any case, the non-applicability of the MFN clause may be irrelevant if the Central American countries and the Dominican Republic transpose the FTA standards to the domestic legislation and make them applicable to local nationals, since the national treatment principle mandates to treat any foreign national (including from non-parties to the FTAs) no less favourably than the former.

(iv) Such agreements are notified to the Council for Trade-Related Aspects of Intellectual Property Rights.

Meeting the conditions enumerated in (i) to (iii) would not exempt the parties of the relevant agreements from the MFN clause. Such agreements must be notified to the Council for TRIPS. The Agreement is silent about the action that the Council might take in cases of notification, but it seems clear that the Council has not authority to object to a notification that meets the requirements of Article 4.

The European Communities and their Member States, the Andean Community, MERCOSUR, and NAFTA have all made notifications under Article 4(d) to the Council for TRIPS.[190] While Article 4(d) refers to prior agreements, such notifications (except that for NAFTA) also apply to *future* acts or regulations made in the course of the integration process. The EC notification states:

Notification of these agreements covers not only those provisions directly contained therein, as interpreted by the relevant jurisprudence, but also existing or future acts adopted by the Community as such and/or by the Member States which conform with these agreements following the process of regional integration.[191]

The notification by MERCOSUR refers to:

the Treaty of Asunción and the Ouro Preto Protocol, with reference not only to the provisions contained therein but also all agreements, protocols, decisions, resolutions and guidelines adopted or to be adopted in the future by MERCOSUR or its States Parties in the course of the regional integration process that are of relevance to TRIPS, pursuant to the Agreement.[192]

---

[189] This applies to all categories of IPRs, whether covered by the TRIPS Agreement or not.

[190] See, for the texts of such notifications, UNCTAD–ICTSD op. cit. (2005), pp 80–1.

[191] Notification under Article 4(d) of the Agreement, European Communities and their Member States, IP/N/4/EEC/1, 29 January 1996.

[192] Notification under Article 4(d) of the Agreement, Argentina, Brazil, Paraguay, Uruguay, IP/N/4/ARG/1, IP/N/4/BRA/1, IP/N/4/PRY/1, IP/N/4/URY/1, 14 July 1998.

The grandfathering of future acts (arguably including amendments of existing agreements) seems to be justified by the plain wording of Article 4(d), as it refers to advantages, favour, privilege, or immunity 'deriving from' such international agreement.

The reservation with regard to future regional or national rules adopted in the course of the process of integration would mean that if, for example, Decision 486 of the Andean Community (which establishes the Common Regime on Industrial Property) was amended and broader IPRs were granted in certain areas, the Andean countries would not be bound to apply the MFN clause. While the justification for the exception in this case can be the pre-existence of the agreements, this argument would not work in case of negotiations for the establishment of new regional agreements, such as the FTAA, if this area were established and a chapter on intellectual property were finally included in the agreement.[193]

The State practice followed so far, hence, indicates that the agreements mentioned in Article 4(d) need not be confined to special agreement on intellectual property (albeit they should certainly contain regulations thereon), and they may include post-TRIPS agreements deriving from agreements notified under Article 4(d).

The requirement of notification applies to the international agreements themselves, and not to particular provisions therein. The notification, in addition, suffices to comply with that requirement, as it is not subject to further examination or approval by the Council for TRIPS, without prejudice to individual Members' rights to seek clarifications with regard to agreements concerning the subject matter of the TRIPS Agreement which are in force between the government or a governmental agency of a Member and the government or a governmental agency of another Member (Article 63.1 of the TRIPS Agreement).

Article 4(d) does not address the issue of late notification of agreements and its effect. The issue, if raised, would have to be solved according to general principles of international law. It is arguable that the absence of timely notification does not prevent a Member from invoking an agreement as of the date of its notification. A more difficult issue is whether the agreement may be attributed retroactive effects. However, since decisions by the DSB have no such effects, the question may not have significant practical implications.[194]

(v) The notified agreements should not constitute an arbitrary or unjustifiable discrimination against nationals of other Members

This last condition requires a judgement about the discrimination that a notified agreement entails. It should not be 'arbitrary or unjustifiable'. It is unclear how such a judgement would be made. There are no standards to determine arbitrariness or whether the discrimination is justifiable. Nor is it clear whether such determination could be made by the Council for TRIPS, or by the DSB upon a

---

[193] Although the initial draft texts incorporated such a chapter, Brazil and other countries have refused to further negotiate the FTAA, mainly due to the reluctance of the US to deal with agricultural protection.   [194] Pires de Carvalho op. cit. (2002), p 89.

complaint by one or more Members. However, as the word 'discrimination' itself conveys the idea of unjustified differentiation,[195] the wording of this provision suggests that it could only be applied in blatant cases of arbitrary differential treatment among nationals of WTO members.

There is the risk that the MFN clause be invoked to nullify the flexibilities retained by a party, for instance, through exceptions to certain rights specified in a bilateral agreement and not recognized in an agreement with other parties. Thus, if an agreement between A and B specified that parties may exclude plants from patentability, and an agreement between A and C did not, nationals of B might claim patent rights based on the agreement between A and C. In the area of investment treaties, the tribunals have cautioned in some cases against importing into an agreement rights recognized in other agreements that may be inconsistent with the clear intent of or significantly impact the substantive rights agreed upon by the parties.[196] A similar caution is required in the area of IPRs. The question is, however, the extent to which it may be applied in the light of the limited nature of the exceptions allowed under Article 4.

Finally, an interesting issue that has been raised[197] is what an 'advantage' for the purposes of the MFN principle may be in the context of IPR law. The 'advantages' Article 4 refers to are those that benefit IPR title-holders, in the form of higher or broader rights. However, in some cases, nationals of some Members may consider advantageous a lower or narrower level of protection given in other Members. For instance, the availability of a 'Bolar exception'[198] in a Member would be a distinct advantage for generic companies of other Members who may initiate procedures for the marketing approval of a drug before the expiry of the relevant patent.

Multilateral agreements on acquisition or maintenance of protection

5. The obligations under Articles 3 and 4 do not apply to procedures provided in multilateral agreements concluded under the auspices of WIPO relating to the acquisition or maintenance of intellectual property rights.

Article 5 carves out an exception to Articles 3 and 4 for 'procedures provided in multilateral agreements' relating to 'the acquisition or maintenance' of IPRs. Its purpose was to avoid Members who are not parties to such agreements enjoying the advantages they confer (for instance, simplified procedures for acquisition of

---

[195] In considering 'discrimination' in the context of Article 27.1, the panel in *Canada—Pharmaceutical Protection Patent*, WT/DS114/R, 17 March 2000, held that 'discrimination' is not the same as 'differentiation', and that WTO members can adopt different rules for particular product areas, provided that the differences are adopted for *bona fide* purposes (para 7.92).

[196] See A Cosbey, H Mann, L Peterson, and K von Moltke, *Investment and Sustainable Development. A Guide to the Use and Potential of International Investment Agreements* (2004: Winnipeg, IISD) p 11.

[197] See, eg, UNCTAD-ICTSD op. cit. (2005), p 78.   [198] See p 304 below.

rights) without granting similar treatment to the nationals of those Members who are parties thereto. The application of this exception is subject to the following conditions:

(i) the *procedures* must relate to the acquisition or maintenance of intellectual property rights. Agreement relating to enforcement procedures as well as agreements regulating substantive aspects are excluded.

(ii) the agreements must have been concluded under the auspices of WIPO.

A number of WIPO agreements clearly fall under this provision. They are:

- Patent Cooperation Treaty (PCT)
- Madrid Agreement (and Protocol) Concerning the International Registration of Marks
- Hague Agreement Concerning the International Deposit of Industrial Designs
- Trademark Law Treaty
- Budapest Treaty on the International Recognition of the Deposit of Micro-organisms for the Purposes of Patent Procedure
- Patent Law Treaty.

A question may arise with regard to WIPO agreements that contain both substantive as well as procedural provisions, such as the Lisbon Agreement for the Protection of Appellations of Origin and their International Registration (1958).[199] Since Article 5 refers to 'procedures provided' in multilateral agreements 'relating to' the acquisition or maintenance of rights, it is arguable that such procedures are also covered by this article.[200]

The limitation to WIPO auspices excludes regional agreements, such as the European Patent Convention.

It is to be noted that this exception may apply to agreements concluded after the entry into force of the TRIPS Agreement. Thus, procedural rules on acquisition and maintenance of rights included in any new WIPO agreement, or in the amendment to an existing WIPO agreement, would also be exempted.

Annex

Negotiating history[201]

In his 23 July 1990 report on the status of work in the TRIPS Negotiating Group, the Chairman (Lars E R Anell) presented two sets of proposals. In an Annex to the report, he presented a composite text that was taken from various proposals by

[199] See WIPO, Provisions of Existing International Conventions Providing Protection for Intellectual Property, Communication from the WIPO Secretariat, MTN.GNG/NG11/W/21, 12 February 1988, para 4.   [200] See, eg, UNCTAD–ICTSD op. cit. (2005), p 82.
[201] For an analysis of the negotiating history, see UNCTAD–ICTSD op. cit. (2005), pp 17–60.

delegations to the Negotiating Group, indicating the source of each proposal by numerical reference to the source document.

Composite text of July 23 1990[202]

1. For the purposes of this agreement, the term 'intellectual property' refers to all categories of intellectual property that are the subject of Sections ... to ... of Part III. This definition is without prejudice to whether the protection given to that subject matter takes the form of an intellectual property right.

2. Parties shall accord the treatment provided for in this agreement to the nationals of other PARTIES. [In respect of the relevant intellectual property right, the term 'nationals' shall be understood as those natural or legal persons meeting the criteria for eligibility for protection under the Paris Convention (1967), the Berne Convention (1971), [the Rome Convention] and the Treaty on Intellectual Property in Respect of Integrated Circuits.[a] [Any PARTY not a party to the Rome Convention and availing itself of the possibilities as provided for in Articles 5.3 or 6.2 of that Convention shall make the notification foreseen in that provision to (the committee administering this agreement).]

3. Unless expressly stated otherwise, nothing in Parts III–V of this agreement shall prevent PARTIES from granting more extensive protection to intellectual property rights than that provided in this agreement.

4. Nothing in this agreement shall derogate from existing obligations of PARTIES to each other under the General Agreement on Tariffs and Trade.

   [a] The relevant provisions would appear to be Articles 2 and 3 of the Paris Convention, Articles 3 and 4 of the Berne Convention, Articles 4, 5 and 6 of the Rome Convention and Art. 5(l) of the Treaty on Intellectual Property in Respect of Integrated Circuits.

1A PARTIES shall comply with the [substantive] provisions [oil economic rights] of the Paris Convention (1967), of the Berne Convention (1971) [and of the Rome Convention].

1. Each PARTY shall accord to the nationals of other PARTIES [treatment no less favourable than] [the same treatment as] that accorded to the PARTY's nationals with regard to the protection of intellectual property, [subject to the exceptions already provided in, respectively,] [without prejudice to the rights and obligations specifically provided in] the Paris Convention [(1967)], the Berne Convention [(1971)], [the Rome Convention] and the Treaty on intellectual Property in Respect of Integrated Circuits.[a] [Any PARTY not a party to the Rome Convention and availing itself of the possibilities as provided in Art. 16(1)(a)(iii) or (iv) or Art. 16(1)(b) of that Convention shall make the notification foreseen in that provision to (the committee administering this agreement)]

[202] Chairman's Report to the GNG, Status of Work in the Negotiating Group, Negotiating Group on Trade-Related Aspects of Intellectual Property Rights, including Trade in Counterfeit Goods, MTN.GNG/NG11/W/76, 23 July 1990, presented by the Chairman of the TRIPS Negotiating Group (Lars E R Anell). Alternatives 'A' correspond to texts from developed countries and 'B' from developing countries.

2A Any exceptions invoked in respect of procedural requirements imposed on beneficiaries of national treatment, including the designation of an address for service or the appointment of an agent within the jurisdiction of a PARTY, shall not have the effect of impairing access (or, aid equality of opportunity on) the market of such PARTY and shall be limited to what is necessary to secure reasonably efficient administration and security of the law.

3A Where the acquisition of an intellectual property right covered by this agreement is subject to the intellectual property right being granted or registered, PARTIES shall provide granting or registration procedures not constituting any *de jure* or *de facto* discrimination in respect of laws, regulations and requirements between nationals of the PARTIES.

4A With respect to the protection of intellectual property, PARTIES shall comply with the provisions of Art.III of the General Agreement on Tariffs and Trade, subject to the exceptions provided in that Agreement).[b]

[a] For the first two and the last of these conventions, the exceptions have been listed by WIPO in document NG11/W/66. For the Rome Convention, the relevant provisions would appear to be Articles 15, 16(1)(a)(iii) and (iv) and (b), and 17.
[b] This provision would be redundant if, as proposed by some participants, the results of the negotiations were to be an integral part of the General Agreement on Tariffs and Trade.

laA PARTIES shall ensure that the protection of intellectual property is not carried out in a manner [which would constitute an arbitrary or unjustifiable discrimination between nationals of a PARTY and those of any other country or which would constitute a disguised restriction on international trade] [that has the effect of impairing access to and equality of opportunity on their markets].

1b.1 With regard to the protection of intellectual property, any advantage, favour, privilege or immunity granted by a PARTY to the nationals of any other [country] [PARTY] shall be accorded [immediately and unconditionally] to the nationals of all other PARTIES.

lb.2 Exempted from this obligation are any advantage, favour, privilege or immunity accorded by a PARTY:

• Deriving from international agreements on judicial assistance and law enforcement of a general nature and not particularly confined to the protection of intellectual property rights.

• Concerning procedures provided under international agreements relating to the acquisition and maintenance of protection for intellectual property in several countries, provided that accession to such agreements is open to all PARTIES.

• Granted in accordance with the provisions of the Berne Convention (1971) [and the Rome Convention] authorising that the treatment accorded be a function not of national treatment but of the treatment accorded in another country.[a]

• Deriving from international agreements related to intellectual property law which entered into force prior to the entry into force of this agreement, provided that such agreements do not constitute an arbitrary and unjustifiable discrimination against nationals of other PARTIES and provided that any such exception in respect of another PARTY does not remain in force for longer than [X] years after the coming into force of this agreement between the two PARTIES in question.

• Exceeding the requirements of this agreement and which is provided in an international agreement to which the PARTY belongs, provided that [such agreement is open for accession by alt PARTIES to this agreement] [any such PARTY shall be ready to extend such advantage, favour, privilege or immunity, on terms equivalent to those under the agreement, to any other PARTY so requesting and to enter into good faith negotiations to this end.]

1.2A With respect to the protection of intellectual property, PARTIES shall comply with the provisions of Art.I of the General Agreement on Tariffs and Trade, subject to the exceptions provided in that Agreement.[b]

The obligations under Articles 3 and 4 do not apply to procedures provided in multi-lateral agreements concluded under the auspices of WIPO relating to the acquisition or maintenance of intellectual property rights.

[a] The relevant provisions would appear to be Articles 2(7), 6(4), 7(8), l4*ter*(1) and (2), 18 and 30(2)(b) of the Berne Convention and Articles 15 and 16(1)(a)(iv) and (b) of the Rome Convention.
[b] This provision would not be necessary if, as proposed by some participants, the results of the negotiations were to be an integral part of the General Agreement on Tariffs and Trade.

Draft text transmitted to the Brussels Ministerial Conference (December 1990)

1. PARTIES shall give effect to the provisions of this Agreement.[a] PARTIES may, but still not be obliged to, implement in their domestic law more extensive protection than is required by this Agreement, provided that such protection does not contravene the provisions of this Agreement. PARTIES shall be free to determine the appropriate method of implementing the provisions of this Agreement within their own legal system and practice.

2. For the purposes of this Agreement, the term 'intellectual property' refers to all categories of intellectual property that are the subject of Sections ... to ... of Part II.

3. PARTIES shall accord the treatment provided for in this Agreement to the nationals of other PARTIES.[b] In respect of the relevant intellectual property right, the nationals of other PARTIES shall be understood as those natural or legal persons meeting the criteria for eligibility for protection under the Paris Convention (1967), the Berne Convention (1971), the Rome Convention and the Treaty on Intellectual Property in Respect of Integrated Circuits. Any PARTY availing itself of the possibilities provided in Articles 5.3 or 6.2 of the Rome Convention shall make a notification as foreseen in those provisions to the Committee established under Part VII below.

1. In respect of Parts II, III and IV of this Agreement, PARTIES shall not depart from the relevant provisions of the Paris Convention (1967).

2. Nothing in this Agreement shall derogate from existing obligations that PARTIES may have to each other under the Paris Convention, the Berne Convention, the Rome Convention and the Treaty on Intellectual Property in Respect of Integrated Circuits.

1. Each PARTY shall accord to the nationals of other PARTIES treatment no less favourable than that it accords to its own nationals with regard to the protection of intellectual property, subject to the exceptions already provided in, respectively, the Paris Convention (1967), the Berne Convention (1971), the Rome Convention and the Treaty on Intellectual Property in Respect of Integrated Circuits. Any PARTY availing itself of the

possibilities provided in Art. 6 of the Berne Convention and Art. 16.1(a)(iii) or (iv) or Art. 16.1(b) of the Rome Convention shall make a notification as foreseen in those provisions to the Committee established under Part VII below.

2. PARTIES may avail themselves of the exceptions permitted under paragraph 1 above in relation to judicial and administrative procedures, including the designation of an address for service or the appointment of an agent within the jurisdiction of a PARTY, only where such exceptions are necessary to secure compliance with laws and regulations which are not inconsistent with the provisions of this agreement and where such practices are not applied in a manner which would constitute a disguised restriction on trade.

[a] When a PARTY gives effect to the provisions of this Agreement through participation in an intergovernmental arrangement, it shall take all reasonable measures as may be available to it to ensure consistency between this Agreement and the arrangement.

[b] When the term 'national' is used in this Agreement, it shall be deemed, in the case of Hong Kong, to mean persons, natural or legal, who are domiciled or who have a real and effective industrial or commercial establishment in Hong Kong.

With regard to the protection of intellectual property, any advantage, favour, privilege or immunity granted by a PARTY to the nationals of any other country shall be accorded immediately and unconditionally to the nationals of all other PARTIES. Exempted from this obligation are any advantage, favour, privilege or immunity accorded by a PARTY:

(a) deriving from international agreements on judicial assistance and law enforcement of a general nature and not particularly confined to the protection of intellectual property rights;

(b) granted in accordance with the provisions of the Berne Convention (1971) or the Rome Convention authorising that the treatment accorded be a function not of national treatment but of the treatment accorded in another country;

(c) deriving from international agreements related to the protection of intellectual property which entered into force prior to the entry into force of this agreement, provided that such agreements are notified to the Committee established under Part VII below and do not constitute an arbitrary or unjustifiable discrimination against nationals of other PARTIES;

[(d) exceeding the requirements of this Agreement and provided in an international agreement to which the PARTY belongs, provided that such agreement is open for accession by all PARTIES to this Agreement, or provided that such PARTY shall be ready to extend such advantage, favour, privilege or immunity, on terms equivalent to those under the agreement, to the nationals of any other PARTY so requesting and to enter into good faith negotiations to this end.]

The obligations under Articles 3 and 4 do not apply to procedures provided in multilateral agreements concluded under the auspices of WIPO relating to the acquisition or maintenance of intellectual property rights.

Chapter 3

INTERNATIONAL EXHAUSTION
OF RIGHTS

Exhaustion

6. For the purposes of dispute settlement under this Agreement, subject to the provisions of Articles 3 and 4 nothing in this Agreement shall be used to address the issue of the exhaustion of intellectual property rights.

Article 6 disclaims any intent in the TRIPS Agreement to limit the Members' freedom to regulate the issue of exhaustion of rights with regard to all types of IPRs. It declares the admissibility of the international exhaustion of rights, that is, the possibility of legally importing into a country a product protected by intellectual property rights, after the product has been legitimately put on the market in a foreign market. These imports—made by a party without the authorization of the title-holder but equally legal—are generally known as 'parallel imports'.

The exclusion of 'the issue of exhaustion of rights' is made '[F]or the purposes of dispute settlement under this Agreement'. This wording suggests that the issue may be subject to the Agreement for other purposes, though it is difficult to imagine a situation in which this would be relevant, as other Members would not be allowed to complain for non-compliance. It may be argued that the intent of this phrase is to make clear that the issue of exhaustion might be subject to dispute settlement under other WTO agreements, such as GATT[1] and GATS. Another possible implication of the 'for the purposes' clause is that it does not preclude actions before national courts on exhaustion of rights.[2]

Notwithstanding the exclusion of the issue of exhaustion of rights, Article 6 obliges Members to apply the non-discriminatory principles contained in Article 3 (national treatment) and Article 4 (MFN principle). Whatever Members decide with regard to the issue of exhaustion of rights, national laws may be subject to dispute settlement for these limited purposes.

Article 6 leaves open to interpretation a number of issues, namely the circumstances in which exhaustion may be deemed to have occurred. It thus provides Members considerable room for manoeuvre in implementing exhaustion policies.

---

[1] As mentioned below, the prohibition of parallel imports may be regarded, under certain circumstances, as contradicting GATT provisions.

[2] See, eg, UNCTAD-ICTSD, *Resource Book on TRIPS and Development* (2005: Cambridge University Press), p 105.

The principle of 'exhaustion of rights' may be applied at the *national* level. In this case, the rights are deemed exhausted domestically and the commercialization in foreign countries is not deemed to have exhausted the patentee's rights. It may also be applied at the *regional* level: exhaustion is deemed to have occurred if commercialization took place in a country member of a regional agreement. The principle was extensively applied in the European Communities—on the basis of jurisprudence elaborated by the European Court of Justice,[3] in order to avoid the partitioning of the internal market and the exercise of discriminatory policies by IPR title-holders within the Community.

Finally, the exhaustion principle may be applied internationally, that is, by allowing parallel imports from any country. The recognition of a principle of *international* exhaustion in the TRIPS Agreement may be seen as a logical reflection of the globalization of the economy. It may help to ensure the competitiveness of local companies, which may be jeopardized if they were bound to buy inputs for their production exclusively from a local distributor that charged higher prices than in foreign markets. Likewise, the consumer should not be denied the right to buy legitimate products from foreign sources at lower prices, except where imported products present substantial differences in the quality or other essential features with respect to those locally available.

Article 6 of the TRIPS Agreement has left Member countries freedom to incorporate the principle of exhaustion of rights into their domestic law with a national, regional, or international reach. The issue as such cannot be the subject matter of a dispute settlement under the Agreement. In a submission to the Council for TRIPS, a number of developing countries stated in this regard that:

Article 6 of the TRIPS Agreement is extremely relevant for Members, especially developing countries, and particularly the least developed and smaller economies among them. Article 6 provides that Members are free to incorporate the principle of international exhaustion of rights in national legislation. Consequently, any Member can determine the extent to which the principle of exhaustion of rights is applied in its own jurisdiction, without breaching any obligation under the TRIPS Agreement.[4]

A similar interpretation was given by the Swiss Federal Supreme Court in *Kodak v Jumbo-Markt*,[5] where the Court persuasively argued that:

Pursuant to Art. 28 of the TRIPS Agreement, the patent holder has inter alia the right to prevent third parties selling patented objects and importing such for this purpose. This provision with its protection of imports merely lays down that the import of products that infringe the patent must be prohibited, without itself laying down a prohibition on parallel imports. This follows not only from Art. 6 of the TRIPS Agreement but is also clarified in a reference to Art. 6 in a footnote to Art. 28 of the Agreement (GATT Message 1, 1994 Federal Gazette IV, p. 301/2; cf. also Bollinger, Die Regelung der Parallelimporte im Recht

---

[3] See, eg, D Graz, *Propriété Intellectuelle et Libre Circulation des Marchandises* (1988: Geneva, Librairie Droz). [4] See IP/C/W/280, p 6.
[5] *Kodak SA v Jumbo-Markt AG*, 4C.24/1999/rnd, 7 December 1999.

der WTO, 1998, p. 548; Alesch Staehelin, Das TRIPS-Abkommen, 2nd ed., Berne 1999, p. 57 et seq. and 148/9; Cottier & Stucki, loc. cit., p. 52; Cohen Jehoram, International Exhaustion versus Importation Right: a Murky Area of Intellectual Property Law, 1996 GRUR Int., p. 284). The claim expressed occasionally in the literature that the substantive protection of importation practically requires national exhaustion through the TRIPS Agreement is not, on the other hand, convincing (argued by Straus, Bedeutung des TRIPS für das Patentrecht, 1996 GRUR Int., p. 193/4); for the attempt to derive the exclusive application of national exhaustion from this agreement ignores and misinterprets the objectives of the agreement to establish the World Trade Organisation dated April 15, 1994, one element of which is the TRIPS Agreement, namely to eliminate all kinds of trade restrictions. On the contrary, TRIPS is intended to balance two sets of interests, namely the demand for the freedom of trade on the one hand and an increased protection of intellectual property rights on the other hand (Bronckers, The Exhaustion of Patent Rights under WTO Law, Journal of World Trade 1998, p. 144). Exhaustion, and hence the question of whether in particular parallel imports can be prohibited by the party entitled to the patent, is not, however, regulated by Art. 28 of TRIPS, but expressly reserved to national law pursuant to Art. 6 of the Agreement (cf. also Kunz-Ballstein, Zur Frage der Parallelimporte im internationalen gewerblichen Rechtsschutz, 1998 GRUR, p. 269/70).

Most importantly, the right to allow parallel imports under Article 6 of the TRIPS Agreement was categorically confirmed by the Doha Declaration on the TRIPS Agreement and Public Health. According to its paragraph 5(d):

Accordingly and in the light of paragraph 4 above, while maintaining our commitments in the TRIPS Agreement, we recognize that these flexibilities include:

(d) The effect of the provisions in the TRIPS Agreement that are relevant to the exhaustion of intellectual property rights is to leave each Member free to establish its own regime for such exhaustion without challenge, subject to the MFN and national treatment provisions of Articles 3 and 4.

The right to parallel import under an international principle of exhaustion has been regarded by many developing countries as a key component of a patent system sensitive to public health needs. This was one of the issues raised by pharmaceutical companies against South African legislation that allowed the Ministry of Health to authorize the parallel importation of medicines.[6]

Developing countries were keen to clarify in the Doha Declaration the Members' right to adopt an *international* principle of exhaustion of rights, in accordance with Article 6 of the Agreement. Paragraph 5(d) provides this sought-after clarification. It specifically states that 'the effect of the provisions in the TRIPS Agreement . . . is to leave each Member free to establish its own regime for such exhaustion *without challenge*' (emphasis added).

Though this paragraph does not add substantively to the TRIPS Agreement, it certainly reassures Members wishing to apply an international exhaustion principle that it would be legitimate and fully consistent with the Agreement to do so.

---

[6] See, eg, S Sell, *Private Power, Public Law: The Globalization of Intellectual Property Rights* (2003: Cambridge University Press) pp 151–3.

This paragraph, however, does not solve all the issues, particularly when the rights of the title-holder may be deemed exhausted in the country of exportation.

The admissibility of parallel imports under the system established by the TRIPS Agreement has been objected to on grounds related to the territorial nature of IPRs, as provided for in the Berne Convention and in the Paris Convention.

Thus, the WIPO Secretariat has argued that Article 16 (seizure of infringing copies not necessarily infringing in the exporting country), Article 13(3) (imported sound recordings produced under a non-voluntary licence) and Article IV(4)(a) of the Appendix to the Berne Convention suggest that the title-holder can prohibit the importation of copies, even if made with his authorization in the exporting country.[7] This position, however, has been widely contested by Berne Contracting Parties, while some countries, such as Australia and New Zealand, have adopted legislation that specifically allows for parallel imports of copyrighted works. In fact, the Berne Convention does not contain distribution or import-ation rights.

With regard specifically to patents, it has been argued that parallel imports are inconsistent with Article 4*bis*(1) of the Paris Convention, which requires Union Members to treat patents obtained in any country of the Union as 'independent of patents obtained for the same invention in other countries'.[8] If this argument were valid, parallel imports of patented products would be banned for Members that are parties to the Paris Convention, but not for those who are not.[9] This argu-ment, however, overlooks, first, that Members are only obliged to comply with the Articles of the Paris Convention (including Article 4*bis*) with regard to Parts II, III, and IV of the TRIPS Agreement, and not with regard to Part I, where Article 6 is included. Second, the argument incorrectly predicates that the exhaustion of rights doctrine affects the principle of independence of the patents. However, the rights in the importing countries are exclusively subject to domestic law and are unaffected by the legal status or changes in the legal status of foreign patents. The treatment given to the sale of the product in the exporting country does not influ-ence the rights and limitations established in the importing country, and vice versa. When parallel imports are admitted, it is because the domestic law of the importing country simply attributes certain effects to *acts* that have taken place in a foreign jurisdiction, independently of how such acts are qualified in the export-ing country. The independence of the respective patents remains untouched. The Supreme Court of Japan thus argued in the *Aluminum Wheels* case[10] that Article 4*bis* of the Paris Convention did not apply to cases of parallel imports, which were only subject to the domestic law of each country.

---

[7] Document prepared for the Committee of Experts on a Possible Protocol to the Berne Convention, BCP/CE/II/2, 12 March 1993, quoted by D Gervais, *The TRIPS Agreement. Drafting History and Analysis* (2003: London, Sweet and Maxwell, 2nd edn), p 114.

[8] Article 4*bis*(2) adds that this provision 'is to be understood in an unrestricted sense'. See N Pires de Carvalho, *The TRIPS Regime of Patent Rights* (2002: The Hague, Kluwer Law International), p 104.

[9] See N Pires de Carvalho op. cit. (2002), p 105.

[10] *Jap-Auto Products v BBS Kraftfarzeug Technik AG*, Hanrei Jiho (Supreme Court, 1 July 1997).

These arguments against an international or regional exhaustion of rights doctrine are, hence, far from convincing. Moreover, the Doha Declaration on the TRIPS Agreement and Public Health, as discussed below, has dissipated any possible doubt about the TRIPS-consistency of a regional or international exhaustion principle and about the admissibility of parallel imports.

The doctrine of exhaustion has been applied with respect to industrial property titles (patents, trademarks) as well as in relation to copyrights.[11] Article 28.1(a) of the TRIPS Agreement specifically allows Member Countries to limit the patent owner's exclusive right to import, as indicated in the footnote to that Article.[12] However, as explained in that footnote, Article 6 applies to 'all other rights conferred' under the Agreement.

Article 6 refers to 'intellectual property rights' without any qualification. A question arises as to whether the exhaustion may be applied in relation to all exclusive rights or only with regard to a subset thereof. It has been argued, based on the footnote to Article 28.1 of the Agreement that, in line with US legal doctrines, the exhaustion would not apply to the exclusive rights to make or reproduce protected subject matter.

According to that footnote, the rights in respect of the 'use, sale, importation or other distribution of goods' are subject to the provisions of Article 6. It notably does not refer to the exclusive right to 'make'—one essential component of the set of exclusive rights conferred by patents—but this seems logical since Article 6 refers to acts of commercialization or distribution of imported goods.

Parallel imports can only take place in relation to 'legitimate' products sold in a foreign country. What is 'legitimate' in this context is susceptible to different interpretations, equally admissible under the broad wording of Article 6.

Some national laws and jurisprudence[13] stipulate that in order for parallel imports to be admissible, the product must have been put on the market in a foreign country by or with the *consent* of the patent owner. Therefore, the supply by a compulsory licensee, or even by a voluntary licensee who is not authorized to parallel export, would not be legitimate.[14]

In some jurisdictions, the sale of goods by an intellectual property owner carries with it an 'implied licence' that the purchaser may use the goods for reasonable contemplated purposes. Exhaustion of the exclusive rights is presumed if the

---

[11] See, eg, Graz op. cit. (1988).

[12] Footnote 6: 'This right, like all other rights conferred under this Agreement in respect of the use, sale, importation or other distribution of goods, is subject to the provisions of Article 6.'

[13] See, eg, Pires de Carvalho op. cit. (2002), p 99, who asserts that '[t]he key element of exhaustion is consent'. Several decisions by the European Court of Justice have held that the application of the doctrine of exhaustion is conditional upon the existence of the right-holder's consent to putting its products on the market (eg *Pharmon v Hoechst*, Case 19/84, 1985 ECR 2281; *Merck & Co v Primecrown Ltd*, joined cases C-267/95 and C-268/95).

[14] See, eg, I Govaere, *The Use and Abuse of Intellectual Property Rights in EC Law* (1996: London, Sweet & Maxwell), pp 161–2.

owner of the IPR abstained from imposing restrictions in the sales contract with regard to the use, sale, or distribution of the product by the acquirer.[15] In the US, for instance, the doctrine of exhaustion has been accepted as a basis for parallel importation, but the patentee may impose contractual limitations to avoid the effects of the doctrine. In other words, parallel importation is authorized in the absence of enforceable contractual restrictions.[16]

Under the 'implied licence' theory, the exhaustion of IPRs ultimately rests on the discretion of the title-holder. This is well illustrated by a case decided by the High Court of Kenya as described in Box 3.1.[17]

The foundation of the consent theory as applied to exhaustion of rights is not clear. The requirement of the right-holder's consent seems to be grounded on the

---

Box 3.1: Parallel imports under the implied licence theory

In *Beecham Group v International Products Ltd*[18] the High Court of Kenya ruled against the importation of the product into Kenya by a local distributor based on territorial restrictions imposed by a UK patentee on a US licensee from whom the local distributor bought the product. The plaintiffs (Beecham Group) licensed the Bristol-Myers Company of New York to sell a new penicillin drug, under the name Pembritim, throughout the world, except in the British Commonwealth. The defendant, a Kenyan distributor, purchased Pembritim directly from the US licensee in New York. The defendant maintained that the Beecham Group's rights were exhausted when they placed the goods in the US market through a licensing agreement. Therefore, although the licensee was not authorized to sell in Kenya, the goods on which a royalty had once been paid were thereafter free in the hands of the purchaser to be sold anywhere in the world.

The Court held, however, that when a patented product is sold, it is free in the hands of the purchaser only from such monopoly rights as the vendor possesses. Therefore, a sale by a patentee, in the absence of any specific reservation, frees the article from the patentee's agents anywhere in the world, and a sale by the patentee's agent confers on the purchaser the same rights as a sale by the patentee. However, in the case of a sale by licensee, the extent to which the article is released from the patentee's rights depends on the extent of the authority conferred and Bristol-Myers had no authority to sell goods in infringement of the Kenyan patent. Hence, the Kenyan distributor could not acquire any better right than those possessed by Bristol-Myers (the US licensee).[19]

---

[15] A Yusuf and A Moncayo Von Hase, 'Intellectual Property Protection and International Trade-Exhaustion of Rights Revisited', (1992) 16 World Competition 1, p 118.

[16] M Barrett, 'The United States' Doctrine of Exhaustion: Parallel Imports of Patented Goods' (2000), 27 Northern Kentucky Law Review (No. 5), p 984.

[17] This decision preceded an amendment to the patent law in 2001 which introduced a provision allowing for parallel imports in broader terms.

[18] Quoted by D Gladwel, 'The Exhaustion of Intellectual Property Rights' (1986) 12 European Intellectual Property Review, p 368.

[19] Based on A Yusuf and A Moncayo von Hase op. cit. (1992), pp 118–19.

assumption that the IPR owner enjoys a *positive* right to the first sale of a protected product. The right of 'first sale' or 'first publication' is established in some countries in the copyright field, as a means of allowing authors control over their works,[20] but it does not apply to other categories of IPR. These are *negative* rights in nature; that is, they only confer the legal ability to exclude unauthorized use of subject matter, but no positive rights.

An interpretation of the scope of Article 6 of the TRIPS Agreement has been suggested, according to which the patent owner's consent will be required as a condition for the legality of parallel imports. This interpretation has been grounded on the footnote to Article 51 and on the approach adopted by the Treaty on Intellectual Property in Respect of Integrated Circuits, Washington DC, on 26 May 1989. However, the footnote to Article 51[21] has a very narrow scope: it only applies to trademarks and copyrights, while the referred to Treaty only deals with semiconductors.

Article 6(5) of the Treaty on Intellectual Property in Respect of Integrated Circuits provides the following:

> *[Exhaustion of Rights]* Notwithstanding paragraph (1)(a)(ii), any Contracting Party may consider lawful the performance, without the authorization of the holder of the right, of any of the acts referred to in that paragraph where the act is performed in respect of a protected layout-design (topography), or in respect of an integrated circuit in which such a layout-design (topography) is incorporated, that has been put on the market by, or with the consent of, the holder of the right.

This is the only express exhaustion of rights clause contained in WIPO-developed treaties.[22] Although this Article explicitly refers to the consent of the holder of the right, there is no basis to consider that this limitation applies to other fields of IPRs covered by the TRIPS Agreement. On the contrary, in the absence

---

[20] See, eg, J Cline, 'Moral Rights: the Long and Winding Road Toward Recognition', (1990), 14 Nova L. Rev, p 121, in A D'Amato and D Long, *International Intellectual Property Anthology* (1996), pp 113–18. In some countries, this right is provided for in the framework of the recognition of authors' moral rights.

[21] Footnote 14: '(b) "pirated copyright goods" shall mean any goods which are copies made without the consent of the right holder or person duly authorized by the right holder in the country of production and which are made directly or indirectly from an article where the making of that copy would have constituted an infringement of a copyright or a related right under the law of the country of importation'.

[22] The Washington Treaty never entered into force, as it failed to obtain the necessary number of ratifications therefor (see Chapter 10). The UPOV Convention, as revised in 1991, also contains an exhaustion of rights clause, which refers to the right-holders' consent. Article 16(1) [Exhaustion of right] stipulates that [T]he breeder's right shall not extend to acts concerning any material of the protected variety, or of a variety covered by the provisions of Article 14(5), which has been sold or otherwise marketed by the breeder or with his consent in the territory of the Contracting Party concerned, or any material derived from the said material, unless such acts (1) (i) involve further propagation of the variety in question; or (ii) involve an export of material of the variety, which enables the propagation of the variety, into a country which does not protect varieties of the plant genus or species to which the variety belongs, except where the exported material is for final consumption purposes.

of such limitation, the conclusion that may be logically arrived at is that the drafters of the TRIPS Agreement, certainly knowledgeable of that provision, opted to give Members more leeway in determining the scope for exhaustion in the fields of IPRs covered by the Agreement. The history of negotiation of this provision seems to confirm this interpretation, as the reference to the right-holder's consent was present in the negotiating drafts (see annex to this chapter), but it was not retained in the finally adopted text.

As the 'consent theory' predicates that exhaustion can only take place when the product is put on the foreign country market by or with the consent of the patent owner, a compulsory licensee could not be the source of legitimate parallel imports. This objection is overcome if exhaustion is construed under what may be called the 'reward theory', which was first formulated by the US Supreme Court in *Adams v Burke*:[23]

When the patentee, or the person having his rights, sells a machine or instrument whose sole value is in its use, he receives the consideration for its use and he parts with the right to restrict that use. The article . . . passes without the limit of the monopoly. That is to say, the patentee or his assignee having in the act of sale received all the royalty or consideration which he claims for the use of his invention in that particular machine or instrument, it is open to the use of the purchaser without further restriction on account of the monopoly of the patentee.

Under this approach, when distributing the protected product in a foreign country, the IPR owner is normally obtaining, as part of the product's price, compensation for the protected subject matter.[24] If the product is sold by a licensee, either voluntary or compulsory, he also receives compensation, generally in the form of a royalty payment. Hence, parallel importation does not deprive the patent owner of income to recoup past investment or impede contributions to future R&D.[25]

Whenever the IPR owner has given consent for distribution of his product or receives adequate remuneration in the country from which a product is imported, he should be deemed to have exhausted his rights over that product. This interpretation provides a sound basis for the application of the exhaustion principle under the TRIPS Agreement, and gives full meaning to all its relevant provisions.

Thus, TRIPS Article 31(f) allows a compulsory licence to be granted 'predominantly' for the domestic market, thereby permitting at least part of the production under licence to be 'parallel exported'. Such exports may take place to countries where there is or where there is no patent protection; the referred provision does not make any distinction in this regard. Excluding parallel exports from a

[23] 84 US 453 (17 Wall) (1873).
[24] Yusuf and Moncayo von Hase (1992), op. cit.; I. Govaere, *The Use and Abuse of Intellectual Property Rights in EC Law*, (1996: London Sweet & Maxwell), p 80.
[25] The net impact of parallel importation on contributions to R&D will depend, among other factors, on the price differential between the exporting and importing countries.

compulsory licensee[26] to a country where there is patent protection would deprive Article 31(f) of its full meaning. There is no basis to assume that Article 31(f) would only apply when the product produced under the compulsory licence is not protected in the importing country.

The underlying concept for allowing parallel imports is, in sum, that since the IPR holder would be normally rewarded through the first sale or distribution of the product, he has no right to control the use or resale of goods put on the market with his consent or in a way that allowed him to obtain compensation.

If parallel imports were outlawed in cases where there is remuneration of, but no consent by the patent owner (as in the case of compulsory licences), the usefulness of parallel imports as a pro-competitive mechanism would be seriously curtailed, since in most instances the patent owner may attach sale limitations to the products that he puts on the market, or impose contractual limitations on his licensees not to export without the patent owner's authorization.

Another controversial question is whether parallel imports would be admissible in cases where there is no IPR protection in the exporting country. Several decisions by the European Court of Justice have, in fact, permitted parallel imports originating from a country where no IPR protection was available.[27] Some national laws declare such imports admissible when the product was put on the market of the exporting country in any *legitimate* manner,[28] such as when patent protection was not available or was not sought for and/or obtained by the holder of the right in the exporting country. In this case, there would be no exhaustion of rights (because they never existed) but there would be no logical basis to apply a different solution if the imported product was put on the foreign market by the title-holder, as determined by the ECJ jurisprudence quoted above.

It is necessary to stress that in order to take advantage of the international exhaustion principle as allowed by the TRIPS Agreement—and confirmed by the Doha Declaration—national laws should incorporate the appropriate provisions. This and other TRIPS flexibilities do not automatically translate into national regimes, and do not protect governments (or private parties) from legal actions based on *national* laws and regulations that fail to make use of such flexibilities. Thus, specific legal provisions allowing for parallel imports would be normally necessary in order to benefit from the principle of international exhaustion of

---

[26] Any compulsory licensee will be bound—according to Article 31(h)—to pay 'adequate remuneration' to the patent holder 'taking into account the economic value of the authorization'. This means that the patent holder will be rewarded whenever his patent is exploited.

[27] See, eg, the *Merck v Primacrown* and *Beecham Group v Europharm* cases, ECJ, 5 December 1996, joined cases C 267/95 and C-268/95.

[28] See, eg, Article 36(i) of Argentine law 24.426 (however, the scope of this provision has been limited by regulation, Decree 260/96). The US complained that Argentina's legislation relating to imports of patented products was inconsistent with Article 28 of the TRIPS Agreement. The complaint was settled by mutual agreement, without amendment to the Argentine law. See *Argentina— Patent Protection for Pharmaceuticals and Test Data Protection for Agricultural Chemicals*, WT/DS171, 6 May 1999, and *Argentina—Certain Measures on the Protection of Patents and Test Data*, WT/DS196, 30 May 2000.

rights. Although in some countries the application of that principle may result from jurisprudential elaboration, it may take a long time to test what the legal solution is. The ensuing uncertainty is likely to discourage or effectively prevent the use of such mechanism as a means to obtain products at lower prices than those available domestically.

Some national laws permit parallel imports on relatively broad terms.[29] However, parallel imports are not allowed under many national laws,[30] or they are only permitted under some conditions. A survey of patent laws in developing countries shows that many such countries have not or have only partially used the flexibilities allowed by the TRIPS Agreement in this regard.[31] Thus, parallel importation is permitted in the Andean Group countries when the product was sold by the patent owner or by another party with his/her consent or by a party economically linked to the patent owner.[32] In Brazil, parallel importation is allowed only if the products are sold with the consent of the owner and provided that the invention is not exploited locally.[33] In Argentina, only a local voluntary licensee is authorized to engage in parallel importation.[34] In the case of South Africa, the scope for parallel importation is also quite limited, since it is subject to a Ministerial order (by the Minister of Health) and only applies to medicines if they were put on the market by the patent owner or with his consent.[35] Despite this narrow scope, the provision of the South African law was vigorously challenged

[29] See, eg, Article 8 of the Kenyan Industrial Property Act, 2001.

[30] Many laws do not clarify whether parallel imports are permitted or not. In the absence of a specific rule allowing them, imports are likely to be subject to the patent owner's exclusive rights.

[31] See P. Thorpe, Implementation of the TRIPS Agreement by Developing Countries, (2002) Commission on Intellectual Property Rights Background Paper 7, available at <http://www. iprcommission.org> (last accessed on 19 June 2005).

[32] Article 54, Decision 486 ('Common Industrial property Regime') of the Andean Community, available at <http://www.comunidadandina.org/ingles/treaties/dec/dec.htm> (last accessed on 19 June 2005).

[33] Article 68.4 of the Brazilian Industrial Property Code Law 9.279, 1996, available at <http:// www.sice.oas.org> (last accessed on 19 June 2005).

[34] Article 36(c) of the Argentine Decree 260/96, 1996.

[35] Article 15C, Medicines Act. Section 15C of the South African Medicines and Related Substances Control Amendment Act, No 90 of 1997, provides as follows:

Measures to Ensure Supply of More Affordable Medicines

15C. The Minister may prescribe conditions for the supply of more affordable medicines in certain circumstances so as to protect the health of the public, and in particular may–

notwithstanding anything to the contrary contained in the Patents Act, 1978 (Act No 57 of 1978), determine that the rights with regard to any medicine under a patent granted in the Republic shall not extend to acts in respect of such medicine which has been put onto the market by the owner of the medicine, or with his or her consent;

prescribe the conditions on which any medicine which is identical in composition, meets the same quality standard and is intended to have the same proprietary name as that of another medicine already registered in the Republic, but which is imported by a person other than the person who is the holder of the registration certificate of the medicine already registered and which originates from any site of the manufacture of the original manufacturer as approved by the council in the prescribed manner, may be imported;

prescribe the registration procedure for, as well as the use of, the medicine referred to in paragraph (b).

by the US government and large pharmaceutical companies.[36] This challenge was one of the main developments that led developing countries to propose a declaration on the TRIPS Agreement and public health, eventually adopted by the Ministerial Conference held in Doha in November 2001.[37]

While it is clear that parallel imports are perfectly legitimate under the TRIPS Agreement, there have been arguments about the benefits and costs of allowing such imports. The US government tends to view parallel imports negatively, although many consumers benefit from parallel imports of medicines from Canada and the permission of such imports has gained growing support in that country. At the Council for TRIPS Special Session of 21 June 2001, the US delegation held that:

In our view, advocates of parallel importation overlook the fact that permitting such imports discourages patent owners from pricing their products differently in different markets based upon the level of economic development because of the likelihood that, for example, products sold for low prices in a poor country will be bought up by middle men and sent to wealthiest country markets and sold at higher prices, for the benefit primarily of the middle men. The lack of parallel import protection can also have significant health and safety implications. Our law enforcement and regulatory agencies, especially FDA, have commented on how very difficult it is for them to keep counterfeit and unapproved drugs out of our country even with the strong parallel import protection provided in the United States. Advocating parallel imports, therefore, could work to the disadvantage of the very people on behalf of whom the advocates purport to be speaking. As Dr Brundtland in Oslo recently noted, 'For differential pricing to work on a large scale, I think we can all agree that there must be watertight ways of preventing lower priced drugs from finding their way back into rich country markets.

This view reflects to a large extent the opinion of the US pharmaceutical industry, which has argued about the risks of the re-exportation of drugs sold at low cost in developing countries to higher-priced markets. Parallel imports, where admitted, it is argued, may affect the industry's ability to fund future R&D.[38] However, trade in medicines is subject to quite stringent national regulations that erect effective barriers to market access. Moreover, parallel imports would only take place where significant price differentials exist. Pharmaceutical firms may reduce such differentials or sell the patented products under different trademarks or packaging in major markets, in order to make parallel importation difficult or unattractive.[39] Further, any developed country may adopt measures to prevent

---

[36] The pharmaceutical industry also argued that the authorization given to the Health Minister was too broadly drafted and unconstitutional. The legal action was withdrawn in April 2001.

[37] See pp 103 and 321 below.

[38] H Bale, 'TRIPS, Pharmaceuticals and Developing Countries: Implications for Drug Access and Drug Development', paper presented at the WHO Workshop on the TRIPS Agreement and its Impact on Pharmaceuticals (Jakarta, 2–4 May 2000) p 18.

[39] J Watal, 'Pharmaceutical patents, prices and welfare losses: a simulation study of policy options for India under the WTO TRIPS Agreement' (2000) The World Economy, vol. 23, No 5, pp 733–52.

parallel imports (provided that such restriction is not found inconsistent with WTO obligations).[40] In fact, the risk of trade diversion into rich markets seems to be often overstated. The European Commission has noted that 'the industry acknowledges that to date there is no re-importation of medicines from the poorest developing countries into the European Union, ie the problem of re-importation is still largely theoretical'.[41]

Parallel imports increase static efficiency, that is, the allocation of products at the lowest possible price. Like the availability of compulsory licences, parallel imports provide an important device to discipline markets and to induce suppliers to commercialize their products on reasonable conditions. Parallel imports may also be a powerful tool to increase allocative efficiency. If consumers can get from a foreign country legitimate products at lower prices than those locally charged by the IPR owner, this increases static efficiency and does not necessarily reduce dynamic efficiency, as the IPR owner has been remunerated (in the foreign market) for the intellectual contribution he has made. Of course, the levels of profit obtained by the IPR owner may be lower than those obtainable if he were able to fragment markets and charge a higher price in the importing country, but this does not mean that he would not be able to recover his R&D expenditures.

It has been suggested that, in order to keep a system of tier pricing and prevent low-priced medicines in developing countries flowing to developed countries, the former should adopt measures to prevent their exportation. The consistency of such export restraints with WTO rules, however, is questionable, notably in the light of Article XI of GATT which prohibits quantitative restrictions.[42] The prohibition to parallel import (deriving from a national exhaustion principle) may, in effect, be regarded as a GATT-inadmissible quantitative restriction, having in view that in the context of WTO the protection of IPRs is subsidiary to the overarching goal of enhancing international trade.[43]

Annex

Negotiating history[44]

In his 23 July 1990 report on the status of work in the TRIPS Negotiating Group, the Chairman (Lars E R Anell) presented two sets of proposals. In an Annex to the report, he

---

[40] See below.

[41] European Commission, DG Trade, Tiered pricing for medicines exported to developing countries, measures to prevent their re-importation into the EC market and tariffs in developing countries. Working Document (2002: Brussels, 22 April), p 10.

[42] See, eg, the ECJ judgment in *EMI Records v CBS Schallplatten GmbH*, 1976 ECR, reproduced in (1976) 7 IIC 275.

[43] See the Preamble of the TRIPS Agreement (first provision) and the Preamble of the Agreement Establishing the WTO. See also S Domenico, 'On parallel importation, TRIPS and European Court of Justice Decisions', (2002) 4 Journal of World Intellectual Property, p 515.

[44] For an analysis of the negotiating history, see UNCTAD-ICTSD op. cit. (2005), pp 92–117.

presented a composite text that was taken from various proposals by delegations to the Negotiating Group, indicating the source of each proposal by numerical reference to the source document.

Composite text of July 23 1990[45]

It is understood that, unless expressly provided to the contrary in this agreement, nothing in this agreement shall limit the freedom of PARTIES to provide that any intellectual property rights conferred in respect of the use, sale, importation and other distribution of goods are exhausted once those goods have been put on the market by or with the consent of the right holder.[46]

Draft text transmitted to the Brussels Ministerial Conference (December 1990)

Subject to the provisions of Articles 3 and 4 above, nothing in this Agreement imposes any obligation on, or limits the freedom of, PARTIES with respect to the determination of their respective regimes regarding the exhaustion of any intellectual property rights conferred in respect of the use, sale, importation or other distribution of goods once those goods have been put on the market by or with the consent of the right holder.

---

[45] Chairman's Report to the GNG, Status of Work in the Negotiating Group, Negotiating Group on Trade-Related Aspects of Intellectual Property Rights, including Trade in Counterfeit Goods, MTN.GNG/NG11/W/76, 23 July 1990, presented by the Chairman of the TRIPS Negotiating Group (Lars E R Anell). Alternatives 'A' correspond to texts from developed countries and 'B' from developing countries.

[46] Footnote to the Article on the right of distribution in the section on copyright.

Chapter 4

OBJECTIVES AND PRINCIPLES

The Interpretive value of Article 7

Objectives

7. The protection and enforcement of intellectual property rights should contribute to the promotion of technological innovation and to the transfer and dissemination of technology, to the mutual advantage of producers and users of technological knowledge and in a manner conducive to social and economic welfare, and to a balance of rights and obligations.

Negotiations on intellectual property in the Uruguay Round were initiated upon the demand of developed countries, with considerable resistance from developing countries. The primary objective of the proponents of the Agreement was to secure the rights of intellectual property owners to exploit their protected assets in the jurisdiction of all parties to the GATT. They emphasized the role of the protection of IPRs as incentives for innovation, and were keen to leave issues relating to the exploitation of the rights to the discretion of title-holders.

In contrast, developing countries feared that a strengthened protection of IPR protection would give too much power to title-holders and limit access to, and transfer of, technology to those countries. They approached these negotiations with a clear understanding of their weakness in the generation of new science and technology. At the time the negotiations took place, only a small fraction of world expenditures on R&D was accounted for by those countries. The situation is not too different today. Ten developed countries account for 84 per cent of global resources spent on R&D annually, control 94 per cent of the technological output in terms of patents taken out in the United States, and receive 91 per cent of global cross-border royalties and technology licence fees.[1]

Article 7 of the Agreement, based on a proposal submitted by developing countries,[2] represents a compromise between these two positions. It reflects the prevailing justification for the granting of IPRs in the technology-related fields, as a tool

---

[1] See, eg, N Kumar, 'Intellectual Property Rights, Technology and Economic Development: Experiences of Asian Countries, Study prepared for the CIPR' (2002), available at <http://www.iprcommission.org> (last accessed on 30 April 2005).

[2] See document MTN.GNG/NG11/W/71, 19 May 1990.

for the promotion of innovation, but also the developing countries' concerns about transfer and dissemination of technology.

Article 7 (jointly with Article 8) of the TRIPS Agreement provides important elements for the interpretation and implementation of the rights and obligations under the Agreement.

As mentioned, Article 7 reflects a compromise between the proponents of the Agreement, who emphasized the role of IPRs on innovation, and developing countries, who were concerned about the impact that IPRs might have on the economic and social development.

Despite that, Article 7 refers to 'the protection and enforcement of intellectual property rights' in general, it only deals with 'innovation' and 'technology'. It thus focuses on certain types of IPR, such as patents, some categories of trade secrets, and integrated circuits' layout-designs. The objectives of IPRs regarding copyright[3] and related rights, treated in Part II, Section 1, of the Agreement, as well as trademarks, geographical indications, and industrial designs (dealt with in Sections 2, 3, and 4 of Part I) are not fully captured in this provision. This imbalance is possibly attributable to developing countries' preoccupation about the impact of higher standards of IPR protection on the access to innovations and the products and services derived therefrom. Negotiations on issues not directly related to access to and use of technology were overall less controversial between the North and the South, while they often created considerable tensions between developed countries themselves.[4]

The focus on technology-related IPRs does not, however, mean that Article 7 is irrelevant for other types of IPRs. The proper balance of rights and obligations is an overriding objective of the WTO system,[5] as it is to enhance Members' social and economic welfare.[6] Thus, Article 7 (read in conjunction with Article 8) may be important to interpret the scope of the exceptions allowed under Article 13 of the TRIPS Agreement in the field of copyright,[7] and to determine the extent of other obligations under the Agreement.[8]

---

[3] Copyright protection not only covers, however, artistic and literary creations, but also works of a functional character and significant technological value, such as computer programs.

[4] See, eg, C Correa, 'TRIPS Agreement: copyright and related rights' (1994) 25 International Review of Industrial Property and Copyright Law, p 543.

[5] See Article 3.5 of the DSU, which refers to settlement of disputes as a means to preserve such a balance between WTO Members.

[6] See the Preamble of the Agreement Establishing the WTO.

[7] See, eg, R Okeidiji, 'Toward an international fair use doctrine' (2000) 39 Columbia Journal of Transnational Law, p 114.

[8] In the case of copyright, the balance between the public interest and private rights is somehow expressed in Article 27 of the Universal Declaration, which provides:

   i) everyone has the right freely to participate in the cultural life of the Community, to enjoy the arts and to share in scientific advancement and its benefits.

   ii) Everyone has the right to the protection of the moral and material interests resulting from any scientific, literary or artistic production of which he is an author.

Article 7 states that IPRs *should* contribute to the promotion of technological innovation and to the transfer and dissemination of technology. Some observers have read 'should' to mean that Article 7 is a mere hortary provision, the interpretative value of which is equivalent to that of any preambular provision. However, the negotiating parties had the option to include the provision in the Preamble but they did it in Part I of the Agreement, under the heading 'General provisions and basic principles'. The interpreter cannot disregard this choice, as a treaty must be interpreted to give meaning and effect to all its terms.[9] This choice indicates that these provisions are to be systematically applied in the implementation and interpretation of the Agreement. The place of this provision in the Agreement heightens its legal status.[10]

Articles 7 and 8 provide the context for the interpretation of other provisions in the TRIPS Agreement.[11] The way in which they define the object and purpose of the Agreement should guide any panel and the Appellate Body for such interpretation. Article 31 of the Vienna Convention on the Law of the Treaties[12]—deemed by GATT/WTO jurisprudence as a codification of customary rules of treaty interpretation[13]—explicitly requires consideration of the 'purpose' of the treaty. If the Agreement itself contains a definition of its purpose, as Article 7 does, panels and the Appellate Body cannot ignore it or create their own definition in interpreting other provisions of the Agreement.

The panel report in *Canada–Patent Protection for Pharmaceutical Products* (relating to the so-called 'Bolar' exception) was particularly important in clarifying the weight to be given to the 'Objectives' (Article 7) (as well as the 'Principles' contained in Article 8) when interpreting the Agreement's other provisions. The panel stated that:

Obviously, the exact scope of Article 30's authority will depend on the specific meaning given to its limiting conditions. The words of those conditions must be examined with particular care on this point. Both the goals and the limitations stated in Articles 7 and 8.1

---

[9] The principle of 'effective interpretation' (or *'l'effet utile'*) has been applied in several GATT/WTO cases. See, eg, Report of the Appellate Body, *Argentina–Safeguard Measures on Imports of Footwear*, WT/DS121/AB/R (2000), p 88. See also P Mengozzi (ed.), 'The World Trade Organization Law: an Analysis of its First Practice', in *International Trade Law on the 50th Anniversary of the Multilateral Trade System 26* (1999: Milano, A. Giuffré).

[10] See, eg, D Gervais, *The TRIPS Agreement. Drafting History and Analysis* (2003: London, Sweet & Maxwell, 2nd edn), p 116.

[11] According to the EC and their Member States, 'although Articles 7 and 8 were not drafted as general exception clauses, they are important for interpreting other provisions of the Agreement, including where measures are taken by Members to meet health objectives'. See IP/C/W/280, 12 June 2001.

[12] A treaty 'shall be interpreted in good faith in accordance with the ordinary meaning to be given to the terms of the treaty in their context and in the light of its object and purpose'. Vienna Convention on the Law of Treaties, 1155 UNTS 331; UKTS (1980) 58, Cmnd 7964; 8 ILM (1969) 679.

[13] See, eg, D Shanker, 'The Vienna Convention on the Law of Treaties, the Dispute Settlement System of the WTO and the Doha Declaration on the TRIPs Agreement' (2002) 36 J World Trade, p 721.

must obviously be borne in mind when doing so as well as those of other provisions of the TRIPS Agreement which indicate its object and purposes.[13a]

However, panels and the Appellate Body may be tempted to introduce their own policy views on IPRs. In the *Canada–Patent Protection for Pharmaceutical Products* case, for instance, the panel advanced its own conception about the 'policy' underpinning patent law. It stated:

The normal practice of exploitation by patent owners, as with owners of any other intellectual property right, is to exclude all forms of competition that could detract significantly from the economic returns anticipated from a patent's grant of market exclusivity... Patent laws establish a carefully defined period of market exclusivity as an inducement to innovation, and the policy of those laws cannot be achieved unless patent owners are permitted to take effective advantage of that inducement once it has been defined (para 7.55).

Though this statement—developed in the context of the discussion on the concept of 'normal exploitation' of a patent—is too simplistic and does not provide elements for a serious elaboration on the justification and objectives of the patent system, it does hint at the panel's own conception on a matter that raises considerable debate—especially among economists—and on which different positions and theories have been elaborated.[14] The panels' view, while emphasizing stimulation to innovation, fails to consider other equally essential objectives of the patent grants. Like other IPRs, patents are granted in the public interest, and not merely to allow the patent owners to obtain the 'economic returns anticipated from a patent's grant of market exclusivity'. The diffusion of knowledge and its continuous improvement are equally important objectives of that system.[15]

If the commercial interests of the patent owner were the only ones to be considered, the interpretation of the Agreement would in practice defeat its intended objectives. The TRIPS Agreement must be viewed as a means for the realization of public policy objectives via the 'inducement to innovation' *and* the access to the results thereof by those who need them. In other words, the objectives of the patent system would not be fulfilled if it only served to induce innovations to the benefit of those who control them.[16]

The context provided by Articles 7 and 8 may be of particular importance to correctly interpret the extent of several obligations and exceptions under the

---

[13a] Report of the panel, WT/DS114/R (2000), para 7.26.

[14] See, eg, A Gutterman, *Innovation and Competition Policy: A Comparative Study of Regulation of Patent Licensing and Collaborative Research & Development in the United States and the European Community* (1999: London, Kluwer Law International), pp 36–70.

[15] See P Welfens, J Addison, D Audretsch, T Gries, and H Grupp, *Globalization, Economic Growth and Innovation Dynamics* (1999: New York, Springer), p 138.

[16] 'The TRIPS Agreement is not *only* about protecting pharmaceutical industry profits. It is also about the health of the global economy, and about the health of individuals. F Abbott, 'The TRIPS-legality of measures taken to address public health crises: a synopsis' (2001, paper presented at the MSF Working Group on IP and access to Medicines, New Delhi, 5–6 June), p 14.

TRIPS Agreement, such as the concepts of 'third party' and 'legitimate interests' in Article 30, 'unfair commercial use' under Article 39.3, and 'abuse' in Articles 40 and 50.3, among others.

IPRs and innovation

In accordance with Article 7, 'the protection and enforcement of intellectual property rights should contribute to the promotion of technological innovation...'. The relationship between IPRs protection and innovation is not straightforward. The use of 'should', in fact, indicates that IPRs do not necessarily lead to innovation.

Intellectual property rights (IPRs) retard imitation. They are intended to stimulate innovation and creation by offering the prospects of a monetary reward that would allow title-holders to recover investments in research and development (R&D) and make a profit. The objective of IPRs is generally achieved by conferring *exclusive* rights for the exploitation of the protected subject matter. Exclusive rights empower title-holders to prevent third parties from commercially using the protected knowledge without authorization, thereby erecting barriers to the diffusion and use of knowledge.

IPRs create scarcity of knowledge despite the fact that, by its very nature, it is a *non-rival* good.[17] Non-rival goods have the property that they can—usually at modest costs, and sometimes even at zero cost—be available for public use. Though non-rivalrous in nature, knowledge is *excludable* by action of its possessor, or by legal means.

A company may prevent its competitors from knowing how a particular manufacturing process operates by, for instance, tightly controlling access to its physical premises and preventing the disclosure of any relevant data by its own employees. Similarly, the development of digital protection technologies, generally known as 'rights management systems' provide technical means[18] to prevent unauthorized access to stored information. In the area of biotechnology, the genetic use restriction technologies (GURTs) would render sterile the subsequent generation of seeds. The use of these types of physical measures may be encouraged or supported by legal means.[19]

In some cases, third parties are excluded from using certain information—which would be otherwise accessible—purely by legal means, such as in the case of published copyright works and patents (which require disclosure of the protected

[17] See, eg, J Stiglitz, 'Knowledge as a global public good', in I Kaul, I Grunberg, and M Stern (eds), *Global Public Goods. International Cooperation in the 21st Century* (1999: New York, Oxford University Press), p 309.

[18] Such as 'password codes' for computer programs, encryption, or scrambling for cable programming, videocassettes, CD-ROMs, and DVDs.

[19] Thus, the protection of trade secrets ('undisclosed information') is a distinct obligation under the TRIPS Agreement. The US 'Digital Millennium Copyright Act' (DMCA) prohibits the sale and use of any devices intended to defeat technical barriers established to protect digitized information.

invention). In these cases, the society creates a deliberate mode of exclusion for the reproduction or use of knowledge by *policy design*, based on the recognition of an intellectual *property*.[20]

Though the notions of intellectual property were known in ancient cultures and developed in the Middle Ages,[21] different forms of protection gradually obtained universal recognition in the course of the twentieth century. During the past twenty years, in particular, large industrial and knowledge-based companies and governments of industrialized countries joined forces in order to expand the boundaries and strengthen the rights available to the owners of knowledge.[22] A noticeable result of this concerted action was the adoption, as part of the Final Act of the Uruguay Round, of the TRIPS Agreement, an important manifestation of the 'pro-patent movement' that emerged in the 1980s in the USA.[23]

Patents, in particular, offer the incentive of a (minimum) twenty years' control over the protected subject matter and, in the appropriate contexts, may encourage investment in R&D. However, one increasingly widespread view is that the role of patents in promoting innovation is less substantial than usually claimed,[24] and that 'incremental increases in patent protection are unlikely to influence inventive activity significantly and incremental reductions might actually enhance economic welfare'.[25]

Patents may even stifle the very innovation they are supposed to foster, such as in the case of upstream scientific outcomes, research tools, or overbroad claims that impede follow-on research. More generally, according to some analysts in the US, 'the patent system is generating waste and uncertainty that hinders and threatens the innovative process'.[26]

Moreover, the argument that a 'strong' patent system would foster local innovation in developing countries is not supported by evidence, even in countries with large markets and considerable industrial development. In the case of Mexico, for instance, a study found no increase in domestic patent applications after ten years of the enactment of strong patent protection, but rather residents' share of total

---

[20] On the application of the concept of property to knowledge, see, eg, C May, *A Global Political Economy of Intellectual Property Rights. The New Enclosures?* (2000: London and New York, Routledge/RIPE) pp 47–9.

[21] On the history of IPRs, see, eg, P David, 'Knowledge, property and the system dynamics of technological change' (1992), World Bank Annual Conference on Development Economics, Washington, DC.

[22] See, eg, M Ryan, *Knowledge Diplomacy. Global Competition and the Politics of Intellectual Property*, (1998: Washington, DC, Brooking Institution Press).

[23] See, eg, O Granstrand, *The Economics and Management of Intellectual Property* (1999: Clentenham and Northampton, Edwar Elgar), p 38.

[24] See, eg, the analysis in R Levin, A Klevorick, R Nelson, and S Winter, 'Appropriating the Returns from Industrial Research and Development' (1987) Brookings Papers on Economic Activity No 3.

[25] W Landes and R Posner, *The Economic Structure of Intellectual Property Law* (2003: Cambridge, The Belkup Press of Harvard University Press), p 327.

[26] See A Jaffe and J Lerner, *Innovation and Its Discontents: How Our Broken Patent System is Endangering Innovation and Progress, and What to Do About It* (2003: Princeton University Press), p 3.

patent applications fell by half, dropping to only 0.67 per cent in 2000 compared to 1.27 per cent in 1996.[27]

As noted by the US Federal Trade Commission, patents 'can enable firms to increase their expected profits from investments in research and development, thus fostering innovation that would not occur but for the prospect of a patent'.[28] However, the role of patents in innovation should not be taken as an article of faith, as it is very dependent on the context in which the rights are conferred and on the extent of rights granted. The standards of patentability applied and the quality of the examination process are also critical. Low standards of patentability and poor examination can lead, as illustrated by the case of the US, to the proliferation of patents on trivial developments, defensive patenting strategies, and the use (or abuse) of patents to limit legitimate competition.[29]

Transfer and dissemination of technology

The use of 'should' in Article 7 seems to indicate that IPRs do not necessarily promote innovation and the dissemination and transfer of technology, but that they should do so in order to satisfy the overall objectives of the TRIPS Agreement, as stated in the first provision of the Preamble. That wording suggests that Members must implement their obligations under the Agreement in a way that effectively contributes to the objectives of promoting innovation *and* the transfer and dissemination of technology. Article 7 (and Article 8) may serve to justify exceptions to exclusive rights where the right-holder has failed to participate in social and economic development.

There are multiple definitions and modalities of 'transfer of technology'. It may take place through non-equity and equity forms, informal and formal mechanisms. The use of different forms of transfer varies as the firms and the industry evolve through different technological stages. At the initiation stage in the industrialization process, mostly 'mature' technologies are incorporated by firms in developing countries through non-equity forms of technology transfer, such as the acquisition of machinery and equipment, imitation through reverse engineering and other means, and technical assistance provided by Original Equipment Suppliers (OEM).[30] Though informal modes of transfer predominate at earlier stages of industrial development, technologies need to be acquired through more formal modes, including turn-key agreements and licences, in cases relating to

---

[27] See J Aboites, 'Innovación, patentes y globalización', in J Aboites and G Dutrénit (eds), *Innovación, aprendizaje y creación de capacidades tecnológicas* (2003: Mexico; UAM), pp 163–206.
[28] Federal Trade Commission (FTC) (2003), To promote innovation: the proper balance of competition and patent law policy (2003) Summary, p 3 (available at <htpp://www.ftc.gov>, last accessed on 28 February 2005).   [29] Idem, p 7.
[30] L Kim and C Dahlman, 'Technology policy for industrialization: an integrative framework and Korea's experience' (1992) 21 Research Policy, p 439.

large-scale industries (eg steel, petrochemicals) where complex processes and plant layouts are difficult to imitate. Foreign direct investment (FDI) is also a usual mode of technology transfer at an early development stage, when local absorptive capabilities for unbundled technologies are limited, as well as for modern technologies that holders want to keep under secure control.[31]

Despite the expectations created by the proponents of the TRIPS Agreement about the increase in technology transfer to developing countries that it would bring about, such countries have become increasingly sceptical about the existence of a virtuous relationship between increased protection of IPRs and technology transfer. This scepticism underpins the request by these countries to establish a Working Group on Trade and Technology Transfer in the WTO, as agreed upon by the Doha Ministerial Conference, in November 2001.[32] Developing countries have noted at the Working Group, that most provisions in WTO agreements relating to transfer of technology were of 'best endeavour' nature rather than binding obligations, and that they should be made operational. Developed countries, however, have argued that the WTO provisions were underpinned by several priorities such as integrating countries into world trade, protecting IPRs, increasing the flow of investment and promoting sustainable development. They also observed that some of these provisions identified technical assistance, training, provision of information and other forms of developmental cooperation as the principal means of promoting transfer of technology (TOT). They were reluctant to introduce any negotiating aspect into the Working Group.[33]

Argentina and Brazil, supported by a number of other developing countries,[34] also made a quest for specifically addressing the issue of transfer of technology within WIPO at the 31st Session of the WIPO General Assembly (27 September–5 October 2004). In view of those countries, the development dimension of intellectual property policy requires that WIPO, through a dedicated process, explores the type of policies, initiatives, and reforms necessary to contribute to the transfer and dissemination of technology to the benefit of all countries.[35]

A number of studies have been conducted to assess the impact of IPRs on technology transfer.[36] However, the available evidence is limited and ambiguous, as is the case with regard to studies of the implications of IPR regimes on the flows of foreign direct investment. Some countries with 'weak' IPR protection schemes, such as South Korea, Taiwan, and Brazil, had been among the major technology

---

[31] See generally C Correa, 'Emerging trends: new patterns of technology transfer', in S Patel, P Roffe, and A Yusuf (eds), *The International Transfer of Technology. The Origins and Aftermath of the United Nations Negotiations on a Draft Code of Conduct* (2000, The Hague: Kluwer Law International).'
[32] Document WT/MIN(01)/DEC/1, 20 November 2001.
[33] See Report of the Working Group on Trade and Transfer of Technology to the General Council. Geneva, World Trade Organization, WT/WGTTT/5, 14 July 2003.
[34] See Document WO/GA/31/11, submitted by Argentina, Bolivia, Brazil, Cuba, Dominican Republic, Ecuador, Egypt, Iran, Kenya, Peru, Sierra Leone, South Africa, Tanzania, and Venezuela.
[35] Ibidem.
[36] See especially Keith Maskus, *Intellectual Property Rights in the Global Economy* (2000: Washington DC, Institute for International Economics).

borrowers in the pre-TRIPS era. The reverse situation can also be found. Countries (including many African countries) with standards of protection comparable to those in force in developed countries have recorded a poor or insignificant performance as technology importers. The simple explanation is, of course, that IPRs are but one of many factors—and arguably not the most important factor—that affect cross-border flows of technology.

IPRs should, in accordance with Article 7, also promote the 'dissemination' of technology. This concept is close to but different from the 'transfer' of technology,[37] as it suggests that access to knowledge takes place through informal mechanisms and reaches an undetermined number of possible users. The word 'dissemination' reinforces the idea contained in the last part of the provision, in the sense that the ultimate purpose of IPRs as a tool to promote innovation is to get used. As innovation economists widely recognize, the innovative process cannot be separated from the diffusion process.[38]

Whatever the importance of different forms of transfer and dissemination of technology may be, in the context of the TRIPS Agreement, Article 7 needs to be read as referring to the transfer and dissemination of IPR-protected technology, since intellectual property protection is the specific subject matter of the Agreement.

The concept of 'mutual advantage of producers and users of technological knowledge' suggests that the recognition of IPRs should not erect a barrier to the use of the protected knowledge. It reinforces the idea that IPRs are a means to promote both the creation and the diffusion of technologies, and explains the incorporation of important provisions of the Agreement, such as Article 31 on compulsory licences. 'Users' in this article can be interpreted as encompassing final consumers as well as producers of goods and services that utilize technological knowledge.

Social and economic welfare

In addition, IPRs should work 'in a manner conducive to social and economic welfare'. This means that the recognition and enforcement of intellectual property rights are subject to higher social values (as further developed in Article 8.1 of the Agreement). The UN Commission on Human Rights has, in fact, addressed the tension between the TRIPS Agreement and human rights,[39] but little recognition of human rights values in international intellectual property instruments can be found.

---

[37] 'To disseminate' means to 'scatter about, sow in various places', *Concise Oxford Dictionary*, (1982: Oxford University Press, 7th edn), p 278.

[38] See, eg, OECD, *Technology and the Economy. The Key Relationships* (1992: Paris).

[39] See Sub-Commission on the Promotion and Protection of Human Rights, 'The impact of the Agreement on Trade-Related Aspects of Intellectual Property Rights on human rights', E/CN.4/ Sub.2/2001/13, June 2001.

An important issue is the extent to which WTO panels and the Appellate Body should consider international human rights law in the interpretation of the provisions of the TRIPS Agreement. In a progress report on 'Globalization and its Impact on Full Enjoyment of Human Rights'[40] submitted to the Sub-Commission on the Promotion and Protection of Human Rights, two UN Special Rapporteurs stated that the UN Charter and its obligations override all international agreements before and after the Charter, and to the extent of any inconsistencies, the Charter prevails.[41] The WTO, they argued, and also the World Bank and the International Monetary Fund, as international organizations, are bound by the UN Charter to respect fundamental principles of international human rights law covering civil, political, economic, social, and cultural rights enshrined in the Universal Declaration of Human Rights and the two international covenants.[42] They called for the strengthening of the provisions of the TRIPS (Articles 7, 8, 30, and 31) seeking to provide a balance of the public interest with the rights and incentives for innovation. Further, they asked WTO Members to come out with a 'specific and unequivocal undertaking to the effect that no provision of the agreement prohibits members from taking measures to provide access to medicines at affordable prices, promote public health and nutrition'.[43]

In the view of Chapman, of the American Association for the Advancement of Science,

Intellectual property law should incorporate explicit human rights and ethical provisions as criteria for the evaluation of applications for patents and trademarks and develop an institution mechanism capable of making these determinations. In most cases, patent and trademark offices are not competent to undertake such a review and are inclined to subordinate human rights considerations to an economic calculus.[44]

The High Commissioner reported to the Fifty-second Session of the Commission on Human Rights (Sub-Commission on the Promotion and Protection of Human Rights),[45] that 'there are potential links between human rights and the TRIPS Agreement' and pointed out that the objectives set out in Article 7 of the TRIPS Agreement 'recognize a need for balance'.[46] It noted that:

while links between the promotion and protection of human rights on the one hand and the rights covered by the TRIPS Agreement exist, there remain fundamental differences of approach. First of all, the overall thrust of the TRIPS Agreement is the promotion of innovation through the provision of commercial incentives. The various links with human rights' subject matter—the promotion of public health, nutrition, environment and

---

[40] See E/CN.4/Sub.2/2001/10.
[41] See SUNS, No. 4952, 8 August 2001 (electronic journal).   [42] Ibidem.
[43] Ibidem.
[44] A Chapman, 'Approaching Intellectual Property as a Human Right: Obligations Related to Article 15(1)(c)', Discussion paper, E/C.12/2000/12, para 33.
[45] See Sub-Commission on the Promotion and Protection of Human Rights, 'The impact of the Agreement on Trade-Related Aspects of Intellectual Property Rights on human rights', E/CN.4/Sub.2/2001/13, June 2001.   [46] Idem, para 16.

development—are generally expressed in terms of exceptions to the rule rather than the guiding principles themselves and are made subject to the provisions of the Agreement. A human rights approach on the other hand would explicitly place the promotion and pro-tection of human rights, in particular those in the ICESCRs, at the heart of the objectives of intellectual property protection, rather than as only permitted exceptions that are subor-dinated to the other provisions of the Agreement. This is not to say that the protection of commercial objectives is necessarily incompatible with the promotion of human rights. Nonetheless, if we truly wish to factor the promotion and protection of human rights into the objectives of the TRIPS Agreement, different ways and strategies of promoting and protecting scientific progress and its results should be explored in particular cases.[47]

Second, while the Agreement identifies the need to balance rights with obligations, it gives no guidance on how to achieve this balance. On the one hand, the Agreement sets out in considerable detail the content on intellectual property *rights*—the requirements for the grant of rights, the duration of protection, the modes of enforcement. On the other hand, the Agreement only alludes to the *responsibilities* of IP holders that should balance those rights in accordance with its own objectives. The prevention of anti-competitive practices and the abuse of rights, the promotion of technology transfer, special and differential treat-ment for least developed countries are merely referred to—but unlike the rights it sets out, the Agreement does not establish the content of these responsibilities, or how they should be implemented. To illustrate the difference, a human rights approach might set out the minimum standards required for protection against anti-competitive practices or for the promotion of technology transfer to developing countries in much the same way as the Agreement now sets out minimum standards for the protection of patents or trade marks. Consequently, the balance identified in the TRIPS Agreement might not equate with the balance required under Article 15 of the ICESCR.[48]

The TRIPS Agreement offers significant operational flexibility and the High Commissioner urges Member States of the WTO to use this operational flexibility in ways that would be fully compatible with the promotion and protection of human rights. In this regard, it is important to note that out of 141 Member States of the WTO, 111 have ratified the ICESCR.[49]

Balance of rights and obligations

Finally, Article 7 stipulates that IPR protection should be conducive to 'a balance of rights and obligations'. This is also an important statement, which confirms that IPRs can be seen neither as an end in itself nor as absolute rights, but subject to appropriate balances. In *Canada—Patent Protection of Pharmaceutical Products*, the parties took different views with regard to this provision. Canada held

that one of the key goals of the TRIPS Agreement was a balance between the intellectual property rights created by the Agreement and other important socio-economic policies of WTO Member governments. Article 8 elaborates the socio-economic policies in question, with particular attention to health and nutritional policies. With respect to patent rights,

---

[47] Idem, para 22.   [48] Idem, para 23.   [49] Idem, para 28.

Canada argued, these purposes call for a liberal interpretation of the three conditions stated in Article 30 of the Agreement, so that governments would have the necessary flexibility to adjust patent rights to maintain the desired balance with other important national policies.[50]

On its side, the EC did not dispute the stated goal of achieving a balance within the intellectual property rights system between important national policies. But,

in the view of the EC, Articles 7 and 8 are statements that describe the balancing of goals that had already taken place in negotiating the final texts of the TRIPS Agreement. According to the EC, to view Article 30 as an authorization for governments to 'renegotiate' the overall balance of the Agreement would involve a double counting of such socio-economic policies. In particular, the EC pointed to the last phrase of Article 8.1 requiring that government measures to protect important socio-economic policies be consistent with the obligations of the TRIPS Agreement. The EC also referred to the provisions of first consideration of the Preamble and Article 1.1 as demonstrating that the basic purpose of the TRIPS Agreement was to lay down minimum requirements for the protection and enforcement of intellectual property rights.[51]

The panel held the view that there was a 'basic balance' in the Agreement, but accepted that patent rights, as defined in the Agreement, needed 'certain adjustment' without going as far as 'renegotiation' of such basic balance. It stated that in its view

Article 30's very existence amounts to a recognition that the definition of patent rights contained in Article 28 would need certain adjustments. On the other hand, the three limiting conditions attached to Article 30 testify strongly that the negotiators of the Agreement did not intend Article 30 to bring about what would be equivalent to a renegotiation of the basic balance of the Agreement. Obviously, the exact scope of Article 30's authority will depend on the specific meaning given to its limiting conditions. The words of those conditions must be examined with particular care on this point. Both the goals and the limitations stated in Articles 7 and 8.1 must obviously be borne in mind when doing so as well as those of other provisions of the TRIPS Agreement which indicate its object and purposes (7.26).[52]

The panel, however, avoided elaboration of the content and implications of Articles 7 and 8.1, despite the specific reference that the parties made thereto in their submissions. It remains unclear, hence, what the panel's understanding of those provisions was, a matter of particular importance given the room for interpretation that Members preserved under the general language of Article 30.[53]

A number of developing country Members have emphasized the importance of Article 7 for the interpretation of the Agreement. They considered it

a key provision that defines the objectives of the TRIPs Agreement. It clearly establishes that the protection and enforcement of intellectual property rights do not exist in a vacuum.

[50] WT/DS114/R, Report of the Panel, 17 March 2000, para 7.24.   [51] Idem, para 7.25.
[52] Idem, para 7.26.   [53] See pp 302–11 below.

They are supposed to benefit society as a whole and do not aim at the mere protection of private rights . . . Article 7 states that the protection and enforcement of intellectual property rights '*should*' contribute to the aforementioned objectives. Such language stems from a recognition by Members that the mere existence and the exercise of IPRs, such as patents, do not necessarily result in the fulfilment of the objectives of the Agreement . . . The objective of the promotion of technological innovation and the transfer and dissemination of technology places the protection and enforcement of IPRs in the context of the interests of society.[54]

In the Declaration on the TRIPS Agreement and Public Health,[55] the Ministerial Conference confirmed the interpretive value of Article 7 for 'each provision of the Agreement'. According to the Declaration:

In applying the customary rules of interpretation of public international law, each provision of the TRIPS Agreement shall be read in the light of the object and purpose of the Agreement as expressed, in particular, in its objectives and principles.[56]

Paragraph 19 of the Declaration adopted at the Doha WTO Fourth Ministerial Conference[57] further confirmed the importance of Article 7 (and Article 8) of the TRIPS Agreement as guidance for the implementation of the Agreement. The Ministerial Conference instructed the Council for TRIPS to examine, inter alia, the relationship between the TRIPS Agreement and the CBD, the protection of traditional knowledge (TK) and folklore, and other relevant new developments raised by Members pursuant to Article 71, and indicated that

in undertaking this work, the TRIPS Council shall be guided by the objectives and principles set out in Articles 7 and 8 of the TRIPS Agreement and should take into account the development dimension.

In sum, Article 7 (read in conjunction with Article 8) recognizes Members' right to implement the obligations under the TRIPS Agreement in a manner consistent with public policies conducive to social and economic welfare. In particular, it may be instrumental in legitimizing exceptions to exclusive rights, such as for fair use in the copyright field, and research and humanitarian access to drugs in the context of patent rights.

Principles

8.1. Members may, in formulating or amending their laws and regulations, adopt measures necessary to protect public health and nutrition, and to promote the public interest in sectors of vital importance to their socio-economic and

---

[54] See the submission to the Council of TRIPS by the African Group, Barbados, Bolivia, Brazil, Dominican Republic, Ecuador, Honduras, India, Indonesia, Jamaica, Pakistan, Paraguay, Philippines, Peru, Sri Lanka, Thailand, and Venezuela, IP/C/W/296, 19 June 2001.

[55] WT/MIN(01)/DEC/W/2, 14 November 2001.   [56] Idem, para 5(a).

[57] Document WT/MIN(01)/DEC/1, 20 November 2001.

technological development, provided that such measures are consistent with the provisions of this Agreement.

2. Appropriate measures, provided that they are consistent with the provisions of this Agreement, may be needed to prevent the abuse of intellectual property rights by right holders or the resort to practices which unreasonably restrain trade or adversely affect the international transfer of technology.

Article 8 is also an important provision for framing national laws that respond to particular public health and other public interests. It makes clear that measures may be adopted in order to prevent or remedy abuses of intellectual property rights. In all cases, however, national laws must be consistent with the provisions of the TRIPS Agreement. This consistency should be assessed in the light of Article 7 and of the Preamble, that is, taking the balance of rights and obligations and the social and economic welfare into account. In particular, nothing in the TRIPS Agreement should be read as preventing Members from adopting measures to protect public health, as well as from pursuing the overarching policies defined in Article 8.[58]

Article 8.1 broadly recognizes Members' rights 'in formulating or amending their laws and regulations'. Unlike the developing countries' proposal on which it was based,[59] it does not only refer to laws and regulations on IPRs but to measures adopted in other fields, for instance, those that restrict the manufacture or commercialization of IPR-protected goods. Issues concerning the application of Article 8.1 may, hence, arise in two contexts, one fully within the IPR realm, and another one outside it, but with implications on the protection of IPRs.

The purpose of the measures referred to under 8.1 may be twofold: (a) to protect public health and nutrition; or (b) to promote the public interest in sectors of vital importance to their socio-economic and technological development.

The 'measures necessary to protect public health and nutrition' may include a whole range of measures specifically allowed by the TRIPS Agreement, such as exceptions to the exclusive rights (Article 30), compulsory licences (Article 31) and the disclosure to the public of test data (Article 39.3). They also include non-IPR measures that may affect in some way the use of IPRs, such as marketing approval and price controls of medicines.[60]

The fourth WTO Ministerial Conference stated, in Paragraph 4 of the Doha Declaration on the TRIPS Agreement and Public Health of 14 November 2001,[61] that

[W]e agree that the TRIPS Agreement does not and should not prevent members from taking measures to protect public health. Accordingly, while reiterating our commitment to the TRIPS Agreement, we affirm that the Agreement can and should be interpreted and

---

[58] See IP/C/W/296, 19 June 2001.

[59] See document MTN.GNG/NG11/W/71, 9 May 1990.

[60] Price controls for pharmaceuticals are applied in a number of developing and developed countries, such as in many European countries. In Canada, prices of patented drugs are subject to permanent scrutiny.   [61] See document WT/MIN(01)/DEC/W/2 (14 November 2001).

implemented in a manner supportive of WTO members' right to protect public health and, in particular, to promote access to medicines for all.

In this connection, we reaffirm the right of WTO members to use, to the full, the provisions in the TRIPS Agreement, which provide flexibility for this purpose.

There are different possible interpretations for this paragraph. On the one hand, it may be viewed as a statement of fact rather than a rebalancing of the Agreement.[62] On the other, it may be regarded as an indication that in cases where there is conflict, IPRs should not be an obstacle to the realization of public health.

Members may also adopt measures to promote the public interest in sectors of vital importance to their socio-economic and technological development. There is a wide variety of measures that can be taken for this purpose, as such interest varies from country to country and may evolve over time. They may include, for instance, measures excluding foreign direct investment in certain sectors,[63] and the regulation of royalty rates and other conditions in licensing agreements. These regulations were applied by many developing (and some developed) countries during the 1970s and 1980s but were gradually abandoned in the context of more liberal policies towards foreign direct investment.[64]

The wording in Article 8.1 allows Members considerable room for interpretation. First, it refers to measures 'to promote'[65] public interest. Members that invoke this provision need not prove that such measures actually achieve their intended objectives, but that they are suitable to do that in the particular context where they apply.

Second, the definition of what constitutes the 'public interest' rests with the concerned Member. It is clearly a domestic issue. Members cannot challenge what 'public interest' is in accordance with the views of a particular Member. 'Public interest' is a concept broader than 'ordre public' used in Article 27.2 of the TRIPS Agreement.[66] It may be deemed to encompass any matter that affects the public. As noted by one commentator:

Whether a particular act is 'in the public interest'.... is probably not subject to any objective tests. Inherent in the noble motive of the public good is the notion that, in certain

---

[62] For example, the USTR Industry Functional Advisory Committee on Intellectual Property Rights for Trade Policy Matters (IFAC-3) has noted that the Doha 'Declaration did not amend the TRIPS Agreement, particularly Article 8.1'. See Advisory Committee Report to the President, the Congress and the United States Trade Representative on the US–Morocco Free Trade (6 April 2004) 14, available at <http://www.ustr.gov/assets/Trade_Agreements/Bilateral/Morocco_FTA/Reports/asset_upload_file164_3139.pdf> (last accessed on 30 March 2005).

[63] Such limitation is not precluded by WTO rules, which only address performance requirements as trade-related investment measures in the context of the TRIMs Agreement. The proposals to negotiate investment rules in WTO have been unsuccessful so far. See C Correa and N Kumar, *International Rules for Foreign Investment. Trade-Related Investment Measures (TRIMS) and Developing Countries* (2003: London and New Delhi, ZED Books/Academic Foundation).

[64] See, eg, C Correa, 'Innovation and technology transfer in Latin America: A review of recent trends and policies', in Lall, Sanjaya (ed.), *The Economics of Technology Transfer* (2002: Cheltenham/Northampton, Elgar Reference Collection).

[65] 'Promote means 'advance ... help forward, encourage ... ', *Concise Oxford Dictionary*, (1982: Oxford University Press, 7th edn), p 824.   [66] See pp 287–92 below.

circumstances, the needs of the majority override those of the individual, and that the citizen should relinquish any thoughts of self-interest in favor of the common good of society as a whole.[67]

Third, which the 'sectors of vital importance to their socio-economic and technological development' are, is also a matter for the particular Members to decide. On the one hand, 'sectors' may refer to economic activities at different levels of aggregation (eg agriculture, maize production), as well as to certain groups of economic agents (eg, small and medium enterprises). Although the adjective 'vital importance' would seem to limit the scope of the provision to specially significant sectors, which sector is important or not is also subject to determination by the concerned Member in the light of its 'socio-economic and technological development'.

Fourth, and finally, the concept of 'socio-economic and technological development' is broad enough to encompass any sector, socially, economically, or technologically relevant. Thus, the importance of a sector may be measured by its contribution to GNP; but it may be also socially important, despite a low contribution thereto.

The broad room for implementation of national measures left by the wording we have examined is limited by two aspects of the provision: (a) the measures referred to must be 'necessary'; and (b) 'consistent with the provisions' of the TRIPS Agreement.

The reference to 'necessary' echoes the wording in the *chapeau* of Article XX of GATT, generally called the 'necessity test'. A possible line of interpretation is that 'necessary' in the context of Article 8.1 alludes to the least trade-restrictive measure, as interpreted by GATT/WTO jurisprudence. In the *Thai Cigarette case* [68] (1990), the panel examined the application of Article XX(b) to an import ban of cigarettes imposed by the government of Thailand, grounded on public health considerations. Despite the evidence supplied, and the technical support given by WHO, the panel concluded that alternatives less trade-restrictive than banning imported cigarettes would be available to achieve the intended public health objectives.

The panel dismissed the justification of the Thai government on the basis of Article XX(b) as a measure 'necessary to protect human . . . life or health'. It held that

there were various measures consistent with the General Agreement which were reasonably available to Thailand to control the quality and quantity of cigarettes smoked and which, taken together, could achieve the health policy goals that the Thai government pursues by restricting the importation of cigarettes inconsistently with Article XI:1. The Panel found therefore that Thailand's practice of permitting the sale of domestic cigarettes while not

---

[67] G Davis, *Copyright and the Public Interest* (2002: London, Sweet & Maxwell, 2nd edn) p 4.
[68] See BISD 37th Supp 200.

permitting the importation of foreign cigarettes was an inconsistency with the General Agreement not 'necessary' within the meaning of Article XX(b).

The panel thus disregarded the various constraints, including institutional and fiscal, that the Thai government would have to face for the implementation of the less restrictive alternatives.[69] In other words, the panel did not examine whether the less trade-restrictive measures also were *reasonably available* to Thailand, as a developing country and given the particular problems faced by the government.

In fact, prior to *EC–Asbestos*, no measure evaluated under GATT Article XX(b) survived the necessity test, giving an indication of how strictly it was applied in dispute settlement. In the *EC–Asbestos* case, however, the AB accepted that the ban on asbestos was necessary as a matter of public policy, and developed a strict scrutiny doctrine for analysing the potential effectiveness of less trade-restrictive measures under the necessity test. This doctrine provides a basis for defending non-compliant GATT measures.[70]

As illustrated by the concept of similarity under GATT,[71] the same term need not be identically interpreted in different provisions or agreements.[72] The meaning of 'necessary' in Article 8.1 of the TRIPS Agreement is not arguably as limited as interpreted in the context of Article XX of GATT, as the necessity is to be judged in the former in relation to very broad concepts, such as 'public interest' and 'socio-economic and technological development'. It would be unreasonable to give a restrictive interpretation to the concept in this context, as Members have significant room to define domestically the content and scope of the measures they can adopt. However, the Member that has invoked it would be bound to demonstrate that a particular measure relates to the objectives set forth in Article 8.1 of the Agreement and that there is a link of necessity between the measure and the objective.[73]

The second limitation ('provided that such measures are consistent with the provisions of this Agreement') restrains Members' freedom to adopt measures in the context of Article 8.1, and is more difficult to interpret. It has been argued

---

[69] M Trebilcock and R Howse, *The regulation of international trade* (1999: London, Routledge, 2nd edn) p 165.

[70] See *European Communities—Measures Affecting Asbestos and Asbestos-Containing Products*, Appellate Body Report, 12 Mar 2001, WT/DS135/AB/R.

[71] The AB held that the meaning of 'similar' in GATT changes in its different provisions: '[T]he concept of "likeness" is a relative one that evokes the image of an accordion. The accordion of "likeness" stretches and squeezes in different places as different provisions of the WTO Agreement are applied. The width of the accordion in any one of those places must be determined by the particular provision in which the term "like" is encountered as well as by the context and the circumstances that prevail in any given case to which that provision may apply' (*EC-Asbestos*, para 88).

[72] See WTO Secretariat, 'Necessity tests' in the WTO, S/WPDR/W/27 of 2 December 2003.

[73] Idem, paras 5–7.

that, in the light of its final proviso, Article 8.1 'in no way permits exceptions to the rights conferred by TRIPS provisions'.[74]

Article 8.1, however, plays three complementary roles. First, Article 8, as mentioned above, constitutes jointly with Article 7, a central piece for the implementation and interpretation of the TRIPS Agreement.[75] The considerations made in this regard in connection with Article 7 are also relevant here. The nature of Articles 7 and 8, however, is quite different. While the former states the objectives of IPR protection, the latter confirms the Members' discretion to adopt measures that may affect the availability or exercise of IPRs, when necessary for certain public purposes, including the control of abuses of IPRs. Article 8 thus confirms the broad and unfettered discretion that Members have to pursue public policy objectives.

Second, Article 8.1 is likely to be important in limiting the potential range of non-violation nullification or impairment causes, if allowed in the context of the TRIPS Agreement,[76] as it makes clear that a wide range of public policy measures eventually changing the balance of concessions should be reasonably expected.[77] Given the broad powers recognized to Members under Article 8.1, a Member challenging a measure adopted by another Member in pursuance of public policy objectives should have the initial burden of proof of inconsistency with the provisions of the TRIPS Agreement.

Third, the 'consistency' requirement may not be deemed to outlaw any government action necessary to protect the interests mentioned in Article 8.1, if such action required the adoption of TRIPS-inconsistent measures. If that were the case, IPRs would assume an overriding preponderance in national policies, far beyond what is actually possible under GATT, which allows for the derogation of Members' obligations.

The extent to which the final proviso of Article 8.1 ('provided that such measures are consistent with the provisions of this Agreement')[78] would mean that IPRs could override public health measures, was a major reason why developing countries proposed the adoption of a declaration on TRIPS and public health, finally adopted by the Doha Ministerial Conference. In the light of paragraph 4 of

---

[74] N Pires de Carvalho, *The TRIPS Regime of Patent Rights*, (2002: The Hague, Kluwer Law International), p 118.

[75] These provisions are of particular relevance for the interpretation of the Articles of the TRIPS Agreement that leave considerable room for national legislations, such as Articles 17 and 30 relating to exceptions to the exclusive rights of trademark and patent owners, respectively.

[76] See pp 488–90 below.

[77] See, eg, UNCTAD-ICTSD, *Resource Book on TRIPS and Development* (2005: New York, Cambridge University Press) p 127.

[78] It should be noted that the draft of this text of 23 July 1990 did not include this proviso. In the Brussels draft text, however, it was added 'provided that PARTIES do not derogate from the obligations arising under this Agreement', which sets out a limitation similar to the consistency text finally adopted. For the history of the negotiation, see UNCTAD-ICTSD op. cit. (2005), pp 119–25.

the already mentioned Doha Declaration on the TRIPS Agreement and Public Health, it may be argued that Article 8.1 would not prevent derogation from certain obligations under the TRIPS Agreement if necessary to address public health needs. The realization of public health has become, with the Doha Declaration, a clearly stated *purpose* of the Agreement. In particular, paragraph 4 of the Declaration provides guidance to panels and the Appellate Body for the interpretation of the Agreements' provisions in cases involving public health issues. In cases of ambiguity, or where more than one interpretation were possible, panels and the Appellate Body should opt for the interpretation that is effectively supportive of WTO Members' right to protect public health.

Thus, if local situations posed such unusual problems as to merit a public interest exception, Members may find it necessary to override or limit some provisions of the Agreement. For instance, Members might determine patentability exclusions in cases of distinct public health emergencies as defined by the national government, and as distinct from ordinary or everyday health and nutrition measures. Emergency cases could trigger the application of a different test of 'inconsistency' (as provided for under Article 8.1) or qualify as a situation not 'conducive to social and economic welfare' (as provided for under Article 7). In such a case, a suspension or exclusion from patentability might be linked to and justified by a specific emergency. Once the emergency subsides, the TRIPS requirement of patentability could be restored.

A key consideration is clearly the purpose for which any subject matter exclusion was adopted. If, for example, the same objective could be obtained by imposing permissible compulsory licences under Article 31, an exclusion of patentability could be seen as merely an attempt to circumvent the pre-conditions of Article 31.

A further issue that deserves exploration is whether an exception to TRIPS obligations may be justified under the general GATT exception to trade disciplines, when the exception is necessary to protect public health (Article XX(b)).[79] This article recognizes that, under some circumstances, Members are able to advance domestic interests, even if contrary to their general obligations under the GATT. However, it remains doubtful whether GATT Article XX(b) would apply in the TRIPS context. In the view of a panel, as mentioned before, the TRIPS Agreement has a relatively self-contained, *sui generis* status within the WTO, even though 'it is an integral part of the WTO system, which itself builds upon the experience of over nearly half a century'[80] under the GATT. In another case, the

---

[79] 'Subject to the requirement that such measures are not applied in a manner which would constitute a means of arbitrary or unjustifiable discrimination between countries where the same conditions prevail, or a disguised restriction on international trade, nothing in this Agreement shall be construed to prevent the adoption or enforcement by any contracting party of measures:

(b) necessary to protect human, animal or plant life or health; . . .'

[80] See the Panel Report on *India–Patent Protection for Agricultural and Chemical Products*, WT/DS50/R, 16 January 1998, para 7.19.

panel affirmed that 'the TRIPS Agreement does not contain any provision corresponding to Article XX of GATT 1994',[81] and further noted that

there is no hierarchy between the TRIPS Agreement and GATT 1994, which appear in separate annexes to the WTO Agreement. The ordinary meaning of the texts of the TRIPS Agreement and GATT 1994, as well as Article II:2 of the WTO Agreement, taken together, indicates that obligations under the TRIPS Agreement and GATT 1994 can co-exist and that one does not override the other. This is analogous to the finding of the Panel in *Canada—Periodicals*, with which the Appellate Body agreed, concerning the respective scopes of GATS and GATT 1994 (*footnote omitted*). Further, a 'harmonious interpretation' does not require an interpretation of one that shadows the contours of the other. It is well established that the covered agreements apply cumulatively and that consistency with one does not necessarily imply consistency with them all (*footnote omitted*).[82]

> **8.2. Appropriate measures, provided that they are consistent with the provisions of this Agreement, may be needed to prevent the abuse of intellectual property rights by right holders or the resort to practices which unreasonably restrain trade or adversely affect the international transfer of technology.**

Article 8.2 is also an important provision for framing national laws that respond to public interests. It makes clear that measures may be adopted in order to prevent or remedy abuses of IPRs and practices that unreasonably restrain trade or the transfer of technology. However, national laws must be consistent with the provisions of the TRIPS Agreement. This consistency should be assessed in the light of Articles 7 and 8.1 and of the Preamble; that is, taking social and economic welfare into account. In particular, nothing in the TRIPS Agreement should be read as preventing Members from adopting measures to protect public health, as well as from pursuing the overarching policies defined in Article 8.[83]

Article 8.2 refers to three types of behaviour by IPR-holders:

(a) abuse of intellectual property rights by right-holders;
(b) practices which unreasonably restrain trade; or
(c) practices which adversely affect the international transfer of technology.

Abuse of IPRs

IPR-holders may use their rights in a manner that unjustifiably restrains trade. Anti-competitive practices may include, for instance, tying the sales of patented products to the purchase of off-patent products and abusive pricing.[84]

---

[81] *European Communities—protection of trademarks and geographical indications for agricultural products and foodstuffs*, WT/DS174/R, 15 March 2005, para 7.114.   [82] Idem, para 7.208.
[83] See IP/C/W/296, 19 June 2001.
[84] See, eg, Article 21(XXIV) of Brazilian Law No 8.884/94, 'to impose excessive prices' may be an abuse of economic power.

The abuse, or misuse, of IPRs may or may not constitute, at the same time, an anti-competitive practice. The Paris Convention, for instance, refers to the failure to work a patented invention as an 'abuse' (Article 5.A) independently of whether the patent owner enjoys or not a dominant position. In the US, the doctrine of patent misuse has developed in parallel to the application of antitrust law to remedy anti-competitive practices emerging from the use of IPRs.[85]

Practices which unreasonably restrain trade

Currently, purely private business practices restricting trade that are not supported by the government cannot be attacked under WTO rules. Further, there is no requirement that WTO Members have a competition policy. In fact, many developing countries have no or weak competition policies. They were required, under the TRIPS Agreement, to strengthen and expand IPRs despite the lack of such policy, which constitutes an essential component of the legal framework applicable to IPRs in developed countries.

The European Union attempted to get consensus for the development within the WTO Round of core principles and rules on competition. Although this initiative did not entail a possible harmonization of national competition law—a task that would face insurmountable obstacles given the differences in national laws, even among developed countries—it failed to obtain sufficient support.

A number of anti-competitive practices may be particularly harmful to developing countries. Thus, export cartels are not controlled or exempted from regulation in many developed countries. Developing countries also are at a disadvantage to deal with the effects of mergers that take place in other jurisdictions, but which may affect their economies. The effects of those operations in developing countries are normally disregarded in the evaluation and control made by developed countries' authorities.

An effective control of anti-competitive practices such as predatory pricing, collusive tendering, tied purchases and sales, may be an important target for developing countries. Since a growing number of firms exert global market power, it becomes increasingly difficult to deal with their conduct and to avoid abuses of market power. The international coordination of competition policies in order to act against anti-competitive practices of global suppliers may be a significant step for developing countries. A notification/consultation approach may contribute to increased account being taken of global welfare in national competition law and practice.

The extent to which it would also be desirable to develop multilateral principles and rules on competition is more controversial, since most developing countries

---

[85] See, eg, P Merges, *Patent Law and Policy. Case and Materials* (1992: Charlottesville, Virginia, The Michie Company), pp 908–10.

have little experience in the application of competition laws, and the objectives and scope of possible WTO disciplines on the matter are unclear. The best option for such countries may be to keep the possibility of establishing their competition regimes, according to their own situation and policy objectives, without being bound to rules that may be enforced through the WTO settlement mechanism.

Practices which adversely affect the international transfer of technology

Transfer of technology ranks high in the priorities of developing countries. Article 8.2 is also an important provision for the discussion of transfer of technology in the context of the TRIPS Agreement. It recognizes the need to adopt 'appropriate measures' to prevent 'the resort to practices which adversely affect the international transfer of technology'. There is a caveat, however, that limits the reach of possible State measures: they must be 'consistent with the provisions' of the Agreement.

Although Article 8.2 addresses the right of Members to adopt legislation aimed at correcting certain practices of IPR owners, it is not limited to the control of restrictive practices in voluntary licensing agreements, as stipulated in Article 40. For instance, unreasonably high royalties may deter the transfer of technology and—as many developing countries did in the past under 'transfer of technology' laws[86]—Members may establish policies to deal with technology pricing and other aspects of transfer of technology transactions. Nevertheless, the extent to which such policies, if adopted, may be successful remains unclear, given that technology owners, in principle, enjoy under IPRs the right to refuse the transfer of their technologies.[87]

Questions may arise as to the threat posed by possible 'non-violation' complaints in the case of measures regulating certain aspects of licensing agreements. However, the admissibility of such complaints in the context of TRIPS is still under debate. There are solid reasons to consider that they should not be admitted.[88]

The strengthening of international and domestic rules and mechanisms to curb restrictive business practices in licensing agreements may be an important step to facilitate transfer and use of technologies. However, as reviewed below, Article 40 of the TRIPS Agreement, rather than empowering governments to take positive action, limits the possible State intervention on such practices.[89]

---

[86] See, eg, Correa, 'Innovation and Technology Transfer in Latin America: a Review of Recent Trends and Policies', (1995) 10 Int'l J Tech Mgmt. p 815.

[87] *See* p 318 below, however, compulsory licences on grounds of 'refusal to deal'.

[88] See, eg, F Abbott, 'Non-Violation Nullification or Impairment Causes of Action under the TRIPS Agreement and the Fifth Ministerial Conference: A Warning and Reminder', QUNO Occasional Paper 11 (2002: Geneva), available at <www.quno.org> (last accessed on 26 May 2005). See also Chapter 14.   [89] See Chapter 12 below.

Annex

Negotiating history[90]

In his 23 July 1990 report on the status of work in the TRIPS Negotiating Group, the Chairman (Lars E R Anell) presented two sets of proposals. In an Annex to the report, he presented a composite text that was taken from various proposals by delegations to the Negotiating Group, indicating the source of each proposal by numerical reference to the source document.

Composite text of July 23 1990[91]

2. *Objective of the Agreement*

2A The PARTIES agree to provide effective and adequate protection of intellectual property rights in order to ensure the reduction of distortions and impediments to [international (68)] [legitimate (70)] trade. The protection of intellectual property rights shall not itself create barriers to legitimate trade. (68, 70)

2B The objective of the present Agreement is to establish adequate standards for the protection of, and effective and appropriate means for the enforcement of intellectual property rights; thereby eliminating distortions and impediments to international trade related to intellectual property rights and foster its sound development. (74)

2C With respect to standards and principles concerning the availability, scope and use of intellectual property rights, PARTIES agree on the following objectives:

(i) To give full recognition to the needs for economic, social and technological development of all countries and the sovereign right of all States, when enacting national legislation, to ensure a proper balance between these needs and the rights granted to IPR holders and thus to determine the scope and level of protection of such rights, particularly in sectors of special public concern, such as health, nutrition, agriculture and national security. (71)

(ii) To set forth the principal rights and obligations of IP owners, taking into account the important inter-relationships between the scope of such rights and obligations and the promotion of social welfare and economic development. (71)

(iii) To facilitate the diffusion of technological knowledge and to enhance international transfer of technology, and thus contribute to a more active participation of all countries in world production and trade. (71)

(iv) To encourage technological innovation and promote inventiveness in all countries. (71)

---

[90] For an analysis of the negotiating history see UNCTAD-ICTSD, op. cit. (2005), pp 118–34.

[91] Chairman's Report to the GNG, Status of Work in the Negotiating Group, Negotiating Group on Trade-Related Aspects of Intellectual Property Rights, including Trade in Counterfeit Goods, MTN.GNG/NG11/W/76, 23 July 1990, presented by the Chairman of the TRIPS Negotiating Group (Lars E R Anell). Alternatives 'A' correspond to texts from developed countries and 'B' from developing countries.

(v) To enable participants to take all appropriate measures to prevent the abuses which might result from the exercise of IPRs and to ensure intergovernmental co-operation in this regard. (71)'

8. *Principles*

8B.1 PARTIES recognize that intellectual property rights are granted not only in acknowledgement of the contributions of inventors and creators, but also to assist in the diffusion of technological knowledge and its dissemination to those who could benefit from it in a manner conducive to social and economic welfare and agree that this balance of rights and obligations inherent in all systems of intellectual property rights should be observed.

8B.2 In formulating or amending their national laws and regulations on IPRs, PARTIES have the right to adopt appropriate measures to protect public morality, national security, public health and nutrition, or to promote public interest in sectors of vital importance to their socio-economic and technological development.

8B.3 PARTIES agree that the protection and enforcement of intellectual property rights should contribute to the promotion of technological innovation and enhance the international transfer of technology to the mutual advantage of producers and users of technological knowledge.

8B.4 Each PARTY will take the measures it deems appropriate with a view to preventing the abuse of intellectual property rights or the resort to practices which unreasonably restrain trade or adversely affect the international transfer of technology. PARTIES undertake to consult each other and to co-operate in this regard.

Draft text transmitted to the Brussels Ministerial Conference (December 1990)
Objectives

7. The protection and enforcement of intellectual property rights should contribute to the promotion of technological innovation and to the transfer and dissemination of technology, to the mutual advantage of producers and users of technological knowledge and in a manner conducive to social and economic welfare, and to a balance of rights and obligations.

Principles

8.1. Provided that PARTIES do not derogate from the obligations arising under this Agreement, they may, in formulating or amending their national laws and regulations, adopt measures necessary to protect public health and nutrition, and to promote the public interest in sectors of vital importance to their socio-economic and technological development.

8.2 Appropriate measures provided that they do not derogate from the obligations arising under this Agreement may be needed to prevent the abuse of intellectual property rights by right holders or the resort to practices which unreasonably restrain trade or affect the international transfer of technology.

Chapter 5

COPYRIGHT AND RELATED RIGHTS

Section 1 of the TRIPS Agreement deals with 'copyright and related rights'. It contains six Articles that supplement the Berne Convention.

Unlike the section relating to patents, which raised strong North–South divergences, negotiations on the copyright area were characterized by a North–North confrontation on a number of issues that concern the fundamentals of intellectual works protection. The main differences arose from the diverging views prevailing in common law countries, on the one hand, and in continental law countries, on the other, on the underlying philosophy and scope of protection conferred under copyright and authors' rights, respectively. The title of Section 1 (Part II) itself reflects a compromise between the common law and continental law conceptions on the nature of rights relating to the so-called 'neighbouring rights'. Although there is growing convergence between the copyright and authors' rights approaches,[1] the TRIPS Agreement contributed little to narrowing down the gap between them.[2]

'The premise for copyright (or authors' rights) protection is that creation and cultural activities are stimulated by the granting of exclusive rights. In the absence of such rights, it is argued, the production and distribution on new works for the public would be jeopardized. As in the case of patents, several theories have been proposed to justify copyright protection, namely natural law, a just reward for labour, the stimulation of creativity, and the social usefulness of copyright.[3] It is necessary to bear in mind, however, that a large portion of creative works are developed without pursuing any protection against copying. The 'open source' model for software development is just an example of alternative paths to encourage creativity and innovation.

---

[1] With regard, for instance, to the level of originality required, the absence of formalities for the acquisition of rights, and the protection of 'neighbouring' or 'related' rights.

[2] See, eg, G Davies, 'The Convergence of Copyright and Authors' Rights–Reality or Chimera?' [1995] 26 IIC, p 964.

[3] See, eg, G Davies, *Copyright and the Public Interest* (2002: London, Sweet & Maxwell, 2nd edn), pp 15–16.

Relation to the Berne Convention

9.1. Members shall comply with Articles 1 through 21 of the Berne Convention (1971) and the Appendix thereto. However, Members shall not have rights or obligations under this Agreement in respect of the rights conferred under Article 6 *bis* of that Convention or of the rights derived therefrom.

Article 9.1 establishes, in terms similar to Article 2.1 for the Paris Convention, the Members' obligation to comply with specified articles of the Berne Convention and its Appendix. While the negotiating texts referred to 'substantive provisions',[4] the direct reference to 'Articles 1 through 21' eliminated any possible controversy[5] regarding whether some provisions (eg Article 20 relating to special agreements) constituted a 'substantive provision'.[6]

This 'friendly takeover' of the Berne Convention[7] means that even Members that are not parties thereto are obliged to abide by its substantive provisions.[8] The specific inclusion of Article 20 of the Berne Convention is also noticeable, as it would seem to indicate the negotiating parties' understanding that nothing in the TRIPS Agreement would diminish the rights conferred under the Convention.[9] This is particularly relevant for interpretation of the exception contained in Article 9.1 and of Article 9.2.

The reference to 'Articles' also indicates that Members can apply the limitations[10] and exceptions specifically allowed in Articles 1–21 of the Berne Convention. Moreover, Members will be obliged to apply the mandatory exception

---

[4] See the main negotiating texts in the annex to this chapter.

[5] The inclusion of a reference to the Berne Convention standards was not contentious during the negotiations. The developing countries, who objected to some Berne-plus provisions, such as rental rights, did not question the general applicability of the Convention. See, eg, Katzenberg, 'TRIPS and copyright law', F Beier and G Schricker (eds), in *From GATT to TRIPS–The Agreement on Trade-Related Aspects of Intellectual Property Rights*, (1996 Munich, IIC Studies Max Planck Institute for Foreign and International Patent, Copyright and Competition Law), p 64; J Watal, *Intellectual Property Rights in the WTO and Developing Countries* (2001: The Hague, Kluwer Law International) op. cit. (1996), p 210.

[6] See, eg, O Gervais, *The TRIPS Agreement. Drafting History and Analysis* (2003: London; Sweet & Maxwell, 2nd edn), p 124.

[7] Following the expression used by P Katzenberger, op. cit. (1996), fn 5.

[8] The provisions of the Berne Convention not referred to in Article 9(1) relate to the creation and administration of the Berne Union and such matters as applicability, acceptance, denunciation and entry into force of the Convention.

[9] As noted by Okediji, the 'systematic expansion of copyright interests' can be traced to this Article of the Berne Convention. 'It was not the TRIPS Agreement that set the stage for the "one-way ratchet" of intellectual property rights which has elicited tremendous concern.' See R Okediji, 'Fostering access to education, research and dissemination of knowledge through copyright', UNCTAD-ICTSD Dialogue on Moving the pro-development IP agenda forward: Preserving Public Goods in health, education and learning, Bellagio, 29 November–3 December 2004 (available at <http://www.ictsd.org>, last accessed on 2 April 2005), p 3.

[10] Article 2(8) of the Berne Convention excludes news of the day and miscellaneous facts having the character of mere items of press information.

provided for in Article 10(1) of the Convention for quotations from a work which has already been lawfully made available to the public.[11]

The main proponent of the exception contained in Article 9.1 was the US, where moral rights are not recognized as such, except in the case of some works of visual arts not made for hire.[12]

The different philosophies underpinning the common law and the continental law approaches on copyright/authors' rights, significantly influence the scope of conferred rights. While copyright in the common law world aims to protect investments of time, effort, and capital in the production of works, under the 'authors' rights' conception, the protection is rather justified in terms of an author's inherent entitlements, as a reward for the personal contributions he has made.[13] The issue of moral rights is, perhaps, one of the outstanding divergences between the two approaches.[14]

Continental European law has paid particular attention to the recognition of 'moral' rights in addition to the 'economic' rights bestowed on the author. The latter include the right to authorize the reproduction, translation, and adaptation of the work, its performance in public, fixation in a sound recording or motion picture, and its broadcasting. The former, which remain even after the author has transferred his economic rights and are, in some jurisdictions, inalienable, may include the following:[15]

- the right of divulgation, that is, to decide if a work is completed and when to publish it:[16]
- the right to paternity, that is, the right to claim authorship, including the right to have the author's name attached to his work;
- the right of integrity, which allows the author to prohibit modification, mutilation or distortion of his work without his permission;
- the right of withdrawal, which allows an author to retrieve his work after publication.[17]

---

[11] See, eg, S Ricketson, WIPO study on limitations and exceptions of copyright and related rights in the digital environment, WIPO document SCCR/9/7 (5 April 2003), p 46.

[12] Limited rights of attribution and integrity are afforded with regard to certain visual artistic works and photographs. See the US Visual-Artists Rights Act 1990, Public Law 101–650, 104 Stat 5089 (1 December 1990), Section 106A of the US Copyright Act. The main reason for the US opposition was its fear that moral rights could unjustifiably interfere with the adaptation of copyrighted works. See, eg, Watal op. cit. (2001), p 212.

[13] See, eg, T Dreier, 'Authorship and New Technologies from the Viewpoint of Civil Law Traditions', WIPO World-wide Symposium on the Future of Copyright and Neighbouring Rights, Paris (June 1994), p 3.

[14] It should be noted, however, that the United Kingdom introduced moral rights in 1988 (Copyright, Designs and Patents Act 1988, Chapter IV).

[15] See, eg, J Cline, 'Moral Rights: The Long and Winding Road Toward Recognition', (1990) 14 Nova L Rev., p 435.

[16] The analog under US copyright is the 'right of first sale' or the 'right of first publication'.

[17] Where this right is recognized, the author is generally required to pay a compensation for any losses that withdrawal may cause.

Moral rights are provided for, as independent from economic rights, under Article 6*bis* of the Berne Convention,[18] as follows:

(1) Independently of the author's economic rights, and even after the transfer of the said rights, the author shall have the right to claim authorship of the work and to object to any distortion, mutilation or other modification of, or other derogatory action in relation to, the said work, which would be prejudicial to his honor or reputation.

(2) The rights granted to the author in accordance with the preceding paragraph shall, after his death, be maintained, at least until the expiry of the economic rights, and shall be exercisable by the persons or institutions authorized by the legislation of the country where protection is claimed. However, those countries whose legislation, at the moment of their ratification of or accession to this Act, does not provide for the protection after the death of the author of all the rights set out in the preceding paragraph may provide that some of these rights may, after his death, cease to be maintained.

(3) The means of redress for safeguarding the rights granted by this Article shall be governed by the legislation of the country where protection is claimed.

This Article does not cover the right to disclose and to withdraw. It does not provide either for the inalienability of the covered rights, which, along with the duration of such rights after the author's death, is an issue left to domestic law.

Despite these limitations, the differences of approach regarding the protection of moral rights clearly emerged in the process of implementation of the Berne Convention in the United States, which became a Member to the Convention on 1 March 1989. The US Berne Convention Implementation Act did not introduce moral rights. It is interpreted that foreigners are not able to claim such rights on the basis of Article 6*bis* of the Berne Convention since its provisions are not deemed to be self-executing in that country.[19]

Article 9.1 of the TRIPS Agreement does not oblige Members to recognize moral rights and it is, in this sense, a 'Berne-minus' solution. However, the exception does not derogate from the rights and obligations that the Contracting Parties to the Berne Convention have under Article 6*bis*. Such rights and obligations remain in force, but are obviously not applicable to WTO Members who have not adhered to the Convention, and cannot in any case ground a complaint under WTO dispute settlement rules.

Although the exception in Article 9.1 is crafted in terms broader than Article 6 of the TRIPS Agreement,[20] its main effect is also to protect Members that are parties to the Berne Convention from complaints under the WTO DSU.

The intention to fully exclude the issue of moral rights from the TRIPS Agreement is reaffirmed by the wording encompassing not only 'the rights conferred under Article 6*bis*' of the Berne Convention, but also 'the rights derived therefrom'. The rights 'derived' from moral rights may be deemed to include the

---

[18] This Article was introduced in the Rome Act of the Berne Convention (1928).

[19] See A Nordemann and A Scheuermann, 'Adherence of the United States to the Berne Convention—Report on a Berlin Copyright Conference' (1992), IIC, Vol. 23, No 1, pp 79–80.

[20] See above.

author's right provided for in Articles 10(3)[21] and 11*bis*(2)[22] of the Berne Convention, and in Article IV(3) of the Appendix to the Convention.[23]

9.2. Copyright protection shall extend to expressions and not to ideas, procedures, methods of operation or mathematical concepts as such.

Neither in the Berne Convention nor in the TRIPS Agreement is there a general definition of what the subject matter of copyright protection is. Article 2(1) of the Berne Convention contains a non-exhaustive list of protected works.

The expression 'literary and artistic works' shall include every production in the literary, scientific and artistic domain, whatever may be the mode or form of its expression, such as books, pamphlets and other writings; lectures, addresses, sermons and other works of the same nature; dramatic or dramatico-musical works; choreographic works and entertainments in dumb show; musical compositions with or without words; cinematographic works to which are assimilated works expressed by a process analogous to cinematography; works of drawing, painting, architecture, sculpture, engraving and lithography; photographic works to which are assimilated works expressed by a process analogous to photography; works of applied art; illustrations, maps, plans, sketches and three-dimensional works relative to geography, topography, architecture or science.

The drafters of the TRIPS Agreement felt no need to provide for a general characterization of protectable works, as a reference was made in Article 10.1 to the articles of the Berne Convention (including Article 2). They rather introduced an innovation in international copyright law by establishing, in Article 10.2, what is *not* protectable.

It is generally agreed that copyright protects 'only the form of expression of ideas, not the ideas themselves.[24] The creativity protected by copyright law is in the choice and arrangement of words, musical notes, colours, shapes and so on.'[25] This principle, however, has been implemented in different ways in various countries, which eventually leads to different results in close cases. Protection may, thus, extend not only to literally similar elements but also to non-literal elements if they are 'comprehensive' relative to the overall texture of the work.[26]

---

[21] Article 10(3): '(3) Where use is made of works in accordance with the preceding paragraphs of this Article, mention shall be made of the source, and of the name of the author if it appears thereon.'

[22] Article 11*bis*(2): 'It shall be a matter for legislation in the countries of the Union to determine the conditions under which the rights mentioned in the preceding paragraph may be exercised, but these conditions shall apply only in the countries where they have been prescribed. They shall not in any circumstances be prejudicial to the moral rights of the author, nor to his right to obtain equitable remuneration which, in the absence of agreement, shall be fixed by competent authority.'

[23] See WIPO, Implications of the TRIPS Agreement on Treaties Administered by WIPO (1997: Geneva), p 14.

[24] This has been the general understanding under the Berne Convention, although it did not contain this clarification. According to WIPO, the dichotomy may be deduced from the basic meaning of the word 'works'. See *WIPO, Implications of the TRIPS Agreement on Treaties Administered by WIPO* (1997: Geneva), p 15; *WIPO, Guide to the Copyright and Related Rights Treaties Administered by WIPO and Glossary of Copyright and Related Rights Terms* (2003: Geneva), p 23.

[25] See *WIPO, Intellectual Property Reading Material* (1988: Geneva), p 36.

[26] P Geller, *International Copyright Law and Practice* (1991: Matthew Bender, Vol. 1) INT. 33–4.

The Berne Convention is silent on this dichotomy and, therefore, leaves national legislation room to draw the dividing line. Article 9.2 of the TRIPS Agreement has instead opted for an explicit rule according to which 'copyright protection shall extend to expressions and not to ideas, procedures, methods of operation or mathematical concepts as such'.

Article 9.2 of the TRIPS Agreement may be regarded as a shortened and simplified version of the dichotomy idea/expression as contained in the US copyright law.[27] According to Dratler, under such law

[T]he primary purpose for the dichotomy is to distinguish patents from copyright and to prevent authors and others from circumventing the strict requirements for patent protection by seeking copyright protection for the ideas and concepts explained in their works... A secondary purpose of the idea/expression dichotomy is to facilitate free speech by allowing anyone to repeat an author's ideas and facts, without fear of civil liability for copyright infringement, as long as she uses different words to do so.[28]

Article 9.2 was introduced as a counterproposal to the Japanese demand to include an exception of this kind in Article 10. The Japanese text, however, only related to the protection of computer programs and explicitly referred to the non-protectability of algorithms. While under the Japanese text this provision would have been restricted to such programs, the finally proposed text is applicable to all areas of copyright and related rights. The reference to 'procedures'. 'method of operations' and 'mathematical concepts' reflect, however, the origin of the provision, as they are relevant for functional works like computer programs.

The free availability of ideas, despite the protection of the form in which they are expressed, is a basic aspect of copyright law.[29] While the expression may be appropriated, copyright protection preserves the ideas in the public domain. This is essential for intergenerational justice and the developments of science and arts. It has been noted in this regard that

the explicit incorporation of the idea/expression dichotomy in an international agreement is precedential, and sets an important boundary for the scope of proprietary rights in creative works. Ideas are the basic building blocks of creative works and reserving them from the scope of copyright is an important policy strategy to ensure that copyright protection does not operate to confer monopoly rights on the basic elements of creative endeavours. The delimitation is also important because it serves to channel certain creative works in to the realm of copyright and others in to the realm of patent law. Finally, the idea/expression

---

[27] 17 USC section 102(b). A similar concept was incorporated in Article 1(2) of the European Directive 91/250/EEC on the legal protection of computer programs.

[28] J Dratler Jr, *Intellectual Property Law: Commercial, Creative and Industrial Property* (1996: New York, Law Journal Seminars Press), paras 1A-52–1A-53.

[29] This issue is also particularly relevant in the digital context. See generally J Liu and F Fang, 'The Idea/Expression Dichotomy in Cyberspace: A Comparative Study of Web Page Copyrights in the United States and in China', (2003) EIPR 11, pp 504–6.

dichotomy ensures that future authors are not hindered from engaging in creative activity due to a monopoly by previous authors on the underlying ideas of their work.[30]

In Dratler's view,

the dichotomy serves the purpose of providing a rational line of demarcation between copyright and other forms of intellectual property. It also no doubt will serve the purpose of convincing signatories to the TRIPS Agreement that providing copyright protection for these new forms of expression will not curtail progress in those fields.[31]

Ideas (as well as procedures, methods of operation or mathematical concepts) are not protectable 'as such'. This clarification suggests that the idea/expression dichotomy is not clear-cut in all circumstances, such as when an idea has been expressed in a particular form and it is problematic to separate both.[32] In United States copyright law, when an *idea* and the way to *express* it are so intricately linked that the ways of expression have little possible variation, there will not be copyright infringement, nor does the copyright prevent others from using or expressing the same idea. This is generally known as the 'the merger doctrine'.[33]

The 'expression' of a copyrighted work is the perceptible manifestation of an idea, fixed in a material form. With the advancement of technology, a work can also be expressed in digital form (eg computer program). Since copyright protection is limited to the expression, the exclusive rights conferred relate to the reproduction, the communication to the public, and the transformation of the protected works.

Article 9.2 neither creates a new exception nor clarifies existing ones;[34] it rather establishes the boundaries of copyright protection.[35] The intent of this provision is not to exclude from protection subject matter that would have been otherwise copyrightable.

Unlike Article 27.1 of the TRIPS Agreement, which specifies the requirements for the protection of inventions (novelty, inventive step, and industrial applicability),

---

[30] UNCTAD–ICTSD, *Resource Book on TRIPS and Development* (2005: New York, Cambridge University Press), pp 139–40. [31] See Dratler op. cit. (1996), para 1A-53.

[32] See D Lipszyc, 'La protección del derecho de autor y los derechos conexos en el Acuerdo sobre los ADPIC', (2004), Revista Temas de Derecho Industrial y de la Competencia No 6, p 205.

[33] One case involving this doctrine was, for example, *Ets-Hokin v Skyy Spirits Inc*, 225 F 3d 1068 (9th Cir 2000) [1], 'in which the court ruled that the whole vodka bottle in that case was driven by function, was not subject to copyright, and could not be protected by copyright law for that reason. While the label might have been protected by copyright, it was ruled to be incidental to the use and not significant' (referenced at <http://en.wikipedia.org/wiki/Merger_doctrine> (last accessed on 20 July 2005). [34] See WIPO, op. cit. (1997), p 15.

[35] It cannot be regarded either as a positive obligation to protect all expressions of artistic and literary works. See, however, Gervais op. cit. (2003), p 131 (suggesting this interpretation) and Watal op. cit. (2001), p 215 (arguing such an interpretation is overreaching as Article 9.2 was only intended to clarify the ambiguities in the Berne Convention).

Article 9.2 broadly refers to the protection of 'expressions' without any qualification.[36] This cannot be interpreted, however, as requiring Members to protect any expression whether original or not.[37] Nor can this be interpreted as implying that Members subjecting protection to an originality requirement (however defined) violate the TRIPS Agreement. In accordance with Article 9.1 Members shall comply with Articles 1–21 of the Berne Convention, which protects 'every production in the literary, scientific and artistic domain' (Article 2(1)), while it leaves Contracting Parties leeway to determine the *level* of creativity required. Similarly, the Agreement leaves it to domestic law to decide where the appropriate line lies between idea and expression.

This flexibility confirms that the TRIPS Agreement cannot be regarded as a uniform or harmonized law, but as a basic platform for IPR protection. In fact, the concept of originality has been differently applied in various countries.[38] Under continental law, the degree of creativity required has generally been higher than in common law countries.[39] Germany, for instance, traditionally applied a high standard of originality. In contrast, in the US it was deemed sufficient to prove that the work was not copied but was the result of the author's own effort ('sweat of the brow').[40] In other jurisdictions, originality requires at least the presence of choices made by the author.[41] The European standard has moved towards a middle ground, thereby narrowing down the differences between common law and continental law approaches. The European Directive on the Legal Protection of

[36] The only provision where 'intellectual creation' is mentioned is Article 10(2) in relation to databases.

[37] The requirement of an 'intellectual creation' has been deemed implicit in the Berne Convention. Thus, in the 1948 Brussels Revision Conference it was stressed that while 'speaking of literary and artistic works, we are already using a term which means that we are talking about...an intellectual creation' (*WIPO Guide to the Copyright and Related Rights Treaties Administered by Wipo and Glossary of Copyright and Related Rights Terms* (2003: Geneva), p 23). This is applicable to all kinds of works, including computer programs, which should exhibit more than a simple response to functional requirements in order to be deemed protected under copyright.

[38] Guidance on this matter may be found in looking at the right of adaptation and the manner in which adaptations may acquire copyright on their own. Where the adaptation begins and where the original ends is one example of establishing originality sufficient to copyright.

[39] In some of these countries 'original' is understood as simply indicating 'origin', that is merely that the author has originated the work and not copied it, whatever the intellectual creativity expressed therein is. According to one opinion, 'the definition of the key notion of originality, as expressed in the famous UK case of *University of London Press v University Tutorial Press Ltd* of 1916 and based on the skill and labour of the author, is incompatible with the Berne Convention and possibly also with the TRIPS Agreement'. See D Gervais, 'The Compatibility of the "Skill and Labour" Originality Standard with the Berne Convention and the TRIPs Agreement' (2004) EIPR 2, p 75.

[40] This approach has been somehow qualified, however, in the *Feist Publications, Inc v Rural Telephone Service Co*, 111 S Ct 1282 (1991), where the Supreme Court considered that a minimal display of creativity was required.

[41] For instance, the Canadian Court of Appeal in *Tele-Direct (Publ'ns) Inc v American Bus Infor Inc* (1997) stated that 'the basis of copyright is the originality of the work in question so long as work, taste, and discretion have entered in to the composition, that originality is established'. (76 CPR 3d, p 296).

Computer Programs[42] defines original 'in the sense that it is the author's own *intellectual* creation' (emphasis added).[43]

It should be noted, finally, that the WIPO Copyright Treaty contains a provision (Article 2) almost identical to Article 9.2 of TRIPS on the scope of copyright protection.

Computer programs and compilation of data

10.1. Computer programs, whether in source or object code, shall be protected as literary works under the Berne Convention (1971).

The recognition of computer programs as copyrightable works has been actively sought by major software producers and the US government since the 1980s. Under the Special Section 301 of the Trade Act, the United States Trade Representative (USTR) initiated several procedures against developed and developing countries that did not adequately protect, in the USTR view, such programs.

Many experts and courts had sustained the applicability of the Berne Convention to software, even in the absence of an express legislative reference to that effect. However, a good part of legal and economic literature had questioned the appropriateness of copyright protection for functional works such as software,[44] and some influential institutions advocated the development of a 'new category of law'.[45] The treatment of software as the part of the TRIPS Agreement has also been criticized.[46]

While copyright as a basis of protection of computer programs was accepted by a large number of countries—in part as a result of US government action under the Special Section 301 of the Trade Act—many were reluctant to consider software as a literary work. During the 1980s, the possibility of protecting computer programs under the category of literary works was hotly disputed. Different solutions were reached by national courts, many of which denied object code the status of literary work. Some countries opted for modalities of protection of computer programs distinct from literary works. Thus, France applied the concept of applied arts, while South Korea and Brazil adopted *sui generis* regimes.

---

[42] Directive 91/250/EEC on the legal protection of computer programs.

[43] The same concept is incorporated in other Euroepan Directives (Directive 93/98/EEC harmonizing the term of protection of copyright and certain related rights; Directive 96/9/EC on the legal protection of databases). See also Article 3.2(a) of the Washington Treaty, whereunder protection is conferred to 'original' layout-designs/topographies, understanding 'original in the sense that they are the result of their creators' own intellectual effort'.

[44] See, eg, A Mody, *New Environment for Intellectual Property* (1989: Washington DC, World Bank).

[45] See *Office of Technology Assessment, Intellectual Property Rights in Age of Electronics and Information* (1986: Washington, DC), p 14.

[46] See, eg, U Uchtenhagen, 'The GATT Negotiations Concerning Copyright and Intellectual Property Protection' (1990), International Review of Industrial Property and Copyright Law, Vol. 21, No 6.

The recognition of copyright as a main modality for the protection of computer programs[47] was a major objective of industrialized countries in the TRIPS negotiations. Article 10.1 provides that 'computer programs, whether in source or object code, shall be protected as literary works under the Berne Convention (1971)'. This provision settled a long debate about the status of computer programs in that Convention. For some, such programs were among the 'productions' referred to in Article 2(1) of the Convention, a view disputed by many experts and policy makers. The applicability of 'moral rights' to computer programs has also been debated, and in some national laws, explicitly limited or excluded.[48]

The essence of Article 10.1 is an obligation to protect computer programs 'as literary works' under the Berne Convention (1971).[49] The wording in Article 9.1 ('as' literary works) suggests that computer programs can be assimilated to literary works, although intrinsically they may not be so. Interestingly, the WIPO Copyright Treaty Article 10.1 requires protection of computer programs 'in source or object code', but is silent with respect to cases where they are embedded in microelectronic devices. Likewise, no specific rule is established in connection with reverse engineering, one of the most controversial issues in this field.

The main implication of the assimilation to literary works is the extension of the term of protection, since the rights conferred by the Berne Convention are essentially the same for all categories of rights, while some aspects (eg number and type of permitted copies for a legitimate user) need to be addressed taking the specificity of computer programs into account.[50]

As mentioned, the TRIPS Agreement does not set forth a specific standard of originality. Since in the case of computer programs choices are limited by their functional nature, the originality requirement can be easily met in some countries (such as in the US) where a low standard of originality has been applied. Many of such programs, however, could remain outside copyright protection in countries (such as Germany) where a higher standard of originality was applied before the adoption of the European Directive on the matter,[51] which only requires that works be the author's own intellectual creation.

As a result of the idea/expression dichotomy,[52] the production of an identical copy of a program is prohibited by law, if it is the result of access to the pre-existing program. There is no infringement if an identical program is independently created without such access. Likewise, there is no infringement if a program has the

---

[47] The terms 'computer programs' and 'software' are used interchangeably in this volume.

[48] See, eg, Watal op. cit. (2001), p 212.

[49] This formulation encountered strong opposition from developing countries, which did not want to accept copyright as the main mode of protection for computer programs. See, eg, Watal op. cit. (2001), p 216.

[50] Many countries, including the United States, have explicitly determined in their national laws the extent to which copies of computer programs can be made.

[51] G Davies, *Copyright and the Public Interest* (2002: London, Sweet & Maxwell, 2nd edn), p 346.

[52] See above, Article 9.2 of the TRIPS Agreement.

same function but a different expression, even if the new program has been created on the basis of access to and reverse engineering of a pre-existing one.[53]

It should be noted that computer programs are not only protectable as copyrightable works. The 'source code' can also be protected as trade secret or undisclosed information. Such code, which contains the most valuable information for software producers, is not made available to the public through the distribution of copies in digital form. In addition, in the USA and some other jurisdictions software has become patentable.[54]

> **10.2. Compilations of data or other material, whether in machine readable or other form, which by reason of the selection or arrangement of their contents constitute intellectual creations shall be protected as such. Such protection, which shall not extend to the data or material itself, shall be without prejudice to any copyright subsisting in the data or material itself.**

The subject matter of protection under Article 10.2 of the TRIPS Agreement is 'compilations of data or other material'. This may include data of a factual nature, as well as collections of literary or artistic works (whether in the public domain or subject to copyright), such as anthologies. The material form of the compilation is irrelevant for protection. The provision applies to paper-based as well as to digital compilations.

The Berne Convention enumerated 'collections' of works among the protected subject matter in Article 2.5. While according to one interpretation,[55] collections of mere data are protected under Article 2(1) of said Convention, it only explicitly protects 'collections of literary or artistic works'.[56]

The eligibility for protection under Article 10.2 of the TRIPS Agreement is based on a standard different from the one contained in Article 2(5) of the Berne Convention. While the TRIPS Agreement protects compilations that constitute 'intellectual creations' by reason of the selection *or* arrangement of their contents, Article 2(5) of the Berne Convention requires creativity with regard to the selection *and* the arrangement of the contents; that is, these elements are cumulative and not alternative. As a result, compilations that may not be protectable under the Convention are, however, covered by Article 10.2 of the TRIPS Agreement. This relaxation of the standard obviously expands the scope of protection.

Article 10.2 of the TRIPS Agreement states ambiguously that, to the extent that compilations constitute 'intellectual creations', they will be protected 'as such'. One

---

[53] The admissibility of reverse engineering of computer programs has given rise to an intense debate. Admitted by the EC Directive on the Protection of Computer Programs (91/250/EEC)—at least for the development of interoperable programs—it has not found a clear treatment under national legislation or case law. In *Sega v Accolade* (CA 9, No 92-15655, 20.10.92) a US court held that intermediate copying necessary for disassembly of computer object code was 'fair use' where it was the only way to get access to the ideas and functional elements embodied in a copyrighted computer program to make compatible programs.   [54] See Chapter 9 below.
[55] Based on the concept of 'production' in Article 2(1) of the Berne Convention. See, eg, Gervais op. cit. (2003), p 136.   [56] See, eg, Watal op. cit. (2001), p 219.

interpretation of 'as such' is that covered compilations are subject to protection as a literary or artistic work. If this were the case, the obligations under the Berne Convention would apply. However, should this have been the intention of the drafters, they could have used a more straightforward wording, like in Article 10.1 with regard to computer programs. Another interpretation, more in line with the Vienna Convention, is that 'as such', as referred to 'intellectual creations', does not subject compilations to the Berne Convention, but leaves Members freedom to determine the level of protection as they see fit.[57]

Article 10.2 also indicates that the protection of compilations 'shall not extend to the data or material itself'. This clarification was necessary due to the coverage under the provision of compilations of mere data which do not themselves constitute copyrightable works. Similarly, artistic and literary works that have fallen into the public domain do not regain copyright protection by virtue of their inclusion in a compilation.

Article 2(5) of the Berne Convention contains a proviso ('without prejudice to the copyright in each of the works forming part of such collections') that Article 10.2 of the Agreement has not reiterated. Since the Agreement does not derogate from obligations under the Convention (Article 2.2 of the Agreement) and Members are bound to comply with Articles 1–21 thereof (Article 9.1 of the Agreement), Members are in any case subject to the same condition.

While Article 10.2 of the TRIPS Agreement may be seen as a 'Berne-plus solution', it remains within the boundaries of accepted copyright principles, as some level of intellectual creation—determined in accordance with domestic legislation—is required for protection. The drafters of the Agreement were not seduced by the concept, promoted at the time of negotiations by the database industry, of expanding protection to non-original databases. This idea underpinned the already-mentioned European Council Directive 96/9/EC, which adopted a *sui generis* form of protection for a database[58] if it is shown that qualitatively and/or quantitatively a 'substantial investment in either obtaining, verification or presentation of the contents' has been made (Article 7.1). The EC Directive provides, in addition, for an 'extraction right', ie the right to prevent 'the extraction or reutilization of the whole or substantial part, evaluated quantitatively or qualitatively, of the contents of the database' (Article 7.1).[59]

---

[57] See S Ricketson, 'WIPO study on limitations and exceptions of copyright and related rights in the digital environment', WIPO document SCCR/9/7 (5 April 2003), p 55.

[58] Defined as 'a collection of independent works, data or other materials arranged in a systematic or methodical way and individually accessible by electronic or other means' (Article 1.2).

[59] The Directive's sections on the *sui generis* right define two categories of restricted acts: extraction and re-utilization. The right applies to the whole or a substantial part of a database. On 9 November 2004, the European Court of Justice (ECJ) decided four cases on the scope of database protection: *British Horseracing Board Ltd v William Hill Organization Ltd Case C 203/02, Fixtures Marketing Ltd v Svenska Spel Ab Case C 338/02, Fixtures Marketing Ltd v Organismos Prognostikon Agonon Podosfairou AE (OPAP) Case C 444/02* and *Fixtures Marketing Ltd v Oy Veikkaus Ab Case C-46/02.* These cases clarified the concept of 'investment', and of the 'extraction right', which covers any act of appropriation, including for non-commercial purposes, that deprives the database owner of revenue (*British Horseracing Board Ltd v William Hill Organization Ltd,* pp 48–51).

This Directive provides a conspicuous example of the emerging paradigm of IPR protection, whereunder the main goal is not to protect creativity and ingenuity,[60] but investments.[61] Databases are, in effect, protected under the *sui generis* right without requiring originality in the selection or arrangement of their contents. In accordance with the European Commission, the main feature of the Directive is

to create a new economic right to protect the substantial investment of a database maker. Considering the considerable investment of human, technical and financial resources necessary to create a database, and given that those databases can be copied at a much lower cost than that of their development, such legal change is important. Unauthorised access to a database and the extraction of its contents are thus acts which can have grave technical and economic consequences.[62]

WIPO convened a Diplomatic Conference to develop a treaty on databases that was held in December 1996. One of the basic proposals considered by the Conference was the protection of non-original databases the production of which entailed a 'substantial investment'.[63] The Conference failed, however, to reach consensus, in part due to the opposition of developing countries as well as librarians and the scientific community within the US.

Despite the fact that the US has championed an across-the-board expansion and strengthening of IPRs, in the area of databases it has not gone as far as the European Union. The US Supreme Court ruled in *Feist Publication Inc v Rural Telephone Services* (499 US 340, 1991) that information consisting solely of facts arranged in a straightforward manner (an alphabetical arrangement of telephone subscribers' names and numbers) were not 'original works of authorship' within the meaning of the Copyright Act. This decision was viewed by some authors as endangering the vitality of the US information industries: '[T]o a nation that counts information as an important asset and a principal export, the outcome is (or should be) extremely worrisome'.[64]

After *Feist*, the 'Collection of Information Antipiracy Bill' was introduced into US Congress in order to expand protection for databases, based on a model of unfair competition rather than property. With the purpose of offering a less restrictive, alternative regulation, a second bill (the 'Consumer and Investor Access to Information Act') was also introduced. So far, no legislation on databases has been adopted in the US.

---

[60] The *sui generis* protection is conferred in addition to any other existing rights.
[61] Protection lasts for 15 years, a period that may be renewed if there has been substantial new investment. See generally, E Derclaye, 'Database Sui Generis Right: What Is a Substantial Investment? A Tentative Definition', (2005) 36 International Review of Industrial Property and Copyright Law 1, pp 2–27; G Westkamp, 'Protecting Databases Under US and European Law—Methodical Approaches to the Protection of Investments Between Unfair Competition and Intellectual Property Concepts', (2003) 34 International Review of Industrial Property and Copyright Law 7, pp 768–803.
[62] Commission of the European Communities, *Green Paper. Copyright and Related Rights in the Information Society* (1995: Brussels), p 32.   [63] See document WIPO CRNR/DC/6, 30.8.96.
[64] R Dreyfuss, 'A Wiseguy's Approach to Information Products: Muscling Copyright and Patent Into a Unitary Theory of Intellectual Property', Supreme Court Review 1992, University of Chicago, p 197.

Rental rights

11. In respect of at least computer programs and cinematographic works, a Member shall provide authors and their successors in title the right to authorize or to prohibit the commercial rental to the public of originals or copies of their copyright works. A Member shall be excepted from this obligation in respect of cinematographic works unless such rental has led to widespread copying of such works which is materially impairing the exclusive right of reproduction conferred in that Member on authors and their successors in title. In respect of computer programs, this obligation does not apply to rentals where the program itself is not the essential object of the rental.

Article 11 of the TRIPS Agreement contains one of the main innovations in the copyright section of the Agreement. It introduces—for the first time in an international agreement—a minimum standard requiring the recognition in some cases of 'rental rights'. This standard is 'Berne-plus'. It contains, however, exceptions and limitations that reflect outstanding differences among developed countries in the field of copyright/authors' rights.

Article 11 confers rights in respect of 'at least' computer programs and cinematographic works. While computer programs were internationally recognized as copyrightable only with the adoption of the TRIPS Agreement, as examined above, cinematographic works had been formally incorporated into the Berne Convention by the Rome Conference in 1928. 'Cinematographic works' should be deemed to include works 'expressed by a process analogous to cinematography'.[65] 'At least' means that the same rights could be conferred in relation to other works, a clarification that is unnecessary, since the TRIPS Agreement contains minimum standards and does not prevent Members from granting a more extensive protection, unless it is inconsistent with the provisions of the Agreement.[66]

The right conferred under Article 11 is 'to authorise or to prohibit the commercial rental to the public of original or copies of their copyright works'.[67] Only 'commercial' rental is subject to the newly created rental rights, thereby excluding not-for-profit rentals. In addition, such rights apply in relation to rental 'to the public', excluding rental made, even against a price, on an individual basis. Rental rights apply both in relation to the 'original' and 'copies' of copyrighted works.

Notwithstanding the general rule incorporated in Article 11, in respect of the rental of cinematographic works exclusive rights need not be granted 'unless such rental has led to widespread copying of such works which is materially impairing the exclusive right of reproduction conferred in the Member on authors and their successors in title'. This part of Article 11 in fact establishes that Members are only obligated to grant exclusive rights if certain conditions are met. In this sense, such

---

[65] See Article 2(1) of the Berne Convention.   [66] See Article 1.1, pp 22–31 above.
[67] Despite some proposals made during negotiations, Article 11 does not provide for an alternative right to obtain an equitable remuneration for rental.

exclusive rights are the exception to the rule, rather than the rule itself. Hence, Members are free to provide or not for exclusive rental rights for cinematographic works, and the burden would be on the complaining party to prove that

(a) rental has led to 'widespread copying';
(b) such copying is 'materially impairing the exclusive right of reproduction conferred in the Member'.

Whether these two conditions are met will depend on the circumstances of each case. There is a significant room for Members to determine when a country would be bound to grant exclusive rental rights on cinematographic works. In implementing this provision several aspects need to be taken into account. First, copying may affect certain cinematographic works (for instance, films popular among youngsters) but not all works falling in that category. It may be difficult to sustain the claim in this case that copying is 'widespread'. Second, even if widespread copying were established, the obligation only arises if it is 'materially impairing' the exclusive right of reproduction. The alleged impairment should take place with regard to the right to control the reproduction of a work, not the rental or distribution of the work. Third, the right-holder will be bound to prove that widespread copying affects the diffusion by any means of an audiovisual work;[68] that is, that such copying affects both his ability to authorize and to prohibit reproduction.

Members may, in view of the obligation imposed under Article 11, adopt flexible approaches. They may not grant exclusive rental rights at all if they deem that the conditions set forth therein are not met. They may only grant such rights in particular cases where it is proven that such conditions are met (administration of this system may be, however, rather complex), or with regard to certain categories of works in respect of which there is proven widespread copying that is materially impairing the exclusive right of reproduction.

Since the situation may change over time, Members may also adopt temporary legislation, as the US did. The origin of Article 11 can, in fact, be traced in US legislation[69] (which the TRIPS Agreement's text mirrored to a large extent) that specifically recognized rental rights for computer programs and sound recordings (and not for visual works).[70]

---

[68] See, eg, Gervais op. cit. (2003) p 140.

[69] The proposal to include a provision of rental rights—with regard, in fact, to all copyrights—was originally submitted by the US. See Watal op. cit. (2001), p 221.

[70] See the Record Rental Amendments Act and the Software Rental Amendments Act. While the TRIPS Agreement established a permanent minimum right, the referred legislation was conceived as temporary due to the US Congress's unwillingness to create a perpetual exception to the 'first sale' doctrine. See, eg, G Peterson and C Makay, 'The US Software Rental Act', (1992) 22 Copyright World, May–June. Dratler reports, however, that in order to implement the TRIPS Agreement's provisions, the US Congress repealed the sunset provision that would have extinguished the rental rights on 1 October 1997, thereby making them permanent. See Uruguay Round Agreements Act 511, Pub L No 103-465, 108 Stat 4809, 4974 (8 December 1994), striking first sentence of Section 804(c) of the Computer Software Rental Amendments Act of 1990, Pub L No 101-650, 804 (c), 104 Stat 5089, 5136 (1 December 1990); 6.01(3)(b)(ii) (Dratler op. cit. (1996), para IA-56).

While rental rights entail an exception to the 'first sale' doctrine that prevails in common-law countries, the exclusive right to rent may be deemed as a part of full distribution rights as recognized under the law of many continental law countries.[71] The EU Commission also felt the need to adopt an EC Directive to harmonize rental rights belonging to authors, performing artists in respect of fixations, phonogram producers, and producers of the first fixation of films.[72]

Both the US legislation and the above-mentioned EC Directive on rental rights have explicitly provided for exceptions for non-profit lending by libraries and other institutions. Such an exception is not provided for under the TRIPS Agreement. However, without prejudice to the application of Article 13, as noted, Article 11 only grants exclusive rights with regard to the 'commercial' rental of computer programs and cinematographic works. Therefore, non-profit lending is outside the scope of the conferred rights.

Article 11 also provides for an exception with regard to the rental rights of computer programs, 'where the program itself is not the essential object of the rental'. This exception would apply, for example, to software embedded in microelectronic devices incorporated in rented cars and other vehicles, and to the commercial rental of computers preloaded with software at airports and hotels. The exception seems broader than the one authorized under US law, which requires that the computer be configured so as to prevent copying or that the software be licensed.[73]

Since Article 11 provides for exclusive rental rights for cinematographic works as an exception, rather than a limitation or exception to a granted right, the three-step test contained in Article 13 of the TRIPS Agreement would be inapplicable to a situation in which national law has opted not to grant such rights. If a Member, however, granted exclusive rental rights in order to comply with the obligations under the Agreement (that is, because rental has led to widespread copying of such works which is materially impairing the exclusive right of reproduction), exceptions to such rights may be deemed covered by Article 13, which, as examined below,[74] applies to all 'exclusive rights'. However, should a Member adopt rental rights for cinematographic works without being obliged thereto, such rights would be a 'TRIPS-plus' advantage not subject to the protection conferred under the Agreement and, therefore, exempted from the three-step test of Article 13. If a Member could grant or not such rights, a fortiori it may impose

---

[71] The TRIPS Agreement does not recognize a general right of distribution. Such a right was introduced by the WCT (Article 6(1)).

[72] See Directive 92/100/EEC on the rental right and lending right and on certain rights related to copyright in the field of intellectual property. Rental rights were recognized for computer programs by the Directive 91/250/EEC on the legal protection of computer programs.

[73] See Dratler op. cit. (1996), para IA-55.   [74] See pp 134–55 below.

thereon the limitations and restrictions it considers suitable in the light of the local circumstances and public policies.

An open question is the extent to which panels and the Appellate Body may interfere with national discretion in determining when the conditions set out by Article 11 requiring the granting of exclusive rental rights for cinematographic works have been met. An 'activist' approach by panels and the Appellate Body in the interpretation of the TRIPS Agreement would be likely to imperil the dispute settlement system. The Agreement has neither addressed nor resolved all issues in IPR law. Article 11 has deliberately left considerable leeway to Members for implementation of their obligations. If panels or the Appellate Body make expansive interpretations or choices that the Members did not make themselves during the negotiations, the credibility of the dispute settlement system would be seriously undermined.

Article 14.4 of the Agreement extends exclusive rental rights to phonograms,[75] but authorizes countries which may have in force a system of equitable remuneration on the date of adoption of the Final Act of the Uruguay Round, to maintain such a system 'provided that the commercial rental of phonograms is not giving rise to the material impairment of the exclusive rights of reproduction of right holders'.[76] It should be noted that rental rights for phonograms are not contemplated under the Rome Convention.

Term of protection

12. Whenever the term of protection of a work, other than a photographic work or a work of applied art, is calculated on a basis other than the life of a natural person, such term shall be no less than 50 years from the end of the calendar year of authorized publication, or, failing such authorized publication within 50 years from the making of the work, 50 years from the end of the calendar year of making.

Article 12 settles a difficulty encountered in the application of the Berne Convention in countries whose legal systems[77] do not allow a juridical person (eg a corporation) to be considered as an 'author'.[78]

The general rule under the Berne Convention is a minimum term of copyright for the life of the author plus fifty years (Article 7(1)). There are three situations

---

[75] See pp. 164–6 below.

[76] One of the main aims of this compromise was to allow Japan to maintain its mixed rental rights system: Japanese law recognized exclusive rights for one year and a right to remuneration thereafter.

[77] Under the author's rights approach, in principle, only natural persons can be 'authors'. The law establishes in some cases that rights are assigned *ex lege* to a juridical person (eg a film producer). In common law countries, in contrast, copyrights can be originally held by juridical persons.

[78] Those cases had been dealt with under Article 7.3 of the Berne Convention, which refers to 'anonymous or pseudonimous' works.

contemplated in Article 7 of the Convention in which the term of protection is not counted on the basis of the author's life:[79]

(a) in the case of cinematographic works, the countries of the Union may provide that the term of protection shall expire fifty years after the work has been made available to the public with the consent of the author, or, failing such an event within fifty years from the making of such a work, fifty years after the making.

(b) In the case of anonymous or pseudonymous works, the term of protection granted by this Convention shall expire fifty years after the work has been lawfully made available to the public.[80]

(c) In the case of photographic works and works of applied art, it shall be a matter for legislation in the countries of the Union to determine the term of protection in so far as they are protected as artistic works; however, this term shall last at least until the end of a period of twenty-five years from the making of such a work.

Article 12 makes clear that it refers to works held by juridical persons as it alludes to a term 'calculated on a basis other than the life of a natural person'. In addition, it clarifies that failing publication of the protected work within fifty years from the making of the work, protection shall extend for fifty years from the end of the calendar day of the making.

Previous drafts of Article 12 included an explicit reference to computer programs. It was deleted once the assimilation of said programs to literary works was incorporated in Article 10.1. That assimilation makes irrelevant a specific rule on duration of rights for such programs.

While Article 7(1) and Article 7(2) of the Berne Convention refer to the 'made available to the public' concept that may include public performances, broadcasting or other communication to the public, Article 12 of the Agreement uses the word 'publication', which has a narrower meaning.

The Berne Convention indirectly defines 'publication' in Article 3(3),[81] which states:

The expression *'published works'* means works published with the consent of their authors, whatever may be the means of manufacture of the copies, provided that the availability of such copies has been such as to satisfy the reasonable requirements of the public, having regard to the nature of the work. The performance of a dramatic, dramatico-musical, cinematographic or musical work, the public recitation of a literary work, the communication

---

[79] See Article 7(2), (3) and (4) of the Berne Convention.

[80] However, when the pseudonym adopted by the author leaves no doubt as to his identity, or discloses his identity during the above-mentioned period, the term of protection shall be that provided in Article 7(1).

[81] Although Members, as well as WTO panels and the Appellate Body, may always resort to the ordinary meaning of publication (as mandated by Article 31 of the Vienna Convention), the fact that the Berne Convention has been incorporated into the TRIPS Agreement lends support to the use of this definition. See, eg, UNCTAD–ICTSD, op. cit. (2005), p 181.

by wire or the broadcasting of literary or artistic works, the exhibition of a work of art and the construction of a work of architecture shall not constitute publication.

As a result of the differences in the rules of the Berne Convention[82] and the TRIPS Agreement, in cases where a work was made available before 'publication', the term of protection under the TRIPS Agreement will be longer than under the Convention.

Article 12 of the TRIPS Agreement leaves untouched the general term of protection based on the author's life plus fifty years, as well as the minimum term (twenty-five years) provided for by the Berne Convention for photographic works and works of applied art. The Agreement, instead, makes mandatory the minimum term of Article 7(2) of the Berne Convention for cinematographic works (other than those copyright works whose terms are based on the life of a natural person).[83]

Article 12 explicitly excludes photographic works or works of applied arts and, hence, leaves unchanged their situation in respect of the term of protection as counted in the Berne Convention. The situation of cinematographic works is affected by the TRIPS Agreement, when a Member makes use of the faculty of calculating the term not from the author's death but from the cinematographic works having been made available to the public or, failing such event, from its making.[84]

Although, as noted, the TRIPS Agreement would in general lead to a term of protection longer than the Berne Convention, there are, according to WIPO's analysis, some (though not typical) cases in which:

the minimum term of protection will be longer under the Berne Convention than under the TRIPS Agreement; namely when no authorized publication takes place within 50 years from the end of the calendar year of the making of the work, but the work is made available to the public, with the consent of the author, within that period in another form (such as public performance). In such a case, the 50-year term of protection would expire under the TRIPS Agreement when 50 years from the making of the work has elapsed, while under the Berne Convention it expires as much later (up to 50 years minus one day) as the time elapsed from the making of the work until its making available to the public, with the consent of the author, in a form different from publication.[85]

The bilateral agreements and FTAs promoted by the US have extended the term of protection to seventy years. This is compatible with the Berne Convention[86] and

---

[82] The expression in Article 3(3) 'whatever may be the means of manufacture of the copies', provides flexibility as to the type of copies that are made available to the public.

[83] With the observed difference between 'publication' and 'made available to the public'. See Dratler op. cit. (1996), para IA-58.   [84] See WIPO op. cit. (1997), p 20.

[85] Idem, p 21. The same applies in respect of anonymous and pseudonymous works (idem, p 22).

[86] Article 7(6): 'The countries of the Union may grant a term of protection in excess of those provided by the preceding paragraphs.'

the nature of the provisions of the TRIPS Agreement. It is questionable, however, whether there is a social and economic justification[87] for such an extension, which delays the entry of knowledge into the public domain, without any clear benefits in terms of incentives or rewards to authors. Thus, in *Eldred v Ashcroft*,[88] where the US Supreme Court examined the constitutionality of a law extending the duration of copyright for twenty years, Justice Breyer elaborated on the costs of an extension and questioned whether longer periods of protection would promote creation, as 'no potential author can reasonably believe that he has more than a tiny chance of writing a classic that will survive commercially long enough for the copyright extension to matter'.[89]

The economic analysis tends to indicate that

changes to copyright law that are expected to assist artists do not work because of the unintended consequences; for example, they strengthen the bargaining power of firms in the cultural industries more than they help artists. That is a testable hypothesis, though it would be difficult to test it. If true, it suggests that policy-makers should abandon the cry to 'strengthen' copyright law as a major part of cultural policy for stimulating creativity and instead offer direct grants or loans to artist. What would be preferable is reducing the term of copyright to 20 years from the date of a work's publication, which with modern IT is not so costly to register. That would enable authors to benefit more from their creations.[90]

Limitations and exceptions

13 Members shall confine limitations or exceptions to exclusive rights to certain special cases which do not conflict with a normal exploitation of the work and do not unreasonably prejudice the legitimate interests of the right holder.

Article 13 determines some of the circumstances under which Members can provide for exceptions to exclusive rights. It is an important provision in the international copyright system, as based on the Berne Convention and the TRIPS Agreement. As noted by one commentator, limitations and exceptions play a key role, because they

serve as the principal means by which national governments strike a balance between the right of copyright owners and other important societal goals, including the proliferation of

---

[87] On the economics of copyright, see generally W Gordon and R Watt, *The Economics of Copyright. Developments in Research and Analysis* (2003: Cheltenham, Edward Elgar); M Einhorn, *Media, Technology and Copyright. Integrating Law and Economics* (2004: Cheltenham, Edward Elgar); B Andersen, Z Kozul-Wright, and R Kozul-Wright, *The Case of the Music Industry* (2000: UNCTAD Discussion Papers No 145).

[88] 537 US 186. In this case, Internet publishers seeking to exploit old works, such as early Mickey Mouse cartoons, constitutionally challenged the twenty years' extension of protection introduced by the 1998 Copyright Extension Act. The action was dismissed by the Court.   [89] Ibidem.

[90] R Towse, 'Copyright policy, cultural policy and support for artists', in W Gordon and R Watt op. cit. (2003), p 78.

knowledge and art, freedom of expression, and the enhancement of culture. Were these exceptions and limitation clauses interpreted restrictively, they might well preclude member states from tailoring their copyright laws to achieve these vital objectives.[91]

The need to strike the balance between copyright protection and public interest has been emphasized by courts in many countries[92] and by legal doctrine.[93] The very general wording of Article 13 raises difficult issues of interpretation about the scope of the provision, the meaning of the conditions its sets forth, and how such balance can be reached in particular cases.

The first and complex interpretive issue that this provision generates is what rights can be subject to these exceptions and what is the relationship between this provision and Article 9(2) of the Berne Convention and the specific exceptions contained in the Convention. It should be remembered that the Berne Convention contains a number of limitations (eg news of the day, official texts) and exceptions, some of them uncompensated (that is, applicable without any payment) and others subject to payment of a remuneration to the right-holder. Such limitations and exceptions (unlike the rights conferred under the Convention) are not mandatory and are worded in general terms.

The wording of Article 13 of the TRIPS Agreement is clearly inspired by Article 9(2) of the Berne Convention, in fact, one of the most controversial provisions in the Convention. The exact meaning of this provision has been extensively debated and was uncertain at the time of the TRIPS negotiations and continues to be so today.[94]

During the negotiations Japan submitted that the limitations on copyright should 'follow the line of the Berne Convention'.[95] The US also proposed to apply the standards of the Convention, adding that any limitations and exemptions to exclusive economic rights

---

[91] L Helfer, 'World music on a US stage: an analysis of the section 110(5) WTO dispute', in H Hansen (ed.), *International Intellectual Property Law & Policy*, vol. 6, (2001: Huntington, Juris Publishing), para 48–3. See also generally Rochelle Cooper Dreyfuss and Andreas Lowenfeld, 'Two Achievements of the Uruguay Round: Putting TRIPs and Dispute Settlement Together' (1997), 37 Va J Int'l L, pp 275, 297.

[92] In the decision by the Supreme Court of Canada in *Theberge v Galeries d'Art du Petit Champlain Inc* [2002] 2 SCR 336, for instance, Justice Binnie, speaking on behalf of the majority, stated: 'The proper balance among these and other public policy objectives lies not only in recognizing the creator's rights but in giving due weight to their limited nature. In crassly economic terms it would be as inefficient to overcompensate artists and authors for the right of reproduction as it would be self-defeating to undercompensate them' (quoted in D Gervais, 'The Compatibility of the "Skill and Labour" Originality Standard with the Berne Convention and the TRIPs Agreement' (2004) European Intellectual Property Review 2, p 79, footnote 49.

[93] See eg, G Davies op. cit. (2002).

[94] G Dworkin, '*Exceptions to Copyright Exclusivity: Is Fair Use Consistent With Article 9.2 Berne And The New International Order?*', in H Hansen (ed.), *International Intellectual Property Law & Policy*, Vol. 6, (2001: Huntington, Juris Publishing), pp 66–5.

[95] See MTN.GNG/NG11/W/17/Add. 1, 6.

in any event shall be confined to clearly and carefully defined special cases which do not impair actual or potential markets for, or the value of, copyrighted works.[96]

Despite the origin of Article 13 of the TRIPS Agreement and its resemblance to Article 9(2) of the Berne Convention, there are important differences between the two provisions.

First, Article 13 states that Members 'shall confine' exceptions to those allowed therein. This wording seems more restrictive than the wording in Article 9(2) of the Berne Convention.[97]

Second, while the Berne Convention only refers to the 'reproduction' right of literary and artistic works, Article 13 of the TRIPS Agreement applies to all exclusive rights conferred, thereby expanding the room for exceptions beyond what the Convention provides for. For this reason, this provision may be viewed as a 'Berne-minus' solution. The covered rights, in addition to reproduction, include:

- translation (Article 8)
- public performance (Article 11)
- broadcasting and other communications (Article 11*bis*)
- public recitation (Article 11*ter*)
- adaptation (Article 12).

Moreover, Article 13 applies to the rental right provided for under Article 11 of the Agreement. Such a right is not stipulated in the Berne Convention.

Third, the Berne Convention refers to the 'legitimate interests of the author'. The TRIPS Agreement has broadened the interests to be taken into account (and correspondingly narrowed the scope of potential exceptions) by referring to the interests of 'the right-holder' who is not necessarily the author (eg a juridical person that has been assigned rights in a work).

While Article 13 may be regarded as a public interest limitation to exclusive rights, in reality it is

a limitation on the *scope of limitations* that member states can implement to promote access and dissemination of works domestically. In sum, what appears to be a limitation to copyright, is actually a limit on the discretion and means by which member states can constrain the exercise of exclusive rights . . . In essence, a member state's *inaction* on public interest issues is not a violation of the Berne Convention and by extension, the TRIPS Agreement. Where a country does not establish any limits or exceptions, the international system does not consider this to be a violation of the treaty. Only the failure to protect rights—not the failure to promote the public interest—is an actionable matter under international copyright law. There is no affirmative duty to implement the discretion available under the

---

[96] See MTN.GNG/NG11/W/14/Rev. 1, 8.

[97] Article 9(2): 'It shall be a matter for legislation in the countries of the Union to permit the reproduction of such works in certain special cases, provided that such reproduction does not conflict with a normal exploitation of the work and does not unreasonably prejudice the legitimate interests of the author.'

international treaties. Conversely, a state who acts to exercise its discretion by creating limitations and exceptions to rights is circumscribed by the provisions of the three-step test.[98]

There seems to be no dispute about the applicability of Article 13 to the newly exclusive rights created by the TRIPS Agreement in Article 11 (rental rights).[99] However, the scope of application of Article 13 of the TRIPS Agreement and, particularly, its relationship with the exceptions allowed under the Berne Convention raise complex issues.

One interpretation is that Article 13 would only effectively apply to rights that are not contemplated in the Berne Convention, ie the rental rights provided for in Article 11 of the Agreement.[100] It is hard, however, to reconcile this narrow scope with the general wording ('exclusive rights') used in the provision, and with the principle of 'effective interpretation' (or *l'effet utile*) applied in several GATT/WTO cases,[101] which requires that a treaty be interpreted to give meaning and effect to all the terms of the treaty. Accordingly, whenever more than one interpretation is possible, preference should be given to the interpretation that will give full meaning and effect to other provisions of the same treaty. As noted by Senftleben,

The scope of Article 13 can be confined to the rights which were newly introduced into international copyright law by the TRIPs Agreement. This interpretation, indeed, leaves the system of the Berne Convention untouched. However, it unduly minimizes the scope of Article 13 and can hardly be reconciled with its wording. The terms used in Article 13 TRIPs do not point towards any such restriction of scope. By contrast, as already elaborated, the wording evokes the impression of universal applicability by simply referring to 'limitations or exceptions to exclusive rights'. Undoubtedly, it would have been possible to lay down the confinement to newly introduced rights in the wording of Article 13 itself, if this was really intended. Hence, this line of reasoning must fail.[102]

In *United States–Section 110(5) of the US Copyright Act*,[103] the panel categorically argued that

In our view, neither the express wording nor the context of Article 13 or any other provision of the TRIPS Agreement supports the interpretation that the scope of application of Article 13 is limited to the exclusive rights newly introduced under the TRIPS Agreement.[104]

---

[98] R Okediji, 'Fostering access to education, research and dissemination of knowledge through copyright', UNCTAD-ICTSD Dialogue on Moving the pro-development IP agenda forward: Preserving Public Goods in health, education and learning, Bellagio, 29 November–3 December 2004 (available at <http://www.ictsd.org>, last accessed on 2 April 2005).

[99] See, eg, Gervais op. cit. (2003), 147; S Ricketson, 'WIPO study on limitations and exceptions of copyright and related rights in the digital environment', WIPO document SCCR/9/7 (5 April 2003), 50; M Senftleben, *Copyright, Limitations and the Three-step Test. An Analysis of the Three-step Test in International and EC Copyright Law* (2004: The Hague, Kluwer Law International), p 90.

[100] See also Article 14.4 of the Agreement.   [101] See 93 above.

[102] M Senftleben op. cit. (2004), p 90.

[103] WT/DS160/R, 15 June 2000.   [104] Para 6.80.

Another interpretation is based on the assumption that Article 13 of the TRIPS Agreement might permit more generous exceptions than Article 9(2) of the Convention. However, since Members are obliged under Articles 2.2 and 9.1 of the TRIPS Agreement to comply with Article 20 of the Convention, the limitations imposed by the Convention, it is argued, would always prevail in case of divergence. Senftleben has observed in this sense that

> [T]heoretically, the establishment of the TRIPs Agreement could have been used to do away with the obligation resulting from Article 20 BC [Berne Convention]. The parties of the TRIPs Agreement, however, obviously did not intend to deviate from the rule set out in Article 20, but manifestly countenanced and even underscored the commitment to the standard of protection reached in the Berne Convention. In contrast to Article 6*bis* BC, Article 20 was not excluded from the reference to provisions of the Convention made in Article 9(1) TRIPs. Furthermore, Article 2(2) TRIPs underlines the intention of the parties not to derogate from existing obligations under the Berne Convention. It would appear schizophrenic to allege that the TRIPs Agreement, by means of a reference to Article 20 BC, places the obligation on its parties to vest authors with more extensive rights when entering into an additional agreement, while at the same time not meeting the standard of protection reached in the Berne Convention itself. Therefore, it can be concluded that Article 20 BC does affect the TRIPs Agreement. Its provisions are to be construed in the light of the obligation to safeguard the Berne standard of protection. This obligation is central to the determination of the function of Article 13 TRIPs.[105]

According to Ricketson's analysis,[106] any exceptions or limitations in relation to the exclusive rights granted under the Berne Convention 'will need to be consistent with what is already allowed under Articles 1–21 of Berne.[107] As a result, provisions that extend the scope of existing Berne Convention limitations and exceptions, 'even though otherwise sustainable under Article 13 of TRIPS, would be unacceptable because they will place Berne members in breach of Article 2(2) of TRIPS'.[108] In the case of the limitation and exceptions in the Convention that simply make no explicit reference to the kind of factors contained in the three-step test, the Berne Convention provision and Article 13 'are to be applied cumulatively' and 'an exception that is made under national law will need to comply with both Articles (this will only be of relevance for TRIPS compliance, not compliance under Berne)'.[109] Finally, if the three-step requirement in Article 13 of TRIPS provides a more rigorous set of criteria, 'in principle, it might be said that there is nothing wrong with requiring members to comply with both sets of requirements, as restricting the scope of an exception or limitation under Berne can hardly be in derogation of Berne members' obligations towards each other under Article 2(2)'.[110]

---

[105] M Senftleben op. cit. (2004), p 88.   [106] S Ricketson op. cit. (2003), pp 48–54.
[107] See S Ricketson, idem , p 50. See also Watal op. cit. (2001), p 226.
[108] Ricketson, op. cit. (2003), p 51.   [109] Ibidem.   [110] Idem, 50.

According to this interpretation, the exceptions provided for by the Berne Convention with regard to reproduction and other exclusive rights, as well as any other exception different from those admitted by the Convention (for instance, in the digital environment), would be subject to the three-step test of Article 13. Thus, according to the US submission in *United States–Section 110(5) of the US Copyright Act*[111] Article 13 would be the standard for reviewing the so-called 'minor exceptions' under the Berne Convention.[112]

The interpretation that the exceptions provided for under the Berne Convention can additionally be scrutinized under Article 13 of the TRIPS Agreement (that is, that Article 13 imposes *additional* conditions for the permissibility of exceptions already allowed by the Berne Convention),[113] would probably not correspond either to the intention of the drafters or to the literal meaning of Article 13 and its status as a free-standing clause. Article 13 is a restatement of Berne Article 9. It seems clear that the TRIPS Agreement intended to incorporate the Berne exceptions as well as the rights. If that is the case, there is no ground to argue for a change in interpretation of the pre-existing treaty's meaning on the same subject matter without explicit intent to do so, which is absent in this case.

The argument that Article 13 would be an additional requirement, a 'Berne plus' solution,[114] would also certainly defeat those who have argued for keeping (if not expanding) the room for socially valuable acts, such as fair use. Despite its narrow wording, Article 13 is the only window left in Section 1 of the TRIPS Agreement for allowing members certain flexibility in recognizing and enforcing rights covered (through incorporation of the Berne Convention) in the Agreement, and the capacity to balance private and public interests. As in the case of patents, important public policies are at stake in the area of copyright, such as access to information and education and the promotion of scientific research. As noted by Helfer, the application of Article 13 to narrow down the discretion States enjoyed under the Berne Convention to enact limitations and exceptions 'would significantly constrain the ability of national governments to preserve balanced intellectual property regimes tailored to local needs and conditions'.[115] Moreover, a

---

[111] WT/DS160/R, 15 June 2000.

[112] See Responses of the US to Written Questions from the Panel—First Meeting, WT/DS160/R, para 166–7 (19 November 1999). The panel had requested the US to explain 'how, absent express wording to that effect in the TRIPS agreement, Article 13 'constitutes the articulation' of the 'minor reservations' doctrine under the Berne Convention . . .' Idem. See J Oliver, 'Copyright in the WTO: The Panel Decision on the Three-Step Test' (2002) 25 Colum J L & Arts, p 119, fn 155. As noted by Oliver, there is no evidence in the negotiating history of the TRIPS Agreement that the negotiating parties intended such an outcome (idem, p 145).

[113] S Ricketson op. cit. (2003), p 52; Gervais op. cit. (2001), 145; Senftleben op. cit. (2004), pp 89–90; N Netanel, 'The Next Round: The Impact of the WIPO Copyright Treaty on TRIPs Dispute Settlement', (1997) 37 Va J Int'l L 441.

[114] See, eg, M Senftleben op. cit. (2004), p 90.

[115] L Helfer, 'World music on a US stage: an analysis of the section 110(5) WTO dispute', in H Hansen (ed.), op. cit. (2001), pp 48–4.

restriction to sovereign power cannot be handed away implicitly; such an interference must be explicitly bargained away.

An interpretation of Article 13 of the TRIPS Agreement in line with the Vienna Convention arguably leads to the conclusion that such article is not applicable to the limitations and exceptions which are specifically allowed by the Berne Convention, but that it can be the basis of new exceptions to the exclusive rights conferred under the Convention as well as with regard to the new rights established by the TRIPS Agreement.

Although the framers of the Berne Convention did not seem extremely concerned about the balance between authors and the public but anxious to proclaim authors' rights,[116] the purpose of copyright is not to ensure the holder a maximum economic return, but to balancing authors' rights to obtain a fair return and society's interest in access to and use of information. More than 100 years ago Numa Droz, one of the founders of the Berne Convention, stated that 'limits to absolute protection are rightly set by the public interest'.[117] In order to reach such balance, copyright laws have normally incorporated a variety of limitations to the authors' exclusive rights, in particular reproduction. Almost every copyright law based on the 'authors rights' conception has contained exceptions for copying for personal use (scientific, educational, or other private use), archival copying, library use, education, freedom of news reporting, and reporting of current events.

These limitations are generally formulated as specific exceptions for particular uses or situations defined in advance. Thus, though the right to prevent unauthorized reproduction of a protected work has been one of the pillars of copyright protection, exceptions were carved in most national laws for private or personal use. These exceptions, however, have not generally allowed for reproduction which might seriously affect the author's primary market. The exceptions have, therefore, been limited in different ways.[118]

Under Anglo-American copyright law, exceptions are generally formulated on a case-by-case basis, and are grounded on the application of broad general principles. The exceptions refer to acts of 'fair dealing' or 'fair use', such as copying for purposes of research, teaching, journalism, criticism, parody, and library activities.

[116] See eg, G Dworkin, 'Exceptions to Copyright Exclusivity: Is Fair Use Consistent With Article 9.2 Berne And The New International Order?', in H Hansen (ed.), vol. 6, op. cit. (2001), pp 66–3.
[117] S Ricketson, 'Simplifying copyright law: proposals from down under', (1999) 11 European Intellectual Property Review, p 540.
[118] In Europe, for instance, these limitations are subject to conditions such as the following:
• Copies should be made of mere parts of the work. Complete works may be copied only where originals are not available on the market.
• Copies may be produced by reprographic processes only, because those copies are of lesser quality.
• Only single copies may be reproduced. Copies may not be used for other than private purposes and not be given to third parties.
• The private use must be intended by the copier himself or the copier must act in a non-commercial way.
• If there are exemptions for the benefit of libraries and archives, those institutions must be accessible to the public and act in a non-commercial way.

A good example is the US doctrine of 'fair use', which only provides general legislative guidelines and conditions[119] and largely leaves to courts the task of elaborating what is permissible on specific instances.[120] 'Fair use' is defined as an equitable rule of reason that permits copyrighted materials to be used under certain conditions without the consent of the copyright owner.

Developing countries have been particularly concerned about maintaining in the TRIPS Agreement enough flexibility to deal with public interest issues (such as education,[121] dissemination of knowledge and research), and would probably question an interpretation of Article 13 that would limit the use of exceptions to what is permitted under the Berne Convention. At the twelfth session of the WIPO Standing Committee on Copyright and Related Rights (SCCR), the Delegation of Chile—which was supported by a number of other delegations—argued that

[N]ew technologies presented new opportunities to facilitate access to education, culture and knowledge for the general public, particularly for the most vulnerable groups in society. For that purpose, specific limitations and exceptions needed to be established in the public interest, while maintaining a balance with other stakeholders' rights . . . The lack of regulation and harmonization of limitations and exceptions at international level made

- 'The legitimate interest of the right-holder must be taken into account.' See T Hoeren and U Decker, 'Electronic archives and the press: copyright problems of mass media in the digital age' (1998) 7 European Intellectual Property Review, p 261.

[119] Such conditions, according to section 107 of the US Copyright Law, as developed by case law, include:

- the purpose and character of the use, including whether the use is commercial or for non-profit educational purpose, transformative and productive or duplicative;[119]
- whether the original work is published or unpublished (taking material from an unpublished work weighs against a finding of fair use);
- the nature of the copyrighted work (the scope of fair use is broader for factual works than it is for works of fantasy);
- the amount and substantiality of the portion used in relation to the copyrighted work as a whole (the greater the taking of copyrighted material, the weaker the claim of fair use); and,
- the effect of the use on the potential market for or value of the copyrighted work. See, eg, D Shiply, 'Property Rights in Cyberspace: Copyright Law in the Internet Era', (1996) Journal of Agricultural and Ford Information, vol. 3 (3), p 10.

[120] In the US Supreme Court decision in *Campbell v Acuff-Rose* (92–1292), 510 US 569 (1994), also known as the 'Pretty Woman' case, the Court held that there are no bright lines, and that fair use involves a sensitive balancing of interests.

[121] The flexibility allowed by the Berne Conventions is quite limited. Thus, Article 10(2) of the Berne Convention provides that '[I]t shall be a matter for legislation in the countries of the Union, and for special agreements existing or to be concluded between them, to permit the utilization, to the extent justified by the purpose, of literary and artistic works by way of illustration in publications, broadcasts or sound or visual recordings for teaching, provided such utilization is compatible with fair practice'. However, the right to use materials 'by way of illustration' would not allow full copies to be made available to teachers and students. In South Africa, for example, lecturers intended to distribute non-governmental printed materials (on a not-for-profit basis) to their students about HIV and sex education. Foreign publishers required to be paid royalty charges. See A Story, 'Don't Ignore Copyright, the "Sleeping Giant" on the TRIPS and International Educational Agenda', in P Drahos and R Mayne (eds), *Global Intellectual Property Rights: Knowledge, Access, and Development*, (2002: London, Palgrave Macmillan) p 126.

difficult any initiative for the benefit of the above mentioned people which had to be a social priority, particularly in developing countries.[122]

The concerns about the implications of copyright on access to knowledge, particularly in a digital environment,[123] are shared by developed countries and, particularly, many consumer organizations and other non-governmental organizations (NGOs). Thus, the US has been careful to ensure that Article 13 of the TRIPS Agreement is not read in a way that undermines its fair use exception, as developed by case law in that country,[124] and has 'stoutly defended' the compatibility of its fair use doctrine with the TRIPS Agreement at the Council for TRIPS.[125] It has been noted that

As the control of rightholders has strengthened steadily to cover most uses of copyright material, a growing number of voices are questioning whether the drive for stronger rights is overstepping the mark and weakening important social, economic and cultural interests. The public domain is shrinking, perhaps there should be more, not less, opportunity for the public, in pursuit of education, news and culture, to utilize freely the creative works of others.

The whole of human development is derivative. We stand on the shoulders of the scientists, artists and craftsmen who preceded us. We borrow and develop what they have done, not necessarily as parasites, but simply as the next generation. It is at the heart of what we know as progress. When we are asked to remember the Eighth Commandment, 'thou shalt not steal', bear in mind that borrowing and developing have always been acceptable.[126]

The debates during the negotiation of the WCT are also revealing of concerns about the impact on the public domain and public interests of the trends towards strengthening and expanding copyright protection. As Senftleben commented:

Not surprisingly, the concern about sufficient breathing space for socially valuable ends played a decisive role in the deliberations concerning limitations. The Minutes of Main Committee I mirror the determination to shelter exemptions. The US sought to safeguard the 'fair use' doctrine. Denmark feared that the new rules under discussion could become 'a "straight jacket" for existing exceptions in areas that were essential for society'.

---

[122] See WIPO document SCCR/12/4.

[123] See generally N Braun, 'The Interface between the Protection of Technological Measures and the Exercise of Exceptions to Copyright and Related Rights: Comparing the Situation in the United States and in the European Community' (2003) European Intellectual Property Review 11, pp 496–503.

[124] According to the official US position 'Article 13 of [TRIPS] widens the scope of . . . [Article 9.2 of Berne] to all exclusive rights in copyright and related rights, thus narrowly circumscribing the limitation and exceptions that WTO member countries may impose. This approach is consistent with 107 of [US Copyright Act] relating to fair use of copyrighted works.' (Uruguay Round Agreements Act, Statements of Administrative Action in Relation to Intellectual Property Rights, HR Doc pp 103–316, 103 Cong 2d Session (1994) (quoted in G Dworkin, 'Exceptions to Copyright Exclusivity: Is Fair Use Consistent With Article 9.2 Berne And The New International Order?', in H Hansen (ed.), op. cit. (2001), pp 66–21.

[125] See, eg, Watal op. cit. (2001), p 228. Japan has also extensively provided for compulsory licences in situations that could only be justified under the Appendix of the Berne Convention to developing countries (idem, pp 228–9).   [126] Dworkin op. cit. (2001), note 124, pp 66–1.

Many delegations opposed the second paragraph of the draft provision set out in the basic proposal which additionally subjects current limitations under the Berne Convention to the three-step test. Korea unequivocally suggested the deletion of paragraph 2—a proposal which was approved by several other delegations. Singapore, for instance, elaborated that the second paragraph was 'inconsistent with the commitment to balance copyright laws, where exceptions and limitations adopted by the Conference were narrowed, and protection was made broader'.[127]

The final text of Article 10 adopted by the WIPO Conference on the WCT reads as follows:

(1) Contracting Parties may, in their national legislation, provide for limitations of or exceptions to the rights granted to authors of literary and artistic works under this Treaty in certain special cases that do not conflict with a normal exploitation of the work and do not unreasonably prejudice the legitimate interests of the author.

(2) Contracting Parties shall, when applying the Berne Convention, confine any limitations of or exceptions to rights provided for therein to certain special cases that do not conflict with a normal exploitation of the work and do not unreasonably prejudice the legitimate interests of the author.

The Agreed Statement concerning Article 10 clarifies the following:

It is understood that the provisions of Article 10 permit Contracting Parties to carry forward and appropriately extend into the digital environment limitations and exceptions in their national laws which have been considered acceptable under the Berne Convention. Similarly, these provisions should be understood to permit Contracting Parties to devise new exceptions and limitations that are appropriate in the digital network environment.

It is also understood that Article 10(2) *neither reduces nor extends the scope of applicability of the limitations and exceptions permitted by the Berne Convention* (emphasis added).

Although Article 10 of the WCT has been interpreted as confirming that the three-step test underlying Article 13 of the TRIPS Agreement sets out *additional* criteria that the exceptions allowed under the Berne Convention should meet,[128] the Agreed Statement clearly indicates that the intention of the contracting parties was not to restrict in that way the scope of applicability of such limitations and exceptions. Even if this were not the case and the thesis of the additional requirements were correct, the difference in wording between Article 13 of the TRIPS Agreement ('Members shall confine limitations or exceptions to exclusive rights...') and Article 10(2) of the WCT ('Contracting Parties shall, when applying the Berne Convention, confine any limitations of or exceptions to rights provided for therein...') is noticeable. While the latter specifically refers to the application of the exceptions and limitations of the Berne Convention, the former alludes to 'exclusive rights' in general.

---

[127] M Senftleben op. cit. (2004), pp 96–97 (*footnotes omitted*).　　[128] Idem, p 97.

It is also to be noted that, despite the fact that the perceived need to adapt and strengthen copyright law to the digital environment was the driving force for the negotiation and adoption of the WCT, the Preamble proclaims

the need to maintain a balance between the rights of authors and the larger public interest, particularly education, research and access to information, as reflected in the Berne Convention.

Samuelson has deemed this statement a 'major development in international copyright policy' since '[I]f copyright policy on an international scale had seemed to be veering away from traditional purposes such as the promotion of knowledge in the public interest and toward a solely trade-oriented set of purposes, this treaty can be seen as a timely correction in the course of international copyright policy'.[129]

Article 13 unambiguously refers to 'exclusive rights' without limitation either to the reproduction right, or to the exceptions already provided for in the Berne Convention. Based on its literal text, a logical reading of this provision is that it allows for the establishment of exceptions not present in the Berne Convention.

While the maxim *lex specialis lege generali derogat* has been invoked as one of the justifications for the prevalence of the Berne Convention over Article 13 of the TRIPS Agreement,[130] the fact is that the *general* obligation to comply with the Convention—imposed through Articles 2.2 and 9.1 of the TRIPS Agreement—is subject to the *special* rule contained in Article 13 of the same Agreement, which allows for exceptions under certain circumstances. Moreover, it is important to bear in mind that the Berne Convention did not limit the availability of exceptions. It simply left it to States to determine them. The drafting history of the Convention shows, in fact, that it took into account the many different kinds of exceptions States were already applying and would apply.

In the *United States–Section 110(5) of the US Copyright Act* case,[131] the EC argued that compliance with both Article 11*bis*(2) of the Berne Convention and Article 13 was required under the TRIPS Agreement. The panel, however, found that these provisions allowed exceptions of different scope. It held:

On the one hand, Article 11*bis*(2) authorizes Members to determine the conditions under which the rights conferred by Article 11*bis*(1)(i)–(iii) may be exercised. The imposition of such conditions may completely replace the free exercise of the exclusive right of authorizing the use of the rights embodied in sub-paragraphs (i)–(iii) provided that equitable remuneration and the author's moral rights are not prejudiced. However, unlike Article 13 of the TRIPS Agreement, Article 11*bis*(2) of the Berne Convention (1971) would not in any case justify use free of charge.[132]

---

[129] P Samuelson, 'The US Digital Agenda at WIPO', (1997) 369 Vanderbilt Journal of International Law, reproduced in F Abbott, T Cottier, and F Gurry, *The International Intellectual Property System: Commentary and Materials* (1999: The Hague, Kluwer Law International) p 926.

[130] See S Ricketson op. cit. (2003), pp 51 and 53.

[131] WT/DS160/R, 15 June 2000.   [132] Idem, para 6.87.

In other words, the panel argued that Article 11 *bis*(2) of the Berne Convention is not applicable to exceptions—like those established by the US law—that allow use of the work *free of charge*. The application of Article 13 of the TRIPS Agreement was, hence, justified, because the exception provided under the US law was not expressly incorporated in the Convention.

The reasoning and ruling of the panel does not support, hence, the argument that Article 13 of the TRIPS Agreement superimposes new requirements on the exceptions provided for in the Convention. Applying Article 13 of the TRIPS Agreement to exceptions expressly allowed under the Berne Convention will unduly narrow down their scope.[133]

Members may not be deemed to be obliged beyond what the Convention requires; they are subject to the obligations set out in the Convention read in conjunction with the exceptions provided for therein. The incorporation of the Convention by the TRIPS Agreement does not derogate the right that Contracting Parties have to implement in their domestic laws the exceptions, as provided for in the Convention. In incorporating Articles 1–21 of the Berne Convention (Article 9.1 of the TRIPS Agreement), the Agreement requires compliance with the obligations of the Convention *to the extent* that they are not subject to exceptions or limitations set out in the Convention itself. Thus, the TRIPS Agreement does not modify the ability of the Berne Union members to craft exceptions allowed under the Convention including, for instance, compulsory licences for the broadcast of literary and artistic works, and communication to the public of dramatic and musical works through wire or wireless means.

In the *United States–Section 110(5) of the US Copyright Act* case, the panel argued that:

As regards situations that would not meet the above-mentioned three conditions, a government may not justify an exception, including one involving use free of charge, by Article 13 of the TRIPS Agreement. However, also in these situations Article 11 *bis*(2) of the Berne Convention (1971) as incorporated into the TRIPS Agreement would nonetheless allow Members to substitute, for an exclusive right, a compulsory licence, or determine other conditions provided that they were not prejudicial to the right holder's right to obtain an equitable remuneration.[134]

Hence, the panel admitted that Members need not comply with both the conditions of an exception allowed by the Berne Convention (in this case Article 11 *bis*(2)) and the conditions set out in Article 13 of the TRIPS Agreement. Moreover, as noted—with some concern—by one commentator, Article 13 may be 'a very elastic minimum standard' and far from confining exceptions, it has become 'the sole minimum standard for free-of-charge exceptions to a variety of existing Berne rights, including the exclusive right to authorize the broadcast of works'.[135]

---

[133] See, eg, P Samuelson, 'The US Digital Agenda at WIPO', (1997) 37 Va J Int'l L, pp 369, 370, 402–3.　　　　　　　　　　　　　　　　　　　　　　　　[134] WT/DS160/R, para 6.89.

[135] D Brennan, 'The three step test frenzy–why the TRIP panel decision might be considered per incuriam', (2002) IPQ 2, p 224.

The three-step test

In order to be exempted under Article 13, limitations to the exclusive rights must meet a three-step test. Members should confine limitations or exceptions to exclusive rights (1) to certain special cases; (2) which do not conflict with a normal exploitation of the work; and (3) do not unreasonably prejudice the legitimate interests of the right-holder.

One situation in which the applicability of the three-step test of Article 13 would be at stake would arise, for instance, if a compulsory licence were granted where unreasonably high prices charged by the copyright owner[136] prevented the public from getting access to educational material. It has been noted that it seems clear that under the TRIPS Agreement compulsory licences can be issued when a copyright owner undersupplies the market or charges unreasonable prices, since Members have the authority to regulate against abuses of market power.[137]

The panel's analysis on the scope of application and the standards set forth by the three-step test contained in Article 13 in *United States–Section 110(5) of the US Copyright Act*[138] is a useful, but not definitive basis for understanding the legal implications of that provision.[139] The case was brought by the EC on the ground that subparagraphs (A) (the 'homestyle exception') and (B) (the 'business exception') of Section 110(5) of the US Copyright Act were in violation of the United States' obligations under Article 9.1 of the TRIPS Agreement and under Articles 11*bis*(1)(iii) and 11(1)(ii) of the Berne Convention (1971).[140]

---

[136] See Article 8.2 of the TRIPS Agreement.

[137] See also R Okediji, 'Fostering access to education, research and dissemination of knowledge through copyright', UNCTAD-ICTSD Dialogue on Moving the Pro-development IP Agenda Forward: Preserving Public Goods in Health, Education and Learning, Bellagio, 29 November–3 December 2004 (available at <http://www.ictsd.org>, last accessed on 2 April 2005).

[138] WT/DS160/R, 15 June 2000.

[139] According to one view, the panel was wrong in examining whether the exception provided under US law was consistent with Article 13 of the TRIPS Agreement, as it would have been sufficient to demonstrate that it was incompatible with the bare minimum requirements of the Berne Convention. See L Helfer, 'World music on a US stage: an analysis of the section 110(5) WTO dispute', in H Hansen (ed.), op. cit. (2001), pp 48–6.

[140] The provisions of the US law at stake were the following:

'Section 110. Limitations on exclusive rights: Exemption of certain performances and displays

Notwithstanding the provisions of section 106, the following are not infringements of copyright:

. . .

(5)(A) except as provided in subparagraph (B), communication of a transmission embodying a performance or display of a work by the public reception of the transmission on a single receiving apparatus of a kind commonly used in private homes, unless—

(A) a direct charge is made to see or hear the transmission; or
(B) the transmission thus received is further transmitted to the public;

(B) communication by an establishment of a transmission or retransmission embodying a performance or display of a nondramatic musical work intended to be received by the

The panel found that US law was TRIPS-consistent with regard to the home-style exception, since it applied to a small number of establishments, in relation only to dramatic musical works (a type of work that right-holders do not normally attempt to license) and the loss of revenue was minimal. However, it found a violation with regard to the business exception, which, in the panel's view, did not meet the requirements of Article 13 of the TRIPS Agreement and was thus inconsistent with Articles 11*bis*(1)(iii) and 11(1)(ii) of the Berne Convention (1971) as incorporated into the TRIPS Agreement by Article 9.1 of that Agreement.[141]

Although the US informed the DSB that it intended to implement the recommendation and rulings of the DSB, disagreement emerged about the 'reasonable time' in which to amend the legislation. Both this issue, and later on the level of

general public, originated by a radio or television broadcast station licensed as such by the Federal Communications Commission, or, if an audiovisual transmission, by a cable system or satellite carrier, if—

(i) in the case of an establishment other than a food service or drinking establishment, either the establishment in which the communication occurs has less than 2,000 gross square feet of space (excluding space used for customer parking and for no other purpose), or the establishment in which the communication occurs has 2,000 or more gross square feet of space (excluding space used for customer parking and for no other purpose) and—

(I) if the performance is by audio means only, the performance is communicated by means of a total of not more than 6 loudspeakers, of which not more than 4 loudspeakers are located in any 1 room or adjoining outdoor space; or

(II) if the performance or display is by audiovisual means, any visual portion of the performance or display is communicated by means of a total of not more than 4 audiovisual devices, of which not more than 1 audiovisual device is located in any 1 room, and no such audiovisual device has a diagonal screen size greater than 55 inches, and any audio portion of the performance or display is communicated by means of a total of not more than 6 loudspeakers, of which not more than 4 loudspeakers are located in any 1 room or adjoining outdoor space;

(ii) in the case of a food service or drinking establishment, either the establishment in which the communication occurs has less than 3,750 gross square feet of space (excluding space used for customer parking and for no other purpose), or the establishment in which the communication occurs has 3,750 gross square feet of space or more (excluding space used for customer parking and for no other purpose) and—

(I) if the performance is by audio means only, the performance is communicated by means of a total of not more than 6 loudspeakers, of which not more than 4 loudspeakers are located in any 1 room or adjoining outdoor space; or

(II) if the performance or display is by audiovisual means, any visual portion of the performance or display is communicated by means of a total of not more than 4 audiovisual devices, of which not more than one audiovisual device is located in any 1 room, and no such audiovisual device has a diagonal screen size greater than 55 inches, and any audio portion of the performance or display is communicated by means of a total of not more than 6 loudspeakers, of which not more than 4 loudspeakers are located in any 1 room or adjoining outdoor space;

(iii) no direct charge is made to see or hear the transmission or retransmission;

(iv) the transmission or retransmission is not further transmitted beyond the establishment where it is received; and

(v) the transmission or retransmission is licensed by the copyright owner of the work so publicly performed or displayed . . . '

[141] WT/DS160/R, 15 June 2000, para 7.1(b).

compensation to be paid to EC composers and performers, was submitted to arbitration[142] as the US did not amend its legislation at the end of the period determined by the arbitrator (27 July 2001).

The main arguments of the parties may be summarized as follows. The EC argued for a narrow interpretation of exceptions permitted under Article 13:

(1) Article 13 applies only to the rights newly introduced into TRIPS and does not apply to the Berne rights incorporated by Article 9(1) of TRIPS.

(2) Even if Article 13 does apply to the Berne rights, it can only confine, and not enlarge, the scope of limitations and exceptions that were previously allowed by the minor exceptions doctrine under Berne.

(3) Section 110(5) does not fall within the bounds of what was a permissible minor exception under the Berne Convention.[143]

The US responded, arguing that

(1) The minor exceptions doctrine, which allows some implied exceptions to certain rights under the Berne Convention, is incorporated into TRIPS.

(2) Article 13 of TRIPS clarifies and articulates the scope of the minor exceptions doctrine as it appears in TRIPS.

(3) The exceptions in Section 110(5) should be judged only against Article 13.

(4) Article 11*bis*(2) of the Berne Convention is not relevant because it does not apply to exceptions that are free of charge to the user.[144]

The panel did not hesitate in adopting the 'Berne acquis' for the consideration of the issues at stake, as well as to consider the preparatory works of the Berne Convention as a supplementary means of interpretation. The panel initiated its analysis by ascertaining the legal status of the minor exceptions doctrine in relation to Articles 11*bis*(1) and 11(1) of that Convention. It argued that

in addition to the explicit provisions on permissible limitations and exceptions to the exclusive rights embodied in the text of the Berne Convention (1971), the reports of successive revision conferences of that Convention refer to 'implied exceptions' allowing member countries to provide limitations and exceptions to certain rights. The so-called 'minor reservations' or 'minor exceptions' doctrine is being referred to in respect of the right of public performance and certain other exclusive rights (*footnote omitted*). Under that doctrine, Berne Union members may provide minor exceptions to the rights provided, *inter alia*, under Articles 11*bis* and 11 of the Berne Convention (1971) (*footnote omitted*).[145]

Despite having concluded that

in the absence of any express exclusion in Article 9.1 of the TRIPS Agreement, the incorporation of Articles 11 and 11*bis* of the Berne Convention (1971) into the Agreement

---

[142] The amount of compensation for the 'nullification or impairment of benefits' to EC rightholders was determined to be U$S 1,219,900 per year. See, eg, J Oliver, 'Copyright in the WTO: The Panel Decision on the Three-Step Test' (2002) 25 Colum J L & Arts 119, pp 123–4.
[143] Idem, pp 139–40 (*footnotes omitted*).   [144] Idem, p 139 (*footnotes omitted*).
[145] WT/DS160/R, 15 June 2000, para 6.48.

includes the entire *acquis* of these provisions, including the possibility of providing minor exceptions to the respective exclusive rights[146]

the panel did not address the question of whether Section 110(5) of the US law was permissible under the 'minor exceptions' doctrine.[147] It instead subsequently examined the applicability of Article 13 of the TRIPS Agreement.

As mentioned above,[148] it rejected the EC argument that Article 13 applied only to those rights added by the TRIPS Agreement.[149] It held that Article 13 of the Agreement was applicable to the exclusive rights alluded in Articles 11*bis*(1)(iii) and 11(1)(ii) of the Berne Convention (1971) as incorporated into the TRIPS Agreement;[150] that is, to the exclusive right of authorizing the public communication by loudspeaker or any other analogous instrument transmitting, by signs, sounds or images, the broadcast of the work, and the exclusive right of authorizing any communication to the public of the performance of their works, respectively.

The panel did not cumulatively apply the conditions set out in Article 13 of the TRIPS Agreement to Article 11*bis*(2), the contours of which are defined in the Berne Convention itself. It held that

As regards situations that would not meet the above-mentioned three conditions, a government may not justify an exception, including one involving use free of charge, by Article 13 of the TRIPS Agreement. However, also in these situations Article 11*bis*(2) of the Berne Convention (1971) as incorporated into the TRIPS Agreement would nonetheless allow Members to substitute, for an exclusive right, a compulsory licence, or determine other conditions provided that they were not prejudicial to the right holder's right to obtain an equitable remuneration.[151]

On the premise that the challenged exceptions in the US law were not subject to an express exception in the Berne Convention, the panel undertook a detailed analysis about the three-step test in the context of this particular case. That premise has been criticized as a 'fundamental error' that led the panel to erroneously apply the three-step standard of Article 13.[152]

The panel made clear from the outset that the three steps were to be applied cumulatively, and that Article 13 should be narrowly interpreted. It stated:

The principle of effective treaty interpretation requires us to give a distinct meaning to each of the three conditions and to avoid a reading that could reduce any of the conditions to 'redundancy or inutility' (*footnote omitted*). The three conditions apply on a cumulative

---

[146] Idem, para 6.63.
[147] According to Oliver, such analysis 'would have given more credibility to the panel's holding, or may have revealed that the three-step test in fact allows wider exceptions than would have been allowed under Berne', J Oliver, op. cit. (2002), p 146. See also D Brennan, 'The Three-Step Frenzy: Why the TRIPs Panel Decision might be considered Per Incuriam', (2002) 2 Intellectual Property Quarterly.   [148] See p 137 above.
[149] WT/DS160/R, 15 June 2000, para 6.75.   [150] Idem, para 6.94.
[151] Idem, para 6.89.   [152] See, eg, D Brennan op. cit. (2002), p 212.

basis, each being a separate and independent requirement that must be satisfied. Failure to comply with any one of the three conditions results in the Article 13 exception being disallowed. Both parties agree on the cumulative nature of the three conditions. The Panel shares their view. It may be noted at the outset that Article 13 cannot have more than a narrow or limited operation. Its tenor, consistent as it is with the provisions of Article 9(2) of the Berne Convention (1971), discloses that it was not intended to provide for exceptions or limitations except for those of a limited nature. The narrow sphere of its operation will emerge from our discussion and application of its provisions in the paragraphs which follow.[153]

The panel also noted that

the wording of Article 13 derives largely from Article 9(2) of the Berne Convention (1971) which applies, however, to reproduction rights only. Given the similarity of the wording, we consider that the preparatory works of Article 9(2) of the Berne Convention and its application in practice may be of contextual relevance in interpreting Article 13 of the TRIPS Agreement.[154]

In examining the first step—whether the exceptions under the US law could be one of the 'certain special cases' referred to in Article 13 of the Agreement—the panel enquired about the ordinary meaning of 'certain', 'special' and 'case'. The panel refused to equate 'special case' with 'special purpose' and the interpretation according to which

an exception or limitation must be justified in terms of a legitimate public policy purpose in order to fulfil the first condition of the Article. We also recall in this respect that in interpreting other WTO rules, such as the national treatment clauses of the GATT and the GATS, the Appellate Body has rejected interpretative tests which were based on the subjective aim or objective pursued by national legislation (*footnote omitted*).[155]

In the panel's view,

the first condition of Article 13 requires that a limitation or exception in national legislation should be clearly defined and should be narrow in its scope and reach. On the other hand, a limitation or exception may be compatible with the first condition even if it pursues a special purpose whose underlying legitimacy in a normative sense cannot be discerned. The wording of Article 13's first condition does not imply passing a judgment on the legitimacy of the exceptions in dispute. However, public policy purposes stated by law-makers when enacting a limitation or exception may be useful from a factual perspective for making inferences about the scope of a limitation or exception or the clarity of its definition.[156]
    . . . We reject the idea that the first condition of Article 13 requires us to pass a value judgment on the legitimacy of an exception or limitation. However, we also observed that stated public policy purposes could be of subsidiary relevance for drawing inferences about the scope of an exemption and the clarity of its definition. In our view, the statements from the legislative history indicate an intention of establishing an exception with a narrow scope.[157]

---

[153] WT/DS160/R, 15 June 2000, para 6.97.   [154] Idem, fn 105.
[155] Idem, para 6.111.   [156] Idem, para 6.112.   [157] Idem, para 6.157.

Although the concept that the exception must be necessarily 'narrow in its scope and reach' is questionable as a matter of principle, the panel was right in not interfering with national discretion in determining the purpose of exceptions to copyright exclusive rights. There is nothing, in fact, in Article 13 suggesting that WTO bodies are authorized to scrutinize public policies of Member countries in adopting such exceptions.

Although panel interpretations lack precedential value in the WTO system, it is interesting to note the meaning accorded to the different elements of the first test in Article 13:[158]

- '*certain*': this term means that, under the first condition, an exception or limitation in national legislation must be clearly defined. However, there is no need to identify explicitly each and every possible situation to which the exception could apply, provided that the scope of the exception is known and particularized. This guarantees a sufficient degree of legal certainty.[159]

- '*special*': The term 'special' connotes 'having an individual or limited application or purpose', 'containing details; precise, specific', 'exceptional in quality or degree; unusual; out of the ordinary' or 'distinctive in some way' (*footnote omitted*). This term means that more is needed than a clear definition in order to meet the standard of the first condition. In addition, an exception or limitation must be limited in its field of application or exceptional in its scope. In other words, an exception or limitation should be narrow in a quantitative as well as a qualitative sense. This suggests a narrow scope as well as an exceptional or distinctive objective. To put this aspect of the first condition into the context of the second condition ('no conflict with a normal exploitation'), an exception or limitation should be the opposite of a non-special, ie, a normal case.[160]

- '*case*': The ordinary meaning of the term 'case' refers to an 'occurrence', 'circumstance' or 'event' or 'fact' (*footnote omitted*). For example, in the context of the dispute at hand, the 'case' could be described in terms of beneficiaries of the exceptions, equipment used, types of works, or by other factors.

The panel examined the effect of the contested US law exception on the 'normal exploitation' of *each* right granted to the copyright owner:

[W]e agree with the European Communities that whether a limitation or an exception conflicts with a normal exploitation of a work should be judged for each exclusive right individually. We recall that this dispute primarily concerns the exclusive right under Article 11*bis*(1)(iii) of the Berne Convention (1971) as incorporated into the TRIPS Agreement, but also the exclusive right under Article 11(1)(ii). In our view, normal exploitation would presuppose the possibility for right holders to exercise separately all three exclusive rights guaranteed under the three subparagraphs of Article 11*bis*(1), as well as the rights conferred

---

[158] It is also interesting to note the panel's reluctance to give these terms the meaning that they had already acquired under the Berne Convention. Surely the fact that the same terms were used provided an indication that the same meanings were intended.　　[159] Idem, para 6.108.
[160] Idem, para 6.109.

by other provisions, such as Article 11, of the Berne Convention (1971). If it were permissible to limit by a statutory exemption the exploitation of the right conferred by the third subparagraph of Article 11*bis*(1) simply because, in practice, the exploitation of the rights conferred by the first and second subparagraphs of Article 11*bis*(1) would generate the lion's share of royalty revenue, the 'normal exploitation' of each of the three rights conferred separately under Article 11*bis*(1) would be undermined *(footnote omitted)*.[161]

It is also interesting that the factual analysis conducted by the panel included whether technological changes brought about by the Internet could fall outside a 'special case' in the terms of Article 13.[162]

The analysis by the panel of the first step led it to the conclusion that the 'business exception' (subparagraph (B) of Section 110(5) of the US Copyright law) did not satisfy the first step in Article 13 and that, moreover, it

did not satisfy the requirements of Article 13, given that its three conditions are cumulative. Thus it would appear that subparagraph (B) is in violation of Articles 11*bis*(1)(iii) and 11(1)(ii) of the Berne Convention (1971), as incorporated into the TRIPS Agreement by reference in Article 9.1, and not justified by Article 13.[163]

At the same time, the panel found that the 'homestyle exception' (subparagraph (A) of Section 110(5) of the US Copyright law) was consistent with the first step. Although in this case it was justified to pursue the analysis under the two additional tests in Article 13, the panel did not need to continue such analysis for the 'business exception', which was disallowed altogether by application of the first test. The arguments given about why the principle of 'judicial economy' was not followed[164] are not convincing, since the panel's finding secured anyway 'a positive solution' to the dispute and could not be characterized as a 'partial resolution'. Whether its findings were correct or not is another matter.

With regard to the second step—'not conflict with a normal exploitation of the work'—the panel drew a distinction between the empirical and the normative concept of 'normal'. It held:

We note that the ordinary meaning of the term 'normal' can be defined as 'constituting or conforming to a type or standard; regular, usual, typical, ordinary, conventional . . .'.[165] In our opinion, these definitions appear to reflect two connotations: the first one appears to be of an empirical nature, ie, what is regular, usual, typical or ordinary. The other one reflects a somewhat more normative, if not dynamic, approach, ie, conforming to a type or

---

[161] Idem, para 6.173.

[162] The panel stated that 'based on the information provided to us by the parties, there seems to be no experience to date of the application of the homestyle exemption in its original or amended form to the transmission of "dramatic" musical works over the Internet. In these circumstances, we cannot see how potential repercussions in the future could affect our conclusions concerning subparagraph (A) at this point in time in relation to the first condition of Article 13, of the TRIPS Agreement. But we also do not wish to exclude the possibility that in the future new technologies might create new ways of distributing dramatic renditions of 'dramatic' musical works that might have implications for the assessment of subparagraph (A) as a 'certain special case' in the meaning of the first condition of Article 13 (idem, para 6.153). [163] Idem, para 6.160.

[164] Idem, para 6.162.   [165] *Oxford English Dictionary*, p 1940.

standard. We do not feel compelled to pass a judgment on which one of these connotations could be more relevant. Based on Article 31 of the Vienna Convention, we will attempt to develop a harmonious interpretation which gives meaning and effect to both connotations of 'normal'.[166]

The panel focused on the economic aspects of copyright exploitation:

We believe that an exception or limitation to an exclusive right in domestic legislation rises to the level of a conflict with a normal exploitation of the work (ie, the copyright or rather the whole bundle of exclusive rights conferred by the ownership of the copyright), if uses that in principle are covered by that right but exempted under the exception or limitation enter into economic competition with the ways that right holders normally extract economic value from that right to the work (ie, the copyright) and thereby deprive them of significant or tangible commercial gains.[167]

The US had argued that 'uses from which an owner would not ordinarily expect to receive compensation are not part of the normal exploitation'.[168] While acknowledging that 'the extent of exercise or non-exercise of exclusive rights by right-holders at a given point in time is of great relevance for assessing what is the normal exploitation with respect to a particular exclusive right in a particular market', the panel considered, however, that

in certain circumstances, current licensing practices may not provide a sufficient guideline for assessing the potential impact of an exception or limitation on normal exploitation. For example, where a particular use of works is not covered by the exclusive rights conferred in the law of a jurisdiction, the fact that the right holders do not license such use in that jurisdiction cannot be considered indicative of what constitutes normal exploitation. The same would be true in a situation where, due to lack of effective or affordable means of enforcement, right holders may not find it worthwhile or practical to exercise their rights.[169]

The panel also indicated that what is 'normal' may vary over time according to prevailing commercial and technological conditions:

[W]hat is a normal exploitation in the market-place may evolve as a result of technological developments or changing consumer preferences. Thus, while we do not wish to speculate on future developments, we need to consider the actual and potential effects of the exemptions in question in the current market and technological environment.[170]

These dynamic elements were considered by the panel as part of the 'normative' analysis of 'normal exploitation'. It argued as follows:

We have to give meaning and effect also to the second aspect of the connotation, the meaning of 'conforming to a type or standard'. We described this aspect of normalcy as reflecting a more normative approach to defining normal exploitation, that includes, *inter alia*, a dynamic element capable of taking into account technological and market developments. The question then arises how this normative aspect of 'normal' exploitation could be given meaning in relation to the exploitation of musical works.[171]

---

[166] WT/DS160/R, 15 June 2000, para 6.166.   [167] Idem, para 6.183.
[168] Idem, para 6.177.   [169] Idem, para 6.188.   [170] Idem, para 6.187.
[171] Idem, para 6.178.

... it appears that one way of measuring the normative connotation of normal exploitation is to consider, in addition to those forms of exploitation that currently generate significant or tangible revenue, those forms of exploitation which, with a certain degree of likelihood and plausibility, could acquire considerable economic or practical importance.[172]

In sum, the analysis of the second tests heavily relied on essentially economic considerations. This approach has raised concerns about the room for exceptions conferred on social grounds, such as uses for educational purposes or quotations for news reporting.[173]

In examining the application of the third step ('not unreasonably prejudice the legitimate interests of the right holder'), the panel made a number of interesting observations.

First, the panel did not

find any indication in the express wording of the third condition of Article 13 that the assessment of whether the prejudice caused by an exception or limitation to the legitimate interests of the right holder is of an unreasonable level should be limited to the right holders of the Member that brings forth the complaint.[174]

Second, the panel examined in detail the concept of 'legitimate interests'. It concluded that 'interest'

may encompass a legal right or title to a property or to use or benefit of a property (including intellectual property). It may also refer to a concern about a potential detriment or advantage, and more generally to something that is of some importance to a natural or legal person. Accordingly, the notion of 'interests' is not necessarily limited to actual or potential economic advantage or detriment.[175]

'Legitimate, in turn,

relates to lawfulness from a legal positivist perspective, but it has also the connotation of legitimacy from a more normative perspective, in the context of calling for the protection of interests that are justifiable in the light of the objectives that underlie the protection of exclusive rights.[176]

Thirdly, and most importantly, the panel argued that when the third test is applied,

a certain amount of 'prejudice' has to be presumed justified as 'not unreasonable' (*footnote omitted*). In our view, prejudice to the legitimate interests of right holders reaches an unreasonable level if an exception or limitation causes or has the potential to cause an unreasonable loss of income to the copyright owner.[177]

---

[172] Idem, para 6.180.   [173] See, eg, Oliver op. cit. (2002), p 157.
[174] WT/DS160/R, 15 June 2000, para 6.231.
[175] Idem, para 6.223.   [176] Idem, para 6.224.
[177] Idem, para 6.229. The panel also noted that '[N]ot unreasonable' connotes a slightly stricter threshold than 'reasonable' (idem, para 6.225).

Finally, it is to be noted that the panel seemed to agree with previous analyses suggesting that an exception may be conferred, even if it causes an 'unreasonable prejudice to the legitimate interests' of the copyright owner, in cases where a system of compulsory licensing or equitable remuneration is available.[178] This is, perhaps, the only point (not specifically addressed in the ruling, though) where the panel seemed to allow for some flexibility in an otherwise narrow reading of Article 13 of the TRIPS Agreement.

Related rights

The protection of the so called 'neighbouring rights'[179] has been one of the most divisive issues, at least as a matter of principle,[180] in the relationship between the copyright and authors' rights conception. Unlike the Paris and Berne Conventions, the Rome Convention is not incorporated into the TRIPS Agreement. The reasons for that differentiation probably lie in the smaller number of members of the Rome Convention, as compared to the other two Conventions,[181] the fact that the US did not ratify it, and the specific approach—not shared in many common-law countries—that the Rome Convention has taken with regard to the protection of 'neighbouring' rights.

Article 14 of the TRIPS Agreement protects the rights of:

(a) 'performers', that is, actors, singers, musicians, dancers, and other persons who act, sing, deliver, declaim, play in, or otherwise perform literary or artistic works;

(b) 'producers of phonograms', persons who, or the legal entities which, first fix the sounds of a performance or other sounds; and

(c) 'broadcasting organizations', that is, those which transmit by wireless means for public reception sounds or images and sounds.[182]

Continental law countries have been reluctant to admit the rights of performers, producers of phonograms (sound recordings), and broadcasting organizations on the same footing as the rights of authors.[183] This reluctance reflected authors' fears of loss of control over their works. For this reason, the concept of 'related'

---

[178] Idem, fn 205.

[179] This concept was first used at the Brussels Diplomatic Conference for the Revision of the Berne Convention (1948), which refused to consider the rights of performers within the Convention, and only expressed the wish that studies should be actively pursued on the matter. See G Bodenhausen, 'Protection of Neighbouring Rights' (1954) 19 Law and Contemporary Problems, pp 156–7.

[180] In practice, the scope of protection conferred has become closer over time. See G Davies op. cit. (2002), p 338.

[181] The Rome Convention had 79 members (as of 4 November 2004) many of which became so after the adoption of the TRIPS Agreement. The Berne Convention had 159 members, and the Paris Convention 169.　　　　　[182] These definitions are based on Article 3 of the Rome Convention.

[183] See Watal op. cit. (2001), p 233.

rights was developed and retained in the TRIPS Agreement. In common-law countries, this distinction has not been made, and those rights are simply incorporated (such as in the US and the United Kingdom) under the general rubric of copyright.[184]

A particularly thorny issue during the TRIPS negotiations was the protection of phonograms (sound recordings),[185] as they are subject to copyright in common-law countries but not recognized as such in continental law countries. Phonograms (sound recordings) are not covered by the Berne Convention. The only express obligation established in the TRIPS Agreement relates to their direct or indirect reproduction under Article 14.2.

Article 14 heavily relies on the Rome Convention. The most significant difference with the latter is the omission of a rule similar to Article 12 of the Convention, one of the key provisions therein. Article 12 provides that

> If a phonogram published for commercial purposes, or a reproduction of such phonogram, is used directly for broadcasting or for any communication to the public, a single equitable remuneration shall be paid by the user to the performers, or to the producers of the phonograms, or to both. Domestic law may, in the absence of agreement between these parties, lay down the conditions as to the sharing of this remuneration.

Although Article 14 covers three categories of rights—performers, producers of phonograms (sound recordings), and broadcasting organizations—even in common-law countries differences are recognized between the protection of the artistic achievement of performers on the one hand, and the rather technical and financial interests protected in relation to phonogram producers and broadcasters on the other.[186] The phonogram producers, however, have been successful in gradually elevating the status of their rights with the adoption of the Rome Convention in 1961, the Phonograms Convention of 1971 and, more recently, of the TRIPS Agreement.

In some jurisdictions, such as in Germany, other types of neighbouring rights beyond those mentioned in Article 14 of the TRIPS Agreement are recognized, such as the rights of organizers of performances, film producers, and editors of

---

[184] See, eg, UNCTAD–ICTSD op. cit. (2005), p 199.

[185] Although the title of Article 14 suggests that 'phonograms' and 'sound recordings' are equivalent terms, they have traditionally had different meanings. For a discussion of these concepts under common law and continental law systems, see Gervais op. cit. (2003), p 157.

[186] This distinction is, for instance, noted by the WIPO Guide to the Rome Convention and to the Phonogram Convention, where it is said: '[T]rue, the purist may complain that, notwithstanding the skill and talent of a recording engineer or a broadcast producer, the making of a record or of a broadcast is, after all, an essentially industrial act, whereas the performances of artistes are of their nature acts of spiritual creation; and to mix them up together in one convention creates a hotchpotch. Nevertheless, the Rome Convention has done so, always with the guide-line of stopping the unfair appropriation of the labor of other (*Guide to the Rome Convention and to the Phonogram Convention* (1981: Geneva), p 12).

works no longer protected.[187] In the United Kingdom, some form of copyright protection is recognized in respect of cinematographic films, cable-transmission, and the typographical format of published editions.[188] These rights are, however, outside the scope of the TRIPS Agreement.

> **14.1. In respect of a fixation of their performance on a phonogram, performers shall have the possibility of preventing the following acts when undertaken without their authorization: the fixation of their unfixed performance and the reproduction of such fixation. Performers shall also have the possibility of preventing the following acts when undertaken without their authorization: the broadcasting by wireless means and the communication to the public of their live performance.**

Performers' rights, as recognized by the first sentence of Article 14.1 of the TRIPS Agreement, can be exercised in respect of the first fixation of their performance on a phonogram.

There is no definition in Article 14.1 of 'performers' or 'performances'. However, the definition as developed in the context of the Rome Convention may be applicable. First, Article 1.3 of the TRIPS Agreement, as examined above,[189] refers to the Rome Convention for determining the beneficiaries of protection. Second, Article 2.2 of the Agreement stipulates that '[N]othing in Parts I to IV of this Agreement shall derogate from existing obligations that Members may have to each other under the . . . Rome Convention'.[190] Third, Article 14.6 of the Agreement allows Members to apply the 'conditions, limitations, exceptions . . . ' provided for under the Rome Convention.

In the title of Article 14 'phonograms' are equated to 'sound recordings'.[191] The Rome Convention contains a definition of 'phonogram' ('any exclusively aural fixation of sounds of a performance or of other sounds'). This definition, if applied to Article 14.1, would seem to exclude digital representations of sounds,[192] and would clearly not apply to videograms. However, the concept of 'phonogram' could be interpreted on the basis of its ordinary meaning,[193] in accordance with

---

[187] B Teller, 'Toward Better Protection of Performance In The United States: A Comparative Look At Performers' Rights in the United States, Under The Rome Convention' (1990) 28 Colum J Transnat'l L, p 775.   [188] Ibidem.

[189] See above, p 40.

[190] This obligation, however, does not apply to non-parties to the Convention.

[191] In the US the definition of sound recordings excludes sounds 'accompanying a motion picture or other audiovisual work' (Section 101, US Copyright Act 1976). In 1995 the US Digital Performance Rights in Sound Recordings Act was enacted. See M Einhorn, *Media, Technology and Copyright. Integrating Law and Economics* (2004: Cheltenham, Edward Elgar), p 104.

[192] The definition in the WPPT, adopted after the TRIPS Agreement, is broader: 'phonogram' means the fixation of the sounds of a performance or of other sounds, or of a representation of sounds, other than in the form of a fixation incorporated in a cinematographic or other audiovisual work (Article 2(b)).

[193] It should be noted (see p 151 above), that in *United States–Section 110(5) of the US Copyright Act*, WT/DS160/R, 15 June 2000, the panel opted for the ordinary meaning of 'certain special cases' in Article 13 of the TRIPS Agreement, in line with prior GATT/WTO jurisprudence, despite accepting that the 'Berne acquis' and the negotiating history of the Berne Convention were part of the context for interpretation of the Agreement (see paragraphs 6.72 and footnote 95; paras 6.107–6.110).

the interpretation criteria set forth by the Vienna Convention, eventually encompassing any medium from which sounds may be reproduced.[194]

The Rome Convention defines 'performers' as 'actors, singers, musicians, dancers, and other persons who act, sing, deliver, declaim, play in, or otherwise perform literary or artistic works' (Article 3(a)). According to the negotiating history of the Convention[195] and the generally accepted interpretation of this definition,[196] only performances of 'artistic and literary' works, if fixed in 'phonograms', are covered under this provision.

'Artistic and literary works', in turn, are to be understood, as defined in the Berne Convention.[197] This means that performances by variety artists, circus performers, and sportspersons are not covered by Article 14.1. Under this definition, the performance of expressions of folklore would not be covered either. This issue was raised and addressed during the preparation of the WPPT. The Memorandum prepared by the International Bureau of WIPO for the first meeting of the Committee of Experts for the WPPT held that:

expressions of folklore do not correspond to the concept of literary and artistic works (and, thus, should, be granted *sui generis* protection). At the same time, it is hardly questionable that the performances of expressions of folklore (such as folk songs, instrumental folk music, folkdances, folk plays, folk poetry and folk tales) deserve the same protection as the performances of literary and artistic works.[198]

'Expressions of folklore' were finally incorporated in Article 2(a) of the WPPT, which provides that

'performers' are actors, singers, musicians, dancers, and other persons who act, sing, deliver, declaim, play in, interpret, or otherwise perform literary or artistic works or expressions of folklore.

A question arises as to whether it would be legitimate to interpret Article 14.1 of the TRIPS Agreement in the light of this expanded definition of the WPPT.[199] While action has been taken at the national level in some countries,[200] and work

---

[194] See Gervais op. cit. (2003), p 159 arguing that the protection under Article 14.1 only applies to performers of music. For the contrary position, see O Morgan op. cit. (2002), p 159.

[195] See Report of the Rapporteur-General, Records of the Diplomatic Conference on the International Protection of Performers, Producers of Phonograms and Broadcasting Organisations (ILO, UNESCO and BIRPI, Geneva, 1968), p 46.

[196] See, eg, O Morgan op. cit. (2002), p 138.   [197] See above.

[198] International Bureau of WIPO, Questions concerning a possible instrument for the protection of the rights of performers and producers of phonograms', INR/CE/1/2, June 1993, p 17.

[199] This definition also included 'interpret' among the acts that qualify as a protected performance. For the interpretation of this addition, see O Morgan op. cit. (2002), p 144.

[200] See, eg, WIPO Secretariat, 'The protection of traditional cultural expressions/expressions of folklore: outline of policy options and legal mechanisms', WIPO/GRTKF/IC/7/4, 27 August 2004, Annex I, pp 15–18.

for the development of a *sui generis* regime on the protection of traditional cultural expressions/expressions of folklore has been undertaken by the WIPO Intergovernmental Committee on Intellectual Property and Genetic Resources, Traditional Knowledge and Folklore,[201] the international legal status of expressions of folklore remains still unsettled.

It may be argued that the interpretation of the TRIPS Agreement should be made with an evolutionary view, and take into account new developments in the IPR field. This could permit consideration of performances of expression of folklore as covered under Article 14.1. As discussed below,[202] in *United States–Section 110(5) of the US Copyright Act*, the panel stated that the WIPO Copyright Treaty of 1996 should be viewed as 'relevant to seek contextual guidance . . . when developing interpretations that avoid conflicts within the overall multilateral copyright framework . . .'.[203] Although the coverage of expression of folklore would be desirable on equity grounds, an evolutionary interpretation of the TRIPS Agreement may endanger its carefully achieved balance in some areas and stretch the Members' obligations beyond what they have actually agreed to. The issue of the protection of expressions of folklore, including performances thereof, should be addressed in the context of the mandate given to the Council for TRIPS by paragraph 19 of the Doha Ministerial Declaration (2001).[204]

'Fixation' is defined neither in the Rome Convention nor in the TRIPS Agreement. It is the process of reducing a work to a material form (eg music on a phonorecord[205]). 'Reproduction' means, in accordance with the Rome Convention, 'the making of a copy or copies of a fixation' (Article 3(e)).

Article 14.1 is ambiguous as to whether infringement of the exclusive rights would take place when *both* fixation and reproduction without authorization occur. The use of 'and' ('fixation of their unfixed performance *and* the reproduction of such fixation') suggests that performers would not have a separate right to authorize the reproduction of already-authorized fixations of their performance[206] but only a right of 'first fixation'.[207]

---

[201] Ibidem. See, eg, WIPO International Bureau, 'The protection of traditional cultural expressions/expressions of folklore: outline of policy options and legal mechanisms', WIPO/GRTKF/IC/7/4, 27 August 2004.   [202] See p 487 below.

[203] WT/DS160/R 15 June 2000, para 6.70.

[204] 'We instruct the Council for TRIPS . . . to examine, *inter alia*, . . . the protection of traditional knowledge and folklore . . .'.

[205] Under US law, 'phonorecords are material objects in which sounds, other than those accompanying a motion picture or other audiovisual work, are fixed by any method now known or later developed, and from which the sounds can be perceived, reproduced, or otherwise communicated, either directly or with the aid of a machine or device. The term "phonorecords" includes the material object in which the sounds are first fixed' (17 USC §101), encompassing cassette tapes, CDs, LPs, 45 r.p.m. disks, as well as other formats (US Copyright Office Circular 56, 'Registration of Sound Recordings').

[206] See Dratler op. cit. (1996), para IA-59.

[207] The interpretation seems consistent with the history of the Rome Convention. See O Morgan op. cit. (2002), p 166. It should also be noted that neither the Rome Convention nor the TRIPS Agreement grants a right of distribution.

The coverage of Article 14.1 is narrower than Article 7.1 of the Rome Convention, since the former only covers the fixation of an unfixed performance *on a phonogram*, while, under Article 7.1(b) of the Convention, performers must be given the possibility of preventing fixation *on any medium*.[208] As a result, the TRIPS Agreement does not confer on performers the right to control the first fixation and further reproduction of their performances in a visual or audiovisual work. In addition, the Convention stipulates other cases in which performers may prevent reproduction, without their consent, of a fixation of their performance.[209]

Performers are given 'the possibility of preventing' the fixation[210] of their unfixed performance and the reproduction of such fixation, when undertaken without their authorization. This wording, based on Article 7(1) of the Rome Convention, makes clear that the right conferred under Article 14.1 is *not* an exclusive right, like the one recognized under other sections of the TRIPS Agreement, for instance, with regard to patents and trademarks.[211] It leaves WTO Members freedom to determine the means through which such rights will be implemented. Although such means have only included, under the Rome Convention, criminal and administrative measures,[212] there is nothing in Article 14.1 forbidding other means, notably civil remedies. In fact, as examined below, the TRIPS Agreement requires Members to make available civil proceedings concerning 'any intellectual property right covered by the Agreement' (Article 42).[213]

Finally, it is to be noted that the right of first fixation and reproduction under Article 14.1 is subject, in accordance with Article 14.6, to Article 15(1)(c) to the Rome Convention, which provides an exception, under certain conditions, for the ephemeral fixation of a performance by broadcasting organizations.

The second sentence of Article 14.1 provides for the 'possibility of preventing'

(a) the broadcasting by wireless means of their live performance, and
(b) the communication to the public of their live performance.

---

[208] See WIPO, Implications of the TRIPS Agreement on Treaties Administered by WIPO, p 23.

[209] Article 7.1(c) of the Rome Convention stipulates that the protection provided for performers shall include the possibility of preventing the reproduction, without their consent, of a fixation of their performance:

(i) if the original fixation itself was made without their consent;
(ii) if the reproduction is made for purposes different from those for which the performers gave their consent;
(iii) if the original fixation was made in accordance with the provisions of Article 15 and the reproduction is made for purposes different from those referred to in those provisions.

[210] The Berne Convention (Article 2(2)) permits, but does not oblige, to subject copyright protection to fixation of the work, as established, for instance, under Anglo-American law. See, eg, D Brennan and A Christie, 'Spoken Words and Copyright Subsistence in Anglo-American Law' (2000) 4 Intellectual Property Quarterly.

[211] The WPPT, however, has recognized exclusive rights of broadcasting and communication to the public in favour of performers. See Articles 6, 7, 8, 9, and 10.

[212] See, eg, Gervais op. cit. (2003), p 159, UNCTAD-ICTSD op. cit. (2005), p 205.

[213] See pp 417–19 below.

As in the case of fixation, the Agreement does not recognize an exclusive right with regard to these acts.

'Broadcasting' means, according to Article 3(f) of the Rome Convention,[214] 'the transmission by wireless means for public reception of sounds or of images and sounds'.[215] It does include terrestrial and satellite transmission, but excludes making works and objects of related rights available interactively over computer networks (where the time and place of reception may be individually chosen by members of the public).[216]

'Communication to the public' is not defined in the Rome Convention.[217] There are differences in the concept used in this Convention vis-à-vis the Berne Convention.[218] The interpretation to be given to this concept in the context of the TRIPS Agreement is unclear. The wording of the second sentence of Article 14.1 suggests, however, that 'broadcasting' refers only to transmission by wireless means while 'communication to the public' refers to transmission by wire.[219]

Article 14.1 alludes in its second sentence to 'live' performance, a term not used in the Rome Convention. This reference has been deemed 'unfortunate' as 'live' and 'unfixed' performances are not synonymous.[220] In any case, it seems clear that the rights conferred under Article 14.1 do not extend to the rebroadcast of a performance, since in that case it would no longer be a 'live' performance.[221]

---

[214] A definition of 'broadcasting', in relation to copyrighted works, may also be deduced from Article 11*bis*(1)i) of the Berne Convention.

[215] The lack of precision of this definition, however, has been observed. For a transmission to qualify as 'broadcasting', it is not necessary that its reception be 'public', that is, that it takes place in the presence of a group of people corresponding to the concept of 'public' or at least at a place open to the public. See WIPO op. cit. (2003), p 271. As noted below, however, the definition of the WPPT has retained the expression 'for public reception'.

[216] WIPO, op. cit. (2003), p 270. Article 2(f) of the WPPT has included a more updated definition of 'broadcasting', which takes into account recent technological developments: 'broadcasting' means the transmission by wireless means for public reception of sounds or of images and sounds or of the representations thereof; such transmission by satellite is also 'broadcasting'; transmission of encrypted signals is 'broadcasting' where the means for decrypting are provided to the public by the broadcasting organization or with its consent.

[217] The WPPT includes the following definition in Article 2(g): ' "communication to the public" of a performance or a phonogram means the transmission to the public by any medium, otherwise than by broadcasting, of sounds of a performance or the sounds or the representations of sounds fixed in a phonogram. For the purposes of Article 15, "communication to the public" includes making the sounds or representations of sounds fixed in a phonogram audible to the public.'

[218] Although in some sense the concept in the Rome Convention is deemed narrower than in the Berne Convention, it is broader than the latter in that it includes 'not only communication to the public at a place other than from where the communication is originated, but also communication to the public in the presence of the public, or, at least, at a place open to the public, of a phonogram or a broadcast' (WIPO op. cit. (2003), p 276). See also a discussion on the relationship between Article 14.1 (second sentence) and Article 7.1(a) of the Rome Convention in WIPO, *Implications of the TRIPS Agreement on Treaties Administered by WIPO* (1997: Geneva), pp 24–5.

[219] See O Morgan op. cit. (2002), p 158.   [220] Ibidem.   [221] Idem, p 158–9.

It is to be noted that the TRIPS Agreement does not recognize performers' rights to an equitable remuneration in respect of the broadcasting and communication to the public of a phonogram published for commercial purposes or a reproduction thereof, as established by Article 12 of the Rome Convention.[222]

14.2. Producers of phonograms shall enjoy the right to authorize or prohibit the direct or indirect reproduction of their phonograms.

Article 14.2 literally reproduces Article 10 of the Rome Convention. 'Reproduction' is defined in this Convention as 'making of a copy or copies of a fixation' (Article 3(e)). In the Berne Convention, it is clarified that reproduction 'in any manner or form' is subject to an exclusive right (Article 9(1)).

Phonogram producers provide the setting for recording, compiling, and editing musical works. Their contribution is of a technical and financial rather than of an artistic nature. For this reason, the recognition of copyrights to phonogram producers and, in particular, of 'authorship' has been contested.[223]

'Direct reproduction' alludes to copying directly from a phonogram. 'Indirect' reproduction may take place when a work is broadcast from a phonogram, eg by radio transmission. Both acts are subject to the producers of phonograms' exclusive right recognized under this provision.[224]

14.3. Broadcasting organizations shall have the right to prohibit the following acts when undertaken without their authorization: the fixation, the reproduction of fixations, and the rebroadcasting by wireless means of broadcasts, as well as the communication to the public of television broadcasts of the same. Where Members do not grant such rights to broadcasting organizations, they shall provide owners of copyright in the subject matter of broadcasts with the possibility of preventing the above acts, subject to the provisions of the Berne Convention (1971).

Broadcasting organizations are recognized under Article 14.3 with 'the right to prohibit' certain 'acts when undertaken without their authorization'. The acts subject to the control of broadcasting organizations are:

- the fixation,
- the reproduction of fixations,
- the rebroadcasting by wireless means of broadcasts,
- the communication to the public of television broadcasts.

The rights conferred to broadcasting organizations in relation to the communication to the public of television broadcasts are more absolute than under Article 13(d) of the Rome Convention, as they are not confined to establishments

---

[222] Such rights may be subject, however, to reservations narrowing the scope of the obligation or completely excluding its application (Article 16.1(a) of the Rome Convention).

[223] See, eg, B Teller, op. cit. (1990), p 775.

[224] It refers to the right 'to authorise or prohibit' in contrast to 'the possibility of preventing', as in Article 14.1.

that charge an entrance fee.[225] However, according to one interpretation,[226] Article 14.3 does not appear to subject *simultaneous* cable rebroadcast to the conferred rights but only subsequent rebroadcasts, in a way that would legitimize US provisions for compulsory licences of certain simultaneous rebroadcasts.[227]

Despite the rights conferred, Article 14.3 exempts Members from complying with this obligation if they provide 'owners of copyright in the subject matter of broadcasts' with the possibility of preventing the acts described therein, 'subject to the provisions of the Berne Convention (1971)'.[228] This exemption—which again seems to be specifically tailored to safeguard US law—is more apparent than real, though. Only those Members that recognize copyright protection with regard to broadcast programmes may deny the specific right to broadcasting organizations provided for in Article 14.3.[229] The phrase 'subject to the provisions of the Berne Convention (1971)' would permit those Members to resort to the possibility admitted in Article 11*bis*(2) of the Berne Convention—and implemented in some countries, such as the US and the Netherlands—of establishing compulsory licences, against an 'equitable remuneration', for broadcasting copyrighted works.[230]

Most terms ('fixation', 'reproduction', 'communication to the public') used in Article 14.3 have been examined above. Article 3(g) of the Rome Convention defines 'rebroadcasting' as 'the simultaneous broadcasting by one broadcasting organisation of the broadcast of another broadcasting organisation'.[231]

The TRIPS Agreement does not clarify the scope of 'broadcasts', particularly whether satellite broadcasting is covered.

The reference in Article 14.3 (second sentence) to 'the possibility of preventing the above acts, subject to the provisions of the Berne Convention (1971)' may be interpreted as allowing Members to adopt criminal or other measures, and not necessarily conferring exclusive rights. It has been argued, however, that the only way of implementing such a possibility is through an 'exclusive right', since the Berne Convention requires the granting of such rights in Article 11*bis*.[232]

A new 'Treaty on the protection of broadcasting organizations' is under discussion at the WIPO Standing Committee on Copyright and Related Rights

---

[225] See Watal op. cit. (2001), p 236.   [226] Dratler op. cit. (1996), para 1A-60.
[227] Ibidem.
[228] As explained by WIPO International Bureau, Article 13 of the Rome Convention provides that the 'right of broadcasting organizations "to authorize or prohibit" also extends to the fixation, the reproduction of fixation (without their consent) and the rebroadcasting by wireless means of their broadcast but, in the case of communication to the public, it only covers communication to the public, of television broadcasts and only under certain conditions; in the latter case, the State where protection is claimed may determine conditions under which this right may be exercised and Article 16.1(b) even allows a reservation to completely exclude the application of the right, in such a case' (WIPO, op. cit. (1997), p 26).   [229] Idem, p 27.
[230] Dratler casts doubts about the compatibility of US compulsory licence provisions with Article 14.3 of the TRIPS Agreement (Dratler op. cit. (1996), para 1A-61).
[231] There is no definition of this concept in Article 2 of the WPPT.
[232] WIPO op. cit. (1997), p 28.

(SCCR).[233] The 2004 WIPO General Assembly indicated that the SCCR should accelerate its work with a view to a diplomatic conference, despite the fact that several issues, including technological protection measures (TPMs) and webcasting, remain highly controversial. Many developing countries emphasized the need to ensure that any international instrument considers their particular needs, as well as the needs of copyright holders, consumers, and the public in general.[234]

> **14.4. The provisions of Article 11 in respect of computer programs shall apply** *mutatis mutandis* **to producers of phonograms and any other right holders in phonograms as determined in a Member's law. If on 15 April 1994 a Member has in force a system of equitable remuneration of right holders in respect of the rental of phonograms, it may maintain such system provided that the commercial rental of phonograms is not giving rise to the material impairment of the exclusive rights of reproduction of right holders.**

This Article extends *mutatis mutandis* the rental rights provided in respect of computer programs to producers of phonograms and any other right-holders in phonograms. This obligation is subject to a broad exception that benefits countries (like Japan) that on the date of signing of the TRIPS Agreement had in place 'a system of equitable remuneration of right holders in respect of the rental of phonograms'.

One key interpretive issue with regard to Article 14.4 is who the 'other right holders' are. The wording in Article 14.4 'as determined in a Member's law' seems to indicate that the obligation to grant rental rights will arise only with regard to those who are deemed 'right holders in phonograms' by the national law. Moreover, it has been interpreted that the obligation to grant rental exclusive rights applies 'provided that the domestic law of a TRIPs Member confers any rights at all upon performers in phonograms'.[235]

It is particularly controversial whether the obligation to extend rental rights in this form would apply in countries such as the US, where the phonogram itself is considered a work and the phonogram producer its sole author, while composers, librettists, etc do not own rights in phonograms but in works recorded therein.[236]

---

[233] See the Revised Consolidated Text for a Treaty on the protection of broadcasting organizations prepared by the Chairman of the Standing Committee on Copyright and Related Rights, WIPO document SCCR/12/2, 4 October 2004.

[234] See, eg, the interventions of the African Group, Brazil, India, Iran, and China at the 12th Session of the Standing Committee on Copyright and Related Rights (SCCR). The draft report is available at <http://www.wipo.int/edocs/mdocs/sccr/en/sccr_12/sccr_12_ 4_prov.doc> (last accessed on 16 May 2005). See also 'WIPO Broadcasting Treaty Discussions end in Controversy, Confusion,' available at <http://www.ip-watch.org> (last accessed on 16 May 2005); South Centre and CIEL IP quarterly update: first quarter 2005. Intellectual property and development: overview of developments in multilateral, plurilateral, and bilateral fora, available at <http://www.southcentre.org> (last accessed on 16 May 2005).

[235] P Katzenberger op. cit. (1998), 'TRIPS and copyright law', in F Beier and G Schricker (eds) op. cit. (1996), p 91.

[236] See Katzenberger op. cit. (1998), p 87. This author is of the opinion that such countries should not be exempted from the obligation to accord rental rights in these cases (idem, p 88).

It has been argued that an additional rental right for authors whose work is embodied in a phonogram,[237] or for performers in relation to fixations of performances on phonograms,[238] may be based on Article 14.4. In accordance with the International Bureau of WIPO, Members are free to extend rental rights to authors and performers whose works and performances, respectively, are fixed in phonograms.[239]

It is to be noted that, like Article 11 of the TRIPS Agreement, the rental rights mentioned in Article 14.4 thereof only apply with regard to 'commercial rental to the public'. In addition, the exception related to computer programs that are not essential to the object of the rental must be applied, *mutatis mutandis*, to the commercial rental of phonograms, such as in cases, for instance, of a CD containing instructions for the operation of rented equipment.

Countries that on the date of signing of the TRIPS agreement had a system of equitable remuneration of right-holders in respect of the rental of phonograms can maintain it subject, however, to a factual condition: the commercial rental of phonograms must not give rise to the material impairment of the exclusive rights of reproduction of right-holders. The way in which Article 14.1 is worded suggests that, whenever a system of equitable remuneration was in place at such date, the burden of proof that there is 'material impairment of the exclusive rights of reproduction of right holders' will be on the complaining party. This provision makes clear that it only applies in relation to the 'exclusive rights of reproduction of right holders'. It leaves open, like the first sentence of Article 14.1, who the 'right holders' are,[240] thereby leaving the issue for resolution under the domestic law.

The determination of the circumstances in which there is 'material impairment' of the rights of reproduction will depend on what the domestic law of the concerned country stipulates and on the way the courts evaluate the existence of acts that damage such exclusive rights. The use of 'material' in this provision suggests that rental should in practice prevent the right-holders from exercising such rights.

Finally, the wording of Article 14.4 ('[I]f on 15 April 1994 a Member has in force a system of equitable remuneration . . .') indicates that Members that did not have such a system on that date cannot in the future establish it as a substitute for the recognition of rental rights. There is no sound logic for this temporal differentiation. This suggests that Article 14.4 was the result of a negotiating compromise (mainly with Japan, which insisted on maintaining an equitable remuneration provision for rental rights) rather than of a reasoned consideration

---

[237] See, eg, M Senftleben op. cit. (2004), p 90 and bibliography cited in fn 466.
[238] See, eg, O Morgan op. cit. (2002), p 187.
[239] See WIPO op. cit. (1997), p 28.
[240] According to Morgan, this provision is 'more obviously directed to the protection of producers of phonograms, who are the named beneficiaries under Article 14(4)' (O Morgan op. cit. (2002), p 188). However, there is no reason to introduce a limitation that the provision does not contain.

of what kind of regime was desirable to protect rental rights in respect of phonograms. Thus, Members will not be allowed to apply a system of equitable remuneration if they had not adopted it at that date.

> **14.5. The term of the protection available under this Agreement to performers and producers of phonograms shall last at least until the end of a period of 50 years computed from the end of the calendar year in which the fixation was made or the performance took place. The term of protection granted pursuant to paragraph 3 shall last for at least 20 years from the end of the calendar year in which the broadcast took place.**

The protection for performers and phonogram producers was set out under the TRIPS Agreement at fifty years. There is no clear economic justification for the introduction of this long period, obviously welcomed by the phonogram industry and performers. It can only be understood as part of the philosophy—which generally inspired the TRIPS Agreement—that more protection is necessarily better. This philosophy, however, fails to consider the interests of the public, as it aims at increasing the rents generated by the extended rights without any evidence indicating that it will generate more or better artistic outcomes and products for the consumers.

The term of protection of the rights of broadcasting organizations is the same as already provided for under the Rome Convention.

> **14.6. Any Member may, in relation to the rights conferred under paragraphs 1, 2 and 3, provide for conditions, limitations, exceptions and reservations to the extent permitted by the Rome Convention. However, the provisions of Article 18 of the Berne Convention (1971) shall also apply, *mutatis mutandis*, to the rights of performers and producers of phonograms in phonograms.**

Article 14.6 authorizes, but does not obligate, Members to apply the 'conditions, limitations, exceptions and reservations to the extent permitted by the Rome Convention' in relation to the three first paragraphs of Article 14. Article 14.6 does not apply, hence, in relation to the rental rights recognized under Article 14.4.

Article 14.6 has an asymmetrical effect on Members, such as the US, who have not adhered to the Rome Convention, since although they are not obliged to comply with the Convention's requirements, they have 'the benefit of all its exemptions'.[241]

As a result of Article 14.6, Members may apply, as appropriate,[242] the exceptions contained in Article 15 of the Rome Convention, as well as the limitation

---

[241] See Dratler op. cit. (1996), para 1A-61. Nationals of such Members, however, do not necessarily benefit from the Rome Convention standards, but only from the rights conferred under the TRIPS Agreement.

[242] Some exceptions provided for in the Rome Convention may not be relevant, such as Article 16(1)(a) relating to equitable remuneration for secondary uses, which was not incorporated in the TRIPS Agreement. See, eg, O Morgan op. cit. (2002), p 210.

provided for in Article 7(1) of the Convention with regard to Article 14.1 of the TRIPS Agreement. The exceptions allowed under the Rome Convention are quite limited. They include:

(a) private use;
(b) use of short excerpts in connection with the reporting of current events;
(c) ephemeral fixation by a broadcasting organization by means of its own facilities and for its own broadcasts;
(d) use solely for the purposes of teaching or scientific research.

Irrespective of these exceptions, Contracting States may provide for the same kinds of limitations with regard to the protection of performers, producers of phonograms, and broadcasting organizations, as it provides for, in its domestic laws and regulations, in connection with the protection of copyright in literary and artistic works. However, compulsory licences may be provided for only to the extent to which they are compatible with the Rome Convention (Article 15.2).

Whether Article 13 of the TRIPS Agreement applies in relation to 'related' rights provided for under the Agreement has raised some controversy. For some commentators (as well as the US Administration) Article 13 applies to related rights.[243] This is the conclusion that could be drawn from the location of this provision in Section 1 on 'Copyright and related rights', without any distinction between the two categories of rights.

However, although Article 13 refers to the 'rightholder' rather than 'author', it alludes to 'works', not to 'works and related rights'. Moreover, Article 13 refers to 'exclusive rights' and Article 14.1 does not confer such rights. The only category of rights that may be subject to Article 13 are the rental rights established in Article 14.4 of the TRIPS Agreement (by reference to Article 11) not covered in the Rome Convention. Hence, there is no solid ground to argue that the Agreement generally subjects related rights and the limitations and exceptions provided therein to the conditions set out in Article 13.[244]

The last sentence of Article 14.6—referring to Article 18 of the Berne Convention—essentially means that the TRIPS Agreement provides for the retroactive application in respect of the right of performers and producers of phonograms with the possible exceptions and under the conditions provided for in Article 18 of the Berne Convention.[245] As a result, the Agreement recognizes the rights conferred in paragraphs 1–3 of Article 14 in respect of producers of phonograms and performers in existing phonograms for which the fifty-year

---

[243] See, eg, M Basso, *O direito internacional da propriedade intelectual* (2000: Porto Alegre, Livraria do Advogado), pp 196–7; Watal op. cit. (2001), p 225.

[244] See on this issue G Dworkin, 'Exceptions to Copyright Exclusivity: Is Fair Use Consistent With Article 9.2 Berne And The New International Order?', in H Hansen (ed) op. cit. (2001), pp 66–13.   [245] WIPO op. cit. (1997), p 31.

terms of protection had not expired at the date of application of the TRIPS Agreement for the Member in question.[246] Despite this, the Agreement does not give rise to obligations in respect of acts which occurred before the date of application of the Agreement for the Member in question (Article 70.1). Hence, acts that occurred before that date cannot substantiate claims by the right-holders that may benefit from the conferred retroactive protection.[247]

Annex

Negotiating history[248]

In his 23 July 1990 report on the status of work in the TRIPS Negotiating Group, the Chairman (Lars E R Anell) presented two sets of proposals. In an Annex to the report, he presented a composite text that was taken from various proposals by delegations to the Negotiating Group, indicating the source of each proposal by numerical reference to the source document.

Composite text of July 23 1990[249]

1A PARTIES shall grant to authors and their successors in title the [economic] rights provided in the Berne Convention (1971), subject to the provisions set forth below.

1B 'PARTIES shall provide to the nationals of other parties the rights which their respective laws do now or may hereafter grant, consistently with the rights specially granted by the Berne Convention.'

2. *Protectable Subject Matter*

2.1 PARTIES shall provide protection to computer programs [,as literary works for the purposes of point 1 above,] [and to databases]. Such protection shall not extend to ideas, procedures, methods [, algorithms] or systems.

2.2B.1 For the purpose of protecting computer programs, PARTIES shall determine in their national legislation the nature, scope and term of protection to be granted to such works.

2.2B.2 In view of the complex legal and technical issues raised by the protection of computer programs, PARTIES undertake to cooperate with each other to identify a suitable method of protection and to evolve international rules governing such protection.'

---

[246] Such rights are, hence, restored in relation to phonograms created after 1945, in the case of developed countries, and 1950 for developing countries.

[247] The application of Article 14.6 gave rise to one of the first complaints under the DSU. See Watal op. cit. (2001), p 237.

[248] For an analysis of the negotiating history, see UNCTAD–ICTSD op. cit. (2005), pp 135–265.

[249] Chairman's Report to the GNG, Status of Work in the Negotiating Group, Negotiating Group on Trade-Related Aspects of Intellectual Property Rights, including Trade in Counterfeit Goods, MTN.GNG/NG11/W/76, 23 July 1990, presented by the Chairman of the TRIPS Negotiating Group (Lars E R Anell). Alternatives 'A' correspond to texts from developed countries and 'B' from developing countries.

Rental Rights

3A.2.1 [At least in the case of computer programs [, cinematographic works] [and musical works,]] PARTIES shall provide authors and their successors in title the [right to authorise or prohibit the rental of the originals or copies of their copyright works] [or, alternatively,] [the right to obtain an equitable remuneration] [corresponding to the economic value of such a use] [whenever originals or copies are rented or otherwise made available against payment]. [It is understood that granting to authors the right to authorise or prohibit the rental of their works for a certain period of time and to claim an equitable remuneration for the remaining period is sufficient to fulfil this provision.]

3A.2.2 For the purposes of the previous point, rental shall mean the disposal [for a limited period of time] of the possession of the original or copies for [direct profit-making purposes] [direct or indirect commercial advantage].

3A.2.3 There shall be no obligation to provide for a rental right in respect of works of applied art or architecture.'

(Right of Importation and Distribution)

3A.1 *Economic rights shall include:*

3A.1.1 the right to import or authorize the importation into the territory of the PARTY of lawfully made copies of the work as well as the right to prevent the importation into the territory of the PARTY of copies of the work made without the authorization of the right-holder;

3A.1.2 the right to make the first public distribution of the original or each authorized copy of a work by sale, rental, or otherwise except that the first sale of the original or such copy of, at a minimum, a computer program shall not exhaust the rental or importation right therein.[1]

'7. *Term of Protection*

7A.1 The term of protection of a work whose author is a legal entity shall be no less than 50 years from the end of the year of authorised publication, or, failing such authorised publication within 50 years from the making of the work, 50 years from the end of the year of making.

7A.2 The term of protection of computer programs shall be no less than 50 years after the end of the year of creation.'

'8. *Limitations, Exemptions and Compulsory Licensing*

8A.1 In respect of the rights provided for at point 3, the limitations and exemptions, including compulsory licensing, recognised under the Berne Convention (1971) shall also apply mutatis mutandis. [Limitations made to the rights in favour of private use shall not apply to computer software.] [PARTIES may also provide for other limited

---

[1] It is understood that, unless expressly provided to the contrary in this agreement, nothing in this agreement shall limit the freedom of PARTIES to provide that any intellectual property rights conferred in respect of the use, sale, importation and other distribution of goods are exhausted once those goods have been put on the market by or with the consent of the right holder.

exceptions to rights in respect of computer programs, consistent with the special nature of these works.]

8A.2 PARTIES shall confine any limitations or exemptions to exclusive rights (including any limitations or exceptions that restrict such rights to 'public' activity) to clearly and carefully defined special cases which do not impair an actual or potential market for or the value of a protected work.

8A.3 Translation and reproduction licensing systems permitted in the Appendix to the Berne Convention (1971):

8A.3.1 shall not be established where legitimate local needs are being met by voluntary actions of copyright owners or could be met by such action but for intervening factors outside the copyright owner's control; and

8A.3.2 shall provide an effective opportunity for the copyright owner to be heard prior to the grant of any such licences.

8A.4 Any compulsory licence (or any restriction of exclusive rights to a right of remuneration) shall provide mechanisms to ensure prompt payment and

10. *Relation to Rome Convention*

10A PARTIES shall, as minimum substantive standards for the protection of performers, broadcasting organisations and producers of phonograms, provide protection consistent with the substantive provisions of the Rome Convention. [Articles 1 to 20 of the Rome Convention could be considered to constitute the substantive provisions.]

11. *Rights of Producers of Phonograms (Sound Recordings)*

11A.1 PARTIES shall extend to producers of phonograms the right to authorise or prohibit the direct or indirect reproduction of their phonograms [by any means or process, in whole or in part].

11A.2a [In regard to the rental of phonograms,] the provisions of point 3 in respect of computer programs shall apply mutatis mutandis in respect of producers of phonograms [or performers or both].

11A.2b The protection provided to producers of phonograms shall include the right to prevent all third parties not having their consent from putting on the market, from selling, or from otherwise distributing copies of such phonograms.

11A.3 The provisions of point 4A shall apply mutatis mutandis to the producers of phonograms.

12. *Rights of Performers*

12A The protection provided for performers shall include the possibility of preventing:

12A.1 the broadcasting [by any technical means or process such as by radio wave, by cable or by other devices] [by wireless means and the communication to the public of their live performance];

12A.2 the fixation of their unfixed performance [on phonograms or data carriers and from reproducing such fixations];

12A.3 the reproduction of a fixation of their performance;

12A.4 the production of their performance in any place other than that of the performance;

12A.5 the offering to the public, selling, or otherwise distributing copies of the fixation containing the performance.

13. *Rights of Broadcasting Organisations*

13.1 Broadcasting organisations shall have the possibility of preventing:

13A.1 the fixation of their broadcasts [on phonograms or data carriers, and from reproducing such fixations];

13A.2 the reproduction of fixations;

13A.3 the communication to the public of their [television] broadcasts;

13A.4 the rebroadcasting by wireless means of their broadcasts;

13A.5 the retransmitting of their broadcast;

13A.6 the putting on the market, sale, or other distribution of copies of the broadcast.

14. *Public Communication of Phonograms*

14A If a phonogram published for commercial purposes, or a reproduction of such a phonogram, is used directly for broadcasting or for any communication to the public, a single equitable remuneration shall be paid by the user to the performers, or to the producers of the phonogram, or to both.

15. *Term of Protection*

15A.1a The term of protection granted to producers of phonograms, performers and broadcasting organisations shall last at least until the end of a period of [20] [50] years computed from the end of the year in which the fixation was made or the performance or broadcast took place.

15A.2a PARTIES may, however, provide for a period of protection of less than 50 years provided that the period of protection lasts at least for 25 years and that they otherwise assume a substantially equivalent protection against piracy for an equivalent period.

15Ab Point 7 shall apply mutatis mutandis to the producers of phonograms.

16. *Exceptions*

16Aa PARTIES may, in relation to the rights conferred by points 11, 12, 13 and 14, provide for limitations, exceptions and reservations to the extent permitted by the Rome Convention.

16Ab Points 8A.2–4 of this Part shall apply mutatis mutandis to phonograms.

16B (See Section 8 of this Part.)

17. *Acquisition of Rights*

17A.1 The provisions of points 6 and 9 of this Part shall apply mutatis mutandis to the producers of phonograms.

17A.2 PARTIES shall protect phonograms first fixed or published in the territory of another PARTY, including phonograms published in the territory of a PARTY within thirty days of their publication elsewhere; and phonograms the producer of which is a national of a PARTY, or is a company headquartered in the territory of a PARTY.

17A.3 The acquisition and validity of intellectual property rights in phonograms shall not be subject to any formalities, and protection shall arise automatically upon their creation.'

Draft text transmitted to the Brussels Ministerial Conference (December 1990)

Article 9
Relation to Berne Convention

PARTIES shall comply with the substantive provisions [on economic rights] of the Berne Convention (1971). [However, PARTIES shall not have rights or obligations under this Agreement in respect of the rights conferred under Article 6*bis* of that Convention or of the rights derived therefrom].

Article 10
Computer Programs and Compilations of Data

1. Computer programs, whether in source or object code, shall be protected as [literary] works under the Berne Convention (1971). [Such protection shall not extend to ideas, procedures, methods of operation or mathematical concepts.] [This shall not prevent PARTIES from requiring, as a condition of protection of computer programs, compliance with procedures and formalities consistent with the principles of Part IV of this Agreement or from making adjustments to the rights of reproduction and adaptation and to moral rights necessary to permit normal exploitation of a computer program, provided that this does not unreasonably prejudice the legitimate interests of the right holder.]

2. Compilations of data or other material, whether in machine readable or other form, which by reason of the selection and arrangement of their contents constitute intellectual creations shall be protected as such. Such protection, which shall not extend to the data or material itself, shall be without prejudice to any copyright subsisting in the data or material itself.

Article 11
Rental Rights

In respect of at least computer programs and cinematographic works, a PARTY shall provide authors and their successors in title the right to authorise or prohibit the commercial rental to the public of originals or copies of their copyright works [, or alternatively the right to obtain an equitable remuneration corresponding to the economic value of such use] [, where circumstances arise by which the commercial rental of originals or copies of copyright works has led to [unauthorised] copying of such works which is materially impairing the exclusive right of reproduction conferred in that PARTY on authors and their successors in title].

Article 12
Term of Protection

Whenever the term of protection of a work, other than a photographic work or a work of applied art [or a computer program], is calculated on a basis other than the life of a natural person, such term shall be no less than 50 years from the end of the calendar year of authorized publication, or, failing such authorized publication within 50 years from the making of the work, 50 years from the end of the calendar year of making.

Article 13
Limitations and Exceptions

1. PARTIES shall confine limitations or exceptions to exclusive rights to certain special cases which do not conflict with a normal exploitation of the work and do not unreasonably prejudice the legitimate interests of the right holder.

[2. Translation and reproduction licences permitted under the Appendix to the Berne Convention (1971) shall not be granted where the legitimate local needs of a PARTY could be met by voluntary actions of right holders but for obstacles resulting from measures taken by the government of that PARTY].

Article 14
Definition of public

The term 'public' shall not be defind in the domestic law of PARTIES in a manner that conflicts with a normal commercial exploitation of a work and unreasonably prejudices the legitimate interests of right holders.]

Article 15
Protection of Works Existing at Time of Entry into Force

The provisions of the Berne Convention (1971) concerning the protection of works existing at the time of entry into force shall apply in respect of the rights secured under that Convention.

Article 16
Protection of Performers, Producers of Phonograms

[1. In respect of a fixation of their performance on a phonogram, performers shall have the possibility of preventing: the fixation of their unfixed performance; and the reproduction of such fixation. Performers shall also have the possibility of preventing the broadcasting by wireless means and the communication to the public of their live performance.]

2. Producers of phonograms shall enjoy the right to authorize or prohibit the direct or indirect reproduction of their phonograms.

[3. Broadcasting organizations shall have the right to authorise or prohibit the fixation, the reproduction of fixations, and the rebroadcasting by wireless means of broadcasts, as well as the communication to the public of television broadcasts of the same. Where PARTIES do not grant such rights to broadcasting organizations, they shall provide right holders in the subject matter of broadcasts with the possibility of preventing the above acts.]

4. The provisions of Article 11 shall apply *mutatis mutandis* to right holders in phonograms.

5. The term of the protection available under this Agreement to performers and producers of phonograms shall last at least until the end of a period of [50] years computed from the end of the calendar year in which the fixation was made or the performance or broadcast took place. The term of protection granted pursuant to paragraph 3 above shall last for at least [25] years from the end of the calendar year in which the broadcast took place.

6. Any PARTY to this Agreement may, in relation to the rights conferred under paragraphs 1–3 above, provide for conditions, limitations, exceptions and reservations to the extent permitted by the Rome Convention. [However, the provisions of Article [–217] of this Section shall also apply *mutatis mutandis* to the rights of performers and producers of phonograms in phonograms.]

Chapter 6

TRADEMARKS

Section 2, Part II, of the TRIPS Agreement relates to trademarks. In addition to the substantive rules contained in said section, the Agreement incorporates provisions to ensure the enforcement of rights (Part III) and, particularly, procedures to be followed by customs authorities with regard to counterfeit trademark goods (Part III, Section 4).

The negotiation of this section (probably with the exception of the issue of use requirement for the registration of a trademark) was not as controversial as other areas of the TRIPS Agreement, particularly the copyright and patent sections.

This section significantly strengthens the rights of trademark owners as compared to those available under the Paris Convention.[1] The main innovation brought about by the TRIPS text in the trademark area probably relates to the expanded protection conferred on well-known trademarks. Another area of potential significant impact is the limitation and conditions imposed with regard to the use requirement to maintain registration, and the flexibility accorded to assign trademarks unrelated to the respective business.

The enforcement rules in Part III are likely to be, however, the most significant components of the Agreement in terms of impact on trademark law.

Trademarks are 'relational', in the sense that 'it is a right created by the confluence of a mark, the goods or services to which the mark refers, and the identification of the source of the product by the mark'.[2] Source identification, understood as the communication of information about a source from where previously satisfactory goods have emanated,[3] has traditionally been deemed the primary purpose of trademark law. Other functions relate to the protection of consumers against confusion and deceiving practices, and the protection of an undertaking's goodwill. As examined below, the 'source identification' function has been to some extent diluted by the provisions of the TRIPS Agreement.[4]

---

[1] See, J Dratler Jr, *Intellectual Property Law: Commercial, Creative and Industrial Property* (1996: New York, Law Journal Seminars Press), paras 1A-73–1A-80.

[2] N Wilkof, 'Trademarks and the public domain: generic marks and domain names', in H Harser (ed.), *International Intellectual Property Law & Policy*, vol. 6, (2001: Huntington, Juris Publishing), pp 21–7.

[3] See, eg, C Pickering, *Trade Marks in Theory and Practice* (1998: Oxford, Hart Publishing) p 43.

[4] UNCTAD-ICTSD Project on IPRs and Sustainable Development, *Resource Book on TRIPS and Development* (2005: New York, Cambridge University Press), p 229. The differentiation of the goods or services of one undertaking from those of others may be regarded as a corollary of the 'source identification' function. See C Pickering op. cit. (1998), p 45.

This section of the Agreement is to a large extent based on the EC submission made during the TRIPS negotiations.[5] It supplements various provisions in the Paris Convention relating to trademarks, with additional obligations that, to some extent, reflected pre-existing law and jurisprudence on the matter.[6] The TRIPS Agreement contains in Part III other provisions that specifically refer to trademarks, such as Article 51 (border measures in case of counterfeiting), Article 61 (criminal sanctions for willful counterfeiting)) and Article 62.3 (priority period of Article 4 of the Paris Convention extended to service trademarks).

Subject matter

15.1. Any sign, or any combination of signs, capable of distinguishing the goods or services of one undertaking from those of other undertakings, shall be capable of constituting a trademark. Such signs, in particular words including personal names, letters, numerals, figurative elements and combinations of colours as well as any combination of such signs, shall be eligible for registration as trademarks. Where signs are not inherently capable of distinguishing the relevant goods or services, Members may make registrability depend on distinctiveness acquired through use. Members may require, as a condition of registration, that signs be visually perceptible.

Article 15.1 of TRIPS defines the subject matter which is to be protected under trademark law. It represents a significant step in international trade law. Under the Paris Convention, fundamental disputes arose around the scope of the obligation to register a foreign trademark 'as is' (*telle quelle*), imposed by Article 6*quienquies* of that Convention, particularly with regard to whether it concerned only the form or also the content of trademarks and its applicability to other requirements (such as use or intention to use).[7]

Trademarks for goods and for services are equally protectable under the TRIPS Agreement, in line with the generalized trend to allow for the protection of marks for services. Though national laws may still determine the conditions of sufficient distinctiveness and specificity of service marks,[8] this provision ensures a 'Paris-plus' protection, since the Paris Convention obliged Contracting Parties to protect service marks, but not 'to provide for the registration of such marks' (Article 6*sexies*). Member countries assume under Article 15.1 of TRIPS the obligation to permit the registration of service marks.

---

[5] MTN.GNG/ NG11/W/68, which in turn relied on the Council Directive on Trademarks (89/104/EEC). See J Watal, *Intellectual Property Rights in the WTO and Developing Countries* (2001: The Hague, Kluwer Law International), p 244. [6] Idem, p 260.

[7] See, eg, A Kur, 'TRIPs and trademarks', in F-K Beier and G Schricker, *From GATT to TRIPs— The Agreement on Trade-Related Aspects of Intellectual Property Rights* (1996: Munich, Max Planck Institute for Foreign and International Patent, Copyright and Competition Law) p 99.

[8] In the UK, for instance, the registration of service marks has been refused for ancillary activities of a retailer which are not definite enough to be adequately specified (see, eg, Dee Corporation's Application, 1989, Fleet Street Patent Law Reports, 1989).

The single criterion set out by Article 15.1 for the eligibility of a sign as a trade-mark is its capacity to distinguish the goods or services of one party from those of other parties. Article 15.1 has followed in this respect the approach of the US Landham Act,[9] and recognizes both inherent distinctiveness and secondary mean-ing.[10] However, a sign that allows consumers to distinguish or differentiate among providers is not the same as a sign that identifies a particular provider as the source of goods or services. Hence, Article 15.1 does not require that the consumer be able to identify the specific source of the goods or services; he should just be able to determine that goods or services identified by the mark are distinct from other goods or services.[11]

The distinctiveness requirement is not to be exclusively judged on the basis of the inherent distinctive features of a sign. Article 15.1, third sentence, extends the eligibility to signs that 'are not inherently capable of distinguishing the relevant goods or services', when distinctiveness was acquired through use. This is, how-ever, a facultative rule ('Members may require') and not an obligation.

The enumeration of signs that may be registered as trademarks is of an illustra-tive nature, as clearly indicated by the second sentence in Article 15.1: '[S]uch signs, in particular . . .'. Hence, any sign which complies with the distinctiveness requirement is eligible for protection, whether it is mentioned in Article 15.1 or not. In *United States–Section 211 Omnibus Appropriations Act of 1998*, the Appellate Body stated that

Article 15.1 defines which signs or combinations of signs are *capable of* constituting a trade-mark. These signs include words such as personal names, letters, numerals, figurative elements and combinations of colours, as well as any combination of such signs. This defin-ition is based on the distinctiveness of signs as such, or on their distinctiveness as acquired through use. If such signs are capable of distinguishing the goods or services of one undertak-ing from those of other undertakings, then they become *eligible for* registration as trademarks (*footnote omitted*). To us, the title of Article 15.1—'Protectable Subject Matter'—indicates that Article 15.1 embodies a *definition* of what can constitute a trademark. WTO Members are obliged under Article 15.1 to ensure that those signs or combinations of signs that meet the distinctiveness criteria set forth in Article 15.1—and are, thus, *capable of constituting a trademark*—are *eligible for registration* as trademarks within their domestic legislation.[12]

Members, however, may require that such signs be visually perceptible. This allows a country to exclude from protection audible and olfactory signs.[13] The question may arise regarding the protection of one letter or one colour as a mark.

---

[9] Sect 45, 15 USC. 1127.   [10] See Dratler op. cit. (1996), para 1A-74.

[11] UNCTAD-ICTSD op. cit. (2005), p 230.

[12] WT/DS176/AB/R, 2 January 2002, para 154.

[13] These signs may, however, be protected under 'passing of' or unfair competition law. See WIPO, *Background Reading Material on Intellectual Property* (1988: Geneva), p 145. They may also be visually represented through musical language and description of the chemical formulae. See Watal op. cit. (2001), p 249. In the EC, however, neither the formula, nor a description in written words, nor a deposit of an odour sample or a combination of these elements is deemed to satisfy the require-ment of graphic representability. See, eg, UNCTAD-ICTSD op. cit. (2005), p 262.

Although the commented text refers to 'letters' (in plural) and 'combinations of colours') they are only mentioned in an illustrative way, without excluding other possibilities. The protection of individual letters or colours has been admitted (for instance, with respect to pharmaceutical capsules) but generally based on a very substantial proof of use as trademark which led to a secondary meaning for the public.[14]

There is no explicit reference to three-dimensional trademarks consisting of the shape or container of products. To the extent that they are a distinctive sign they should, in principle, be deemed to be protectable under TRIPS.[15] Members could, however, determine the conditions for such a protection, in order to exclude, for instance, configurations that are dictated by functional rather than by aesthetic considerations. Protection of shapes of goods or of their container ensures a protection *sine die*, unlike the case where such forms are only protectable as industrial designs.[16]

Members may be flexible about the requirement of distinctiveness, when a sign is not 'inherently' distinctive but it has become so through use. It is generally accepted under trademark law that the lack[17] of inherent distinctiveness does not necessarily mean that protection is excluded, if it has acquired distinctiveness through use. In some countries (eg USA, United Kingdom) a different register exists for marks not inherently distinctive.

Article 15.1 alludes to 'undertakings' and not to 'parties', as elsewhere in the Agreement. The absence of detailed proceedings on the negotiations makes it difficult to identify the reasons behind this terminological choice, but it does not limit national laws' freedom to determine who can legally become a trademark owner. There are no limitations in TRIPS with regard to the protection of trademarks by persons not carrying out trading activities, as required by some laws. Trademark rights might, thus, be granted to non-profit organizations. Likewise, countries remain free to recognize 'collective' marks (trademarks used by members of a cooperative, association or other group of firms), as well as 'certification' marks (used by different enterprises on or in connection with products or services complying with defined standards).

---

[14] The satisfaction of the distinctiveness requirement in these cases is difficult to make out even in systems where the acquisition of rights in trademarks is possible through use.

[15] In some countries the registration of the 'get-up' of products, such as the 'Coca-Cola' bottle, has been restricted or excluded (see, eg, W Cornish, *Intellectual Property. Patents, Copyrights, Trade Marks and Allied Rights* (1989: London, Sweet & Maxwell), p 439. There is also an exclusion in the European Trademark Regulation (Article 7(1)(e)) and in the European Trademark Directive (Article 3(1)(e)) relating to shapes resulting from the nature of goods necessary to obtain a technical effect or which give substantial value to products. On the compatibility of this exclusion with Article 15.1 of the TRIPS Agreement, see A Kur op. cit. (1996), p 100.

[16] For this reason, the protection of three-dimensional trademarks has been restrictively considered in some countries, such as Germany. See Watal op. cit. (2001), p 250.

[17] Article *6quinquies* C(1) of the Paris Convention states that 'in determining whether a mark is eligible for protection, all the factual circumstances must be taken into account, particularly the length of time the mark has been in use'.

An application for registration as a trademark of a sign that is *eligible* for protection in accordance with Article 15.1 may be refused, however, in a number of cases specified in the Paris Convention (and, by reference, in the TRIPS Agreement) as well as for other reasons, such as ownership in the trademark.[18] In considering the application of Article 15.1 in *United States–Section 211 Omnibus Appropriations Act of 1998*, the Appellate Body argued that Article 15.1 does not mean that distinctive signs must be accorded protection as trademarks, but only that they qualify for such protection, which may be subject to additional criteria, in line with the discretion granted by Article 6(1) of the Paris Convention.[19] The AB concluded that Article 6*quinquies* of the Paris Convention applies to the *form* of a trademark, but not to other conditions of eligibility.[20]

> 15.2. Paragraph 1 shall not be understood to prevent a Member from denying registration of a trademark on other grounds, provided that they do not derogate from the provisions of the Paris Convention (1967).

Trademark laws typically specify several grounds for denying trademark protection. The Paris Convention admits a number of such grounds in Articles 6*bis* and 6*ter*.

Article 6*bis* requires the refusal of third-party registration of well-known trademarks,[21] and Article 6*ter* refers to prohibitions concerning State emblems, official hallmarks and emblems of intergovernmental organizations.[22]

In addition, Article 6*quinquies* of the Paris Convention stipulates a number of exceptions to the obligation to accept trademarks for registration *telle quelle* ('as is'); that is, as registered in the country of origin. Refusal of 'as is' registration may take place when the trademarks

(a) are of such a nature as to infringe rights acquired by third parties in the country where protection is claimed;

(b) are devoid of any distinctive character, or consist exclusively of signs or indications which may serve, in trade, to designate the kind, quality, quantity, intended purpose, value, place of origin, of the goods, or the time of production, or have become customary in the current language or in the bona fide and established practices of the trade of the country where protection is claimed;

(c) are contrary to morality or public order and, in particular, of such a nature as to deceive the public. It is understood that a mark may not be considered contrary to public order for the sole reason that it does not conform to a provision of the legislation on marks, except if such provision itself relates to public order. This provision is subject, however, to the application of Article 10*bis*.[23]

---

[18] See commentary on Article 15.2 below.

[19] Article 6(1): 'The conditions for the filing and registration of trademarks shall be determined in each country of the Union by its domestic legislation.'

[20] WT/DS176/AB/R, 2 January 2002, para 144. See, eg, UNCTAD-ICTSD op. cit. (2005), p 251.

[21] See pp 188–92 below.   [22] See also below, commentary on Article 15.5.

[23] The text of Article 6*quinquies*(B) of the Paris Convention is as follows:

'Trademarks covered by this Article may be neither denied registration nor invalidated except in the following cases:

(i) when they are of such a nature as to infringe rights acquired by third parties in the country where protection is claimed;

Article 6*quinquies* B of the Paris Convention enumerates the cases in which a trademark can be denied registration or, if granted, can be subsequently cancelled. They refer to infringement of prior rights, lack of distinctive character or customary use, and where the marks are contrary to 'morality or public order', including when they are likely to deceive the public. It is of note that refusal of a mark due to 'morality or public order' may be grounded on the characteristics of the trademarks, and not on the nature of the products as such.[24]

In *United States–Section 211 Omnibus Appropriations Act of 1998*, the Appellate Body interpreted the meaning of 'other grounds' in Article 15.2 of the TRIPS Agreement. It confirmed that Members may define such other grounds, subject to the limitation of the grounds that are explicitly prohibited by the Paris Convention.[25] Thus, refusal of registration of a trademark may be linked to issues relating to its ownership, and upheld a decision of the US government that had refused to register a trademark alleging that the applicant was not the rightful owner. It stated:

Thus, in our view, the European Communities sees an obligation in Article 15.1 that is not there. Identifying certain signs that are *capable of* registration and imposing on WTO Members an obligation to make those signs *eligible for* registration in their domestic legislation is not the same as imposing on those Members an obligation to register *automatically* each and every sign or combination of signs that are *capable of* and *eligible for* registration under Article 15.1. This Article describes which trademarks are 'capable of' registration. It does not say that all trademarks that are capable of registration 'shall be registered'. This Article states that such signs or combinations of signs 'shall be *eligible* for registration' as trademarks. It does not say that they 'shall be registered'. To us, these are distinctions with a difference. And, as we have said, supporting these distinctions is the fact that the title of this Article speaks of subject matter as 'protectable', and not of subject matter 'to be protected'. In this way, the title of Article 15 expresses the notion that the subject matter covered by the provision is subject matter that *qualifies* for, but is not necessarily *entitled to*, protection.[26]

It follows that the wording of Article 15.1 allows WTO Members to set forth in their domestic legislation conditions for the registration of trademarks that do *not* address the definition of either 'protectable subject matter' or of what constitutes a trademark.[27]

   (ii) when they are devoid of any distinctive character, or consist exclusively of signs or indications which may serve, in trade, to designate the kind, quality, quantity, intended purpose, value, place of origin, of the goods, or the time of production, or have become customary in the current language or in the bona fide and established practices of the trade of the country where protection is claimed;

   (iii) when they are contrary to morality or public order and, in particular, of such a nature as to deceive the public. It is understood that a mark may not be considered contrary to public order for the sole reason that it does not conform to a provision of the legislation on marks, except if such provision itself relates to public order. This provision is subject, however, to the application of Article 10*bis*.'

[24] See p 182 below.
[25] WT/DS176/AB/R, 2 January 2002, paras 157–9; 169. Although the non-derogation clause in Article 15(2) seems redundant in the light of Article 2.2 of the TRIPS Agreement (except in that it does not identify a specific Act of the Convention), it was relied on and instrumental in the reasoning of the AB in this case.
[26] WT/DS176/AB/R, 2 January 2002, para 155.   [27] Idem, para 156.

The right of Members under Article 15.2 to deny registration of trademarks on grounds other than the failure to meet the distinctiveness requirements set forth in Article 15.1 implies that Members are not obliged to register any and every sign or combination of signs that meet those distinctiveness requirements.[28]

As with our interpretation of Article *6quinquies*, here, too, we recall that Article 6(1) of the Paris Convention (1967), which has become a WTO provision by incorporation through Article 2.1 of the *TRIPS Agreement*, reserves to each country of the Paris Union the right to determine the 'conditions' for filing and registration of trademarks in its domestic legislation (*footnote omitted*). If Article 15.1 required the registration of any and every sign or combination of signs that meets the distinctiveness criteria specified in that Article, then WTO Members would be deprived of the legislative discretion they enjoy under Article 6(1) of the Paris Convention (1967). In our view, Article 15.1 of the *TRIPS Agreement* limits the right of Members to determine the 'conditions' for filing and registration of trademarks under their domestic legislation pursuant to Article 6(1) *only* as it relates to the distinctiveness requirements enunciated in Article 15.1.[29]

Entitlement is not, however, the only important issue on which the TRIPS is moot, and defers the legal solution to national legislation. As mentioned, the Agreement does not address either who can apply for and obtain registration of a trademark, notably whether the applicant should undertake a commercial activity to be entitled to do so. This requirement, present—but often loosely applied—in many national laws, aims (like, in fact, the prior use of a trademark) to avoid speculative registration of trademarks and the ensuing barriers to legitimate trade.

Could a domestic law that permits refusal of trademarks in such circumstances be regarded as incompatible with Article 15.2 of the TRIPS Agreement? Such refusal would not proceed in this case on grounds related to the characteristics of the trademarks and would not be covered under Article *6quinquies* of the Paris Convention. It would not conflict with Article 7 of the Paris Convention (and Article 15.4 of the TRIPS Agreement) either, as refusal would not be linked to the nature of the products and services, but to the activities of the applicant. The reply to that question seems, hence, negative.

It is interesting to note that the Trademark Law Treaty did address the nature of the applicant's activities and established a TRIPS-plus provision in this regard. Article 3(7)(iii) of the Treaty stipulates that no Contracting Party may demand in respect of the application throughout its pendency:

> (iii) an indication of the applicant's carrying on of an activity corresponding to the goods and/or services listed in the application, as well as the furnishing of evidence to that effect.

Requirement of use for application and registration

15.3. Members may make registrability depend on use. However, actual use of a trademark shall not be a condition for filing an application for registration. An

---

[28] Idem, para 159.   [29] Idem, para 165.

application shall not be refused solely on the ground that intended use has
not taken place before the expiry of a period of three years from the date of
application.

One of the most controversial issues in the negotiation of the trademarks section
of the TRIPS Agreement was the 'use requirement'. This requirement may arise
out in relation to four main issues: a) use as a condition for registration; b) use as a
basis for the availability of rights; c) use as a condition to maintain registration;
and d) use of a trademark with other signs or in a special form. The first issue is
considered here, while issues b), c), and d) are dealt with below.

Under Anglo-American law, rights in trademarks could traditionally be created
by using a trademark without a registration procedure.[30] Moreover, actual use, or
the intention to use, has traditionally been required for the registration of a trademark, in order to avoid the protection of trademarks not effectively linked to
traded products or services. This system—applied, for instance, in the US and
Canada—is in contrast with the registration system predominant in civil law
countries, where trademarks rights are acquired through registration.

Although the two systems tended to converge over time, when the Uruguay
Round negotiations started the US continued to require the prior use of a trademark as a condition for negotiation. During the Round, through an amendment
of the Lanham Act in 1988, the US moved to a modified use-based registration
system, which though still based on use allows for registration grounded on an
'intent to use'.[31]

The confrontation between the use-based and the registration-based approaches
posed a significant challenge to TRIPS negotiators. While the US aimed at preserving a system allowing for a declaration of intent to use,[32] the EC and Japan suggested, instead, that the Agreement explicitly state that use of a trademark prior to
registration shall not be a condition for registration. The finally adopted text reflects
a compromise between the two positions, but also the extent to which the US was
able to preserve its own legal approach in this and other areas.[33] Article 15.3 'exactly
accommodates the structure of the United States' intent-to-use system'.[34]

Article 15.3 allows Members to make registration, but not the application for a
trademark, dependent on actual use. It thus allowed the US to maintain its system.

In addition, the third sentence of Article 15.3 limits a Member's ability to
refuse a trademark application solely on the grounds that intended use has not
taken place before the expiry of a period of three years from the date of application. An implication of this provision is that a trademark may be refused *solely* on
the grounds of lack of use for more than three years after the date of application,

---

[30] See, eg, D Burge, *Patent and Trademark Tactics and Practice* (1984: New York, Wiley Interscience,
2nd edn), p 133.
[31] See, eg, UNCTAD-ICTSD op. cit. (2005), p 233.
[32] See Article 1(b) of the Lanham Act.
[33] See, eg, the commentary on the exclusion of moral rights in the field of copyright p 117 above.
[34] Dratler op. cit. (1996), para 1A-78. The US was obliged, however, to introduce some changes
in its legislation to adapt to the section on trademarks of the TRIPS Agreement, such as the extension
of the time period for presuming abandonment from two to three years (ibidem).

although non-use is not one of the admitted grounds for rejection under the Paris Convention.[35]

During the three-year period, the trademark is to be deemed as used for the purposes of the application. This provision is only relevant to countries in which the use of a trademark can be a condition for registration. Article 15.3 does not require the granting of any other right during that three-year period.

The prohibition to refuse a trademark solely on grounds of lack of use during the specified three-year period raises the question whether a term of less than three years, subject to extension if lack of use is justified, would comply with Article 15.3 of the TRIPS Agreement.[36]

15.4. The nature of the goods or services to which a trademark is to be applied shall in no case form an obstacle to registration of the trademark.

This provision is a replica of Article 7 of the Paris Convention, with an important difference: it applies to both trademarks in goods and services. The registration of a trademark cannot be limited or prevented on the basis of the 'nature of the goods and services' to be protected. This shall 'in no case form an obstacle to registration of the trademark' (Article 15.4).

This provision avoids any discrimination with regard to the availability of trademark protection based on the types of products or services involved. The compatibility of this rule with other possible legal requirements or limitations needs to be considered. In case, for instance, that a country allows the sale of certain medicines only under a generic name, an infringement to Article 15.4 might be claimed. Similarly, Article 15.4 would not allow a Member to deny registration of trademarks for products which are not in the public interest, such as by being harmful to health.[37] This limitation is more restrictive of State sovereignty than the equivalent provision for patents, which allows Members to refuse patents, under certain circumstances, when it is necessary to prevent the commercial exploitation of inventions that are contrary, inter alia, to morality or *ordre public*.[38]

However, unlike Article 27.1 relating to patents, Article 15.4 does not refer to the enjoyment of rights, but only to their availability. Article 16, on the other hand, defines the exclusive rights of the trademark owner in a negative way (the right to exclude others). Article 15.4, hence, cannot be interpreted as preventing a Member from limiting or prohibiting the use of trademarks for the commercialization of goods or services based on public health, security, or other reasons.[39]

---

[35] The reason for rejection may be linked in this case to lack of distinctiveness. See D Gervais *The TRIPS Agreement. Drafting history and analysis* (2003: London; Sweet & Maxwell, 2nd edition), p 169.

[36] See A Kur op. cit. (1996), p 103 (arguing that the US law could be in conflict with the TRIPS Agreement, as US law required a special justification to extend the term during which non-use is allowed).

[37] See W Kingston, 'Why harmonisation is a Trojan horse' (2004) European Intellectual Property Review 10, p 460 (suggesting that countries must be allowed to deny registration in cases where products are not in the public interest, as the TRIPS Agreement allows in respect of inventions).

[38] See Article 27.2, p 287 below.

[39] Some countries, for instance, have considered mandatory regulations for 'plain packaging' of tobacco products (Kur op. cit. (1996), p 114).

15.5. Members shall publish each trademark either before it is registered or promptly after it is registered and shall afford a reasonable opportunity for petitions to cancel the registration. In addition, Members may afford an opportunity for the registration of a trademark to be opposed.

Transparency in the process of registering trademarks is crucial to reduce the likelihood of confusion and to protect legitimate interests of third parties.

Article 15.5, first sentence, imposes an obligation with respect to the publication of a trademark 'before it is registered or promptly after it is registered'. Members shall also afford 'a reasonable opportunity' for petitions to cancel the registration (Article 15.5). National laws normally include provisions to this effect.

The wording of this provision leaves Members with considerable flexibility in various respects. First, Members may decide how to 'publish' each trademark, including by cost-saving digital means (eg through a web page). Second, they can determine what is meant by 'promptly' after registration.[40] Finally, the wording 'reasonable opportunity' leaves many aspects to Members' discretion, such as when and how such opportunity is to be given, and on which grounds. It does not specify either against which standard the reasonableness of the afforded opportunity will be judged. Since the procedures relating to the acquisition of rights are specifically addressed in Part IV of the TRIPS Agreement,[41] it may be presumed that 'reasonable' refers here to the conditions under which a third party may exercise a right to petition the cancellation of a registration. The Agreement is silent about the grounds that may determine such cancellation, leaving the matter to the determinants contained in the Paris Convention and domestic law.

The Paris Convention prescribes a number of grounds for the refusal (or cancellation of a trademark). According to Article 6*quinquies*, a trademark must be refused in the following cases:

B. . . . 1. when they are of such a nature as to infringe rights acquired by third parties in the country where protection is claimed;

2. when they are devoid of any distinctive character, or consist exclusively of signs or indications which may serve, in trade, to designate the kind, quality, quantity, intended purpose, value, place of origin, of the goods, or the time of production, or have become customary in the current language or in the bona fide and established practices of the trade of the country where protection is claimed;

3. when they are contrary to morality or public order and, in particular, of such a nature as to deceive the public. It is understood that a mark may not be considered contrary to public order for the sole reason that it does not conform to a provision of the legislation on marks, except if such provision itself relates to public order. This provision is subject, however, to the application of Article 10*bis*.'

---

[40] 'Promptly' is also used in the TRIPS Agreement's Article 31(b) (regarding information on governmental non-commercial use of a patent), Articles 54 and 58 (the importer the applicant, and the importer and right-holder, respectively, shall be promptly notified of the suspension of the release of goods).   [41] See Chapter 14 below.

In addition, trademarks must be denied in the case of well-known marks (Article 6*bis*),[42] and when they are in conflict with state flags and symbols (Article 6*ter*).

Domestic laws may, in addition, establish other grounds for the refusal of a trademark registration, such as when use has not taken place within a period exceeding three years from the date of application,[43] or lack of entitlement of the applicant, as ruled in the *United States–Section 211 Omnibus Appropriations Act of 1998* case, where the panel and the AB endorsed the US interpretation that Articles 15 and 16 of the TRIPS Agreement do not regulate the issue of ownership of trademarks, a matter entirely left to national legislation.[44]

Moreover, in line with Article 6(1) of the Paris Convention, the Members' right to determine, according to its national legislation, the conditions for the filing and registration of trademarks, was confirmed by the AB.[45]

Opposition procedures are generally established by national laws, in order to provide an opportunity to challenge an application before the granting of the trademark. This possibility is explicitly recognized, as a faculty of Member countries, by Article 15.5, second sentence, without any limitation with respect to whom may exercise the right to oppose.

It is interesting to note that, although pre-grant opposition is also applicable in the case of patents (and many countries in fact have established it), in the TRIPS Agreement's section on patents there is no equivalent to Article 15.5, second sentence. Pre-opposition procedures may significantly contribute to avoiding the wrong granting of patents. However, the US has succeeded in banning that possibility in some recent FTAs.[46]

Rights conferred

16.1. The owner of a registered trademark shall have the exclusive right to prevent all third parties not having the owner's consent from using in the course of trade identical or similar signs for goods or services which are identical or similar to those in respect of which the trademark is registered where such use would result in a likelihood of confusion. In case of the use of an identical sign for identical goods or services, a likelihood of confusion shall be presumed. The rights described above shall not prejudice any existing prior rights, nor shall they affect the possibility of Members making rights available on the basis of use.

---

[42] See pp 188–92 below.   [43] See commentary on Article 15.3 above.

[44] See Appellate Body Report, WT/DS176/AB/R, 2 January 2002, paras 189–95.

[45] Idem, paras 122–48.

[46] See, eg, Article 15.9.5 ('Where a Party provides proceedings that permit a third party to oppose the grant of a patent, a Party shall not make such proceedings available before the grant of the patent') of the US–Morocco FTA, available at <http://www.ustr.gov/assets/Trade_Agreements/Bilateral/ Morocco_FTA/FInal_Text/asset_upload_file797_3849.pdf> (last accessed on 28 September 2005).

Article 16.1 explicitly defines the exclusive rights of the trademark owner. Like other provisions in the TRIPS Agreement, this article sets out minimum standards.[47]

Article 16.1 is clearly a 'Paris-plus' provision, as the Paris Convention had left the definition of trademark rights to the Contracting Parties and only provided, in Article 10*bis*(3), protection against unfair competition—which by definition does not confer exclusive rights—against acts that create confusion with the goods, establishment, or activities of a competitor.

The exclusive rights are only granted, according to the first sentence of Article 16.1, to 'the owner of a registered trademark'.[48] However, the third sentence provides that the exclusive rights shall not 'affect the possibility of Members making rights available on the basis of use'. This provision allows countries where use confers trademarks' rights to continue with that possibility. As the third sentence refers to 'rights' and not 'exclusive rights', there is no obligation to grant exclusive rights on the basis of use.

It has been suggested that protection of unregistered trademarks should only be conferred when use has resulted in a certain degree of public awareness or 'trade recognition'.[49] However, the extent to which Members can make *use* of the basis for the granting of rights is not subject to any particular characteristics of use, thereby deferring to the national law the determination of the conditions under which use can create rights.

The use of the term 'owner' and the reference to his 'consent' reinforces the notion that trademark owners enjoy the right to exclude others from the use of their property.[50] However, as indicated by the AB in *United States–Section 211 Omnibus Appropriations Act of 1998*, this provision (nor any other provision in the TRIPS Agreement) does not set out the conditions to claim ownership of a trademark, a matter exclusively subject to national law. The AB held in this regard that

As we read it, Article 16 confers on the *owner* of a registered trademark an internationally agreed minimum level of 'exclusive rights' that all WTO Members must guarantee in their domestic legislation. These exclusive rights protect the owner against infringement of the registered trademark by unauthorized third parties (*footnote omitted*).[51]

We underscore that Article 16.1 confers these exclusive rights on the 'owner' of a registered trademark. As used in this treaty provision, the ordinary meaning of 'owner' can be defined as the proprietor or the person who holds the title or dominion of the property constituted by the trademark (*footnote omitted*). We agree with the Panel that this ordinary meaning does not clarify how the ownership of a trademark is to be determined (*footnote omitted*). Also, we agree with the Panel that Article 16.1 does not, in express terms, define

---

[47] See WT/DS176/AB/R, 2 January 2002, para 186.
[48] The same sentence *in fine* also refers to goods or services 'in respect of which the trademark is registered'.   [49] Kur op. cit. (1996), p 104.
[50] This emphasis is in contrast to the rights conferred in the sections of the TRIPS Agreement on geographical indications and undisclosed information, whereunder no exclusive rights are mandated. See Chapters 7 and 11 below.   [51] See WT/DS176/AB/R, 2 January 2002, para 186.

how ownership of a registered trademark is to be determined. Article 16.1 confers exclusive rights on the 'owner', but Article 16.1 does not tell us who the 'owner' *is*.[52]

Based on a textual analysis of the Paris Convention and the TRIPS Agreement, the AB concluded that 'neither Article 16.1 of the *TRIPS Agreement*, nor any other provision of either the *TRIPS Agreement* and the Paris Convention (1967), determines who owns or who does not own a trademark'.[53]

The exclusive rights conferred are subject to several conditions and limitations. First, such rights only apply in relation to the use of a trademark 'in the course of trade', that is, in commercial activities. Hence, such rights do not control the use of trademarks, for instance, in writings not intended to promote sales of the trademarked products and services, or as a domain name.[54]

Second, the exclusive right is only conferred with regard to 'identical or similar signs for goods or services which are identical or similar to those in respect of which the trademark is registered'. Counterfeiting is the main threat to trademark owners. The TRIPS Agreement provides, in Part III, for measures (such as criminal sanctions) specifically applicable to trademarks (and copyright).[55]

Article 16.1 leaves ample room to Member countries for determining when two trademarks are to be deemed 'similar'. Similarity may by be judged phonetically, visually, or graphically, but the standards applied vary among countries and generally have been developed by case law.

Third, the use of the trademark should result in a 'likelihood of confusion'. This requirement, which breaks new ground in international trademark law,[56] implies that a mere possibility of confusion is not sufficient for legitimizing the exercise of the exclusive rights. The meaning of 'confusion' should be understood in the light of Article 15.1; that is, in relation to the capacity of a trademark to distinguish identical or similar goods or services of one undertaking from those of another. For an infringement to be found under this rule, the infringing trademark need not be identical to the registered mark; it would also apply if that trademark is similar and a likelihood of confusion exists.

Finally, Article 16.1 does not refer to the possibility of preventing the registration of an identical or similar trademark, but only its use. In fact, Article 15.5, as examined above, stipulates that Members *may* provide for an opposition system, but it does not oblige thereto. It establishes, instead, the obligation to 'afford a reasonable opportunity for petitions to cancel the registration'.

Article 16.1 alludes to the right to exclude the use under certain conditions. It is clearly provided for as a negative right, and not as the right to use the trademark.[57]

---

[52] Idem, para 187.   [53] Idem, para 195.
[54] See, eg, UNCTAD-ICTSD op. cit. (2005), p 236; G Cabanellas de las Cuevas, 'El uso atípico de la marca ajena', (1999) Temas de Derecho Industrial y de la Competencia, No 3, pp 39–77.
[55] See pp 448–50 below.   [56] See Dratler op. cit. (1996), para 1A-75.
[57] In *European Communities–Protection of trademarks and geographical indications for agricultural products and foodstuffs*, WT/DS174/R, 15 March 2005, the panel held that 'the TRIPS Agreement does not generally provide for the grant of positive rights to exploit or use certain subject matter, but

However, Article 20 of the TRIPS Agreement, as examined below, stipulates some positive rights with respect to the mode of use of a trademark.

Article 16.1 leaves Members the determination of the circumstances under which goods or services are 'similar',[58] as well as when 'confusion' is likely to exist. National laws and case law have developed criteria to determine when such confusion may be validly alleged.[59] Under that Article, the likelihood of confusion seems to be, by itself, sufficient to prohibit third parties from using a similar trademark, without the burden to prove that use causes injury to the trademark owner or that there is deception of the public.

Article 16.1 further stipulates that 'in case of the use of an identical sign for identical goods or services, a likelihood of confusion shall be presumed'. The text does not clarify whether this presumption may or may not admit proof to the contrary, unlike Article 34.1 of the Agreement, relating to process patents.[60] However, there is no reason to think that an alleged infringer could not prove that such likelihood does not exist. Hence, this provision may be interpreted as only requiring a *juris tantum* presumption. Further, given the freedom to choose the method of implementing TRIPS obligations, the presumption may be established by law (like in the case of Germany, Australia, New Zealand, India, etc) or applied through courts' interpretation, as in the case of the US and Japan.[61]

Unlike the corresponding provision of the TRIPS Agreement on patents, Article 16.1 does not explicitly refer to the exclusive right to import the protected goods or services (Article 28.1). An important point left to national laws is the extent to which parallel imports may be admissible. Article 6 of the TRIPS Agreement—which applies to all rights covered in the Agreement, including trademarks—has avoided a straightforward definition on the matter, but allows any Member to apply the principle of exhaustion of rights on an international basis and, hence, to admit parallel imports irrespective of its origin. Given that the Agreement stipulates minimum standards, a Member can prevent parallel imports while other Members not doing so could not be considered as infringing the TRIPS Agreement provisions.

The third sentence of Article 16.1, finally, stipulates that the conferred exclusive rights 'shall not prejudice any existing prior rights'. This safeguard may apply to cases in which third parties used a trademark prior to its registration, concurrently with the trademark owner, a possibility often allowed under domestic laws.

---

rather provides for the grant of negative rights to prevent certain acts. This fundamental feature of intellectual property protection inherently grants Members freedom to pursue legitimate public policy objectives since many measures to attain those public policy objectives lie outside the scope of intellectual property rights and do not require an exception under the TRIPS Agreement (at para 7.210).

[58] 'Similar' means 'like, alike; having mutual resemblance or resemblance to; of the same kind, nature or amount; (geom.) shaped alike', *Concise Oxford Dictionary*, (1982: Oxford University Press, 7th edn), p 985.

[59] See, eg, Cornish, op. cit. (1989) p 449; F Polaud-Dulian, *Droit de la proprieété industrielle* (Paris: 1999, Montchrestien) pp 654–6. [60] See pp 344–6 below.

[61] See, eg, Watal op. cit. (2001), p 254.

This provision might also be interpreted to the effect that the rules of Article 16.1 are not intended to have an effect on trademark rights that arose prior to the entry into force of the TRIPS Agreement, and that such uses might continue thereafter. However, similar situations would not be permitted to arise after that date.[62]

It is to be noted that in *United States–Section 211 Omnibus Appropriations Act of 1998* the European Communities held that that there was an equation in Article 16.1 between the owner of the trademark and the 'undertakings' whose goods or services are distinguished by the trademark. The AB rejected this argument and noted that

Article 16.1 of the *TRIPS Agreement* refers to the 'owner of a registered trademark' and to the 'goods or services' in respect of which trademarks are used. Unlike Article 15.1, Article 16.1 does not include the word 'undertakings'. Nor does it mention the owner of the goods or services for which the trademark is used. So, unlike the European Communities, we fail to see any basis in Article 16.1 for the assertion that this provision equates the owner of a trademark with the undertaking whose goods or services are distinguished by the trademark.[63]

> 16.2. Article *6bis* of the Paris Convention (1967) shall apply, *mutatis mutandis*, to services. In determining whether a trademark is well-known, Members shall take account of the knowledge of the trademark in the relevant sector of the public, including knowledge in the Member concerned which has been obtained as a result of the promotion of the trademark.

Perhaps the greatest contribution of TRIPS in terms of higher standards for the protection of trademarks is the clearly 'Paris-plus'[64] provision contained in Article 16.2. This article makes Article *6bis* of the Paris Convention—which only refers to well-known trademarks used in respect of identical or similar *goods*—applicable, *mutatis mutandis*, to services. This extension reflects the growing importance of services in the contemporary economy and of service trademarks in domestic and international trade.[65]

The main innovation of Article 16.2, however, is the broadening vis-à-vis the Paris Convention (Article *6bis*) of the factors to determine the existence of a well-known trademark that is subject to special protection. Rather than introducing a full new provision, the Agreement expanded the application of Article *6bis* of the Convention. This implies that the interpretation given to Article *6bis*, and the history of its negotiation, will have considerable weight in the interpretation of Article 16.2.[66]

[62] See UNCTAD-ICTSD op. cit. (2005), p 238, which stresses the ambiguity of this part of the provision, and that 'prior' may refer to the date of entry into force of the Agreement rather than to the date of trademark registration. However, in cases where the Agreement refers to its date of application it clarifies whether it refers to the general date or the date of application for a Member, a clarification absent here.

[63] WT/DS176/AB/R, 2 January 2002, para 192.

[64] That is, a solution which goes beyond the standards of the Paris Convention for the Protection of Industrial Property.

[65] See, eg, M Kostecki, 'International trade in services', in B Hocking and S McGuire, *Trade Politics. International, Domestic and Regional Perspectives* (1999: London, Routledge) p 68.

[66] Panels and the Appellate Body have extensively used the negotiating history of the Conventions that are specifically referred to by the TRIPS Agreement to confirm the interpretation reached by

'Well-known' trademarks are defined neither in the Paris Convention nor in the TRIPS Agreement. There is, hence, considerable leeway for Members to determine when knowledge of the trademark is sufficient to consider it as 'well-known'. The determination of whether a trademark is well known is left to the government or courts of the Member where protection is sought. The TRIPS Agreement indicates *where* such knowledge should exist ('relevant sector of the public' in the country where protection is sought) and through which *acts* can it be obtained (use and promotion), but it does not define the *level* of knowledge required to obtain the special protection.[67]

Article 16.2 introduces, however, some criteria to determine when a trademark may be regarded as 'well known'. A first significant difference between the protection granted to well-known trademarks in the Paris Convention and the TRIPS Agreement is that under the latter it is sufficient to prove knowledge of the trademark 'in the relevant sector of the public'. This requires Members to grant special protection to signs that may be unknown to the general public, but familiar to a group of consumers. How a 'sector of the public' may be defined is left to domestic law, but may certainly include certain types of users (eg, health providers for medical equipment) or groups of consumers identified by income levels, habits, education, geographical location, etc. Even a small segment of the public may be deemed a 'relevant sector of the public' if certain goods or services are intended to or reasonably expected to be known by it.

A second important difference between Article 16.2 and the Paris Convention lies in that not only the use but also the 'knowledge' in a country resulting from the 'promotion' of the trademark should be taken into account to provide protection.[68] In accordance with one commentator, the latter is

an obvious attempt to resolve a problem that frequently arises in merchandising. Very often a successful property cannot be merchandised in all countries at the same time. It begins to take off in some countries, and is then pirated in other countries by people who see it in the original country and use it without permission. In traditional trademark law this may be difficult to prevent (although recent developments in various countries indicate a new trend disregarding the territorial restrictions in trademark protection).[69]

The existence of promotion, even if intense, of a trademark would not be sufficient to consider it as a well-known sign. Knowledge of the trademark must be a

---

application of Article 31 of the Vienna Convention. See, eg, C Correa, 'The TRIPS Agreement from the perspective of developing countries', in P Macrory, A Appleton, and M Plummer (eds), in *The World Trade Organization: Legal, Economic and Political Analysis* (2005: New York, Springer), vol. II, pp 429–30. See also Chapter 14.

[67] Thus, different parameters may be established with regard, for instance, to the percentage of the 'relevant sector of the public' that should be aware of the trademark.

[68] According to the Trade Marks Ordinance 2001 of Pakistan, for instance, a well-known trademark is protected on the basis of its 'reputation in Pakistan'. The law does not require actual use of the well-known trademark in the country.

[69] S Cohen, 'GATT TRIPS and character merchandising', (1993) Trademark Law, June, p 25.

'result of the promotion of the trademark'. However, the effective knowledge of the trademark is the relevant standard. Hence, it would be immaterial for the recognition of a well-known trademark if such knowledge was reached by other means.[70]

The consideration of the notoriety of a trademark independently of its actual use in the territory where the protection is sought, for the purposes of obtaining the special protection as a well-known trademark, had been rejected in the Conference of Lisbon for the revision of the Paris Convention.[71] The acceptance of mere notoriety under the TRIPS Agreement is consistent with the concept of trademarks as a means to distinguish the marked products from those of other firms. But a trademark will rarely become associated to certain features and quality of a product or services without their actual commercialization in the relevant country. There might be exceptions, for instance, in the case of durable goods, such as certain well-known cars, but this will not be the situation for most consumer goods.

The dissociation of the concept of a well-known trademark from the effective use thereof has implications for determining which is the 'relevant' sector of the public to be taken into account. There is no actual market for a product or service when knowledge thereof is acquired through mere promotion. The question arises whether only potential consumers (those, for instance, with sufficient income to afford the product or service in question) would constitute the 'relevant sector' or whether it could be enlarged to include those that are out of the potential market.

Although the US proposal during the TRIPS negotiations aimed at a determination of the degree of knowledge of a trademark on the basis of its 'use and promotion in international trade',[72] the degree to which the 'promotion' of the trademark makes it well known depends on the knowledge reached in the country where protection is sought. The wording of the examined provision 'can hardly be taken for a sufficient basis to take into account (inter alia) the international fame of the mark in assessing its notoriety'.[73] Article 16.2 makes clear, in fact, that knowledge of the trademark through promotion should exist 'in the Member concerned'. Promotion in a country different from the one where protection is sought would not suffice to consider a trademark as well-known.[74]

Work initiated in WIPO soon after the adoption of the TRIPS Agreement led to the approval of a Joint Recommendation Concerning Provisions on the Protection of Well-Known Marks by the WIPO General Assembly and the Assembly of the

[70] Article 16.2 requires Members to 'take account of the knowledge of the trademark..., *including* knowledge... which has been obtained as a result of the promotion of the trademark' (emphasis added).
[71] See, eg, Kur op. cit. (1996), p 105.   [72] See MTN.GNG/NG11/W/70, 11 May 1990.
[73] See Kur op. cit. (1996), p 106, who notes unjustified attempts to interpret 'knowledge in the Member concerned' as relating not to the country where protection is sought, but to the country of origin of the trademark, with the implication that a trademark well known in a Member would deserve automatic protection in *any* other Member (idem, 107). In some countries, however, case law has permitted the protection of well-known trademarks on the basis of trans-border reputation, even when the trademarks had only been marginally present in the country. See, eg, Watal op. cit. (2001), p 256.
[74] *Contra* Gervais op. cit. (2003), p 174.

Paris Union, in September 1999. This 'soft-law', non-binding instrument, substantially expands the concept of well-known trademarks, beyond the boundaries of the TRIPS Agreement. It states factors that may be considered for determining when a trademark is well known,[75] as well as factors that should not be required.[76] The Joint Recommendation also provides a definition of the concept of 'relevant sector of the public'.[77] The economic case for the broadening of the notion of well-known trademarks is unclear. It may certainly facilitate global marketing strategies of large companies actively engaged in international trade, at the price,

---

[75] Article 2: (1) [*Factors for Consideration*] (a) In determining whether a mark is a well-known mark, the competent authority shall take into account any circumstances from which it may be inferred that the mark is well known.

(b) In particular, the competent authority shall consider information submitted to it with respect to factors from which it may be inferred that the mark is, or is not, well known, including, but not limited to, information concerning the following: 1. the degree of knowledge or recognition of the mark in the relevant sector of the public; 2. the duration, extent and geographical area of any use of the mark; 3. the duration, extent and geographical area of any promotion of the mark, including advertising or publicity and the presentation, at fairs or exhibitions, of the goods and/or services to which the mark applies; 4. the duration and geographical area of any registrations, and/or any applications for registration, of the mark, to the extent that they reflect use or recognition of the mark; 5. the record of successful enforcement of rights in the mark, in particular, the extent to which the mark was recognized as well known by competent authorities; 6. the value associated with the mark.

(c) The above factors, which are guidelines to assist the competent authority to determine whether the mark is a well-known mark, are not pre-conditions for reaching that determination. Rather, the determination in each case will depend upon the particular circumstances of that case. In some cases all of the factors may be relevant. In other cases some of the factors may be relevant. In still other cases none of the factors may be relevant, and the decision may be based on additional factors that are not listed in subparagraph (b), above. Such additional factors may be relevant, alone, or in combination with one or more of the factors listed in subparagraph (b), above.

[76] Article 2(3): [*Factors Which Shall Not Be Required*] (a) A Member State shall not require, as a condition for determining whether a mark is a well-known mark: (i) that the mark has been used in, or that the mark has been registered or that an application for registration of the mark has been filed in or in respect of, the Member State; (ii) that the mark is well known in, or that the mark has been registered or that an application for registration of the mark has been filed in or in respect of, any jurisdiction other than the Member State; or (iii) that the mark is well known by the public at large in the Member State. (b) Notwithstanding subparagraph (a)(ii), a Member State may, for the purpose of applying paragraph (2)(d), require that the mark be well known in one or more jurisdictions other than the Member State.

[77] Article 2(2): [*Relevant Sector of the Public*] (a) Relevant sectors of the public shall include, but shall not necessarily be limited to: (i) actual and/or potential consumers of the type of goods and/or services to which the mark applies; (ii) persons involved in channels of distribution of the type of goods and/or services to which the mark applies; (iii) business circles dealing with the type of goods and/or services to which the mark applies.

(b) Where a mark is determined to be well known in at least one relevant sector of the public in a Member State, the mark shall be considered by the Member State to be a well-known mark.

(c) Where a mark is determined to be known in at least one relevant sector of the public in a Member State, the mark may be considered by the Member State to be a well-known mark.

(d) A Member State may determine that a mark is a well-known mark, even if the mark is not well known or, if the Member States applies subparagraph (c), known, in any relevant sector of the public of the Member State.

however, of limiting the room for domestic firms to select and use in good faith their own trademarks, and possibly increasing litigation. As a soft-law instrument, countries are not obliged to apply the Joint Resolution. However, some FTAs signed by the US require the partner countries to be guided by or apply it.[78]

It should be noted, finally, that the use of a trademark in advertising or other promotional material has not been established beyond doubt as sufficient ground to prevent expungement for non-use of a trademark.[79]

> **16.3. Article *6bis* of the Paris Convention (1967) shall apply, *mutatis mutandis*, to goods or services which are not similar to those in respect of which a trademark is registered, provided that use of that trademark in relation to those goods or services would indicate a connection between those goods or services and the owner of the registered trademark and provided that the interests of the owner of the registered trademark are likely to be damaged by such use.**

Under the TRIPS Agreement protection of well-known trademarks is not limited, as in the Paris Convention, to the use of the trademark in respect of identical or similar goods, but it extends to goods or services which are not similar to those in respect of which a trademark is used.[80]

The approach of this article is similar to Article 16.2. It extends, *mutatis mutandis*, the application of Article *6bis* of the Paris Convention (1967) beyond its original boundaries. Its aim is to prevent confusing uses of trademarks and thereby protect a trademark against 'dilution' of its distinguishing merit.

There are three conditions for the application of this provision.

First, the trademark in question must be registered ('... not similar to goods or services which are not similar to those in respect of which a trademark is *registered*') (emphasis added). Registration is not a requirement under Article *6bis* of the Paris Convention, nor under Article 16.2 of the TRIPS Agreement. Article 16.3, hence, significantly departs from the concept underlying the protection of unregistered well-known trademarks. Although the rationale for the reference to Article *6bis* of the Paris Convention is unclear, the limitation of Article 16.3 to

---

[78] For instance, the US–Chile FTA—which includes a TRIPS-plus protection of well-known trademarks—explicitly recognizes the importance of the Joint Recommendation, and requires the Parties to be guided by the principles contained therein. The US–Singapore FTA, moreover, obliges the Parties to comply with Articles 1 to 6 of the Joint Recommendation. See, eg, P Roffe, *Bilateral Agreements and a TRIPS-Plus World: the Chile–USA Free Trade Agreement*, TRIPS Issues paper 4, QUNO, Geneva, 2004. Available from <http://www.geneva.quno.info> (last accessed on 25 September 2005), p 39.

[79] See, eg, WIPO, op. cit. (1988), p 162.

[80] One example of legislation providing for this broad protection is Article 136(h) of Decision 486 (December 2000) of the Andean Community, which prohibits the registration of signs which 'constitute a reproduction, imitation, translation, transliteration or transcription of all or part of a well-known distinctive sign the owner of which is a third party, regardless of the goods or services to which the sign is applied, where their use would be liable to create a risk of confusion or association with that third party or with his goods or services, constitute misappropriation of the prestige of the sign or dilution of its distinctive power or commercial or advertising value'.

registered trademarks cannot be seen, in the light of the interpretive principles of the Vienna Convention, just as a drafting mistake.[81]

Second, the use of the trademark in relation to non-similar goods or services should indicate a connection between those goods or services and the owner of the registered trademark. Indicating a connection does not necessarily mean that there should be confusion, or likelihood of confusion, with the products or services of the owner of the registered trademark for this provision to apply. However, given that Article 6*bis* of the Paris Convention applies '*mutatis mutandis*', Article 16.3 of the TRIPS Agreement read in conjunction with said Article of the Convention may be interpreted as requiring both that the use indicates a connection to the trademark owner[82] and that a likelihood of creating confusion exists.

Third, the protection is only conferred where the interests of the owner of the registered trademark are likely to be damaged by such use. Only the likelihood of damages arising from a use that suggests a connection with the trademark owner is to be taken into account. The provision requires a likelihood of damage, not actual damage. The mere possibility of damage, however, would not be sufficient to sustain a case. It will be up to the owner of the well-known trademark to prove that such likelihood of damage exists (since this cannot be presumed), and to the courts of the country where protection is sought to determine what proof should be produced in order to substantiate such a claim.

The concept of damage to the interests of the trademark owner suggests that the aim of protection is the *reputation* of the trademark,[83] rather than its distinctive function.[84] As noted above, however, the likelihood of confusion also comes into the picture via the reference to Article 6*bis* of the Paris Convention.

Exceptions

17. Members may provide limited exceptions to the rights conferred by a trademark, such as fair use of descriptive terms, provided that such exceptions take account of the legitimate interests of the owner of the trademark and of third parties.

---

[81] See the arguments in this sense of Kur, based on the history of the negotiation of Article 16.3 (Kur op. cit. (1996), p 106).

[82] It is to be noted that the indication of connection with the trademark owner under this provision should stem from the *use* of the trademark. Other types of indications that suggest such a connection could be dealt with under other rules, such as passing off and unfair competition, or constitute a trademark or trade name infringement.   [83] See, eg, UNCTAD-ICTSD op. cit. (2005), p 241.

[84] Some national laws distinguish between 'well-known' trademarks, which are to be protected when used with regard to identical or similar goods, and 'famous' trademarks, which need to be protected against use in any class of goods and services. 'Defensive' registration of trademarks, with weaker use requirements, is also allowed in some countries for preventing wrongful registration of well-known trademarks by third parties for non identical or similar goods or services. See Watal op. cit. (2001), pp 256–7.

Exceptions to exclusive rights may be determined by national laws, provided that they are 'limited' and that they 'take into account of the legitimate interests of the owner of the trademark and of third parties'. A typical exception (explicitly referred to by Article 17) is the case of fair use of descriptive terms.

The wording in this provision echoes that of Articles 13 and 30 of the TRIPS Agreement, but it does not encompass the three-step test. Article 17 does not establish an exception per se; it only allows Members to do so subject to three conditions:

(a) The exception must be 'limited'. Article 17 follows the wording of Article 30, which was examined in detail in the *Canada—Patent Protection for Pharmaceutical Products*,[85] where the panel provided a narrow interpretation of what 'limited' means in Article 30. It argued that 'the word "exception" by itself connotes a limited derogation, one that does not undercut the body of rules from which it is made ... The term "limited exception" must therefore be read to connote a narrow exception—one which makes only a small diminution of the rights in question'.[86]

The Panel concluded that the text should be read literally, focusing on the extent to which legal rights have been curtailed, rather than the size or extent of the economic impact. In support of this conclusion, the Panel noted that the following two conditions of Article 30 ask more particularly about the economic impact of the exception, and provide two sets of standards by which such impact may be judged.[87] Only one of such conditions, however, is mentioned in Article 17.

A question arises as to the extent to which the interpretation in *Canada–Patent Protection for Pharmaceutical Products* may be applied to Article 17. There is no compelling reason to adopt the panel's interpretation in that case—which dealt with patents—in the area of trademarks, and the analysis of 'limited' may well take into account the extent of the economic implications thereof. Hence, an exception with little economic effects might be permitted under Article 17.

(b) The exception should 'take account of the legitimate interests of the owner of the trademark and of third parties. In *Canada–Patent Protection for Pharmaceutical Products* and in *United States–Section 110(5) of the US Copyright Act*, the concept of 'legitimate interests' was addressed.

In the Canada case, the panel stated that:

To make sense of the term 'legitimate interests' in this context, that term must be defined in the way that it is often used in legal discourse—as a normative claim calling for protection of interests that are 'justifiable' in the sense that they are supported by relevant public policies or other social norms. This is the sense of the word that often appears in statements such as 'X has no legitimate interest in being able to do Y'.[88]

---

[85] WT/DS114/R (2000).   [86] Idem, para 7.30.
[87] The interpretation of the second and third conditions of Article 30 are explained below.
[88] WT/DS114/R (2000), para 7.69.

In *United States–Section 110(5) of the US Copyright Act,* the panel adopted a more positivist perspective. It argued that 'one—albeit incomplete and thus conservative—way of looking at legitimate interests is the economic value of the exclusive rights conferred by copyright on their holders'.[89] However, it observed that the term 'legitimate' also had 'the connotation of legitimacy from a more normative perspective, in the context of calling for the protection of interests that are justifiable in the light of the objectives that underlie the protection of exclusive rights'.[90]

(c) The exception should 'take account of the legitimate interests ... of third parties'.

The legitimate interests of third parties are put in Article 17 on the same footing as the legitimate interests of the owner of the trademark. This means that in case of tension between those interests, the trademark owner's legitimate interest should not be deemed to necessarily prevail over third parties' interests.

Article 17 illustrates a 'limited exception' with the case of 'fair use of descriptive terms'. Legal doctrine generally defines this exception (or defence) as the reasonable and good faith use of a descriptive term that is another's trademark to describe rather than to identify the user's goods, services or business,[91] such as the use of the trademark in news, magazines, commentaries, and other writings. Other possible exceptions include the good faith use of one person's name, address or pseudonym, the use of a name that indicates the purpose of a product,[92] and the use of a trademark for comparative advertising, which is deemed legal in many countries. Exceptions may also be grounded on public interest considerations. For instance, disputes have arisen in some countries with regard to the registration and use as a trademark of the colour of medicines, which helps patients to distinguish some pills from others. Although it may be argued that in this case the colour performs a *function* that trademark law does not protect, the use of the colour by a competitor may be deemed safeguarded as an exception based on public health reasons.[93]

The exceptions allowed under Article 17 may apply with regard to both registered and unregistered trademarks, as it would be illogical to differentiate between them for this purpose.

The applicability of Article 17 to some cases involving public health interest was discussed in Canada, in relation to the government's initiative to require plain packaging for tobacco products, and to standardize the size, shape, and colour of bioequivalent oral dosage forms of medicines, notwithstanding any trademarks' rights in the products' appeararence.[94]

---

[89] WT/DS114/R (2000), para 6.227.   [90] Idem, para 6.224.
[91] See, eg, L Rich, Fair Use of Trademarks (2002), available at <http://www.publaw.com> (last accessed on 28 June 2005).   [92] See Kur op. cit. (1996), p 108.
[93] See, eg, UNCTAD-ICTSD op. cit. (2005), pp 242–3.
[94] See J Keon, 'Intellectual property rules for trademarks and geographical indications: important parts of the New World Trade Order', in C Correa and A Yusuf op. cit. (1998), p 172.

Term of protection

18. Initial registration, and each renewal of registration, of a trademark shall be for a term of no less than seven years. The registration of a trademark shall be renewable indefinitely.

Unlike the Paris Convention, which contains no minimum term of protection, the TRIPS Agreement stipulates that the initial and successive renewals of trademarks shall be at least for seven years.[95] National laws have differed on this issue, and they may continue to do so to the extent that the minimum seven-year term is respected.

The registration of a trademark shall be renewable indefinitely. In fact, a trademark may potentially last forever, although ownership may change over time (by succession or assignment). An important question is whether national authorities may require proof of use in order to renew a trademark, or accept third parties' opposition to renewal due to lack of use. The TRIPS Agreement does not forbid any of these possibilities. If use can be required—after a certain period—to maintain registration (see the commentary on Article 19 of the TRIPS Agreement that follows), Members can equally require use as a condition for renewal,[96] to the extent that they are not interested in keeping in force unused trademarks.

Use as a condition to maintain registration

19.1. If use is required to maintain a registration, the registration may be cancelled only after an uninterrupted period of at least three years of non-use, unless valid reasons based on the existence of obstacles to such use are shown by the trademark owner. Circumstances arising independently of the will of the owner of the trademark which constitute an obstacle to the use of the trademark, such as import restrictions on or other government requirements for goods or services protected by the trademark, shall be recognized as valid reasons for non-use.

19.2. When subject to the control of its owner, use of a trademark by another person shall be recognized as use of the trademark for the purpose of maintaining the registration.

The maintenance of trademarks which are not effectively used creates a burden for national registration offices and may block the eventual registration of signs by potential users. Many national laws impose use as a condition to keep a trademark

---

[95] Developed countries argued during the TRIPS negotiations for a ten-year minimum term, while developing countries wanted that the matter be deferred entirely to national laws (see Annex).

[96] However, in a TRIPS-plus provision, the Trademark Law Treaty prevents the competent authorities from requesting proof of use of a trademark for its renewal. See Article 13(4)(iii) of the Treaty.

in force. The Paris Convention legitimized such a requirement,[97] subject to some general conditions which are further developed in Article 19 of the TRIPS Agreement.

Article 19 specifies the 'reasonable period' of the Paris Convention by requiring an uninterrupted period of at least three years of non-use in order to cancel a registration. However, said article does not define from which date that period should be counted. Members may, hence, opt for different solutions, such as to count it from the date of registration of the trademark or of its renewal. It may also be required, as is the case under some national laws,[98] that a trademark be cancelled if it had not been used during an interrupted period before a request for cancellation was filed.

Article 19 is also more precise than the Paris Convention on the possible excuses for non-use. The non-use cannot lead to the cancellation of a trademark if the trademark owner can show valid reasons for non-use 'based on the existence of obstacles to such use'. Several conditions emerge from this provision.

First, the alleged reasons must be 'valid', thereby suggesting that there might be reasons that need not be taken into account (eg, if non-use was imposed by a court in order to deter an illegal conduct).

Second, there must be an 'obstacle' and not merely inconvenience or commercial preferences. An 'obstacle' is a 'thing that obstructs progress',[99] such as a commercial barrier that impeded commercialization of a marked good or service.[100]

Third, the valid reasons must be proven by the trademark owner. This could be done either before an administrative authority or a court, according to the applicable procedures (subject to the provisions in Part III of the Agreement).

The burden of proof that a trademark has been used entirely lies with the trademark owner.[101] Members have retained considerable flexibility to establish under which conditions 'use' of a trademark may be deemed to have occurred, depending on the evidence produced. Thus, it would be up to the competent authority or

---

[97] Article 5C(1) of the Paris Convention: 'If, in any country, use of the registered mark is compulsory, the registration may be cancelled only after a reasonable period, and then only if the person concerned does not justify his inaction.'

[98] See, eg, Article 26 of Argentine Law on Trademarks No 22.632 (Boletin Oficial, 2 January 1981).

[99] *The Concise Oxford Dictionary* (1982: Oxford University Press, 7th edn), p 701.

[100] An issue open to interpretation is whether the generally long procedures needed to obtain marketing approval of a medicine could be considered an 'obstacle' under this provision. See, eg, Dratler op. cit. (1996), para 1A-79.

[101] In *United States–Section 110(5) of the US Copyright Act* the European Communities argued—as they did in relation to Article 16.1—that Article 19.1 seems also to equate the 'owner of the trademark' with the 'undertaking' using it. The AB rejected this argument: 'we note that Article 19.1 addresses the situation where a Member's domestic legislation requires use of the trademark for the purposes of maintaining its registration and those circumstances when use by a person other than the owner of the trademark is recognized as use for the purposes of maintaining a registration. Here, as well, there is no mention of the "undertaking" that uses the trademark for its goods or services. Thus, here, too, unlike the European Communities, we find no basis for viewing this provision as relevant to the argument the European Communities is making' (WT/DS114/R (2000), para 193).

courts to consider when the use has been effective. They may eventually regard occasional minimal uses or uses only in promotion, as insufficient to justify the preservation of a trademark. The use of trademarks on the Internet may be recognized as valid use insofar as it is effectively associated with electronic commerce.

Article 19 mandates the recognition of 'circumstances arising independently of the will of the owner of the trademark which constitute an obstacle to the use of the trademark' as valid reasons for non-use. It also provides the example of 'import restrictions on or other government requirements for goods or services protected by the trademark'.

This provision means that permissible obstacles independent of the will of the trademark owner must be considered as valid reasons for non-use.[102] Logically excluded are circumstances deliberately generated by the trademark owner, for instance, a decision to postpone the marketing of a product for commercial reasons. However, such obstacles are not limited to 'force majeure', that is, to circumstances that could not have been foreseen or that, even if foreseen, could not have been prevented.

Article 19 also implies that to the extent that import restrictions or other government requirements cause the non-use, the trademark owner will have no need to prove that these are 'valid' reasons. This would seem to be the case even if the government restrictions were motivated by public interest, such as the prohibition to commercialize a pharmaceutical product found to have toxic effects. However, the trademark owner may be required to prove that there is an actual cause–effect relationship between the government restrictions and non-use.

The use of a trademark for the purpose of this article may be undertaken by a person different from the title-holder, provided that such a use is 'subject to the control' of the latter (Article 19.2). The expression 'subject to the control' is rather ambiguous,[103] since there may be different criteria to consider when such a situation arises, as in the case of corporate control. Thus, the granting of a licence may not necessarily fulfil this requirement, if it does not encompass the exercise of an actual control by the licensor over the use of the trademark. While the use by a wholly owned subsidiary of the parent company's trademark may be considered to meet such requirement, this may not be clear in cases where other forms of equity or non-equity participation are present. Members have ample room to determine when the control requirement is deemed to be met.

Under some national laws, the lack of appropriate quality control measures enforced by the title-holder may have other direct consequences, as it may be

---

[102] Under the Paris Convention, governments' acts that impeded use of a trademark could arguably be deemed as not sufficient to 'justify' the trademark owners' inaction. See UNCTAD-ICTSD op. cit. (2005), p 245.

[103] In the case of the US, it may be interpreted in the light of the 'related-company doctrine' (Dratler op. cit. (1996), para 1A-79).

deemed as constituting a fraud on the public and lead to the cancellation of the registration.[104]

Although Article 19 does not refer to the situation in which a trademark is used in a modified form, Article 5C(2) of the Paris Convention applies by virtue of Article 2 of the Agreement.[105]

Other requirements

20. The use of a trademark in the course of trade shall not be unjustifiably encumbered by special requirements, such as use with another trademark, use in a special form or use in a manner detrimental to its capability to distinguish the goods or services of one undertaking from those of other undertakings.

This will not preclude a requirement prescribing the use of the trademark identifying the undertaking producing the goods or services along with, but without linking it to, the trademark distinguishing the specific goods or services in question of that undertaking.

National laws have sometimes established obligations to be observed while using registered trademarks. For instance, some developing countries (such as Brazil, Mexico, and India) tried in the past to improve the bargaining power of local joint-venture partners or licensees by requesting that a licensed trademark be used together with a trademark owned by the licensee or another local party. In other cases, trademarks applied to specific products needed, in accordance with legal requirements, to be used jointly with trade-names identifying the enterprises producing them. In certain fields (eg pharmaceuticals), regulations may determine special forms of using trademarks or linking them to the generic names of the relevant products (eg, by imposing that trademarks on the labels appear with the same or a smaller size than that required for the generic names).

Article 20 of the TRIPS Agreement limits the scope of this type of requirement, but only to the extent that they are detrimental to the capability of a trademark to perform its distinguishing function. Several conditions are relevant for the application of this provision.

First, Article 20 refers to use 'in the course of trade'; that is, in commerce. It may be interpreted that uses of a trademark in non-commercial channels (for instance free distribution in hospitals of medicines) would not be subject to the limitation imposed by this Article.

---

[104] D Burge op. cit. (1984), p 141.

[105] Article 5C(2) stipulates that 'Use of a trademark by the proprietor in a form differing in elements which do not alter the distinctive character of the mark in the form in which it was registered in one of the countries of the Union shall not entail invalidation of the registration and shall not diminish the protection granted to the mark.'

Second, the provision applies when 'special' requirements are imposed. If a country would apply general requirements—such as specifications on labelling for tax control or other purposes on all products—Article 20 would arguably not be applicable.

Third, the requirements should *encumber*[106] the use of the trademark. It is an open question whether all special requirements, particularly those enumerated in Article 20 (use with another trademark, use in a special form, or use in a manner detrimental to its capability to distinguish the goods or services of one undertaking from those of other undertakings), would be regarded as banned per se under this provision, or whether a Member could be given the opportunity to demonstrate that the requirement is justified. This latter interpretation seems logical. 'Such as' only seems to indicate what 'special requirements' might exist, but not that they are necessarily unjustifiable.[107] In any case, given the ambiguity of the provision, any Member could legitimately sustain this interpretation.

Fourth, and most importantly, the examined provision only applies when the use of a trademark is 'unjustifiably' encumbered by special requirements.[108] It clearly suggests that there are special requirements that can be justified. For instance, limitations on the size of a trademark in order to give prominence to the generic name of a medicine is justifiable for public health reasons. The same would apply to conditions imposed with an aim to warn the public about the effects of the use of a product (eg tobacco) or restricting the use of trademarks.[109]

The TRIPS Agreement should not stand in the way of measures applied by Members to protect public health or other public interests.[110] According to paragraph 4 of the Doha Declaration on the TRIPS Agreement and Public Health,[111] 'the TRIPS Agreement does not and should not prevent Members from taking measures to protect public health. Accordingly, ... the Agreement can and should be interpreted and implemented in a manner supportive of WTO Members' right to protect public health...'. Moreover, even 'hybrid' marks obliging the use of a local trademark with a foreign trademark may be deemed justified in certain circumstances, if necessary to 'promote the public interest in sectors of vital importance' to the socio-economic and technological development of a Member.[112]

A Member claiming that the use of a trademark is unjustifiably encumbered by special conditions about its use will bear the initial burden of proof in a dispute under the DSU.

---

[106] 'Encumber' means 'hamper (person, movement, action with burden difficulty, etc). *Concise Oxford Dictionary* (1982: Oxford University Press, 7th edn), p 317.

[107] See Gervais op. cit. (2003), p 181.

[108] This concept (as an adjective 'unjustified') is only used in the TRIPS Agreement in Article 4(d) (relating to the MFN clause) and in this Article 20.

[109] Some countries introduced legislation that restricts the use of tobacco trademarks for other products (Kur op. cit. (1996), p 114).

[110] See J Keon, 'Intellectual property rules for trademarks and geographical indications: important parts of the New World Trade Order', in C Correa and A Yusuf op. cit. (1998), p 172.

[111] See pp 104–5 above.

[112] See Article 8.1 of the TRIPS Agreement and Watal op. cit. (2001), p 252.

The second sentence of Article 20 in no case precludes the establishment of a requirement that a trade name[113] be used for the commercialization of goods or services. It clarifies that the limitation imposed in the first sentence of Article 20 does not prevent a Member from prescribing the use of the trade name of the firm that effectively produces the goods or services jointly with the trademark that identifies the latter, provided that they are not linked. The assumption of this sentence is that the trade name and trademark belong to different undertakings, and the precaution about the absence of linkage reflects developed countries' concerns about the possibility of local firms unfairly obtaining advantages from foreign-owned trademarks.[114]

The interpretation of Article 20 was addressed by a panel in the *Indonesia–Cars* case.[115] Under the Indonesian National Car Program, beneficiary companies were required to acquire and maintain an Indonesian-registered trademark in order to obtain the benefits from the Program. The US argued that this requirement and the limitation to use a trademark outside the program amounted to a violation of Article 20. The panel, however, dismissed this aspect of the complaint (which essentially questioned the compatibility of said Program with the Agreement on Subsidies and Countervailing Measures). It held, in synthesis, that there was not a 'requirement' banned under Article 20, since foreign companies entered into collaboration agreements with national companies under the Program on a voluntary basis, and the owner of a trademark would be well aware in advance that the use of the trademark would be restricted. The panel also said that while only Indonesia-owned marks would benefit from the Program, this was not a fact tied to the trademark as such, but rather was a condition of participating in the program.[116]

Licensing and assignment

21. Members may determine conditions on the licensing and assignment of trademarks, it being understood that the compulsory licensing of trademarks shall not be permitted and that the owner of a registered trademark shall have the

---

[113] The TRIPS Agreement does refer to the concept of 'trade name'. The AB, however, found in *United States–Section 211 Omnibus Appropriations Act of 1998* that 'Article 2.1 explicitly incorporates Article 8 of the Paris Convention (1967) into the *TRIPS Agreement*' (para 336) and that 'Article 8 of the Paris Convention (1967) covers only the protection of trade names; Article 8 has no other subject. If the intention of the negotiators had been to exclude trade names from protection, there would have been no purpose whatsoever in including Article 8 in the list of Paris Convention (1967) provisions that were specifically incorporated into the *TRIPS Agreement*. To adopt the Panel's approach would be to deprive Article 8 of the Paris Convention (1967), as incorporated into the *TRIPS Agreement* by virtue of Article 2.1 of that Agreement, of any and all meaning and effect . . .' (para 338). It concluded, in reversing the panel's finding, that 'WTO Members do have an obligation under the *TRIPS Agreement* to provide protection to trade names' (para 341).

[114] See, eg, UNCTAD-ICTSD op. cit. (2005), p 247.

[115] See Report of the Panel, WT/DS54/R, WT/DS55/R, WT/DS59/R, WT/DS64/R, 2 July 1998.

[116] See, eg, UNCTAD-ICTSD op. cit. (2005), p 255; Watal op. cit. (2001), p 252.

right to assign the trademark with or without the transfer of the business to which the trademark belongs.

Finally, the TRIPS Agreement regulates certain aspects of the licensing and assignment of trademarks. It recognizes, as a general principle, that national laws may define the conditions applicable to those acts. Thus, national legislation may establish the obligation to register any license agreement in order to recognize its validity, as in countries that follow British law.

Article 21, however, sets two limits to national legislation:

a) Trademarks cannot be subject to compulsory licensing.

Although there are precedents of compulsory licensing of trademarks,[117] such licences have very rarely been provided for in the field of trademarks. Hence, Article 21 is just a preventive measure against future (in any case, unlikely) regulations allowing for non-voluntary licences for trademarks.

b) A registered trademark can be assigned with or without the transfer of the business to which the trademark belongs.

This standard is a clearly 'Paris-plus' solution, since the Paris Convention allowed contracting parties to establish that in cases where, in accordance with the domestic law, the assignment of a mark is valid only if it takes place at the same time as the transfer of the business or goodwill to which the mark belongs, it shall suffice for the recognition of such validity that the portion of the business or goodwill located in that country be transferred to the assignee, together with the exclusive right to manufacture in the said country, or to sell therein, the goods bearing the mark assigned (Article 6*quater*(1)). This restriction was motivated by the concern that consumers may be deceived about of the source of goods for which the origin may have changed without their knowledge. Accordingly, Article 6*quater*(2) of the Convention does not impose upon the countries of the Union any obligation to regard as valid the assignment of any mark the use of which by the assignee would, in fact, be of such a nature as to mislead the public, particularly as regards the origin, nature, or essential qualities, of the goods to which the mark is applied.

Article 21 of the TRIPS Agreement enshrines the principle of free assignability of trademarks, recognized already in many national laws. A trademark can be transferred independently of the business to which it belonged. The admission of this principle represents, however, a significant departure from the Paris Convention and the concept of trademarks as identifiers of the source of goods and services that is, in fact, reflected in Article 15.1 of the TRIPS Agreement.

---

[117] The US Federal Trade Commission (FTC) proposed in *FTC v Cereal Companies* the creation of five completely new companies and required the major existing firms (Kellogg, General Mills and General Food) to license their trademarks. In *FTC v Borden Company*, the FTC found market dominance in the lemon juice market and the judge decided to compulsorily license the 'Realemon' trademark. See S Goldstein, 'A study of compulsory licensing' (1977) LES, p 124.

The 'business' associated to a trademark may be interpreted as the 'undertaking' or 'enterprise'.[118] Unlike Article *6quater* of the Paris Convention, Article 21 does not refer to the transfer of 'goodwill' but only of 'the business'. 'Goodwill' is the benefit and advantage of the good name, reputation, and connection of a business. It may be protected under unfair competition law (which condemns dishonest commercial practices) or, in common-law countries, under the doctrine of 'passing-off' (the wrong of misrepresenting one's business goods or services as another's, to the latter's injury, generally by using a confusing trademark or trade name). Its protection often encompasses not only the use of trademarks, but also of a particular packaging, 'get up' or 'trade dress' and advertising styles.[119] As a result of that omission in Article 21, it may be argued that Members may subject the assignment of a registered trademark to the transfer of goodwill,[120] particularly where that assignment without the business to which it belonged would mislead the public with regard to the origin, nature, or essential qualities of the goods to which the assigned trademark is applied.[121] Members may also adopt other measures to protect consumers in the context of laws on consumers' protection, such as imposing labelling requirements.

It is to be noted that while the first part of Article 21 refers to trademarks in general, the free assignability principle only applies with regard to *registered* trademarks. Unregistered trademarks, hence, continue to be governed by the more restrictive provision of Article *6quater* of the Paris Convention.

Annex

Negotiating history[122]

In his 23 July 1990 report on the status of work in the TRIPS Negotiating Group, the Chairman (Lars E R Anell) presented two sets of proposals. In an Annex to the report, he presented a composite text that was taken from various proposals by delegations to the Negotiating Group, indicating the source of each proposal by numerical reference to the source document.

---

[118] See, eg, Gervais op. cit. (2003), p 184.

[119] See, eg, L Bently and B Sherman, *Intellectual Property Law* (2001: New York, Oxford University Press), pp 673–8.   [120] See, eg, Gervais op. cit. (2003), p 184.

[121] In some countries, the transfer of a trademark without the goodwill is only possible if the mark had been used in good faith by the assignor in the country. See Watal op. cit. (2001), p 259.

[122] For an analysis of the negotiating history, see UNCTAD-ICTSD op. cit. (2005), pp 214–66.

[123] Chairman's Report to the GNG, Status of Work in the Negotiating Group, Negotiating Group on Trade-Related Aspects of Intellectual Property Rights, including Trade in Counterfeit Goods, MTN.GNG/NG11/W/76, 23 July 1990, presented by the Chairman of the TRIPS Negotiating Group (Lars E R Anell). Alternatives 'A' correspond to texts from developed countries and 'B' from developing countries.

Composite text of July 23 1990[123]

SECTION 2: TRADEMARKS

1. *Protectable Subject Matter*

1A.1 A trademark is a sign capable of distinguishing goods or services of one undertaking from those of other undertakings. It may in particular consist of words and personal names, letters, numerals, the shape of goods and of their packaging, combinations of colours, other graphical representations, or any combination of such signs.

1A.2 Trademarks which are:
- (i) devoid of any distinctive character;
- (ii) of such a nature as to deceive the public, for instance as to the nature, quality or geographical origin of the goods or services; or
- (iii) in conflict with earlier rights,

[shall not be protected] [cannot be validly registered]. Protection may also be denied in particular to trademarks contrary to morality or public order.

1A.3 The term 'trademark' shall include service marks, as well as collective [and] [or] certification marks.

1B PARTIES shall provide protection for trademarks and service marks registered in their territories in compliance with the formalities and requirements laid down in their respective national legislation.

2. *Acquisition of the Right and Procedures*

2A.1 PARTIES shall enable the right to a trademark to be acquired by registration or by use. For the acquisition of the right to a trademark by use, a PARTY may require that the trademark is well-known among consumers or traders of the PARTY.

2A.2 A system for the registration of trademarks shall be provided. The nature of the goods [or services] to which a trademark is to be applied shall in no case form an obstacle to registration of the trademark.

2A.3 [[Actual] use of a trademark prior to [the application for] registration shall not be a condition for registration.] [Use of a trademark may be required as a prerequisite for registration.]

2A.4 PARTIES are encouraged to participate in a system for the international registration of trademarks.

2A.5 PARTIES shall publish each trademark either before it is registered or promptly after it is registered and shall afford other parties a reasonable opportunity to petition to cancel the registration. In addition, PARTIES may afford an opportunity for other parties to oppose the registration of a trademark.

2B Parties shall provide protection for trademarks and service marks registered in their territories in compliance with the formalities and requirements incorporated or laid down in their respective national law.

3. *Rights Conferred*

3.1 [The owner of a registered trademark shall have exclusive rights therein.] The owner of a registered trademark [or service mark] shall be entitled to prevent all third parties not having his consent from using in the course of trade identical or similar signs for goods or services which are identical or similar to those in respect of which the trademark registration has been granted [where such use would result in a likelihood of confusion.] [However, in case of the use of an identical sign for identical goods or services, a likelihood of confusion shall be presumed.]

3.2A Protection for registered or unregistered trademarks shall extend under trademark law or other law to the use in the course of trade of any sign which is identical with, or similar to, the trademark in relation to goods or services which are not similar to those in respect of which the right to the trademark has been acquired, where the latter has a reputation and where use of that sign without due cause takes unfair advantage of, or is detrimental to, the distinctive character or the repute of the trademark.

3.3A PARTIES shall refuse to register or shall cancel the registration and prohibit use of a trademark likely to cause confusion with a trademark of another which is considered to be well-known [in that country]. [This protection shall be extended inter alia against the use of such marks for goods or services which are dissimilar to original goods or services.] [In determining whether a trademark is well-known, the extent of the trademark's use and promotion in international trade must be taken into consideration. A PARTY may not require that the reputation extend beyond the sector of the public which normally deals with the relevant products or services.]

3.4A The owner of a trademark shall be entitled to take action against any unauthorised use which constitutes an act of unfair competition.

4. *Exceptions*

4A Limited exceptions to the exclusive rights conferred by a trademark, such as fair use of descriptive terms, may be made, provided that they take account of the legitimate interests of the proprietor of the trademark and of third parties.

4B Rights shall be subject to exhaustion if the trademarked goods or services are marketed by or with the consent of the owner in the territories of the PARTIES.

5. *Term of Protection*

5A Initial registration of a trademark shall be for a term of no less than ten years. The registration of a trademark shall be renewable indefinitely.

5B It shall be a matter for national legislation to determine the duration of the protection granted.

6. *Requirement of Use*

6.1 If use of a registered trademark is required to maintain the right to a trademark, the registration may be cancelled only after [an uninterrupted period of at least [five years] [three years]] [a reasonable period] of non-use, unless valid reasons based on the existence of obstacles to such use are shown by the trademark owner.

6.2A Use of the trademark by another person with the consent of the owner shall be recognized as use of the trademark for the purpose of maintaining the registration.

6.3A Valid reasons for non-use shall include non-use due to circumstances arising independently of the will of the proprietor of a trademark which constitute an obstacle to the use of the trademark, such as import restrictions on or other governmental requirements for products protected by the trademark.

7. *Other Requirements*

7A The use of a trademark in commerce shall not be [unjustifiably] encumbered by special requirements, such as use with another trademark, a use requirement which reduces the function of the trademark as an indication of source, [or use in a special form].

7B It shall be a matter for national legislation to determine the conditions for the use of a mark.

8. *Licensing and Compulsory Licensing*

8A Compulsory licensing of trademarks shall not be permitted.

8B It will be a matter for national legislation to determine the conditions for the use of a mark. (See also Section 8 below)

9. *Assignment*

9A The right to a [registered] trademark may be assigned with or without the transfer of the undertaking to which the trademark belongs. [PARTIES may require that the goodwill to which the trademark belongs be transferred with the right to the trademark.] [PARTIES may prohibit the assignment of a registered trademark which is identical with, or similar to, a famous mark indicating a state or a local public entity or an agency thereof or a non-profit organisation or enterprise working in the public interest.]

9B It will be a matter for national legislation to determine the conditions for the use or assignment of a mark. (See also Section 8 below)'[124]

Draft text transmitted to the Brussels Ministerial Conference (December 1990)

SECTION 2: TRADEMARKS

Article 17
Protectable Subject Matter

1. Any sign, or any combination of signs, capable of distinguishing the goods or services of one undertaking from those of other undertakings, shall be capable of constituting a trademark. Such signs, in particular words including personal names, letters, numerals, figurative elements and combinations of colours as well as any combination of such signs, shall be eligible for registration as trademarks. Where signs are not inherently capable of distinguishing the relevant goods or services, PARTIES may make registrability depend on distinctiveness acquired through use. PARTIES may require, as a condition of registration, that signs be capable of graphical representation.

---

[124] MTN.GNG/NG11/W/76, 23 July 1990.

2. Paragraph 1 above shall not be understood to prevent a PARTY from denying registration of a trademark on other grounds, provided that they do not derogate from the provisions of the Paris Convention (1967).

3. PARTIES may make registrability depend on use. However, actual use of a trademark shall not be a condition for filing an application for registration. An application shall not be refused solely on the ground that intended use has not taken place before the expiry of a period of 3 years from the date of application.

4. The nature of the goods or services to which a trademark is to be applied shall in no case form an obstacle to registration of the trademark.

5. PARTIES shall publish each trademark either before it is registered or promptly after it is registered and shall afford a reasonable opportunity for petitions to cancel the registration. In addition, PARTIES may afford an opportunity for the registration of a trademark to be opposed.

Article 18
Rights Conferred

1. The owner of a registered trademark shall have the exclusive right to prevent all third parties not having his consent from using in the course of trade identical or similar signs for goods or services which are identical or similar to those in respect of which the trademark is registered where such use would result in a likelihood of confusion. In case of the use of an identical sign for identical goods or services, a likelihood of confusion shall be presumed.

2. Article 6*bis* of the Paris Convention shall apply, mutatis mutandis , to services. In determining whether a trademark is well-known, account shall be taken of the knowledge of the trademark in the relevant sector of the public including knowledge in that PARTY obtained as a result of the promotion of the trademark in international trade.

3. Article 6*bis* of the Paris Convention shall apply, mutatis mutandis, to goods or services which are not similar to those in respect of which a trademark is registered, provided that use of that trademark in relation to those goods or services would unfairly indicate a connection between those goods or services and the owner of the registered trademark.

Article 19
Exceptions

PARTIES may provide limited exceptions to the rights conferred by a trademark, such as fair use of descriptive terms, provided that such exceptions take account of the legitimate interests of the owner of the trademark and of third parties.

Article 20
Term of Protection

Initial registration, and each renewal of registration, of a trademark shall be for a term of no less than seven years. The registration of a trademark shall be renewable indefinitely.

Article 21
Requirement of Use

1. If use is required to maintain a registration, the registration may be cancelled only after an uninterrupted period of at least three years of non-use, unless valid reasons based on the

existence of obstacles to such use are shown by the trademark owner. Circumstances arising independently of the will of the owner of the trademark which constitute an obstacle to the use of the trademark, such as import restrictions on or other government requirements for goods or services protected by the trademark, shall be recognised as valid reasons for non-use.

2. When subject to the control of its owner, use of a trademark by another person shall be recognised as use of the trademark for the purpose of maintaining the registration.

Article 22
Other Requirements

A. The use of a trademark in commerce shall not be unjustifiably encumbered by special requirements, such as use with another trademark, use in a special form or use in a manner detrimental to its capability to distinguish the goods or services of one undertaking from those of other undertakings.

B. It shall be a matter for national legislation to determine the conditions for the use of a mark.

Article 23
Licensing and Assignment

PARTIES may determine conditions on the licensing and assignment of trademarks, it being understood that the compulsory licensing of trademarks shall not be permitted and that the owner of a registered trademark shall have the right to assign his trademark with or without the transfer of the business to which the trademark belongs.

Chapter 7

GEOGRAPHICAL INDICATIONS

The adoption of the TRIPS Agreement represented an important step for the international recognition of geographical indications. Although such indications were covered under some prior international conventions, the scope and membership of such conventions offered a protection considerably more limited than the one granted by the TRIPS Agreement. However, significant controversies still dominate the discussion of this issue at WTO. In particular, disagreement exists about the modes of implementing the registration of geographical indications under Article 23.4 of the Agreement. Moreover, as examined below, a number of developed and developing countries have proposed to expand to other products the special protection only available today for wines and spirits.[1]

Interestingly, unlike the case of public health, in the area of geographical indications there is no North–South divide, but different groups—inclusive of developed and developing countries alike—hold diverging positions on several critical issues.[2] This reflects different perceptions on the economic value of geographical indications to promote the commercialization of domestic products, as well as on the implications of the recognition, of foreign geographical indications on the local economy.

Geographical indications have three basic functions.[3] They provide information about

- the name of a product;
- the geographical origin of the product;
- a given quality, reputation, or characteristics attributable to a geographical area.

As in the case of trademarks, the use of a geographical indication permits the consumer to associate a name or other sign to directly unobservable attributes of a

[1] This issue is to be addressed as part of the 'Implementation-related issues and concerns' defined by the WTO Doha Ministerial Conference (see Ministerial Declaration, WT/MIN(01)/DEC/1, paras 12 and 18).

[2] See, eg, D Rangnekar, 'Geographical Indications: A Review of Proposals at the TRIPS Council' (2002: UNCTAD/ICTSD Capacity Building Project on Intellectual Property Rights and Sustainable Development, Geneva).

[3] See, eg, F Gevers, 'Conflicts Between Trademarks and Geographical Indications. The Point of View of the International Association for the Protection of Industrial Property (AIPPI)', Symposium on the International Protection of Geographical Indications, Melbourne, 5–6 April, (1995: Geneva, WIPO), pp 148–9.

product. In both cases, the 'information asymmetry'[4] that prevails in most markets can be addressed. Consumers' transaction costs are reduced as far as the consumer can rely on his previous experience (or on the experience transmitted by others) to choose a product among other options.

Although geographical indications and trademarks perform similar functions, there are also important differences: a geographical indication identifies a geographical area where one or several enterprises are located that produce the product for which the geographical indication is used, while a trademark identifies the enterprise which offers certain products or services on the market. Thus, the use of a geographical indication may be combined with a trademark which identifies a *specific* producer within the geographical area.[5]

A basic feature of a geographical indication is that each and every producer which is located in the area to which the geographical indication refers has the right to use the said indication for the products originating in the said area, generally subject to compliance with certain quality and other requirements. A geographical indication is the *generic* designation of a product, pointing out that it comes from a specific area, as long as the product enjoys certain qualities or reputation essentially deriving from that area.

A geographical indication successful in the market becomes an asset of the producers authorized to use it, since it generates accumulated goodwill. Without such protection, it would be difficult for such producers to appropriate the benefits derived from maintaining the quality or other attributes of their products and they would, hence, have little or no incentive to invest for that purpose. The connection between product and geographical area allows for niche marketing, brand development, and extracting value from reputable indications.[6] According to WIPO,

Geographical indications are understood by consumers to denote the origin and the quality of products. Many of them have acquired valuable reputations which, if not adequately protected, may be misrepresented by dishonest commercial operators. False use of geographical indications by unauthorized parties is detrimental to consumers and legitimate producers. The former are deceived and led into believing to buy a genuine product with specific qualities and characteristics, while they in fact get a worthless imitation. The latter suffer damage because valuable business is taken away from them and the established reputation for their products is damaged.[7]

Geographical indications are increasingly recognized as a tool for securing consumers' loyalty by establishing the link between product attributes and the

---

[4] This asymmetry exists because sellers have much better information with regard to the unobservable features of a product than the buyer (P Goldstein, *Copyright, Patent, Trademark and Related State Doctrines. Cases and Materials on the Law of Intellectual Property* (1993: Westbury, revised third edn, The Foundation Press Inc, p 16). See also G Grossman and C Shapiro, 'Counterfeit-product trade', (1988) 78(1) American Economic Review, pp 59–75.

[5] See, eg, F Gevers op. cit. (1995), p 148.   [6] Rangnekar op. cit. (2002), p 6.

[7] WIPO, *What is a Geographical Indication?* (2002: Geneva), available at <http://www.wipo.int/about-ip/en/index.html>, (last accessed on 27 June 2004).

geographical origin. In economic terms, a geographical indication essentially permits as increase in producers' rents based on *product differentiation*; that is, a form of *monopolistic competition* prevalent in the modern economy where there are elements of both monopoly and perfect competition.[8]

Of course, the economic value of geographical indications is not limited to the additional rents they may generate to producers. There are also other, less quantifiable, benefits such as the possibility of generating employment, increasing income, or retaining population in certain regions.[9]

Some developing countries have shown considerable enthusiasm about the possible benefits that could be derived from an increased protection of geographical indications. While, as discussed below, there are some examples of geographical indications from developing countries that have gained recognition in world markets, the largest number of such indications belongs to developed countries, notably European countries.[10] A key issue is, therefore, whether developing countries with different production structures and natural endowments may be better off or not with a broader protection of geographical indications.

Terminology

There are few areas of intellectual property law where definitions are as diverse as in the area of geographical indications. Any study on the matter, therefore, needs to clarify the concepts used in order to avoid misunderstandings and permit to adequately assess the available policy options under the TRIPS Agreement.

A geographical indication of source is a sign used in connection with goods in order to indicate their geographical origin. Conceptually, two main types of geographical indications of source may be distinguished:

(a) Simple, quality-neutral geographical indications of source (like 'made in . . . '), where there is no suggestion of a direct linkage between attributes of the products and their geographical origin. The use of an indication of source on a given product is merely subject to the condition that this product originates from the place designated by the indication of source.

---

[8] See, eg, E Mansfield, *Applied Microeconomics* (1994: New York and London; WW Norton & Co), p 385.

[9] 'Thanks to the designation of origin which gives more value to the product and thus makes it possible to obtain a selling price higher than the one of a standard cheese, there is maintenance on the spot of the population which would otherwise leave the mountain area to seek work in the urban centers'. F Vital, 'Protection of geographical indications: The approach of the European Union' in *WIPO Symposium on the International Protection of Geographical Indications*, Somerset West, Cape Province, 1–2 September (1999: Geneva, WIPO), p 52.

[10] There are 518 denominations of origin registered in Europe, distributed by products as follows: 138 cheeses; 106 fruits and vegetables; 80 fresh meat category; 58 fatty materials (essentially olive oils); 52 processed meat products. See also F Vital op. cit. (1999), p 53.

(b) Qualified geographical indications having a particular descriptive meaning because the characteristics, quality, or reputation of products are essentially attributable to a country, region, or locality. These indications consist of a name which is used to *designate* a product.[11] They are often called 'appellations of origin'.

Geographical indications may also be classified as *direct* and *indirect*. Though geographical indications generally consist of geographical names ('direct' indications), they may also be based on non-geographical names[12] or symbols,[13] if perceived by the public as identifying certain geographical origin. These are generally called 'indirect' geographical indications.

In accordance with the European approach—which has significantly influenced the provisions in the TRIPS Agreement—geographical indications constitute a component of *intellectual property* if the designated product possesses characteristics, reputation, or quality that are essentially attributable to its geographical origin.[14] That is, this concept applies only to *qualified* indications. Simple geographical indications not possessing such attributes may also be protected against misuse, under the discipline of unfair competition, consumer protection, or trademark law,[15] but they are not one of the categories of intellectual property that WTO Members are bound to protect.

There are significant differences in the terminology used in national laws and international treaties on this subject. The expression 'geographical indication'— which appeared only recently in international negotiations—is, as defined in the TRIPS Agreement, very similar to the concept of 'appellation of origin' as defined in Article 2 of the Lisbon Agreement for the Protection of Appellations of Origin and their International Registration (hereinafter the 'Lisbon Agreement') of 1958. It also probably covers the so-called 'designation of origin'[16] and the 'protected geographical indication' as provided for in EC Council Regulation No 2081/92 on the Protection of Geographical Indications and Designations of Origin for Agricultural Products and Foodstuffs.[17] There are, however, differences

---

[11] Geographical indications or appellations of origin are often considered a sub-category of the indications of source. See, eg, WIPO, *Intellectual Property. Reading Material* (1998: Geneva) pp 115–16.

[12] This is the case, for instance, with 'Mozart-Kugeln', which are associated by the consumer with Austria, and 'Ouzo' and 'Grappa', associated with Greece and Italy, respectively.

[13] Some symbols may be capable of indicating the origin of goods without literally naming its place of origin. Examples are the Eiffel Tower for Paris, the Matterhorn for Switzerland, the Tower Bridge for London, the colours of the French flag for cigarettes, the statue of Liberty, etc. See, eg, *Actes du Colloque de Lausanne, Les indications de provenance et les appellations d'origine en droit comparé* (1983: Geneve; Librairie Droz).

[14] F Beier and R Knaak, 'The Protection of Direct and Indirect Geographical Indications of Source in Germany and the European Community', (1994) 25 Int'l Rev Industrial Property & Copyright Law 1–38, p 28.

[15] By preventing, in the latter case, the registration of geographical marks (see Article 6.1 and 6*quinquies* B of the Paris Convention).   [16] 'Appellation d'origine' in French.

[17] This Regulation provides for the protection as intellectual property of indications of origin which are used for products whose quality or characteristics are primarily or exclusively dependent upon the respective geographical region.

Table 7.1 Definition of geographical indication

LISBON 1958	TRIPS 1994	EC 1992
Product	Good	Agricultural Product Foodstuff
Geographical name: country, region, locality	Geographical indication: country, region, locality	Name: country (exceptional cases), region, specific place
Quality or characteristics due exclusively or essentially to geographical environment: natural and human factors	Quality or reputation or other characteristics attributable to geographical origin	Quality or characteristics due exclusively or essentially to geographical environment: natural and human factors production, processing, and preparation in defined area

Source: based on J Audier, 'Protection of Geographical Indications in France and Protection of French Geographical Indications in Other Countries', in *Symposium on the International Protection of Geographical Indications in the Worldwide Context*, Hungary (1997: Geneva, WIPO), pp 241–2.

between the concepts provided for in these three instruments, as indicated by Table 7.1.

In contrast, 'geographical indication' as defined in these three instruments does not cover the wider concept of 'indication of source' as contained in the Madrid Agreement for the Repression of False or Deceptive Indications of Source on Goods (hereinafter 'the Madrid Agreement') of 1981, nor does it cover the words 'geographical indication' such as provided in Article 1712 of the NAFTA Agreement, which seems to be equivalent to the concept of 'indication of source'.[18]

Prior conventions

Three international conventions established before the TRIPS Agreement contain rules relating to geographical indications or appellations of origin: the Paris Convention, the Madrid Agreement, and the Lisbon Agreement.[19]

---

[18] See F Gevers op. cit. (1995), pp 147–8. It should be noted, however, that WIPO has opted to use the term 'geographical indication' in its widest possible meaning to describe names and symbols regardless of whether they indicate that the qualities of a given product are due to its geographical origin (such as appellations of origin), or they merely indicate the place of origin of a product (such as indications of source).

[19] There are also several other plurilateral and bilateral agreements on specific products (for instance, the Stressa Convention on Cheese, 1951).

Paris Convention

The Paris Convention (as revised in 1925, 1934, 1958, and 1967) includes the protection of 'indications of source or appellations of origin' (Article 1.2) but does not define these concepts,[20] and only provides for the level of protection accorded to domestic indications.[21]

The obligation to protect indications of source is specifically provided for in Article 10 of the Convention, but there are no special provisions therein for the protection of appellations of origin. Nevertheless, it has been interpreted that Articles 9, 10, and 10*ter* are applicable to appellations of origin since each appellation of origin, by definition, constitutes an indication of source under said Convention.[22]

Article 10(1)—the basic provision of the Paris Convention on indications of source—provides that the sanctions prescribed by Article 9 in respect of goods unlawfully bearing a trademark or trade name apply to any use of a 'false indication of the source' of a product. 'False indication of source' means, in this context, that no indications of source (or appellations of origin) can be used if they refer to a geographical area from which the products in question do not originate.[23] Article 10(1), however, does not apply to indications which may mislead the public, but are not false.

Article 9 establishes that seizure upon importation must be provided for, or at least prohibition of importation or seizure inside the country but, if those sanctions did not exist in a particular country, the actions and remedies available in such cases are to be applied. In the case of indications of source, requests for the seizure of such infringing goods can be made by any producer, manufacturer, or merchant established in the locality falsely indicated as the source (Article 10.2), or by federations and associations representing them when the action by such entities is allowed by the national legislation (Article 10*ter* 2).

Article 10*bis* of the Paris Convention on the protection against unfair competition is also relevant. It provides a basis for protection against the use of confusing, false, or misleading geographical indications.

As examined above,[24] WTO Members are obliged to comply with the provisions of the Paris Convention. They are, hence, subject to the provisions described above.

---

[20] According to WIPO, 'indication of source' means any expression or sign used to indicate that a product or service originates in a country, a region or a specific place, whereas 'appellation of origin' means the geographical name of a country, region or specific place which serves to designate a product originating therein the characteristic qualities of which are due exclusively or essentially to the geographical environment, including natural or human factors or both natural and human factors' (WIPO op. cit. (1998), pp 115–16).

[21] See, eg, R Knaak, 'The protection of geographical indications according to the TRIPs Agreement', in F-K Beier and G Schricker, *From GATT to TRIPs—The Agreement on Trade-Related Aspects of Intellectual Property Rights* (1996: Munich, Max Planck Institute for Foreign and International Patent, Copyright and Competition Law), p 120.   [22] See, eg, WIPO op. cit. (1998), p 120.

[23] Ibidem.   [24] See pp 44–6 above.

Madrid Agreement

The Madrid Agreement is a special agreement within the framework of the Paris Union that aims at the repression not only of false but also of deceptive indications of source.[25] This agreement provides that any product bearing a false or deceptive[26] indication by which one of the States party to it or place situated therein is directly or indirectly indicated as being the country or place of origin must be seized on importation into any of the States party to the Madrid Agreement (Article 1).

Articles 1 and 2 of the Agreement specify the cases and the manner in which seizure or similar measures may be requested and carried out. However, there is no provision allowing private parties to directly request such measures. States party to the Agreement may provide that such parties apply through a public prosecutor or any other competent authority.

Article 3*bis* obliges the States party to the Madrid Agreement to prohibit the use, in connection with the sale or display or offering for sale of any goods, of all indications capable of deceiving the public as to the source of the goods.[27] Article 4 provides that the courts of each country have to decide what appellations, on account of their generic character, do not fall within the provisions of the Madrid Agreement. Only regional appellations concerning the source of products of the vine are excluded from this reservation, leading to an 'absolute' protection for the latter.[28]

Lisbon Agreement

The Lisbon Agreement protects *appellations of origin*, that is, indications in respect of products that possess special characteristics and features of quality

---

[25] The Madrid Agreement has thirty member States. WTO Members that are not parties to the Madrid Agreement are not bound by its obligations.

[26] Deceptive indications are those that are literally true, but nevertheless misleading: 'where two geographical areas, possibly in two different countries, have the same denomination but only one of them so far has been used for the purposes of an indication of source for certain products, and such indication is used for products originating from the other geographical area in a way that the public believes that the products originate from the first area . . . then such use is considered as a deceptive use because the public believes that the products originate from the geographical area for which the indication traditionally has been used' (L Baeumer, 'Protection of geographical indications under WIPO treaties and questions concerning the relationship between those treaties and the TRIPS Agreement', WIPO, *Symposium on the International Protection of Geographical Indications in the Worldwide Context*, Eger (Hungary), 23–25 October 1997 (1999: Geneva, WIPO) p 17.

[27] Article 3 authorizes a vendor to indicate his name or address on goods coming from a country other than that in which the sale takes place, but obliges him, if he does so, to have his name or address accompanied by an exact indication in clear characters of the country or place of manufacture or production, or by some other indication sufficient to avoid any error as to the true source of the wares.

[28] See, eg, WIPO op. cit. (1998), p 121.

attributable to their geographical origin. For the purposes of this Agreement, appellation of origin means

the geographical name of a country, region, or locality which serves to designate a product originated therein, the quality and characteristics of which are due exclusively or essentially to the geographical environment, including natural and human factors (Article 2(1)).

There are three important elements in this definition:

- the appellation must be the geographical name of a country, region, or locality, thus excluding *indirect* geographical indications;
- the appellation of origin must serve to designate a product originating in the country, region, or locality referred to;
- the 'quality and characteristics' must be due exclusively or essentially to the geographical environment.

The Lisbon Agreement provides that the countries party to it undertake to protect on their territories, in accordance with the terms of the Agreement, the appellation of origin of products of the other countries party to the Lisbon Agreement, recognized and protected as such in the country of origin[29] and registered at the International Bureau of the World Intellectual Property Organization (WIPO). It is not sufficient for the country involved to protect its appellations under a general law. Each appellation has to benefit from distinct and express protection, stemming from a specific official or administrative act (see Box 7.1). The reason for such a requirement is that specific elements of the protection such as the geographical area, the lawful users of the appellation, and the nature of the product linked to a given quality, must be determined.[30]

The Lisbon Agreement has only been ratified by a very limited number of countries,[31] and has been largely ignored in current debates on the implementation of Article 23 of the TRIPS Agreement. Its registration system is, in fact, available to only a small number of geographical indications.[32] As noted by one commentator, 'one problem was that accession was confined to those nations which protected appellations of origin "as such". Thus, states which protected this form of intellectual property under unfair competition or consumer protection laws were locked out. Also the Agreement did not make exception for geographic indications which had already become generic in member states.'[33]

---

[29] Article 2(2) defines the country of origin as being 'the country whose name, or the country in which is situated the region or locality whose name, constitutes the appellation of origin which has given the product its reputation'. [30] WIPO op. cit. (1998), p 122.

[31] Twenty-four States are party to the Lisbon Agreement (see <http://www.wipo.int/treaties/en/ShowResults.jsp?lang=en&treaty_id=10>, last accessed on 17 March 2006).

[32] Knaak op. cit. (1996), p 121.

[33] M Blakeney, *Geographical Indications and TRIPS* (2001: Geneva; Quaker United Nations Office), Occasional Paper 8, available at <www.quno.org> (last accessed on 22 June 2005).

Box 7.1: International registration under the Lisbon Agreement

International registration must be applied for by the competent Office of the country of origin, in the name of any natural persons or legal entities, public or private, having a right to use the appellation according to the applicable national legislation. The International Bureau of WIPO has no competence to examine the application with respect to substance; it may only make an examination as to form. Under Article 5(2) of the Lisbon Agreement, the International Bureau notifies the registration without delay to the Offices of the countries party to the Lisbon Agreement.

In accordance with Article 5(3) to (5), the Office of any State party to the Lisbon Agreement may, within a period of one year from the receipt of the notification of registration, declare that it cannot ensure the protection of a given appellation, indicating the grounds for refusal as discretionally determined by each country. The registered appellation enjoys protection in all countries not having refused it. However, if third parties had been using the appellation prior to the notification of the registration, the Office of that country may grant them a maximum of two years in which to terminate such use (Article 5(6)).

The protection conferred by international registration is unlimited in time. Article 6 provides that an appellation that has been granted protection cannot be deemed to have become generic, as long as it is protected as an appellation of origin in the country of origin. Article 7 provides that the registration need not be renewed and is subject to payment of a single fee. An international registration ceases to have effect only in two cases: either the registered appellation has become a generic name in the country of origin, or the international registration has been cancelled by the International Bureau at the request of the Office of the country of origin.

Source: WIPO op. cit. (1998), pp 122–3.

Protection of geographical indications under TRIPS

22.1. Geographical indications are, for the purposes of this Agreement, indications which identify a good as originating in the territory of a Member, or a region or locality in that territory, where a given quality, reputation or other characteristic of the good is essentially attributable to its geographical origin.

Article 22.1 contains the concept of 'geographical indications' for the purposes of the TRIPS Agreement. Several features of this concept must be highlighted.

First, protection only applies with regard to goods.[34] There is no limitation with regard to the nature of goods for which geographical indications can be protected.

---

[34] During the negotiations the proponed definitions included the concept of 'products', finally replaced for goods. Note also that Article 24.4 refers to goods and services (see pp 248–9 below).

Unlike some national or regional regulations that apply only to some categories of agricultural products, the TRIPS Agreement also covers other products.

Geographical indications historically originated and their protection evolved in relation to wines and spirits. Thus, around 70 per cent of the indications registered under the Lisbon Agreement come from two product categories: wines and wine products and spirits.[35]

However, geographical indications may be applied to a wide range of products which are 'land-based' other than wines and spirits, such as dairy products, poultry, and plant products. For instance, agricultural products account for 6.7 per cent of the registration under the Lisbon Agreement, and cheese for 6.5 per cent of the total.[36] Manufactured products or handicrafts (eg, watches, textiles) may also be distinguished with geographical indications. Examples of protected geographical indications are provided in Box 7.2.

Box 7.2: Examples of protected geographical indications

Bulgaria: Bulgarian yoghurt, Traminer from Khan Kroum (wine), Merlou from Sakar (wine)

Canada: Canadian Rye Whisky, Canadian Whisky, Fraser Valley, Okanagan Valley, Similkameen Valley, Vancouver Island

Czech Republic: Pilsen and Budweis (beers), various vines, liqueurs, Saaz hops, Auscha hops, Jablonec jewellery, Bohemia crystal, Vamberk lace

European Union: Champagne, Sherry, Porto, Chianti, Samos, Rheinhessen, Moselle Luxembourgeoise, Mittelburgenland (all wines); Cognac, Brandy de Jerez, Grappa di Barolo, Berliner Kümmel, Genièvre Flandres Artois, Scotch Whisky, Irish Whiskey, Tsikoudia (from Crete) (all spirits); and a range of other products, such as Newcastle Brown Ale, Scottish beef, Orkney beef, Orkney lamb, Jersey Royal potatoes, Cornish Clotted Cream, Cabrales, Roquefort, Gorgonzola, Aziete de Moura, Olive de Kalamata, Opperdoezer Ronde, Wachauer Marille, Danablu, Lübecker Marzipan, Svecia, Queijo do Pico, Coquille Saint-Jacques des Côtes-d'Amour, Jamón de Huelva, Lammefjordsgulerod

Hungary: Eger (wine), Szatmar (plum)

Liechtenstein: Malbuner (meat products), Balzer (hi-tech products)

Slovak Republic: Korytnická minerálna voda (mineral water), Karpatská perla (wine), Modranská majolika (hand-painted pottery), Piešťanské bahno (healing mud)

United States: Idaho, (potatoes and onions), Real California Cheese, Napa Valley Reserve (still and sparkling wines), Pride of New York (agricultural products), Ohio River Valley (viticulture area).

Source: WTO News—1998 News Items (<http://www.wto.org>); Rangnekar op. cit. (2002), p 6.

---

[35] See S Escudero, International protection of geographical indications and developing countries. TRADE Working Papers No 10 (2001: Geneva, South Centre) available at: <http://www.southcentre.org> (last accessed on 22 June 2005).   [36] Ibidem.

Second, in order to qualify as a geographical indication, the sign must 'identify' a good 'as originating' from some specific territory. Therefore, its function is different from that of a trademark, which must permit to distinguish the products of one enterprise from those of others.[37] A geographical indication does not fulfill this latter role. On the contrary, many suppliers can use the same indication.

Third, the identification must relate to a 'territory', without any geographical or political limitation. Thus 'territory' may include a locality, a province, or a country. However, protection is not limited to the name of a territory, but extends to 'indirect' indications (such as images), which evoke rather than name a territory, as defined above.

Fourth, the goods must originate from the identified territory; that is, they must be mined, grown or manufactured therein. This means that a geographical indication cannot be assigned or licensed to producers established in another territory, although part of the work involved may take place outside the designated territory.[38]

Finally, it is essential to establish a relationship between the goods'

- quality;
- reputation; or
- other characteristics,

and the originating territory.

The determination of whether such relationship exists is left to the Member where protection is sought. Article 22.1 requires that the quality, reputation, or other characteristics only be 'essentially', and not exclusively, attributable to its geographic origin. 'Essentially'[39] may be understood as implying that the production of the relevant goods may partially take place outside the designated territory. There is significant room for the Member where protection is sought to independently decide when the conditions for acquiring protection are met.[40]

There is nothing in the TRIPS Agreement obliging a Member to protect geographical indications merely on the basis that they are protected in another Member.

While the concept of 'quality' refers to objective properties of the goods,[41] 'reputation' refers to perceptions that may influence purchasing decisions by the public, whether related to measurable qualitative properties or not.[42] Establishing

[37] See Chapter 6 above.

[38] See, eg, UNCTAD-ICTSD, *Resource Book on TRIPS and Development* (2005: New York, Cambridge University Press), p 290.

[39] 'Essential' means 'of or constituting a thing's essence; fundamental; indispensable (to); exceedingly important'. 'Essentially' is 'indispensable or fundamental element or thing' *Concise Oxford Dictionary*, (1982: Oxford University Press, 7th edn), p 329.

[40] See, eg, Knaak op. cit. (1996), p 128, who also notes that there has hardly been any international experience with the examination of the necessary link between certain goods and their geographical origin.

[41] 'Quality' is 'degree of excellence, relative nature or kind or character', *Concise Oxford Dictionary*, (1982: Oxford University Press, 7th edn), p 843.

[42] See the European Court Decision in the *Turron* case, which emphasized that simple indications of goods not produced according to specific quality requirements may be protected (OJ EC No L 232, of 9 August 1989, p 13).

the reputation of an indication can be considerably more difficult than proving objective physical properties attributable to a given geographical origin. Reputation may not necessarily be linked to certain quality or other properties of the goods, as it may be built upon consistent advertising efforts. In any case, the reputation should be 'essentially attributable' to a geographical origin.

The use of a geographical indication does not create an automatic presumption that a relationship between quality, reputation, or other characteristics and the geographical origin exists.[43] Such relationship must be proven according to the law of the jurisdiction where protection is sought.

It is important to note that the identification may be based on quality or reputation, or on any other characteristic that the Agreement does not define. The latter may include, for instance, taste, texture, design, appearance, etc of the goods, as well as the absence of elements that consumers may deem undesirable. Whatever the characteristic is, it must be sufficient to identify a good as originating in a given territory, through a certain quality, reputation, or other characteristic of the good, provided that the identifying factor is 'essentially attributable to its geographical origin'. This definition, hence, excludes cases where there is a relationship between quality, reputation, or other characteristic of the product and its geographical origin, but neither of them can be 'essentially attributed' to such origin.

Moreover, a geographical indication, unlike a trademark, is perceived as such rather than 'created'. The same term may be differently perceived by different linguistic communities across countries or within one country. The fundamental question is, in effect, the extent to which a certain name (or symbol) serves to *identify a good as originating in a certain location*. Any claim for protection of a geographical indication critically hinges on whether it effectively indicates a link between certain goods and a location.[44] For instance, some developing countries have in the last few years identified geographical indications, such as 'Basmati' rice (India), 'Nuoc mam' (fish-based sauce from the island of Fu Quoc, Vietnam), 'Long Jin' tea (China),[45] 'Chuau cacao' and 'Cocuy Pecayero' spirit (Venezuela).[46]

As a result of the above-mentioned conditions, protection is limited to *qualified* geographical indications. As mentioned, for the purposes of the TRIPS Agreement protection needs only to be granted to 'indications which identify a good as originating in the territory of a Member, or a region or locality in that territory, where a

---

[43] For the opposite view, see Knaak op. cit. (1996), 130.

[44] See A Taubman, 'The way ahead: developing international protection for geographical indications: thinking locally, acting globally', *Symposium on the International Protection of Geographical Indications*, WIPO/GEO/MVD/01/9, Montevideo, 28–29 November, (2001: Geneva, WIPO), pp 6–7.

[45] See, eg, J Girardeau, 'The use of geographical indications in a collective marketing strategy: The example of Cognac', *Symposium on the International Protection of Geographical Indications*, Somerset West, Cape Province, 1–2 September (1999: Geneva; WIPO), p 75.

[46] See D Vivas Eugui and M Ruiz Muller, *Handbook on Mechanisms to Protect the Traditional Knowledge of the Andean Region Indigenous Communities*, prepared for the UNCTAD BIOTRADE Initiative (2001: Geneva, UNCTAD), p 14 (available at <http://www.unctad.org>, last accessed on 25 June 2005).

given quality, reputation, or other characteristic of the good is essentially attributable to its geographical origin' (Article 22.1). Though this definition resembles the one contained in the Lisbon Agreement, it adds 'reputation' as one of the conditions that (like quality *or* other characteristic) an indication needs to meet in order to attract protection under the Agreement.

It has also been debated whether geographical indications, as defined in the TRIPS Agreement, may cover *services* and not only physical goods.[47] Though such an interpretation is unlikely to prevail if a dispute were brought to a panel in WTO, Members may consider to extend protection of geographical indications to services, as currently provided for in a few countries.[48]

> 22.2. In respect of geographical indications, Members shall provide the legal means for interested parties to prevent:
>
> (a) the use of any means in the designation or presentation of a good that indicates or suggests that the good in question originates in a geographical area other than the true place of origin in a manner which misleads the public as to the geographical origin of the good;
>
> (b) any use which constitutes an act of unfair competition within the meaning of Article 10*bis* of the Paris Convention (1967).

Not only are there deep terminological differences in the area of geographical indications, there are also significant divergences with regard to the modes of protection. Various modalities have been developed in national and international law for the protection of geographical indications:

- 'absolute' protection against use by any non-authorized party whether the public may be misled or not, as established, for instance, by the French law of 6 May 1919 (which recognized 'appellations of origin' and laid down the conditions for their protection), the EC Council Regulation No 2081/92, the Lisbon Agreement, and Article 23 of the TRIPS Agreement (only for wines and spirits). This special title or *sui generis* protection is based on a public or administrative act.[49]

- protection against the use of an indication which is deceptive or misleads the public, as provided for by the Madrid Agreement and by Article 22.2 (a) of the TRIPS Agreement;

- protection against acts of unfair competition committed with the use of geographical indications, as provided for under Article 10*bis* of the Paris Convention;

- protection against acts of 'passing-off', as recognized in common-law countries;[50]

---

[47] See, eg, L Beresford, 'The protection of geographical indications in the United States of America', *Symposium on the International Protection of Geographical Indications*, WIPO, Somerset West, Cape Province, South Africa, 1–2 September, (1999: Geneva, WIPO), p 45.

[48] Such as in Peru, Liechtenstein, and Switzerland. See IP/C/W/253, available at <http://www.wto.org> (last accessed on 20 June 2005).   [49] See, eg, WIPO op. cit. (1998), pp 118–19.

[50] 'Passing-off' is misrepresenting one's business goods or services as another's, to the latter's injury. This approach has been followed, for instance, in the United Kingdom.

- protection against the 'false' use of an indication, when it does not indicate the true origin of the product. This protection—established, for instance, under Article 10(1) of the Paris Convention—does not extend to indications which may mislead the public but are not false (for example, where certain geographical areas in different countries have the same name but only one of those areas is known for particular products).

- protection as collective or certification mark,[51] which may be registered by the government or by a private entity.[52]

The available modes of protection have been classified by the WTO Secretariat[53] in three categories, as summarized in Box 7.3.

Generally, these different categories of protection coexist in a single country. For instance, the legal forms of protection for geographical indications available in the US include measures of categories (1) and (2).[54] In that country protection is conferred in a variety of ways, including unfair competition, federal (such as trademark law), and state statues and regulations. In particular, the US Trademark Act of 1946, as amended, provides for the protection of geographical indications

[51] 'Collective marks' are owned and used by a group of producers—generally the members of an association—and may serve to distinguish the geographical origin or other common characteristics of certain products. The group or collectivity that owns the mark does not use it directly, but via its members. These marks are principally designed to guarantee certain product characteristics (quality, nature or origin) for consumers. The submission of regulations for the use of the mark is normally required for the acquisition of a collective mark.

'Certification marks' are generally found in common-law countries. They also aim at guaranteeing certain characteristics or quality of products, and may be used by any person (even if not belonging to a particular group or association) that complies with specified standards. The use of a certification mark is subject to the authorization of its owner, who does not trade himself with the mark but should ensure that the relevant standards are complied with by the authorized users. The verification by the owner of a certification mark of compliance with specified standards means that this instrument in the common law system comes closest to the *sui generis* system established in some countries regarding 'appellations of origin'; OECD, *Appellations of Origin and Geographical Indications in OECD Member Countries: Economic and Legal Implications*, Working Party on Agricultural Policies and Markets of the Committee for Agriculture Joint Working Party of the Committee for Agriculture and the Trade Committee, COM/AGR/APM/TD/WP (2000) 15/FINAL (2000: Paris, OECD), p 9. In some countries (eg the USA) when a certification mark consists solely or essentially of a geographical term, normally the authority that exercises control over its use is a governmental body or a body operating under governmental authorization. Examples of registered certification marks in the USA include 'Idaho', 'Real California Cheese', 'Napa Valley Reserve', 'Pride of New York', 'Ohio River Valley'. See Beresford op. cit. (1999), pp 42–43.

[52] While in principle a geographical name is not protectable (unless distinctive of the products or services) as a trademark, the US law allows for this possibility. Under section 45 of the Lanham Act, it is possible to register a certification mark of 'regional or other origin' of goods. The registration must be accompanied by the criteria that need to be met to use the certification.

[53] See IP/C/W/253 of 4 April 2001.

[54] With respect to registration of geographical indications as certification marks, applicants must submit a copy of the standards established to determine whether others may use the certification mark on their goods and/or in connection with their services (37 CFR 2.61 (b)). The standard need not be original with the applicant. They may be standards established by another party, such as specifications promulgated by a government agency or standards developed through research of a private research organization.

Box 7.3: Categories of protection for geographical indication

---

(1) Regulations focusing on business practices
The basic issue under these regulations (such as unfair competition, consumer protection, trade descriptions, labelling, and food standards) is not whether the geographical indication as such is eligible for protection but, rather, whether a specific act involving the use of a geographical indication has contravened standards contained in laws covering such acts.

(2) Trademark law
Trademark law may provide two types of protection for geographical indications: against the registration and use of geographical indications as trademarks, or through collective, guarantee, or certification marks.

(3) *Sui generis* protection
A third category of regulations comprises of laws and regulations specifically dedicated to the protection of geographical indications.

Source: D De Sousa, 'Protection of geographical indications under the TRIPS Agreement and related work of the World Trade Organization (WTO)', *Symposium on the International Protection of Geographical Indications*, WIPO/GEO/MVD/01/2, Montevideo, 28–29 November (WIPO: 2001, Geneva), p 4.

---

as certification marks.[55] In other countries (eg in Europe) there are also regulations of type (3) especially for foodstuffs, wines, and spirits.

According to Article 22.2 of the TRIPS Agreement, the protection of geographical indications may be enforced by 'interested parties'. This broad expression leaves room for Members to determine who such parties may be, and eventually to limit who may assert rights. They may only include, for instance, producers of a territory identified by a geographical indication or an association thereof, the owner of collective trademarks, or the States.

The main differences between a *sui generis* regime, as provided for in continental Europe, and the application of a common-law approach based on certification trademarks and other regulations on business conduct, are summarized in Table 7.2.

One key difference between certification marks and geographical indications protected under a *sui generis* regime (such as European appellations of origin), is that in the latter case the group or association of producers must demonstrate the existence of a special link between the characteristics of the product and its geographical origin, and

must also undertake that production, processing and preparation will take place in the geographical area specified. These conditions do not apply for registration of a certification mark which is based on the intention of the group and which is free to define the rules for users in line with the characteristics it chooses. This does not exclude the possibility that the owner of a certification mark includes, should he so wish, the existence of a special tie

---

[55] Beresford op. cit. (1999), p 42.

Table 7.2 Differences between the *sui generis* and the certification trademark systems

Sui generis protection	Certification trademark (CTM)
The indication belongs to the State and the administration corresponds to the regulating authority. It is a public or a private property right.	It is a private right, but governments may own CTM. The property and the administration belongs to an association of manufacturers or producers, or to government.
Mainly designed to protect identification of the origin and its link with quality and reputation.	They are designed to certify quality, characteristics, origin, materials, etc.
Must be protected as from date of registration up until the conditions that justified protection persist.	They have to be renewed after a certain period of time. Fees have to be paid for each renewal.
Protection for GIs is based on *ex officio* and private actions.	The protection of CTM is based on actions by CTM owners.
They have regulation for homonymous GI.	The issue of homonymous CTMs does not exist. There must be just one right-holder.
Inspection is performed by an independent agency or government.	Inspection is performed by the CTM owner, government, or another authorized party.
There is no automatic collateral protection against use in other products.	They have collateral protection, against use in other products.

Source: based on D Vivas Eugui, 'Negotiations on geographical indications in the TRIPS Council and their effect on the WTO agricultural negotiations: implications for developing countries and the case of Venezuela', 4 The Journal of World Intellectual Property (2001), p 703; and OECD, Appellations of origin and geographical indications in OECD Member Countries: economic and legal implications, Working Party on Agricultural Policies and Markets of the Committee for Agriculture, Joint Working Party of the Committee for Agriculture and the Trade Committee, COM/AGR/APM/TD/WP (2000)15/FINAL (2000: Paris; OECD), pp 9–10.

between the characteristics of the product and its geographical origin in the certification standards of the product.[56]

Though in the case of certification marks, the owner may perform verification of compliance with users' rules, this is often done by the government or a government-authorized agency. Geographical indications are deemed to belong (under a special regime or certification marks) to governments and not private parties. Public intervention is important for three main reasons:

- preserving the freedom of all producers in the region to use the geographical indication, provided they comply with the established requirements for that purpose;
- preventing abuses or illegal uses of the indication, including non-conformity of products with norms, a task that generally rests with (regional or local) governments;

[56] OECD, *Appellations of Origin and Geographical Indications in OECD Member Countries: Economic and Legal Implications*, Working Party on Agricultural Policies and Markets of the Committee for Agriculture Joint Working Party of the Committee for Agriculture and the Trade Committee, COM/AGR/APM/TD/WP (2000)15/FINAL (2000: Paris, OECD), p 10.

• enforcing the rights domestically and in foreign countries, either by the producers themselves or through the government (eg a public prosecutor).

In the USA, for instance, it is normally considered that a private individual is not in the best position to preserve the freedom of all persons in the region to use the term, and to prevent abuses or illegal uses of the mark which would be detrimental to all those entitled to use the mark. Hence,

The government of a region would be the logical authority to control the use of the name of the region. The government, either directly or through a body to which it has given authority, would have power to preserve the right of all persons and to prevent abuse or illegal use of the mark.[57]

Another important aspect to comparatively examine *sui generis* protection against certification marks is the extent to which any producer in the designated geographical area is able to use the protected indication, provided that the user rules (for the certification mark) or the product specifications (for the appellation of origin) are complied with. While *sui generis* systems, in principle, provide for such a possibility, laws on certification marks may offer similar opportunities. For instance, in Canada, one section of the trademark law deals specifically with *certification marks descriptive of the place of origin*. If a certification mark is descriptive of the place of origin, the owner (the administrative authority of a country, state, province, or municipality, or a commercial association having an office or representative in that area) shall permit the use of the mark in association with any wares or services produced or performed in the area of which the mark is descriptive.[58]

However, under any of such systems collusive conduct to limit entry by new producers, or to perform other anti-competitive practices, is possible and has been found in a number of cases in European countries.[59] This suggests that the establishment of protection for geographical indications—like other titles of intellectual property—should be accompanied by *effective competition policies*, an area in which most developing countries are still rather weak.[60]

The protection to be accorded under Article 22.2(b) means that the use of designations that are similar to protected geographical indications may be prohibited, if such use amounts to unfair competition. However, it is not a convincing argument[61] that protection may also be conferred against the use of lower-quality products, even if originating from the territory rightly identified by an indication, unless an act of unfair competition can be proven.

---

[57] H Rademeyer, 'The Protection of Geographical Indications in South Africa', *Symposium on the International Protection of Geographical Indications*, Somerset West, Cape Province, 1–2 September (1999: Geneva, WIPO) pp 42–3. [58] OECD op. cit. (2000), p 20.
[59] OECD op. cit. (2000), pp 15–20.
[60] In many developing countries, no competition laws have been enacted, while in many others there is little tradition in effectively applying competition laws.
[61] See Knaak op. cit. (1996), p 130.

'Protection' of a geographical indication may mean:

(a) the right to prevent unauthorized persons from using geographical indications, for products that do not originate from the geographical place indicated;

(b) the right to prevent a geographical indication from becoming a generic expression.[62] This aspect of protection is dealt with, for example, by the Lisbon Agreement.[63]

Under the TRIPS Agreement, Members have considerable leeway to determine the 'legal means' to protect geographical indications, which may include a variety of measures, such as unfair competition, certification marks, administrative registration of geographical indications, and other means available under certain legal systems, such as the doctrine of passing off. The Agreement determines, however, in Article 22, which *acts* must be prevented.

Paragraph a) of Article 22.2 makes clear that protection is not limited to 'direct' indications of origin, but embraces 'the use of any means in the designation or representation of a good that indicates or suggests' a certain geographical origin. This is an important clarification, since it permits the protection as geographical indications of non-geographical names, as well as of graphical or pictorial representations that evoke a certain geographical origin.[64]

Whatever the domestic form of protection is, given that no true international protection exists for geographical indications, any country wishing to protect its own indications abroad would have to comply with the laws and regulations of *each* country where protection is sought. This implies accommodation of the demand for protection to the particular legal system applied in the targeted country. The acquisition of rights over geographical indications in foreign countries, therefore, requires dealing with different legal systems, and is likely to require substantial resources and sophisticated expertise.

In some cases, protection requires a formal application and registration of the indication. In others (including countries where special protection is available) no registration is needed. The procedures to be followed, the substantive provisions to be complied with, as well as the remedies available for cases of infringement, may also vary according to the products involved. For instance, in Europe there exist only two specialized regulations at the European level, one for wines and

---

[62] Once its distinctiveness is lost, the indication loses its protection. In many cases, a geographical name is regarded in one country as a protected geographical indication while it is considered to be generic in another country. Thus, 'Champagne' and 'Chablis' are only allowed in Europe to be used for products originating from a certain geographical area and produced according to certain quality standards, while in the United States of America they are regarded as being semi-generic names. 'Port' and 'Sherry' have been deemed customary terms in South Africa. See A Stern, 'The protection of geographical indications in South Africa', in WIPO, *Symposium on the International Protection of Geographical Indications*, Somerset West, Cape Province, South Africa, 1–2 September (1999: Geneva, WIPO), p 33.   [63] See, eg WIPO op. cit. (1998), p 116.

[64] See, eg, UNCTAD-ICTSD op. cit. (2005), p 292.

spirits and the other on agricultural products and foodstuffs.[65] There is no general European protection for geographical indications; therefore, national laws should be complied with for other products.[66]

The USA requested consultations under the WTO dispute settlement rules regarding the protection of trademarks and geographical indications for agricultural products and foodstuffs in the European Communities. The US stated in its request that 'the European Communities' Regulation 2081/92, as amended, does not provide national treatment with respect to geographical indications, and does not provide sufficient protection to pre-existing trademarks that are similar or identical to a geographical indication. This situation appears to be inconsistent with the European Communities' obligations under the TRIPS Agreement, including but not necessarily limited to Articles 3, 16, 24, 63 and 65 of the TRIPS Agreement.'[67] The ruling of the panel in *European Communities–Protection of trademarks and geographical indications for agricultural products and foodstuffs* (WT/DS174/R) of 15 March 2005 found, inter alia, that the Regulation was inconsistent with Article 3.1 of the TRIPS Agreement with respect to (a) the equivalence and reciprocity conditions, as applicable to the availability of protection for GIs; (b) the application procedures, insofar as they require examination and transmission of applications by governments; (c) the objection procedures, insofar as they require verification and transmission of objections by governments; and (d) the requirements of government participation in the inspection structures under Article 10, and the provision of the declaration by governments under Article 12a(2)(b).[68]

In the US, as mentioned, geographical indications are protected under the trademark law, but wine-related geographical indications are regulated under the Federal Alcohol Administration Act and the regulations issued by the Federal Bureau of Tobacco, Alcohol & Firearms.[69] In the case of the Andean Community

---

[65] Foodstuffs include beer, natural mineral waters and spring waters, beverages made from plant extracts, bread, pastry, cakes, confectionery, biscuits and other baker's wares, natural gums and resins; agricultural products include hay, essential oils, cork, cochineal (raw product of animal origin): Council Regulation (EEC) No 2081/92 of 14 July 1992 on the protection of geographical indications and designations of origin for agricultural products and foodstuffs (Annexes I and II).

[66] Some national laws also contain provisions with regard to particular types of *use* of geographical indications, such as advertising, labelling, and the sale of products that do not meet the requirements for use of a geographical indication (see IP/C/W/253, para 107, available at <http://www.wto.org>, last accessed on 31 May 2005).

[67] See WTO document IP/D/19, available at <http://www.wto.org> (last accessed on 18 February, 2006).

[68] A proposal to amend the Regulation was approved in January 2006 by the European Commission. One of its objectives is to put the European regime in line with the TRIPS Agreement, by formally deleting the requirement for 'reciprocity and equivalence' from the regulations and by allowing third-country operators to submit applications and objections directly rather than through their governments. The deadline for implementing the ruling of the panel was set to expire in April 2006. See <http://europa.eu.int/rapid/pressReleasesAction.do?reference=IP/06/2&format=HTML&aged=0&language=EN&guiLanguage=en> (last accessed on 20 February 2006).

[69] See, eg, V O'Brien, Protection of Geographical Indications in the United States of America, *Symposium on the International Protection of Geographical Indications in the Worldwide Context*, Eger (Hungary), 24–25 October (1997: Geneva, WIPO), p 163. The Bureau of Alcohol, Tobacco and Firearms (ATF) controls the terms that may be used on the label of any wine or spirits sold in the United

Regime Decision 486,[70] there is both a special protection for geographical indications and certification marks. This permits the protection of foreign geographical
indications as such and foreign certifications marks as certifications marks only.
Cross-protection is not allowed.[71]

The protection conferred under Article 22.2(a) of the TRIPS Agreement is
against indications that mislead as to the 'true place of origin' of the product.
There is no specification in the TRIPS Agreement on which are the conditions to
consider that a product truly originates from a particular location. As mentioned,
the concept of geographical indication assumes that a product has been mined,
grown, or manufactured in the named or evoked locality, but it is uncertain the
extent to which materials or other inputs form other localities could be incorporated without affecting the nature of the indication. However, the use of geographical indications would not seem admissible in situations where the connection
between location and product is lost, such as when a producer located in the
named or evoked locality or region partially or totally subcontracts production
outside that locality or region.

 Whether the public is misled by the use of a geographical indication depends
on the facts involved in a particular situation. The use of a similar or identical
indication is not sufficient, as the determinant factor is whether it misleads the
public or not. Interestingly, unlike the case of trademarks (Article 16)[72] there is no
presumption in Article 22, thereby imposing on the 'interested party' the burden
of proof of such misleading effect, even in cases where the use of an identical indication may be at stake. This burden represents a major difference with the treatment afforded to geographical indications for wines and spirits, as discussed
below, and explains the interest of some countries in obtaining a general protection to geographical indications based on the standards provided for wines and
spirits. In fact, proving that the public is misled with regard to the origin of some
products may be difficult, since often the general public lacks knowledge about
the 'true origin' of certain products. It has been noted in this regard that:

confusion presupposes that the consumer in fact identifies a particular good with a place of
origin. Establishing such a connection may be difficult for many of those interested parties
asserting rights in geographical indications. By way of illustration, many cheeses are marketed in the United States under names of European origin. However, it is very doubtful
that a significant part of the consuming public in the United States draws a link between
these cheeses and any geographic location. Assuming solely for argument's sake that
American consumers have some vague sense that a type of cheese at some point was made

States. ATF maintains a list of geographical indications that have been notified by third countries. There
are more than 400 geographical indications from Europe on their list. No one, except the listed owner,
can use such a geographical indication on a label approved by ATF. See Beresford op. cit. (1999), p 45.

[70] Andean Community's Common Regine on Industrial Property (Decision 486), 14 September
2000, available at <http://www.sice.org/int_prop.asp> (last accessed on 30 May 2005).

[71] See, eg, Vivas Eugui op. cit. (2001), p 201.   [72] See pp 184–8 above.

in Europe, specific knowledge as to a geographical link is likely to be limited to a very small portion of consumers.[73]

The decision about the extent to which the public is deceived will be generally made by courts. It is foreseeable that they would apply different criteria to evaluate when the public should be considered to know that an association exists between a product and a locality or region, and that its designation or representation is misleading.

Article 22.2(b) refers to 'any use which constitutes an act of unfair competition within the meaning of Article 10*bis* of the Paris Convention (1967)' as acts distinguishable from those that mislead the public. Paragraph 3(iii) of Article 10*bis* of the Paris Convention (1967) prohibits

indications or allegations the use of which in the course of trade is liable to mislead the public as to the nature, the manufacturing process, the characteristics, the suitability for their purpose, or the quantity, of the goods.

Since the central concept under the quoted article is also the misleading effect on the product, it may be unclear what it adds to what is provided for under Article 22.2(a). However, the customary principles of interpretation require that Article 22.2(b) be given an 'effet utile'. One difference between the two provisions is that while Article 22.2(a) refers to indications misleading as to the 'geographical origin' of the good, Article 10*bis* alludes to 'the nature, the manufacturing process, the characteristics, the suitability for their purpose, or the quantity, of the goods', a specification that is absent in Article 22.2(a). In addition, while Article 22.2(a) refers to cases where the public is actually misled ('in a manner which misleads...'), the language in the Paris Convention includes potential misleading effects ('...is liable to mislead'). Hence, the incorporation of article 10*bis* provides a broader basis for action than what may be deemed allowed under Article 22.2(a), including cases where a disclaimer about the origin is made but confusion may exist about the nature and characteristics of the good, and where there is potential for confusion, although it may have not actually occurred.

It should be noted, finally, that the potential use of geographical indications to protect traditional (including indigenous) knowledge has been raised in many fora and examined by many commentators.[74] However, though the use of a geographical indication may be associated with the use of certain traditional knowledge (for instance, a particular process that determines peculiar characteristics of a product), a geographical indication *does not protect the underlying knowledge as such* which—in the absence of other forms of protection—could be used by third parties without

---

[73] See, eg, UNCTAD-ICTSD op. cit. (2005), p 292.

[74] See, eg, C Correa, 'Traditional Knowledge and Intellectual Property. A Discussion Paper' (2001, Geneva, QUNO) (available at <http://www.quno.org>, last accessed on 31 May 2005); GRULAC, Traditional knowledge and the need to give it adequate intellectual property protection, WO/GA/26/9, 14 September 2000, available at<http://www.wipo.int> (last accessed on 31 May 2005).

restrictions based on the existence of such indication. This means that the title-holder/s of a geographical indication may prevent, where their rights are recognized, the commercialization of the same products under their indication, but not competition from firms that use their knowledge and sell under a different name or trademark.

> **22.3. A Member shall, *ex officio* if its legislation so permits or at the request of an interested party, refuse or invalidate the registration of a trademark which contains or consists of a geographical indication with respect to goods not originating in the territory indicated, if use of the indication in the trademark for such goods in that Member is of such a nature as to mislead the public as to the true place of origin.**

Article 22.3 addresses the tension between trademarks and geographical indications, when the former contains or consists of a geographical indication. In case of conflict, the protection of a geographical indication prevails, provided that the following conditions are met:

(a) the trademark contains or consists of a geographical indication. This provision would only apply when the trademarked sign is a geographical indication as defined in the TRIPS Agreement, and not simply when a territory is (directly or indirectly) designated.

(b) the goods do not originate from the designated territory;[75]

(c) it is proven that the 'use of the indication in the trademark for such goods in that Member is of such a nature as to mislead the public as to the true place of origin'. The fact that a trademark contains or consists of a geographical indication with respect to goods *not* originating in the indicated territory is not sufficient per se to refuse or invalidate it. In other words, the protection conferred in favour of the geographical indications is not absolute, but subject to determination, in the respective Member, that the use of the indication as a trademark is able to mislead the public specifically with regard to the 'true origin' of the goods.[76] Unlike the wording in Article 22.2(a) that refers to indications used 'in a manner which misleads the public', Article 22.3 refers to a use that 'is of such nature as to mislead the public', thereby suggesting that the probability of confusion by the public would be sufficient ground for the application of the provision.

---

[75] Although a trademark could not be refused or invalidated on the grounds set out in Article 22.3 when the goods originate from the designated territory, a trademark may be vulnerable to challenges based on other considerations, such as ownership, which are not dealt with in the TRIPS Agreement. See Chapter 6 above.

[76] Misleading with regard to other aspects, such as quality, would not be relevant if not associated by consumers with the geographical origin of the goods.

At the same time, Article 22.3 does not prevent a Member from allowing the registration of trademarks containing or consisting of geographical indications, if they are used with regard to goods originating from the designated territory.

The refusal or invalidation of a trademark under Article 22(3) may operate *ex officio* when the legislation does allow for this procedure, but should always be available upon request of an 'interested party'. As mentioned in connection with Article 22.2, this is a broad expression the specific content of which is to be determined by domestic laws.

A provision with regard to the refusal and invalidation of trademarks considerably stronger than Article 22.3 is stipulated, as mentioned below, for trademarks applied to wines which contain or consist of a protected indication.

An interesting question is whether, in the light of the need to act *ex officio* when the national legislation so permits, governments may be deemed obliged to review existing registrations of trademarks in order to comply with the requirements of Article 22.3. An affirmative reply would impose a heavy burden on trademark and patent offices, difficult to justify in the absence of a request by interested parties, particularly as Article 24.5 creates an exception for trademarks applied for or registered in good faith. If national legislation may provide or not for the *ex officio* faculty to act in these cases, a fortiori it may also reasonably limit it to future registrations of trademarks.

22.4. The protection under paragraphs 1, 2 and 3 shall be applicable against a geographical indication which, although literally true as to the territory, region or locality in which the goods originate, falsely represents to the public that the goods originate in another territory.

This provision addresses the use of so-called 'homonymous' geographical indications. It prevents their use even though literally true as to the territory, region, or locality in which the goods originate,[77] provided that they falsely represent to the public that the goods originate in another territory (Article 22.4). This proviso means that there is not an absolute ban on the use of homonymous geographical indications, but only when it is proven that the public believes that the goods originate in another territory. In these cases, 'delocalizing' additions may be used in order to allude to the true geographical origin of the relevant goods.

Article 22 does not rule out the use of explanatory additions to prevent confusion with a protected geographical indication, such as 'kind', 'type', 'style', 'imitation' or the like.[78] The determination of whether the use of a designation deceives or misleads the public or constitutes an act of unfair competition, exclusively rests with the competent authorities of the Member where protection is sought.

---

[77] One example of the conflict that this issue may raise is the case of 'Champagne', a well-known French designation, which is also used (for products other than wines) by producers in the Swiss locality of Champagne.

[78] See, however, the special treatment conferred to indications for wines and spirits, pp 232–40.

Additional protection for geographical indications
for wines and spirits under TRIPS

23.1. Each Member shall provide the legal means for interested parties to prevent use of a geographical indication identifying wines for wines not originating in the place indicated by the geographical indication in question or identifying spirits for spirits not originating in the place indicated by the geographical indication in question, even where the true origin of the goods is indicated or the geographical indication is used in translation or accompanied by expressions such as 'kind', 'type', 'style', 'imitation' or the like.[4]

> [4] Notwithstanding the first sentence of Article 42, Members may, with respect to these obligations, instead provide for enforcement by administrative action.

Article 23 provides for an enhanced protection for geographical indications relating to wines and spirits. This provision represented a significant achievement for the EC, which has championed a strong protection of indications for such products. A distinct advantage of this strengthened protection—as compared to that generally available for other geographical indications—is that there is no need to prove unfair commercial practices or that the public is misled (as is the case under Article 22). Any person or entity that does not produce within the territory alluded by a geographical indication could be prevented from using the corresponding denomination. This, of course, greatly facilitates the enforcement of rights, though right-holders must still face the substantial costs that litigation in the intellectual property area generally entails. A further advantage of this 'absolute' protection is that it would permit *ex officio* action by WTO Members against false indications of origin, thus reducing the cost of protection in foreign markets.

The concept of 'wines' may be deemed not only to include beverages derived from grapes, but other alcoholic beverages, such as rice and fruit wines.[79] Similarly, the concept of 'spirits' is not entirely clear, as some beverages of low alcoholic content may not be considered included therein.[80]

Article 23.1 requires Members 'to provide the legal means for interested parties to prevent use' of geographical indications identifying wines and spirits. This Article sets out the objective of the measures ('to prevent') but does not spell out how this objective can be achieved. The general wording of this obligation leaves considerable room for Members to determine the nature of the measures to be applied.

Article 23.1 makes clear that geographical indications for wines and spirits deserve a higher level of protection than other goods. Subject to the exceptions discussed below, protection should be granted in order to prevent the use of indications

---

[79] This seems to be confirmed by the specification, in Article 24.6, of 'products of the vine' and 'grape varieties'. See, eg, UNCTAD-ICTSD op. cit. (2005), p 296.   [80] Ibidem.

identifying wines or spirits not originating in the place indicated by the geographical indication in question, even in cases where:

(a) the true origin of the goods is indicated; or
(b) the geographical indication is used in translation;
(c) the indication is accompanied by 'delocalizing' expressions such as 'kind', 'type', 'style', 'imitation', or the like.

The protection conferred means that the use of 'homonymous' indications is prohibited, and that there is no need to prove, as mentioned above, that the public is misled by the use of the indication. An important issue is that the protection under Article 23.1 only applies to the use of *identical* indications, and not *similar* indications, which would be covered under Article 22(2).[81]

Footnote 4 refers to an enforcement issue. In some countries, public authorities have the right, or the duty, to initiate enforcement proceedings, but this is not always available for the benefit of foreign geographical indications.[82] Right-holders would normally need to initiate such proceedings, which are generally very costly and lengthy especially when—as is the case under many national laws—the plaintiff has to prove false or deceptive use, or compliance with the specified conditions for use of a geographical indication. Of course, systems with prior registration may imply significant costs for acquiring the rights, but this may lead to lower costs for enforcement. In the case of geographical indications protectable under Article 23, there is no need to prove that the public is or may be misled, but compliance with the conditions set forth in Article 22.1 may be disputed and require proof by the party seeking protection.

The remedies available against infringement significantly differ across countries. As mentioned, the TRIPS Agreement leaves Members wide flexibility to determine both the mode of protection and the scope of the rights conferred. In some cases, such as when the discipline of unfair competition is applied, no exclusive rights are conferred, but only the right to prosecute those responsible for unfair commercial practices.[83]

Footnote 4 clarifies that Members may provide enforcement exclusively on the basis of administrative procedures, thereby carving out an exception to the general principle of Article 42 that requires the availability of 'civil judicial procedures'. The reason for this limitation is unclear, but probably linked to the fact that some countries may opt for an administrative form of protection for geographical indications. However, final administrative decisions can generally be reviewed by judicial courts.[84]

---

[81] See, eg, Knaak op. cit. (1996), p 132.

[82] See IP/C/W/253, paras 100 and 136; see also De Sousa op. cit. (2001), p 10.

[83] See generally A Kamperman Sanders op. cit. (1997); S Ladas, *Patents, Trademarks, and Related Rights. National and International Protection* (1997: Cambridge, MA, Harvard University Press), vol. III.

[84] Article 41.4 of the TRIPS Agreement stipulates that '[P]arties to a proceeding shall have an opportunity for review by a judicial authority of final administrative decisions and, subject to jurisdictional

23.2. The registration of a trademark for wines which contain or consist of a geographical indication identifying wines or for spirits which contain or consist of a geographical indication identifying spirits shall be refused or invalidated, *ex officio* if a Member's legislation so permits or at the request of an interested party, with respect to such wines or spirits not having this origin.

Article 23.2 addresses the relationship between geographical indications for wines or spirits and trademarks that eventually contain them. It provides for a specific ground for refusing or invalidating a trademark.[85] Members are not obliged to act *ex officio*, unless the domestic law provides for this possibility, but they are obliged to give 'interested parties' an opportunity to request such refusal or invalidation.

This provision allows for the protection of domestic and foreign geographical indications (for wines and spirits) against their use as trademarks. This is not an absolute prohibition, however. It does not prevent the producers of the territory from which the wines or spirits originate to apply for and own trademarks that contain or consist of the respective indications.

Like Article 22.3, this provision applies to trademarks that include, as one of their elements, indications for wines or spirits, but not to the case of the registration of similar or modified indications. An important difference with Article 22.3 is, however, that in the case of wines and spirits there is no need to prove that trademarks are of such a nature as to mislead the public. As noted before, this is the principal advantage conferred to geographical indications that fall under Article 23, as compared to other indications protectable under this Section of the TRIPS Agreement.

23.3. In the case of homonymous geographical indications for wines, protection shall be accorded to each indication, subject to the provisions of paragraph 4 of Article 22. Each Member shall determine the practical conditions under which the homonymous indications in question will be differentiated from each other, taking into account the need to ensure equitable treatment of the producers concerned and that consumers are not misled.

Article 23.3 addresses the same issue as Article 22.4, but puts on Members an additional obligation when the concerned products are wines.[86] They are bound to 'determine the practical conditions under which the homonymous indications in question will be differentiated from each other'. The reference to 'practical' seems to suggest that the conditions should be determined case by case and not in a general form, such as through the use of delocalizing terms or other additions. The adopted conditions should be sufficient to differentiate the goods from different origin.

provisions in a Member's law concerning the importance of a case, of at least the legal aspects of initial judicial decisions on the merits of a case. However, there shall be no obligation to provide an opportunity for review of acquittals in criminal cases.' See pp 415–6 below.

[85] This provision introduced a standard for the protection of geographical indications even higher than the one available under European law at the time of the adoption of the TRIPS Agreement. See Knaak op. cit. (1996), p 133.   [86] There is no reference to spirits in this provision.

Article 23.3 provides for two criteria for the determination of such conditions. They should ensure:

(a) equitable treatment of the producers concerned; and
(b) that consumers are not misled.

The first condition is important because it clarifies that none of the parties in conflict has the right to prevail over the other. The treatment of both parties should be 'equitable'. Hence, the fact that some producers in a territory have used a designation for a longer period than those of another territory would not be, as such, an element that would give the former an advantage over the latter. The key condition is that differentiation should be sufficient to prevent consumers' confusion with regard to the origin of the goods.

The wording 'each Member' points out that the Member where the conflict between the homonymous indications arises is bound to determine the conditions under which the differentiation may be ensured.

In any case, the expression 'subject to the provisions of paragraph 4 of Article 22' indicates that, prior to the application of the referred to conditions, a determination should be made whether any of the indications falsely represent to the public that the goods originate in another territory. Protection may be denied to the indication that induces to such a false representation.

23.4. In order to facilitate the protection of geographical indications for wines, negotiations shall be undertaken in the Council for TRIPS concerning the establishment of a multilateral system of notification and registration of geographical indications for wines eligible for protection in those Members participating in the system.

The TRIPS Agreement requires Members to undertake negotiations for the establishment of a 'multilateral system of notification and registration' for wines. This provision (jointly with Article 24.1) is exceptional in the Agreement, in the sense that it does not set out a specific standard but merely mandates Members to undertake negotiations. Under this provision, Members have not committed themselves to any particular outcome of such negotiations.

Despite the use of 'multilateral', such a system could only be operative in 'those Members participating in the system'; that is, some Members may opt out and decide no to participate therein.

Significant differences exist among WTO Members with regard to the ways of implementing Article 23.4. The coverage of the proposed system has been one of the areas of controversy. While Article 23.4 only refers to *wines*, some Members[87] have sought to develop a system covering *spirits* as well.[88] In fact, the WTO Members

---

[87] Notably Mexico and the United States, on account of their production of tequila and bourbon, respectively (Vivas Eugui op. cit. (2001), p 210).

[88] The Ministerial Declaration of Singapore (1996) had endorsed the Council for TRIPS report, which in its para 34 stated that '... in regard to geographical indications ... The Council will initiate ... preliminary work on issues relevant to the negotiations specified in Article 23.4 of the TRIPS

agreed at the Doha Ministerial Conference 'to negotiate the establishment of a multilateral system of notification and registration of geographical indications for wines and spirits by the Fifth Session of the Ministerial Conference' (para 18).[89]

The European Communities and their Member States proposed[90] an international registration system for such indications whereunder registered indications would be automatically protected in the participating Members, subject to a procedure for dealing with oppositions from each Member who considers that a geographical indication is not eligible for protection in its territory (Box 7.4).

Box 7.4: EC Proposal for a registration and notification system

Submission

Members wishing to avail themselves of the registration facility may send applications to the WTO Secretariat with the list of geographical indications recognized and protected in their country of origin and elements of proof that the geographical indication corresponds to the definition of Article 22.1 of the TRIPS Agreement;

Members will have to notify the WTO Secretariat regional and multilateral agreements as well as the list of geographical indications.

Notification

By the WTO Secretariat of the dossier (list of indications and elements of proof) to all WTO Members.

Opposition procedure

Time limit for opposition: 1 year.

Grounds for refusing protection:

- the name does not fulfill the requirements of a geographical indication under Art. 22.1 of the TRIPS Agreement;
- the geographical indication is not protected in the country of origin;
- the geographical indication has become a generic or is the customary name of a grape variety in the third country on 1 January 1995;
- the grographical indication, although literally true falsely represents that the goods originate from the territory.

Negotiation between the parties

- In case of homonymous indications;
- In case of prior use of trademarks.

Agreement for wines. Issues relevant to a notification and registration system for spirits will be part of this preliminary work . . . [which] would be conducted without prejudice to the rights and obligations of members under the TRIPS Agreement'.

[89] See Ministerial Declaration, WT/MIN(01)/DEC/1, para 18.
[90] See IP/C/W/107, 28 July 1998.

Legal effects

- full and indefinite protection of geographical indications one year after notification in all WTO Members;
- no effect pending opposition procedure;
- opposition mechanism (yet to be developed);
- in case of successful opposition, the Member is not obliged to apply the principle of full and indefinite protection.

Publication

- definitive lists of geographical indications to be published (one for wines and one for spirits), including references to the relevant national legislation;
- updating when additional lists of geographical indications.

Alterations (i.e., changes) in the multilateral register

- addition of new geographical indications;
- possibility for each Member to request re-examination of a geographical indication in two cases: the indication has ceased to be protected or it has fallen into disuse.

Source: T Wasescha, 'Recent developments in the Council for TRIPS (WTO)', WIPO, *Symposium on the International Protection of Geographical Indications*, 1999, Somerset West, Cape Province, 1–2 September, p 25.

The EC proposal would lead to a significant strengthening of the international protection of geographical indications, particularly as it would ensure indefinite protection of all internationally registered indications, one year after notification, in *all* WTO Members.

On the other hand, United States and Japan envisaged the development of an international database of geographical indications to which Members would be expected to have reference in the operation of their national systems. The US–Japanese proposal was later on endorsed by Canada and Chile[91] and supported by other countries. The main characteristics of this system are described in Box 7.5.

This proposal aims at neither creating additional obligations nor diminishing the rights and obligations contained in Section 3 of the TRIPS Agreement, nor imposing burdensome procedures on Members and the WTO Secretariat. The system is based on a voluntary approach.

Hungary suggested the involvement of WIPO in order to alleviate the administrative burden of management of a new possible notification and registration system,[92] and proposed alternative approaches to the system delineated by the EC and their Member States (see Box 7.6).

[91] See IP/C/W/133 of 11 March 1999 and 133/Rev.1 of 26 July 1999.
[92] See T Wasecha, 'Recent developments in the Council for TRIPS (WTO)', WIPO, *Symposium on the International Protection of Geographic Indications*, Somerset West, Cape Province, September 1–2, 1999, p 27.

Box 7.5: US–Japan proposal for a registration and notification system

---

Notification

- The system proposed is voluntary and participation in the system can be terminated at any time;
- A Member wishing to participate submits a list of domestic geographical indications for 'covered products', with an indication of the date, if any, on which protection will expire;
- Notifications are to be made once or twice a year to avoid an administrative burden.

Registration

- The registration system proposed consists in a data base compiling all notified geographical indications for covered products;
- Two identical or similar geographical indications may be submitted by more than one Member, provided the indication is recognized by each notifying Member in accordance with its national regime;
- Transparency is ensured through distribution of lists of geographical indications to all Members and through the WTO web site;
- The WTO Secretariat is in charge of the administrative management of the database (additions, deletions) on the basis of the notifications.

Legal effects

- Participating Members agree to 'refer to' the WTO lists of notified geographical indications for covered products when making decisions to provide protection for geographical indications for such products in accordance with their national legislation;
- Appeals from, or objections to, any decision (grant or rejection) concerning a particular geographical indication must be made at the national level at the request of appropriate interested parties;
- Notwithstanding the above (i.e., whether there is a registration or not in the data base), geographical indications in accordance with national legislation are entitled to protection under Section 3.

Review

After two years from the establishment of the system.

Source: T Wasescha, 'Recent developments in the Council for TRIPS (WTO)', WIPO, *Symposium on the International Protection of Geographical Indications*, 1999, Somerset West, Cape Province, 1–2 September, p 26.

These diverging interests and views on the issue of protection of wines and spirits have led to the emergence of a complex web of alliances involving both developed and developing countries. Members' positions have been largely determined by their own policies and perceptions about the benefits and costs of a broad and strong protection for geographical indications. European countries (including Switzerland),

---

Box 7.6: Hungarian proposal

The system proposed by the EC involving direct bilateral consultations in the case of disagreement regarding registration of a geographical indication should be supplemented with a multilateral procedure that would apply where bilateral negotiations do not yield a settlement. In justification of its proposal, Hungary has stated that, amongst other things, the possibility to seek a solution of a multilateral character is necessary to ensure that smaller WTO Members enjoy the same opportunities for representing their legitimate commercial interests as larger ones. Under the proposal, if, within the 18-month period prescribed under the EC proposal, negotiations following a Member's challenge of a notified geographical indication have not led to a mutually satisfactory result, the dispute will be submitted to binding arbitration. Geographical indications that have been successfully challenged on the basis of the definition contained in Article 22.1 or because they are false pursuant to Article 22.4 will not be registered. Members who successfully challenge protection on the basis of the exception for generic terms (Article 24.6) will not have to protect the geographical indication, even though they cannot prevent entry of the geographical indication in the register on this ground. The same would apply in respect of challenges based on the exceptions contained in Article 24.4 for prior use and Article 24.5 for pre-existing trademarks. Registration will only have effect in Members participating in the system.

Source: A Taubman, 'The way ahead: developing international protection for geographical indications: thinking locally, acting globally', *Symposium on the International Protection of Geographical Indications* (2001: WIPO/GEO/MVD/01/9, Montevideo, 28–29 November), p 6.

---

with a long tradition on the matter and in possession of a large number of geographical indications to be potentially protected globally, not surprisingly favour a multilateral system of notification and registration for wines (and spirits) that facilitates protection and enforcement of such indications in all Member States. Other Members with a shorter history as independent States, which received immigrants who brought with them the names of their places of origin (giving rise to 'homonymous' indications) fear that, on balance, an enhanced protection in this area may prejudice rather than benefit their trade interests. In particular, some Members resist the creation of a system that would grant further trade advantages precisely to those Members that keep high barriers in the field of agriculture. In this context, the following considerations can be made.

First, quality wine production is concentrated in a few countries, such as some European countries,[93] the United States, Chile, South Africa, Australia, and Argentina. Expectedly, other countries may have little interest in a system that (like the one proposed by EC) would significantly improve the possibility of enforcing foreign geographical indications.

---

[93] Thus, out of 831 geographical indications registered under the Lisbon Agreement, 70.3 per cent belong to West European countries, 23.3 per cent to East European countries, and only 6.3 per cent to developing countries (Algeria, Cuba, Mexico, Tunisia) parties to the Agreement.

Second, Article 23.4 asks for a system to 'facilitate protection of geographical indications for wines', and not for a system to strengthen or expand such protection.

Third, the system should consist of 'notification' and 'registration' of geographical indications. Registration of intellectual property rights is, in some cases (eg trademarks, patents), required for the acquisition of rights, but in other cases (eg copyright) only provides a presumption of titlehood and does not create any rights. National laws on geographical indications considerably diverge on this issue, including systems under which special protection is conferred.[94] Notification and registration of such indications may be established for transparency purposes without creating further legal effects.

Fourth, the system should apply to geographical indications 'eligible for protection in those Members participating in the system' (Article 23.4). This wording suggests that the system is to be based on voluntary rather than binding participation.

Fifth, the establishment of the system as proposed by the EC would require, in practice, to conduct trade-related negotiations for just one single tariff-line product, a process that many Members regard as too burdensome and unjustified.[95]

Finally, an opposition system as suggested in the European proposal may be expensive for many developing countries, and may put them in a weak position where homonymous geographical indications exist.[96]

International negotiations: exceptions

24.1. Members agree to enter into negotiations aimed at increasing the protection of individual geographical indications under Article 23. The provisions of paragraphs 4 through 8 below shall not be used by a Member to refuse to conduct negotiations or to conclude bilateral or multilateral agreements. In the context of such negotiations, Members shall be willing to consider the continued applicability of these provisions to individual geographical indications whose use was the subject of such negotiations.

Under Article 24.1 Members also undertake to enter into negotiations, in this case aimed at 'increasing the protection of individual geographical indications under Article 23' (ie, those relating to wines and spirits). This obligation suggests that, for some Members, the Uruguay Round was unable to reach a fully satisfactory agreement on the subject.

The mandate in this provision relates to 'individual' geographical indications, and not to geographical indications in general nor to the development of new standards thereon. The aim of such negotiations should be 'increasing protection'.

The provision does not specify whether the negotiations should be of a bilateral or multilateral nature. Given that negotiations refer to 'individual' indications,

---

[94] See IP/C/W/253, 4 April 2001, p 13.   [95] See Vivas Eugui op. cit. (2001), p 703.
[96] Ibidem.

their outcome would only benefit the parties interested in the protection of such particular indications.

The exceptions provided for in Article 24 shall not be used to refuse to conduct negotiations or to conclude bilateral or multilateral agreements. This means that, despite the fact that Members are not obliged to confer protection in cases subject to an exception (see Article 1 of the TRIPS Agreement), they may not refuse to enter into negotiations that may eventually lead to the elimination or reduction in the scope of such exceptions, although there is no obligation to do so. Nevertheless, the last sentence of Article 24.1 recognizes the Members' right ('... Members shall be willing to consider the continued applicability of these provisions ...') to maintain the exceptions negotiated under the TRIPS Agreement.

Noticeably, this provision goes beyond the multilateral negotiations, as it refers to 'bilateral or multilateral agreements'. It is through bilateral agreements[97] that the EU has been able (eg agreement with South Africa) to expand the protection for European geographical indications.

Although the wording of Article 24.1 refers to 'individual' geographical indications', and to those covered by Article 23 (ie for wines and spirits), some Members have read this article as opening the door for broader negotiations aiming at enhancing the protection of geographical indications in general. The EC and their Member States, not surprisingly, strongly favour this approach. It has also been supported by a number of developing countries in the belief that they could extract benefits from an enhanced protection of some geographical indications. Thus, Egypt proposed that the additional protection conferred for geographical indications for wines and spirits (Article 23.1) be extended to other products, particularly those of interest to developing countries (WT/GC/W/136). Turkey (WT/GC/W/249) and the Czech Republic have demanded an additional protection for specific foodstuffs and handicraft products. In the case of the latter, it especially sought an enhanced protection 'for beers which are particularly vulnerable to imitation, counterfeit and usurpation and whose protection of such indications against consumer deception is insufficient and trademark protection is not satisfactory due to its formal requirements such as registration and the use requirement' (WT/GC/W/206).

The Indian delegation has also argued that

'it is an anomaly that the higher level of protection is available only for wines and spirits. It is proposed that such higher level of protection should be available for goods other than wines and spirits also. This would be helpful for products of export interest like basmati rice, Darjeeling tea, alphonso mangoes, Kohlapuri slippers in the case of India. It is India's belief that there are other Members of the WTO who would be interested in higher level of protection to products of export interest to them like Bulgarian yoghurt, Czech Pilsen beer, many agricultural products of the European Union, Hungarian Szatmar plums and

---

[97] On the implications of the MFN clause on these bilateral agreements, see UNCTAD-ICTSD op. cit. (2005), p 301.

so on. There is a need to expedite work already initiated in the Council for TRIPS in this regard, under Article 24, so that benefits arising out of the TRIPS Agreement in this area are spread out wider' (WT/GC/W/147).

The proposals relating to the expansion of the products covered by an additional protection have been supported by a number of developing countries, such as Cuba, Dominican Republic, Honduras, Indonesia, Nicaragua, and Pakistan (WT/GC/W/208), the African Group (WT/GC/W/302), and Venezuela (WT/GC/W/282). Bulgaria, the Czech Republic, Egypt, Iceland, India, Kenya, Liechtenstein, Pakistan, Slovenia, Sri Lanka, Switzerland, and Turkey made a submission to the Council for TRIPS[98] supporting an extension to other products and proposing a 'basket approach' that would take into consideration the issue of extension as a full component of the built-in agenda.[99]

For another group of countries, there is no mandate under Article 24.1 to extend the 'absolute' protection conferred to wines and spirits to other products. The Doha Ministerial Conference decided to address this issue as part of the 'Implementation-related issues and concerns' defined by the WTO Doha Ministerial Conference.[100] The proposal to increase the protection of geographical indications has been opposed by many developing (notably Argentina, Chile) and developed (eg Australia and the USA) countries.[101] Table 7.3 summarizes the arguments for and against the expansion of protection.

The outstanding differences on this issue are deep and unlikely to be easily overcome. While some developing countries expect to benefit from the extension of protection, if it occurred, European countries (including Switzerland), which are in possession of a large number of geographical indications, may, in the last instance, benefit the most. There are also fears that geographical indications could be used as a substitute for other protectionist measures that developed countries apply in agriculture, and that eventual reductions in agricultural protection be conditioned upon acceptance of an increased protection for geographical indications.

The extent to which developing countries might benefit from an expansion of the protection for geographical indications is doubtful, particularly as they would be required to extend the same enhanced protection to a large number of indications

---

[98] IP/C/W/204/Rev.1   [99] See, eg, Vivas Eugui op. cit. (2001).

[100] Ministerial Declaration, WT/MIN(01)/DEC/1, paras 12 and 18. However, Argentina indicated that the extension of geographical indication to products other than wines and spirits cannot be treated as part of the 'outstanding implementation issues' and that 'consensus will be required to launch negotiations on these issues' (Communication from Argentina, WT/MIN(01)/W/8). Other countries responded that negotiations on the extension of protection did not require additional consensus. See the Communication from Bulgaria, Kenya, India, and Sri Lanka, WT/MIN(01)/W/9, 13 November 2001, and the Communication from Bulgaria, the Czech Republic, the European Communities and its Member States, Hungary, Liechtenstein, Kenya, Mauritius, Nigeria, Pakistan, the Slovak Republic, Slovenia, Sri Lanka, Switzerland, Thailand, and Turkey, WT/MIN(01)/W/11, 14 November 2001.

[101] See, eg, the Communication from Argentina, Australia, Canada, Chile, Guatemala, New Zealand, Paraguay, and the US (IP/C/W/289, para 3).

Table 7.3 Arguments for and against increased protection to products other than wines and spirits

For increased protection	Against increased protection
(a) additional protection of geographical indications for all products adds value for exports because it increases the chances of market access for such goods;	(a) the legal and administrative costs associated with extending the scope of Article 23.1 would be significant;
(b) without the additional protection, free-riding is possible and there is a risk that geographical indications will become generic over time;	(b) there is no evidence of failure of Article 22 to protect geographical indications for products other than wines and spirits;
(c) the test contained in Article 22, which currently applies to products other than wines and spirits, leads to legal uncertainty in the enforcement of protection for geographical indications;	(c) there is no evidence to indicate whether extending the scope of Article 23.1 to products other than wine and spirits would result in more effective protection than is already afforded to those products under Article 22;
(d) Article 22 places a costly burden of proof on the producer entitled to use a geographical indication to show that the public has been misled, or that there has been an act of unfair competition.	(d) additional protection could close off future market access opportunities for emerging industries and result in uncertainty concerning the continued use in existing markets;
	(e) consumer confusion would be caused through the disappearance of terms customarily used to identify products which will, in turn, increase search and transaction costs for consumers and potentially prices as well.

Source: De Sousa op. cit. (2001), pp 8–9.

from Europe.[102] Geographical indications, such as trademarks and other forms of intellectual property rights, permit to charge consumers a 'premium' above marginal costs. How large such a premium could be is dependent on a number of factors, such as market size, degree of competition with substitutes, consumers' perceptions about the linkage of an indication with product attributes, and demand elasticity. Some geographical indications may be suitable, for instance, to address 'niche markets' (such as markets for 'organic' products), though there are obvious limits to the size of such markets.[103]

---

[102] In addition to the 118 already registered geographical indications for agricultural products and foodstuffs, there might be in Italy at least 3,558 products that may potentially seek recognition under geographical indications (interview with the Italian Minister of Agriculture and Forestry Policy, reported by G Pinna, 'Che cosa bolle davvero in pentola', *Panorama* (2002) Year XL, No 32, Italy, p 46.

[103] In the 1990s, locally produced foodstuffs accounted for 10.6 per cent of the total foodstuffs market in France, 10.7 per cent in Italy, 6.7 per cent in Spain, and 5.2 per cent in Portugal. See Rangnekar op. cit. (2002), p 14.

For example, it has been noted that the selling price of the 'Poulet de Bresse' was four times the price of the standard chicken. The olive oil 'Riviera Ligure' (Italy) was sold for 30 per cent more than anonymous olive oil; the price of 'Roccaverano' cheese (from Alto Monferrato, Italy) is reported to have increased by 100 per cent, and the supply was insufficient to satisfy the growing demand.[104]

As illustrated by these examples, there are cases in which consumers exhibit a preference for authentic and distinctive products associated to a particular region, and are willing to pay a premium price. Sales of agricultural products and food-stuffs under European protected designations of origin are reported to grow at a rate of 5–10 per cent a year, and to have reached €7.7 billion in 2001, 56.8 per cent of which corresponds to cheese and 36.9 per cent to salami and ham. Almost 20 per cent of the total (in value) was exported.[105] The growth of market segments like 'organic' is evidence that select consumers recognize and value the product–place association in foodstuffs. It has also been noted, however, that

a range of developments involving packaging and preservation, processing and distribu-tion, production and marketing, have fundamentally weakened the product's territorial and land-based associations embedded in the consumer's mind. The movement of prod-ucts from their territory of origin and their production/processing in other locales suggests that in certain instances technical aspects of production/processing can override features of the product that are intrinsically linked to its area of origin.[106]

Creating value in the market through a geographical indication normally requires investment such as in production methods, development of reliable sup-plies of raw materials, quality controls, etc. Hence, there are costs to be borne which may not be trivial.

Exploiting geographical indications also requires an effective marketing effort to guide and develop consumer perceptions. As noted by Tregear *et al* (1998),

consumer perceptions of regionality are tied closely to perceived authenticity. More specif-ically, official designation of a food as regional may not be sufficient to convey authentic regionality to consumers: consumers also appear to infer regionality from, for example, a product's physical attributes, place of purchase or consumption and communicated heri-tage. Marketing techniques are critical therefore in conveying authenticity and enhancing the attractiveness of regional foods. The success of policy measures such as EU 2081/92 or regional food promotion schemes may therefore hinge upon careful consideration and implementation of wider marketing techniques for regional foods' (p 392).[107]

In addition to direct investment, the use of a geographical indication requires control by an authority (or owner of a certification mark) in order to ensure that the characteristics of the products and quality standards are met. For instance, for

[104] G Pinna op. cit. (2002), p 45; Vital op. cit. (1999), p 52.   [105] Ibidem.
[106] Rangnekar op. cit. (2002), p 14.
[107] A Tregear, S Kuznesof, and A Moxey, 'Policy initiatives for regional foods: some insights from consumer research', (1998) Food Policy 23(5), pp 383–94 (quoted in Rangnekar op. cit. (2002), p 14).

the recognition of a quality wine under an appellation of origin, it is necessary, taking into account the traditional conditions of production, to define and verify for each quality wine:

- the delimitation of the production area;
- vine varieties;
- cultivation methods;
- minimum natural alcoholic strength by volume;
- yield per hectare;
- analysis and assessment of organoleptic characteristics.[108]

The sophistication of a system of verification for quality wines is illustrated by the case of South Africa as described in Box 7.7.[109]

Box 7.7: Certification system for wines in South Africa

Officials who are appointed in terms of the Liquor Products Act are given the right to take random samples of alcohol products from both the premises of producers and from liquor outlets and to analyse these so as to ensure that each product complies with all legal requirements, and that it carries no prohibited indications or indications which the producer is not entitled to use, and no misleading indications. Where such samples are found to contravene the legislation, the officials are entitled to seize the products and call upon the responsible persons to rectify the defects, failing which, criminal proceedings could be instituted. This does not extend only to wines intended for the domestic market, but to all wines intended for export, where origin-related claims must be substantiated and certificates of origin issued by the Wine & Spirits Board. No claims on origin may be made, unless such claim has been verified and certified by the Wine & Spirits Board.

Where a producer intends producing a wine of origin, he is obliged to notify the Board of his intention to do so before harvesting grapes, and to give the relevant officials of the Board an opportunity to verify the origin and cultivar of the grapes concerned. This ensures that the claims of the producer are true from the outset and adhered to throughout the production process. On applying for final certification, the Board requires that samples of all labels are submitted to it and checks each and every indication on the labels to ensure that all legal requirements have been met, correspond with the product, and are not prohibited or misleading.

Source: A Stern, 'The protection of geographical indications in South Africa', *Symposium on the International Protection of Geographical Indications*, (1999: WIPO, Somerset West, Cape Province, 1–2 September), p 34.

---

[108] F Vital op. cit. (1999), p 56.
[109] See also J Niekerk, 'The use of geographical indications in a collective marketing strategy: the example of the South Africa Wine Industry', WIPO, *Symposium on the International Protection of Geographical Indications*, Somerset West, Cape Province, September 1–2, 1999, pp 79–88.

The verification of compliance with established standards generally requires the regular testing of samples. In some cases, an authority certifies (and marks with a seal) origin and quality. The costs of such activities may be financed via a fee charged on producers or supported by States. However, the implementation of controls may not be simple, since it may require a large number of trained people to undertake inspections and penalize deviations from approved standards, while ensuring that such standards are controlled and applied in a uniform manner.[110]

Finally, in addition to the cost associated with the acquisition of rights over geographical indications, and of those necessary to defend the indication against infringement or loss of its distinctive character, countries introducing protection in this field should consider the possible losses emerging from the closing down of domestic activities based on the use of foreign geographical indications that become protected. Such losses may be more or less significant depending on the circumstances, and on the extent to which the exceptions allowed by the TRIPS Agreement are applied.

> 24.2. The Council for TRIPS shall keep under review the application of the provisions of this Section; the first such review shall take place within two years of the entry into force of the WTO Agreement. Any matter affecting the compliance with the obligations under these provisions may be drawn to the attention of the Council, which, at the request of a Member, shall consult with any Member or Members in respect of such matter in respect of which it has not been possible to find a satisfactory solution through bilateral or plurilateral consultations between the Members concerned. The Council shall take such action as may be agreed to facilitate the operation and further the objectives of this Section.

In accordance with Article 24.2, the Council for TRIPS shall keep under review the *application* of the provisions of this section.[111] The first such review was scheduled for within two years of the entry into force of the WTO Agreement. This provision was obviously intended to accelerate the application of the obligations relating to geographical indications in Member countries. The period of two years provided for was shorter than the general period for review stipulated in Article 71.1 of the Agreement,[112] which only commenced on 1 January 2000. Such shorter period, however, did not derogate the transitional periods provided for in Articles 65 and 66 of the Agreement; that is, Members that could enjoy those transitional periods were not bound to anticipate protection for geographical indications.

---

[110] Some Italian producers of 'zucchine' of Liguria and Sannio have been reported, for instance, to have abandoned their attempts to get recognition of geographical indications, in view of the severe controls required (Pinna op. cit. (2002), p 47).

[111] Unlike Article 27.3(b) of the TRIPS Agreement, which refers to the 'review' of the subparagraph, Article 24.2 is clearly limited to the review of the implementation of the provision of Section 3 of Part II of the Agreement.

[112] Article 71.1: 'The Council for TRIPS shall review the implementation of this Agreement after the expiration of the transitional period referred to in paragraph 2 of Article 65.'

In addition, the Council for TRIPS can also undertake consultations and 'action as may be agreed to facilitate the operation and further the objectives of this Section'. The wording is ambiguous about what 'action' may be taken by the Council. It should certainly be within its ordinary competence, as Article 24.2 does not expand the authority conferred on the Council.

The examination of laws and regulations started in November 1996 for those Members obliged to comply with the TRIPS Agreement at that time. A checklist of questions was prepared concerning national protection of geographical indications, and 37 sets of responses were received. A summary paper based on such responses was prepared by the WTO Secretariat, upon the Council's request. The examination showed significant differences in the way of implementing the provisions on geographical indications at the national level.[113]

Considerable debate has surrounded the scope of the review under Article 24.2 of the TRIPS Agreement. For some developing and developed countries, the mandate to 'review the application of the provisions of this Section' includes not only an examination of the implementation of such provisions by Members but also provide an opportunity for possible changes in those provisions in order to improve available protection.[114] But this view, which does not seem to find support in the text of the provision interpreted in its context, is not shared by all Members. As a result, there are two main positions on Article 24.2.

(1) any review or negotiation must fall under the principles of increasing protection and not refusal of present or future negotiations;
(2) there is no link between the review and negotiations for increased protection or the establishment of a multilateral register on wines.[115]

> **24.3. In implementing this Section, a Member shall not diminish the protection of geographical indications that existed in that Member immediately prior to the date of entry into force of the WTO Agreement.**

Article 24.3 prevents Members from diminishing 'the protection' of geographical indications as granted on the date of entry into force of the WTO Agreement. A similar freezing clause is contained in Article 65.5.[116] A common element of both provisions is that neither of them restrains the Members rights to amend their laws. There are, however, major difference between these two provisions.

First, Article 65.5 only applied during the transitional period and has no effect once that period is over. Article 24.3 is, instead, permanent.

Second, the only restriction imposed by Article 65.5 was that, if the national law was amended, it could not diminish the protection conferred *below* the minimum

---

[113] See Review under Article 24 of the application of the provisions of the section of the TRIPS Agreement on geographical indications. Summary of the responses to the checklist of questions (IP/C/13 and ADD. 1), IP/C/W/253; Wasecha op. cit. (1999), p 23.

[114] See, eg, the Communication (Revision) from Bulgaria, the Czech Republic, Egypt, Iceland, India, Kenya, Liechtenstein, Pakistan, Slovenia, Sri Lanka, Switzerland, and Turkey (IP/C/W/204/Rev.1).

[115] See Vivas Eugui op. cit. (2001).   [116] See pp 495–6 below.

standards provided for by the TRIPS Agreement. If the resulting protection was above or just consistent with the TRIPS standards, no violation of Article 65.5 could be articulated.

In the case of Article 24.3, however, there seems to be an obligation to keep the pre-TRIPS level of protection, even if an amendment to the law that diminished protection resulted in a level of protection above or just consistent with the TRIPS standards. The chilling effect of Article 24.3 is, hence, much more significant that that under Article 65.5.

When the 'protection' for the purposes of Article 24.3 is diminished may be controversial in many instances. For example, if a country moved from a system of *sui generis* protection of geographical indications to a system based on certification marks, could be it argued that there has been a reduction of protection, as the rights conferred will not be exactly the same under both regimes?

> **24.4. Nothing in this Section shall require a Member to prevent continued and similar use of a particular geographical indication of another Member identifying wines or spirits in connection with goods or services by any of its nationals or domiciliaries who have used that geographical indication in a continuous manner with regard to the same or related goods or services in the territory of that Member either (a) for at least 10 years preceding 15 April 1994 or (b) in good faith preceding that date.**

Article 24.4 introduces an important exception to the 'absolute' protection conferred to geographical indications for wines and spirits (Article 23(1)) and to the general prohibition on deception of the public (Article 22(2)). The continued and similar use of a geographical indication of another Member identifying wines and spirits shall not be affected where such a use takes place under certain conditions.

First, the use must be in connection with 'goods or services' in the territory of a Member 'by any of its nationals or domiciliaries'. Note the reference to 'services' in this clause. It may comprise, for instance, the use of a geographical indication in advertising. Most importantly, the exception is confined to the use by the 'nationals or domiciliaries' of the Member where the exception is invoked, and as far as that use takes place in the Member's territory. The reference to 'domiciliaries' extends protection to non-nationals established in the relevant territory, but excludes other non-nationals without domicile in the country concerned. This amounts to a derogation of the national treatment principle[117] mandated by the Agreement.

Second, the exception allows the future use of a particular geographical indication in the same or in a manner 'similar' to the use given in another Member. This means that, for instance, the geographical indication may continue to be used as a trademark, if that was the case. But the continued use may also be in the form of a generic name.

---

[117] See Chapter 2 above.

Third, the use must have taken place in a 'continuous' and 'similar' manner with regard to the same or related goods or services. 'Continuous' means that the use should not have been interrupted, although it might be a matter of interpretation whether non-use for short periods would make the exception inapplicable.

Fourth, the relevant past use may have taken place in any form, as a generic name, a geographical indication, or a trademark. There is no distinction in this regard in Article 24.4. Further, that use may have concerned 'the same or related goods or services', thereby broadening the scope for the exceptions where use did not refer to the *same* goods. What 'related goods or services' may be is left to the interpretation of each Member willing to apply the exception.

Fifth, prior continuous use may provide the basis for an exception according to Article 24.4 in either of the two following cases:

(a) When the use lasted for at least ten years preceding the date of the Ministerial Meeting concluding the Uruguay Round of Multilateral Trade Negotiations (that is, 15 April 2004). There is no qualification about the nature of such use. Even use made knowing that a foreign geographical indication was involved—and possibly benefiting from the market value of such indication—may provide the basis for the exception.

(b) When the use was made in good faith preceding that date, independently of the time during such use continued. The key issue for the application of this condition will be the determination of a subjective element, the good or bad faith of the person using the indication. Use without knowledge of the existence of the foreign indication will most likely be deemed use in good faith in most jurisdictions. If the existence of a foreign indication was known, the determination of bad faith may be based on the intent to benefit from the market value of a foreign indication. It may also be considered, however, that a knowing use of a foreign indication might not be considered in bad faith to the extent that it was legally irreprochable under the law applicable when the use took place.[118]

> 24.5. Where a trademark has been applied for or registered in good faith, or where rights to a trademark have been acquired through use in good faith either: (a) before the date of application of these provisions in that Member as defined in Part VI; or (b) before the geographical indication is protected in its country of origin; measures adopted to implement this Section shall not prejudice eligibility for or the validity of the registration of a trademark, or the right to use a trademark, on the basis that such a trademark is identical with, or similar to, a geographical indication.

The TRIPS Agreement shall not affect the eligibility or validity of trademarks applied for, registered or acquired through use in good faith, which are identical with or similar to a geographical indication, if they were applied for or the rights

---

[118] See, eg, UNCTAD-ICTSD op. cit. (2005), p 304.

acquired before the date of application of the TRIPS Agreement's provisions in the relevant Member[119] or before the geographical indication became protected in its country of origin. A trademark applied for or obtained in good faith under the conditions set forth in Article 24.5 may be maintained unchanged in all Member countries.

The main field of application of Article 24.5 is likely to be in relation to trademarks applied for or acquired before the specified date, since thereafter it would be more difficult to claim good faith. Future trademarks may, however, be protected against challenges when applied for or acquired before a particular geographical indication was recognized in the country of origin.

The second part of this provision ('measures adopted to implement this Section shall not prejudice eligibility for or the validity of the registration of a trademark, or the right to use a trademark, on the basis that such a trademark is identical with, or similar to, a geographical indication') indicates that identity of similarity of a trademark with a protected geographical indication would not be sufficient ground to challenge the former's eligibility for protection or validity. It is also noticeable that this text refers to 'this Section' and not to 'this provision', thereby implying that the eligibility for protection or the validity of the registration or the right to use a trademark is not affected by identity or similarity as such with a geographical indication in all cases, including indications for wines or spirits.[120]

> **24.6. Nothing in this Section shall require a Member to apply its provisions in respect of a geographical indication of any other Member with respect to goods or services for which the relevant indication is identical with the term customary in common language as the common name for such goods or services in the territory of that Member. Nothing in this Section shall require a Member to apply its provisions in respect of a geographical indication of any other Member with respect to products of the vine for which the relevant indication is identical with the customary name of a grape variety existing in the territory of that Member as of the date of entry into force of the WTO Agreement.**

Members are not obliged to recognize rights relating to geographical indications if these are identical with a term 'customary in common language as the common name' for certain goods or services in those countries. This is an important exception, since some geographical indications (such as 'champagne') have become common names in many countries and significant business and consumers interests could be affected if its use were prohibited.

Article 24.6 refers to 'common' rather than 'generic' names as it is the practice under trademark law. It is unclear whether the drafters intended to point out a distinction between the two concepts; it may be perhaps argued that 'common' is narrower than 'generic' as it is possible that the use of the term had become common

---

[119] On the date of application of the Agreement to different categories of Members, see Chapter 14 below.

[120] With regard to trademarks relating to geographical indications for wine and spirits, see Article 23.2 above. This Article mandates refusal or invalidation only in cases where the trademark identifies wines or spirits not having the origin evoked or named by the geographical indication.

but still the public might be aware that it is not the proper 'generic' name of the relevant goods. If this interpretation were correct, the exception would be narrower than a generic-based provision.

What is 'customary in common language' will depend on the fact of each case. An issue that this provision has not taken into account is that in many countries there is a rich cultural diversity, and that a large number of different languages may be spoken, particularly at the local level. In the absence of any specification, it would seem appropriate to consider that a name is common if it is customarily used as such in the country, even though it may not be used in all existing languages.

An exception also applies to the 'products of the vine for which the relevant indication is identical with the customary name of a grape of a variety' existing in the territory of the Member as of the date of entry into force of the TRIPS Agreement. Although alternative interpretations have been suggested for this poorly drafted text,[121] it seems logical to understand it as permitting a Member where grape varieties are named identically to an indication for vine products of another Member, to continue using such name.

As Article 24.6 refers to '[N]othing in this Section', it makes clear that this important exception applies to *all* types of geographical indications, including for wines and spirits.

It is also of note that, unlike Article 24.4, this provision does not limit the right to continued use to the country of domicile, but it extends to all Members where the indication has become a common name.[122]

> **24.7. A Member may provide that any request made under this Section in connection with the use or registration of a trademark must be presented within five years after the adverse use of the protected indication has become generally known in that Member or after the date of registration of the trademark in that Member provided that the trademark has been published by that date, if such date is earlier than the date on which the adverse use became generally known in that Member, provided that the geographical indication is not used or registered in bad faith.**

Article 24.7 contains a rather complicated facultative provision ('[A] Member may provide . . . '), which aims at generating some certainty about the use or eligibility of trademark protection. This provision essentially makes incontestable trademarks that may be in conflict with geographical indications after some specified periods, on the grounds of deception of the public or forbidden use of geographical indications for wines and spirits. These maximum periods, however, would not apply if the trademark that consists of a geographical indication was used or registered in bad faith.

The five-year term may be counted from the date the adverse use of the protected indication has become generally known in the Member. Alternatively, it may be counted from the date of registration of the trademark in the Member (provided

---

[121] See UNCTAD-ICTSD op. cit. (2005), pp 305–6.
[122] See Knaak op. cit. (1996), p 136.

that the trademark has been published by that date) if such date is earlier than the date on which the adverse use became generally known in that Member. The determination of the 'date on which the adverse use became generally known' is critical for the application of this provision. Since an identifier becomes generally known through a process of diffusion of the relevant products, advertising and other forms of communication, and not instantly, it may be quite difficult to establish when such general knowledge has been attained. The application of this provision, if incorporated in national laws, may be, hence, very controversial.

> **24.8. The provisions of this Section shall in no way prejudice the right of any person to use, in the course of trade, that person's name or the name of that person's predecessor in business, except where such name is used in such a manner as to mislead the public.**

In addition to the exceptions mentioned above, Article 24.8 specifically excludes the application of Section 3 in relation to the use, in the course of trade, of a person's name or of the name of his predecessor in business. However, this right is limited and overridden by the protection of a geographical indication where it is proven that 'such name is used in such a manner as to mislead the public'. This wording suggests the intention to mislead the public, that is, a use in bad faith. If this circumstance is not proven, the right to use the name would remain unfettered.

> **24.9. There shall be no obligation under this Agreement to protect geographical indications which are not or cease to be protected in their country of origin, or which have fallen into disuse in that country.**

Article 24.9 means that the effective protection in the country where a geographical indication originates can be required as a condition of protection, in addition to the requirements in the protecting country.[123] The justification for this provision is quite straightforward: there would be no reason to protect a foreign geographical indication if it is not recognized in the country where it originates, or where it is not actually used in trade. The fact that the indication might be used in other Members could not be invoked, under this provision, to seek protection in a Member. Determination of whether an indication has fallen into disuse would be a matter of proof. The burden of proof would seem to rest with the party that invokes an obligation to protect the indication whose protection is in dispute.

Annex

Negotiating history[124]

In his 23 July 1990 report on the status of work in the TRIPS Negotiating Group, the Chairman (Lars E R Anell) presented two sets of proposals. In an Annex to the report, he presented a composite text that was taken from various proposals by delegations to the

---

[123] Idem, p 128.
[124] For an analysis of the negotiating history, see UNCTAD-ICTSD op. cit. (2005), pp 267–321.

Negotiating Group, indicating the source of each proposal by numerical reference to the source document.

Composite text of July 23 1990 [125]

SECTION 3: GEOGRAPHICAL INDICATIONS

1. *Definition*

1.1 Geographical indications are any designation, expression or sign which [aims at indicating] [directly or indirectly indicates] that a product [or service] originates from a country, region or locality.

1.2 [Geographical indications] [Appellations of origin] are for the purpose of this agreement [geographical] indications which designate a product as originating from the territory of a PARTY, a region or locality in that territory where a given quality, reputation or other characteristic of the products is attributable [exclusively or essentially] to its geographical origin, including natural [and] [or] human factors. [A denomination which has acquired a geographical character in relation to a product which has such qualities, reputation or characteristics is also deemed to be an appellation of origin.]

1.3 PARTIES agree that the provisions at point 2b.1 and 2b.2 below shall also apply to a geographical indication which, although literally true as to the territory, region or locality in which the goods originate, falsely represents to the public that the goods originate in the territory of another PARTY.

2. *Protection*

2a PARTIES shall provide protection for geographical indications by complying with the provisions under the Madrid Agreement for the Repression of False or Deceptive Indications of Source on Goods of 1891, as last revised in 1967.

2b.1 PARTIES shall protect [, at the request of an interested party,] geographical [or other] indications [denominating or suggesting the territory of a PARTY, a region or a locality in that territory] against use with respect to products not originating in that territory if that use [constitutes an act of unfair competition in the sense of Article 10*bis* of the Paris Convention (1967), including use which] [might mislead] [misleads] the public as to the true origin of the product.

[Such protection shall notably be afforded against:
– any direct or indirect use in trade in respect of products not originating from the place indicated or evoked by the geographical indication in question;
– any usurpation, imitation or evocation, even where the true origin of the product is indicated or the appellation or designation is used in translation or accompanied by expressions such as 'kind', 'type', 'style', 'imitation' or the like;
– the use of any means in the designation or presentation of products likely to suggest a link between those products and any geographical area other than the true place of origin.]

[125] Chairman's Report to the GNG, Status of Work in the Negotiating Group, Negotiating Group on Trade-Related Aspects of Intellectual Property Rights, including Trade in Counterfeit Goods, MTN.GNG/NG11/W/76, 23 July 1990, presented by the Chairman of the TRIPS Negotiating Group (Lars E R Anell). Alternatives 'A' correspond to texts from developed countries and 'B' from developing countries.

2b.2 PARTIES shall [, at the request of an interested party,] refuse or invalidate the registration of a trademark which contains or consists of:
[an indication denominating or suggesting a geographical indication,]

[a geographical or other indication denominating or suggesting the territory of a PARTY, or a region or locality in that territory,]

with respect to products not originating in the territory indicated [, if use of such indication [for such products] is of such a nature as to mislead or confuse the public [as to the true place of origin]]. [National laws shall provide the possibility for interested parties to oppose the use of such a trademark.]

2b.3 Appropriate measures shall be provided by PARTIES to enable interested parties to impede a geographical indication [, generally known in the territory of the PARTY to consumers of given products or of similar products as designating the origin of such products manufactured or produced in the territory of another PARTY,] from developing, as a result of its use in trade for [identical or similar] products of a different origin, into a designation of generic character [for these products or for similar products] [, it being understood that appellations of origin for products of the vine shall not be susceptible to develop into generic designations].

2c.1 PARTIES shall protect geographical indications that certify regional origin by providing for their registration as certification or collective marks.

2c.2 PARTIES shall provide protection for non-generic appellations of origin for wine by prohibiting their use when such use would mislead the public as to the true geographic origin of the wine. To aid in providing this protection, PARTIES are encouraged to submit to other PARTIES evidence to show that each such appellation of origin is a country, state, province, territory, or similar political subdivision of a country equivalent to a state or country; or a viticultural area.

2d PARTIES undertake to provide protection for geographical indications including appellations of origin against any use which is likely to confuse or mislead the public as to the true origin of the product.

3. *International Register*

PARTIES agree to cooperate with a view to establishing an international register for protected geographical indications, in order to facilitate the protection of geographical indications including appellations of origin. In appropriate cases the use of documents certifying the right to use the relevant geographical indication should be provided for.

4. *Exceptions*

4.1 No PARTY shall be required to apply the provisions for the protection of geographical indications:

(a) to the prejudice of holders of rights relating to an indication identical with or similar to a geographical indication or name and used or filed in good faith before the date of the entry into force of this agreement in the PARTY;

(b) with regard to goods for which the geographical indication or name is in the common language the common name of goods in the territory of that PARTY, or is identical with a term customary in common language.

4.2a PARTIES agree that the preceding paragraphs shall not prevent the conclusion pursuant to Article 19 of the Paris Convention (1967) of bilateral or multilateral agreements concerning the rights under those paragraphs, with a view to increasing the protection for specific geographical or other indications, and further agree that any advantage, favour, privilege or immunity deriving from such agreements are exempted from the obligations under point 7 of Part II of this agreement.

4.2b Given the country specific nature of [geographical indications] [appellations of origin], it is understood that in connection with any advantage, favour, privilege or immunity stemming from bilateral agreements on such [indications] [appellations] and exceeding the requirements of this agreement, the most-favoured nation treatment obligations under point 7 of Part II of this agreement shall be understood to require each PARTY belonging to such an agreement to be ready to extend such advantage, favour, privilege or immunity, on terms equivalent to those under the agreement, to any other PARTY so requesting and to enter into good faith negotiations to this end.'

Draft text transmitted to the Brussels Ministerial Conference (December 1990)

SECTION 3: GEOGRAPHICAL INDICATIONS

Article 24
Protection of Geographical Indications

1. Geographical indications are, for the purposes of this Agreement, indications which identify a good as originating in the territory of a PARTY, or a region or locality in that territory, where a given quality or other characteristic on which its reputation is based is essentially attributable to its geographical origin.

2. In respect of geographical indications, PARTIES shall provide in their domestic law the legal means for interested parties to prevent:

   (a) the use of any means in the designation or presentation of a good that indicates or suggests that the good in question originates in a geographical area other than the true place of origin in a manner which misleads the public as to the geographical origin of the good;

   (b) any use which constitutes an act of unfair competition within the meaning of Article 10*bis* of the Paris Convention (1967).

3. A PARTY shall, at the request of an interested party, refuse or invalidate the registration of a trademark which contains or consists of a geographical indication with respect to goods not originating in the territory indicated, if use of the indication in the trademark for such goods in that PARTY is of such a nature as to mislead the public as to the true place of origin.

4. The provisions of the preceding paragraphs of this Article shall apply to a geographical indication which, although literally true as to the territory, region or locality in which the goods originate, falsely represents to the public that the goods originate in another territory.

Article 25
Additional Protection for Geographical Indications for Wines

1. Each PARTY shall provide in its domestic law the legal means for interested parties to prevent use of a geographical indication identifying wines for wines not originating in the place indicated by the geographical indication in question, even where the true origin of

the goods is indicated or the geographical indication is used in translation or accompanied by expressions such as 'kind', 'type', 'style', 'imitation' or the like.

2. The registration of a trademark for wines which contains or consists of a geographical indication identifying wines shall be refused or invalidated at the request of an interested party with respect to such wines not having this origin.

3. In the case of homonymous geographical indications for wine, protection shall be accorded to each indication, subject to the provisions of paragraph 4 of Article 24 above. Each PARTY shall determine the practical conditions under which the homonymous indications in question will be differentiated from each other, taking into account the need to ensure equitable treatment of the producers concerned and that consumers are not misled.

Article 26
Exceptions

1. Where a geographical indication of a PARTY has been used with regard to goods originating outside the territory of that PARTY in good faith and in a widespread and continuous manner by nationals or domiciliaries of another PARTY, including use as a trademark, before the date of application of these provisions in the other PARTY as defined in Article 68 below, nothing in this Agreement shall prevent such continued use of the geographical indication by those nationals or domiciliaries of the said other PARTY.

2. A PARTY shall not take action to refuse or invalidate registration of a trademark first applied for or registered:

(a) before the date of application of these provisions in that PARTY as defined in Article 68 below;

(b) before the geographical indication is protected in its country of origin;

on the basis that the trademark is identical with, or similar to, a geographical indication.

3. No PARTY shall be required to apply the provisions of this Article in respect of a geographical indication of any other PARTY with respect to goods for which the relevant indication is identical with the term customary in common language as the common name for such goods or of the process for their production in the territory of that PARTY, or where the goods are products of the vine, is the name of a grape variety.

4. There shall be no obligation under this Agreement to protect geographical indications which are not or cease to be protected in their country of origin, or which have fallen into disuse in that country.

5. On the request of a PARTY, each PARTY shall be willing to enter into good faith negotiations aimed at [sic] The provisions of the preceding paragraphs shall not prevent PARTIES from concluding bilateral and multilateral agreements concerning the protection under this Section, with a view to increasing the protection for specific geographical indications.

Article 27
Notification of Geographical Indications

In order to facilitate the protection of geographical indications, the Committee shall examine the establishment of [sic] establish a multilateral system of notification and registration of geographical indications eligible for protection in the PARTIES participating in the system.

Chapter 8

INDUSTRIAL DESIGNS

Industrial designs are generally defined as features of ornamentation applied to an article. They consist of the shape, configuration, pattern, or ornament—or a combination thereof—of a product that gives it eye-appeal. Industrial designs normally exclude those designs determined solely by their utilitarian function on an article.[1]

The protection of industrial designs is addressed in the TRIPS Agreement by only two Articles. Article 25 defines the requirements for protection, and Article 26 the extent of exclusive rights and the admissible exceptions. This scant treatment reflects the fact that the protection of industrial designs had a low priority in the TRIPS negotiations[2] for the US and other countries, except perhaps the EC, which aimed at enhancing such protection, of particular value, for instance, for fashion industries.

Industrial property statistics show[3] that industrial designs, where a *sui generis* regime of protection exists, are applied for much less frequently than patents, trademarks and utility models (where recognized).[4] Several reasons may explain this: the level of protection given to designs is generally narrow and can be circumvented by minor changes to the protected design;[5] protection of the function (eg by patents) or trademarks is more easily enforceable;[6] designs are often short-lived and, hence, there is little incentive to initiate lengthy and costly litigation and, perhaps more importantly, small and medium enterprises (SMEs), which are major users of designs, generally do not see any form of intellectual property protection—such as registered designs and patents—as important to protect their innovations.[7] A survey in the United Kingdom, for instance, indicated that for

---

[1] Functional designs are protected in some countries by 'utility models' or by a special system of law. In the United Kingdom, for instance, a distinction is made between 'design rights', which mainly apply to functional designs and 'registered designs', which protect aesthetic designs. See D Bainbridge, *Intellectual Property* (1992: London, Pitman), p 312.

[2] See J Phillips, 'Protecting values in industrial designs', in C Correa and A Yusuf, *Intellectual Property and International Trade. The TRIPS Agreement* (1998: London, Kluwer Law International), pp 179–80.

[3] These statistics do not reflect protection conferred by copyright, which is acquired without formalities, nor the protection granted in some countries (eg, United Kingdom, Hong Kong, New Zealand, the European Union) to *unregistered* designs.

[4] See J Phillips op. cit. (1998), p 180.   [5] Ibidem.   [6] Ibidem.

[7] A noticeable exception is the case of small biotechnology firms that often heavily depend on their patented inventions.

more than 70 per cent of the surveyed firms, registered designs brought about little or no benefit; trademarks and trade secrets were marginally better valued than registered designs.[8]

Industrial designs is probably the area of intellectual property rights with the greatest diversity in the forms of available protection. Most countries have adopted *sui generis* systems of protection, but in some cases they are based on registration procedures while in others designs are protected without registration. Moreover, both the subject matter and the requirements for protection significantly vary. Thus, some countries require novelty, either absolute or merely limited to the country of registration; others require originality, aesthetic merit, or distinctiveness. In some cases, industrial design protection is close to patent law protection (such in the US), while in others (eg France) is close to copyright law. The term of protection also presents differences before the implementation of the TRIPS Agreement, ranging from 5–10 years to an indefinite term.

Disparities also stem from the applicability of various types of protection, either co-existing in parallel or in a cumulative way. Co-existence means that the creator of a design may choose to be protected by one regime or by another. Cumulative protection, instead, allows for simultaneous and concurrent protection by two or more regimes. Coexistence or accumulation in the case of industrial designs generally takes place on the basis of a *sui generis* industrial design law and copyright law,[9] but other combinations also exist.[10] Protection of industrial designs by a *sui generis* system[11] or by copyright law also often overlaps with trademark law, to the extent that the latter allows the protection of a distinguishing guise of products.[12] Designs that combine aesthetic and functional aspects may also be protected under patent law, where both aspects are inseparable and the patentability requirements are met.[13] Finally, overlapping may also take place under unfair competition law, trade dress protection[14] and passing off.[15]

---

[8] See S Macdonald, 'Exploring the hidden costs of patents', in P Drahos and R Mayne (eds), *Global Intellectual Property Rights: Knowledge Access and Development* (2002: New York, Palgrave and Oxfam GB); C Correa, 'Do small and medium enterprises benefit from patent protection?', in C Pietrobelli and Á Sverrisson (eds), *Linking Local and Global Economies. Organisation, Technology and Export Opportunities for SMEs* (2003: London and New York, Routledge), pp 220–39.

[9] See, eg, WIPO, *Intellectual Property Reading Material* (1988: Geneva), p 202.

[10] In the USA, for instance, industrial designs may be protected separately or in combination under design patents, trade dress and copyrights. See J Hudis and P Signore, 'Protection of industrial designs in the United States', (2005) EIPR 7, pp 256–64.

[11] In some countries, in addition to the general *sui generis* regimes of protection of industrial designs, special systems for particular types of designs have been established, such as in France for the fashion industry.

[12] In Canada, for instance, copyright and trademark law co-exist for the protection of industrial designs. See also, with regard to the French system, D Cohen, *Le droit des dessins et modeles* (1997: Paris; Economica), pp 77–87.   [13] See, eg, Cohen op. cit. (1997), p 89.

[14] The 'trade dress' of a product is its total image and overall appearance, including features such as size, shape, colour, texture, etc. See J Hudis and P Signore op. cit. (2005), p 259.

[15] 'Passing off' is the common law form of a trade mark law, and usually protects business 'goodwill' involving a wider scope of materials than trademark law.

International conventions and TRIPS

The Paris Convention specifically mentions industrial designs as a subject matter of protection.[16] Hence, their protection is subject to the principle of national treatment, priority rights, and other provisions of the Convention. It stipulates that such designs cannot be forfeited by reason of failure to work or by the importation of articles corresponding to the protected design (Article 5B). However, the Paris Convention does not require a *sui generis* or any other particular form of protection; countries of the Union can protect them, for instance, under copyright.[17] The granting of protection on the basis of unfair competition disciplines is also a possibility.[18]

Designs are protectable, under the Berne Convention, as 'works of applied art'[19] for a period of at least 25 years from the making of such works (Article 7.4). Article 2.7 of the Convention recognized the hybrid nature of such works, and permitted contracting parties to determine whether to protect, and if so, the extent of protection of industrial designs and models. Moreover, it established a substantive reciprocity clause:

Works protected in the country of origin solely as designs and models shall be entitled in another country of the Union only to such special protection as is granted in that country to designs and models; however, if no such special protection is granted in that country, such works shall be protected as artistic works.

Given that Article 3.1 of the TRIPS Agreement preserves the exceptions to the national treatment principle of the Berne Convention and the other intellectual property treaties referred to by the Agreement,[20] Members may only confer special protection when designs and models are subject to such special protection in the country of origin.[21]

Moreover, despite the Swiss negotiating proposal to make copyright a mandatory form of protection,[22] Section I, Part II of the TRIPS Agreement does not contain any specific obligation regarding the protection of designs under such modality. Hence, a Member can comply with its obligations under the Agreement by means of other modalities, provided that the minimum requirements set forth in the TRIPS Agreement are complied with.

---

[16] See, in particular, Articles 1(2), 5B and 5*quinquies*.

[17] See eg, A Kur, 'TRIPs and design protection' in F-K Beier and G Schricker, *From GATT to TRIPs—The Agreement on Trade-Related Aspects of Intellectual Property Rights* (1996: Munich, Max Planck Institute for Foreign and International Patent, Copyright and Competition Law), p 144.

[18] See below the discussion on Article 26.1.

[19] This term is generally intended to refer to artistic works, often three-dimensional designs, which have been industrially applied to an article, which is subsequently commercially exploited. See UNCTAD-ICTSD, *Resource Book on TRIPS and Development* (2005: New York, Cambridge University Press), p 324.   [20] See Chapter 2 above.

[21] Within the European Union, however, this possibility has been precluded after the decision of the European Court of Justice in *Phil Collins* (OJ EC N C312/3 of 18 November 1993). See Kur op. cit. (1996), p 146.   [22] See MTN.GNG/NG11/W/73, 14 May 1999.

The Hague Agreement Concerning the Deposit of Industrial Designs (1960),[23] established within the framework of the Paris Convention, permits persons entitled to make an international deposit to obtain protection for their industrial designs in a number of States with a minimum of formalities and reduced cost, by means of a single deposit made with the International Bureau of WIPO.[24] Subject to the provisions on the protection in the State of origin, an international deposit may have effect in all contracting States. The Hague Agreement contains a few substantive provisions (such as a minimum term of protection),[25] and it is essentially aimed at countries where design protection is granted without substantive examination.

Although the TRIPS Agreement entails a 'Paris-plus' solution, it does not significantly help to diminish the disparities in national regulations referred to. The negotiation of the relevant Articles reflected major differences in approaches among industrialized countries. Draft proposals included, in some cases, functional as well aesthetic designs. In particular, the EC wanted the United States to expand the coverage of protection granted by US law, which was limited by the application of a non-obviousness test.[26] The possible expansion of industrial designs protection as an outcome of the Uruguay Round generated concerns in the United States and opposition from replacement part manufacturers and insurance companies. They feared that the proposed TRIPS Agreement would allow for the protection of replacement parts by automobile companies, thus reducing or eliminating competition in that market.

Requirements for protection

25.1. Members shall provide for the protection of independently created industrial designs that are new or original. Members may provide that designs are not new or original if they do not significantly differ from known designs or combinations of known features. Members may provide that such protection shall not extend the designs dictated essentially by technical or functional considerations.

In accordance with Article 25.1, Members are obliged to protect independently created industrial designs which meet the requirement of novelty *or* originality. Unlike the case of trademarks and geographical indications, there is no definition[27] on what an industrial design is, nor any precise reference to the mode of

---

[23] Despite efforts to make the Convention acceptable to United States, Japan, and other countries, its membership remains limited. The Convention had 42 members as of 15 April 2006.

[24] See, eg, WIPO op. cit. (1988), p 203.   [25] See Article 11 of the Convention.

[26] The EC proposed to protect industrial designs and models which are 'original or novel', while the United States proposed to limit protection to designs which are 'new, original, ornamental and non-obvious'. This requirement had led to the registration of designs in the United States that is numerically much lower than in Japan and other countries. See J Phillips op. cit. (1998), p 180.

[27] Despite some proposals during the negotiations to refer to bi-dimensional or three-dimensional forms of products.

protection to be conferred (copyright, *sui generis* regime, etc). This broad room for manoeuvre was most probably retained in recognition of the wide diversity of regimes of industrial design protection that Members had at the time the TRIPS Agreement was negotiated. Thus, after the adoption of the TRIPS Agreement many countries (such as the United States) with diverging regimes did not change the pre-existing mode of design protection.

In addition, Article 25.1 does not specify whether a system of unregistered or registered protection (with or without examination) is required. Both are equally admissible separately or in combination.[28]

Despite this room for manoeuvre, Members are under the general obligation to implement the minimum standards set forth by the Agreement.[29] An important question arises in the case where two or more modalities are applied to industrial designs:[30] should all the applicable modalities comply with TRIPS minimum requirements or would it be enough for one of such modalities to be TRIPS-compliant? It would seem reasonable to argue that a Member will be TRIPS-compliant to the extent that at least one of the modalities of protection complies with the Agreement's minimum standards and foreigners can resort to protection on a national treatment basis and without discrimination. Other forms of protection may be deemed supplementary or TRIPS-extra.[31]

Article 25.1 also leaves Members considerable flexibility to determine the requirements of protection: it must be accorded when an industrial design has been independently created *and* is new *or* original.

The first condition—independent creation—is of a subjective nature: it requires that the person seeking protection proves, if needed, that the design has been the result of his own acts and *not copied*. Under *sui generis* regimes inspired by or close to patent law, it is immaterial whether a third party's design results from an independent act of creation or not; the title holder may in any case prevent its exploitation. In the case of copyright, however, independent creation may be sufficient to attribute originality to a work and generate an autonomous title to protection. A basic rule under copyright is that 'if a third party *independently* creates a design that resembles the protected design, the copyright in the protected design does not provide for the right to prevent the third party exploiting his independently created design'.[32]

---

[28] While some countries have opted for one of these modalities, others apply both. This is the case, for instance, of European law (Council Regulation EC No 6/2002 of 12 December 2001 on Community designs, OJ L 3, 5.1.02). In some countries, such as the United Kingdom, copyright applies in addition to registered and unregistered designs protection.

[29] See Article 1.1 above.

[30] In some cases such modalities are ostensibly not TRIPS-compliant. For instance, Japan protects unregistered designs under an unfair competition regime for three years; the same term of protection is conferred (from the date on which a design was first made available to the public) under the unregistered Community design right (Council Regulation EC No 6/2002 of 12 December 2001 on Community designs, OJ L 3, 5.1.02).   [31] See UNCTAD-ICTSD op. cit. (2005), pp 341–2.

[32] UNCTAD-ICTSD op. cit. (2005), p 324.

The second condition requires showing either novelty or originality. These are non-cumulative but alternative requirements.[33] During the negotiations, the US and other countries advocated for the cumulative application of both criteria,[34] but finally the European approach ('new or original') prevailed.[35]

As in the case of patents (Article 27.1 of the TRIPS Agreement), Article 25.1 does not provide a definition of novelty[36] and, in particular, it does not specify whether the novelty requirement is absolute or local. This requirement as applied in the area of industrial designs significantly varies across countries.

The possibility of relying on 'originality' alone as a requirement of protection opens the door for the protection of designs under copyright law. If this option were chosen, compliance with both the Berne Convention and the provisions on the matter in the TRIPS Agreement should be ensured.

In practice, the concept of 'new' or 'original' may be near to either in most situations.[37] However, an artistic work may, under the requirement of originality, be deemed protectable even if previously developed or used, to the extent that it was independently created;[38] instead, novelty requires that the same design was not publicly available before the date of application for protection.[39] The originality requirement would, hence, seem to be easier to comply with than the novelty requirement.

One interesting interpretive issue is whether 'independently created' and 'originality' refer both to one and the same requirement, or whether they constitute separate requirements that reinforce each other, thereby indicating that 'more of a creative contribution than mere independent creation' is needed to obtain protection.[40] To 'create' means 'to bring into existence, give rise to, make by one's action'.[41] A literal reading of Article 25.1, hence, would not suggest that the concept of 'independently created' requires a certain level of aesthetic contribution. However, the fact that it is used in addition to 'original' does point to a differentiation between the two concepts and would support the view that they demand

[33] See, eg, D Gervais, *The TRIPS Agreement. Drafting History and Analysis* (2003: London, Sweet & Maxwell, 2nd edn), p 213. In the view of other commentators, however, a combination of novelty and originality may be established by national laws. See, eg, Phillips op. cit. (1998), p 184.

[34] The US proposed the addition of 'ornamental and non-obvious' in line with its domestic legislation.

[35] The US also failed in its attempt to incorporate a requirement of 'non-obviousness' in Article 25.1. According to one view, this failure may have created a conflict between the TRIPS disciplines and US law. See J Reichman, 'Universal Minimum Standards of Intellectual Property Protection under the TRIPS Component of the WTO Agreement' (1995) 29 International Lawyer, p 376.

[36] See Chapter 9 below.

[37] Cohen notes that in France, in nearly fifty years of case law and thousands of decisions on the matter, in no case was it found that a design met the novelty and not the originality requirement or vice versa. He concludes that novelty and originality are in this context 'simply the same concept' (Cohen op. cit. (1997), p 96).

[38] See, eg, W Cornish, *Intellectual property: Patents, Copyright, Trade Marks and Allied Marks* (1989: London, Sweet & Maxwell), pp 371–2.

[39] According to the patent law and practice in some countries, the prior art includes disclosures by prior secret commercial use of the invention, but this is not a generalized approach.

[40] See J Reichman, op. cit. (1995), p 376.

[41] *Concise Oxford Dictionary*, (1982: Oxford University Press, 7th edn), p 222.

something else than mere originality in the sense of 'origin'.[42] Given the ambiguity of the provision, both interpretations may be deemed reasonable and TRIPS-compatible, if deference is given to Member States. As stated in *Canada–Patent Protection for Pharmaceutical Products*, WTO panels and the Appellate Body should not 'decide, through adjudication, a normative policy issue that is still obviously a matter of unresolved political debate'.[43] More generally, it is not within the competence of panels and the Appellate Body to fill in the gaps or cure the ambiguities of the TRIPS Agreement.[44]

The relationship between independent creation and novelty is clearer. A Member may establish a local novelty requirement, which would allow a third party, in principle, to legitimately copy and register a foreign industrial design. However, protection may be refused or cancelled in this case as the design does not meet the requirement of independent creation.[45]

In addition to independently created, new or original, Members *may* require that designs significantly differ from known designs or combinations of known designs.[46] The faculty conferred by Article 25.1 to add this requirement (which is not mandatory) shows how pragmatic and accommodating of different views the TRIPS negotiators were in this section.[47] Of course, since Members have the option to require or not this additional requirement, a fortiori, they can determine the degree of differentiation (or objective originality) necessary for an industrial design to be eligible for protection.

Finally, Members *may* exclude from protection designs which are dictated essentially by technical or functional reasons; that is, protection may only be conferred to designs that have an aesthetic merit. The US[48] strongly argued for an exclusion of functional designs (such as spare or 'crash' automobile parts). It succeeded in obtaining a facultative clause, but not a mandatory exclusion. Members can, however, protect both aesthetic and functional designs under one and the same regime,[49] or can implement separate regimes. Thus, functional designs may be specifically protected as 'utility models' or 'petty patents'.[50] These titles may be

---

[42] See, eg, Kur op. cit. (1996), p 150, fn 43.

[43] See para 7.82.

[44] See, eg, C Correa, 'The TRIPS Agreement from the perspective of developing countries', in Macrory A Appleton and M Plummer (eds), *The World Trade Organization: Legal, Economic and Political Analysis* (2005: New York, Springer), p 435.   [45] See, eg, Phillips op. cit. (1998), p 185.

[46] A similar concept was incorporated by the TRIPS Agreement, via Article 3 of the Washington Treaty, with regard to layout-designs/topographies of integrated circuits. See Chapter 10 below.

[47] See, eg, Reichman op. cit. (1995), pp 345–88.

[48] In the US designs can be protected under copyright law as 'pictorial, graphic and sculptural works' only if, and only to the extent that they incorporate pictorial, graphic, or sculptural features that can be identified *separately from, and are capable of existing independently of,* the utilitarian aspects of the article' (Section 101 of the US Copyright Act; emphasis added).

[49] See, eg, K Levin and M Richman, 'A survey of industrial design protection in the European Union and the United States', (2003) EIPR 3, p 111.

[50] Utility model protection is granted in Argentina, Armenia, Austria, Belarus, Belgium, Bulgaria, China, Colombia, Costa Rica, Czech Republic, Denmark, Estonia, Ethiopia, Finland, France, Georgia, Germany, Greece, Guatemala, Hungary, Ireland, Italy, Japan, Kazakhstan, Kenya, Kyrgyzstan,

useful to protect minor or incremental innovations, particularly in the mechanical field. They may be especially suited to protect minor innovations that predominate in developing countries.[51]

Legislators have had a hard time differentiating designs of aesthetic value from those that have a functional purpose since in many cases they are intimately interlinked. Some regimes have addressed this issue by excluding protection of designs that are necessarily determined by the function of the product it applies to.[52] Members have a broad leeway to determine whether to exclude functional designs and, if so, under what circumstances.

A debatable issue is whether Members can provide for *other* exclusions, such as those necessary to protect morality or *ordre public*. An exclusion of this kind is contemplated for patents.[53] The absence of a specific provision, however, would not be a sufficient basis for an objection to an exclusion of this kind, as one basic responsibility of States is anyway to protect morality and *ordre public*.[54]

> **25.2. Each Member shall ensure that requirements for securing protection for textile designs, in particular in regard to any cost, examination or publication, do not unreasonably impair the opportunity to seek and obtain such protection. Members shall be free to meet this obligation through industrial design law or through copyright law.**

While Article 25.1 applies to all kinds of designs, Article 25.2 particularly refers to 'textile designs'. The provision does not refer to 'industrial' designs, but the title of Section 4 does. 'Textile' means 'of weaving...woven, suitable for weaving'.[55] Hence, Article 25.1 may be deemed applicable to bi-dimensional or three-dimensional designs applied to any woven material, independently of the products (clothes, furniture, luggage, etc) bearing or embodying such designs.

Textile designs, which are particularly important for many SMEs, generally have a short-lived economic value, as tastes and fashion change fast. Textile companies may need to quickly protect a large number of designs, only a limited number of which may be actually exploited.[56] Article 25.2 reflects concerns about the possible deleterious impact of the delays and costs to be incurred for applying for and obtaining protection.

Malaysia, Mexico, Netherlands, members of the African Organization of Intellectual Property (OAPI), Peru, Philippines, Poland, Portugal, Republic of Korea, Republic of Moldova, Russian Federation, Slovakia, Spain, Tajikistan, Trinidad & Tobago, Turkey, Ukraine, Uruguay, and Uzbekistan.

[51] See, for a discussion on this subject, U Suthersanen, *Utility Models and Innovation in Developing Countries* (2006: Geneva, UNCTAD–ICTSD); available at <http://www.ictsd.org> (last accessed on 12 May 2006).

[52] See, eg, Article 7(1) of the European Directive 98/71 IEC on the Legal Protection of Designs, which excludes from protection registered designs 'solely dictated by the product's technical function'.

[53] See Chapter 9 below.

[54] See Kur op. cit. (1996), (who mentions that this exclusion was only proposed during the TRIPS negotiations by Peru), p 153.

[55] *Concise Oxford Dictionary* (1982: Oxford University Press, 7th edn), p 1107.

[56] See, eg, Gervais op. cit. (2003), p 214.

While Members are subject to the general obligation established by Article 41.2 of the TRIPS Agreement regarding the *procedures for enforcement* of intellectual property rights,[57] Article 25.2 refers to 'requirements for securing protection'; that is, to conditions that may be imposed with regard to the *acquisition* of rights. 'Cost, examination or publication' are only illustrative of the factors that may 'unreasonably impair' such acquisition, but singling out these factors does not mean that they should necessarily be deemed as impairments, nor that these are the only factors to be taken into account.

Hence, Members can impose reasonable fees regarding applications for or grants of industrial designs, and they can require their examination and publication as a condition of protection.[58] Some countries have addressed the special needs of the textile industry by allowing the registration of multiple designs in one application, deferring publication, or providing for provisional protection.[59] Article 25.2, however, only imposes a standard regarding the reasonableness of such costs and conditions. 'To impair' means 'to damage, weaken';[60] therefore, a violation of such standard would require not only proof that a damage occurs as a result of the imposed requirements and costs, but also that it is unreasonable.

Article 25.2 explicitly leaves Members the option to protect textile designs under industrial design law or copyright.[61] Although the same choice of system applies to any other designs, as elaborated above, this provision presents an important difference: it seems to rule out the application of other systems, such as unfair competition. If copyright is chosen, problems associated with cost and time for acquiring protection dissipate, since copyright is vested automatically, without formalities.

Protection

26.1. The owner of a protected industrial design shall have the right to prevent third parties not having his consent from making, selling or importing articles bearing or embodying a design which is a copy, or substantially a copy, of the protected design, when such acts are undertaken for commercial purposes.

---

[57] Article 41.2: 'Procedures concerning the enforcement of intellectual property rights shall be fair and equitable. They shall not be unnecessarily complicated or costly, or entail unreasonable time-limits or unwarranted delays.' See Chapter 13 below.

[58] For instance, registered designs can be acquired in the United Kingdom in about two or three months with a fee of £ 35–60. Procedures before the Office of Harmonization for the Internal Market last for an estimated period of three months, with a fee of about € 350, for obtaining a Community registered design under the Council Regulation on Community Designs of 12 December 2001. See Levin and Richman op.cit. (2003), p112.   [59] See eg, Kur op.cit. (1996), p 154.

[60] *Concise Oxford Dictionary* (1982: Oxford University Press, 7th edn), p 499.

[61] The advantages of copyright generally refer to the lack of registration formalities and to the long duration of protection. In some countries, however, copyright protection may not be extended to the reproduction of a design by making a copy.

26.2. Members may provide limited exceptions to the protection of industrial designs, provided that such exceptions do not unreasonably conflict with the normal exploitation of protected industrial designs and do not unreasonably prejudice the legitimate interests of the owner of the protected design, taking account of the legitimate interests of third parties.

26.3. The duration of protection available shall amount to at least ten years.

The extent of minimum protection to be conferred is stipulated in Article 26, which also contains a general provision on admissible exceptions, similar to the provisions found in other sections of the Agreement.

The wording of Article 26.1 '[T]he owner of a protected industrial design shall have the right to prevent third parties not having his consent . . .' echoes the wording used in Articles 16.1, with regard to trademarks, and 28.1 with regard to patents, with at least three important differences.

First, while the provisions on trademarks and patents refer to the granting of 'exclusive' rights, this word is absent in the case of industrial designs. This omission, which cannot be deemed accidental, indicates that TRIPS drafters intended to leave a wide range of possibilities for the protection of industrial designs, including unfair competition and liability rules, which do not rely on the granting of exclusive rights.

Second, consistently with the lack of reference to exclusiveness, Article 26.1 confers a right against the copying of protected designs (' . . . a design which is a copy, or substantially a copy, of the protected design . . .'). This confirms that an independently created industrial design may be deemed as not infringing a protected identical (or substantially identical) design, and situates the TRIPS Agreement protection of industrial designs closer to copyright than to patent law.

Third, the list of acts subject to the designer's rights (making, selling, or importing articles) is shorter than for patents (which also apply to acts of 'using' and 'offering for sale') with the additional qualification that such acts are only prevented when 'undertaken for commercial purposes'. This excludes, for instance, the importation of products bearing or embodying a design if done for non-commercial purposes such as charity or personal use.

It is of note that the anti-copying rights granted under Article 26.1 apply in cases of both slavish copying and where minor changes are made that are not sufficient to differentiate the copied design from the original one. This provision, however, does not provide guidance as to when a design could be considered 'substantially a copy' of a protected design. The general appearance of the products would certainly be the main criterion. Unlike the case of trademarks, no reference is made to the likelihood of consumers' confusion arising from the use of the same or substantially the same design; hence, the determination of infringement would seem independent of whether the designs in conflict are applied to competing products or to products with different functions and unrelated markets (eg jewellery and furniture).

The protection against copying, or substantial copying, however, would not apply with regard to foreign designs not registered in a Member, where the Member requires registration as a condition for protection (a possibility that is not in any way foreclosed by the TRIPS Agreement) and only requires local novelty for granting protection. In this situation, a foreign design might be legally copied and the applicant still benefit from protection under national law.

With the same wording used in Article 30 of the TRIPS Agreement in relation to patents, Article 26.2 allows for 'limited exceptions' to the rights conferred by industrial designs. The exceptions shall be admissible if such exceptions:

- do not unreasonably conflict with the normal exploitation of protected industrial designs; and
- do not unreasonably prejudice the legitimate interests of the owner of the protected design;
- taking account of the legitimate interests of third parties.

The interpretation of Article 30, as elaborated below [62] is, hence, relevant to the understanding and implementation of Article 26.2. One important difference, however, is that the rights conferred by industrial designs are subject to the general principle that their protection is limited to 'acts undertaken for commercial purpose'. Thus, use for scientific research and experimentation, private use and other non-commercial uses would be outside the scope of the protection granted in accordance with the Agreement, and there would be no need to apply the three-step test of Article 26.2. Acts of research or experimentation done by third parties with commercial intent can also be exempted provided, however, that they meet the three-step test.

It is worth noting that despite the fact that industrial designs can be protected, as is the case in many countries, through copyright, Article 26.2 refers to 'limited exceptions' and not to the rather narrower concept of 'special cases' like Article 9(2) of the Berne Convention and Article 13 of the TRIPS Agreement.[63] In addition, Article 26.2 mandates to take account of the 'legitimate interests of third parties', a requirement which is absent in those provisions. However, where a Member has opted to protect industrial designs through copyright, it would be bound to apply the Berne Convention.[64]

A controversial exception to industrial designs is the so-called 'repair clause'; that is, an exclusion of protection of spare parts in the aftermarket. This clause has particular importance for the automobile industry, car insurers, and consumers. Conflicting views have been expressed, for instance, in Europe, where the European Commission has promoted such an exception to offer consumers a larger spectrum of spare parts, open business opportunities for SMEs, and allow

---

[62] See Chapter 9 below.   [63] See Chapter 5 above.
[64] See Article 9.1 of the TRIPS Agreement; see also UNCTAD-ICTSD op. cit. (2005), p 330.

new entrants to emerge, among other reasons.[65] While some have opined that a repair clause would conflict with the three-step test of Article 26.2 in the light of European and WTO jurisprudence,[66] others hold that the exception is justified. Drexler, Hilty, and Kur have correctly noted that under Article 26 of the TRIPS Agreement 'it would even be admissible to exclude design protection for spare parts altogether' and have suggested a compromise based on a remuneration right or a short exclusivity period (three years) after which the repairs clause would apply.[67]

Section 4 does not refer—unlike Section 5 on patents[68]—to compulsory licences. Several countries (eg, Cuba, Sweden, Brazil, and the United Kingdom) have provided for such licences for industrial designs under the general rules of the Paris Convention.[69] The absence of any specific provision in the TRIPS Agreement cannot certainly be interpreted as a prohibition to provide for and grant compulsory licences.[70] These licences—which are fairly common under copyright law—may be deemed a particular case of the 'limited exceptions' allowed under Article 26.2.[71] Moreover, if TRIPS drafters wanted to exclude compulsory licences in the area of industrial designs, they could have included an express prohibition as in Article 21 of the Agreement[72] in relation to trademarks.[73]

Finally, the minimum duration of industrial designs rights should be ten years, in accordance with Article 26.3. This term is much shorter than the term provided for 'works of applied art' (25 years) under copyright but longer than that offered by some national regimes. This provision is much more flexible than other provisions in the Agreement referring to terms of protection (such as Articles 18 and 33) since it does not specify whether the term:

- is to be counted from the date of the design, the application, or its publication, or from the date of its grant or any other date;
- could be divided in a shorter original term plus a renewal totalling at least ten years;
- may be subject to renewal.

[65] See Explanatory Memorandum of the European Commission's Proposal to amend Article 14 of the European Directive 98/71 IEC on the Legal Protection of Designs (COM (2004) 582 final, 2004/2003 (CODE)).

[66] See, eg, J Straus, 'Design protection for spare parts gone in Europe? Proposed changes to the EC Directive: the Commission's mandate and its doubtful execution', (2005) European Intellectual Property Review 11, pp 391–402.

[67] J Drexler, R Hilty, and A Kur, 'Design protection for spare parts and the Commission's Proposal for a Repairs Clause, (2005) 36 IIC 4, p 454.					[68] See Chapter 9 below.

[69] See Phillips op. cit. (1998), p 187.

[70] This conclusion seems to be confirmed by the negotiating history of this provision. Some countries (Switzerland, Austria, and Hong Kong) suggested a ban on compulsory licences for industrial designs, but this position did not find its way into the adopted text. The USA proposed to apply the same conditions as patents. See Kur op. cit. (1996), p 156, fn 73.					[71] Idem, p 186.

[72] '... it being understood that the compulsory licensing of trademarks shall not be permitted...'. See Chapter 6 above.

[73] Article 5B of the Paris Convention, as mentioned above, only prohibits forfeiture of an industrial design by reason of failure to work or by the importation of articles corresponding to the protected design. No reference is made to compulsory licences.

All these possibilities seem permissible. The lack of reference to the date of application or grant is understandable: some of the modalities (copyright; unregistered designs) of industrial designs' protection do not contemplate an application. This latitude means that the harmonizing effect of the TRIPS Agreement with regard to the term of protection will be less significant than in other areas, such as patents.

As mentioned above, in case a Member offers protection under more than one modality, it would be sufficient for one of them to comply with the minimum term established by the TRIPS Agreement.[74]

Annex

Negotiating history[75]

In his 23 July 1990 report on the status of work in the TRIPS Negotiating Group, the Chairman (Lars E R Anell) presented two sets of proposals. In an Annex to the report, he presented a composite text that was taken from various proposals by delegations to the Negotiating Group, indicating the source of each proposal by numerical reference to the source document.

Composite text of July 23 1990[76]

SECTION 4: INDUSTRIAL DESIGNS

1. *Requirements for Protection*

   1.1 PARTIES shall provide for protection for industrial designs which are new [and] [or] original [, ornamental and non-obvious].

   1.2 PARTIES [may] [shall] condition such protection on registration [or other formality].

   1.3 PARTIES may provide that protection shall not extend to features required by technical reasons.

   1.4 Such protection shall be provided without affecting any protection under copyright law [or other law].

2. *Textiles Designs*

   2A The acquisition of industrial design rights in textiles or clothing shall not be encumbered by any special requirements such as ex officio examination of novelty

---

[74] See, eg, UNCTAD-ICTSD op. cit. (2005), p 341.

[75] For an analysis of the negotiating history, see UNCTAD-ICTSD op. cit. (2005), pp 322–50.

[76] Chairman's Report to the GNG, Status of Work in the Negotiating Group, Negotiating Group on Trade-Related Aspects of Intellectual Property Rights, including Trade in Counterfeit Goods, MTN.GNG/NG11/W/76, 23 July 1990, presented by the Chairman of the TRIPS Negotiating Group (Lars E R Anell). Alternatives 'A' correspond to texts from developed countries and 'B' from developing countries.

before registration, compulsory publication of the design itself or disproportionate fees for multiple users of the registration.

3. *Industrial Design Rights*

3. The owner of a [protected] [registered] industrial design shall have the right to prevent third parties not having his consent from:

manufacturing; [selling] [offering, putting on the market]; using; or importing for commercial purposes; [an object which is the subject matter of the industrial design right] [their industrial designs] [articles the appearance of which does not differ substantially from that of the protected design] [articles bearing a design which is a copy or substantially a copy of the protected design].

4. *Obligations of Industrial Design Owners*

4B With respect to the obligations of an industrial design owner, the requirements for patent inventions under point 3 of Section 5 below shall apply.

5. *Term of Protection and Renewal*

5A.1 The term of protection available shall be at least ten years.

5A.2 PARTIES shall provide for an initial term of protection of registered industrial designs of at least five years [from the date of application], with a possibility of renewal for [at least another period] [two consecutive periods] of five years.

5B The term of protection shall be provided under national legislation.

6. *Remedial Measures under National Legislations; Compulsory Licensing of Industrial Designs*

6A.1 [PARTIES shall not issue compulsory licences for industrial designs except to remedy adjudicated violations of competition law to which the conditions set out at point 3 of Section 5 below shall apply *mutatis mutandis*.] [The compulsory licensing of an industrial design shall not be permitted.]

6A.2 The protection of industrial designs shall not be subject to any forfeiture by reason of failure to exploit.

Draft text transmitted to the Brussels Ministerial Conference (December 1990)

1. PARTIES shall provide for the protection of industrial designs which are new [and] [or] original. PARTIES may provide that designs are not new [and] [or] original if they do not significantly differ from known designs or combinations of known design features. PARTIES may provide that such protection shall not extend to designs dictated essentially by technical or functional or technical considerations.

2. Each PARTY shall ensure that requirements for securing protection for textile designs, in particular in regard to any cost, examination or publication, do not unreasonably impair the opportunity to seek and obtain such protection. PARTIES shall be free to meet this obligation through industrial design law or through copyright.

3B With respect to the obligations of the owner of a protected industrial design, the provisions set forth in paragraph 3 (b) of Article [29] below shall apply.

4. The duration of protection available shall amount to at least 10 years.

Chapter 9

PATENTS

Patentable subject matter

27.1. Subject to the provisions of paragraphs 2 and 3, patents shall be available for any inventions, whether products or processes, in all fields of technology, provided that they are new, involve an inventive step and are capable of industrial application.[4] Subject to paragraph 4 of Article 65, paragraph 8 of Article 70 and paragraph 3 of this Article, patents shall be available and patent rights enjoyable without discrimination as to the place of invention, the field of technology and whether products are imported or locally produced.

[4] For the purposes of this Article, the terms 'inventive step' and 'capable of industrial application' may be deemed by a Member to be synonymous with the terms 'non-obvious' and 'useful' respectively.

The issue of patentability and the exclusions thereto was one of the main areas of controversy in the TRIPS negotiations. At the time the Round started, nearly fifty countries did not confer patent protection on medicines and, in some cases, on other products such as food and beverages. It was quite evident from the outset of the Round that the extension of patentability, particularly to pharmaceuticals, in those countries that did not recognize it, was a major objective of the proponents of GATT disciplines on intellectual property. The very existence of the TRIPS Agreement can probably be attributed to the active lobbying of the pharmaceutical industry and its ability to convince the US government to link intellectual property and trade matters.

Article 27.1 of the TRIPS Agreement stipulates that 'patents shall be available for any inventions...'. It further adds that 'patents shall be available and patent rights enjoyable without discrimination as to...the field of technology'.[1]

As with most patent laws in the world, the Agreement does not define what an invention is.[2] The plain wording of Article 27.1 suggests that Members have been

---

[1] The notion of 'non-discrimination' as to subject matter was suggested in UNICE, 'Basic framework of GATT provisions on intellectual property. Statement of views of the European, Japanese, and United States Business Communities', (1988: The Intellectual Property Committee, Keidanren, UNICE), p 32.

[2] Some patent laws include a definition of 'invention', but this is rather exceptional. For instance, the Mexican patent law considers as an invention all human creation that permits the transformation of matter or energy that exists in nature, for the benefit of man and to satisfy his concrete needs (Article 15). The same concept is contained in the Argentine patent law (Article 4(a)).

left room to define 'invention' within their legal systems,[3] in good faith, subject only to the application of the method of interpretation set out by the Vienna Convention.

The ordinary meaning of 'invention' suggests the output of an intellectual activity in the form of new knowledge of a technical nature. To invent is 'to create by thought, originate (new method, instrument, etc)'.[4] It also suggests a distinction between creations and mere discoveries and, more generally, between inventions and other subject matter that does not qualify as such.[5]

The interpretation of the obligation to patent 'any inventions' raises many important policy issues, such as the extent to which Members are bound to confer patents over discoveries, particularly over substances found in nature such as genes. Although it may be argued that Article 27.1 is intended to permit the patentability of any subject matter that meets the patentability criteria, the text employs the substantive notion of 'invention' whereas, if a broader scope was intended, another formulation could have been used, such as 'any subject matter that is new, involve an inventive step and is capable of industrial application'.

Although Members can adopt a more expansive concept at the national level, they are not obliged to grant patents to what is not ordinarily considered an 'invention'. Thus, they are not obliged to grant patents over genes. The Nuffield Council on Bioethics has stated that

genes are naturally occurring entities that are there to be discovered, like new species or new planets. They are not invented. In our common usage of the term, a 'discovery' is the acquisition of knowledge of a new but already existing fact about the world. An 'invention', on the other hand, is something that someone creates or develops which did not previously exist. Thus, on the usual interpretation of the words, it seems apparent that the identification of a gene is a discovery, since genes exist in the world, in our bodies.[6]

Despite that in some jurisdictions, such as in the United States, isolated genes are deemed patentable,[7] genes do not become an 'invention' by the mere process

---

[3] J Straus, 'Implications of the TRIPs Agreement in the field of patent law', in F-K Beier and G Schricker, *From GATT to TRIPs—The Agreement on Trade-Related Aspects of Intellectual Property Rights* (1996: Munich, Max Planck Institute for Foreign and International Patent, Copyright and Competition Law).   [4] *Concise Oxford Dictionary* (1982: Oxford University Press, 7th edn), p 527.

[5] Many patent laws make such a distinction. For instance, Article 52(2) of the European Patent Convention stipulates that '[T]he following in particular shall not be regarded as inventions within the meaning of paragraph 1: (a) discoveries, scientific theories and mathematical methods; (b) aesthetic creations; (c) schemes, rules and methods for performing mental acts, playing games or doing business, and programs for computers; (d) presentations of information'.

[6] Nuffield Council on Bioethics, *The ethics of patenting DNA. A discussion paper* (2002: London), p 23.

[7] In the United States, a substance cannot be claimed as it exists in nature, but an isolated or purified form thereof is patentable. Hence, only a very thin line separates invention from discovery, and many patents have been granted on purified or crystallized products obtained from a natural source of impure material. The European Directive on Biotechnological Inventions (No 96/9/EC of 11 March 1996) stipulates that 'biological material which is isolated from its natural environment or processed by means of a technical process may be the subject of an invention even if it already occurred in nature' (Article 3.2).

of isolation.[8] In addition, many countries have explicitly excluded genes from patentability even if isolated.[9] Hence, the extension of the concept of invention to genes and other matters found in nature cannot be deemed universally accepted or incorporated into the TRIPS Agreement. WTO Members can legitimately exclude the patentability of genes claimed in various forms, including human genes, as found in nature, even if isolated or purified.

Could a WTO panel or the Appellate Body, if a case under the DSU were brought, provide their own interpretation of what an 'invention' is? The competence of such bodies is limited to the clarification of WTO rules;[10] they are not permitted to resolve ambiguities deliberately left in the text by the drafters of the Agreements and alter the delicate balance reached and the various compromises made as an outcome of difficult negotiations.[11] The existence of gaps and ambiguities in the TRIPS Agreement indicates that Members retained a certain amount of room for manoeuvre at the national level, which should not be limited by interpretations by panels or the Appellate Body.[12]

Article 27.1 further requires to patent inventions 'whether products or processes'. 'Products' include machines and other devices, chemical compounds, etc. A 'process' is a 'course of action, proceeding, especially series of operations in manufacture, printing, photography, etc'.[13] Processes are generally deemed to encompass in patent law the sequence of steps required to manufacture or otherwise obtain a product. In some countries, in addition to these processes, 'methods of use' are patentable independently of the patentability of the product and of the process of manufacture as such.[14] In the USA, for instance, 'method-of-use'

---

[8] A report published by the World Health Organization (WHO) observed in this regard: 'It is argued that a normal or abnormal gene sequence is, in effect, naturally occurring information which cannot therefore be patentable. The counter-argument which has been used widely by patent lawyers, that DNA sequence identification is a form of purification "outside the body," and therefore analogous to the purification of naturally occurring pharmacological agents, is specious; the DNA molecule is not, in this context, important as a substance and its value resides in its information content.' See WHO, *Genomics and World Health. Report of the Advisory Committee on Health Research* (2002: Geneva), p 136.

[9] For instance, Decision 486 of the Andean Community considers non-patentable substances that pre-exist in nature. Similarly, the Mexican and Argentine laws exclude the patentability of substances existing in nature, although it is unclear the extent to which isolated materials may be deemed patentable in the case of Mexico. The 1996 Brazilian Industrial Property Code (No 9.279, 14 May 1996) is more precise in this respect. It excludes the patentability of living beings or 'biological materials found in nature', even if isolated, including the 'genome or germplasm' of any living being (Article 10.IX). The Biodiversity Law of Costa Rica (1998) establishes the non-patentability of sequences of DNA *per se*.

[10] Article 3.2 of the DSU expressly prevents panels and the Appellate Body from adding rights and obligations when adjudicating disputes.

[11] In *Canada–Patent Protection for Pharmaceutical Products*, the panel alerted against interpretations that 'would be equivalent to a renegotiation of the basic balance of the Agreement' (WT/DS114/R, 2000, para 7.26).

[12] See J Jackson, *The Jurisprudence of GATT and the WTO* (2000: Cambridge University Press), pp 184 and 186.   [13] *Concise Oxford Dictionary* (1982: Oxford University Press, 7th edn), p 820.

[14] See, eg, H Wegner, *Patent Law in Biotechnology, Chemicals & Pharmaceuticals* (1994: Chippenham, Stockton), p 302.

patents allow for the protection of inventions consisting of the use of a product not suggested by the prior art, despite that the product is known and not patentable.[15] A literal interpretation of Article 27.1, however, does not permit us to sustain that there is an obligation under the TRIPS Agreement to recognize the patentability of such methods.

A closely related issue is the patentability of the 'second indication' of a pharmaceutical product; that is, its use for a treatment different from that previously known for the same compound.[16] This is an important issue for the design of a patent policy sensitive to public health concerns. Admitting such patentability expands the scope of protection where no new product has been developed. It is in the interest of consumers to keep patent protection limited to products and processes that make real contributions to the state of the art,[17] and to avoid the granting of patents that may otherwise affect legitimate competition and better access to medicines.

Some patent offices (eg the European Patent Office) have admitted the protection of second indications of a pharmaceutical product on the basis of a legal fiction: claims are framed under the so-called 'Swiss formula' ('use of x for the manufacture of product y to treat disease z'). However, this formula suffers from 'the logical objection that it lacks novelty, since it claims the use of the compound for preparation of a medicament, and normally the medicament itself will be the same as that already used for the first pharmaceutical indication'.[18]

Article 27.1 does not address the issue of second indications. Since it only obliges to protect 'products and processes' Members are free to consider such indications as non-patentable. Moreover, the Agreement allows Members to exclude the patentability of therapeutic methods to which second indications claims are essentially equivalent,[19] as they contain instructions to the physician about how to employ a known drug to treat a particular disease.

[15] See, eg, R Merges, *Patent Law and Policy. Cases and Materials* (1992: Boston, Contemporary Legal Educational Series), p 489.

[16] Significant resources are devoted by the pharmaceutical industry to identify—and patent—new therapeutic uses of existing drugs. This may be the result of a substantial decline in the invention of new chemical entities of pharmaceutical use. See, eg, Commission on Intellectual Property Rights, Innovation and Public Health (CIPIH) (2006), *Public Health, Innovation and Intellectual Property Rights*, available on<http://www.who.int> (last accessed on 15 May 2006).

[17] This is the approach adopted by a recent reform (2005) to the Indian Patent Act, which stipulated that the following shall not be treated as an invention within the meaning of the Act: 'the mere discovery of a new form of a known substance which does not result in the enhancement of the known efficacy of that substance or the mere discovery of any new property or new use for a known substance or of the mere use of a known process, machine or apparatus unless such known process results in a new product or employs at least one new reactant' (Section 3(d)).

[18] P Grubb, *Patents for Chemicals, Pharmaceuticals and Biotechnology. Fundamentals of Global Law, Practice and Strategy* (1999: Oxford, Clarendon Press), p 221.

[19] It has been noted in this regard that '[T]here is no real difference between patent claims relating to a use of a substance and those relating to a therapeutic procedure: in both cases a new medical activity is patented, ie a new way of using one or more known products. Thus the difficulties in European patent law of protecting a new medical indication for a known substance are due to the combination of the novelty requirement (which impedes products claims) and the ban on patents for

In accordance with Article 27.1, finally, patents shall be available 'in all fields of technology'. This provision may be deemed as one of the major concessions made by developing countries during the TRIPS negotiations, both in the light of these countries' original negotiating position and of the legislation of many of such countries that excluded the patentability of pharmaceuticals and agrochemicals at the inception of the Uruguay Round.

One of the main arguments for the recognition of patents for pharmaceuticals is that in order to ensure future R&D it is essential that patent protection be conferred universally. The argument is based on the undeniable contributions that the industry's R&D has made to the development of products for curative or preventive purposes[20] for a vast array of human diseases. Such contributions would not be possible if companies could not recover their investments in R&D and make a profit thereon. Patents provide, thus, one of the mechanisms that encourage future R&D on new products, in exchange for the exclusive use of the R&D outcomes for a certain period. However, patents only provide incentives where profitable markets exist; they do not stimulate R&D for diseases that prevail in the poor countries (such as malaria and tuberculosis), nor are they likely to have any significant impact in fostering pharmaceutical innovation in developing countries.[21]

In accordance with Article 27.1, patents should be granted if claimed inventions meet the requirements of novelty, inventive step, and industrial applicability.

The *universal* novelty requirement, as applied in most countries, prevents the patentability of an information which belongs to the 'prior art'; that is, which has been published in a written form or has been made otherwise available to the public, for instance, through public use, *in any country* before the date of filing of a patent. Nevertheless, WTO Members are not constrained to apply a particular concept of the patentability requirements. In the case of novelty, this flexibility has permitted, for instance, the US to maintain a double novelty standard depending on whether the disclosure of the invention has taken place within or outside the territory of the US (35 USC section 102 (a)).[22] The US held in this regard that in

---

medical procedures (which impedes use claims)'. See B Domeij, *Pharmaceutical Patents in Europe* (2000: Stockholm, Kluwer Law International/Norstedts Juridik), p 178.

[20] It has been noted that '[V]accines are the most cost-effective technologies known in health care, preventing illness in a one-time dose. But they generate smaller profits and have higher potential liabilities than treatments used repeatedly. As a result a consortium of US pharmaceutical companies has united to develop antiviral agents against HIV, but not to produce a vaccine against AIDS' (UNDP, *Human Development Report* (1999: New York, Oxford University Press), p 69.

[21] See, eg, Commission on Intellectual Property Rights, Innovation and Public Health (CIPIH) op. cit. (2006).

[22] According to this section 'A person shall be entitled to a patent unless the invention was known or used by others in this country, or patented or described in a printed publication in this or a foreign country, before the invention thereof by the applicant for patent, or the invention was patented or described in a printed publication in this or a foreign country or in public use or on sale in this country, more than one year prior to the date of the application for patent in the United States . . . '.

the TRIPS Agreement there was 'no prescription as to how WTO Members define what inventions are to be considered 'new' within their domestic systems' and, hence, that its legislation was 'perfectly consistent with the provisions of the TRIPS Agreement'.[23]

Article 27.1 permits the application of grace periods (as admitted in the USA and in many other countries). Differences in the treatment of disclosures that take place before the filing date also illustrate the limited role of the TRIPS Agreement as a harmonizing instrument.[24]

Similarly, the TRIPS Agreement does not define the concept of 'non-obviousness/inventive step'. Members can consider 'inventive step' to be synonymous with the term 'non-obvious'. The former is applied, for instance, in Europe and the latter in the USA. Although Members can consider them synonymous, there are some differences between them, as 'inventive step' connotes that a intellectual process has taken place to develop a new product or process; non-obviousness may be predicated with regard to subject matter, even if found and not 'invented'.

There is ample room for Members to establish the level of 'non-obviousness/inventive step', according to the policies they opt to apply. They may opt for a strict standard aimed at rewarding substantive departures from the prior art, as applied in the USA in the past.[25] On the other extreme, a low standard would allow the patenting of a broad range of minor, incremental, developments,

---

[23] See document IP/Q3/USA/1, 1 May 1998. As a result of the relative novelty requirement of the US, several patents have been granted to researchers or firms of developed countries by the US Patent and Trademark Office relating to or consisting of genetic materials or traditional knowledge acquired in developing countries. This appropriation (or 'biopiracy') has involved resources protected 'as is'; that is, without any further improvement (eg US Patent No 5.304.718 on quinoa granted to researchers of the Colorado State University) and on products based on plant materials and knowledge developed and used by local/indigenous communities. A telling case was the patent on *ayahuasca* (*Banisteriopsis caapi*). The US Patent and Trademark Office (PTO) revoked it in November 1999. The PTO based its decision on the fact that publications describing *Banisteriopsis caapi* were 'known and available' prior to the filing of the patent application. However, in 2001 the PTO reinstated the patent because, at the time it was granted, the law did not allow a third party such as COICA standing to object to it.

[24] United States, Japan, and the European Union are suggesting, in the framework of WIPO, the harmonization of legislation with regard to prior art and grace periods. See Annex to document WO/GA/31/9 dated 23 July 2004, available at <http://www.wipo.int/documents/en/document/govbody/index04.htm> (last accessed on 28 May 2005).

[25] In an early precedent Justice Bradley stated that '[I]t was never the object of [the patent] laws to grant a monopoly for every trifling device, every shadow of a shade, of an idea, which would naturally and spontaneously occur to any skilled mechanic or operator in the ordinary progress or manufactures' (*Atlantic Works v Brady*, 107 US (17 Otto) 192, 1883). Fifty years later Justice Douglas stated that a new device, to be patentable, 'must reveal the flash of creative genius' (*Cuno Engineering Corp*, 314 US 84, 51 USPQ 1, 1941), while in another case the Court considered that a combination of old mechanical elements was patentable only if it showed 'unusual or surprising consequences' (*Great Atlantic & Pacific Tea Co v Supermarket Equipment Co*, 340 US 147, 87 USPQ 303, 950). The US Supreme Court's requirement of non-obviousness was so high that Justice Jackson complained, in dissent, 'that the only valid patents were those the Court had not been able to get its hands on' (*Junguersen v Ostby & Barton Co*, 335 US 560, 80 USPQ 32 (1949) dissenting opinion). See D Chisum and M Jacobs, *Understanding Intellectual Property Law* (1995: New York, Matthew Bender), pp 2-14–2-15.

as is currently the case in the USA, mainly as a result of the lax approach adopted by the US Federal Circuit specializing in intellectual property matters.[26]

Inventions marked with considerable originality do not occur frequently,[27] even in highly intensive R&D industries. For instance, while in the pharmaceutical sector, only a small and declining number of 'new chemical entities' (i.e. not pre-existing molecules) are developed and patented each year,[28] thousands of patents are applied for and obtained for processes of manufacture, salts, esters, crystal forms, isomers, formulations, new indications, etc of existing pharmaceutical products. This strategy—often called 'evergreening'—tends to delay the entry of generic competition in the market.

The application of low standards of patentability may, in practice, subject to private control both genuine inventions and minor/incremental innovations that occur in different sectors. It might be argued that, as patents might cover both major and minor innovations, a patent regime based on a low inventive threshold could be functional to the innovation path prevailing in developing countries.

This expansive approach on patentability, however, may have negative consequences. On the one hand, as exemplified by the case of pharmaceuticals, large firms with experienced patent lawyers are much better prepared, financially and technically, to exploit a patent regime with a low patentability threshold than domestic firms, and there is a risk of blocking innovation and competition rather than promoting it. In addition, the public will be bound to pay monopoly prices for access to knowledge and product that should be, and remain, in the public domain.

On the other, the cost of acquisition and, particularly, exercise of patent rights is too high for most local innovators, generally small and medium enterprises (SMEs). While SMEs could opt in many cases to seek patent protection, they should bear the costs of filing, registration, and maintenance. If there is litigation (either to enforce the patent against infringers or to defend it from validity challenges), victory in courts is not assured, damage claims by counterparts may be high, and litigation costs prohibitive.

---

[26] Scherer noted almost two decades ago: 'As the bleary-eyed reviewer of some 15,000 patent abstracts in connection with research... I was struck by how narrowly incremental (adaptive?) most 'inventions' are' (F Scherer, 'Comment' on RE Evenson, 'International Invention: Implications for Technology Market Analysis', in Zvi Griliches (ed.) *R&D, Patents, and Productivity* (1987: University of Chicago and National Bureau of Economic Research), pp 123–6. See also A Jaffe and J Lerner, *Innovation and Its Discontents: How Our Broken Patent System is Endangering Innovation and Progress, and What to Do About It* (2004: Princeton University Press).

[27] See R Merges and R Nelson, 'On limiting or encouraging rivalry in technical progress: the effect of patent-scope decisions', in *The Sources of Economic Growth* (1996: Cambridge/London, Harvard University Press), p 128.

[28] See, eg, Commission on Intellectual Property Rights, Innovation and Public Health (CIPIH) op. cit. (2006).

   The third patentability requirement relates to the industrial applicability of the invention. 'Industrial' must be interpreted in the sense of Article 1(3) of the Paris Convention:

Industrial property shall be understood in the broadest sense and shall apply not only to industry and commerce proper, but likewise to agricultural and extractive industries and to all manufactured or natural products, for example, wines, grain, tobacco leaf, fruit, cattle, minerals, mineral waters, beer, flowers, and flour.

   In accordance with footnote 4 to Article 27.1, for the purposes of this Article, the terms 'capable of industrial application' may be deemed by a Member to be synonymous with the term 'useful'. However, 'useful' is much broader than industrial applicability. Thus, research tools, business and other methods[29] and computer programs may be patentable under the former, while they do not meet the industrial patentability requirement. This difference is one of the factors explaining the significant increase in the number of patents in the USA vis-à-vis other jurisdictions, such as the European countries.

   Given the latitude of Article 27.1, Members can determine when an invention is deemed to be capable of industrial application or useful. Many national laws consider that the former requirement is met when the invention can be *used* in any kind of industry; other laws, however, qualify such use and more explicitly require that the invention be capable of industrial use as a manufacturing process or by materializing into an industrial product. 'Useful', on the other hand, may be deemed to include an assessment of 'efficacy', as in the case of the already quoted Section 3(d) of the Indian Patent law (as amended in 2005).

   Based on a broad concept of utility, thousands of patents on computer programs have been granted in the United States. US courts distinguished, in early cases on patent protection of software, between non-patentable, purely mathematical algorithms, and inventions in which such an algorithm is 'applied'. However, after *Diamond v Diehr* and *Diamond v Bradley* (both decided in 1981), the US Supreme Court applied a liberal rule permitting the patenting of software algorithms. The US Patent and Trademark Office followed suit by issuing software patenting guidelines that have expanded the definition of patentable software subject matter. A patent attorney suggested that the language was 'so sweeping as to allow Newton to receive a patent on the calculus'.[30] Hence, in the US, patents have been routinely granted in cases where there is no transformation of physical substances into a different physical state, and only manipulation of data is involved.

---

   [29] See, eg, US Patent 6,076,070, 'On-line price comparison of competitor's goods and/or services over a computer network'; US Patent 5,443,036 on a 'Method of exercising a cat'; US Patent 5,616,989 on a 'Method of putting golfer's hand'.
   [30] S Graham and D Mowery, 'Intellectual property in the US software industry', in WM Coher and S A Merill (eds), *Patents in the Knowledge-Based Economy* (2003: Washington DC, Committee on Intellectual Property Rights in the Knowledge-Based Economy, National Research Council).

In *In re Alappat* (33 F 3d 1526, Fed Cir 1994), the court held that data transformed by a machine through a series of mathematical calculations to produce a smooth wave from display on a . . . monitor, constituted a practical application of an abstract idea a mathematical algorithm, formula, or calculation), because it produced a useful concrete and tangible result. In *State Street Bank v Signature Financial Group*, 149 F 3d 1368, Fed Cir 1998 the definition of protectable software was expanded. The Court of Appeals for the Federal Circuit (CAFC) validated a software patent awarded on a data-processing system used in financial transactions.[31] The court held that the transformation of data, representing discrete dollar amounts, by a machine through a series of mathematical calculations into a final share price, constitutes a practical application of a mathematical algorithm, formula, or calculation, because it produces 'a useful, concrete, and tangible result'.

According to one commentator,

the court acknowledges that by a patent monopoly on the software to implement the mutual fund structure, the patent owner may in effect monopolize that mutual fund structure itself. Yet this is no bar to patentability . . . If calculating a share price for a trade is adequately 'tangible' for patentability, as is a monitor display, then all functioning software must pass this 'tangible' test. Indeed, practically speaking, this tangible test is now dead . . . This reading is so broad and so favorable for software patents in financial service industries, that it would be difficult to conceive of any software developed in the financial industry that would not be patentable subject matter, if it merely satisfied the minimal requirements for novelty, non-obviousness, notice, and disclosure. This would be the case even if the software were so broadly claimed as to monopolize all practical computer methods necessary for keeping the books and records for the product offering.[32]

The *State Street Bank v Signature Financial Group* opened the way for the controversial patenting of 'business methods' in the USA. This was later confirmed in *AT&T Corp v Excel Communications, Inc*, 172 F3d 1352, Fed Cir 1999, in relation to a patent that protected a message record used by a long-distance carrier in providing a differential billing treatment for subscribers. On appeal the Federal Circuit found again that no 'physical transformation' was necessary for a mathematical algorithm to be patentable subject matter.[33] Because of the low inventive standard (if any) and broad coverage, 'business method patenting raises the specter of an explosion of litigation focused on technical methods long in use, but patented only recently'.[34]

[31] US Patent No 5,193,056 protects a computerized accounting system used to manage a particular type of mutual fund investment structure, specifically the 'hub and spoke' structure for mutual funds that simultaneously invest in stocks in different national stock exchanges, priced in different currencies.

[32] Stephen Glazier, *E-Patent Strategies for Software, e-Commerce, the Internet, Telecom Services, Financial Services, and Business Methods* (2000: Washington DC, LBI Institute), pp 29–32.

[33] Idem, p 40.

[34] B Steil, D Victor, and R Nelson, *Technological Innovation & Economic Performance* (2002: Princeton and Oxford; A Council on Foreign Relations Book; Princeton University Press), p 22.

Software patents—to the extent that, unlike copyright, they protect ideas—may have significant implications, independent from the technical importance of the involved 'invention'. Thus, Warshofsky reported that Cadtrak Corporation applied for a patent on a computer screen display and included the exclusive-or statement as one of fifteen claims. 'They were granted US Patent No 4,197,590, and as a result, anyone who wanted to put a cursor on a computer screen either paid Cadtrak or ran the infringement gauntlet. More than three hundred hardware and software companies, including IBM, Texas Instruments, and Fujitsu, chose the easy way and paid royalties to license that single patent.' In another case, 'Paul Heckel, a California programmer, was granted US Patent Nos 4,486,857 and 4,736,308 for a system that displays records or strings of information and then allows the operator to scroll, or browse, through them. Heckel sued Apple computer, alleging their Hypercard program violated those patents. Despite the fact that scrolling and sub-windows, the techniques incorporated in the patents, were quite well known, using them in a combination could be considered illegal. Rather than fight what is considered a nuisance suit, Apple simply took out a license.'[35]

The European Patent Convention forbids the patenting of computer programs as such.[36] Patents have not been granted in cases where the program only undertakes mathematical operations, analyses or tests data, or permits the graphic presentation of data, among others. In exchange, computer programs that generate a transformation in physical reality by guiding the operation of other means have been deemed patentable, such as a computer-operated radiologic device, a system to automatically manage the order of the supply of services to clients at different sites.[37]

However, the US permissive approach on software patents seems to have influenced European law.[38] In a decision by the Board of Appeals of the European Patent Office (EPO) relating to an IBM patent on 'a method and system in a data processing system windowing environment for displaying previously obscured information', the Board noted that Article 52(c) of the EPC 'establishes an

---

[35] F Warshofsky, *The Patent Wars, The Battle to Own the World's Technology* (1994: New York, John Wiley & Sons, Inc), pp 163–4.

[36] The Guidelines for Examination of the EPO state that 'a computer program claimed by itself or as a record on a carrier or in the form of a signal' is not patentable and 'programs for computers' are included among the items listed in Article 52(2) of the European Patent Convention; that is, they are not patentable (available at <http://www.european-patent-office.org/legal/gui_lines/>, last accessed on 28 June 2005).

[37] Giovanni Guglielmetti, A Giuffré (ed.), *L'invenzione di Software. Brevetto e Diritto D'Autore* (1996: Dott), pp 78–89.

[38] It is to be noted, however, that the Diplomatic Conference for the Revision of the European Patent Convention, Munich, 20–29 November 2000, rejected (by 16 out of 20 votes) the proposal to delete computer programs from Article 52(2)(c) of the Convention. See generally R Nack and B Phélip, Report. Diplomatic Conference for the Revision of the European Patent Convention (2001), Munich, 20–29 November 2000, 32 IIC. However, the European Ministers approved an amendment to EU law that would allow (if finally adopted by the European Parliament) to obtain patents over computer programs. See <http://news.bbc.co.uk/go/pr/fr/-/1/hi/technology/4325215.stm> (last accessed on 2 April 2005).

important limitation to the scope of this exclusion'. The Board narrowly inter-preted and determined that software programs excluded from patentability are those that are 'mere abstract creations lacking in technical character', and that therefore all programs for computers 'must be considered as patentable inven-tions when they have a technical character', which can be found when the soft-ware is used to solve a 'technical problem'.[39]

Software patents can create several problems. First, a patented program cannot be used as a basis for further development without the authorization of the patent holder. This may block a whole area of possible innovation. Unlike chemical patents, it may be difficult in some cases to 'invent around' software patents, since mathematical rules are logical and precise, and in some cases there may be no alternative way for obtaining the same effect. Second, if a licence is sought and obtained on a piece of software, royalties may be too high—particularly for a small firm—to ensure the feasibility of a development project. Third, even if patents may be 'by-passed' and new technical solutions may be found, serious problems still remain. It may be impossible to design a program that at a certain point will not infringe an existing patent. Patents searches to establish whether patents would be infringed are extremely costly and difficult to make. What is even worse, a patent search does not guarantee that a patent would not be infringed; if this is the case, litigation costs may force a small firm out of business.[40]

Non-discrimination

Article 27.1, *in fine*, contains a non-discrimination clause that is unique in the whole Agreement. It was introduced in the text just before the submission of the Dunkel proposal in December 1991, as a compromise solution aimed at essen-tially addressing the conflicting views about the possible granting of compulsory licences in cases of lack of or insufficient working of patented inventions.

The application of the non-discrimination clause is subject to three provisions of the Agreement:

- paragraph 4 of Article 65 allowing a Member to discriminate, until 1 January 2005, with regard to areas of technology for which product patents were not conferred on the general date of application of the Agreement for that Member;
- paragraph 8 of Article 70, which establishes the so called 'mail box' for patent applications relating to pharmaceutical and agricultural chemical products, applicable where a Member did not make available as of the date of entry into force of the WTO Agreement patent protection for such product; and
- paragraph 3 of Article 27, which allows for some exceptions in the biotechno-logical field.

---

[39] See, eg, Glazier op. cit. (2000), p 42.   [40] See Warshofsky op. cit. (1994), p 168.

The obligation not to discriminate applies both to the *availability* and *enjoyment* of patent rights, meaning that neither the acquisition of patent rights nor the means for their enforcement can be subject to discrimination. Although the provision is broad in this respect, it is only applicable when discrimination takes place on the basis of one out of the following grounds:

* the place of invention;
* the field of technology; and
* whether products are imported or locally produced.

The discrimination addressed in this clause is not related to the nationality of the title-holder, as in the case of the national treatment and the most-favoured-nation clauses. Non-discrimination about the place of invention in fact expands the anti-discrimination protection conferred under those clauses, as it does not allow a Member to provide differential treatment based on the location where the invention was made. Thus, preferential treatment given to persons who have locally developed their inventions, would not violate the national treatment principle[41] but would violate Article 27.1.

Non-discrimination with regard to the 'field of technology' reiterates what the first sentence of Article 27 already stipulates with regard to the availability of patents ('patents shall be available for any inventions... in all fields of technology...') but adds that the conferred rights should also be *enjoyable* without discrimination. This means that availability and scope of enforcement measures should not unjustifiably differentiate on the basis of the field of technology.[42]

This aspect of the non-discrimination clause has been mentioned in some complaints before the WTO. For instance, a discrimination about the field of technology was argued by the EC in the case against Canada on the so-called 'Bolar exception'.[43] The EC unsuccessfully argued that the Canadian provision violated Article 27.1 of the TRIPS Agreement. In an interesting statement, the panel made a distinction between 'discrimination' and 'differentiation'. It held that

Article 27 prohibits only discrimination as to the place of invention, the field of technology, and whether products are imported or produced locally. Article 27 does not prohibit *bona fide* exceptions to deal with problems that may exist only in certain product areas. Moreover, to the extent the prohibition of discrimination does limit the ability to target certain products in dealing with certain of the important national policies referred to in Articles 7 and 8.1, that fact may well constitute a deliberate limitation rather than frustration of purpose.[44]

---

[41] As discussed above, there may be *de jure* and *de facto* violations of such principle. See Chapter 2 above.

[42] In the area of industrial designs, on the contrary, there are special provisions for a peculiar sector (textiles). See Chapter 8 above.

[43] *See* Report of the WTO Panel, *Canada–Patent Protection for Pharmaceutical Products*, WT/DS114/R (2000). See a more detailed analysis of this case below in this chaper.

[44] Idem, para 7.92.

In order to discourage 'evergreening' after the adoption of the Australia–USA Free Trade Agreement, the Australian Labour Party was able to include an amendment to the US Free Trade Agreement Implementation Bill 2004[45] that permits an AU 10 million penalty for drug patent litigation in bad faith. The US warned of a challenge under WTO non-discrimination rules. The US argument would be that Australia's amendment discriminates against the field of drug patents, since the provision does not apply to non-drug patents.[46]

A critical issue in addressing Article 27.1, especially for developing countries, is whether the non-discrimination clause in this Article governs Article 31 (conditions for the granting of compulsory licences).[47] If so, compulsory licences could not be established to address public interests in certain fields of technology (eg pharmaceuticals, environmental protection, or remediation). Developing countries have argued that:

As regards the relationship of the provisions related to compulsory licenses with Articles 27.1 and 28 of TRIPS, we believe that both set of provisions address different matters and circumstances. In no way do Articles 27.1 and 28 limit the right of Members to issue compulsory licenses.[48]

In *Canada–Patent Protection for Pharmaceutical Products* the panel held that Articles 30 (exceptions) and 31 (compulsory licences) of the TRIPS Agreement were subject to Article 27.1 of the Agreement.[49] However, the factual and legal basis for this finding are unconvincing, since it would seem logical to limit certain exceptions or modalities of compulsory licences to certain fields of technology, rather than being forced to apply them to fields where such measures are not required.

One example—unchallenged by other WTO Members—of compulsory licences limited to a particular field of technology is provided by French law, which provides that:

Where the interests of public health demand, patents granted for medicines or for processes for obtaining medicines, for products necessary in obtaining such medicines or for processes for manufacturing such products may be subject to ex officio licences in accordance with Article L 613–17 in the event of such medicines being made available to the public in insufficient quantity or quality or at (abnormally high prices) by order of the Minister responsible for industrial property at the request of the Minister responsible for health.[50]

---

[45] Amendment (2), The Senate, The Parliament of the Commonwealth of Australia (codified as new Section 26C of the Therapeutic Goods Act 1989).

[46] See K Outterson, 'Agony in the Antipodes: The Generic Drug Provisions of the Australia–US Free Trade Agreement' (2005), Journal of Generic Medicines, Vol. 2, No 4, July 2005, pp 316–26.

[47] See pp 311–24 below.

[48] See *TRIPS and Public Health*, IP/C/W/296 (29 June 2001), paper submitted by the African Group, Barbados, Bolivia, Brazil, Cuba, Dominican Republic, Ecuador, Honduras, India, Indonesia, Jamaica, Pakistan, Paraguay, Philippines, Peru, Sri Lanka, Thailand, and Venezuela, para 8.

[49] WT/DS114/R (2000), para 7.91.　　　[50] Article L 613–16.

Under US legislation[51] and in accordance with the FTAs signed by the USA with a number of countries,[52] special provisions apply for the extension of the term of pharmaceutical patents to compensate for delays in the marketing approval of medicines. The same advantage is not conferred, however, to other products that are also subject to marketing approval, such as agrochemicals. Whether this divergent treatment is compatible with the non-discrimination clause is debatable.[53]

A differentiation between fields of technology may also take place *de facto*. Thus, US courts treat differently non-obviousness in biotechnological and software inventions. While the level of inventive step is low for the former, software inventions are deemed patentable if not obvious for extremely skilled programmers.[54] In exchange, DNA sequences must be disclosed under a stringent written description rule (the actual sequence in hand), while applicants need to disclose virtually nothing about the detailed workings of their invention in the case of software patents.[55]

While differentiation based on fields of technology may be possible, as mentioned, it may also be argued that 'problem areas' are distinct from 'fields of technology'. Hence, differential treatment (including compulsory licences) could be established, for instance, to address public health problems, involving products originating from different technological fields, such as equipment, software, diagnostic kits, medicines, and a large variety of other products required for public health purposes.

Article 27.1 of the Agreement stipulates that 'patent rights shall be enjoyable without discrimination ... whether the products are imported or locally produced'. The interpretation of this part of the provision is perhaps the most controversial. Although this proposition has been understood as prohibiting any obligation to locally work a patented invention and the possibility of granting compulsory licences due to lack of or insufficient working, this interpretation is not based on a literal reading of the text.

During the Uruguay Round negotiations developing countries advocated the right to impose working requirements.[56] In fact, several developed and

---

[51] Under the US law the extension to compensate for delays in the marketing approval process shall not exceed five years and the effective protection shall not exceed fourteen years from the date of approval by the Food and Drug Administration (35 USC § 156).

[52] See Singapore FTA, Article 16.8.4(a); Chile FTA, Article 17.10.2(a); Morocco FTA, Article 15.10.3; Bahrain FTA, Article 14.8.6(b)(i); CAFTA, Article 15.9.6(b)). These provisions do not contain, however, the caps provided for under US law.

[53] The FTAs referred to curiously reproduce in their intellectual property chapters the first part of Article 27.1, but omit the non-discrimination clause.

[54] D Burk and M Lemley, 'Is Patent Law Technology-Specific?' (2003), 17 Berkeley Tech LJ 1155, pp 1155–206.   [55] Idem.

[56] See, eg, Negotiating Group on Trade-Related Aspects of Intellectual Property Rights, including Trade in Counterfeit Goods, Meeting of Negotiating Group of 2, 4 and 5 April 1990, Note by the Secretariat MTN.GNG/NG11/20, 24 April 1990, para 34; Negotiating Group on Trade-Related Aspects of Intellectual Property Rights, Including Trade in Counterfeit Goods, Existence, Scope and Form of Generally Internationally Accepted and Applied Standards/Norms for the Protection of

developing countries that are WTO Members have adopted and maintain local working obligations.[57]

Article 27.1 of the Agreement does not specify whether the products that are 'imported or locally produced' are those of the patent owner or third parties' infringing products. The 'patent rights' referred to in Article 27.1 are defined in Article 28.1,[58] which only requires the granting of *negative* rights with regard to the exploitation of the invention; that is, the right to prevent third parties from using (without authorization) the patented invention. Hence, an interpretation of Article 27.1 read in conjunction with Article 28.1, and based on the rules of the Vienna Convention, suggests that the products mentioned in Article 27.1 are *infringing* products, not the products of the patent owner himself, since patents only confer exclusionary rights in relation to the former. In other words, Article 27.1 forbids discrimination between *infringing* imported and *infringing* locally made products, but it does not prevent the establishment of differential obligations with regard to non-infringing imported and locally made products (ie, products made or imported by the patent owner or with his/her consent).

Thus, the non-discrimination clause of Article 27.1 applies in cases where the rights enjoyed by patent owners are different (substantially or procedurally) depending on the foreign or domestic origin of the products. For instance, Section 337 of the US Tariff Act was found inconsistent with the GATT in *United States–Section 337 of the Tariff Act of 1930*,[59] since it accorded less favourable treatment to imported products challenged as infringing US patents

Intellectual Property, Note Prepared by the International Bureau of WIPO, MTN.GNG/NG11/W/24, 5 May 1988, p 2; Negotiating Group on Trade-Related Aspects of Intellectual Property Rights, including Trade in Counterfeit Goods, Meeting of Negotiating Group of 11, 12, and 14 December 1989, Note by the Secretariat, MTN.GNG/NG11/17, 23 January 1990, para 41; Negotiating Group on Trade-Related Aspects of Intellectual Property Rights, including Trade in Counterfeit Goods, Meeting of Negotiating Group of 11–12 May 1989, Note by the Secretariat, MTN.GNG/NG11/12, 13 June 1989, para 5; Negotiating Group on Trade-Related Aspects of Intellectual Property Rights, including Trade in Counterfeit Goods, Meeting of Negotiating Group of 11–12 May 1989, Note by the Secretariat, MTN.GNG/NG11/12, 13 June 1989, para 36; Negotiating Group on Trade-Related Aspects of Intellectual Property Rights, including Trade in Counterfeit Goods, Meeting of Negotiating Group of 30 October–2 November 1989, Note by the Secretariat, MTN.GNG/NG11/16, 4 December 1989, para 24; Negotiating Group on Trade-Related Aspects of Intellectual Property Rights, including Trade in Counterfeit Goods, Meeting of Negotiating Group of 12–14 July 1989, Note by the Secretariat, MTN.GNG/NG11/14, 12 September 1989, pp 75, 83.

[57] A review of comparative law made by Oxfam found working obligations in the patent laws and regulations of Indonesia and Cuba (similar to Brazil); Ghana, Ireland, South Africa, Sudan, and Zimbabwe (based on former United Kingdom laws); Greece and Lesotho (compulsory licensing linked to local working); Turkey, Spain, and Portugal (certificate of working required); Sweden, Norway, Finland, and Iceland (local working tied to reciprocity); India; Israel; Zaire; Thailand; Pakistan; Liberia. Oxfam, *Local Working Requirements and the TRIPS Agreement: Using Patent Law as a Means of Ensuring Affordable Access to Essential Medicines. A Case Study from the US–Brazil Dispute* (2001), available at <http://www.field.org.uk/papers/pdf/twrta.pdf> (last accessed on 18 June 2005).

[58] See pp 294–9 below.

[59] See M Haedicke, 'US Imports, TRIPS and Section 337 of the Tariff Act of 1930' (2000), 31 (7/8) International Review of Industrial Property and Copyright Law p 774.

than the treatment accorded to similarly challenged products of United States origin.[60]

It should also be noted that Article 5(A)(2) of the Paris Convention provides that each party to the Convention 'shall have the right to take legislative measures providing for the grant of compulsory licenses to prevent the abuses which might result from the exercise of the exclusive rights conferred by the patent, for example, *failure to work*' (emphasis supplied).

In addition, Article 7 of the TRIPS Agreement makes it clear that one of the objectives of the Agreement is to promote technology transfer, which may be ensured, in some circumstances, by means of compulsory licences for non-working.

The United States initiated in January 2001 a case against Brazil[61] arguing that Article 68 of the Brazilian patent law was inconsistent with the TRIPS Agreement. This provision[62] authorizes the government to grant a compulsory licence if the patent owner fails to work the subject matter of the patent in Brazil. The dispute ended several months later, when the US complaint was withdrawn.[63] In a separate case, Brazil requested consultations against the United States with regard to provisions of the US patent law that limits the right to use or sell any federally owned invention to a licensee that agrees that any products embodying the invention or produced through the use of the invention will be manufactured substantially in the United States.[64]

The scope of the discrimination clause was also examined in other contexts. During the negotiations of the International Treaty on Plant Genetic Resources for Food And Agriculture (IPGRFA), for instance, a concern voiced was whether Article 14.2.d.(iv) of the treaty could be banned as discriminatory

[60] The USA 'hesitantly effected an amendment of Section 337 in 1994 in order to improve the position of foreign respondents, but left the substance of the proceedings unchanged', Haedicke op. cit. (2000), p 774.

[61] *See Brazil—Measures Affecting Patent Protection*, Request for the Establishment of a Panel by the United States, 9 January 2001, WT/DS199/3. Cuba, the Dominican Republic, Honduras, India, and Japan reserved third-party rights.

[62] Article 68 (1) of the Brazilian Industrial Property Code (Law 9.279) provides as follows:

Art. 68. A patent shall be subject to compulsory licensing if the owner exercises his rights therein in an abusive manner or if he uses it to abuse economic power under the terms of an administrative or judicial decision.

(1) The following may also be grounds for compulsory licensing:

I. Failure to work the subject matter of a patent on the territory of Brazil, failure to manufacture or failure to completely use a patented process, except for failure to work due to the lack of economic viability, in which case importing shall be admitted; or

II. Marketing that does not satisfy the needs of the market.

[63] On 1 February 2001, the DSB authorized establishment of a panel, although no panel members had been appointed by the time the complaint was withdrawn. Without prejudice to their respective positions, the United States and Brazil agreed to enter into bilateral discussions before Brazil makes use of Article 68 against a US patent holder. *Brazil—Measures Affecting Patent Protection*, Notification of Mutually Agreed Solution, WT/DS199/4, G/L/454, IP/D/23/Add.1, 19 July 2001.

[64] *United States–US Patents Code*, WT/DS224/1, 7 February 2001. This case was not pursued.

under Article 27.1 of the TRIPS Agreement. That provision requires a payment to be made to an international mechanism when the recipient of materials within the Multilateral System that the treaty establishes, acquires rights on such materials that restrict their utilization for further research and plant breeding. This may particularly be the case of patents. The wording of Article 27.1, however, only bans discrimination when one of the three specific grounds stated therein is involved. It does not prevent Member countries from adopting other measures that—without conflicting with the national treatment principle—may impose differential conditions on the acquisition or exercise of patent rights when justified by other reasons, such as particular characteristics of the protected inventions. Moreover, there is no obligation under the TRIPS Agreement to provide patent protection for plants and plant varieties.[65] If, despite such possibility, patent protection were provided but the exploitation of patent rights were subject to certain obligations, no serious objection of inconsistency could be raised. Since a Member can exclude patent protection altogether, a fortiori a Member that grants patents but imposes certain conditions on their exploitation will be above the applicable minimum standard established by the Agreement.

Exclusions to patentability

27.2 Members may exclude from patentability inventions, the prevention within their territory of the commercial exploitation of which is necessary to protect ordre public or morality, including to protect human, animal or plant life or health or to avoid serious prejudice to the environment, provided that such exclusion is not made merely because the exploitation is prohibited by domestic law.

Article 27.2 specifies some of the exclusions to patentability that any country may (but is not obliged to) establish in its domestic law. This provision incorporates as a ground for non-patentability EEC, Japanese, and developing countries' proposals on 'ordre public and morality'.[66] The exception is complemented with a possible exclusion to 'protect human, animal or plant life or health', in line with but in broader terms than the Japanese and the developing countries' suggestions.

There is no generally accepted notion of 'ordre public'. The provision employs the French words for 'public order'. This is, perhaps, an indication that TRIPS drafters had in mind a particular concept, which is probably much narrower than 'public order' or 'public interest'.

Under the Guidelines for Examination of the European Patent Office, 'ordre public' is linked to security reasons, such as riot or public disorder, and inventions

---

[65] Member countries are bound to protect plant varieties under an effective *sui generis* system *or* patents, or a combination of both (Article 27.3.b). See pp 292–4 below.

[66] Another element that did not appear in the formal proposals referred to above is the possible exclusion to avoid 'serious prejudice to the environment'.

that may lead to criminal or other generally offensive behaviour (Part C, Chapter IV, 3.1). The EPO has clearly distinguished the concept of 'ordre public', as relating to the protection of the public interest and of the physical integrity of individuals, from morality grounds.[67] In decision T.356/93 (Plant Genetic Systems), it reasoned that it needs to be established in each individual case whether a particular invention relates to an improper use or has destructive effects on plant biotechnology. The Board held that 'inventions the exploitation of which is likely to breach public peace or social order (for example, through acts of terrorism) or to seriously prejudice the environment are to be excluded from patentability as being contrary to ordre public'.

However, there is no reason to apply an interpretation of the concept which has not been internationally accepted. WTO Member countries have considerable flexibility to define which situations are covered under 'ordre public', depending upon the Members' conception about what public values need to be protected. For instance, a country devastated by an epidemic may consider that adopting measures to combat it may be a matter of 'ordre public'.

Morality judgements depend on the values prevailing in a particular society at a particular time. Such values are not the same in different cultures and countries, and change over time. Like 'ordre public', morality is a vague and evolutive concept,[68] and their content will be dependent on national perceptions by patent offices or judges.

It is a matter of national public policy to determine when a certain conduct may be deemed contrary to fundamental values of a society, and whether this is an aspect relevant for the grant or refusal of a patent. Article 27.2 is a 'may' provision; it does not mandate Members to provide for an exception based on moral grounds. There have been different views about the role that patent offices should have with regard to morality issues in examining and granting patents. According to one view, such offices should not be charged with the task of assessing whether inventions or the description thereof are moral or not. For others, 'it is inadmissible to think that patent offices may grant patents to any kind of invention, without considering ethical issues whatsoever'.[69]

There is limited experience with the application of morality clauses under national patent laws. The European Patent Office (EPO) has decided—on the basis of Article 53(a) of the European Patent Convention (EPC)[70]—some cases involving genetically engineered products. Morality is deemed to include the 'totality of the accepted norms which are deeply rooted in a particular culture'.[71]

---

[67] See Decision T.356/93.

[68] F Pollaud-Dulian, *La Brevetabilité des inventions. Etude comparative de jurisprudence*, France-OEB (1997: Paris, Le Droit des Affaires, No 16), p 166.

[69] A Bercovitz, 'Panel Discussion on Biotechnology', in K Hill and L Morse (eds), *Emergent Technologies and Intellectual Property. Multimedia, Biotechnology & Other Issues* (1996: Seattle, ATRIP-CASRIP Publications Series No 2), p 53.

[70] A similar provision is contained in the 1998 European Directive on Biotechological inventions 98/44/EC (Article 9).   [71] See Decision T.356/93.

The EPO has employed two methods to assess the applicability of Article 53(b) of the EPC to particular patent applications: the balancing on interests at stake and the opinion of the vast majority of the public.

The balancing of interests takes into consideration the advantages and disadvantages of an invention including, for instance, the possible environmental risks due to the eventual dissemination of genes in nature. In a case relating to a patent on a genetically modified mouse (the so-called 'oncomouse') the balancing of interest approach led to the view that the advantages for humanity of a genetically modified animal exceeded its eventual inconveniences (Decision T.19/90). The patentability was deemed to depend 'mainly on a careful weighing up of the suffering of the animals and possible risks to the environment on the one hand, and the invention's usefulness to mankind on the other'. With regard to the ecological risks, the Board held that it was not a task of the EPO to regulate the use of dangerous materials, but a matter subject to competent national authorities. In the Plant Genetics System case the Board of Appeals considered that the adverse ecological effects were not proven and, hence, it was not possible to balance the advantages and disadvantages of the invention, since one of the terms for comparison was missing.

The opinion of the majority of the public was considered by the Opposition Division of the EPO in a decision of 12 October 1994 in the case of 'Relaxine'. The patent related to a DNA fragment codifying for a human protein. The Office examined whether the invention would appear immoral for the vast majority of the public. The decision held that there was nothing immoral with the isolation of mRNA from the tissue of pregnant women, and that the majority of the public accepts and desires the research on the use of human materials for therapeutic applications. The Office added that the patent in question did not give control over the human being and concluded that DNA is not equal to 'life'.

The arguments developed by the EPO illustrate how the public order and moral considerations may affect the granting or validity of patents. The EPO philosophy and criteria may not be followed in other jurisdictions, where other values and social perceptions may prevail.

Article 27.2 also refers to the protection of 'human, animal or plant life or health'. This is not incorporated as an autonomous ground for the refusal of a patent application, but as a sub-species of ordre public and morality ('... including to protect human, animal or plant life or health'). The issues at stake in the protection of life and health are, however, so important that it is difficult to consider a situation in which the need to ensure such protection could be subject to additional considerations relating to ordre public or morality. Rather, the right interpretation seems to be that when it is necessary to protect such interests, there is no need to prove the existence of ordre public or morality grounds as such to grant an exception.

Article 27.2 contains one of the flexibilities that Members can use 'to the full' to protect public health as stated by paragraph 4 of the Doha Declaration on the TRIPS Agreement and the Public Health:

We agree that the TRIPS Agreement does not and should not prevent members from taking measures to protect public health. Accordingly, while reiterating our commitment to the TRIPS Agreement, we affirm that the Agreement can and should be interpreted and implemented in a manner supportive of WTO members' right to protect public health and, in particular, to promote access to medicines for all.

In this connection, we reaffirm the right of WTO members to use, to the full, the provisions in the TRIPS Agreement, which provide flexibility for this purpose.

As in the case of health, serious prejudices to the environment are considered within the context of ordre public or morality. This is consistent with the European approach, under which ordre public also encompasses the protection of the environment.[72] However, the EPO refused to assume a regulatory role on the introduction of genetic engineering inventions and its environmental impact. In dealing with this issue, an EPO opposition decision stated that

A patent does not give a positive right to its proprietor to use the invention but rather only confers the right to exclude others from using the invention for a limited period of time. If the legislator is of the opinion that certain technical knowledge should be used under limited conditions only it is up to him to enact appropriate legislation.[73]

Article 27.2 allows Members to consider the effects of an invention on the environment as a ground for denying a patent application. In addition to the general conditions for the applicability of that article examined below, the wording employed suggests that such refusal may be justified in limited circumstances. On the one hand, the provision refers to 'avoid' prejudice, which would seem to exclude cases in which the aim of the refusal would be to mitigate or control such prejudice. On the other, the text alludes to 'serious' prejudice, thereby implying that not all prejudice may justify refusal.

Despite the restrictive wording of this provision, it represents a step forward that may influence future legislation on the matter. In addition, the seriousness of damage to the environment provides an imprecise standard, since Members may apply different levels of environmental protection; some may consider 'serious' what is tolerable for others. As in the case of the determination of when a public health emergency exists,[74] it will be up to the Members to establish when a prejudice is 'serious' or not. The prejudice to the environment may be actual or potential, a distinction that Article 27.2 does not make, suggesting that it applies to both.

Notwithstanding the apparent broadness of the exceptions allowed under Article 27.2, its application is subject to three important conditions.

---

[72] See Pollaud-Dulian op. cit. (1997), p 173.
[73] Decision T.0019/90, in the 'oncomouse' case.
[74] See the Doha Declaration on the TRIPS Agreement and Public Health, para 5.

First, non-patentability can only be established if the commercial exploitation of the invention that is deemed non-patentable is prevented in the territory of the respective Member. Since the refusal of patent protection does not necessarily lead to the exclusion of commercialization of the invention, the obvious purpose of this condition is to prevent a situation in which an invention is declared non-patentable but its commercialization is permitted. Generally, patent offices have no powers to prevent the commercialization of a product. Article 27.2, therefore, seems to require a decision by another competent authority to prevent the commercialization of the invention at stake.

It is debatable whether the exceptions under this Article can only be applied when there is an actual ban on commercialization. According to one opinion, an effective ban should exist in order to make the exception viable.[75] It has been held, however, that the TRIPS Agreement

does not require an actual ban of the commercialization as a condition for exclusions; only the necessity of such a ban is required. In order to justify an exclusion under Art 27 (2) TRIPs, a member state would therefore have to demostrate that it is necessary to prevent— by whatever means—the commercial exploitation of the invention. Yet, the member state would not have to prove that under its national laws the commercialization of the invention was or is actually prohibited.[76]

Second, the general final proviso ('provided that such exclusion is not made merely because the exploitation is prohibited by domestic law') would not permit exclusions which are not based on the specific grounds set forth in Article 27.2 even if they are prescribed by a national law. The existence of a legal prohibition, if based on other reasons, will not be sufficient to sustain the non-patentability of an individual invention or of a category of them. The rationale for this limitation is the presumption that legal prohibitions unrelated to ordre public or morality, as discussed above, would not be of sufficient entity to exclude patent protection altogether. Thus, the prohibition to commercialize a patented invention (for instance, a medicine for which negative side effects were found after initial approval) would not be sufficient ground to deny a patent.

Unlike the case of compulsory licences, which must be granted case-by-case, there is no impediment under Article 27.2 to determine that a certain type or category of inventions (eg all inventions relating to cloning of humans) are not patentable.

Article 27.2 permits the denial of patentability without specifying when that decision can be made. It may take place on the occasion of the examination of the patent application or after the patent has been granted, via revocation, if, for

---

[75] See, eg, A Otten, Viewpoint of the WTO, in M Swaminathan (ed), *Agrobiodiversity and Farmers' Rights—Proceedings of a Technical Consultation on an Implementation Framework for Farmers' Rights* (1996: Madras, MS Swaminathan Research Foundation).
[76] D Leskien and M Flitner, 'Intellectual Property Rights and Plant Genetic Resources: Options for a Sui Generis System' (1997) Issues in Genetic Resources No 6, IPGRI, Rome, p 15.

instance, the reasons of ordre public or morality were not taken into account at the time of the grant of the patent or arose after the grant of the patent.

27.3. Members may also exclude from patentability:

(a) diagnostic, therapeutic and surgical methods for the treatment of humans or animals;

(b) plants and animals other than micro-organisms, and essentially biological processes for the production of plants or animals other than non-biological and microbiological processes. However, Members shall provide for the protection of plant varieties either by patents or by an effective *sui generis* system or by any combination thereof. The provisions of this subparagraph shall be reviewed four years after the entry into force of the Agreement Establishing the WTO.

An exception with regard to therapeutic and surgical methods was proposed by a number of developing countries[77] in their communication of 14 May 1990.

Most countries do not grant patents on therapeutic, diagnostic, and surgical methods. Even in the absence of specific provisions excluding the patentability of the methods referred to, they may be deemed non-eligible for protection in many countries due to the lack of industrial applicability. However, in the United States, patent practice increasingly favours the patenting of medical methods if they satisfy the definition of process and the other conditions of eligibility. A bill enacted in 1996 (amending US patent law, 35 USC 287.c) determined, however, that the use of patented surgical procedures is protected from infringement suits.[78]

Diagnostic, therapeutic, and surgical patents, even if rarely granted, may negatively affect low-income patients' access to required diagnosis[79] or treatments, particularly in new areas such as gene-therapy.[80]

In any case, the non-patentabilty of methods would not affect the patentability of equipments and substances necessary to execute them.[81] Likewise, although gene therapy methods may not be patentable as such, relevant genes, vectors and constructs may be patentable, as well as *ex vivo* process steps not involving the administration of the transformed cells to the patient.

The exclusion under Article 27.3.(a), if correctly interpreted, would not extend either to any apparatus used for diagnostic or treatment or to products such as

---

[77] The Agreement explicitly refers—unlike said communication—to 'diagnostic methods' and not only to methods of medical or surgical treatment. The patentability of therapeutic methods was not admitted under the European Patent Convention. However, the EC proposals were silent on this point.   [78] See, eg, Grubb op. cit. (1999), p 220.

[79] A telling example is the case of the Myriad patent on a breast cancer gene that was revoked by the European Patent Office in May 2004. See, eg, <http://www.newscientist.com/article.ns?id=dn5016>.   [80] See, eg, Grubb op. cit. (1999), p 244.

[81] In cases where the protection of such equipment and/or substances could lead to a *de facto* monopolizaton of the non-patented method, governments may have recourse to compulsory licences. See pp 311–24 below.

'diagnostic kits', one of the main biotechnology-based products currently on the market.

The exception contained in Article 27.3(b) reflects the outstanding differences, among industrialized countries themselves and between them and developing countries, existing at the time of the TRIPS negotiations about the patenting of plants and animals. The EC proposals aimed at maintaining the position—later confirmed by the Directive on biotechnological inventions (98/44/EC)—of European countries which are members of the European Patent Convention which excludes the patentability of plant varieties and animal races, as well as essentially biological processes for their obtention.[82]

Various elements of Article 27.3(b) need to be considered. First, unlike European law and other national laws that follow the same approach, this Article refers to 'plants and animals' and not to a certain classification thereof ('varieties', 'races' or 'species').[83] In the absence of any distinction—and in the light also of the second sentence of the same Article, which introduces an exception for one particular classification ('plant varieties')—the exclusion is to be interpreted in broad terms, inclusive of animals and plants as such, plant varieties, as well as animal races and animal and plant species.

Second, the exclusion of 'essentially biological processes' is limited by the reference to processes 'other than non-biological and microbiological'. The concept of microbiological processes as an exception to the exception is present in the European legislation and in the laws of various other countries. Its main aim in the TRIPS context is probably to limit the exclusion of patentability to traditional breeding methods, while preserving the possibility to obtain protection, for instance, on developments based on cell manipulation or, with the advances in biotechnology, the transfer of genes. Under the text commented on, processes employing micro-organisms (such as fermentation) are also patentable, in accordance with current practice in most countries.

The concept of 'non-biological' processes may include, for instance, the use of irradiation to obtain certain transformation in plants.

Third, and as an exception to the generally authorized exclusion, Members must provide protection for 'plant varieties' either by patents or by 'an effective *sui generis* system or by a combination or both'. This obligation has been an important basis for the expansion of intellectual property protection in a field that had remained outside such protection in many developing countries before the TRIPS Agreement. Although there is flexibility as regards to the form of protection, the fact is that all WTO Member countries are bound to protect plant varieties.

---

[82] It should be noted that the interpretation of the non-patentability of 'essentially biological processes' tends to be narrowly construed. Illustrative of this trend was the decision by the European Patent Office in the *Lubrizol* case (T320/87 Hybrid Plants/LUBRIZOL OJ EPO 1990, p 71) in connection with the concept of 'essentially biological processes' for the production of plants or animals.

[83] The distinction is important. Thus, the prohibition to patent a 'variety' does not prevent in European countries to patent a plant as such. The acceptance of the 'Harvard mouse' was, similarly, based on the judgment that it is not a 'race' but a specifically altered animal which is patented.

While in the United States, Australia and Japan a plant variety may be patentable as such, this is not the case in Europe and other countries. The reference to a '*sui generis* system' opens the possibility of combining the patent with the breeders' rights protection,[84] or to develop other '*sui generis*' forms of protection not necessarily modelled under the UPOV Convention.[85] Hence, Members have considerable room to develop their own systems of protection.

Fourth, Article 27.3(b) is the single provision in the whole TRIPS Agreement subject to an early revision—four years after the entry into force of the Agreement that created the World Trade Organization. This period is even shorter than the transitional period contemplated for developing countries (Article 65). It suggests how difficult a compromise on the biotechnology-related issues was.

The African Group has been particularly active in relation to the review of Article 27.3(b). It wants this provision to be harmonized with the CBD. One of the proposals of the African Group demanded that such harmonization also be made with the FAO International Undertaking on Plant Genetic Resources, which 'seeks to protect and promote Farmers' Rights and to conserve plant genetic resources'.[86] The group argued that:

by mandating or enabling the patenting of seeds, plants and genetic and biological materials, Article 27.3(b) is likely to lead to appropriation of the knowledge and resources of indigenous and local communities.[87]

Moreover, the African Group submitted that a review of Article 27.3(b) should preserve the room existing at the national level to develop specific modalities of protection for traditional knowledge, and clarify that plants, animals, microorganisms, their parts and natural processes cannot be patented.[88]

Rights conferred

28.1. A patent shall confer on its owner the following exclusive rights:

(a) where the subject matter of a patent is a product, to prevent third parties not having the owner's consent from the acts of: making, using, offering for sale, selling, or importing for these purposes that product;

(b) where the subject matter of a patent is a process, to prevent third parties not having the owner's consent from the act of using the process, and from the

[84] The UPOV Convention, in its 1978 version, banned the 'double protection' of plant varieties through patents and breeders' rights. This ban was removed by the 1991 amendment to the Convention.
[85] Neither the UPOV Convention is mentioned nor are breeders' rights considered a form of 'intellectual property' under the TRIPS Agreement.
[86] This Understanding has been superseded by the FAO Treaty on Plant Genetic Resources for Food and Agriculture adopted in November 2001. See <http://www.fao.org> (last accessed on 18 June 2005).   [87] WT/GC/W/202 of 14 June 1999.
[88] WT/GC/W/302 of 6 August 1999 and IP/C/W/206 of 20 September 2000.

acts of: using, offering for sale, selling, or importing[6] for these purposes at least the product obtained directly by that process.

28.2. Patent owners shall also have the right to assign, or transfer by succession, the patent and to conclude licensing contracts.

[6] This right, like all other rights conferred under this Agreement in respect of the use, sale, importation or other distribution of goods, is subject to the provisions of Article 6.

Article 28 sets forth the rights that a patent should confer to its title-holder by separately referring to the two traditional categories of inventions: products and processes.[89]

The provision clearly states that rights to be conferred are 'exclusive',[90] which is further confirmed (perhaps unnecessarily) by the phrase indicating that such rights confer the ability 'to prevent third parties not having the patentee's consent' from executing certain acts. In conformity with accepted principles of patent law, this provision requires Members to grant *negative* rights. A patent, hence, does not confer on the holder any positive right to act on the basis of a patent. There are some important implications of this concept.

First, the acquisition of patent rights on a product or process does not entitle the patent owner to produce or use them if other requirements should be met, for instance approval for the cultivation of a transgenic variety or for the commercialization of agrochemicals or medicines. Clearly, a patent would not allow the commercialization of an invention, if otherwise prohibited by law.

Second, Article 28 provides the context for the interpretation of other provisions relating to patents in the TRIPS Agreement, notably the concept of 'patent rights' in Article 27.1 which, strictly interpreted, should be understood in relation to products subject to the patentee's *ius excluendi* and not to the products made or commercialized by the patent holder himself.

Third, in the case of product patents, the patent owner has the right to exclude the making, etc of the product independently of the process used by a third party to obtain it. Unlike the case of trade secrets, a patent allows the exercise of the conferred exclusive rights even against a third party who has independently reached the same invention. Possible conflicts need to be solved under the first-to-apply or the first-to-invent rule.[91]

Fourth, the *ius excluendi* may be exercised independently of the purpose of the acts covered by Article 28.1 performed by third parties. This Article does not require that such acts be made with commercial intent. It is an open issue whether

[89] National legislation and case law will have to address particular cases, such as when a microorganism capable of producing a product is patented. In *Amgen v Chugai*, for instance, US courts were required to judge whether a product (erythropoietin) manufactured abroad using certain cells infringed a US patent on those cells. A bill (Biotechnology Patent Protection Act of 1991) was submitted to Congress in order to clarify the patentee's rights in these cases.

[90] 'Exclusive' means 'shutting out, not admitting of', *Concise Oxford Dictionary*, (1982: Oxford University Press, 7th edn), p 336.

[91] The first-to-invent rule is applied in the US, while other countries follow the first-to-apply rule.

a Member may exclude acts made without such intent, for instance, importation for humanitarian reasons.

The granting of exclusive rights represents a drastic derogation to the principle of free access and usability of knowledge as a public good.[92] The enumeration in Article 28 of the acts that the patent owner can prevent is exhaustive, and should be narrowly interpreted. The acts that the patent owner can prevent are the following:

(a) 'making' means 'constructing, framing, creating, from parts or other substances'.[93] The use of a process different from that used by the patent owner does not avoid infringement. It is also irrelevant what kind of process of making is used (extraction, chemical synthesis, assembly, etc) and whether a large or small number of products are made. Many laws, however, exempt the preparation in a pharmacy or by a medical doctor, of a medicine in accordance with a medical prescription and for individual uses.

Although the application of the concept of 'making' seems straightforward, special consideration may be required in the case of repair or modification of a patented product,[94] as well as when a product is manufactured for exportation, which is not specifically mentioned as an act subject to exclusive rights by Article 28.1. In the US some case law has differentiated the treatment of the acts of making and exportation, but the dominant view seems to hold that making an entire patented product for export infringes the patent.[95] The adoption of the WTO Decision of 30 August 2003[96] pursuant to paragraph 6 of the Doha Declaration on the TRIPS Agreement and Public Health,[97] would seem to confirm this approach, since a compulsory licence is needed in order to export a patented medicine.[98]

(b) Using: the patent owner can prevent third parties from using a patented process or an infringing product. The exclusionary right obviously does not extend to uses of the products marketed by the patent owner or with his consent domestically, or internationally, where subject to exhaustion of rights.[99]

---

[92] See, eg, J Stiglitz, 'Knowledge as a global public good', in I Kaul, I Grunberg, and M Stern (eds), *Global Public Goods. International Cooperation in the 21st Century* (1999: New York, UNDP-Oxford University Press).

[93] *Concise Oxford Dictionary*, (1982: Oxford University Press, 7th edn), p 611.

[94] Infringement would depend in this case on the extent of repair or modification and on the circumstances of the particular case. See, eg, L Bently and B Sherman *Intellectual Property Law* (2001: New York, Oxford University Press), p 488.   [95] See, eg, Chisum and Jacobs (1995), pp 2–219.

[96] See WT/L/540, available at <http://www.wto.org> and C Correa *Implementation of the WHO General Council Decision on Paragraph 6 of the Doha Declaration on the TRIPS Agreement and Public Health* (2004: Geneva, WHO), available at <http://www.who.int/medicines/areas/policy/WHO_EDM_PAR_2002.3.pdf> (last accessed on 25 May 2005).

[97] WT/MIN(01)/DEC/W/2, 14 November 2001.

[98] The Decision was incorporated on 6 December 2005 into the TRIPS Agreement as Article 31*bis*, but the amendment is subject to ratification by Members in accordance with WTO rules.

[99] See Chapter 3 above.

Uses that the patent owner may prevent include acts of commercialization which do not entail a sale, such as renting or leasing, and sales demonstrations. However, mere acts of possession or display have not been deemed subject to the patentee's rights.[100] The utilization of a patented product as part of a land vehicle, aircraft, or vessel may also be considered a 'use' subject to such rights, but most laws provide an exception for this use in accordance with Article 5*ter* of the Paris Convention.[101]

(c) 'Offering for sale': it includes acts made with the intent of selling patented products. Offers to licsense or lease would not be subject to this right. With the inclusion of this right, the TRIPS Agreement has gone beyond what many national laws provided for at the time of the negotiation.[102]

An issue that has given rise to some disputes at the national level is whether requesting or obtaining an authorization to sell a product is an infringing act. The 'Bolar exception', as elaborated below,[103] casts an exception for the compliance with regulatory requirements. Hence, where this exception is established, it might be difficult to argue that an infringement exists. Moreover, applying or even obtaining market authorization is not equivalent to 'offering for sale' in accordance with a literal interpretation of the wording in the Agreement.

Another controversial situation may arise when a third party offers to sale (for instance, in the context of tendering procedures) with the expectation of subsequently obtaining a compulsory licence.

(d)'selling': this is one of the key components in the set of exclusive rights granted to the patent holder. The concept is narrower than 'commercializing'. The exclusive right to sell can be exercised to prevent the sale and resale of infringing products, but it does not extend to the resale of products first put on the market by the patent owner[104] or in an otherwise legitimate manner, such as by a voluntary or compulsory licensee. Based on the wording of Article 28.1 ('. . . or importing for these purposes that product . . .') the exclusive right to sell may be deemed to ban an importation for sale. The footnote to this provision indicates, however, that this right is subject to Article 6 on exhaustion of rights.[105]

---

[100] See, eg, Chisum and Jacobs op. cit. (1995), pp 2–217.

[101] Article 5*ter*: 'In any country of the Union the following shall not be considered as infringements of the rights of a patentee: (i) the use on board vessels of other countries of the Union of devices forming the subject of his patent in the body of the vessel, in the machinery, tackle, gear and other accessories, when such vessels temporarily or accidentally enter the waters of the said country, provided that such devices are used there exclusively for the needs of the vessel; (ii) the use of devices forming the subject of the patent in the construction or operation of aircraft or land vehicles of other countries of the Union, or of accessories of such aircraft or land vehicles, when those aircraft or land vehicles temporarily or accidentally enter the said country.'

[102] For instance, in the USA, the patent law did not provide for penalties for the offer to sell a patented product. See, eg, R Neff and F Smallson, *NAFTA, Protecting and Enforcing Intellectual Property Rights in North America* (1994: Colorado, Shepard's), p 86.   [103] See p 304.

[104] Under the doctrine of 'first sale' it is considered that the patent owner has exhausted his rights and cannot control successive transactions after the product has been first sold.

[105] See Chapter 3 above.

(e) 'importing': this is another aspect where the TRIPS Agreement went beyond many laws, including of developed countries, under which importation as such, not followed by sales, was not deemed an infringement.[106] As noted, the exclusive right to import is subject, according to footnote 6 to Article 6 on the principle of exhaustion of rights.[107]

Article 28.1(b) specifies the acts that are subject to the control of the patent owner in the case of process patents. Given the territoriality of patent rights, as a general principle, such patents can be used to prevent third parties from using the patented process in the country where the patent has been granted. The patent owner cannot prevent the making and sale of the same product resulting from the patented process if obtained with a different process[108] or if the patented process was applied in a foreign country.

However, the TRIPS Agreement also went in this case beyond what many patent laws established at the time of its adoption. It extended the protection to the acts of using, offering for sale, selling, or importing for these purposes at least the product *obtained directly* by the patented process. This extension—introduced by German law in 1891—confers an extraterritorial effect to the use of the process in a foreign jurisdiction, thereby significantly strengthening the protection conferred by process patents.

The interpretation of this extension has raised several issues in the countries that have applied this concept, for instance, whether it applies in cases where the product obtained by the process is further processed,[109] where allegedly infringing products are not mentioned in the patent claims, where the effectively used process involves different steps and only some of them are covered by the patent,[110] and where the obtained product is excluded from patentability, such as in the case of plants and animals.[111]

The provision of Article 28.1(b) with regard to products directly obtained with a patented process excludes cases where the product is *obtainable* by that process but evidence of the use of the patented product is not produced.[112]

---

[106] See, eg, Bently and Sherman op. cit. (2001), p 490; Chisum and Jacobs op. cit. (1995), pp 2–220).

[107] See Chapter 3 above.

[108] If an infringement is invoked, courts would normally determine whether the alternative process can be deemed 'equivalent' to the patented process or not (see, eg, Wegner (1994), p 526).

[109] According to the 'loss of identity test'—developed through case law in some European countries—the concept of 'directly obtained' applies in cases where the directly obtained product is further processed but does not lose its identity. See, eg, B Hansen and F Hirsch, *Protecting Inventions in Chemistry. Commentary on Chemical Case Law under the European Patent Convention and the German Patent Law* (1997: Weinheim, WILEY-VCH), p 357.

[110] See, eg, Hansen and Hirsch op. cit. (1997), p 357.

[111] When a unique process of obtention is known, the extension would be tantamount to the protection of the product as such, thereby *de facto* overriding the prohibition to patent the product.

[112] Providing this evidence is difficult in many cases, such as when the differences in the chemical processes used for the obtention of the same product are not traceable therein. On the reversal of the burden of proof, see UNCTAD-ICTSD, *Resource Book on TRIPS and Development* (2005: New York, Cambridge University Press) pp 496–504 .

The reference to 'at least' in the last sentence of Article 28.1(b) would indicate that Members *may* extend the protection conferred under process patents to products not directly obtained by the claimed process. However, it does not mandate Members to go beyond what it provides for and doing so would dangerously blur the line differentiating process from product patents.

Finally, it is worth mentioning that Article 28.1 applies with regard to granted patents. There is no obligation under this provision to recognize any exclusive rights before the grant, as established by some national laws in order to give the applicant the possibility of preventing infringement of a would-be patent. This extension of the exclusive rights may be particularly harmful for competition in a context of proliferation of patent applications on trivial developments resulting from 'evergreening' and other patenting strategies.[113]

> 28.2. Patent owners shall also have the right to assign, or transfer by succession, the patent and to conclude licensing contracts.

Article 28 refers to rights of patent owners that are normally uncontested: the right to:

- assign;
- transfer by succession; and
- conclude licensing contracts.

Unlike the case of trademarks, the assignment of which has generally been subject to restrictions under national laws,[114] patents are generally assignable without limitations. They are also transferable by succession. Article 28.2, however, shall not be read as precluding requirements imposed by national laws about registration of any assignment or transfer of rights in order to produce effects with regard to third parties.

It should be noted that this provision does not touch on the issue of assignment of the right to a patent (as opposed to the right over a granted patent), which is entirely subject to the applicable national law.

Patents are often voluntarily licensed. The right 'to conclude licensing contracts' confirms this possibility. This right, however, is not tantamount to a right to absolutely control the use of the patented invention. Patents can be subject, in accordance with Article 31 of the TRIPS Agreement, to compulsory licences, which can be granted without or against the consent of the patent owner.[115] A compulsory licence is only an authorization to use the patented invention. It does not establish a contractual relationship with the patent owner, despite the fact that he may eventually agree with the compulsory licensee on the royalty rate and payment modalities.

This provision also indicates that it is within the patent owner's discretion to enter or not into a licensing agreement; that is, he enjoys the *freedom to contract*.

---

[113] On various patent strategies, see O Granstrand, *The Economics and Management of Intellectual Property: Towards Intellectual Capitalism* (1999: Northampton, EE).
[114] See Article 21 of the TRIPS Agreement and Chapter 6.   [115] See pp 311–24 below.

Nevertheless, this provision does not exclude the possibility of prescribing certain conditions under which such contracts may be established, both with regard to formalities and substance. Thus, Article 40 of the TRIPS Agreement expressly recognizes (although subject to some limitations) the Members' right to control restrictive practices in licensing agreements.[116] Other conditions (eg with regard to guarantees, applicable law, etc) can also be established by national laws.

Conditions on patent applicants

29.1. Members shall require that an applicant for a patent shall disclose the invention in a manner sufficiently clear and complete for the invention to be carried out by a person skilled in the art and may require the applicant to indicate the best mode for carrying out the invention known to the inventor at the filing date or, where priority is claimed, at the priority date of the application.

29.2. Members may require an applicant for a patent to provide information concerning the applicant's corresponding foreign applications and grants.

Article 29 deals with one of the pillars of the patent system: the disclosure of the claimed invention. Disclosing an invention that could otherwise remain secret has been considered as one of the basic trade-offs of patent grants, and even the very reason why patents are issued.[117]

The lack of full disclosure to execute the invention is under most national laws sufficient ground to refuse a patent application or to revoke a patent.[118] The reproducibility of the invention may indeed be considered on the same footing as the patentablity requirements for the grant of a valid patent. In countries where pre-grant or post-grant opposition procedures exist, third parties may generally invoke the failure to properly comply with the disclosure requirement as a ground for revocation,[119] and this is often a ground for the judicial invalidation of patents.

The disclosure obligation is contemplated with various qualifications. Generally, the disclosure should be sufficient for a person skilled in the art to execute the invention. The concept of 'a person skilled in the art' is normally equivalent to that applied to establish the existence of inventive step/non-obviousness, but this does not need to be always the case. Patents allow access to

[116] See Chapter 12 below.
[117] See, eg, E Penrose, *The Economics of the International Patent System* (1951: Baltimore, The Johns Hopkins Press), pp 31–2; A Gutterman, *Innovation and Competition Policy: A Comparative Study of Regulation of Patent Licensing and Collaborative Research & Development in the United States and the European Community* (1997: London, Kluwer Law International).
[118] As discussed below, the TRIPS Agreement does not limit the grounds for revocation of a patent.
[119] Under the European Patent Convention, however, the failure to adequately disclose an invention cannot be articulated during post-grant procedures.

valuable information through the publication of patent specifications, although such information cannot be freely used in countries where protection has been acquired. However, in order to be useful, the information must be presented in a form comprehensible for people working in different technological contexts, including in developing countries with unsophisticated innovation systems. Mere translations of patent applications as originally filed in developed countries may be insufficient to adequately disclose an invention in developing countries.[120]

Under Article 29, Members are bound to require that disclosure of the invention be made 'in a manner sufficiently clear and complete for the invention to be carried out by a person skilled in the art'. There is nothing in this provision requiring that the concept of 'a person skilled in the art' be the same to assess inventive step and the extent of disclosure. Hence, Members may apply different concepts, for instance, to require a strict inventive step through a concept of a 'skilled person' with qualified knowledge, while promoting the accessibility to the disclosed information by applying a concept of 'skilled person' with only ordinary knowledge. In fact, significant inter-sectoral differences in the application of the concept of a 'person having ordinary skills in the art' have been found in the United States, in relation to software and biotechnological inventions: as mentioned, while in the case of DNA patents sequences must be disclosed under a stringent written description rule, in that of software patents, applicants need to disclose virtually nothing about the detailed workings of their invention.[121]

In practice, patent specifications often include the minimum information necessary for an expert in the respective technical field to execute the invention. Experienced patent applicants disclose as little as they can in order to make inventing around and follow-on innovation more difficult for competitors.

Article 29 does not provide guidance, nor does it impose any restrictions, on how to solve the problem of disclosure in the case of inventions that consist of or are based on biological materials which, by their very nature, cannot be fully described. Countries can establish for these cases the obligation to deposit the relevant materials in order to supplement their written characterization as well as the rules whereunder third parties could obtain access to them.[122]

Members may (but are not obliged to) require the applicant 'to indicate the best mode for carrying out the invention known to the inventor' at the filing or priority date. This requirement is aimed at facilitating the use of the invention at the expiry of the patent term. In certain cases, such as when a compulsory licence is granted, it may help to permit the execution of the invention by the licensee

---

[120] See UNCTAD, *The TRIPS Agreement and Developing Countries* (1996: Geneva and New York), p 33.   [121] See, eg, Burk and Lemley op. cit. (2003).
[122] See, eg, the Budapest Treaty on the International Recognition of the Deposit of Microorganisms for the Purposes of Patent Procedure (1977, as amended in 1980) available at <http://www.wipo.int/treaties/en/registration/budapest/trtdocs_wo002.html> (last accessed on 26 May 2006).

during the lifetime of the patent. Since the information to be provided is that available on the filing date, specialist skills, know-how and ancillary technology, which are generally required for that purpose, will not be generally disclosed, as it is normally acquired through experimentation and production after that date. The best mode requirement is currently in force under US law,[123] but the Federal Circuit has essentially excused software inventions from compliance with this requirement.[124]

Finally, Members may also require applicants to provide information concerning their corresponding foreign applications and grants. This requirement may be important to facilitate the examination of applications as well as the adoption of decisions on the eventual invalidation of patents, if such decisions have been taken elsewhere. Patent offices and courts in developing countries in general lack the human resources and infrastructure to deal with the increasingly complex problems of patent granting and judicial review. While not affecting the principle of territoriality of patents, Article 29.2 leaves the door open to establish obligations to supply that information as of the date of the application till the expiry of the patent.

Since the TRIPS Agreement does not limit the grounds for revocation of a patent, as discussed below,[125] Members may establish procedures, including *ex officio*, for review of the validity of a patent if a parallel patent or particular claims have been invalidated in a foreign jurisdiction.

Exceptions to rights conferred

A group of developing countries, including the megadiverse countries, has proposed an amendment to Article 29 of the TRIPS Agreement[126] in order to introduce an obligation to disclose the origin of biological resources in patent applications. One of the purposes of the proposal is to ensure that better prior art information is available to the patent examiners on genetic resources and associated traditional knowledge. The main aim of the proposal is, however, to help interested parties monitoring patent applications involving such resources, and thereby promote compliance with the benefit-sharing provisions of the Convention on Biological Diversity. An obligation of disclosure of the type proposed is contained in the Biodiversity Law No 7.788 of Costa Rica (Article 80), in Decision 486 (Article 26(h)), and in the Brazilian Provisional Measure 2.186–16 (Article 31).

---

[123] A coalition of patent lawyers and corporations, however, are currently lobbying for the derogation by Congress of the best mode requirement. See <http://www.aipla.org/Template.cfm?Section=By_Topic&template=/ContentManagement/ContentDisplay.cfm&ContentID=9895> (last accessed on 24 October 2005). The Advisory Commission on Patent Law Reform had also recommended its elimination in 1992.   [124] Burk and Lemley op. cit. (2003), p 1156.
[125] See pp 342–3.   [126] IP/C/W/474.

30. Members may provide limited exceptions to the exclusive rights conferred by a patent, provided that such exceptions do not unreasonably conflict with a normal exploitation of the patent and do not unreasonably prejudice the legitimate interests of the patent owner, taking account of the legitimate interests of third parties.

The very general wording of Article 30 indicates how difficult it was for the negotiating Parties to agree on the nature and extent of the exceptions to the patent rights.[127] Three conditions need to be met by the referred exceptions. First, they must be 'limited', without specifying whether in scope, duration, or otherwise. Second, they should not 'unreasonably conflict with a normal exploitation of the patent'. And, third, the exceptions should not 'unreasonably prejudice the legitimate interests of the patent owner'. All these three conditions are to be applied, however, 'taking account of the legitimate interests of third parties'.

This text necessarily leads to a case-by-case assessment of the exceptions that can be granted. It provides 'little more than flexible guidelines for the legislatures and courts of the Member countries' based on 'extremely manipulable requirements'.[128] In the light of current comparative patent law and on other proposals made on the subject,[129] at least the following exceptions may be deemed legitimate within the scope of Article 30:

  i) importation of a product that has been put in the market elsewhere by the patentee, with his consent or by an otherwise authorized person;
 ii) acts done privately and on a non-commercial scale or for a non-commercial purpose;
iii) using the invention for research and experimentation and for teaching purposes;
 iv) seeking regulatory approval for marketing of a product before the expiry of the patent;
  v) preparation of medicines for individual cases according to a prescription;
 vi) use of the invention by a third party who started—or undertook *bona fide* preparatory acts—before the application for the patent (or of its publication).

Some of these exceptions are particularly important from the perspective of technological policies, such as the 'experimental' exception, and to promote

---

[127] Some of the proposals made during the negotiations included more specific provisions. See the EEC submission as contained in MTN.GNG/NG11/W/26 of 7.7.88.

[128] J Straus op. cit. (1996), p 203.

[129] See, eg, alternative B, Article 19, of the WIPO draft Treaty Supplementing the Paris Convention as far as Patents are Concerned presented to The Hague Diplomatic Conference in June 1991.

competition and access to medicines on competitive terms, such as the so-called 'Bolar' exception. These exceptions are considered below.

Experimental use

Exceptions relating to research and experimentation on the invention may be an important tool to create a favourable context for innovation. The adoption of an experimental exception may permit innovation based on 'inventing around' of or improving on the protected invention, as well as evaluation of an invention in order to request a licence, or for other legitimate purposes, such as to test whether the invention works, and has been sufficiently disclosed.

In the United States, research without the authorization of the patent owner is narrowly admitted for scientific purposes only. The Federal Circuit Court of Appeals held in *Madey v Duke*[130] that

regardless of whether a particular institution or entity is engaged in an endeavor for commercial gain, so long as the act is in furtherance of the alleged infringer's legitimate business and is not solely for amusement, to satisfy idle curiosity, or for strictly philosophical inquiry, the act does not qualify for the very narrow and strictly limited experimental use defense. Moreover, the profit or non-profit status of the user is not determinative.

In European and other countries, experimentation *on* an invention (as opposed to *with* an invention) is allowed even for commercial purposes.[131] Case law—which relates to pharmaceutical or agrochemical products—in European countries has accepted research done to find out more information about a product—provided that it is not made just to convince licensing authorities or customers about the virtues of an alternative product, and to obtain further information about the uses of a product and its possible side effects and other consequences of its use.[132]

With the exception of a few countries, most developing countries have aparently not explicitly used the room left by the TRIPS Agreement to provide for an experimentation exception, including for commercial purposes.

Bolar exception

The so-called 'Bolar' or 'early working' exception deals with the use of an invention relating to a pharmaceutical product to conduct tests and obtain the approval

[130] 64 USPQ 2d 1737 (Fed Cir 2002).

[131] The Community Patent Convention, for instance, provides that there is no infringement in case of 'acts done for experimental purposes relating to the subset-matter of the patented invention' (Article 27.b).

[132] W Cornish, 'Experimental Use of Patented Inventions in European Community States', (1998), 29 IIC 7, p 736. See also C Correa, International Dimension of the Research Exception, (2004), SIPPI Project, AAAS, Washington DC, available at <http://sippi.aaas.org/intlexemptionpaper.shtml> (last accessed on 15 May 2006).

from the health authority, before the expiry of a patent, for commercialization of a generic version, just after such expiry. This exception is named after the case *Roche Products Inc v Bolar Pharmaceutical Co*,[133] in which a US court denied Bolar the right to begin the FDA approval process before the expiry of the patent. Subsequently, the US Drug Price Competition and Patent Term Restoration Act (1984) permitted the initiation of procedures for the marketing approval of generic products before the expiry of the relevant patent. The purpose of this exception was to help generic drug producers to place their products on the market as soon as a patent expired, and thereby allow consumers to obtain medicines at lower prices immediately thereafter. In exchange, the patent term of the original drug could be extended up to five years. An analysis of the welfare implications of this Act indicated that

from the perspective of economic welfare, the Act is the source of large potential positive gains of two types. First, it eliminated costly scientific testing which served no valid purpose. Second, the Act lowered prices to consumers with some elimination of deadweight losses and large transfers from producers to consumers.[134]

'Bolar'-like exceptions which have been established in numerous countries allow consumers to get access to medicines at a lower price as soon as the patent expires and to support the development of a generic pharmaceutical industry.

The consistency of the 'Bolar exception' with Article 30 of the TRIPS Agreement was tested in a case initiated in November 1998 by the European Communities and their member States against Canada *(Canada–Patent Protection for Pharmaceutical Products)*. Canada had adopted a 'Bolar'-like provision in 1991 explicitly allowing a third party to produce and stockpile the product for release immediately after the expiry of the patent.

In March 2000, the panel concluded that Canada was not in violation of the TRIPS Agreement in terms of its practice of allowing the development and submission of information required to obtain marketing approval for pharmaceutical products carried out without the consent of the patent holder. However, Canada was found to be acting inconsistently with the Agreement in terms of its practice of manufacturing and stockpiling pharmaceutical products during the six months immediately prior to the expiry of the 20-year patent term.[135]

In this case, the panel addressed the TRIPS-consistency of Section 55(2)(1) and (2) of the Canadian Patent with Article 30 of the Agreement. The admissibility of exceptions to patent rights is subject, under Article 30, to three conditions which, in the view of the panel, are 'cumulative, each being a separate and independent requirement that must be satisfied. Failure to comply with any one of the three

---

[133] 733 F 2d 858, Fed Cir, cert denied 469 US 856, 1984.
[134] W Viscusi, J Vernon, and J Harrington, *Economics of Regulation and Antitrust* (1997: Cambridge, The MIT Press, 2nd edn), p 857.   [135] WT/DS114/R, para 8.1.

conditions results in the Article 30 exception being disallowed'.[136] The panel added that:

The three conditions must, of course, be interpreted in relation to each other. Each of the three must be presumed to mean something different from the other two, or else there would be redundancy. Normally, the order of listing can be read to suggest that an exception that complies with the first condition can nevertheless violate the second or third, and that one which complies with the first and second can still violate the third. The syntax of Article 30 supports the conclusion that an exception may be 'limited' and yet fail to satisfy one or both of the other two conditions. The ordering further suggests that an exception that does not 'unreasonably conflict with normal exploitation' could nonetheless 'unreasonably prejudice the legitimate interests of the patent owner.[137]

The first condition to be met is that the exception must be 'limited'. According to its ordinary meaning, 'limited' is 'confined within definite limits; restricted in scope, extent, amount, etc'. It is also 'small' in relation to an amount or number; or 'low' in relation to an income.[138]

The panel provided an interpretation of what 'limited' means in Article 30:

The word 'exception' by itself connotes a limited derogation, one that does not undercut the body of rules from which it is made. When a treaty uses the term 'limited exception', the word 'limited' must be given a meaning separate from the limitation implicit in the word 'exception' itself. The term 'limited exception' must therefore be read to connote a narrow exception—one which makes only a small diminution of the rights in question.[139]

In the absence of other indications, the Panel concluded that it would be justified in reading the text literally, focusing on the extent to which legal rights have been curtailed, rather than the size or extent of the economic impact. In support of this conclusion, the Panel noted that the following two conditions of Article 30 ask more particularly about the economic impact of the exception, and provide two sets of standards by which such impact may be judged. The term 'limited exceptions' is the only one of the three conditions in Article 30 under which the extent of the curtailment of rights as such is dealt with.[140]

In adopting a narrow concept of 'limited', the panel focused on the extent of the curtailment and not on the extent of the economic implications thereof. Hence, an exception with little economic effects might be disallowed under this doctrine even if the patent owner is not negatively affected in practice. In the panel's view, the economic impact of the exception must be evaluated under the other conditions of Article 30. Given that panel reports do not create binding precedents (and the fact that this particular report was not subject to appeal), nothing would prevent future panels and the AB from adopting a broader concept on this matter, as suggested by Canada in its submission.[141] An exception may be

---

[136] Idem, para 7.20.				[137] Idem, para 7.21.
[138] *New Shorter Oxford Dictionary*, p 1592.			[139] WT/DS114/R, para 7.30.
[140] Idem, para. 7.31.
[141] See Canada's submission relating to the limited nature of the products, the persons that may invoke the exception and its duration, and the panel's critical position on these arguments in relation to Article 52.2(2) of the Canadian Patent law (para 7.37).

deemed limited when it is subject to certain boundaries, for instance, with regard to the *acts* involved (eg importation, exportation, evaluation), the *purpose* of the use (eg for private purposes or education), the *outcome* of the invention's use (eg preparation of individual medicinal prescriptions), the *persons* that may invoke the exception, or its *duration*. An exception may be limited in relation to a *field of technology* as well (eg food or pharmaceuticals). While the consistency of this latter kind of limitation with the non-discrimination clause of Article 27.1 was addressed by the panel in the *EC–Canada* case, the panel did not give a definite interpretation on the issue.[142]

The second condition established by Article 30 is that the exception should not 'unreasonably conflict with the normal exploitation' of the patent. This language, substantially borrowed from Article 9(2) of the Berne Convention, requires a determination of whether there is a conflict with the 'normal' exploitation of a patent and, if a conflict exists, whether it is unreasonable. The literal method of interpretation followed by GATT/WTO panels requires a careful understanding of these key elements.

As mentioned above,[143] two approaches have been suggested for the interpretation of this test under Article 9(2) of the Berne Convention: an *empirical* meaning of 'normal' as a reference to the usual or regular course of events, and a *normative* connotation in the sense of what 'normal' is according to a certain standard.[144] The empirical approach requires an investigation into what are the ways in which the title-holder can exploit his IPRs in the normal course of events, possibly leading to the conclusion that there are certain modes of exploitation for which he would not ordinarily receive a remuneration. This approach puts an emphasis on actual markets. In contrast, the normative approach also includes potential markets.[145] If the concept of 'potential' markets, however, is drawn too widely, this test may be insuperable and the exception rendered meaningless, since it would cover each and every possibility of deriving profit from protected subject matter.[146]

Canada took the position in the *EC–Canada* case that 'exploitation' of the patent involves the extraction of commercial value from the patent by 'working' the patent, either by selling the product in a market from which competitors are excluded, or by licensing others to do so, or by selling the patent rights outright. The European Communities also defined 'exploitation' by referring to the same three ways of 'working' a patent. The parties differed primarily on their interpretation of the term 'normal'.[147]

---

[142] See para 7.92.   [143] See Chapter 5.

[144] M Senftleben, *Copyright, Limitations and the Three-step Test. An Analysis of the Three-step Test in International and EC Copyright Law* (2004: The Hague, Kluwer Law International), p 168.

[145] According to the study group which tabled the proposals for revising the substantive provisions of the Berne Convention at the 1967 Stockholm conference, 'all forms of exploiting a work, which have, or are likely to acquire, considerable economic or practical importance, must be reserved to the authors' (quoted by Senftleben, op. cit. (2004), p 177).   [146] Idem, pp 178, 181, 185.

[147] WT/DS114/R, para 7.51.

The panel noted that, literally interpreted, 'normal' is 'regular, usual, typical, ordinary, conventional'.[148] The panel did not take a position with regard to the empirical or normative connotation of the concept. It held that

the term can be understood to refer either to an empirical conclusion about what is common within a relevant community, or to a normative standard of entitlement. The Panel concluded that the word 'normal' was being used in Article 30 in a sense that combined the two meanings (para 7.54).

The panel's reluctance to opt for one of the approaches left this important aspect without clarification and open to controversy. It also stated that

The normal practice of exploitation by patent owners, as with owners of any other intellectual property right, is to exclude all forms of competition that could detract significantly from the economic returns anticipated from a patent's grant of market exclusivity. The specific forms of patent exploitation are not static, of course, for to be effective exploitation must adapt to changing forms of competition due to technological development and the evolution of marketing practices. Protection of all normal exploitation practices is a key element of the policy reflected in all patent laws.[149]

The panel's reasoning is questionable. The right to exclude the use of the patented subject matter by third parties is not a form of exploitation of the patent, but a legal power established by law that may be exercised or not. The exploitation consists of the acts of making, using, or commercializing the inventions without third parties' competition. In addition, the panel went too far in considering 'all forms of competition' since competition may legitimately proceed through the improvement of the patented technology.

Another important interpretive issue is whether the encroachment upon the economic value of the patent is to be assessed as a whole or separately for each individual exclusive right. In the *Section 110(5) of the US Copyright Act* case, the panel stated that 'whether a limitation or an exception conflicts with a normal exploitation of a work should be judged for each exclusive right individually' (para 6.173). It also argued that an exception raises to the level of conflict with a normal exploitation of the work 'if uses, that in principle are covered by that right but exempted under the exception or limitation, enter into economic competition with the ways that right holders normally extract economic value from that right to the work (ie, the copyright) and thereby deprive them of significant or tangible commercial gains' (para 6.183).

However, it is unclear the rationale for this opinion. Not all exclusive rights generate the same level of income. A 10 per cent limitation to an important income-generating exclusive right (eg right to sell) may be more significant than a 100 per cent limitation to another exclusive right (eg the right to make when products are imported). Instead of considering different exclusive rights separately,

---

[148] *New Shorter Oxford English Dictionary*, p1940.   [149] Idem, para 7.55.

it would be more appropriate to evaluate the extent to which an exception impairs the overall exploitation of the subject matter.[150]

Finding a 'conflict with the normal exploitation' of a patent does not mean, however, that an exception is proscribed. The conflict must be 'unreasonable'. The panel in the *Canada–Patent Protection for Pharmaceutical Products* case did not address what 'unreasonable' means in this context, since its analysis led to the conclusion that there was not conflict with the normal exploitation of a patent and, therefore, it was not necessary to elucidate whether the Canadian exception was reasonable or not. If a conflict of such kind were found, however, the way in which 'unreasonable' is to be interpreted would acquire crucial importance.

Member countries have considerable latitude to interpret what 'unreasonable' is. In the last instance, the unreasonableness of an exception will depend on the conceptual framework that underpins the granting of patents in a given jurisdiction and at a certain point in time. The panel in the *Canada–Patent Protection for Pharmaceutical Products* case took the view that

Patent laws establish a carefully defined period of market exclusivity as an inducement to innovation, and the policy of those laws cannot be achieved unless patent owners are permitted to take effective advantage of that inducement once it has been defined.[151]

This statement hints at the panel's conception on the role and objectives of the patent system. The panel seems to have ignored the fact that there is no *universal* patent system, and that the national patent laws have historically reflected different philosophies and objectives[152] largely correlated to different levels of economic and technological development. Moreover, while emphasizing the stimulation to innovation, the panel's view failed to consider other essential objectives of the patent system, such as the diffusion of knowledge and its continuous improvement. In the last instance, patents were instituted to serve the public interest and not to benefit individual inventors.[153]

It is also important to note that in the Doha Ministerial Declaration on the TRIPS Agreement and Public Health,[154] Members stated that

In applying the customary rules of interpretation of public international law, each provision of the TRIPS Agreement shall be read in the light of the object and purpose of the Agreement as expressed, in particular, in its objectives and principles [paragraph 5 (a)].

Developing countries have stressed the need to construe the 'purpose' of the Agreement and of the protection conferred thereunder on the basis of Article 7 of

---

[150] Senftleben op. cit. (2004), p 193.   [151] See, eg, WT/DS114/R, para 7.55.
[152] See, eg, Gutterman op. cit. (1997).
[153] P Welfens, J Addison, D Audretsch, T Gries, and H Grupp, *Globalization, Economic Growth and Innovation Dynamics* (1999: Berlin, Springer), p 138.
[154] Doha Ministerial Declaration on the TRIPS Agreement and Public Health, WT/MIN(01)/DEC/W/2, 14 November 2001.

the Agreement.[155] The panel seems to have focused, however, on the protection of private rights and overlooked the social objectives that underpin the recognition of patents.

The third condition of Article 30 requires that the exception does 'not unreasonably prejudice the legitimate interests of the patent owner'. This condition puts on the same footing the 'legitimate interests' of the patent owner and those of third parties in using the invention. Only the patent owners' interests that are 'legitimate' require protection. In addition, they may be deemed harmed to the extent that the prejudice caused by the exception is unreasonable.

This condition raises, on the one hand, the issue of what 'legitimate interests' are and, on the other, of when such interests are 'unreasonably' prejudiced.

The EC argued in the *EC–Canada* case that 'legitimate interests' were essentially 'legal' interests. The panel rightly rejected this interpretation. It considered that

To make sense of the term 'legitimate interests' in this context, that term must be defined in the way that it is often used in legal discourse—as a normative claim calling for protection of interests that are 'justifiable' in the sense that they are supported by relevant public policies or other social norms. This is the sense of the word that often appears in statements such as 'X has no legitimate interest in being able to do Y'.[156]

The panel added that 'a definition equating "legitimate interests" with legal interests makes no sense at all when applied to the final phrase of Article 30 referring to the "legitimate interests" of third parties' (para 7.68).

Proof that a prejudice is caused to the patent owner's legitimate interests is not sufficient to outlaw a 'limited exception' (provided it fulfils the second condition

---

[155] See the submission by the African Group Barbados, Bolivia, Brazil, Cuba, Dominican Republic, Ecuador, Honduras, India, Indonesia, Jamaica, Pakistan, Paraguay, Philippines, Peru, Sri Lanka, Thailand, and Venezuela (IP/C/W/296): 'Each provision of the TRIPS Agreement should be read in light of the objectives and principles set forth in Articles 7 and 8. Such an interpretation finds support in the Vienna Convention on the Law of Treaties (concluded in Vienna on 23 May 1969), which establishes, in Article 31, that "[a] treaty shall be interpreted in good faith in accordance with the ordinary meaning to be given to the terms of the treaty in their context and in the light of its object and purpose" (para 17). 'Article 7 is a key provision that defines the objectives of the TRIPS Agreement. It clearly establishes that the protection and enforcement of intellectual property rights do not exist in a vacuum. They are supposed to benefit society as a whole and do not aim at the mere protection of private rights. Some of the elements in Article 7 are particularly relevant, in order to ensure that the provisions of TRIPs do not conflict with health policies: the promotion of technological innovation and the transfer and dissemination of technology; the mutual advantage of producers and users of technological knowledge; social and economic welfare; and the balance of rights and obligations' (para 18).

[156] WT/DS114/R, para 7.69. It should be noted that, as examined in Chapter 5 in *United States–Section 110(5) of the US Copyright Act*, the panel adopted a more positive perspective regarding the concept of 'legitimate interests' based on 'the economic value of the exclusive rights conferred by copyright on their holders' (para 6.227). It also observed, however, that the term 'legitimate' also had 'the connotation of legitimacy from a more normative perspective' (para 6.224).

referred to above). A test of reasonableness also needs to be applied. Such a test may be equated to the principle of *proportionality* as developed under EC law, which requires that the means used to achieve an end bear a reasonable relationship with the end achieved.[157] However, WTO Members have significant leeway to define how such a test will be defined and applied. They have the right to craft the exceptions they deemed necessary for public policy purposes, whatever the economic or non-economic importance of the legitimate interests of the patent owner are. The only limitation is that the scope of the exception should not be excessive in relation to its intended objective.

The last part of Article 30 ('taking account of the legitimate interests of third parties') is absent in Article 9(2) of the Berne Convention, which inspired the drafters of Article 30. However, said Article has been understood as calling for a weighing process between the interests of authors and third parties. Thus, it has been suggested that although strong user interests may underlie a limitation, the prejudice to the legitimate interests of the author must be proportionate.[158]

In the *EC–Canada* case, the panel alluded to the new wording introduced by Article 30. It noted that

> [A]bsent further explanation in the records of the TRIPS negotiations, however, the Panel was not able to attach a substantive meaning to this change other than what is already obvious in the text itself, namely that the reference to the 'legitimate interests of third parties' makes sense only if the term 'legitimate interests' is construed as a concept broader than legal interests.[159]

Clearly, the legitimate interests of the third parties at stake must be in competition with the legitimate interests of the patent owner, in order for this part of the provision to apply. The interests to be taken into account may include those of follow-on innovators, competitors, and users, as well as the interests of society at large, for instance, in addressing a public health crisis or in ensuring the advancement of science and technology.

Compulsory licences

Other use without authorization of the right-holder

31. Where the law of a Member allows for other use[160] of the subject matter of a patent without the authorization of the right holder, including use by the government or third parties authorized by the government, the following provisions shall be respected: (a) authorization of such use shall be considered on its

---

[157] Senftleben op. cit. (2004), p 211.   [158] Idem, p 153.
[159] WT/DS114/R, para 7.71.
[160] 'Other use' refers to use other than that allowed under Article 30.

individual merits; (b) such use may only be permitted if, prior to such use, the proposed user has made efforts to obtain authorization from the right holder on reasonable commercial terms and conditions and that such efforts have not been successful within a reasonable period of time. This requirement may be waived by a Member in the case of a national emergency or other circumstances of extreme urgency or in cases of public non-commercial use. In situations of national emergency or other circumstances of extreme urgency, the right holder shall, nevertheless, be notified as soon as reasonably practicable. In the case of public non-commercial use, where the government or contractor, without making a patent search, knows or has demonstrable grounds to know that a valid patent is or will be used by or for the government, the right holder shall be informed promptly; (c) the scope and duration of such use shall be limited to the purpose for which it was authorized, and in the case of semi-conductor technology shall only be for public non-commercial use or to remedy a practice determined after judicial or administrative process to be anti-competitive; (d) such use shall be non-exclusive; (e) such use shall be non-assignable, except with that part of the enterprise or goodwill which enjoys such use; (f) any such use shall be authorized predominantly for the supply of the domestic market of the Member authorizing such use; (g) authorization for such use shall be liable, subject to adequate protection of the legitimate interests of the persons so authorized, to be terminated if and when the circumstances which led to it cease to exist and are unlikely to recur. The competent authority shall have the authority to review, upon motivated request, the continued existence of these circumstances; (h) the right holder shall be paid adequate remuneration in the circumstances of each case, taking into account the economic value of the authorization; (i) the legal validity of any decision relating to the authorization of such use shall be subject to judicial review or other independent review by a distinct higher authority in that Member; (j) any decision relating to the remuneration provided in respect of such use shall be subject to judicial review or other independent review by a distinct higher authority in that Member; (k) Members are not obliged to apply the conditions set forth in subparagraphs (b) and (f) where such use is permitted to remedy a practice determined after judicial or administrative process to be anti-competitive. The need to correct anti-competitive practices may be taken into account in determining the amount of remuneration in such cases. Competent authorities shall have the authority to refuse termination of authorization if and when the conditions which led to such authorization are likely to recur; (l) where such use is authorized to permit the exploitation of a patent ('the second patent') which cannot be exploited without infringing another patent ('the first patent'), the following additional conditions shall apply: (i) the invention claimed in the second patent shall involve an important technical advance of considerable economic significance in relation to the invention claimed in the first patent; (ii) the owner of the first patent shall be entitled to a cross-licence on reasonable terms to use the invention claimed in the second patent; and (iii) the use authorized in respect of the first patent shall be non-assignable except with the assignment of the second patent.

The TRIPS Agreement does not refer to the widely accepted notion of 'non-voluntary' or 'compulsory' licences. Most countries in the world allowed for one form or another of compulsory licenses at the time of negotiation of the TRIPS Agreement.[161] Article 31 on 'Other use without the authorisation of the right holder' contains a detailed set of conditions and limitations for the granting of such licences. Through this article industrialized countries tried to limit the room for the use of the compulsory licensing system, even though its actual application has been rather limited in the past, except in the United States.[162] However, Article 31 'leaves untouched the principles on compulsory licensing laid down in Art 5A(2)–(4) Paris Convention' subject to a number of additional requirements'.[163]

Compulsory licences can enhance static efficiency, for instance, when they are granted to remedy anti-competitive practices, or to address public health emergencies by ensuring access to cheaper drugs. The granting of one or more of such licences[164] will force prices down, thus increasing consumers' welfare. Such licences may also increase dynamic efficiency, when production is undertaken by the licensee.[165] The use of the patented process or the manufacturing of the patented product may lead to follow-on innovations or new innovative concepts in the relevant technical field. As the evolutionary theory on innovation has convincingly demonstrated, routine productive activities and cumulative learning at the plant level are important sources of innovation.[166] Hence, while improving allocative efficiency, compulsory licences may, in some cases, also have a positive effect on the future flows of innovations. As noted by Gutterman,

Compulsory licensing might be considered as a means for reducing some of the adverse costs of the patent system. For example, requiring compulsory licensing at reasonable rates may reduce the underutilization costs of the patent system; however, uses of lesser value than the royalty rate would still not be covered. Compulsory licensing might also reduce to

---

[161] See D Cohen, 'Applications for licences of right in the United Kingdom' (1990), Patent World, pp 28–9.

[162] '...compulsory patent licensing has been used as a remedy in more than 100 antitrust case settlements, including cases involving Meprobamate, the antibiotics tetracycline and griseofulvin, synthetic steroids, and most recently, several basic biotechnology patents owned by Ciba-Geigy and Sandoz, which merged to form Novartis' (F Scherer, 'The patent system and innovation in pharmaceuticals', (2001), Revue Internationale de Droit Economique, Special Edition, p 119). The US Government has also made an extensive use of compulsory licences for governmental use, in a manner that has raised the complaints of the European Union (European Commission, 1997 Report on United States Barriers to Trade and Investment, Brussels); J Reichman and C Hasenzahl, *Non voluntary licensing of patented inventions: history, TRIPs, and Canadian and United States Practice* (2002), *Bridges*, UNCTAD/ICTSD, vol. 6, No 7.   [163] J Straus, in Beier et al, op. cit, (1996).

[164] According to the Paris Convention (Article 5A) and the TRIPS Agreement (Article 31) compulsory licences must be non-exclusive. This means that licences to use a patent may be given to more than one company.

[165] A compulsory licence may be worked through manufacturing or importation of the protected product. Both options are admissible under the TRIPS Agreement.

[166] See, eg, C Cooper (ed.), *Technology and Innovation in the International Economy* (1994: Cambridge, Edward Elgar United Nations University Press), p 8.

some extent the contribution of the patent system to monopoly power, the wasteful duplication of research efforts, the problem of blocking patent strategies, and the concerns
about research in areas that may well already be covered by patents.[167]

It has been argued that to the extent that a compulsory licence would reduce
the prices of the patented products and the expected profits of the patent owner,
granting such licences would undermine the incentives to undertake future
R&D. This is the view held by the research-based pharmaceutical industry.[168]
However, Scherer analysed the extent to which the granting of compulsory
licences affected R&D expenditures and, particularly, whether such licences
diminished or destroyed the incentives to undertake R&D by patent holders. His
statistical findings relating to seventy companies showed no negative effect on
R&D in companies subject to compulsory licences but, on the contrary, a significant rise in such companies' R&D relative to companies of comparable size not
subject to such licences.[169] According to Tandon, moreover,

Firms spend large sums of money on efforts to 'invent around' the patents of their competitors. Under generalized compulsory licensing, these expenditures would be unnecessary, which might increase the welfare benefits.[170]

Article 31 allows Members to determine the grounds for granting compulsory
licensing. Although it refers to some specific grounds (national emergency, anti-
competitive practices, public non-commercial use, dependent patents), it does
not limit the Members' right to establish such a remedy for different situations.
The text only sets out the conditions to be met 'where the law of a Member allows
for other use' without the authorization of the right-holder. The only exception
relates to 'semi-conductor technology', which can only be subject to compulsory
licences for public non-commercial use and to remedy anti-competitive practices.

Article 31 applies when a country has established a compulsory licensing or a
government use system. This indicates that the TRIPS Agreement simply *recognizes* the right of WTO Members to limit the patent owners' rights under compulsory licences and government use, as indicated by the wording of the *chapeau* of
Article 31.

Article 31, therefore, does not limit in any way the capacity of governments to
grant compulsory licences or undertake government use. WTO Members can

[167] Gutterman op. cit. (1997), p 69.
[168] See, eg, R Rozek and R Rainey, 'Broad-based compulsory licensing of pharmaceutical
technologies—Unsound public policy', (2001), The Journal of World Intellectual Property, vol. 4,
No 4, p 463.
[169] See F Scherer, 'Comments', in R Anderson and N Gallini (eds), *Competition Policy and
Intellectual Property Rights in the Knowledge-based Economy* (1998: Alberta, University of Calgary
Press), pp 107–8. Scherer's studies also indicated a decline in patenting activities of firms subjected to
compulsory licensing. However, such a result does not necessarily mean that the overall expenditures
of the firms on research declined, but rather that the firms could rely on alternative methods of protection, such as trade secrets.
[170] P Tandon, 'Optimal Patents with Compulsory Licensing', (1982), Journal of Political
Economy, vol. 90, No 3, p 485.

determine the *grounds* under which such licences can be granted. Said Article, as discussed below, only stipulates the *conditions* that governments must comply with. Paragraph 5 (b) of the Doha Declaration categorically confirmed this interpretation. It stated that:

Each member has the right to grant compulsory licences and the freedom to determine the grounds upon which such licences are granted.

Although this paragraph does not add anything substantively to the understanding of the TRIPS Agreement, it specifically employs the expression 'compulsory licence' which, as mentioned, is not found in the Agreement itself. There is nothing in Article 31 limiting the possible grounds of compulsory licences to cases where an *abuse* can be determined, as suggested by one interpretation,[171] nor are Members bound to apply the terms provided for in Article 5A(4) of the Paris Convention,[172] except in the case of compulsory licences granted to remedy failure to work or insufficient working of the patented invention. Ladas held in this regard that

The compulsory licence for nonworking or for insufficient working can be granted only after the expiration of four years from the date of filing or three years from the date of grant of the patent, whichever is later, and the patentee can always justify his inaction. Since this period is provided for only in the case of nonworking or insufficient working, it follows that a compulsory licence for other reasons of abuse or public interest or dependent patent can be granted at any time.[173]

In determining the grounds for the grant of compulsory licences, it is necessary to comply with the general principles of national treatment and most-favoured-nation clause (Articles 3 and 4 of the TRIPS Agreement). Article 31 includes a non-exhaustive reference to some of the possible grounds:

- national emergency or extreme urgency;
- public non-commercial use;
- remedy to anti-competitive practices;
- dependency of patents.

Members can determine when situations of 'national emergency or extreme urgency' justify the granting of a compulsory licence. The Doha Declaration on TRIPS and Public Health unambiguously confirmed this prerogative.[174] In accordance with paragraph 5(c) of the Declaration

---

[171] See J Straus, in Beier et al op. cit. (1996), p 204.
[172] Article 5A(4): 'A compulsory license may not be applied for on the ground of failure to work or insufficient working before the expiration of a period of four years from the date of filing of the patent application or three years from the date of the grant of the patent, whichever period expires last;...'.
[173] S Ladas, *Patents, Trademarks and Related Rights: National and International Protection*, vol. 1 (1975: Cambridge, Harvard University Press), p 538.
[174] For instance, in May 2002, the Minister of Justice, Legal and Parliamentary Affairs of Zimbabwe issued a Declaration of Period of Emergency (HIV/AIDS) (Notice, 2002). In view of the

Accordingly and in the light of paragraph 4 above, while maintaining our commitments in the TRIPS Agreement, we recognize that these flexibilities include: . . .

c. Each member has the right to determine what constitutes a national emergency or other circumstances of extreme urgency, it being understood that public health crises, including those relating to HIV/AIDS, tuberculosis, malaria and other epidemics, can represent a national emergency or other circumstances of extreme urgency.

This clarification is important for several reasons. First, it suggests that 'public health crises' can represent 'a national emergency or other circumstances of extreme urgency', thereby allowing for the granting of compulsory licences or government use when provided for under national law and, pursuant to TRIPS Article 31(b), without the obligation for prior negotiation with the patent owner.

Second, the reference to 'HIV/AIDS, tuberculosis, malaria and other epidemics' indicates that an 'emergency' may not only be a short-term problem, but a long-lasting situation, as is the case with the epidemics specifically mentioned, merely for illustrative purposes. This recognition implies that specific measures to deal with an emergency may be adopted and maintained as long as the underlying situation persists, without time constraints.

Third, the wording in paragraph 5(c) seems to place the burden on a potentially complaining Member to prove that an emergency or urgency invoked by another Member does *not* exist. This represents an important difference with respect to earlier GATT/WTO jurisprudence about the 'necessity test' in the context of Article XX (b) of GATT.[175]

Finally, there are no formalities or prescribed criteria for the determination of what constitutes a national emergency or other circumstances of extreme urgency. A formal declaration by the Member is not required. The determination can be made upon granting the compulsory licence or authorizing government use, or in any other manner.

'Public non-commercial use' (hereinafter 'government use')[176] is an act by the government authorizing a government department to exploit by itself or through a contractor a patented invention without the consent of the title-holder, with a non-commercial purpose. Government use may in many cases be the simplest and fastest way of addressing a public need, notably because it can be decided by the government *ex officio*, without the need of a third party's request, and there is no

---

rapid spread of HIV/AIDS among the population of Zimbabwe, the Minister declared 'an emergency for a period of six months, with effect from the date of promulgation of this notice, for the purpose of enabling the State or a person authorized by the Minister under section 34 of the Act (a) to make or use any patented drug, including any antiretroviral drug, used in the treatment of persons suffering from HIV/AIDS or HIV/AIDS related conditions; (b) to import any generic drug used in the treatment of persons suffering from HIV/AIDS or HIV/AIDS-related conditions'.

[175] See C Correa, Implementing national public health policies in the framework of the WTO Agreements', (2000), *Journal of World Trade*, vol. 34, No 5.

[176] Also called 'Crown use' under British and Commonwealth legislation.

need of a prior negotiation with the patent holder, as discussed below.[177] The administrative act authorizing government use of a patent does not need to specify a determined quantity or value of the product to be produced or imported.

The 'non-commercial' nature of the use does not prevent the government from appointing a *commercial* contractor or agent to exploit the relevant patents on behalf of the government, as is common and extended practice in the United States.[178] It is also important to note that in accordance with Article 44.2 of the TRIPS Agreement, national laws can limit the remedies available against government use to payments of remuneration in accordance with subparagraph (h) of Article 31; that is, no injunctions may be admitted.

Although in the United States the patent law does not expressly provide for compulsory licences, this is probably the country with the largest experience in the granting thereof to remedy anti-competitive practices. More than one hundred such licences have been granted.[179] They have included both present and future patents. Generally such licences have been granted against a reasonable royalty, generally determined on the basis of the 'willing-buyer, willing-seller' formulation.[180] However, in some cases the compulsory licences were conferred royalty-free,[181] and the patentee required to make the results of its research readily available to other industry members,[182] or to transfer the know-how actually used in production.[183]

A very detailed provision on compulsory licences grounded on the dependency of patents is contained in Article 31(l). It stipulates a number of conditions for its granting, relating to the technical and economic importance of the 'second patent' (it shall involve 'an important technical advance of considerable economic significance'), the granting of 'a cross licence on reasonable terms' to the owner of the 'first patent', and the non-transferability of the licence (except with the assignment of the 'second patent'). These conditions tend to limit the more flexible ways in which compulsory licences for dependent patents were admissible in some countries,[184] often in order to promote access to patented technology by local enterprises. Key in the actual operation of the system will be the interpretation of the economic and technical importance of the second

---

[177] See p 177.
[178] See J Reichman, *Nonvoluntary Licensing of Patented Inventions: The Law and Practice of the United States* (forthcoming: Geneva, UNCTAD-ICTSD).
[179] See, eg, F Scherer, 'Comments' in Anderson, Robert and Gallini, Nancy, (eds) op. cit. (1998).
[180] See M Finnegan, 'The folly of compulsory licensing', (1977; Licensing Executive Society), p 140.
[181] For instance, in *FTC v Xerox Corporation* (S Goldstein, 'A study of compulsory licensing', (1977, Licensing Executive Society), p 124.
[182] *Hartford-Empire* case, M Finnegan op. cit. (1977), p 139.
[183] For instance, in *FTC v Xerox Corporation* (Goldstein op. cit. (1977), p 124.
[184] Such as in many European countries where the owner of the dependent patent could get a licence upon request (Netherlands) or showing only a 'substantial contribution to the art'. See J Straus, op. cit. (1996), p 207.

invention. What is 'of considerable economic significance' is a relative concept, and will depend on the parameters established by the national law. The assessment of what is important may be different in developing and developed countries, as well as for small and large companies.

Another important aspect is that the Agreement does not limit the purpose for which a compulsory licence can be granted. It can be conferred to import or to locally produce a patented product.[185] In some cases, such as compulsory licences to remedy abuses of a market dominant position or to protect public health, importation may be, in fact, the sole or main way to comply with the purposes for which the authorization is given.

Compulsory licences may be contemplated and granted for grounds other than those explicitly referred to above, such as the following.

Article 8 ('Principles') of the TRIPS Agreement states the right of Parties to 'adopt measures necessary to protect public health and nutrition, and to promote public interest in sectors of vital importance to their socio-economic and technological development, provided that such measures are consistent with the provisions of this Agreement'. Based on this provision, and subject to the condition set forth by Article 31, compulsory licences could be granted, for instance, for reasons of 'public interest' (as under German law), or to satisfy objectives of public health (as under French law).[186]

A compulsory licence may be granted—in line with the British tradition—in cases where the patent owner refuses to grant a voluntary basis on reasonable commercial conditions. In some cases compulsory licences grounded on a 'refusal to deal' have been justified on the basis of the 'essential facilities' doctrine.[187]

The obligation to work a patented invention has historically been—together with disclosure requirements—one of the foundations of the patent system. During the twentieth century—as evidenced by the successive amendments to the Paris Convention—industrialized countries have tended to interpret such an obligation flexibly in order to facilitate transnational activities of large corporations in increasingly globalized markets. For most developing countries, however, such an obligation (understood as actual industrial application and not just as importation of the protected product) has been one of the essential counterbalances of the patent system, and viewed as a possible inducement to the transfer of technology.

Not surprisingly, the extent of the working obligation was one of the most controversial issues in TRIPS negotiations. The difficulties encountered to reach an agreement are evidenced by the language of the compromise contained in Article 27.1, as examined above.[188] As also discussed above,[189] the US

---

[185] The authorization could also refer to the importation of a product directly made with a patented process.   [186] See French Patent Law, Article L. 613–16.
[187] See, eg, C Correa, 'Refusal to deal and access to an essential facility: balancing private and public interests in intellectual property law', in *Mélanges Victor Nabhan* (2004: Québec; Ed. Yvon Blais, Série les cahiers de propriété intellectuelle).   [188] See pp 281–7 above.
[189] See p 286 above.

complained against Brazil in relation to the compulsory licence for lack of local working contemplated by Brazilian law. In a complaint initiated by the US against Argentina in May 2000 pursuant to Article 4 of the Understanding on Rules and Procedures Governing the Settlement of Disputes ('DSU') and Article 64 of the TRIPS Agreement, the USA requested consultations with the Government of Argentina, inter alia, in relation to the 'availability of certain safeguards for the granting of compulsory licenses, including timing and justification safeguards for compulsory licenses granted on the basis of inadequate working'. The case was settled following two years of consultations[190] and no inconsistency with the TRIPS Agreement was determined in relation to this issue.

Environmental protection

One of the most pressing problems in the world is the degradation of the environment. Important efforts are underway at the international and national level to prevent harmful activities and to develop effective measures of environment protection. In the patent field, compulsory licensing may contribute to expanding the use of environmentally sound technologies as well as of technologies available for environmental protection,[191] in line with the international instruments that promote the transfer to and use of such technologies in developing countries.[192]

Despite the undoubted legitimacy of compulsory licences and government use,[193] some countries that have provided for one or more of them in their legislation have faced the threat of unilateral retaliations, or the suspension of aid.[194] Of particular interest was the case brought by a number of pharmaceutical companies, supported by the US government, against South Africa in relation to its legislation allowing for parallel imports for medicines and compulsory licences.[195]

[190] See WT/DS171/3, WT/DS196/4, IP/D/18/Add.1, IP/D/22/Add.1, 20 June 2002.

[191] For instance, under 42 USC Sec 7608, and the regulations to implement this Act, compulsory licences can be granted for technologies required for compliance with the US Clean Air Act; see <http://www.epa.gov/docs/fedrgstr/EPA-AIR/1994/December/Day-30/pr-251.html> (last accessed on 26 May 2006), p 3.

[192] See, eg, the Convention on Biological Diversity and Chapter 34 of 'Agenda 21', para 34.18.

[193] In accordance with US Law (28 USC 1498), 'the use or manufacture of an invention described in and covered by a patent of the United States by a contractor, a subcontractor, or any person, firm, or corporation for the Government and with the authorization or consent of the Government, shall be construed as use or manufacture for the United States'.

[194] The US Trade Representative 'watch lists' have included many countries that could be subject to trade sanctions under Special Section 301 of the US Trade Act due to the provision of certain forms of compulsory licences.

[195] See eg, S Sell, *Private Power, Public Law: The Globalization of Intellectual Property Rights* (2003: Cambridge University Press).

Conditions for the granting of compulsory licences

The TRIPS Agreement has paid particular attention to the conditions under which a compulsory licence may be granted. They include the following:

i) Compulsory licences should be granted or government use authorized taking into consideration the 'individual merits' of the proposed use (Article 31(a)). This means that decisions cannot involve sets of patents defined by its subject matter, title-holder or otherwise. However, this would not be an impediment to establish parameters for the granting of compulsory licences regarding, for instance, certain categories of products that are needed to address a specific need (such as a disease or epidemics). In addition, Article 31(a) would not prevent a Member from authorizing the use of several patents (even if not precisely determined) relating to a given product or process. In many cases, it may be difficult to establish the patent status of particular products, since often several patents are obtained on variants of the same product (such as in the case of pharmaceuticals). In these cases, the application for a compulsory licence can be made with regard to *all* patents that may be infringed by the production, commercialization, or importation and use of the required product/s.

ii) Prior to granting a compulsory licence the proposed licensee should have made 'efforts to obtain authorisation from the right holder on reasonable terms and conditions' provided that 'such efforts have not been successful within a reasonable period of time'. This provision makes compulsory a prior negotiation with the title-holder. The determination of what the 'reasonable terms and conditions' are is left to national laws. Article 31 allows, nevertheless, for exceptions in cases of:

- national emergency or other circumstances of extreme urgency;
- public non-commercial use;
- licences granted to remedy anti-competitive practices.

In the case of national emergency or other circumstances of extreme urgency, the title-holder should be notified as soon as reasonably practicable. In the case of government use, moreover, he should be informed when there are demonstrable grounds that his patent is or will be used.

iii) The scope and duration of the authorization 'shall be limited to the purpose for which it was authorized' (Article 31(c)). This clause may imply the limitation of the licence, both in terms of scope (eg to certain claims or kind of products) and of duration. However, nothing will prevent a potential licensee from asking for and being granted a licence covering all the claims of a patent and extending until its expiry. This has been, in fact, the generally accepted practice under the Paris Convention. For a licensee that has to undertake investments in production or marketing it will be often essential to obtain a licence for the lifetime of the patent.

iv) Any authorization shall be—as established in most national laws—non-exclusive and non-assignable, except with that part of the enterprise or goodwill that uses it.

v) A compulsory licence should be granted 'predominantly for the supply of the domestic market' (Article 31(f)). This limitation—which may not be applied in connection with licences to remedy anti-competitive practices—implies that a compulsory licence or government use cannot be given exclusively or principally for exportation. The vague wording used does not provide specific guidance as to when the domestic market is to be deemed 'predominantly' supplied. National laws may adopt different standards in this respect, based on sales value or volume (eg exports should not exceed an annual average of 50 per cent of net income generated by the product under licence).

Developing countries argued in their submission of 12 June 2001 to the Council for TRIPS that 'nothing in the TRIPS Agreement prevents Members from granting compulsory licenses for foreign suppliers to provide medicines in the domestic market... In this respect, the reading of Article 31(f) should confirm that nothing in the TRIPS Agreement will prevent Members to grant compulsory licenses to supply foreign markets'.[196] However, other Members regarded Article 31(f) as a barrier to such supply. The limitation contained in Article 31(f) was a central factor in the adoption of paragraph 6 of the Doha Declaration, as examined below.

The rationale for this paragraph 6 was as follows. Only a few developing countries have some manufacturing capacity in pharmaceuticals; hence after the TRIPS Agreement became fully operative (on 1 January 2005), many countries could face difficulties in acquiring medicines at affordable prices. Before that date some countries, such as India, produced generic versions of medicines at a fraction of the price of the patented products and could export them to other countries. As a result, a Member country where the price of the patented product was high had the option of issuing a compulsory licence to import it from such countries. The problem was that as these countries became bound to comply fully with the TRIPS Agreement after 2005, they were no longer able to produce and export cheap generic versions of patented medicines. Consequently, countries with insufficient manufacturing capacity could not ensure access to medicines even if they granted a compulsory licence, since they would not be able to find a source for their importation.

In order to address this problem, after protracted negotiations, the General Council adopted the Decision of 30 August 2003, which gave rise to an amendment to the TRIPS Agreement as discussed below.[197]

vi) Article 31(g) sets forth the principle that a compulsory licence is liable to be terminated when 'the circumstances which led to it cease to exist and are

---

[196] See IP/C/W/296.   [197] See p 325–42.

unlikely to recur'. Competent authorities shall have, therefore, the authority to review, upon motivated request, the continued existence of such circumstances. The eventual termination is subject, however, to 'adequate protection of the legitimate interests of the persons' authorized to use the invention. Without this proviso, this paragraph should have completely diluted the potential of use of the compulsory licensing system, since if a reasonable degree of certainty is not assured, nobody would be interested in applying for a licence that could be terminated at any time. The protection of the legitimate interests of the licensee may be interpreted as meaning that he could not be deprived of his right to the licence once he has made serious preparations for putting the invention into use, or established productive or marketing capabilities.

vii) The title-holder shall be paid 'adequate remuneration in the circumstances of each case, taking into account the economic value of the authorisation' (Article 31(h)). This provision would apply, in principle, to any kind of compulsory licence.[198]

Considerable room is left for interpretation at the national level on the criteria to determine when a remuneration is to be deemed 'adequate'.[199] The same provision provides two elements for said interpretation: on the one hand, the adequateness is to be judged according to the circumstances of each case and, on the other, it is necessary to take into account—as one but not as the sole or determining factor—'the economic value of the authorisation'. Thus, the circumstances of the licensee and of the country where it operates, as well as the purpose of the licence should be considered to establish the remuneration due. The 'economic value' will significantly differ depending, inter alia, on the size of the market to be supplied (predominantly the domestic market), the newness or maturity of the technology, and its rate of obsolescence, the degree of competition by substitute products, and the coverage of the patent.

The meaning of 'adequate' needs to be clarified in order to give more precise guidance to national judicial and administrative authorities. One possible understanding is that it simply means that the title-holder should be able to obtain a remuneration comparable to what it would have obtained in a voluntary arm's-length transaction. An alternative interpretation would take into account factors such as the subsidies or other contributions that the title-holder eventually received to develop the invention, the degree to which development costs have been amortized and the R&D commitment of the patent owner.

---

[198] In the case of licences to remedy anti-competitive practices, the need to correct them 'may be taken into account in determining the amount of remuneration' (Article 31(k)). The objective being to restore a healthy competition, this provision would allow for a reduced remuneration. See C Correa, *Intellectual Property Rights and the Use of Compulsory Licenses: Options for Developing Countries*, Trade-Related Agenda, Development and Equity, Working Papers (1999: Geneva, South Centre).

[199] It is interesting to note that this is the sole provision in the Agreement that refers to 'adequate' remuneration. Articles 14.4 and 70.4 use, instead, the expression 'equitable' remuneration.

According to the *Remuneration Guidelines for Non-voluntary Use of a Patent on Medical Technologies*[200] the following are some of the methods of calculation that may be reasonably applied to determine an adequate level of remuneration:

a) The 1998 Japan Patent Office Guidelines (applicable to government-owned patents) allow for normal royalties of 2 to 4% of the price of the generic product, and can be increased or decreased by as much as 2%, for a range of 0 to 6%.

b) The 2001 UNDP Human Development Report proposed a base royalty rate of 4% of the price of the generic product. This can be increased or decreased by 2%, depending upon such factors as the degree to which a medicine is particularly innovative or the role of governments in paying for R&D.

c) The 2005 Canadian Government royalty guidelines for compulsory licensing of patents for export to countries that lack the capacity to manufacture medicines in accordance with the WTO Decision of August 30, 2003. These guidelines establish a sliding scale of 0.02 to 4% of the price of the generic product, based upon the country rank in the UN Human Development Indicator. For most developing countries, the royalty rate is less than 3%. For most countries in Africa, the rate is less than 1%.

d) The Tiered Royalty Method (TRM) method is different from the 2001/UNDP, 1998/JPO or 2005/Canadian methods in that the royalty rate is not based upon the price of the generic product. Instead, the royalty is based upon the price of the patented product in the high-income country. The base royalty is 4% of the high-income country price, which is then adjusted to account for relative income per capita or, for countries facing a particularly high burden of disease, relative income per person with the disease.[201]

viii) Finally, the title-holder should be given the possibility of review, by a judicial or other 'distinct higher authority', of the 'legal validity' of any decision relating to the granting of a licence as well as of the determined remuneration (Article 31(i) and(g)). Such a right will not prevent a Member, however, from giving immediate effect to a decision conferring a licence, subject to a later review. This will be particularly important in cases involving public interests or the correction of anti-competitive practices.

Members may establish that the required review be made by an administrative authority, if 'distinct' from and 'higher' than the authority that conferred the compulsory licence or authorization for government use. The adjective 'distinct' may be interpreted as 'independent' but, according to a literal interpretation, the intervention of a different authority would seem to be sufficient.

[200] Document prepared by James Love, WHO/TCM/2005.1 Geneva, 2005.
[201] Idem, pp 83–85.

It is also of note that the obligation to provide for a 'review' is limited to the 'legal validity' of the decision. This means that Members are not bound to require the review of the opportunity of granting a compulsory licence or authorizing government use, nor of the conditions under which they are granted, including the remuneration stipulated in favour of the patent owner.

Lack of manufacturing capacity in pharmaceuticals

31*bis*.1. The obligations of an exporting Member under Article 31(f) shall not apply with respect to the grant by it of a compulsory licence to the extent necessary for the purposes of production of a pharmaceutical product(s) and its export to an eligible importing Member(s) in accordance with the terms set out in paragraph 2 of the Annex to this Agreement.

2. Where a compulsory licence is granted by an exporting Member under the system set out in this Article and the Annex to this Agreement, adequate remuneration pursuant to Article 31(h) shall be paid in that Member taking into account the economic value to the importing Member of the use that has been authorized in the exporting Member. Where a compulsory licence is granted for the same products in the eligible importing Member, the obligation of that Member under Article 31(h) shall not apply in respect of those products for which remuneration in accordance with the first sentence of this paragraph is paid in the exporting Member.

3. With a view to harnessing economies of scale for the purposes of enhancing purchasing power for, and facilitating the local production of, pharmaceutical products: where a developing or least-developed country WTO Member is a party to a regional trade agreement within the meaning of Article XXIV of the GATT 1994 and the Decision of 28 November 1979 on Differential and More Favourable Treatment Reciprocity and Fuller Participation of Developing Countries (L/4903), at least half of the current membership of which is made up of countries presently on the United Nations list of least-developed countries, the obligation of that Member under Article 31(f) shall not apply to the extent necessary to enable a pharmaceutical product produced or imported under a compulsory licence in that Member to be exported to the markets of those other developing or least-developed country parties to the regional trade agreement that share the health problem in question. It is understood that this will not prejudice the territorial nature of the patent rights in question.

4. Members shall not challenge any measures taken in conformity with the provisions of this Article and the Annex to this Agreement under subparagraphs 1(b) and 1(c) of Article XXIII of GATT 1994.

5. This Article and the Annex to this Agreement[202] are without prejudice to the rights, obligations and flexibilities that Members have under the provisions of this Agreement other than paragraphs (f) and (h) of Article 31, including those

---

[202] Reproduced in Annex II of this chapter.

reaffirmed by the Declaration on the TRIPS Agreement and Public Health (WT/MIN(01)/DEC/2), and to their interpretation. They are also without prejudice to the extent to which pharmaceutical products produced under a compulsory licence can be exported under the provisions of Article 31(f).

Article 31*bis*, agreed upon on 6 December 2005, incorporates the WTO Decision of 30 August 2003 (hereinafter 'the Decision'). It is the first amendment introduced to the TRIPS Agreement, subject to ratification in accordance with the WTO rules (Article X of the Marrakesh Agreement Establishing the WTO).

The Decision[203] applies when the required pharmaceutical products are patented, at least in the exporting country.[204] Given the territoriality of the patent system and that the same patents are not necessarily applied for and obtained in all countries, and that the scope of the approved claims (with regard to the same invention) may also vary from country to country, the set of patents to be subject to compulsory licences may not be exactly the same in the exporting and importing countries. In addition, it will be necessary to determine whether the relevant patents are in force. They not only elapse due to the expiry of the term of protection, but also due to the lack of timely payment of maintenance fees.[205]

The Decision may be applied when the required pharmaceutical product is subject to one or more patents validly in force in *the exporting country*. However, if the relevant patents are subject in *the exporting country* to a compulsory licence to remedy anti-competitive practices that allows the licensee to export (Article 31(k) of the TRIPS Agreement) or to a compulsory licence under which the licensee is predominantly supplying the domestic market, there would be no need to apply the Decision.

The Decision does not apply either if the relevant product is off-patent in the exporting country, since a waiver of Article 31(f) is not required. In this case, and if the product were patented in the importing country, a compulsory licence should only be granted in the latter, under the ordinary terms allowed by the applicable national law.

---

[203] The following analysis is based on C Correa, *Implementation of the WHO General Council Decision on Paragraph 6 of the Doha Declaration on the TRIPS Agreement and Public Health* (2004: Geneva; WHO). The analysis refers to the Decision, and not to Article 31*bis* of the Agreement, because at the time of writing that Article has not been ratified, as required by WTO rules.

[204] Patents may be obtained not only in relation to active ingredients, but in respect of formulations, pharmaceutical salts, isomers, polymorphs, combinations, manufacturing processes, etc. In some countries the *new use* of a known product may also be patented (as a 'second indication'). There are cases in which an active ingredient is off-patent, but the pharmaceutical product that contains it, its method or manufacture or use, is patented, even many years after the expiry of the original patent. In other cases, a patent on the active ingredient may coexist (though not necessarily for exactly the same period) with many other patents on the product.

[205] Most countries in the world provide for the automatic expiry of patents when the patent owner fails to pay the specified maintenance fees. Some laws allow for the rehabilitation of expired patents, but this is facultative (see Article 5*bis* of the Paris Convention).

The Decision would be applicable if in *the importing country* either of these two situations exists:

(a) *Off-patent products and processes*

The required pharmaceutical product, or the process for its manufacture, is not patented in the importing country or the patent has expired or revoked. In this case, by definition, there is no need to grant a compulsory licence there, but the Decision applies in order to allow the granting of such a license in the exporting country.

A particular case may arise in LDCs, which can delay the recognition of pharmaceutical patents until 2016. Subject to national laws, LDCs that make use of this extension may consider granted pharmaceutical patents non-enforceable until that date.

(b) *Patented products and processes*

The product or process for its manufacture is patented. The granting of a compulsory licence is needed under the special conditions set forth in the Decision.

According to paragraph 1(a) of the Decision, a 'pharmaceutical product' is 'any patented product, or product manufactured through a patented process of the pharmaceutical sector needed to address the public health problems as recognized in paragraph 1 of the Declaration'. Several elements in this paragraph are important.

First, the Decision may apply either when a patent covers a product or a manufacturing process.

Second, it applies to products 'of the pharmaceutical sector' in general, without any limitation as to the types of products (eg synthesized chemical products or biologicals), their characterization as 'essential medicines', or the kind of diseases they are intended to treat. The Decision clarifies that this concept includes 'active ingredients necessary for its manufacture'. The Decision may be applied in relation to a patent covering a pharmaceutical formulation or the process for its manufacture. The Decision also clarifies that 'diagnostic kits needed for its use would be included'. This wording may be interpreted as including reagents, diagnosis and monitoring kits. Microbiocides can also be considered as covered products.

Vaccines are not specifically mentioned in the Decision. It may be argued that if the drafters had the intention to exclude them, an exception would have been expressly established. According to its ordinary meaning 'pharmaceutical' means 'of or engaged in pharmacy; of the use or sale of medicinal drugs'.[206] Vaccines are delivered at a pharmacy, are produced by pharmaceutical firms, and are crucial to address public health problems in developing countries. In view of the very

---

[206] *Concise Oxford Dictionary* (1982: Oxford University Press, 7th edn), p 768.

purpose of the Declaration, the term 'product...of the pharmaceutical sector' should, hence, be read as including vaccines.[207]

Third, reference is made in the examined definition to paragraph 1 of the Doha Declaration, which recognizes ' the gravity of the public health problems afflicting many developing and least developed countries, *especially* those resulting from HIV/AIDS, tuberculosis, malaria and other epidemics' (emphasis added). As the negotiation of the Decision made clear, it applies to pharmaceutical products for *any* disease. The three mentioned epidemics are only special cases—which certainly deserve particular attention—but the system established by the Decision is not limited to products related to them. Similarly, the Decision is not limited to 'grave' diseases, since 'gravity' in paragraph 1 of the Declaration is generally referred to 'the public health problems' and is not intended to qualify the type of diseases to be addressed. Moreover, the level of gravity is to be determined by each Member, as it is its prerogative to do so.[208]

It is unclear whether a patent covering a therapeutic use (generally called 'second indication') is covered by the Decision. The protected invention in this case is a *method of treatment* and not a product as such.[209] However, such patents can be effectively used to restrict access to the products for important therapeutic purposes. In the absence of an exception, and in view of the intended objectives of the Decision, it seems reasonable to interpret that the Decision can be applied in these cases too.

The Decision defines the 'eligible importing Members' as follows:

(a) any least-developed country Member. The only qualification is that the LDC must be a WTO Member;

(b) any other Member that has made a notification to the Council for TRIPS of its intention to use the system as an importer. As discussed below, the notification may be unqualified or qualified.

The Chair's statement issued upon approval of the decision indicates that the following Members have agreed to opt out of using the system as importers: Australia, Austria, Belgium, Canada, Denmark, Finland, France, Germany, Greece, Iceland, Ireland, Italy, Japan, Luxembourg, Netherlands, New Zealand, Norway, Portugal, Spain, Sweden, Switzerland, the United Kingdom, and the United States of America. Until their accession to the European Union, the Czech Republic, Cyprus, Estonia, Hungary, Latvia, Lithuania, Malta, Poland, the Slovak Republic, and Slovenia agreed that they would only use the system as importers in

---

[207] See, eg, Paul Vandoren and Jean Charles Van Eeckhaute, 'The WTO Decision on Paragraph 6 of the Doha Declaration on the TRIPS Agreement and Public Health', (2003), The Journal of World Intellectual Property, vol. 6, No 6, p 784.

[208] *European Communities-Measures Affecting Asbestos and Asbestos-Containing Products*, WT/DS135/AB/R, 12 March 2001, para 168.

[209] For instance, AZT—an important antiretroviral—was developed in the 1950s, and later on its use for HIV/AIDS was patented in many countries.

situations of national emergency or other circumstances of extreme urgency. These countries further agreed that upon their accession to the European Union, they would opt out of using the system as importers.

Other Members have agreed that they would only use the system as importers in situations of national emergency or other circumstances of extreme urgency: Hong Kong, China, Israel, Korea, Kuwait, Macao China, Mexico, Qatar, Singapore, Chinese Taipei, Turkey, United Arab Emirates.

For what purposes can the system be used?

LDCs can use the system to import pharmaceutical products under a compulsory licence granted according to any ground determined by their national laws. As the Doha Declaration has expressly confirmed, WTO Members are free to determine such grounds, which may include, inter alia, non-working, public interest, remedying anti-competitive practices, emergency, and refusal to deal. It is clear that while a public health emergency may be one of the grounds for granting a compulsory licence, Member countries may invoke any other ground for that purpose.

The same applies to any other Member, with two exceptions:

(a) Members that, as noted above, have stated at the time of adoption of the Decision that, if they use the system, it would only be in situations of national emergency or other circumstances of extreme urgency;

(b) Members that have notified the Council for TRIPS that they will use the system in a limited way, for example only in the case of a national emergency or other circumstances of extreme urgency or in cases of public non-commercial use. This notification can be made at any time.

A question arises as to the extent to which the wording in the Statement may limit the reasons for which a compulsory licence could be issued. The Statement indicates that the system 'should be used in good faith to protect public health and, without prejudice to paragraph 6 of the Decision, not be an instrument to pursue industrial or commercial policy objectives'.

At the same time, paragraph 7 of the Decision states that 'Members recognize the desirability of promoting the transfer of technology and capacity building in the pharmaceutical sector in order to overcome the problem identified in paragraph 6 of the Declaration'. Paragraph 6 of the Decision aims at 'harnessing economies of scale for the purposes of enhancing purchasing power for, and facilitating the local production of, pharmaceutical products' in the context of some regional trade agreements.

This wording suggests that industrial and commercial policy objectives should not be pursued by Member countries under the system established by the Decision, but such objectives are not excluded altogether therefrom. Thus, eligible importing Members may grant compulsory licences to foster the development of capacity in their pharmaceutical industry as a sustainable way to address their public health problems,[210] for instance by importing active ingredients under the Decision for the local formulation of medicines.

Further, it seems clear that prospective suppliers of pharmaceutical products under the Decision include private companies, notably from countries where a strong generic industry has developed. Such companies would not make the investments needed nor bear the opportunity costs of supplying products under the Decision, if they are not able to obtain some commercial benefit.

Notification of intention to use the system

There are two kinds of notifications to the Council for TRIPS: a general notification about the intention to be an eligible importing Member, and a specific notification about the products, quantities, etc that it intends to import.[211] This second type of notification is examined below. In both cases, 'these notifications are for the sake of transparency and information only . . . [They] do not amount to authorization requests; Members concerned will not need be approved by any WTO body in order to be able to use the system. They can automatically use the system once they have made the notifications'.[212]

The notification to the Council for TRIPS by a prospective importer Member is about *the intention to use* the Decision, and not about its actual use. This notification seems to be a condition to qualify as an 'eligible importing Member'. It does not apply, however, to LDCs.

The notification may be unqualified, when the Member does not notify any limitation to its possible use of the system, or qualified, when the Member voluntarily states that it will use the system in a limited way. This limitation may be expressed in terms of the grounds of the compulsory licences (eg national emergency or other circumstances of extreme urgency) or otherwise. There is nothing in the Decision preventing a Member from changing, at any time, the terms of its notification. Thus, a Member that notified a limited use of the system may later notify its intention to expand its use.

The effect of the notification is declaratory. A Member can self-declare an 'eligible importing Member'. Footnote 2 of the Decision clarifies that this notification 'does not need to be approved by a WTO body in order to use the system set out in this Decision'. This means that neither the Council for TRIPS nor any other

---

[210] See in Chapter 14 other WTO decisions relating to the transfer of technology to LDCs.

[211] Except as required by Article 31(b), where applicable, there is no obligation to notify the patent owner about the intention to grant a compulsory licence and the conditions thereof. Likewise, there is no obligation to offer the patent owner the option to supply himself the required products under the terms and conditions established for the compulsory licence.

[212] Vandoren and Van Eeckhaute, op. cit. (2003), p 789.

WTO body is entitled to review, approve, or reject a notification and the specific terms under which it is made.

Notification about needed products, compulsory licence

The second notification to be made by the eligible importing Member[213] relates to the importation of particular products.[214]

The would-be importing country is bound to notify:

(i) the names of the needed product(s): the generic names of the required pharmaceuticals are to be mentioned.

(ii) the 'expected quantities': the notified quantities may not exactly correspond to the quantity of product finally requested or purchased. However, importing countries should carefully assess the quantities needed since, as mentioned below, the compulsory licence can be granted in the exporting country for a specified amount only.

The specification of quantities may be made in different ways. It may refer to number of pills or other doses, to a quantity of active ingredients (eg 50 kilograms of drug X), to the number of patients to be treated over a period of time, or to other parameters.

The obligation to specify the expected quantity only applies to the notification. It does not refer to the specific terms of the compulsory licence. The compulsory licence issued in the importing country may not establish a determined quantity. The authorization could be given to import whatever is required over the duration of the compulsory licence. It would be too cumbersome for the importing country to issue a compulsory licence each time it needs to import a given quantity of a product.

A situation may arise in which the notified 'expected' quantities may not correspond to the quantities effectively imported. A country may need, in particular, to import more than expected because it had underestimated its needs. This discordance would not affect the validity of the issued compulsory licence nor the application of the system established by the Decision.

The application of the Decision does not exclude tendering procedures by the importing country. Moreover, there is no obligation to determine a specific time in which importation would take place. However, the use of such procedures is complicated by the fact that 'offering for sale' constitutes an infringement of

---

[213] This notification also is for transparency purposes only and does not amount to an authorization request.

[214] Joint notifications providing the information required under this subparagraph may be made by the regional organizations referred to in para 6 of this Decision on behalf of eligible importing Members using the system that are parties to them, with the agreement of those parties (fn 4 of the Decision).

patent sights[215] and a potential supplier is not likely to undergo the cumbersome procedures to obtain a compulsory licence if he has no certainty about getting the order to supply the requested products.

Establishing lack of, or insufficient, manufacturing capacity

This requirement does not apply to LDCs. The insufficient or no manufacturing capacity is not to be assessed in general, but only for the particular pharmaceutical product(s) required.

There are two alternative ways to establish these circumstances, as set out in the Annex to the Decision:

(i) The first option applies when the Member has established that it has *no* manufacturing capacity in the pharmaceutical sector.

(ii) The second option applies when the Member has some manufacturing capacity in this sector, it has examined this capacity and found that, excluding any capacity owned or controlled by the patent owner, it is currently insufficient for the purposes of meeting its needs.

What manufacturing capacity means in either of the options is open to interpretation. In a market economy such a capacity has two dimensions: the *technical* capability (dependent on availability of technology, trained personnel, equipment, access to raw materials, etc) and the *economic feasibility* of production. The technical capability alone does not make it possible to undertake production. The Decision recognizes this limitation and, in particular, the importance of economies of scale in its paragraph 6,[216] thereby suggesting that the assessment of the existence of manufacturing capacity is not limited to technical aspects.

A Member may establish the lack of or insufficient manufacturing capacity and use the system to import an active ingredient, even though it may have manufacturing capacity to formulate the corresponding product.

It is important to note that the Decision does not determine particular criteria or methods to establish the lack of or insufficient capacity. This is a matter of self-assessment[217] the outcome of which cannot be challenged by another Member or subject to review, reversed, or rejected by the Council for TRIPS. The Chair's statement indicates that 'to promote transparency and avoid controversy, notifications under paragraph 2(a)(ii) of the Decision would include information on how the Member in question had established, in accordance with the Annex, that it has insufficient or no manufacturing capacities in the pharmaceutical sector'.

---

[215] See Article 28.1 of the TRIPS Agreement.

[216] 'With a view to harnessing economies of scale for the purposes of enhancing purchasing power for, and facilitating the local production of, pharmaceutical products . . .'.

[217] See Vandoren and Van Eeckhaute op. cit. (2003), p 785.

The statement, however, does not amend the Decision. It only suggests the communication of information, for instance, about the type of analysis made, but not about the criteria or method employed, the data used, or the way in which conclusions were reached.[218]

Confirming the intention to grant a compulsory licence

Finally, the importing country must notify, where a pharmaceutical product is patented in its territory, that it has granted or intends to grant a compulsory licence. This means that the compulsory licence may have been granted or not, and that procedures for that purpose may have initiated or not at the time the notification is made. It would be sufficient to notify that the competent authority *intends* to grant a compulsory licence. There is no specified term for issuance of the compulsory licence after the notification was made.

The only condition imposed on the compulsory licence to be granted is that it must be 'in accordance with Article 31 of the TRIPS Agreement'.[219] Hence, the importing country has to respect the conditions set out in this Article, and is not bound to apply more stringent conditions. In particular, there will be no obligation to limit the compulsory licence to a limited quantity of the required product/s. The compulsory licence may be granted—as in any other situation—for the lifetime of the patent, and could only be terminated in accordance with Article 31(g) 'subject to adequate protection of the legitimate interests' of the compulsory licence.

In addition, there is no obligation to provide a compensation to the patent holder, as the application of Article 31(h) is waived by the Decision.

As mentioned, the notification is for informational purposes only. The importing country is not bound to prove that the conditions provided for by Article 31 have been met, nor can the Council for TRIPS review or contest the content of the notification.[220]

---

[218] The following types of notifications would indicate *how* the assessment was made:

'The Department/Ministry of...has [reviewed information in its possession and] [, upon consultations with experts in the field of pharmaceuticals,] found that there is currently no capacity to manufacture [product/s] in the country.'

'The Department/Ministry of...has undertaken an enquiry among pharmaceutical producers established in [country] and determined that, excluding the patent owner's facilities, there is currently no capacity in the country to manufacture [product/s] for the purposes of meeting its needs.'

[219] A question may be raised as to whether this condition means that a compulsory licence may be granted to import pharmaceutical products under Article 31 even in cases where the national legislation does not provide for such grant or for the execution of a compulsory licence through importation. The adopted waiver means that a Member State will not have the right to complain against another Member not complying with Article 31(f) or (h) but would not prevent, in principle, the patent owner from interfering with the granting of a compulsory licence if inconsistent with national law.

[220] However, the Chair's Statement indicates that:

• In accordance with the normal practice of the TRIPS Council, notifications made under the system shall be brought to the attention of its next meeting.

The notification will be made publicly available by the WTO Secretariat through a page on the WTO website dedicated to the Decision. If the notification was made before the granting of the compulsory licence by the importing country, there is no need to make another notification thereafter.

It is to be noted, finally, that though paragraph 6 of the Doha Declaration and the Decision refer to 'compulsory licenses', the system established by the Decision applies to any use without authorization of the right-holder as contemplated in Article 31 of the TRIPS Agreement. This means that the importing country (as well as the exporting country) may apply the system on the basis of an authorization for *public non-commercial use*, and not necessarily under a compulsory licence granted to a third party. This type of use without the authorization of the patent holder has, vis-à-vis compulsory licences, the advantage that the obligation under Article 31(b) is waived in all cases, and that Members may limit the remedies available against such use by the government or third parties authorized by the government (Article 44.2).

Compulsory licence in the exporting country

The Decision requires the granting of a compulsory licence in the exporting country. It does not waive the need to request a voluntary licence to the patent owner, as prescribed by Article 31(b).[221] However, the exporting country may invoke a health emergency in a foreign country.[222]

If the request of the voluntary licence is unsuccessful, the interested supplier would have to apply for a compulsory licence under the applicable national rules. The competent national authority would have to decide on the application and determine the remuneration to be paid. This would require that the national law in the exporting country provide for the possibility of issuing a compulsory licence to satisfy a demand on the terms set out in the Decision.

The patent owner may appeal the government's decision to grant a compulsory licence. Depending on procedural rules, the appeal may not interfere with the immediate execution of the licence, or may prevent the applicant from using it until the decision is confirmed. If the appeal does not suspend the execution of the

---

- Any Member may bring any matter related to the interpretation or implementation of the Decision, including issues related to diversion, to the TRIPS Council for expeditious review, with a view to taking appropriate action.
- If any Member has concerns that the terms of the Decision have not been fully complied with, the Member may also utilise the good offices of the Director General or Chair of the TRIPS Council, with a view to finding a mutually acceptable solution.

[221] See above situations in which the application of this paragraph is exempted.

[222] In accordance with by Vandoren, and Van Eeckhaute '[...] procedures to grant compulsory licenses are not necessarily cumbersome and lengthy. The procedural requirements of Article 31 TRIPS are minimal and flexible, and also provide for a fast-track procedure as regards situations of extreme urgency or national emergency (which covers, in any event, AIDS, tuberculosis and malaria, but also potentially a range of other situations or diseases)' (op. cit. (2003), p 783).

licence, the applicant may start production and export but at the risk of a later claim for damages by the patent owner, if the decision to grant the compulsory licence were reversed.

The Decision sets out with some detail the conditions under which a compulsory licence can be issued by the exporting Member.

Amount necessary to meet needs

The compulsory licence must be granted only to produce and export 'the amount necessary to meet the needs of the eligible importing Member(s)'. In addition, the *entirety of the production* under licence shall be exported to the Member(s) which has notified its needs to the Council for TRIPS.

The 'needs' are established by the importing country. The amount to be supplied is the one actually agreed upon with the importing country (which autonomously determines what its needs are) and not necessarily what was indicated in the notification by the importing country (which should only contain the 'expected' quantities, as mentioned above). The 'amount necessary to meet the needs' may be established on the basis of several criteria, depending on the degree to which the 'needs of the eligible importing country' can be determined *ex ante*. For instance, it may be based on a specified number of units of products when the needs can be precisely determined, or on the basis of patients to be treated or hospitals to be supplied over a period of time. Given that one of the concerns underpinning the Decision is the risk of diversion, the criteria to determine quantities to be supplied should be established in good faith and be sufficient to determine the extent of use of the patented invention.

Identification of product(s)

Labelling and marks

The Decision requires that the products to be supplied under the Decision be *clearly* identified as being produced thereunder. The purpose of the label or mark is to make the products *identifiable* in case there is diversion to other markets. The required identification should be made 'through specific labeling or marking'. This requirement may be satisfied by literally stating in the label that a product has been produced under the Decision,[223] but the requirement does not impose any specific indication. Hence, the supplier may choose what phrase or sign to utilize to make the products identifiable.

---

[223] For instance, by indicating in the label 'Product made for country X under the WTO General Council Decision of 30 August 2003'.

Packaging, colouring, and shaping

Products should not only be identifiable but also *distinguishable*, presumably from the branded products. This is to be achieved, according to the Decision, through special

- packaging; and/or
- colouring/shaping of the products themselves.

Despite the apparent ambiguity of the expression 'colouring/shaping', it is clear that these requirements are not cumulative.[224] It will be up to the supplier to choose whether distinction will be achieved through packaging, colouring, or shaping.

The differences in packaging, colouring, or shaping should be those reasonably necessary to permit the distinction to be made. The Decision does not state, however, who should be able to distinguish the products. The requirements may be differently implemented depending on whether the products are to be distinguishable to customs authorities, distributors and retailers, medical doctors, or the general public. Since the objective of this provision is not to protect consumers but pharmaceutical companies against diversion,[225] the differences should be those sufficient for customs authorities or pharmaceutical manufacturers (in the case of active ingredients) to distinguish the products.

The Decision seems to refer to differentiation of finished products only. However, the statement indicates that 'the provisions of paragraph 2(b)(ii) apply not only to formulated pharmaceuticals produced and supplied under the system but also to *active ingredients* produced and supplied under the system and to finished products produced using such active ingredients' (emphasis added). Whatever the legal value of the statement is, the differentiation of an active ingredient by shape may be impossible (since it would normally be provided in powder, liquid, or other amorphous form), while differentiation by colour would require to include unnecessary additives and change the chemical composition of the product. Packaging would seem the only reasonable option for differentiation of active ingredients. Since they are traded between specialized companies, however, such differentiation may not be relevant—as in the case of finished products—to prevent diversion.

---

[224] See the second paragraph of the Statement where reference is explicitly made to 'packaging, colouring *or* shaping' (emphasis added).

[225] See the second paragraph of the Statement, which indicates that 'Members recognize that the purpose of the Decision would be defeated if products supplied under this Decision are diverted from the markets for which they are intended. Therefore, all reasonable measures should be taken to prevent such diversion in accordance with the relevant paragraphs of the Decision.'

The obligation to distinguish the products is not absolute. There are two situations in which the distinction can be omitted altogether. This will occur when such distinction:

- is not feasible; or
- it has a significant impact on price.

There are no parameters in the Decision to determine what a 'significant impact on price' means. Since the Decision's aim is to address public health needs of Member countries—in the framework of the overall objective of the Doha Declaration to ensure access to drugs to all (paragraph 4)—the significance of the increase in price is to be assessed from the perspective of the purchaser. Any increase in price may be 'significant' for the purchaser and limit its capacity to address public health needs, particularly in the case of expensive products or purchases in big volumes.

The Decision does not specify either who is going to assess whether the impact is significant or not. It is the supplier who is expected to make this judgement. Though the burden to distinguish the products is on him, the assessment of its impact on price should take the purchasers' interests into account.

The statement indicates that 'it is the understanding of Members that in general special packaging and/or special colouring or shaping should not have a significant impact on the price of pharmaceuticals'. This ambiguous statement may be read as a recognition that special packaging, colouring, or shaping *does not generally have* a significant impact, or as a normative statement emphasizing the idea that the use of such distinction *should not have* such negative impact. This second reading corresponds to the literal wording of the text. Though it may be seen as redundant, it does clarify that colouring and shaping are alternative and not cumulative, and expresses the Member's concern that the distinction of products must not significantly increase prices.

It is important to note that obtaining a compulsory licence may not be sufficient for a company to be able to export a pharmaceutical product under the system, as national health regulations generally require prior approval for the production of medicines for export.

Notification by the supplier

Under the terms of the compulsory licence granted in the supplying country, the supplier should post on a website certain information before shipment begins. The licensee may use for this purpose its own website or the page on the WTO website dedicated to the Decision to be developed by the WTO Secretariat. The information to be posted is the following:

- the quantities being supplied to each destination; and
- the distinguishing features of the product(s) referred to above.

The obligation to provide information is limited to the 'distinguishing features', and does not encompass other information about the product. It may include, for instance, an image showing the product as packaged or its label, or indication of its colour or shape, depending on the distinguishing characteristic chosen by the supplier.

Notification by the exporting country

In addition to the supplier's notification, the exporting country must make a notification to the Council for TRIPS of the grant of the licence. As in the case of the notification of the importing country, this notification does not need to be approved by a WTO body in order to use the system set out in the Decision (footnote 8). The Council for TRIPS has neither competence to review the notification nor to object to the grounds and conditions under which the compulsory licence has been granted. It cannot observe deficiencies in the notification either (for instance, if some of the required information was missing).[226] The notification will be made available publicly by the WTO Secretariat through a page on the WTO website dedicated to the Decision.

The notification must contain the following:

- the name and address of the licensee;
- the product(s) for which the licence has been granted;
- the quantity(ies) for which it has been granted;
- the country(ies) to which the product(s) is (are) to be supplied;
- the duration of the licence;
- the address of the website where the supplier will post the information referred to in paragraph 2.(b)(iii) of the Decision.

The specified content of the notification suggests that though a compulsory licence is to be granted for a limited quantity only, a single compulsory licence may cover the production and export to more than one country. Several importing countries may, in fact, pool their purchasing power of certain pharmaceutical products, in order to obtain better prices. The Decision also allows a country member of a regional trade agreement at least half of the current membership of which is made up of LDCs, to re-export products acquired under the system established by the Decision to other developing or LDC parties of the regional trade agreement that 'share the health problem in question' (paragraph 6(i)). The main advantage created by this provision is that the waiver of Article 31(f) applies to all members of the trade agreement, and that there is no need to notify the

---

[226] The statement, however, indicates as mentioned that any Member may bring any matter related to the interpretation or implementation of the Decision, including issues related to diversion, to the TRIPS Council for expeditious review.

Council for TRIPS each time that an exportation is made. However, this exception only applies to some regional trade agreements in Africa, and not to the bigger regional markets in Asia and Latin America, thereby limiting the effects on economies of scale that could be attained. Moreover, the Decision does not allow the supplier to directly supply all or some of the members of the trade regional agreement eligible under the Decision, but to export to one of its members who could in turn re-export to others.

The duration of the compulsory licence is to be determined by the exporting country's government. It would be logical to provide for its termination upon the effective supply of the required quantities of a given product, in order to avoid the burden and cost of requiring a new compulsory licence if delivery takes place over a period of time.

As mentioned, the compulsory licence may need to cover more than one patent, in cases where the active ingredients, formulations, crystalline forms, salts, or other variants of the relevant product or process are subject to different patents (belonging to the same or different companies).

Anti-diversion measures

According to paragraph 4 of the Decision, 'in order to ensure that the products imported under the system set out in this Decision are used for the public health purposes underlying their importation, eligible importing Members shall take reasonable measures within their means, proportionate to their administrative capacities and to the risk of trade diversion to prevent re-exportation of the products that have actually been imported into their territories under the system. In the event that an eligible importing Member that is a developing country Member or a least-developed country Member experiences difficulty in implementing this provision, developed country Members shall provide, on request and on mutually agreed terms and conditions, technical and financial cooperation in order to facilitate its implementation.'

The statement emphasizes 'that the purpose of the Decision would be defeated if products supplied under this Decision are diverted from the markets for which they are intended' and indicates that 'all reasonable measures should be taken to prevent such diversion in accordance with the relevant paragraphs of the Decision'. Though the wording here appears somehow stronger than in the Decision, it does not alter the content nor the nature of the *best efforts* obligation imposed by the latter. It will be the prerogative of the importing country to determine what is:

- reasonable within the Member's means;
- proportionate to its administrative capacities; and
- proportionate to the risk of trade diversion.

Measures should be adopted not in general, but specifically in relation to 'products that have actually been imported into their territories under the system'.

Suspension of the system

The second alternative in the Annex to the Decision indicates that '[W]hen it is established that such [manufacturing] capacity has become sufficient to meet the Member's needs, the system shall no longer apply'. This condition does not apply when the determination has been based on the lack of manufacturing capacity (as opposed to insufficient capacity).

This Decision does not mention who is to make this determination nor the applicable procedures. Since it is the importing county itself that determines insufficient capacity, and the Council for TRIPS has no power to review this determination, it is logical to interpret that the determination that capacity has become sufficient is also to be made by the importing country. Given that lack of or insufficient capacity is to established per product, and that compulsory licences are issued to import a specified quantity of a needed pharmaceutical product/s, the determination that capacity has become sufficient would not affect the future use of the system with regard to other product/s.

Operation of the system

It is important to note that the system under paragraph 6 of the Doha Declaration will operate in a scenario in which there is only one world supplier of a patented drug and, therefore, there will be no available sources of generic products. The use of such a system will be necessary when the patent owner *refuses to supply* a patented drug in a country (with insufficient or no manufacturing capacity in pharmaceuticals) at a price or under other conditions acceptable to the interested country. The basic assumption for the application of the system is, therefore, a situation where (a) a drug is available and *could* be sold to the country in need by the patent owner; and (b) the patent owner refuses to do so.

This means that whatever humanitarian reasons underlay the country's demand of a given drug, nothing in the adopted system will compel the patent owner to supply the needed drugs. He may just passively watch how the country in need strives to fulfil the conditions imposed by the Decision, while people remain without treatment. He may also facilitate the process by conferring a voluntary licence to a potential exporter. It may also occur that the patent owner exploits the intricacies and complexities of the system, and exercises his rights under the relevant national laws to block the unauthorized use of his patent. The system under paragraph 6 may, in fact, be applied *in a context of conflict* between the demanding country and the patent owner unwilling to supply.

Under the adopted system, for instance, the possibility is recognized (fully consistent with the TRIPS Agreement) of granting a compulsory licence to *import* a patented drug. The problem, however, is that many developing countries provide for the granting of compulsory licences for the *manufacture* of patented subject matter, and not for importation. Hence, in order to make operative any solution under paragraph 6, those developing countries would need to amend their national patent laws accordingly. This may be unnecessary, however, if the national laws included provisions for non-commercial government use of patented inventions, allowing for either local manufacturing or importation.[227]

Similarly, amendments to national laws will be necessary in the potential exporting countries. Compulsory licences are granted under grounds specified by national laws. The supply of export markets is not an accepted ground in most national laws.[228] Moreover, in implementing Article 31(f) of the TRIPS Agreement, WTO Members have established compulsory licences to supply 'predominantly' the domestic market. If a company receives a request under paragraph 6 to supply a foreign country, it would not be able to obtain a compulsory licence exclusively to export, unless the national law has been amended accordingly. So far Canada, Norway, Netherlands, India, and the European Union have introduced legislative changes to implement the Decision.

The effective use of a compulsory licence in both the importing and exporting country will also depend on procedures. In some countries (eg Argentina) an appeal by the patent owner against the grant of a compulsory licence does not suspend its immediate execution (eg Article 49, Argentine Patent Law No 24.481, as amended). But in other countries, this may not be the case. The patent owner may file an appeal or obtain an injunction and thereby stop exports under a compulsory licence until a final administrative or judicial decision is taken, perhaps a few years later. National patent laws, hence, will have to be amended, as necessary, in order to make the use of compulsory licences for export an effective mechanism to address public health needs.

As discussed elsewhere,[229] in order to be effective, a solution to the problem described in paragraph 6 should be economically viable, and not only diplomatically acceptable. In addition to complying with the legal procedures involved in the application of a compulsory licence and the marketing approval of the product, the potential exporters will have (when produced for the first time) to develop the chemistry and formulate the drug, and then produce the active ingredients and/or formulations with shape, colour, label and packaging different from of the

[227] It is to be noted that the Decision as mentioned, only refers to 'compulsory licences' but equally applies to government use for non-commercial purposes.

[228] However, Article 168 of the Australian Patent Act and Article 55(2) of the Patent Act of New Zealand permits exports under an agreement with a foreign country to supply products required for the defence of that country. Section 48B(d)(i) of the UK Patents Act provides for a compulsory licence in respect of a patent whose proprietor is not a WTO proprietor when the owner's failure to license the patent on reasonable grounds means that a market for the export of a patented product made in the UK is not being supplied. Article 45(g) of the Argentine patent law permits the granting of a compulsory licence not predominantly for the domestic markets when necessary to remedy anti-competitive practices or in cases of health emergencies or national security.

[229] See eg, C Correa, *Implications of the Doha Declaration on the TRIPS Agreement and Public Health*, World Health Organization, Geneva (2002), available at <http://www.who.int> (last accessed on 25 September 2005), p 33; Commission on Intellectual Property Rights, Integrating intellectual property rights and development policy, London, 2002 (available at <http://www.iprcommission.org> (last accessed on 25 September 2005).

patent owner's product, and at a price that is affordable to the purchaser. Pharmaceutical firms are unlikely to make the required investment if there is no reasonable profit expectation.

The Decision recognizes that the viability of the 'solution' largely depends on the existence of economies of scale that justify production. However, given the requirement about participation of least-developed countries, the exception for regional trade agreements will only apply to some regional agreements in Africa but not in other regions,[230] thereby limiting the effect on economies of scale that could have been obtained.

As noted by Maskus, though overall needs in the poor nations are immense,

even if some poor countries in a trade agreement covered by this exception pooled their demands for a particular medicine, the scale may be still too low to become attractive for potential suppliers... [B]ecause the eligible import markets in really small countries will not be large, generic producers may not be interested in producing such small volumes and foregoing chances for economies of scale.[231]

The implementation of the Decision on paragraph 6 of the Doha Declaration will require adaptations in national laws and entail, in particular cases, significant transaction costs. As adopted, it is unlikely to put strong pressure on patent owners to lower their prices or to negotiate voluntary licences, nor is it likely to provide incentives to potential suppliers to make the investments necessary to develop and produce the needed drugs.[232]

Despite the quite obvious limitations of and many constraints imposed by the Decision under discussion, countries in need of acquiring patented drugs should test the viability of the system. The Decision should be interpreted, in line with the Doha Declaration on the TRIPS Agreement and Public Health, in a manner that facilitates an increase in the supply of medicines to poor countries. It is also necessary to elaborate a *permanent* solution to the problem affecting countries with limited or without manufacturing capacities in this field, based on a simpler and more straightforward approach,[233] which provides the economic incentives for the solution to be effective.

It is also important to note that the system under paragraph 6 seems to be built up on the assumption that a patent owner is legitimized to prevent access to products under his control, even in the presence of compelling humanitarian

---

[230] For instance, MERCOSUR and the Andean Community do not qualify under the Decision as a single market for the purposes of the Decision.

[231] K Maskus, 'Prof. Keith Maskus on TRIPS, Drug Patents and Access to Medicines—Balancing Incentives for R&D with Public Health Concerns', in KEDG, at <http://www.developmentgateway.org/knowledge> (last accessed on 25 September 2005).   [232] Ibidem.

[233] For instance, on 3 October 2002, the European Parliament adopted Amendment 196 to the European Medicines Directive, which provides that 'manufacturing shall be allowed if the medicinal product is intended for export to a third country that has issued a compulsory licence for that product, or where a patent is not in force and if there is a request to that effect of the competent public health authorities of that third country'.

reasons. This is certainly not consistent with the Doha Declaration on the TRIPS Agreement and Public Health (particularly paragraph 4), nor with States' commitments under the International Covenant on Economic, Social and Cultural Rights, especially its Article 12 (recognizing the human 'right of everyone to the enjoyment of the highest attainable standard of physical and mental health' and requiring steps to be taken to fully realize this right, including 'those necessary for... the prevention, treatment and control of epidemic, endemic,... and other diseases'). The adoption of the Decision, hence, cannot prevent the use of other means when the owner of the relevant patent or patents refuses to supply a needed drug. Countries should be encouraged to develop disciplines to deal with such refusals to deal in the context of the 'essential facilities' doctrine,[234] or other concepts under competition and public health law.

Finally, it should be recalled that paragraph 6 only describes one of the problems arising in the context of the TRIPS Agreement with regard to public health. The intellectual property protection of pharmaceuticals will continue to pose significant challenges to public health policies in developing countries, even if the agreed 'solution' were proven to be viable and effective. The agreement on paragraph 6 does not mean an end to the controversies around intellectual property and public health. They are likely to continue, especially as developed countries seek TRIPS-plus protection via interpretation[235] or the negotiation of bilateral and regional agreements,[236] and as patents on marginal or trivial developments are granted and used to block or delay generic competition.[237]

Revocation and forfeiture

32. An opportunity for judicial review of any decision to revoke or forfeit a patent shall be available.

Article 32 ensures the availability of a judicial review of any decision to revoke/forfeit a patent. According to a literal interpretation, it would not be sufficient to provide for a review by a higher administrative authority, as allowed in the case of the review of compulsory licences (Article 31(i) but to ensure the intervention of a judicial authority. However, the European Patent Office (EPO) has held that an independent appeal authority (like the EPO Boards of Appeal) is to be regarded as a judicial organ in the sense of Article 32.[238]

---

[234] See, eg J Taladay, and J Carlin Jr, 'Compulsory licensing of intellectual property under the competition laws of the United States and European Community', (2002) 10 George Mason Law Review, p 443.

[235] The USTR, for instance, interprets that Article 39.3 of the Agreement requires the granting of an exclusive period of protection for data submitted for the marketing approval of pharmaceuticals and agrochemicals. See Chapter 11.

[236] See, eg, the US–Chile and US–Singapore free-trade agreements.

[237] See, eg, C Correa, *Trends in Drug Patenting. Case Studies* (2001: Buenos Aires, Corregidor).

[238] See J Straus op. cit. (1996), p 209.

The grounds for revocation/forfeiture of a patent have not been dealt with in the TRIPS Agreement. A patent may, thus, be revoked on the grounds determined by national laws.[239] One of the possible grounds is the lack or insufficient working of the invention, if a compulsory licence was granted and the situation was not remedied in accordance with Article 5A of the Paris Convention.[240]

In addition to preserving the capacity to determine the grounds for revocation, Members can stipulate that patents lapse in the absence of payment of maintenance fees, subject to Article 5*bis*(1) of the Paris Convention.[241]

Term of protection

33. The term of protection available shall not end before the expiration of a period of twenty years counted from the filing date.[8]

[8] It is understood that those Members which do not have a system of original grant may provide that the term of protection shall be computed form the filing date in the system of original grant.

Article 33 establishes, as a minimum, the duration of patents for twenty years counted from the filing date of the patent. This provision outlaws any special duration period determined on the basis of the field of technology, the extent of exploitation of the invention, or on any other grounds. Although the term is counted from the date of filing, there is no obligation to provide for a minimum term of effective protection (available as of the grant of the patent). In particular, Members are not bound to extend the term of protection to compensate for delays in the examination process or in the marketing approval of products subject to governmental regulations. This type of compensation is one of the typical features in the FTAs signed by the USA with several countries, particularly since 2000.[242]

Article 33 forced many Members to amend their legislation, including the US (where patents were granted for seventeen years counted from the date of grant). The US filed a complaint against Canada with respect to the extension of the term of patents granted before the entry into force of the Agreement. The US challenged Section 45 of Canada's Patent Act. It claimed that the patent protection

---

[239] There is no basis either in the TRIPS Agreement or in the Paris Convention for the interpretation (see J Straus op. cit. (1996), p 208) that revocation can only proceed in cases where a compulsory licence was not sufficient to ensure the working of a patent in accordance with Article 5A(3) of the Paris Convention.

[240] Paris Convention, Article 5A(3): 'Forfeiture of the patent shall not be provided for except in cases where the grant of compulsory licences would not have been sufficient to prevent the said abuses. No proceedings for the forfeiture or revocation of a patent may be instituted before the expiration of two years from the grant of the first compulsory licence'.

[241] Article 5*bis*(1): 'A period of grace of not less than six months shall be allowed for the payment of the fees prescribed for the maintenance of industrial property rights, subject, if the domestic legislation so provides, to the payment of a surcharge.'

[242] See, eg, C Correa, 'Implications of bilateral free trade agreements on access to medicines' (2006) 84 Bulletin of the World Health Organization, p 5.

term of seventeen years (counted from the date of grant) accorded to patent applications filed before 1 October 1989 often ended before twenty years from the date of filing. The United States argued that pursuant to Articles 33 and 70.2 of the TRIPS Agreement, Canada was obligated to make available a term of protection that lasted at least twenty years from the date of filing to all inventions which enjoyed patent protection on 1 January1996—the date on which the TRIPS Agreement came into effect for developed countries—including those protected by the old Patents Act. Inventions enjoying protection under that Act were covered by Article 70.2 of the TRIPS Agreement (protection of 'subject matter' existing on the date of application of the TRIPS Agreement). Canada unsuccessfully argued that the seventeen-year period was *de facto* in compliance with Article 33 and that, in some cases, patents could effectively last for more than twenty years counting from the filing date. Canada was found to be in violation to the TRIPS Agreement.[243]

Reversal of the burden of proof

34.1. For the purposes of civil proceedings in respect of the infringement of the rights of the owner referred to in paragraph 1(b) of Article 28, if the subject matter of a patent is a process for obtaining a product, the judicial authorities shall have the authority to order the defendant to prove that the process to obtain an identical product is different from the patented process. Therefore, Members shall provide, in at least one of the following circumstances, that any identical product when produced without the consent of the patent owner shall, in the absence of proof to the contrary, be deemed to have been obtained by the patented process:

(a) if the product obtained by the patented process is new;

(b) if there is a substantial likelihood that the identical product was made by the process and the owner of the patent has been unable through reasonable efforts to determine the process actually used.

34.2. Any Member shall be free to provide that the burden of proof indicated in paragraph 1 shall be on the alleged infringer only if the condition referred to in subparagraph (a) is fulfilled or only if the condition referred to in subparagraph (b) is fulfilled.

34.3. In the adduction of proof to the contrary, the legitimate interests of defendants in protecting their manufacturing and business secrets shall be taken into account.

Article 34 provides for the reversal of burden of proof in civil litigation involving *process* patent claims. This provision is largely framed on German patent law.[244]

---

[243] See Report of the Appellate Body, *Canada—Term of Patent Protection*, WT/DS170/AB/R (2000), para 102(B).   [244] J Straus op. cit. (1996), p 210.

It is unclear why this provision, which is aimed at strengthening the patent protection through a procedural means, has been included in Part II and not in Part III ('Enforcement of Intellectual Property Rights') of the Agreement.[245] Its drafting reflects the difficulties found to reach a consensus on the matter.

According to the first sentence of Article 34.1 it is the judge who will have the authority 'to order the defendant to prove that the process to obtain an identical product is different from the patented process'.[246] It leaves the judge the discretion to assess, in the circumstances of each case, the extent to which the reversal is justified. However, the provision establishes, in addition, an *ex lege, juris tantum* presumption according to which 'any identical product when produced without the consent of the patent owner shall, in the absence of proof to the contrary, be deemed to have been obtained by the patented process'. This presumption only applies when the product is identical; hence, similarity in the composition or function does not suffice to reverse the burden of proof. Article 34.1 requires the defendant to disclose (subject to paragraph 3 of the same article) the process actually used to make the product, in order to demonstrate that it is different from the patented process. It will be the plaintiff's burden, however, to prove that such process effectively infringes the patented process.[247]

There are two options (at the discretion of the Member) in which the presumption referred to must apply. The first option is that the product obtained by the patented process is 'new'. Parties may interpret the degree of newness required. It may involve novelty in the terms which are usual in patent law, even if the product is not patentable as such. Newness can also be considered in terms of the existence or not of similar products on the market when the alleged infringement takes place. The application of the patent law concept of 'new' has a major disadvantage: if assessed at the time of the patent application, it would lead to the consideration as if they were 'new' products that may have been marketed for a long time and for which it may be presumed that alternative processes of manufacture have been developed. In fact, the longer a product is in the market, the higher the probability that competitors have found different methods to make it.[248] Thus, it has been noted that:

it seems to be reasonable to assume that, where subsequent processes have been described for obtaining the product resulting from the claimed patented processes to the extent that such processes may vary to a greater or lesser extent, bring different advantages or simply

---

[245] Article 43 contains rules on 'evidence of proof' addressed to judicial authorities.

[246] This provision applies in cases of patents covering processes for the obtention by synthesis, extraction, purification or any other method, of a particular product.

[247] See the decision of the German Federal Court of 25 June 1976 in *Alkylendiamine* II, which held that a similar rule under German law did not shift the responsibility for determining the scope of the plaintiff's right on the defendant; but merely required the defendant to provide sufficient proof of the process actually used in manufacturing the product: GRUR (1997), p 103.

[248] German case law and doctrine have questioned this solution. See, eg, Vidal-Quadras Trias des Bes, 'Process patents on new products and reversal of the burden of proof: factors contributing to the interpretation of its scope' (2002) 24 European Intellectual Property Review 5, p 242.

be practicable, when the patent invoke is close to expiry and alternative processes have been described, these circumstances must be taken into account in order to undermine the grounds for presuming that the patented process has been used.[249]

In implementing this option Argentine law, for instance, originally opted for a concept of 'new' based on the ordinary patent law concept, but moved to a concept of 'new in the market' in the context of the consultations held with the US under the Dispute Settlement Understanding.[250]

The second option[251] is to apply the presumption when there is 'a substantial likelihood that the identical product was made by the process and the owner of the patent has been unable through reasonable efforts to determine the process actually used'. In this case, the product may not be new in any way and, therefore, the scope of the provision is wider than in the first hypothesis. A 'substantial likelihood' is more than the simple possibility: the plaintiff cannot merely argue that infringement takes place, but must submit evidence suggesting that such is effectively the case. The requirement relating to the 'reasonable efforts' of the patentee is to be assessed by the judge in each case; if appropriately applied, it may contribute to limit eventual abuses of patent holders in demanding the reversal of burden of proof and avoid 'strategic' litigation aimed at blocking legitimate competition.

Annex I: Negotiating history

Negotiating history[252]

In his 23 July1990, report on the status of work in the TRIPS Negotiating Group, the Chairman (Lars ER Anell) presented two sets of proposals. In an Annex to the report, he presented a composite text that was taken from various proposals by delegations to the Negotiating Group, indicating the source of each proposal by numerical reference to the source document.

---

[249] Ibidem.

[250] The agreed-to text (already incorporated into Argentina's legislation) read as follows: 'The courts, however, shall be empowered to order the plaintiff to prove that the process that the defendant is using for obtaining a product infringes the process patent if the product obtained by the patented process is not new. It shall be presumed that, in the absence of proof to the contrary, the product obtained by the patented process is not new if the defendant or if an expert appointed by the court at the request of the defendant is able to show that, at the time of the alleged infringement, there exists in the market a non-infringing product identical to the one produced by the patented process that originated from a source different from the right owner or the defendant.' See Law 25.859, 2004.

[251] This option was not included in the German law but in a number of bilateral agreements signed between the USA and former socialist countries. See J Straus op. cit. (2005), p 210.

[252] For an analysis of the negotiating history, see UNCTAD-ICTSD op. cit. (1996), pp 351–504.

Composite text of July 23 1990 [253]

Exclusive rights

'1A. A patent shall confer on its owner at least the following exclusive rights:

(a) to prevent third parties not having his consent from the acts of: making, using, [putting on the market, offering] [or selling] [or importing] [or importing or stocking for these purposes] the product which is the subject matter of the patent.

(b) where the subject matter of a patent is a process, to prevent third parties not having his consent from the act of using process, and from the acts of: using, [putting on the market, offering] [selling,] [or importing,] [or importing or stocking for these purposes,] at least the product obtained directly by that process.

1B. Once a patent has been granted, the owner of the patent shall have the following rights:

(a) The right to prevent others from making, using or selling the patented product or using the patented process for commercial or industrial purposes.

(b) The right to assign, or transfer by succession, the patent and to conclude licence contracts . . . '

Revocation/Forfeiture

'1A A patent [[may not be revoked or forfeited [merely] on grounds [of non-working] stipulated in [point—]] [may only be revoked on grounds that it fails to meet the requirements of [points].

2A Judicial review shall be available in the case of forfeiture of a patent where applicable.

2B A patent may be revoked on grounds of public interest or where the conditions for the grant of non-voluntary licenses are not fulfilled.'

Term of protection

'1A The term of protection shall be [at least] [15 years from the date of filing of the application, except for inventions in the field of pharmaceuticals for which the term shall be 20 years] [20 years from the date of filing of the application] [or where other applications are invoked in the said application, 20 years from the filing date of the earliest filed of the invoked applications which is not the priority date of the said application].[254]

2A PARTIES are encouraged to extend the term of patent protection in appropriate cases, to compensate for delays regarding the exploitation of the patented invention caused by regulatory approval processes.

---

[253] Chairman's Report to the GNG, Status of Work in the Negotiating Group, Negotiating Group on Trade-Related Aspects of Intellectual Property Rights, including Trade in Counterfeit Goods, MTN.GNG/NG11/W/76, 23 July 1990, presented by the Chairman of the TRIPS Negotiating Group (Lars E R Anell). Alternatives 'A' correspond to texts from developed countries and 'B' from developing countries.

[254] At the initial stages of the TRIPS negotiations, Japan proposed a term of fifteen years from the date of grant, as available in its law; Australia and New Zealand sixteen years from the date of filing a complete specification. The EC and US proposed a higher standard of twenty years from the date of filing, which was finally adopted. Countries supporting a shorter term did not unite to propose any alternative and, hence, the issue was decided by default (J Watal, *Intellectual Property Rights in the WTO and developing countries*, (2001: The Hague, Kluwer Law International), p 114).

1B It shall be a matter for national legislation to determine the duration of protection.'

Reversal of burden of proof

1A.1 If the subject matter of a patent is a process for obtaining a product, the same product when produced by any other party shall, in the absence of proof to the contrary, be deemed to have been obtained by the patented process in [at least one of] the following situation[s]:

(a) if the product is new, [or,

(b) where the product is not new, if there is a substantial likelihood that the product was made by the process [and the owner of the patent has been unable through reasonable efforts to determine the process actually used].

1A.2 In the adduction of proof to the contrary, the legitimate interests of the defendant in protecting his manufacturing and business secrets shall be taken into account.

1B Where the subject matter of a patent is a process for obtaining a product, whether new or old, the burden of establishing that an alleged infringing product was made by the patented process shall always be on the person alleging such infringement.

Draft text transmitted to the Brussels Ministerial Conference (December 1990)

Exceptions

PARTIES may provide limited exceptions to the exclusive rights conferred by a patent, provided that such exceptions do not unreasonably conflict with a normal exploitation of the patent and do not unreasonably prejudice the legitimate interests of the patent owner, taking account of the legitimate interests of third parties.

Revocation/Forfeiture

An opportunity for judicial review of any decision to revoke or forfeit a patent shall be available.

Annex II: Annex to the TRIPS Agreement

Annex to the Trips Agreement

1. For the purposes of Article 31*bis* and this Annex:
'pharmaceutical product' means any patented product, or product manufactured through a patented process, of the pharmaceutical sector needed to address the public health problems as recognized in paragraph 1 of the Declaration on the TRIPS Agreement and Public Health (WT/MIN(01)/DEC/2). It is understood that active ingredients necessary for its manufacture and diagnostic kits needed for its use would be included;[255]

'eligible importing Member' means any least-developed country Member, and any other Member that has made a notification[256] to the Council for TRIPS of its intention to use the system set out in Article 31*bis* and this Annex ('system') as an importer, it being understood that a Member may notify at any time that it will use the system in whole or in a limited way, for example only in the case of a national emergency or other

[255] This subparagraph is without prejudice to subparagraph 1(b).
[256] It is understood that this notification does not need to be approved by a WTO body in order to use the system.

circumstances of extreme urgency or in cases of public non-commercial use. It is noted that some Members will not use the system as importing Members[257] and that some other Members have stated that, if they use the system, it would be in no more than situations of national emergency or other circumstances of extreme urgency;

'exporting Member' means a Member using the system to produce pharmaceutical products for, and export them to, an eligible importing Member.

2. The terms referred to in paragraph 1 of Article 31*bis* are that:

the eligible importing Member(s)[258] has made a notification[2] to the Council for TRIPS, that:

(i) specifies the names and expected quantities of the product(s) needed;[259]

(ii) confirms that the eligible importing Member in question, other than a least-developed country Member, has established that it has insufficient or no manufacturing capacities in the pharmaceutical sector for the product(s) in question in one of the ways set out in the Appendix to this Annex; and

(iii) confirms that, where a pharmaceutical product is patented in its territory, it has granted or intends to grant a compulsory licence in accordance with Articles 31 and 31*bis* of this Agreement and the provisions of this Annex;[260]

the compulsory licence issued by the exporting Member under the system shall contain the following conditions:

only the amount necessary to meet the needs of the eligible importing Member(s) may be manufactured under the licence and the entirety of this production shall be exported to the Member(s) which has notified its needs to the Council for TRIPS;

products produced under the licence shall be clearly identified as being produced under the system through specific labelling or marking. Suppliers should distinguish such products through special packaging and/or special colouring/shaping of the products themselves, provided that such distinction is feasible and does not have a significant impact on price; and

before shipment begins, the licensee shall post on a website[261] the following information:

– the quantities being supplied to each destination as referred to in indent (i) above; and

– the distinguishing features of the product(s) referred to in indent (ii) above;

the exporting Member shall notify[262] the Council for TRIPS of the grant of the licence, including the conditions attached to it.[263] The information provided shall include the

---

[257] Australia, Canada, the European Communities with, for the purposes of Article 31*bis* and this Annex, its member States, Iceland, Japan, New Zealand, Norway, Switzerland, and the United States.

[258] Joint notifications providing the information required under this subparagraph may be made by the regional organizations referred to in para 3 of Article 31*bis* on behalf of eligible importing Members using the system that are parties to them, with the agreement of those parties.

[259] The notification will be made available publicly by the WTO Secretariat through a page on the WTO website dedicated to the system.

[260] This subparagraph is without prejudice to Article 66.1 of this Agreement.

[261] The licensee may use for this purpose its own website or, with the assistance of the WTO Secretariat, the page on the WTO website dedicated to the system.

[262] It is understood that this notification does not need to be approved by a WTO body in order to use the system.

[263] The notification will be made available publicly by the WTO Secretariat through a page on the WTO website dedicated to the system.

name and address of the licensee, the product(s) for which the licence has been granted, the quantity(ies) for which it has been granted, the country(ies) to which the product(s) is (are) to be supplied and the duration of the licence. The notification shall also indicate the address of the website referred to in subparagraph (b)(iii) above.

3. In order to ensure that the products imported under the system are used for the public health purposes underlying their importation, eligible importing Members shall take reasonable measures within their means, proportionate to their administrative capacities and to the risk of trade diversion to prevent re-exportation of the products that have actually been imported into their territories under the system. In the event that an eligible importing Member that is a developing country Member or a least-developed country Member experiences difficulty in implementing this provision, developed country Members shall provide, on request and on mutually agreed terms and conditions, technical and financial cooperation in order to facilitate its implementation.

4. Members shall ensure the availability of effective legal means to prevent the importation into, and sale in, their territories of products produced under the system and diverted to their markets inconsistently with its provisions, using the means already required to be available under this Agreement. If any Member considers that such measures are proving insufficient for this purpose, the matter may be reviewed in the Council for TRIPS at the request of that Member.

5. With a view to harnessing economies of scale for the purposes of enhancing purchasing power for, and facilitating the local production of, pharmaceutical products, it is recognized that the development of systems providing for the grant of regional patents to be applicable in the Members described in paragraph 3 of Article 31*bis* should be promoted. To this end, developed country Members undertake to provide technical cooperation in accordance with Article 67 of this Agreement, including in conjunction with other relevant intergovernmental organizations.

6. Members recognize the desirability of promoting the transfer of technology and capacity building in the pharmaceutical sector in order to overcome the problem faced by Members with insufficient or no manufacturing capacities in the pharmaceutical sector. To this end, eligible importing Members and exporting Members are encouraged to use the system in a way which would promote this objective. Members undertake to cooperate in paying special attention to the transfer of technology and capacity building in the pharmaceutical sector in the work to be undertaken pursuant to Article 66.2 of this Agreement, paragraph 7 of the Declaration on the TRIPS Agreement and Public Health and any other relevant work of the Council for TRIPS.

7. The Council for TRIPS shall review annually the functioning of the system with a view to ensuring its effective operation and shall annually report on its operation to the General Council.

Appendix to the annex to the TRIPS agreement

Assessment of Manufacturing Capacities in the Pharmaceutical Sector

Least-developed country Members are deemed to have insufficient or no manufacturing capacities in the pharmaceutical sector.

For other eligible importing Members insufficient or no manufacturing capacities for the product(s) in question may be established in either of the following ways:

(i) the Member in question has established that it has no manufacturing capacity in the pharmaceutical sector;

or

(ii) where the Member has some manufacturing capacity in this sector, it has examined this capacity and found that, excluding any capacity owned or controlled by the patent owner, it is currently insufficient for the purposes of meeting its needs. When it is established that such capacity has become sufficient to meet the Member's needs, the system shall no longer apply.

Chapter 10

LAYOUT-DESIGNS (TOPOGRAPHIES) OF INTEGRATED CIRCUITS

Relation to the IPIC Treaty

35. Members agree to provide protection to the layout-designs (topographies) of integrated circuits (referred to in this Agreement as 'layout-designs') in accordance with Articles 2 through 7 (other than paragraph 3 of Article 6), Article 12 and paragraph 3 of Article 16 of the Treaty on Intellectual Property in Respect of Integrated Circuits and, in addition, to comply with the following provisions.

WTO Members are bound to accord the treatment provided for in the TRIPS Agreement to the natural or legal persons that meet the criteria of eligibility for protection provided for under the Washington Treaty on Intellectual Property in Respect of Integrated Circuits signed in 1989 (hereinafter 'Washington Treaty') subject to the exceptions to the national treatment principle provided for therein (Article 3.1 of the TRIPS Agreement). In addition, in accordance with Article 2.2 of the TRIPS Agreement, '[N]othing in Parts I to IV of this Agreement shall derogate from existing obligations that Members may have to each other under . . . the Treaty on Intellectual Property in Respect of Integrated Circuits'.[1]

Section 6, Part II, of the TRIPS Agreement essentially obliges Members to comply with the Washington Treaty. This obligation applies irrespective of the fact that the Treaty never entered into force. Although the adoption of a treaty on this matter in the framework of WIPO was actively promoted by the US, an alliance between developing countries and European countries (the main users of integrated circuits) at the Washington Diplomatic Conference led to agreements by the majority of delegations that were unsatisfactory for the US and Japan (the main producers of such circuits at that time), which did not sign the Treaty. Probably as a result of this refusal, very few ratifications, insufficient to make the Treaty operative, took place.

The protection of integrated circuits is the newest chapter in the intellectual property field. The first country to introduce a *sui generis* regime with that purpose was the US in 1984, with the adoption of the Semiconductor Chip Protection Act (SCPA). It was followed by Japan, another major world producer

---

[1] See pp 46–51 above.

of integrated circuits, in May 1985.[2] The Japanese law was framed on the model of the SCPA. In December 1986, Sweden approved a law on layout-designs of integrated circuits (No 1425). Unlike the US and Japanese precedents, no registration system was established. Protection was granted from the time of creation (no fixation of the design in a semiconductor was required) for ten years after the first commercial exploitation of the layout-design. Almost simultaneously, the Council of the European Communities approved a Directive on the legal protection of topographies of semiconductor products.[3] One important innovative feature of the EC Directive was the adoption of a new terminology, 'topography', to define the subject matter of protection, which was subsequently applied in the relevant European laws and adopted by the TRIPS Agreement. The Directive required the existence of 'an intellectual effort' to obtain protection. A major reason for the rapid adoption of *sui generis* regimes after the adoption of the SCPA was the fact that the latter included stringent reciprocity rules which limited protection in the US to integrated circuits originating in countries where an equivalent protection was conferred.

With Section 6 of the TRIPS Agreement, the US and Japan obtained what they were unable to reach with the negotiation of the Washington Treaty. The Agreement gave them an opportunity to correct what they deemed weaknesses of the Washington Treaty, notably the provisions relating to compulsory licences, importation of products containing infringing semiconductors, and innocent infringement. The TRIPS Agreement brought about a significant departure from the Treaty provisions in these areas.

The submissions made by the US[4] and Japan[5] during the Uruguay Round clearly indicated their desire not to consider the Treaty as the basis for an international regulation on the matter. The Treaty was not even mentioned in their proposals. The Japanese proposal to GATT included various texts discussed at length during the Treaty negotiation. They were neatly based on the Treaty provisions, except in areas such as the duration (ten years instead of the eight years provided for by the Treaty) and in respect of the industrial articles that contain infringing chips. This was one important issue for the Japanese government which, in its view, was not appropriately dealt with and solved in the Washington Conference. Another important difference with the Treaty was that the proposal to GATT did not contain provisions on compulsory licences. The US submission also proposed a ten-year duration of protection, and made no reference at all to compulsory licences. It was categorical about the possibility for any country to make protection conditional on fixation or registration of the layout-design. Industrialized countries had opposed this position, held by a number of developing

---

[2] Act concerning the circuit layout of a semiconductor integrated circuit (Law No 43).
[3] See EC Directive 87/54/EC (December 1986), which adopted a *sui generis* legislation on integrated circuits. Other countries (eg Australia, Austria, Poland) also enacted *sui generis* regimes of protection.   [4] MTN.GNG/NG11/W/70, 11 May 1990.
[5] MTN.GNG/NG11/W/74, 15 May 1990.

countries, at the Washington Conference. The EC proposals, on their side, were explicitly based on the Treaty, though it specified a number of additional provisions (relating to duration, innocent infringement, and compulsory licences).

The terminology used in the Washington Treaty and in the TRIPS Agreement ('layout-designs (topographies)') reflects the influence of the EC legislation on the subject which, as noted, opted for the term 'topography' instead of 'design' in order to make clear the tri-dimensional nature of integrated circuits. 'Integrated circuits' are, in effect, tri-dimensional electronic circuits incorporated into a sub-strate, generally semiconductor material, such as silicon.[6] Integrated circuits in the form of microprocessors, dynamic memories, etc, constitute the core components of digital equipment and are present in a large variety of other products (such as automobiles, household equipment, watches). As a result, the intellectual property protection of such circuits, as contained in the TRIPS Agreement, may affect the trade in innumerable items.

In fact, the congressional history of the SCPA shows that copyright protection was considered the main candidate for the protection of integrated circuits. Two considerations seem to have been decisive, however, for the adoption of a *sui generis* regime. On the one hand, strong opposition by publishers emerged in connection with any extension of the concept of 'fair use' to cover 'reverse engineering'. On the other, American industry did not want the US to be constrained under the Universal Copyright Convention to grant protection to chips originating in countries which did not grant similar protection to those of American origin.[7] The *sui generis* regime for integrated circuits established under the SCPA presented various substantial differences with copyright legislation: the term of protection was shortened to ten years; registration is compulsory (within two years of the first 'commercial exploitation' of a mask work); a special provision allowing for 'reverse engineering' is contemplated; defences for an 'innocent infringer' are specifically set forth.

The protection of the layout-designs (topographies) of integrated circuits is to be granted, under the TRIPS Agreement, on the basis of the standards provided for by the Washington Treaty supplemented by a number of obligations, and subject to some exclusions, precisely in those areas that were highly controversial and which explained the rejection of the Treaty by the US and Japan. Thus, Article 35 of the TRIPS Agreement obliges Member States to protect the layout-designs (topographies) of integrated circuits in accordance with Articles 2–7 ('other than' Article 6.3), Article 12, and Article 16.3 of the Washington Treaty. Articles 2–7 provide for the substantive obligations.

---

[6] In the US, due to the properties of the materials used, legislation referred to 'semiconductors'. Materials other than semiconductors (such as sapphire) may also be used as a substrate. See, eg, J Dratler, *Intellectual Property Law: Commercial, Creative, and Industrial Property*, (1997), Intellectual Property Series, Law Journal Seminars-Papers, vol. 2, New York, pp 8–6.

[7] J Fort, 'La protection des semiconducteurs à l'étranger: situation aux Etats Unis et Japon', in *La protection des produits semi-conducteurs* (1988: Paris, Librairies Techniques), p 28.

Article 3(1)(b) of the Washington Treaty states that 'the right of the holder of the right in respect of an integrated circuit applies whether or not the integrated circuit is incorporated in an article'. This insertion, proposed by the Group of 77 during the Washington Treaty negotiations, was a compromise offered in order to avoid an explicit reference in Article 6 to industrial articles that incorporate infringing microchips.[8]

Article 3(1)(c) of the same Treaty allows any contracting party to limit protection to semiconductor integrated circuits. The Treaty definitions do not specify the type of material in which the layout may be incorporated. Most laws in force (in the US, Japan, EC, Denmark, etc) however, specifically refer to 'semiconductors'.

Article 3(2)(a) of the Washington Treaty determines the requirements for protection of a layout-design by combining the concepts of 'originality' and 'intellectual effort' (employed in the US and in the EEC Regulations, respectively). It also adds the condition, expressly provided for in the US and in the UK legislation, that the layout should not be 'commonplace among creators of layout-designs (topographies) and manufacturers of integrated circuits at the time of their creation'.

Article 4—also introduced upon a proposal of developing countries during the preparations for the Diplomatic Conference—expressly allows contracting parties to apply either a *sui generis* regime on layout-designs (topographies) or the law on copyright, patents, utility models, industrial designs, unfair competition, or any other law or a combination of any of those laws. While exercising this freedom, however, the contracting parties are bound to comply with the obligations under the Treaty. The TRIPS Agreement has not diminished such freedom.

According to the interpretation of the Director-General of WIPO, the effect of that Article is that:

if a Contracting Party chose to implement its obligations under the Treaty through a law made, totally or partly, on the basis that layout designs are works under the copyright law or are a subject matter of industrial property law, and that a Contracting Party is a party not only to the proposed Treaty but also to the Berne Convention or the Paris Convention, the said law must be compatible not only with the proposed Treaty but also with that or those Conventions. For example, if a Contracting Party considered layout designs to be works under its copyright law and was a party to both the proposed Treaty and the Berne Convention, layout designs would have to be protected without formalities (even though the proposed Treaty admits formalities) and for 50 years after the death of the author (even though the proposed Treaty admits a shorter period of protection). Or, if the Contracting Party is party to the proposed Treaty and the Paris Convention and protects layout designs by patents for inventions or utility models, layout designs would require the grant of a patent or other official certificate (even though the proposed Treaty admits protection without any procedure before a Government authority).[9]

---

[8] See the commentary on Article 36 of the TRIPS Agreement below.

[9] See WIPO, 1989. Diplomatic Conference for the Conclusion of a Treaty on the Protection of Intellectual Property in Respect of Integrated Circuits. Draft Treaty prepared under Rule 1(1) of the

Article 5 of the Washington Treaty requires the application of the national treatment principle. The SCPA contained a strict material reciprocity clause which had been regarded 'as the most blatant and severe stroke ever led against the principle of international treatment by a developed nation'.[10] That clause triggered, as mentioned, the rapid adoption of *sui generis* regimes of protection in other developed countries.[11] The purpose of the reciprocity clause precisely was

to incite foreign nations to explicitly grant protection for semiconductor chips—and this irrespectively of the question whether traditional laws were in fact inappropriate or not. In this respect, the legislative history contains sufficient material to believe that mere affirmative statements that protection would already be provided for by existing copyright laws would have just as few chances to be accepted as references made to unfair competition law. Consequently, in order not to have the products of their own nationals unprotected within the US and not to lose the US market, other chip-producing industrialised nations didn't have much choice but to comply with the SCPA's legal mechanism.[12]

A question may arise as to whether Members are bound not to apply Article 6.3 of the TRIPS Agreement or whether they are merely authorized not to do so. The wording of Article 35 ('Members agree to provide protection . . . in accordance with Articles 2 through 7 (other than Article 6.3)') suggests the former interpretation; that is, that Members agreed to exclude altogether the application of Article 6.3 of the Washington Treaty.

The non-applicability of Article 6.3[13] addresses one of the main concerns of the US with respect to the Washington Treaty as to the conditions for the grant of compulsory licences. This exclusion, however, does not prevent Members

Draft Rules of Procedure, by the Director-General of WIPO, Washington DC, 8 to 26 May, IPIC/DC/3.

[10] T Dreier, 'The Case of Computer Programs and Integrated Circuits', National Treatment, Reciprocity and Retorsion—New Tendencies for Improving the International Protection of Intellectual Property, Ringberg Castle, 13 to 16 July 1988, p 9.

[11] The regulations enacted in order to respond to the US law, with the exception of the Japanese law, also incorporated that condition.   [12] Dreier op. cit. (1988) above.

[13] Article 6(3): *[Measures Concerning Use Without the Consent of the Holder of the Right]* (a) Notwithstanding *paragraph (1)*, any Contracting Party may, in its legislation, provide for the possibility of its executive or judicial authority granting a non-exclusive license, in circumstances that are not ordinary, for the performance of any of the acts referred to in *paragraph (1)* by a third party without the authorization of the holder of the right ('non-voluntary license'), after unsuccessful efforts, made by the said third party in line with normal commercial practices, to obtain such authorization, where the granting of the non-voluntary license is found, by the granting authority, to be necessary to safeguard a national purpose deemed to be vital by that authority; the non-voluntary license shall be available for exploitation only in the territory of that country and shall be subject to the payment of an equitable remuneration by the third party to the holder of the right. (b) The provisions of this Treaty shall not affect the freedom of any Contracting Party to apply measures, including the granting, after a formal proceeding by its executive or judicial authority, of a non-voluntary license, in application of its laws in order to secure free competition and to prevent abuses by the holder of the right. (c) The granting of any non-voluntary license referred to in *subparagraph (a)* or *subparagraph (b)* shall be subject to judicial review. Any non-voluntary license referred to in *subparagraph (a)* shall be revoked when the conditions referred to in that subparagraph cease to exist.

from granting compulsory licences with regard to integrated circuits' layout-designs/topographies, as examined below.[14]

Like most national laws on the matter, the Washington Treaty spells out in Article 7(1) some conditions on which protection may be made conditional. This provision leaves freedom to grant protection since the creation of the design (as under the UK regulations), to subject it to 'commercial exploitation' (like most laws in force do) or even to registration (as in the US to institute civil actions, in Japan and other countries). Members could even opt, for instance, to require commercialization plus registration within certain periods as in the US and Japan, in order to confer or to maintain protection.

Article 7(2)(b) of the Treaty contains a limitation for those countries that at the same time require commercial exploitation and registration. The latter cannot be imposed before two years counting from the date of first commercialization anywhere in the world. This minimum period was necessary, according to some developed countries' delegations at the Diplomatic Conference, for the title-holder to prepare the information to be supplied or to present the samples of the microchips. That term may be, however, significantly longer than what is really needed for that purpose, particularly in view of the speed with which developments take place in this field.

In addition, Article 35 determines the applicability of Article 12[15] of the Washington Treaty, thereby making it clear that the conferred protection shall not affect the obligations that Members may have under the Paris or the Berne Convention.

Finally, Members are obligated to apply paragraph 3 of Article 16[16] of the Washington Treaty, which contains a provision of transitional nature, relating to the protection of layout-designs/topographies conferred before the entry into force of the Treaty.[17]

Scope of the protection

36. Subject to the provisions of paragraph 1 of Article 37, Members shall consider unlawful the following acts if performed without the authorization of the

[14] See commentary on Article 37.2 below.

[15] Article 12: 'This Treaty shall not affect the obligations that any Contracting Party may have under the Paris Convention for the Protection of Industrial Property or the Berne Convention for the Protection of Literary and Artistic Works.'

[16] Article 16(3) *[Protection of Layout-Designs (Topographies) Existing at Time of Entry Into Force]*: 'Any Contracting Party shall have the right not to apply this Treaty to any layout-design (topography) that exists at the time this Treaty enters into force in respect of that Contracting Party, provided that this provision does not affect any protection that such layout-design (topography) may, at that time, enjoy in the territory of that Contracting Party by virtue of international obligations other than those resulting from this Treaty or the legislation of the said Contracting Party.'

[17] In many countries layout-designs were, and continue to be, protected under copyright. The obligations provided for under the Berne Convention apply in this case.

right holder:[9] importing, selling, or otherwise distributing for commercial purposes a protected layout-design, an integrated circuit in which a protected layout-
design is incorporated, or an article incorporating such an integrated circuit only
in so far as it continues to contain an unlawfully reproduced layout-design.

   [9] The term 'right holder' in this Section shall be understood as having the same meaning
as the term 'holder of the right' in the IPIC Treaty.

Article 36 specifies the rights conferred with regard to layout-designs/ topographies
of integrated circuits. Its content must be examined in the light of the provisions
of the Washington Treaty.

   Article 6(1) of the Treaty enumerates—in a non-exhaustive way[18]—the acts
that require the title-holder's authorization. On the one hand, since non-fixed layout designs are eligible for protection, the reproduction 'by incorporation in an
integrated circuit or otherwise' will be unlawful if made without authorization
(except for non-original parts of the design). This provision, as drafted, comprises
the total or partial reproduction of the layout design on a mask, on a computer
tape, on paper, or by any other means, including the manufacture of a microchip.

   On the other, the Treaty deems unlawful the acts of 'importing, selling or otherwise distributing for commercial purposes a protected layout-design (topography)
or an integrated circuit in which a protected layout-design (topography) is incorporated' (Article 6.1(a)(ii)) if made without authorization.

   Article 6(2)(a) authorizes a third party's acts of 'evaluation, analysis, research or
teaching'. The 'evaluation' (or 'reverse engineering') of integrated circuits has been
common practice in the semiconductor industry and was already allowed, albeit
with some differences, by the SCPA and other national laws enacted on the matter
before the adoption of the Washington Treaty. The reproduction of a layout-
design, for instance, at a university laboratory for purposes of training, is also to be
deemed legal.

   Article 6(2)(b) clarifies the extent of the title-holder rights in respect of another
layout-design which is identical. Those rights cannot be exercised against a third
party if such a design has been independently created. A fortiori, the same rule
would apply if the result is not an identical but a similar or substantially similar
design independently developed. This provision is a strong indication of the rad-
ical difference existing between the rights conferred under the Treaty and the protection granted under patent law and other titles of industrial property. The rights
recognized under the Treaty do not confer exclusivity either on the functionalities
of the design or on a specific expression thereof. They only protect, in essence,
against copying; more precisely, the protection is only against slavish copying and
not against that based on an own 'intellectual effort'.

   [18] In accordance with Article 6.1(b) of the Washington Treaty '[A]ny Contracting Party shall be
free to consider unlawful also acts other than those specified in *subparagraph (a)* if performed without
the authorization of the holder of the right'.

Several observations are relevant with regard to Article 35 of the TRIPS Agreement. First, unlike other provisions in Part II, Article 35 neither refers to 'exclusive' rights nor to the 'owner' of the layout-design. Like Article 6 of the Washington Treaty, Article 36 of the Agreement alludes to 'unlawful acts' leaving Members room to determine the specific nature of the rights to be granted. In addition, Article 35 employs, with regard to the beneficiaries of protection, the same terminology as the Washington Treaty: 'holder of the right'. This concept is defined, in accordance with footnote (9) to Article 35, as the natural person who, or the legal entity which, according to the applicable law, is to be regarded as the beneficiary of the protection referred to in Article 6' (Article 2(iii) of the Washington Treaty).

Second, Article 35 of the TRIPS Agreement reproduces Article 6.1(a)(ii) of the Washington Treaty in determining that the unlawful acts may consist of 'importing, selling, or otherwise distributing for commercial purposes'. In contrast to patent rights, this provision does not cover 'making, using, offering for sale'. In addition, such acts may be unlawful only if made 'for commercial purposes', a qualification absent in the case of patents. Needless to say, although no reference is made to Article 6 of the TRIPS Agreement (as is done in the case of Article 28.1), the rights granted with regard to layout-designs are equally subject to the principle of exhaustion, as determined by the national law. Members are free, in particular, to apply a principle of international exhaustion.[19]

Third, the unlawful acts may refer to

- a protected layout-design;
- an integrated circuit in which a protected layout-design is incorporated; or
- an article incorporating such an integrated circuit only in so far as it continues to contain an unlawfully reproduced layout-design.

While the two first situations are covered in the Washington Treaty, the last one (an article incorporating a protected integrated circuit) represents a Washington-plus provision, since the Diplomatic Conference did not accept the US and Japanese proposals[20] to extend protection to articles incorporating layout-designs. Article 36 thus fixed what was seen by those countries as a gap in the Treaty.

The extension of protection to industrial articles required by the TRIPS Agreement is, however, subject to a determination that said articles continue 'to

---

[19] Article 6(5) of the Washington Treaty introduces the exception of 'exhaustion of rights', as a facultative provision for Contracting States. It stipulates the following: Article 6(5): '*[Exhaustion of Rights]* Notwithstanding *paragraph (1)(a)(ii)*, any Contracting Party may consider lawful the performance, without the authorization of the holder of the right, of any of the acts referred to in that paragraph where the act is performed in respect of a protected layout-design (topography), or in respect of an integrated circuit in which such a layout-design (topography) is incorporated, that has been put on the market by, or with the consent of, the holder of the right'.

[20] With the exception of the regulations on integrated circuits of the United States and Japan, other regulations adopted at the time of the negotiation of the Washington Treaty did not mention the case of industrial articles.

contain an unlawfully reproduced layout-design'. A direct implication of Article 36 is that the title-holder cannot exercise his rights with regard to the import- ation and sale of industrial articles that lawfully contain protected layouts/integ- rated circuits imported, sold, or otherwise distributed with commercial intent; in other words, his rights are exhausted both nationally and internationally with first sale of articles that incorporate a legitimately reproduced layout-design/ topography.

Such extension of protection to articles that incorporate a layout-design/topog- raphy was questioned by developing countries during the negotiation of the Washington Treaty, due to the difficulties that importers and distributors of elec- tronics and other goods containing semiconductors were likely to face to establish whether such goods contain or not infringing layout-designs/topographies. Developing countries considered it unreasonable to treat on the same footing the cases of sale, importation, and other forms of distribution of pirated chips and those where the latter are incorporated in industrial articles. While accepting the principle that the right of the title-holder does not terminate with the incorp- oration of a chip in an article, those countries did not want to accept that the title- holder could have exactly the same legal actions in these two different situations.[21] In fact, it may be extremely difficult to determine whether chips imported or incorporated in imported products are infringing or not. As noted in the case of Canada,

There is also a significant technical hurdle to overcome in demonstrating infringement. Any infringing topography will be contained in an integrated circuit product probably produced in a foreign country and imported into Canada. In order to demonstrate that the integrated circuit product contains a topography that is identical to the plantiff's, the chip must be reverse engineered, a process by which each layer is determined. This is an extremely expensive activity performed by speciality engineering firms. The results are never 100 percent accurate and require significant interpretation by an expert.

The very technical nature of the subject matter also raises considerable uncertainty in the litigation process. Federal Courts judges of varying backgrounds often struggle with technical subject matter presented during patent infringement trials. The unique nature of an integrated circuit will further complicate their lives. Ultimately, any trial will become a "battle between experts" as to the interpretation of an alleged infringing integrated circuit layout, with the judge caught in the middle trying to make sense of the relatively arcane field of integrated circuit design.[22]

Finally, the first sentence of Article 36 makes clear that the conferred rights can- not be exercised in cases of *bona fide* infringement in accordance with Article 37, as examined below.

[21] See C Correa, 'Legal Protection of the Layout Designs of Integrated Circuits: the WIPO Treaty', (1990), European Intellectual Property Review, vol. 12, No 6 (June), p 198.
[22] A Millard, 'Integrated Circuit Topography Protection: Why Bother?', (2004), Canadian Intellectual Property Review, vol. 21 No 1 (NW 2004), p 136.

Acts not requiring the authorization of the right-holder

37.1. Notwithstanding Article 36, no Member shall consider unlawful the performance of any of the acts referred to in that Article in respect of an integrated
circuit incorporating an unlawfully reproduced layout-design or any article incorporating such an integrated circuit where the person performing or ordering such
acts did not know and had no reasonable ground to know, when acquiring the
integrated circuit or article incorporating such an integrated circuit, that it incorporated an unlawfully reproduced layout-design. Members shall provide that,
after the time that such person has received sufficient notice that the layout-
design was unlawfully reproduced, that person may perform any of the acts with
respect to the stock on hand or ordered before such time, but shall be liable to pay
to the right holder a sum equivalent to a reasonable royalty such as would be
payable under a freely negotiated licence in respect of such a layout-design.

2. The conditions set out in subparagraphs (a) through (k) of Article 31 shall
apply *mutatis mutandis* in the event of any non-voluntary licensing of a layout-
design or of its use by or for the government without the authorization of the
right holder.

Article 37.1 carves out an exception to the conferred rights. In accordance with
this provision, after the *bona fide* acquirer has received 'sufficient notice that the
layout-design was unlawfully reproduced', he may continue the acts of importing,
selling or otherwise distributing (for commercial purpose) but only 'with respect
to the stock on hand or ordered before such time' and subject to payment to the
right holder of 'a sum equivalent to a reasonable royalty such as would be payable
under a freely negotiated licence in respect of such a layout-design'.

This provision means that the *bona fide* acquirer cannot continue with the covered acts with respect to integrated circuits or products not in stock at the time of
or ordered after the notification. It sets as the standard to determine 'a reasonable
royalty' what would be payable under a 'freely negotiated licence'. However, this is
an inappropriate standard since an acquirer of industrial goods that incorporate
integrated circuits would very rarely enter into a licensing agreement with the supplier of such circuits. It would have been more logical to require payment of a reasonable royalty from the manufacturer of such goods or of the parts that
incorporate the protected layout-designs.

Article 37.1 also represents a 'Washington-plus' solution. The Washington
Treaty had left this issue open to national legislation, given the resistance of developing countries to accept that the *bona fide* acquirer—and not the supplier—of
the infringing circuits or industrial goods be made subject to an obligation to
compensate the title-holder of the layout-design/topography.

Article 37.2 makes it clear that protected layout-designs/topographies can be subjected to compulsory licences, in accordance with the conditions set out in subparagraphs (a) to (k) of Article 31 of the TRIPS Agreement. These conditions shall apply
mutatis mutandis in the event of any compulsory licensing of a layout-design/

topography or of its use by or for the government without the authorization of the right-holder. It should be recalled that Article 31(c) of the Agreement limits the grounds admissible for the granting of compulsory licences of patents in respect of 'semi-conductor technology' to those relating to anti-competitive practices and use by governments for non commercial purposes.[23] However, this limitation does not apply to layout-designs/topographies since they do not constitute semi-conductor technology, but the form that can be imparted to integrated circuits built on different substrates.

Term of protection

38.1. In Members requiring registration as a condition of protection, the term of protection of layout-designs shall not end before the expiration of a period of 10 years counted from the date of filing an application for registration or from the first commercial exploitation wherever in the world it occurs.

2. In Members not requiring registration as a condition for protection, layout-designs shall be protected for a term of no less than 10 years from the date of the first commercial exploitation wherever in the world it occurs.

3. Notwithstanding paragraphs 1 and 2, a Member may provide that protection shall lapse 15 years after the creation of the layout-design.

Finally, the minimum term of protection is extended by Article 38 of the TRIPS Agreement from eight years (as provided for under the Washington Treaty) to ten years. Ten years was the standard set out by the SCPA and also adopted by the regulations passed in other developed countries. In addition, Article 38 of TRIPS specifies the dates from which such term is to be counted, in cases where registration is required as a condition of protection (from the date of application or first commercial exploitation in the world) and where such a condition is not imposed (from the date of first commercial exploitation in the world).[24] In any case, Members may limit the duration to fifteen years after the creation of the layout-design/topography.

In view of the little judicial activity under the SCPA, Siegle and Laurie[25] may have been right in arguing that it was 'a solution in search of a problem'. One of the few cases brought to the courts in the US involved two American firms, Brooktree Corp and Advanced Micro Devices Inc. The plaintiff claimed that

---

[23] The restriction regarding the grounds for granting compulsory licences in the case of 'semiconductor technology' was one of the few changes introduced in December 1993, in response to a request of the United States, to the compromise draft of the TRIPS Agreement that had been submitted by the Director General of GATT in December 1991.

[24] This is also an important difference with the Washington Treaty, which is silent about the date from which the term is to be counted. This gives contracting parties freedom to apply different solutions, such as from first commercial exploitation, application for registration or registration.

[25] D Siegel and R Laurie, 'Beyond Microcode: *Alloy v Ultrateck*. The First Attempt to Extend Copyright Protection to Computer Hardware', (1989) The Computer Lawyer, vol. 6, No 4, April, p 14.

Advanced Micro Devices had copied two of the former's chips that represented 40 per cent of its sales.[26]

The encouragement of innovation was presented as one of the main reasons for the adoption of a special regime of protection. The argument is, nevertheless, far from being proven. In fact, studies on the semiconductor industry have shown that gaining lead time and exploiting learning curve advantages are the primary methods for appropriating the returns of investments in R&D. According to Levin et al,

the premise that stronger protection will always improve the incentives to innovate is also open to challenge. Unimpeded diffusion of existing technology is immediately beneficial not only for consumers but also for those who would improve that technology. Because technological advance is often an interactive, cumulative process, strong protection of individual achievements may slow the general advance. The semiconductor industry of the 1950s and 1960s provides an excellent example of rapid progress in a cumulative technology that might have been impossible under a regime that strongly protected intellectual property.[27]

Annex

Negotiating history[28]

In his 23 July 1990 report on the status of work in the TRIPS Negotiating Group, the Chairman (Lars E R Anell) presented two sets of proposals. In an Annex to the report, he presented a composite text that was taken from various proposals by delegations to the Negotiating Group, indicating the source of each proposal by numerical reference to the source document.

Composite text of July 23 1990[29]

Any PARTY shall consider unlawful the following acts if performed without the authorisation of the holder of the right:

1A.1 Incorporating the layout-design (topography) in an integrated circuit;

1A.2 Importing, selling, or otherwise distributing for commercial purposes a protected layout-design (topography), an integrated circuit in which a protected layout-design (topography) is incorporated or a product incorporating such an integrated circuit.

---

[26] See C Correa op. cit. (1990), p 196.

[27] R Levin, A Klovorick, R Nelson, and S Winter, *Appropriating the Returns from Industrial Research and Development*, (1987), Brooking Papers on Economic Activity, p 3.

[28] For an analysis of the negotiating history, see UNCTAD-ICTSD, *Resource Book on TRIPS and Development* (2005: New York, Cambridge University Press), pp 505–29.

[29] Chairman's Report to the GNG, Status of Work in the Negotiating Group, Negotiating Group on Trade-Related Aspects of Intellectual Property Rights, including Trade in Counterfeit Goods, MTN. GNG/NG11/W/76, 23 July 1990, presented by the Chairman of the TRIPS Negotiating Group (Lars E R Anell). Alternatives 'A' correspond to texts from developed countries and 'B' from developing countries.

1A PARTIES may exempt from liability under their law the reproduction of a layout-design (topography) for purposes of teaching, analysis, or evaluation in the course of preparation of a layout-design (topography) that is itself original. This provision shall replace Articles (2)(a) and (b) of the Washington Treaty.

2A The act of importing, selling, or otherwise distributing for commercial purposes [an unlawfully reproduced layout-design (topography),] [an integrated circuit incorporating an unlawfully reproduced layout-design (topography) or] a product incorporating an unlawfully reproduced layout-design (topography) [shall] [may] not itself be considered an infringement if, at the time of performance of the act in question, the person performing the act [establishes that he] did not know and had [no reasonable grounds to believe] that the layout-design (topography) was unlawfully reproduced. However, PARTIES [shall] [may] provide that, after the time [of receipt of notice] [that the person comes to know or has reasonable grounds to believe] that the layout-design (topography) was unlawfully reproduced, he may perform any of the acts with respect to the stock on hand or ordered before such time, but shall be liable to pay [a reasonable royalty] [an equitable remuneration] to the right holder.

3Aa Non-voluntary licences shall not be granted for purposes or on terms which could result in a distortion of international trade.

3Ab The conditions set out at point [—] of Section 5 above shall apply *mutatis mutandis* to the grant of any non-voluntary licences for layout-designs (topographies).

3Ac Non-voluntary licences shall not be granted for layout-designs (topographies).

A(i) In PARTIES requiring registration as a condition of protection, layout-designs (topographies) shall be protected for a term of no less than 10 years from the date of [filing an application for registration] [registration] or of the first commercial exploitation wherever in the world it occurs, whichever is the earlier [, except that if neither of the above events occurs within 15 years of the first fixation or encoding there shall no longer be any obligation to provide protection].

(ii) In PARTIES not requiring registration as a condition for protection, layout-designs (topographies) shall be protected for a term of no less than 10 years from the date of the first commercial exploitation wherever in the world it occurs [, except that if a layout-design (topography) is not so exploited within a period of 15 years of the first fixation or encoding, there shall no longer be any obligation to provide protection].

[(iii) If registration is required by law, and no application is filed, the protection of the layout-design (topography) shall lapse after two years from the date of the first commercial exploitation wherever in the world it occurs.

(iv) Notwithstanding (i), (ii) and (iii) above, protection shall lapse 15 years after the creation of the layout-design (topography).]

Draft text transmitted to the Brussels Ministerial Conference (December 1990)

Subject to the provisions of Art. [37](1) below, PARTIES shall consider unlawful the following acts if performed without the authorisation of the holder of the right: importing, selling, or otherwise distributing for commercial purposes a protected layout-design, an integrated circuit in which a protected layout-design is incorporated [, or an article incorporating such an integrated circuit. Rights extend to an article incorporating an integrated circuit only insofar as it continues to contain an unlawfully reproduced layout-design.]

1. Notwithstanding Art. [36] above, no PARTY shall be obliged to consider unlawful the performance of any of the acts referred to in that paragraph in respect of an integrated circuit incorporating an unlawfully reproduced layout-design [or any article incorporating such an integrated circuit] where the person performing or ordering such acts did not know and had no reasonable ground to know, when acquiring the integrated circuit [or article incorporating such an integrated circuit], that it incorporated an unlawfully reproduced layout-design. [PARTIES shall provide that, after the time that such person has received sufficient notice that the layout-design was unlawfully reproduced, he may perform any of the acts with respect to the stock on hand or ordered before such time, but shall be liable to pay to the holder of the right a sum equivalent to a reasonable royalty in a freely negotiated licence in respect of the layout-design.]

2. The conditions set out in sub-paragraphs (a)-(1) and (o) of Art. [31] above shall apply *mutatis mutandis* in the event of any non-voluntary licensing of a layout-design or of its use by or for the government without the authorisation of the right holder.

   1. In PARTIES requiring registration as a condition of protection, the term of protection of layout-designs shall not end before the expiration of a period of 10 years counted from the date of filing an application for registration or from the first commercial exploitation wherever in the world it occurs.

   2. In PARTIES not requiring registration as a condition for protection, layout-designs shall be protected for a term of no less than 10 years from the date of the first commercial exploitation wherever in the world it occurs.

   3. Notwithstanding paragraphs 1 and 2, a PARTY may provide that protection shall lapse 15 years after the creation of the layout-design.

Chapter 11

UNDISCLOSED INFORMATION

Protection under unfair competition

39.1. In the course of ensuring effective protection against unfair competition as provided in Article 10*bis* of the Paris Convention (1967), Members shall protect undisclosed information in accordance with paragraph 2 and data submitted to governments or governmental agencies in accordance with paragraph 3.

Section 7 of Part II of the TRIPS Agreement contains specific provisions on 'undisclosed information'. This is the first international regime on undisclosed information and, in this sense, it is one of the most significant innovations brought about by the TRIPS Agreement. Article 39.1 stipulates that 'in the course of ensuring effective protection against unfair competition as provided in Article 10*bis* of the Paris Convention', parties shall protect undisclosed information and the 'data submitted to governments or governmental agencies' as a condition for approving the marketing of pharmaceutical and agrochemical products.

Although Article 39.1 refers to 'undisclosed information' and to 'undisclosed test' or other 'data submitted' to governments as two separate issues, it seems clear that in the latter case the data also need to be 'undisclosed' in order to be covered under the terms of the Agreement, as elaborated below in this chapter.

According to Article 1.2 of the TRIPS Agreement, undisclosed information is a category of 'intellectual property', like patents, trademarks, and other modalities dealt with by the Agreement. There has traditionally been resistance in some academic circles to consider such information on the same footing as the traditional forms of protection of industrial property.[1] It has rather been seen as one of the cases where unfair competition rules may apply. Moreover, the application of the concept of 'property' in undisclosed information has generally been rejected under continental law concepts.

In contrast, a majority of common-law commentators have adopted the theory of the existence of property rights in secret information (or 'know-how'). This divergence is largely grounded on the different concepts of 'property' predominant in these systems of law. While under continental law the recognition of property

---

[1] See, eg, C Correa, 'Legal nature and contractual conditions in know-how transactions', (1981), The Georgia Journal of International and Comparative Law, vol. 11, No. 3.

rights is limited by the principle of *numerus clausus*,[2] common-law judges are free to recognize new types of property in equity.[3] The concept encompasses both rights *in rem* as well as any legally enforceable claim and interest, including a diversity of rights *in personam*. The concept of property is so broad that it has been deemed applicable even to the expectations and privileges derived from the fact of belonging to the white race,[4] and distinguishing between property and other rights has become extremely difficult.[5]

Despite the fact that the concept of 'property' of trade secrets is prevalent in common-law countries, its application has been controversial there. For instance, it has been held that

neither information in general, nor confidential information in particular, are property in the strict understanding of that term, and that terminology associated with property while maybe useful in a descriptive sense, is best avoided in the interests of conceptual certainty.[6]

Further, in a landmark decision in *Du Pont Powder Company v Masland*, the US Supreme Court stated:

The word property as applied to trademarks and trade secrets is an unanalyzed expression of certain secondary consequences of the primary fact that the law makes some rudimentary requirements of good faith. Whether the plaintiffs have any valuable secret or not, the defendant knows the facts, whatever they are, through a special confidence he accepted. The property may be denied but the confidence cannot be. Therefore, the starting point for the present matter is not the property or due process of law, but that the defendant stood in confidential relations with the plaintiffs, or one of them.[7]

Two general considerations are relevant with regard to Article 39.1. First, the Agreement subjects the legal treatment of 'undisclosed information' to the discipline of unfair competition, as regulated by Article 10*bis* of the Paris Convention. With this approach, the Agreement clearly avoids the treatment of undisclosed information as a 'property', as suggested by the US in some early informal

---

[2] For instance, the Court of Justice of the Andean Community stated—in interpreting the Community law implemeting Article 39 of the TRIPS Agreement—that the protection of trade secrets does not materialize through a property right in the secret information (Proceso No 37-IP-2003, 'Interpretación prejudicial de las disposiciones previstas en los artículos 78 y 79 de la Decisión 344 de la Comisión del Acuerdo de Cartagena, solicitada por el Consejo de Estado de la República de Colombia, Sala de lo Contencioso Administrativo, Sección Primera, e interpretación de oficio de los artículos 72 y 73 *eiusdem* (Parte actora: sociedad PFIZER S.A. Caso: 'Registros sanitarios del producto VINTIX COMPRIMIDOS RECUBIERTOS'. Expediente interno No 6015), available at <http://intranet.comunidadandina.org/Documentos/procesos/37-ip-2002.doc> (last accessed on 24 June 2006).

[3] In the US, for instance, trade secret law is based on court decisions. Although each state can establish its own trade secret law, most states have adopted the definition of *Restatement of the Law of Torts* (see footnote 12 below).

[4] See, eg, S Ackerman, 'The White Supremacist Status Quo: How the American Legal System Perpetuates Racism as Seen Through the Lens of Property Law' (1999) 21 Hamline J Pub & Pol, p 137.

[5] See, eg, KJ Vandele, 'The New Property of Nineteenth Century: The Development of the Modern Concept of Property', (1980) Buffalo LR, pp 325–67.

[6] A Coleman, *The Legal Protection of Trade Secrets* (1992: London; Sweet & Maxwell), p 8.

[7] 244 US 100, 61 L Ed 1016, 37 S Ct 575 (1917).

submissions. The fact that the 'undisclosed information' is deemed to be a 'category' of intellectual property, hence, does not imply the existence of a property right. It is generally accepted that unfair competition is one of the disciplines of industrial property,[8] and Article 1.2 should be interpreted in this sense. Article 39 does not imply any obligation to confer exclusive rights on undisclosed information, but just to protect it against unfair commercial practices.

The non-proprietary nature of the rights recognized under Article 39 seems to be confirmed by the terminology used therein. Unlike the provisions on patents and trademarks, that Article does not refer to the 'owner' of the undisclosed information but to persons who have 'information lawfully within their control'. Control does not imply ownership or property. Strictly speaking, undisclosed information is a mere factual situation eventually subject, under certain circumstances, to the indirect protection conferred by unfair competition law, and to the contractual conditions laid down by the relevant parties to preserve its secret character or implement its transfer. As stated by Laquis, 'unpatented technical knowledge constitutes an objective fact, however devoid of legal status as long as it is not recognized by the law and, hence, cannot be opposed to third parties'.[9]

Second, the text does not use the terms 'know-how' or 'trade-secrets', which are usual to refer to secret information of technical or commercial value, and it does not contain either a definition of 'undisclosed information'. The difficulties in finding a common and acceptable understanding on what those notions mean, favoured the adoption of the terminology used, which does not characterize the contents of the information, but just its 'undisclosed' character.

The way in which Article 10*bis* of the Paris Convention is referenced in Article 39.1 is of critical importance for the interpretation of the content of the obligations set out in paragraphs 2 and 3 of the same Article. The negotiating parties wanted to make clear that such obligations do not add to but develop those already contained in the Paris Convention. In accordance with Article 39.1, in effect, protection should be conferred '[I]n the course of ensuring effective protection against unfair competition as provided in Article 10*bis* of the Paris Convention (1967) . . .'. The text is unusually clear in indicating that the obligations under Article 39 do not go beyond what is already contained in that Convention. Since the Agreement, thus, only develops obligations prescribed in Article 10*bis*, any reading of Article 39 requiring Members to establish some form of exclusive rights (as argued by the US and the pharmaceutical industry with regard to test data[10]) is fundamentally inconsistent with the treaty language.

---

[8] See, eg, S Ladas, *Patents, Trademarks and Related Rights—National and International Protection* (1975: Cambridge, Harvard University Press), p 427.

[9] M Laquis, 'Revisión del Convenio de París en el Marco latinoamericano, La Propiedad Industrial y el Abuso del Derecho: Problemas de la Transferencia de Tecnología (know-how) a los Países/en Desarrollo, La declaración de Méjico', (1976) 9 Revista del Derecho Comercial y de las Obligaciones, p 488.   [10] See p 389 below.

Article 10*bis* of the Paris Convention states:

(1) The countries of the Union are bound to assure to nationals of such countries effective protection against unfair competition.

(2) Any act of competition contrary to honest practices in industrial or commercial matters constitutes an act of unfair competition.

(3) The following in particular shall be prohibited:

    (i) all acts of such a nature as to create confusion by any means whatever with the establishment, the goods, or the industrial or commercial activities, of a competitor;

    (ii) false allegations in the course of trade of such a nature as to discredit the establishment, the goods, or the industrial or commercial activities, of a competitor;

    (iii) indications or allegations the use of which in the course of trade is liable to mislead the public as to the nature, the manufacturing process, the characteristics, the suitability for their purpose, or the quantity, of the goods.

Given the relationship between Article 39 of the TRIPS Agreement and Article 10*bis* of the Paris Convention, the interpretation of the latter, including its negotiating history, are of crucial importance to interpret Article 39 in accordance with the Vienna Convention on the Law of the Treaties.[11]

Conditions for protection

39.2. Natural and legal persons shall have the possibility of preventing information lawfully within their control from being disclosed to, acquired by, or used by others without their consent in a manner contrary to honest commercial practices[10] so long as such information:

(a) **is secret in the sense that it is not, as a body or in the precise configuration and assembly of its components, generally known among or readily accessible to persons within the circles that normally deal with the kind of information in question;**

(b) **has commercial value because it is secret; and**

(c) **has been subject to reasonable steps under the circumstances, by the person lawfully in control of the information, to keep it secret.**

    [10] For the purpose of this provision, 'a manner contrary to honest commercial practices' shall mean at least practices such as breach of contract, breach of confidence and inducement to breach, and includes the acquisition of undisclosed information by third parties who knew, or were grossly negligent in failing to know, that such practices were involved in the acquisition.

Article 39.2 specifies the conditions that the information needs to meet in order to be deemed 'undisclosed' and protectable: it should be secret, possess a commercial value, and be subject to reasonable steps, under the circumstances, to

    [11] See Chapter 14.

be kept secret. The conditions set forth are substantially based on US legislation on the matter, as enacted by many States of the Union.[12]

Unlike other provisions in the TRIPS Agreement, Article 39.2 clarifies that both natural and legal persons can institute legal actions based on unfair competition disciplines regarding undisclosed information. The wording 'shall have the possibility of preventing' is indicative of the broad room that Members enjoy to determine the means to be applied to prevent the enumerated practices. It makes clear that there is no requirement to establish exclusive rights, as such rights are not provided for in the context of unfair competition disciplines. Instead, Members may impose civil or commercial sanctions, or criminal sanctions as is the case in many jurisdictions.

Although Article 39.2 does not define the nature of the rights to be conferred, it indicates which are the acts that holders of undisclosed information should be entitled to prevent. They are:

- disclosure;
- acquisition; or
- use

of the information by others provided that such acts take place without the title-holder's consent and 'in a manner contrary to honest commercial practices'.

The footnote to Article 39.2 specifies some practices that 'at least' are to be considered as 'contrary to honest practices', thus reducing possible divergences in the application of this provision. They include 'breach of contract, breach of confidence and inducement to breach'. The obligation not to disclose aims to protect the very essence of undisclosed information: its secret character. Once this character is lost, by whatever means, including by fraudulent acts, no further protection can be claimed. If disclosure to the public has taken place without the authorization of the person who controlled the information, he can seek compensation of damages or other punishment, as available under the applicable law, but the 'undisclosed' nature of the information cannot be restored, and any person would be authorized to use it freely.

The concept of disclosure as used in Article 39.2 also encompasses, however, cases in which the information is transferred to a third party (eg a competitor)

---

[12] In accordance with the definition provided by the US *Restatement of the Law of Torts* 'a trade secret may consist of any formula, pattern, device or compilation of information which is used in one's business and which gives him an opportunity to obtain an advantage over competitors who do not know or use it'. In addition, the *Restatement* lists certain factors to be considered in determining the existence of a trade secret. These are the following:

  i) the extent to which the information is known outside the business to which it refers;
 ii) the extent to which it is known by employees and others involved in the business;
iii) the extent of measures taken by the owner to guard the secrecy of the information;
iv) the value of the information to the owner and his competitors;
 v) the amount of effort or money expended by him in developing the information; and
vi) the ease or difficulty with which the information could properly be acquired or duplicated by others (Section 757, Comment (b) (1939)).

without losing its secret character. In this case, both the transferor and the trans-feree of the information may be deemed to have engaged in misconduct. Not all disclosures amount, however, to acts of unfair competition. They should be against honest practices.[13]

The footnote to Article 39.2 also refers to the 'acquisition by third parties of undisclosed information knowing—or being grossly negligent in failing to know—that such unfair practices were involved in the acquisition'. An illegitim-ate acquisition may take place through the transfer of the information by some-body in breach of his duty of confidence, or through the acquirer's own means, for instance, espionage. The acquisition of undisclosed information, however, only constitutes an unfair commercial practice when the acquirer knew or should have reasonably known, in the circumstances of the particular case, that access to the information constituted an unfair practice. The concept of gross negligence is used in both common law and continental law systems,[14] but its precise meaning may vary across different jurisdictions.

Finally, the 'use' of undisclosed information might constitute a dishonest prac-tice when it derives from a non-authorized acquisition of the information, and while the information remains secret. After disclosure (for whatever reason) the use of the information would be licit. In addition, the same information can be used by any third party if independently developed or obtained from another source. As mentioned, the protection of undisclosed information does not confer exclusive rights.

In all three cases (disclosure, acquisition, use) the right-holder could take action only if the acts were made (1) without their consent; and (2) 'in a manner contrary to honest commercial practices'. A key element in establishing the existence of unfair competition is what 'honest commercial practice' means in this context.

What is 'honest' depends on the values of a particular society at a given point in time. There is no absolute, universal rule to determine when certain practices should be deemed commercially dishonest and, hence 'unfair'. Ladas addressed this issue as follows.

Morality, which is the source of the law of unfair competition, is a simple notion in theory only. In fact it reflects customs and habits anchored in the spirit of a particular community. There is no clearly objective standard of feeling, instincts, or attitudes toward a certain conduct. Therefore, specific prescriptions involving uniform evaluation of certain acts are extremely difficult... The pressures existing in the various countries for the suppression of acts of unfair competition differ greatly. Generally, the development of the law of unfair competition depends on active and intense competition in the marketplace by competing enterprises. It is the pressure of conflicting interests which leads to the establishment of clear rules of law. This pressure is not uniform in all countries and indeed it is evolving continuously.[15]

---

[13] See below the discussion on this concept.
[14] See, eg, D Gervais, *The TRIPS Agreement. Drafting history and analyst* (2003: London, Sweet & Maxwell, 2nd ed), p 276.   [15] S Ladas op. cit. (1975), vol. III, pp 1685–6.

We look for a standard by which we may judge the act complained of. This is an objective standard: the honest practices in the course of trade in the particular community and at the particular time.[16]

Which practices can be deemed dishonest in relation to undisclosed information, hence, will vary among Members.[17] Different countries can judge certain situations differently, depending on the moral standards that the society applies. This latitude is only limited by the footnote to Article 39.2 which, as mentioned, establishes a non-exhaustive enumeration of practices deemed to be 'contrary to honest commercial practices' (breach of contract, breach of confidence, and inducement to breach, and includes the acquisition of undisclosed information by third parties who knew, or were grossly negligent in failing to know, that such practices were involved in the acquisition).

Except for this limitation, there was no attempt in the negotiation of the TRIPS Agreement to go beyond the Paris Convention in determining minimum standards with regard to unfair competition. Article 39 relies on the Convention for the determination of which conducts may be deemed commercially unfair. Said Article only sets out the *conditions* under which undisclosed information is to be protected against unfair commercial use. The modest reach of the TRIPS Agreement in this regard may be explained by the profound differences in comparative law with regard to the treatment of unfair competition.[18]

There is no secret and, hence, no protectable information, when the information is either (a) generally known by; or (b) readily accessible to 'persons within the circles that normally deal with the kind of information in question'. This means that an information may not be currently known to such persons, but it would not be deemed secret if it is 'readily available', for instance, via reverse engineering of products on the market.[19]

There are three conditions set out by the TRIPS Agreement for the protection of undisclosed information.

First, the information must be 'secret'. This concept is logically understood in relative terms, 'in the sense that it is not generally known . . . among or readily

---

[16] Idem, p 1689.

[17] Bodenhausen held that the judicial or administrative authorities 'will also have to take into account honest practices established in international trade' (G Bodenhausen, *WIPO Guide to the Paris Convention*, 1968 WIPO, p 144). However, these practices refer to those that are internationally accepted in inter-country trade, but not to those that developed in the domestic context, for instance, regarding the treatment of information submitted for the marketing approval of pharmaceutical and agrochemical products.

[18] See, eg, A Kamperman Sanders, *Unfair Competition Law* (1997: Oxford, Clarendon Press), pp 6–65.

[19] Reverse engineering is accepted in many jurisdictions, for instance, in the US, as a legitimate means to obtain access to embedded information. The NAFTA definition of a trade secret also seems to track the majority United States' rule that reverse engineering, if no more than nominally difficult, destroys the secret which is embodied in the goods. See, eg, R Neff and F Smallson, *NAFTA. Protecting and Enforcing Intellectual Property Rights in North America* (1994: Colorado, Shepard's), p 102.

accessible to persons within the circles that normally deal with the kind of information in question'.

Hence, information that is known to a number of persons in a group that normally deals with the kind of information in question may be deemed secret, if such knowledge is not generalized.

In addition, the secret character may be retained if the information is known 'as a body' but not 'in the precise configuration and assembly of its components'.

Second, an essential condition is that the information must have 'commercial value *because* it is secret' (emphasis added). This means that the value of the information must be actual, and not merely potential, and directly derive from its secret character. In the last instance, the aim of the protection is in this case to allow a business entity to preserve competitive advantages based on undisclosed information.

The concept of 'commercial' encompasses information of a technical nature (generally called 'know-how') as well as business information, such as clients' lists and marketing plans.

Third, the information must be 'subject to reasonable steps under the circumstances... to keep it secret'. The nature of the steps will depend on the type of information and the conditions of its use. It may include keys for access to computerized information, encryption, restricted access to laboratories, etc. 'Reasonable' should be judged in accordance with what is normally done in similar circumstances. These measures may be required with regard to third parties as well as to employees of the entity that controls a given undisclosed information.

Article 39.2 does not stipulate any qualification about the creative or inventive nature of the information; it only requires 'commercial value' and secret character. It does not set out either any condition regarding the fixation of the information for that purpose.[20] Since requirements of this type would narrow down the scope of information eligible for protection, their consistency with Article 39.2 is open to question. Instead, it would be logical to require that the information for which protection is claimed be sufficiently identifiable.[21]

Article 39 will, in sum, apply to any kind of business information, provided it meets the requirements set out in Article 39.2. When interpreting this section at the national level an appropriate balance should be sought among the interests of the possessor of secret information and society's interests in the diffusion of technologies. Too stringent an interpretation may hinder, in particular, the mobility of personnel in areas where trade secrets are especially relevant (eg chemical industry, software production).

---

[20] Conditions of this kind can be found in some national laws, such as the Mexican Industrial Property Law of 1991 (see, eg, R Pérez Miranda, *Derecho de la Propiedad Industrial* (2006: Mexico, Editorial Porrúa), pp 284–89). NAFTA Article 1711(2) provides that '[A] Party may require that to qualify for protection a trade secret must be evidenced in documentary, electronic or magnetic means, optical discs, microfilms or other similar instruments'.

[21] See, eg Gervais, op. cit. (2003), p 274.

Test data of pharmaceutical and agrochemical products

39.3. Members, when requiring, as a condition of approving the marketing of pharmaceutical or of agricultural chemical products which utilize new chemical entities, the submission of undisclosed test or other data, the origination of which involves a considerable effort, shall protect such data against unfair commercial use. In addition, Members shall protect such data against disclosure, except where necessary to protect the public, or unless steps are taken to ensure that the data are protected against unfair commercial use.

Before the entry into force of the TRIPS Agreement, countries had full latitude to determine whether or not to confer protection on test data.[22] Said Article introduced the first international standard on the subject. But the Agreement only established broad parameters for national rules, thereby allowing WTO Member countries freedom to apply different models for such protection.

Article 39.3 has been one of the most controversial in the TRIPS Agreement. Despite the fact that Article 39.3 does not provide for the granting of exclusive rights, research-based industry and the governments of some developed countries have argued that investment made for developing test data can only be ensured if a minimum period (eg five years for pharmaceuticals, ten years for agrochemicals) of exclusivity is granted.

The protection to be conferred in accordance with Article 39.3 is twofold: on the one hand, it is against 'unfair commercial use' of the relevant protected information. This means that a third party could be prevented, for instance, from using the results of the test undertaken by another company as background for an independent submission for marketing approval if the respective data were acquired through dishonest commercial practices. Such a party could, obviously, independently develop the relevant data and information or obtain them from other sources. However, from a cost–benefit social point of view the duplication of tests (involving clinical trials with patients) to obtain results that are already known will be questionable. The under discussion provision would permit, thus, the use without payment by the government of the data presented by one enterprise to assess submissions by other enterprises.

On the other hand, protection is to be ensured against disclosure of confidential data. This obligation essentially applies to government authorities that received confidential information. Two exceptions to that obligation are provided for: a) when disclosure is necessary to protect the public; and b) when steps are taken to ensure that the data will not be used in a commercially unfair manner. Under these exceptions, disclosure would be permissible, for example, to allow a compulsory licensee to obtain a marketing approval, particularly when the licence is aimed at remedying anti-competitive practices or at satisfying public health needs.

---

[22] The following analysis is essentially based on C Correa, *Protection of Data Submitted for the Registration of Pharmaceuticals: Implementing the Standards of the Trips Agreement* (2001: Geneva, South Centre).

Given the controversial nature of this provision, a detailed interpretation based on the method set out by the Vienna Convention on the Law of the Treaties is called for.[23]

Test data is the information generated to demonstrate the efficacy and safety of new chemical entities for use as pharmaceuticals or agrochemicals. In the case of pharmaceuticals, such data include the results of pre-clinical studies (pharmaco-dynamic, phamacokinetic, and toxicological tests) and of phases 1 to 3 of clinical studies.[24]

As mentioned, according to Article 1.2 of the TRIPS Agreement, the protection of test data is a category of 'intellectual property'. The structure of Article 39 suggests that the regime for test data has been conceived by the negotiating parties as a *particular* case in the framework of the protection of 'undisclosed' information.

The categorization of test data as a subject matter of 'intellectual property' does not mean, however, that Article 39.3 puts their protection on the same footing as other intellectual property rights. In particular, it cannot be inferred that such protection requires *exclusive* rights. Though in most instances intellectual property rights confer a *ius excluendi*, this is far from being an absolute rule. It is well accepted, for example, that trade secrets protection in the framework of unfair competition does not give rise to a right to exclude. Nor does the protection of geographical indications under the TRIPS Agreement entail the granting of such faculty.[25] Likewise, there are many situations in which copyright protection only allows the title-holder to claim remuneration, but not to prohibit unauthorized acts.

As Article 39.3 itself indicates, test data protection is a reward for the *investment* in data production, rather than for the creativity or inventiveness involved in generating the data. Test data are developed in accordance with standard protocols and procedures, involving a systematic compilation of factual information. Though the testing may refer to a novel drug, the test results themselves are merely the outcome of routine scientific practices.

Thus, the inclusion of test data in the TRIPS Agreement as a category of 'intellectual property' does not determine the nature of the protection conferred. In particular, it does not indicate that such data should be protected through the grant of exclusive rights.

---

[23] There has been no WTO panel or AB interpretation on this provision so far.

[24] In *Phase I* chemical testing, a small group of healthy volunteers receive dosages of the investigational drug for a short period of time. The primary purpose is to look for evidence of toxicity or unexpected undesirable reactions, and to study the bioavailability and pharmacokinetics of the drug applied to patients. *Phase II* of clinical testing has a similar purpose to Phase I, but considering the therapeutic context. Its primary objective is to ascertain the effectiveness of the investigational drug. *Phase III* clinical trials are conducted on a large number of patients: they often involve several hundred human subjects and are conducted for substantial periods. These tests are designed to determine the efficacy of the investigational drug and to uncover any unanticipated side effects that the drug may have, considering age and gender influence, drug interactions, and specific dosage for different indications.   [25] See Article 22.2 of the TRIPS Agreement.

It should be noted that, in its starting positions in the TRIPS negotiations, developing countries rejected any form of protection for know-how under the Agreement. At the other extreme, proposals were made by some industrialized countries in order to establish a minimum period of exclusive protection (five years for pharmaceuticals) for the protection of the tests and data submitted for marketing approval. The text in the Agreement represents a compromise that leaves considerable room for implementation at the national level. It certainly introduces, however, a complex issue and, for many countries, new obligations that not only concern private parties but governmental agencies as well.

In some jurisdictions, the data submitted for the registration of pharmaceutical (and agrochemical products), are subject to a *sui generis* system of protection, based on a temporary right to the exclusive use of such data by the first applicant (generally the company that developed a new product). Thus, the US adopted a regulatory data protection regime for pesticides[26] and regulatory exclusivity provisions for medicines. It provides for five years of exclusivity for new chemical entities, and three years for data filed in support of authorizations based on new clinical research relating to chemical entities which have already been approved for therapeutic use. In the EU, the Member states provided exclusivity protection for the data filed in support of marketing authorizations for pharmaceuticals since 1987. This means that the competent authority will not be able, for a certain period, to use or rely on the data submitted by the first applicant in order to approve subsequent applications by other companies (often 'generic' manufacturers) for the commercialization of a similar product. The rationale for this model would be the need to permit the originator of data to recover the investments made for their development. The underlying assumption is that without such protection, private firms would have no incentive to bear the considerable costs of producing the required data.

In other countries, however, it is possible for authorities to rely on data submitted by the first applicant, or on the registration made by a foreign authority, to process and approve third parties' subsequent applications on the same products. According to this approach the registration of products should not erect barriers to otherwise legitimate competition. The registration system should promote price competition and access to more affordable medicines and agrochemicals. In fact, the exclusivity approach developed in the US and Europe had been adopted by few countries at the time of conclusion of the TRIPS Agreement. Most countries in the world did not provide then for exclusivity and allowed the national health authorities to *rely* on test data submitted by the first applicant to approve subsequent applications on 'similar' products. Moreover, in some countries (eg Argentina, Singapore, Taiwan, and the territory of Hong Kong) in order to obtain

---

[26] This regime limits exclusivity by allowing third parties to use originator's test data against compensation, the amount of which is determined, in case of disagreement, through arbitration.

the registration of a similar product it was sufficient to prove that it had been approved or commercialized in a foreign country.

The issue of protection of data is especially relevant to off-patent products, since in cases where the product is patented, the patent holder can, in principle, exclude *any* competition during the lifetime of the patent. It is also of particular importance to many developing countries that had excluded patent protection for pharmaceuticals until recently. Because of such exclusion, in those countries there is still a large pool of pharmaceutical or agrochemical products that fall outside any patent rights. Data protection systems could, if they provided exclusivity, become a partial substitute for patent protection.

Data necessary for marketing approval

The first sentence of Article 39.3 states that 'Members, when requiring, as a condition of approving the marketing of ... '. Hence, a basic premise for the application of this Article is that a Member country should impose an obligation to submit data as a condition to obtain the marketing approval of such products.

Given the territoriality of the intellectual property system—a feature that the TRIPS Agreement has not altered—the obligation to protect test data only arises in the Member countries where national regulations require the submission of such data. Therefore, this is not a general obligation relating to pharmaceutical and agrochemical products; if a Member country opts not to require those data, such as when the national authority relies on the marketing approval conferred in a foreign country, Article 39.3 does not apply.

In addition, the submission of data must be *necessary* to obtain approval. This means that data voluntarily submitted by an applicant, or in excess of those required for approval, are not subject to protection. An implication of this rule is that the actual set of data protected will vary from country to country, depending on the scope of the requirement imposed by national law.

Undisclosed data

The subject matter of the protection under this Article is written material which details the results of scientific health and safety testing of drugs and agrochemicals, in relation to human, animal and plant health, impact on the environment and efficacy of use. The provision covers tests and other data that may be required by the authorities. These 'other' data may include, for instance, manufacturing, conservation, and packaging methods and conditions, but only to the extent that it is *necessary* to submit them in order to obtain marketing approval.

Section 7 of the TRIPS Agreement relates to 'Undisclosed information'. Article 39 protects 'undisclosed information' and 'undisclosed test' or other 'data submitted' to governments. It thereby distinguishes between general business confidential information, covered under Article 39.2, and the data specifically required to obtain marketing approval of pharmaceutical and agrochemical products, covered under Article 39.3.

It seems clear, hence, that in both cases a basic condition imposed by the Agreement is that the pertinent information must be 'undisclosed' in order to qualify for protection. This means that information that is already public (eg, because it has been published in scientific journals or by another national health authority), does not fall within the scope of this Article.[27] If in certain cases it were necessary to submit published or otherwise disclosed information to a national authority, this shall not generate any right relating to the use of such information by the government or third parties, since the information would be in the public domain.

Given that protection is only conferred to undisclosed information, it will be necessary to determine in cases of controversy which of the materials accompanying an application for marketing approval are confidential and need to be protected, and which are not. The undisclosed or disclosed nature of information is an *objective* feature, and it is not dependent on the qualification given by the applicant to the information that is submitted. Hence, the applicant's declaration that all or certain information is 'confidential' or 'undisclosed', should be subject in due course to scrutiny.

New chemical entities

Another important condition for the application of Article 39.3 is that the data must refer to a 'new chemical entity'. The Agreement does not define what should be meant by 'new'. Presumably it does not impose a patent standard of novelty, but nothing prevents a Member country from assimilating the concept of 'new' used in this Article to the one applied under patent law.

It may also be held that this Article alludes to newness in terms of application for approval. Thus, a chemical entity may be deemed 'new' if there were no prior application for approval of the same product in the Member where protection is sought.

Occasionally, a product which is known and used in a certain field (eg the chemical industry) may find an application in the pharmaceutical sector. Though this would lead to a new therapeutic product (generally known as 'first indication'), it may not be deemed to constitute a 'new chemical entity', since the chemical was already known. It may be understood, however, that the newness of the product should be assessed within a particular regulatory framework, despite the

---

[27] In accordance with two commentators, 'TRIPS Article 39.3 only requires that the data be undisclosed as of the date of submission. There is no express condition that the data remain undisclosed after submission in order to maintain protection' (G Skillington and E Solovy. 'The Protection of Test and Other Data Required by Article 39.3 of the TRIPS Agreement', (2003), Fall, 2003 24 NW J Int'l L & Bus 1, p 35).

fact that the same chemical may have been used in the context of another regulatory framework.[28]

All the above interpretations are equally permissible. The TRIPS Agreement has deliberately avoided defining the concept of 'new chemical entity', thus deferring such definition to national law. This is one of the clear areas in which Member countries enjoy room for manoeuvre to implement the Agreement's provisions.

Based on the ordinary meaning of the terms used, it may be also interpreted that there is no obligation to provide for protection when the test data were developed for a new *use* of a pharmaceutical product (generally called 'second indication'). In this case what is new is the application or method of use of a known chemical entity, but not the entity as such.

Similarly, Article 39.3 would not apply in cases where approval is sought for new dosage forms, combinations, new forms of administration, crystalline forms, isomers, etc of existing products, since there would be no novel chemical entity involved. This issue was indirectly addressed by the European Court of Justice in the '*Squibb*' case.[29] The Court held that a (second) product is 'essentially similar' to an earlier approved product if the second product has 'the same qualitative and quantitative composition in terms of active principles', 'the same pharmaceutical form', and is bio-equivalent to the first product, 'unless it is apparent in the light of scientific knowledge that it differs significantly from the original product as regards safety or efficacy'. In these cases, the original applicant does not receive new periods of so-called 'marketing exclusivity' for each new indication, dosage form, or dosage schedule.

Considerable effort (investment)

The subject matter of the protection under Article 39.3 is test data resulting from clinical trials for the pharmaceutical and field trials for agrochemicals. As mentioned above, this information is not 'invented' or 'created'. For this reason, the TRIPS Agreement does not define any substantive standard for granting protection (like inventive step or novelty), but simply mandates protection when obtaining the data involved 'a considerable effort'.

The requirement of a 'considerable effort' suggests that national authorities may request the applicant to prove that the information for which protection is sought is the result of such effort. However, the text is vague about the type of effort

---

[28] T Cook, *Special Report: The Protection of Regulatory Data in the Pharmaceutical and Other Sectors* (2000: London, Sweet & Maxwell), p 6.

[29] The ECJ decision was given in response to questions referred to it from the English High Court in relation to three cases. In all of them the research-based pharmaceutical companies had made changes to certain aspects of its products and obtained marketing approval for each change. Subsequently, generic companies sought to rely not only on the original versions of the products but also on the products which had been approved more recently. The Medicines Control Agency acceded to certain of the generic companies requests, but not all of them (see, eg, N Jones and R Nittenberg, 'Essentially Similar Despite Being Different: The *Squibb* Case', (1998/1999: BSLR), p 152.

involved (technical, economic?) and also with respect to its magnitude (when would it be deemed 'considerable'?). Quite obviously, the proponents of this formulation aimed at the protection of the *investment* made in producing the test data.

The extension of intellectual property beyond its boundaries so as to protect investment and not intellectual contributions,[30] disrupts the essence of a system conceived to reward the creators of original ideas and new inventions. Even if it may be argued that 'free riding' or 'unfair use' of such data by third parties may create unfair advantages or unjust enrichment, it is not the role of the intellectual property system to solve competition problems that do not relate to the creation or use of intellectual assets.

Non-disclosure obligation

As indicated before, since the protection of test data is established under the TRIPS Agreement in the framework of the protection of undisclosed information, it seems clear that Members' obligations are limited to information effectively requested by and submitted to the government, as long as it was undisclosed at the time of submission to a particular authority. This means that data already disclosed, for instance, by publication of the competent authority in a foreign country is no longer undisclosed in other Members.

The non-disclosure obligation requires that the test data be protected against 'disclosure' unless:

- it is necessary to protect the public; or
- steps are taken to ensure that the data are protected against unfair commercial use.

The application of the first exception is subject to a 'necessity test'. According to the interpretation of such test in other contexts of GATT/WTO rules, deference should be given to Members to determine when such necessity arises, but the Member invoking it will bear the burden of proof, an often difficult task.[31]

The second exception would permit a Member to disclose any information, provided that its unfair commercial use is prevented. The key question is what would constitute such use and how that protection could be guaranteed.

Article 39.3 aims to preserve the confidentiality of the information submitted for marketing approval without any time limit. There is no indication in the provision about the duration of the obligation, certainly a weak point in the text. Under these conditions, the obligation would, in principle, only cease when the information becomes known. It may also be possible for a Member to establish a maximum period of confidentiality.

---

[30] An investment-based system was adopted by the European Community in the form of a *sui generis* regime for the protection of data bases (Directive 96/9/EC of 11 March 1996).

[31] See, eg, M Trebilcock and R Howse, *The Regulation of International Trade* (1999: London and New York, Routledge), p 140.

Acts of unfair commercial use

One of the crucial interpretative issues in Article 39.3 is whether the reliance by a national authority on data submitted by one company (the 'originator') to evaluate a subsequent application by another company (a 'follower'), constitutes an 'unfair commercial use' of the information.

The expression *'unfair commercial use'* is not defined in Article 39. Pursuant to Article 31(1) of the Vienna Convention, its interpretation should be based on the ordinary meaning of the terms of the Treaty in their context and in the light of its object and purpose.

Unfair

The ordinary meaning of 'unfair' is *'not equitable or honest or impartial or according to rules'*.[32] In the case of Article 39.3, this concept must be understood in the light of Article 10*bis* of the Paris Convention.

The concept of 'unfair' is relative to the values of a particular society at a given point in time.[33] It varies among Members, and this variation is in fact one of the premises on which the discipline of unfair competition is grounded. There is no absolute, universal rule to determine when certain practices should be deemed 'unfair'.[34]

Ladas concludes by indicating that:

We look for a standard by which we may judge the act complained of. This is an objective standard: the honest practices in the course of trade in the particular community and at the particular time.

Given this diversity, it is likely that different countries judge certain situations differently, depending on their values and competitive advantages. The fact that a 'follower' company commercially benefits, via a marketing approval system based on 'similarity', from the data produced by the originator may be seen in some countries as an 'unfair practice' or may give rise to claims of 'unjust enrichment' leading to a compensation for the use of the data. In others, it may be regarded as the legitimate exploitation of an externality created during legitimate competition in the market.

Certainly, specific regulations could be adopted at the international level in order to harmonize the treatment of these cases. This is what would have occurred had the US proposal for the TRIPS negotiation reached consensus.[35] Such a proposal, not incorporated in the final text of the TRIPS Agreement, obliged to prevent any use of data, without the consent of the right-holder or on payment of

---

[32] *Concise Oxford Dictionary*, (1982: Oxford University Press, 7th edn).
[33] See Ladas op. cit. (1975).   [34] Idem, p 1689.
[35] See below the history of the negotiation of Article 30.3.

'the reasonable value of the use', if that use led to the 'commercial or competitive benefit of the government or of any person'. If approved, this provision would have obliged the prevention of *any* practice that would create such benefit. There was no reference in that proposal to 'unfair commercial practices'. The rejection of the US proposal indicates that the negotiating parties deliberately opted to mandate the control, under Article 39.3, of certain types of *practice* (those that are commercially *unfair*) and not to prevent any practice based on the *effects* that may arise therefrom.

In other words, Article 39.3 only applies when a competitor obtains a benefit or advantage from the use of the originator's testing data *as the result of unfair commercial practices*. It is the qualification of the practice that counts, not the mere existence of an advantage or benefit. Such qualification is left to Members' discretion; it is part of the room for manoeuvre that they retained when signing the Agreement.

There are many instances in which the production of goods, notably intangibles, in a competitive environment, generate externalities that benefit competitors. In describing the nature of competition, Ladas has noted that

> it is an undeniable fact of modern business life that successful manufacturers or traders have to cope with the danger of having the goodwill of their business, their connection with the purchasing public, interfered with by competitors . . . In a competitive economy is it to be expected that each manufacturer or trader necessarily seeks to maintain and improve his market position by obtaining the benefit of a public demand, even though this demand be created by other manufacturers or traders . . .
>
> . . . where does lawful competition end and unlawful competition begin? The fact that a competitor may derive a profit from his act of competition or cause monetary loss to another is not, in itself, unlawful. The dictum 'no one should reap where he has not sown' requires delicate application. Progress would be paralysed and monopoly would become general if we should attempt to prevent persons from using the work or experience of others. We must encourage people in the same trade or industry to compete for the custom of the public on the most favorable terms. The issue is whether the means employed in such competition are fair and lawful. An act may lack tact or taste but not be dishonest.[36]

Many countries consider, as mentioned, that the commercialization of a 'similar' product approved by reference to a previous registration, or relying on data submitted by the originator company, is *not* an unfair commercial practice. Other countries may have a different perception, and that is also valid. Article 39.3 only mandates to protect against 'unfair commercial practices', but leaves Member countries the freedom to determine which practices will be deemed commercially unfair. As mentioned, differences among countries are likely to exist, consistently with Article 10*bis* of the Paris Convention.

---

[36] Ladas op. cit. (1975), pp 1676; 1677; 1689.

Commercial

In addition, Article 39.3 only covers 'commercial' uses. This clearly excludes the use by the government, notably by the national health authority, to assess the efficacy and toxicity of a pharmaceutical or agrochemical product.

In the view of the European Union, however, there would be a substantial difference between the underlying principle in Article 39.1, which refers to relationships between competitors, and Article 39.3, which would include governmental acts:

> The main question of interpretation is what is meant by 'unfair commercial use'. Clearly, this concept is different from the concept of 'unfair competition', as used in Article 39.1 with a reference to Article 10bis of the Paris Convention on the protection of Industrial Property, and which relates to behaviour among competitors. Protection of registration data is a government function. Article 39.3 does not indicate whether the notion of 'unfair commercial use' refers to unfair commercial use by generic manufacturers to those who have submitted the data (usually research-based pharmaceutical industry) or to use by regulatory authorities of these data to the benefit of competitors. Protecting data against 'unfair commercial use' is also different from protecting them from disclosure, since the latter is a separate and distinct obligation under Article 39.3.[37]

The EU argument, however, disregards that Article 39 *develops* and does not add to Article 10*bis* of the Paris Convention. It only incorporates *examples of the general principle* contained in paragraph (2) of Article 10*bis*.

In addition, though the use by governments will *indirectly* have commercial consequences (the entry of a competitor in the market), it clearly does not represent a *commercial* activity as such, but a legitimate State practice. In order to be 'commercial', the use of the information should be made by somebody who is actually in commerce. As also noted by Ladas,

> The general clause of Article 10*bis*, in establishing as its foundation 'honest usages', looks to the relations between competitors and to the interests of customers, and these provide an objective test which reflects an evolving pattern of competition in most of the present world ... By definition, competition in commerce refers to the efforts of two or more persons, acting independently, to secure the custom of third parties, with the results that one may increase the sale of his goods and reduce the sale of the goods of the other.[38]

The same concept underlies the WIPO 'Model Provisions on Protection Against Unfair Competition' which, in relation to data protection, suggests the adoption by national laws of the following provision:

> Use or Disclosure of Secret Information Submitted for Procedure of Approval of Marketing: Any act or practice, in the course of industrial or commercial activities, shall be considered an act of unfair competition if it consists or results in an unfair

---

[37] European Union, *Questions on TRIPs and Data Exclusivity. An EU Contribution* (2001, Brussels), p 3.
[38] Ladas op. cit. (1975), p 1688.

commercial use of secret test or other data, the origination of which have been sub-mitted to a competent authority for the purposes of obtaining approval of the mar-keting of pharmaceutical or agricultural chemical products which utilize new chemical entities (emphasis added).[39]

Use

Finally, there must be 'use' of the information.[40] This means that the documenta-tion must be utilized in some form in order to give rise to practices regulated under Article 39.3. Depending on the applicable legal system, national health author-ities can follow different approaches for the approval of a second-entry marketing application. The authority may:

a) require the second-entrant to produce its own testing data or to obtain an authorization of use from the 'originator' of the data;
b) allow the second-entrant to rely on the 'originator's' data against payment of compensation;[41]
c) use the 'originator's' data in order to technically examine second-entry appli-cations. In this case, the authority directly relies on the originator's data;
d) require the second-entrant to prove that his product is 'similar' to an already regis-tered product,[42] without having to examine and rely upon the 'originator's' data.

In accordance with a strict interpretation of Article 39.3, none of these situ-ations would fall under the concept of 'unfair commercial use', since in none of them does the authority make a 'commercial' use. Moreover, in case d) there is no 'use' at all, since the authority does not possess (or use) the testing data: it merely relies on public information and on the existence of a foreign marketing approval.

Further, in cases b), c) and d) the competitor does not *use* the data either. He does not need to have access to or to acquire them in any form, since he is not obliged to submit them for approval of his product.

It has been interpreted, however, that in order to protect data against 'unfair commercial use', the data should not be used to support, clear or otherwise review

---

[39] WIPO, *Model Provisions on Protection Against Unfair Competition*, (1996: Geneva).
[40] In one of the texts under consideration by the negotiating parties in July 1990, the broader con-cept of 'exploitation' had been proposed (but not finally adopted). The text read:
   3Aa. Parties, when requiring the publication or submission of undisclosed information consisting of test [or other] data, the origination of which involves a considerable effort, shall protect such data against unfair exploitation by competitors. The protection shall last for a reasonable time commensur-ate with the efforts involved in the origination of the data, the nature of the data, and the expenditure involved in their preparation, and shall take no account of the availability of other forms of protection.
[41] This compulsory licence approach is the one applicable, under certain circumstances, in accord-ance with the US FIFRA.
[42] In some countries, the applicant must provide bio-equivalence tests to prove interchangeability.

other applications for marketing approval for a set amount of time unless authorized by the original submitter of the data.[43]

According to this interpretation, there would be an 'unfair commercial use'
when the national authority relies on the data submitted by the originator in order
to assess a subsequent application. Moreover, even when neither the authority nor
the competitor actually 'use' the data without the originator's authorization (for
instance, when the approval is given without any re-examination of the data) such
unfair use might arise. In the complaint that the US made against Australia, for
instance, the US argued that relying on the innovator's data allowed free-riding by
generic drug companies on

the innovator company's investment in developing the test data and thus puts the innovator company at a competitive disadvantage . . . The US claims that Article 39 para (3)
means that generic companies are not allowed to derive commercial benefit from the innovator's test data.[44]

Under this view, therefore, the fact that a competitor obtains a commercial
benefit or advantage constitutes an 'unfair commercial use' of the data, notwithstanding that actual use may not occur and that the practice as such may not be
'dishonest' or contrary to the prevailing values on what is moral in the course of
commercial activities.

Relying on data

The nature and extent of data exclusivity rights were examined in important decisions by the US Supreme Court (*Ruckelshaus v Monsanto Co*, 467 US 986, 104 S
Ct 2862, 26 June 1984) and by the Canadian Federal Court of Appeal (*Bayer Inc v
The General Attorney of Canada, the Minister of Health, Apotex Inc and Novopharm
Ltd*, 19 May 1999). The second decision, in particular, examined the extent to
which a national health authority can *rely on* the originator's data, *even when an
exclusivity period applies*.

The *Ruckelshaus v Monsanto Co* case related to the protection of data submitted
for the registration of an agrochemical product. Though a subsequent applicant
was obliged to compensate for the use of Monsanto's original data, Monsanto
argued that such use was unconstitutional. A basic argument of the plaintiff was
that the possibility given to a competitor of using the data against payment of
compensation nullified its 'reasonable investment-backed expectation'. However,

---

[43] WHO (2000), The TRIPS Agreement and Pharmaceuticals. Report of an ASEAN Workshop
on the TRIPS Agreement and its Impact on Pharmaceuticals, Jakarta, 2–4 May 2000, p 39.
[44] P Priapantja, 'Trade Secret: How does this apply to drug registration data?', paper presented at
'ASEAN Workshop on the TRIPS Agreement and its Impact on Pharmaceuticals', Department of
Health and World Health Organization (2000) 2–4 May, p 6.

the Supreme Court described the extensive practice of relying on data submitted by the first applicant in the United States, and rejected Monsanto's complaint.

The US Supreme Court in this case recognized that the authority could use the data submitted by the originator to assess second-entrant applications. According to the law applicable at the time of the complaint, Monsanto could be entitled to compensation, but not to the exclusive use of the data. The solution has probably not substantially changed in the USA despite the adoption of the Second Restatement of Unfair Competition Law (1997). In the absence of a specific provision granting an exclusivity period as currently provided by US law, relying on data to approve subsequent applications would not be considered an illegitimate misappropriation of trade secrets.[45]

A second and more significant case was decided by the General Court of Appeal of Canada. Despite the fact that NAFTA provisions provide for a minimum term of exclusivity, the Court found legitimate the approval of a subsequent application on the basis of a prior registration, on the argument that the health authority neither requested undisclosed information again nor examined it; the authority just checked whether the two products were indeed the same. The issue was subject in Canada to the national law and NAFTA Article 1711 on 'Trade Secrets', which establishes the following:

> 5. if a Party requires, as a condition for approving the marketing of pharmaceutical or agricultural chemical products that utilize new chemical entities, the submission of undisclosed test or other data necessary to determine whether the use of such data involves considerable effort, except where the disclosure is necessary to protect the public or unless steps are taken to ensure that the data is protected against unfair commercial use.

> 6. Each Party shall provide that for data subject to paragraph 5 that are submitted to the Party after the date of entry into force of this Agreement, no person other than the person that submitted them may, without the latter's permission, rely on such data in support of an application for the product approval during a reasonable period which shall normally mean not less than five years from the date on which the Party granted approval to the person that produced the data for approval to market its product, taking account of the nature of the data and the person's efforts and expenditures in producing them. Subject to this provision, there shall be no limitation on any Party to implement abbreviated approval procedures for such products on the basis of bioequivalence and bioavailability studies.

> 7. Where a Party relies on a marketing approval granted by another Party, the reasonable period of exclusive use of the data submitted in connection with obtaining the approval relied on shall begin with the date of the first marketing approval relied on.

The Court, in sum, concluded that the Canadian law and NAFTA are responsive to the requirement on innovators of pharmaceutical products of having to

---

[45] Personal communication by Prof J Reichman (Duke University), October 2001.

disclose confidential information to the government. If the health authority actually uses the data submitted by the originator on behalf of the generic manufacturer in order to assess the latter's application, the minimum five years' protection from the competition for the innovator applies. Instead, where the authority does not examine and rely on that confidential or trade secret information on behalf of the generic manufacturer, there is no use of data and the exclusivity provision is not applicable.

If despite the fact that exclusivity is expressly provided for by the law, the mere reliance on a prior registration without use of the data does not allow a claim of exclusivity, a fortiori the same conclusion should be reached when the exclusivity is not specifically established, as in the case of Article 39.3.

In sum, whatever the intention of some of the negotiating parties was, the expression 'unfair commercial use', reasonably interpreted, does not permit us to sustain that Article 39.3 requires the provision of exclusivity, or of compensation. It has left ample room for manoeuvre to Member countries to determine

a) when such a use exists; and
b) which would be the means of protection (see next section).

An 'unfair commercial use' may be determined to exist, for instance, in situations in which a competitor obtains through fraud, breach of confidence, or other 'dishonest' practices, the results of testing data and *uses* them to submit an application for marketing approval in its own benefit. It would also apply in cases where the government provides access to undisclosed testing data in order to provide an advantage to a firm which did not produce them or shared their cost.[46]

Means of protection against unfair commercial use

A key issue for the application of Article 39.3 is to determine what is the nature and extent of the obligation to protect 'against unfair commercial use'. As noted, the interpretation of this rule has created considerable controversy.

The protection of 'undisclosed information' is mandated by the TRIPS Agreement in the framework of the discipline of 'unfair competition'. Article 39.1 of Agreement stipulates that

> in the course of ensuring effective protection against unfair competition as provided in Article 10*bis* of the Paris Convention (1967) Members shall protect . . . the data submitted to governments or governmental agencies in accordance with paragraph 3.

Article 10*bis* of the Paris Convention requires protection against 'unfair competition', defined as

---

[46] This would represent a violation of the non-disclosure obligation as well as an 'unfair commercial use'.

any act of competition contrary to honest commercial practices in industrial or commercial matters.

There are no universal moral values or a unique concept of what is 'honest' in commercial behaviour. As indicated the meaning of what are 'fair' or 'honest' practices is not necessarily the same in the various countries. They may include competitor's misrepresentation, fraud threats, defamation, disparagement, enticement of employees, betrayal of confidential information, and commercial bribery, among others. In many jurisdictions the misappropriation of trade secrets has been deemed a specific hypothesis regulated under unfair competition law, as the TRIPS Agreement does.

Under the discipline of unfair competition, protection is not based on the existence of 'property' rights. Hence, the provision of protection under such discipline does not give rise to claims of property rights in respect of trade secrets and data submitted for marketing approval.[47]

The concept adopted by the TRIPS Agreement clearly avoids the treatment of undisclosed information as a 'property'.[48] The fact that the 'undisclosed information' is deemed to be a 'category' of intellectual property does not imply, as mentioned before, the existence of a property right.[49]

A logical consequence of the legal theory embraced by the Agreement is that Article 39 does not imply any obligation to confer *exclusive* rights in respect of undisclosed information.

The obligation to protect data against unfair commercial practices may be implemented, as some countries have done with a 'TRIPS-plus' approach, through the granting of exclusionary rights.[50] In the absence of mechanisms that permit the use of the data, however, this system leads to the need for competitors to duplicate tests (often involving suffering of animals) in order to reach results that are already known, a solution which is certainly questionable from a social and ethical point of view.

This obligation may also be implemented by other means, such as through the legal faculty to impede the use of information acquired through dishonest practices (eg espionage, breach of confidence), or to prevent the use of test data undertaken by another company as background for an independent submission for marketing approval.

Implementing legislation may also require from the subsequent user the payment of compensation, without providing for exclusive rights. The US FIFRA, for instance, recognizes the possibility of using originator's test data without his

---

[47] See commentary on Article 39.1 above.

[48] On the different approaches in continental and common law with regard to trade secrets, see, eg, Coleman op. cit. (1992), A Font Segura, *La protección internacional del secreto empresarial* (1999: Madrid; Colección Estudios Internacionales, ed. Eurolex, No. XXXI).

[49] See commentary on Article 39.1 above.

[50] The FTAs signed by the USA since 2000 with a number of developing countries and Australia include specific provisions on data exclusivity.

consent for the approval of a subsequent application, against compensation. The law, thus, establishes a form of compulsory licensing for such data.

In summary, Article 39.3 interpreted according to the ordinary meaning of the words used, in their context (notably Article 39.1) and taking into account the object and purpose of the Agreement, does not require the granting of exclusive rights.[51] The obligation that it imposes may be satisfied by other means, not specified in the Agreement. As stated by UNCTAD in relation to data covered by Article 39.3,

authorities are not prevented . . . from using knowledge of such data, for instance, to assess subsequent applications by third parties for the registration of similar products.[52]

The Office of the US Trade Representative has interpreted Article 39.3 of the TRIPS Agreement to mean that

the data will not be used to support, clear or otherwise review other applications for marketing approval for a set amount of time unless authorised by the original submitter of the data. Any other definition of this term would be inconsistent with logic and the negotiating history of the provision.[53]

This is the position that the USA held, for instance, in its complaint (initiated in April 1996), under Special 301 Section of US Trade Act, against Australia,[54] where no exclusivity was granted and generic companies only had to demonstrate bio-equivalence in order to obtain marketing approval of a similar product. In addition, Australian authorities granted certificates of free sale which permitted generic companies to export to other countries where marketing approval was automatically granted on the basis of the Australian certificates. The US argued that Australia violated Article 39.3. This action led to an amendment to the Australian law. Under the Therapeutic Goods Legislation Amendment Act 1998 (No 34, 1998) test data have five years of 'exclusivity'. During this time, another company wishing to register a generic copy of the product will be required to seek

---

[51] See also J Watal, *Intellectual Property Rights in the WTO and Developing Countries* (2001: The Hague/London/Boston, Kluwer Law International), who concludes that 'in the end in the TRIPS text there is no clear obligation not to rely on the test data for the second or subsequent applicants nor a fixed duration of market exclusivity, failing which the first registrant is assured reasonable compensation. This is a clear contrast to the corresponding provisions in NAFTA' (p 199).

[52] UNCTAD, *The TRIPS Agreement and Developing Countries*, UNCTAD/ITE/1 (1996: New York and Geneva), p 48.

[53] Office of the General Counsel, US Trade Representative, 'The protection of Undisclosed Test Data in Accordance with TRIPS Article 39.3', unattributed paper for submission in bilateral discussions with Australia (May 1995).

[54] This case was not brought to a panel resolution under the DSU rules. The US instead threatened the application of unilateral trade sanctions, despite the fact that the TRIPS had already entered into force in both countries. The US also applied economic sanctions against Argentina in 1997 arguing insufficient protection of confidential information. Later the US initiated consultations under the DSU on, *inter alia*, Argentina's compliance with Article 39.3. The case, however, was settled without any change in Argentina's legislation with regard to data protection. See WT/DS171/3, WT/DS196/4, IP/D/18/Add.1, IP/D/22/Add.1.

the agreement of the originator company to use its data, or to develop its own data package.

Further, in the opinion of the European Union:

the only way to guarantee that no 'unfair commercial use' within the meaning of Article 39.3 shall be made is to provide that regulatory authorities should not rely on these data for a reasonable period of time, the determination of what is a reasonable period of time being left to the discretion of the Members.

In theory, Article 39.3 appears to give Members the discretion to provide for different means of data protection, although it is very difficult to imagine other ways than non-reliance over a certain period of time, except for a (temporary) refusal to grant any second market approval to similar products (even if the second applicant submits its own data), as is the case in at least one WTO Member and maybe for an obligation to pay as a compensation for reliance on proprietary data without having to obtain consent from the first applicant. The question remains whether such payment would indeed be sufficient to guarantee that any 'unfair commercial use' of test data takes place. For instance, it would be essential that such payment reflects the investments made by the original applicant—which may not always be easy to establish.

In theory, any country maintaining an effective system to implement obligations under Article 39.3 even if different from non-reliance over time, would not be in breach of its TRIPS obligations, but we are not aware of many alternatives and it is clear that what the TRIPS negotiations had in mind was data exclusivity over a certain period of time. On the other hand, as it does not set any time limit, Article 39.3 would not prevent a country from providing for data exclusivity for an unlimited period of time.[55]

The argument that Article 39.3 established an exclusivity obligation and that it only left Member countries the freedom to determine the *duration* thereof[56] presents several shortcomings.

First, had the negotiating parties agreed to embrace the concept of exclusivity, they would have most probably explicitly indicated it. They did so when they established the obligations in relation to copyrights, trademarks, industrial designs, and patents. It is difficult to explain why, if they had a similar intention with regard to test data, they ostensibly omitted to say so. The EU admits that there was substantial disagreement during negotiations:

It must be admitted that the following of Article 39.3 does not, from a prima facie reading, appear to impose data exclusivity during a certain period of time. This lack of clarity is the obvious result of a difficult negotiation process where divergences of views arose between developing and industrialized countries as to the necessity of EC/US-like type of data protection as well as among industrialized countries on the length of the data exclusivity period.[57]

The disagreement among the parties was, however, more substantial than argued by the EU, and there was no international established practice on which to

---

[55] European Union op. cit. (2001), pp 4–5.   [56] Idem.
[57] European Union, op. cit. (2001), p 3.

rely. As shown by the negotiating history, a text was under consideration for a long time which clearly referred to exclusivity, which is conspicuously absent in the adopted Agreement.

Second, if the negotiating parties only left the Members the freedom to determine the *duration* of the exclusivity period, on what basis could a panel or the Appellate Body establish which is the 'adequate' duration without substituting the Members themselves and violating the basic rule of Article 3.2 of the Dispute Settlement Understanding?[58] The EU itself admits that there was disagreement among the developed countries even about the duration of such period.

As noted by Watal,

It can be argued that if the intention had been to have such exclusive marketing rights, this term, which is used in Article 70.9 of TRIPS, would have been used here too. Further, given the differences in the TRIPS and NAFTA texts of this provision, it is clear that the scope and purpose in TRIPS was intended to be more limited as otherwise the text would have been as specific. No additional obligations, which are not present in the text, can be imported through interpretation. Therefore, a reasonable interpretation would be that the obligation on the authorities would be to keep the test data secret and to prohibit others from accessing this test data for unfair commercial use, such as sale to rival firms.[59]

In summary, Article 39.3 clearly requires some form of protection for test data. Its main purpose is not to prevent the commercial use of such data by governments, but the use thereof by competitors. The wording, context, and purpose of said Article, does not allow to conclude that the required protection can only be implemented on the basis of an *exclusivity* period of protection. This interpretation is confirmed by the history of the negotiation of the TRIPS Agreement. In accordance with the US proposal:

Contracting parties which require that trade secrets be submitted to carry out governmental functions, shall not use the trade secrets for the commercial or competitive benefit of the government or of any person other than the right-holder except with the right holder's consent, on payment of the reasonable value of the use, or if a reasonable period of exclusive use is given to the right-holder.

The negotiating parties also considered the option of protecting data on the basis of a *compensation* to the originator, a concept that vanished during subsequent negotiations. Among the texts on the table as of July 1990, an option read as follows:

PARTIES which require that trade secrets be submitted to carry out governmental functions, shall not use the trade secrets for the commercial or competitive benefit of the government or of any person other than the right-holder except with the right-holder's consent, on

---

[58] Article 3.2: 'Recommendations and rulings by the Dispute Settlement Body cannot add to or diminish the rights and obligations provided in the covered agreements.'

[59] J Watal op. cit. (2001), p 204.

payment of the reasonable value of the use, or if a reasonable period of exclusive use in given the right-holder.

Both these proposals going beyond unfair competition rules were rejected by the majority of negotiating parties.

Annex

Negotiating history [60]

In his 23 July 1990 report on the status of work in the TRIPS Negotiating Group, the Chairman (Lars E R Anell) presented two sets of proposals. In an Annex to the report, he presented a composite text that was taken from various proposals by delegations to the Negotiating Group, indicating the source of each proposal by numerical reference to the source document.

Composite text of July 23 1990 [61]

1A.1 In the course of ensuring effective protection against unfair competition as provided in Art.10*bis* of the Paris Convention (1967), PARTIES shall provide in their domestic law the legal means for natural and legal persons to prevent information lawfully within their control from being disclosed to, acquired by, or used by others without their consent in a manner contrary to honest commercial practices as long as such information:

    1A.1.1 is secret in the sense that it is not, as a body or in the precise configuration and assembly of its components, generally known or readily accessible; and

    1A.1.2 has actual [or potential] commercial value because it is secret; and

    1A.1.3 has been subject to reasonable steps, under the circumstances by the person in possession of the information, to keep it secret.

1A.2 'A manner contrary to honest commercial practices' is understood to encompass, practices such as theft, bribery, breach of contract, breach of confidence, inducement to breach, electronic and other forms of commercial espionage, and includes the acquisition of trade secrets by third parties that knew [, or had reasonable grounds to know] that such practices were involved in the acquisition.

1A.3 PARTIES shall not limit the duration of protection under this section so long as the conditions stipulated at point 1A.1 exist.

2Aa PARTIES shall not discourage or impede voluntary licensing of undisclosed information by imposing excessive or discriminatory conditions on such licences or conditions which dilute the value of such information.

---

[60] For an analysis of the negotiating history, see UNCTAD-ICTSD, *Resource Book on TRIPS and Development* (2005: New York, Cambridge University Press), pp 322–50.

[61] Chairman's Report to the GNG, Status of Work in the Negotiating Group, Negotiating Group on Trade-Related Aspects of Intellectual Property Rights, including Trade in Counterfeit Goods, MTN.GNG/NG11/W/76, 23 July 1990, presented by the Chairman of the TRIPS Negotiating Group (Lars E R Anell). Alternatives 'A' correspond to texts from developed countries and 'B' from developing countries.

2Ab There shall be no compulsory licensing of proprietary information.

3Aa PARTIES, when requiring the publication or submission of undisclosed information consisting of test [or other] data, the origination of which involves a considerable effort, shall protect such data against unfair exploitation by competitors. The protection shall last for a reasonable time commensurate with the efforts involved in the origination of the data, the nature of the data, and the expenditure involved in their preparation, and shall take account of the availability of other forms of protection.

3Ab.1 PARTIES which require that trade secrets be submitted to carry out governmental functions, shall not use the trade secrets for the commercial or competitive benefit of the government or of any person other than the right holder except with the right holder's consent, on payment of the reasonable value of the use, or if a reasonable period of exclusive use is given the right holder.

3Ab.2 PARTIES may disclose trade secrets to third parties, only with the right holder's consent or to the degree required to carry out necessary government functions. Wherever practicable, right holders shall be given an opportunity to enter into confidentiality agreements with any non-government entity to which the PARTY is disclosing trade secrets to carry out necessary government functions.

3Ab.3 PARTIES may require right holders to disclose trade secrets to third parties to protect human health or safety or to protect the environment only when the right holder is given an opportunity to enter into confidentiality agreements with any non-government entity receiving the trade secrets to prevent further disclosure or use of the trade secret.

3Ac.1 Proprietary information submitted to a government agency for purposes of regulatory approval procedures such as clinical or safety tests, shall not be disclosed without the consent of the proprietor, except to other governmental agencies if necessary to protect human, plant or animal life, health or the environment. Governmental agencies may disclose it only with the consent of the proprietor or to the extent indispensable to inform the general public about the actual or potential danger of a product. They shall not be entitled to use the information for commercial purposes.

3Ac.2 Disclosure of any proprietary information to a third party, or other governmental agencies, in the context of an application for obtaining intellectual property protection, shall be subject to an obligation to hear the applicant and to judicial review. Third parties and governmental agencies shall be prevented from further disclosure and commercial use of it without the consent of the proprietor.

Draft text transmitted to the Brussels Ministerial Conference (December 1990)

1A In the course of ensuring effective protection against unfair competition as provided in Art. 10*bis* of the Paris Convention (1967), PARTIES shall protect undisclosed information in accordance with paragraphs 2 and 3 below and data submitted to governments or governmental agencies in accordance with paragraph 4 below.

2A PARTIES shall provide in their domestic law the legal means for natural and legal persons to prevent information lawfully within their control from being disclosed to, acquired by, or used by others without their consent in a manner contrary to honest commercial practices[a] so long as such information:

- is secret in the sense that it is not, as a body or in the precise configuration and assembly of its components, generally known among or readily accessible to persons within the circles that normally deal with the kind of information in question;
- has commercial value because it is secret; and
- has been subject to reasonable steps under the circumstances, by the person lawfully in control of the information, to keep it secret.

3A PARTIES shall not discourage or impede voluntary licensing of undisclosed information by imposing excessive or discriminatory conditions on such licences or conditions which dilute the value of such information.

4A PARTIES, when requiring, as a condition of approving the marketing of new pharmaceutical products or of a new agricultural chemical product, the submission of undisclosed test or other data, the origination of which involves a considerable effort, shall [protect such data against unfair commercial use. Unless the person submitting the information agrees, the data may not be relied upon for the approval of competing products for a reasonable time, generally no less than five years, commensurate with the efforts involved in the origination of the data, their nature, and the expenditure involved in their preparation. In addition, PARTIES shall] protect such data against disclosure, except where necessary to protect the public.]

[a] For the purpose of this provision, 'a manner contrary to honest commercial practices' shall [include] [mean] practices such as breach of contract, breach of confidence and inducement to breach, and includes the acquisition of undisclosed information by third parties who knew, or were grossly negligent in failing to know, that such practices were involved in acquisition.

Chapter 12

CONTROL OF RESTRICTIVE PRACTICES IN CONTRACTUAL LICENCES

Article 40 is the outcome of a proposal originally made by developing countries, which were concerned about the impact of strengthened intellectual property rights on the conditions of voluntary licences.[1]

Technology transfer has been, and will continue to be, one of the main mechanisms through which developing countries may advance in their development processes. During the 1970s developing countries unsuccessfully attempted to generate international rules regarding technology transfer, through the adoption of an International Code of Conduct on Transfer of Technology under the auspices of UNCTAD. They sought the adoption of a voluntary instrument that would contain internationally agreed rules on the specific practices that may be deemed anti-competitive. In addition, the proposed Code included other substantive chapters on obligations and responsibilities of parties engaged in technology transfer transactions, international cooperation, and settlement of disputes.[2]

Many developing countries (eg India, Brazil, Mexico, Nigeria) established during the 1970s and the 1980s specific regulations for the control of transfer of technology transactions and, in particular, of restrictive practices that are common in licensing agreements. Such regulations were largely inspired by US antitrust policies as applied during that period and by the draft International Code of Conduct on Transfer of Technology.[3]

In parallel to the initiative for the establishment of an International Code of Conduct on Transfer of Technology, developing countries promoted the revision of the Paris Convention, and the adoption of a set of rules on the conduct of transnational corporations. Both initiatives, however, also failed. Instead, in December 1980 the UN General Assembly adopted by Resolution 35/63 a 'Set of Multilaterally Equitable Agreed Principles and Rules for the Control of Restrictive

---

[1] See MTN.GNG/NG11/W/71 of 14 May 1999.

[2] On the origin and negotiations of the Code of Conduct, see S Patel, P Roffe, and A Yusuf, *International Technology Transfer. The Origins and Aftermath of the United Nations Negotiations on a Draft Code of Conduct* (2000: The Hague, Kluwer Law International).

[3] See, eg, on the Latin American case, C Correa, 'Innovation and technology transfer in Latin America: A review of recent trends and policies', in S Lall, (ed.), *The Economics of Technology Transfer* (2002: Cheltenham/Northampton, Elgar Reference Collection), pp 339–42.

Business Practices'. The Set of Agreed Principles and Rules is applicable to all transactions in goods and services and to all enterprises (but not to intergovernmental
agreements). It deals with horizontal restraints (such as price-fixing agreements,
collusive tendering, and market or customer allocation agreements), and with the
abuse of dominant position or market power through practices such as discriminatory pricing, mergers, joint ventures, and other acquisitions of control (Section D,
paragraphs 3 and 4). Despite concerns about gaps in the Set of Agreed Principles
and Rules and implementation problems, developing countries promoted its
upgrading to a *binding* instrument.

A main concern of developing countries was that stronger (or expanded) intellectual property rights could entail higher costs in terms of royalties and other
payments by licensees, which may in turn reduce the resources available for local
R&D.[4] Higher levels of protection could also deepen negotiating imbalances and
lead to the imposition of abusive practices.[5] At the same time, technology owners
are unlikely to part with their technology when potential licensees may become
their own competitors in the domestic market or globally.[6]

Arguments on the relevance of adequate intellectual property protection in
connection with transfer of technology may be particularly strong where high, easy-
to-imitate, technology is at stake, such as in the case of biotechnology and computer
software. It is also possible to argue that in cases where 'tacit', non-codified knowledge is essential to put a technology into operation, the transfer is more likely to take
place if it is bundled with the authorization to use patents and other IPRs. If protection of such rights and trade secrets in the potential borrowing country are weak,
the technology owners are unlikely to enter into transfer of technology contracts.

However, the available evidence about the impact of IPRs on technology transfer is limited and ambiguous,[7] as is the case with regard to studies of the implications of IPR regimes on the flows of foreign direct investment.[8] Some countries
with 'weak' IPR protection schemes in the pre-TRIPS era, such as South Korea,
Taiwan, Brazil, have been among the major technology borrowers. The reverse
situation can also be found. Countries (including many African countries) with
standards of protection comparable to those in force in developed countries have

---

[4] See, eg, C Correa, 'Competition law and development policies', in R Zäch (ed.), *Towards WTO
Competition Rules. Key Issues and Comments on the WTO Report (1998) on Trade and Competition*
(1999: The Hague/London/Boston, Staempfli Publishers Ltd, Kluwer Law International), p 372.

[5] The effects of restrictive practices were also a concern in developed countries. For instance, the EC
adopted 'Block exemption' regulations on patent licences and know-how (Commission Regulations
(EC) Nos 2349/84 and 556/89, respectively), now replaced by Commission Regulation (EC) No
772/2004 of 27 April 2004 on the application of Article 81(3) of the Treaty to categories of technology
transfer agreements (OJEU 2004 L 123/11).

[6] See C Correa, 'Emerging trends: new patterns of technology transfer', in Patel, Roffe, and Yusuf
(2000), pp 275–6.

[7] See, eg, K Maskus, *Intellectual Property Rights in the Global Economy* (2000: Washington DC,
Institute for International Economics).

[8] Commission on Intellectual Property Rights, Integrating Intellectual Property Rights and
Development Policy (2002: London) available at <http://www.iprcommission.org>, last accessed on
25 November 2005.

recorded a poor or insignificant performance as technology importers. The simple explanation is, of course, that IPRs are but one of many factors—and arguably not the most important factor—that affect cross-border flows of technology.

Although the impact of the TRIPS Agreement should presumably be felt mainly with regard to innovation, there is no evidence indicating that such has been the case so far.[9] It is also uncertain what the effects of the TRIPS Agreement on the transfer of technology have been after some years of implementation. A study by McCalman revealed that

> patent harmonization has the capacity to generate large transfers of income between countries, with the US being the major beneficiary . . . These transfers significantly alter the perceived distribution of benefits from the Uruguay Round, with the US benefits substantially enhanced, while those of developing countries and Canada considerably diminished. Furthermore, accounting for the increase in dead weight loss from higher standards of patent protection undermines the aggregate benefits of the Uruguay Round package, with the increase in dead weight loss amounting to as much as one fifth of the efficiency gains from trade liberalization.[10]

Global payments for royalties and licensing fees doubled in only six years from $61 billion to $120 billion in 2004. About half of these payments accrued to the US,[11] and between 70 per cent and 80 per cent corresponded to parent–subsidiary payments,[12] which are not significantly influenced by the levels of intellectual property protection.[13] Such an impressive increase in payments may not be associated, hence, to a positive impact of the TRIPS Agreement on the international flows of technology. An econometric study relating to patents and licensing payments found that

> although stronger patent rights induce greater dollar volume of licensing, it is impossible on this evidence to claim that stronger patent rights encourage more licensing contracts and additional transfer of technological information.[14]

Section 8 of the Agreement contains a set of rules aimed at the control of 'anti-competitive practices' in voluntary licences. These rules may be regarded as one of the few concrete applications in said Agreement of the general principle stated in Article 8.2, according to which 'appropriate measures, provided that they are consistent with the provisions of this Agreement, may be needed to prevent the abuse of intellectual property rights by right-holders or the resort to practices

[9] See, eg, F Scherer, 'Global Welfare in Pharmaceutical Patenting' (2004) The World Economy, July. See also P McCalman, 'Who Enjoys "TRIPs" Abroad? An Empirical Analysis of Intellectual Property Rights in the Uruguay Round', (2005) 38 Canadian Journal of Economics 2, p 21.

[10] P McCalman, 'Reaping What You Sow: An Empirical Analysis of International Patent Harmonization'(1999), available at <http://www.innovations.harvard.edu/showdoc.html?id=5075>, p 30 (last accessed on 25 November 2005).

[11] World Development Indicators Database (2000 and 2006).

[12] According to data of the US Bureau of Economic Analysis.

[13] See G Yang and K Maskus, 'Intellectual property rights and licensing: an econometric investigation', in C Fink and K Maskus (eds) *Intellectual property and development. Lessons from recent economic research* (2005: New York, World Bank and Oxford University Press), p 128.   [14] Ibidem.

which unreasonably restrain trade or adversely affect the international transfer of technology'.[15]

Anti-competitive practices in contractual licences

40.1. Members agree that some licensing practices or conditions pertaining to intellectual property rights which restrain competition may have adverse effects on trade and may impede the transfer and dissemination of technology.

Article 40.1 recognizes that some licensing practices pertaining to intellectual property rights which restrain competition 'may have adverse effects on trade and impede the transfer and dissemination of technology'. As drafted, this principle is wider in scope than Article 8.2 as far as it includes 'dissemination' in addition to technology transfer. In contrast, Article 40.1 is worded more restrictively to the extent that the practices considered are only those that 'impede' such a transfer or dissemination. The wording of Article 8.2 in this regard ('adversely affect') would have been broader and more appropriate.

It is worth mentioning that the Havana Charter on an International Trade Organization provided for the obligation of each contracting party to take appropriate measures and cooperate to prevent business practices by private or public commercial enterprises affecting international trade which restrain competition, limit access to markets or foster monopolistic control, whenever such practices have harmful effects on the expansion of production or trade and interfere with the achievement of any of the other objectives set forth in Article 1 of the Charter (Article 46).

As the Charter was not adopted, efforts were made at the GATT, in 1954, to remedy the absence of rules on anti-competitive practices, but this did not get far. In November 1958, GATT Contracting Parties recognized that international cartels might hamper expansion of world trade and economic development of countries and interfere with the objectives of the GATT.[16] Article 40 is, hence, one of the few provisions in WTO agreements that expressly deals with some modalities of restrictive practices.[17]

The title of Section 8 refers to 'practices in contractual licenses', while the wording in Article 40.1 also alludes to 'conditions'. It seems clear that the drafters'

---

[15] Another application of this principle is the already-mentioned Article 31(k) relating to compulsory licensing to remedy anti-competitive practices. See Chapter 9.

[16] The work of a group of experts convened that year concluded in 1960 with a Decision (18 November) according to which 'in present circumstances it would not be practicable for the Contracting Parties to undertake any form of control of such practices nor to provide for investigation'.

[17] See also Articles VIII and IX of the General Agreement on Services (GATS), which provide the following:
Article VIII: Monopolies and Exclusive Service Suppliers
'1. Each Member shall ensure that any monopoly supplier of a service in its territory does not, in the supply of the monopoly service in the relevant market, act in a manner inconsistent with that Member's obligations under Article II and specific commitments.

intention was to limit Article 40 to anti-competitive situations relating to licensing agreements. As a result, with the exception of Article 8.2,[18] the Agreement has not included provisions addressing the anti-competitive effects of intellectual property rights as such, despite the well-established possibility of acquiring and abusively exercising such rights in a way that unduly restrains competition.[19]

Intellectual property rights referred to in Article 40.1 should be broadly understood as relating to any category subject to TRIPS disciplines, as defined in Article 1.2 of the Agreement.[20] Further, the wording 'practices or conditions' suggests that that provision is applicable not only to the clauses in a contract, but to the circumstances surrounding the conclusion or not of a licensing agreement, including situations of refusal to deal and abusive or discriminatory conduct by right-holders.

The wording in Article 40.1 reflects an agreement limited to certain practices or conditions 'which restrain competition' and that, in addition, 'may have adverse effects on trade and may impede the transfer and dissemination of technology'. This means that—unlike the original proposal of developing countries—the restraint of competition is a central element in the definition of the practices and conditions covered in this Section. They do not encompass those that may have 'adverse effects on trade and may impede the transfer and dissemination of technology' as long as they do not restrain trade.

The agreement expressed in Article 40.1 essentially means that Members recognize other Members' right to take measures against the described practices and conditions. An important issue is what the legal effects of this provision are. According to one view, Article 40.1 is non-committal, a non-binding chapeau.[21] However, the Article immunizes Members from violation (or non-violation, if applicable[22])

---

2. Where a Member's monopoly supplier competes, either directly or through an affiliated company, in the supply of a service outside the scope of its monopoly rights and which is subject to that Member's specific commitments, the Member shall ensure that such a supplier does not abuse its monopoly position to act in its territory in a manner inconsistent with such commitments.'

Article IX: Business Practices:
'1. Members recognize that certain business practices of service suppliers, other than those falling under Article VIII, may restrain competition and thereby restrict trade in services.
2. Each Member shall, at the request of any other Member, enter into consultations with a view to eliminating practices referred to in paragraph 1. The Member addressed shall accord full and sympathetic consideration to such a request and shall cooperate through the supply of publicly available non-confidential information of relevance to the matter in question. The Member addressed shall also provide other information available to the requesting Member, subject to its domestic law and to the conclusion of satisfactory agreement concerning the safeguarding of its confidentiality by the requesting Member.'

[18] See Chapter 4 above.
[19] See, eg. Federal Trade Commission, 'To promote innovation: the proper balance of competition and patent law policy', (2003) available at <htpp://www.ftc.gov> (last visited, May 26 2006).
[20] See Chapter 2 above.
[21] See, eg, A Heinemann, 'Antitrust Law of Intellectual Property in the TRIPS Agreement of the World Trade Organization, in F-K Beier and G Schricker (eds), *From GATT to TRIPS—The Agreement on Trade-Related Aspects of Intellectual Property Rights* (1996: Munich, Max Planck Institute for Foreign and International Patent, Copyright and Competition Law), p 245.
[22] See Chapter 14 below.

complaints under the TRIPS Agreement in case they control restrictive practices in licensing agreements subject to the criteria set out in Article 40.2. Moreover, it has been authoritatively held that

If Members have indeed agreed that certain licensing practices should be addressed, it is difficult to see why TRIPS would allow Members to remain inactive with respect to such practices, since these run directly contrary to the objectives of Article 7. Reading Article 40.1 in conjunction with Article 7 may well be understood as imposing an obligation on Members to address certain forms of anticompetitive practices in licensing agreements.

Article 40.1 . . . does not provide for a specific obligation of Members to actively enforce their rules on competition relating to matters covered by Article 40, each time these are violated. It is also true that, as a matter of principle, Article 40.1 and 2 leaves the definition of the anticompetitive practice in question to Members. However, under Article 1.1 (first sentence), Members have obliged themselves 'to give effect to the provisions of this Agreement'. Anticompetitive practices, which adversely affect trade or impede technology transfer, may frustrate the very purpose of the protection of IPRs, as provided for by TRIPS. Therefore, a total absence of rules of competition even as regards such properly abusive practices may be considered as 'inconsistent' with the provisions of the Agreement (Article 40.2, second sentence). Consequently, Members may be considered to contradict the spirit of Article 40.1 if they systematically abstain from taking measures against practices which directly offend the basis and the objectives of TRIPS provisions and/or principles, or if they systematically fail to enforce existing national rules on competition regarding such practices.[23]

An issue for consideration in this context is whether the Member where the licensor is domiciled could be deemed to be under an obligation to control practices or conditions, even if their effects take place in a foreign jurisdiction. Generally, under the 'effects doctrine', countries control restrictive practices that have an anti-competitive effect in their territories, even if they originated in another country.[24] But this extra-territorial application of the law does not encompass interventions of States where the practices originate in their own territories and affect parties in other countries, as Article 40.3 of the TRIPS Agreement suggests.[25]

Finally, an important interpretive issue is whether Article 40 positively disallows Members to adopt measures against restrictive or abusive practices that do not comply with the general definition set out in Article 40.1. This article states what a Member 'may' do and only based on an *a contrario* argument—which provides a very weak basis for legal interpretation—it may be read as excluding the Member's right to consider other practices as void or non-enforceable. Many laws in developing countries[26] have provided in the past for the control of restrictive practices that would not necessarily fall under the category of anti-competitive

---

[23] UNCTAD-ICTSD, *Resource Book on TRIPS and Development* (2005: New York, Cambridge University Press), pp 555–6.

[24] See D Brault, *Droit de la concurrence comparé. Vers un ordre concurrentiel mondial?*(1995: Paris, Economica), p 97.　　　　　　　　　　　　　　　　　　　　　　　[25] See p 404 below.

[26] See, eg, on the Latin American case, C Correa, 'Innovation and technology transfer in Latin America: A review of recent trends and policies', in Lall (ed.), op. cit. (2002), pp 339–42.

in accordance with a conventional competition test. It has been held in this regard that

The link between the restrictive nature of the licensing practice or condition and its effects on trade or technology transfer is important. It means that Article 40.1 does not recognize national measures, whereby Members subject technology transfer to a control in the abstract and regardless of their relationship to competition, or whereby they incriminate certain practices of technology transfer because of perceived general negative effects. Rather, it recognizes only those measures which address technology transfer, specifically cases of harmful effects resulting from a restraint of competition. In that sense, Article 40.1 enshrines a competition approach to the regulation of technology transfer, albeit not to the exclusion of other approaches.[27]

Article 40.1 should not be read, hence, as implying that Members have foregone their right to control practices other than those covered by this Article, such as export restrictions, which may not have a direct effect on competition in their jurisdictions, but limit the development impact of licensing agreements. The sole distinct implication is that States' measures controlling practices not covered under Article 40.1 of the TRIPS Agreement will not be immunized against complaints (including non-violation complaints, if applicable) by other Members. In any case, the complaining Member will bear the burden of proving that his complaint is justified under the Agreement.

40.2. Nothing in this Agreement shall prevent Members from specifying in their legislation licensing practices or conditions that may in particular cases constitute an abuse of intellectual property rights having an adverse effect on competition in the relevant market. As provided above, a Member may adopt, consistently with the other provisions of this Agreement, appropriate measures to prevent or control such practices, which may include for example exclusive grantback conditions, conditions preventing challenges to validity and coercive package licensing, in the light of the relevant laws and regulations of that Member.

Article 40.2, unlike most provisions of the TRIPS Agreement, does not contain specific obligations. It expressly allows countries to adopt measures to control or prevent certain practices or conditions relating to licensing agreements. Judgement of whether they should be controlled or prevented is based on three elements. Contractual practices or conditions should:

• be examined in each particular case;
• constitute an 'abuse' of intellectual property rights;
• have an 'adverse effect on competition in the relevant market'.

Unlike Article 40.1 (and Article 8.2) of the Agreement no specific reference is made in Article 40.2 to adverse effects on technology transfer and dissemination. Further, Article 40.2 refers to an adverse effect on 'competition' rather than trade.

27 UNCTAD-ICTSD op. cit. (2005), p 557.

This wording seems to put the control of licensing practices more squarely into the framework of competition law, and exclude the possibility of considering effects on the transfer and dissemination of technology as sufficient grounds to condemn a practice if it is not abusive and does not affect competition in the relevant market.[28]

Article 40.2, however, should be read in conjunction with Article 40.1 and the concept of relevant market should not be deemed limited to markets for goods, but as encompassing markets for technology[29] and other intellectual assets as such. For instance, the Antitrust Guidelines for the Licensing of Intellectual Property issued by the United States Department of Justice and the Federal Trade Commission (6 April 1995), distinguished between markets for 'goods', markets for 'technology' and markets for 'innovation'.[30] This means that the control of practices and conditions may include those that affect access to the technology as such, and not only, as mentioned, the clauses in a licensing agreement.

The need to examine the effects of licensing practices and conditions 'in each particular case' evokes the so called 'rule of reason' developed under US antitrust law. In accordance with this rule, the competent authority must weigh all circumstances of the case to determine whether a practice *unreasonably* restrains competition.[31] However, Article 40.2 only provides a general indication about the method of examination of such practices, and does not set out a substantive standard. This provision does not exclude the determination under the domestic law of restrictive practices that are prohibited per se; that is, practices that are deemed a priori to be anti-competitive.[32] Practices prohibited per se were defined, for instance, under US law before the substantial changes in the antitrust approach introduced in the 1980s under the influence of the 'Chicago school'[33] and non-challenge clauses are still deemed, at least in principle, unlawful under such law.[34]

The determination of what is an 'abuse of intellectual property rights' is left to national laws. This notion varies across countries and has also evolved over time in some jurisdictions. In the US and the EC, for instance, intellectual property rights were viewed with a certain hostility until the 1980s or 1990s from the perspective of competition law, but this view has more recently evolved towards the idea that it is not to be presumed that intellectual property creates market power in the antitrust context, but rather, as indicated in the US *Antitrust Guidelines for the Licensing of Intellectual Property* of 1995, that intellectual property laws and the antitrust

[28] 'Relevant market' is generally defined as a grouping of sales for which the elasticity of supply and the elasticity of demand are sufficiently low that if a single firm controlled all the sales it could profitably reduce output and charge a price higher than marginal cost. See, eg, H Hovenkamp, *Antitrust* (1993: St Paul, Minnesota, West Publishing Co), p 336.
[29] See an analysis of this concept in A Arora, A Fosfuri, and A Gambardella, *Markets for Technology. The Economics of Innovation and Corporate Strategy* (2001: Cambridge/London, The MIT Press).
[30] Reproduced in *ILM*, vol XXXIV, No 4 (July 1995), pp 1115–49.
[31] See *Blacks' Law Dictionary* (1999: St Paul, Minnesota, West Publishing Co), p 926.
[32] See, eg, Roffe (1998), who considers that the TRIPS Agreement does not preclude blacklisting certain clauses that may still allow for a showing of reasonableness under specific circumstances (p 289). See also UNCTAD-ICTSD op. cit. (2005), p 559; A Heinemann op. cit. (1996), p 492.
[33] See, eg, C Correa, 'Competition law and development policies', in Zäch (ed.) op. cit. (1999), p 364.
[34] See, UNCTAD-ICTSD op. cit. (2005), p 559.

system 'share the common purpose of promoting innovation and enhancing consumer welfare'. This has not prevented, however, the consideration of the use of patents and other regulatory mechanisms as abusive.[35]

Member countries, however, need not attach a particular meaning to the concept of 'abuse' and have considerable room to determine when certain practices restrain trade, as competition law greatly differs across countries[36] and there are no competition rules in the WTO system, despite the efforts of some countries (notably the EU) to generate new multilateral disciplines on the matter.[37]

In the context of patent law, 'abuse' has traditionally been given a broad meaning. Article 5A of the Paris Convention, as mentioned above,[38] refers to the lack or insufficient working of a patent as one of the cases of 'abuses'. During the long and unsuccessful negotiations on an International Code of Conduct on Transfer of Technology, developing countries also aimed at incorporating a concept of restrictive practices encompassing adverse development effects.[39] However, the wording 'abuse of intellectual property rights having an adverse effect on competition' seems to strongly link that concept to conducts restraining competition and to exclude a more expansive interpretation in the context of the TRIPS Agreement.

Article 40.2 provides a few examples of practices which may be deemed restrictive. They include:

a) exclusive grant-back provisions, ie those that oblige the licensee to transfer the improvements made on the licensed technology exclusively to the licensor;
b) obligations imposed on the licensee not to challenge the validity of licensed rights;
c) coercive package licensing, ie the obligation for the licensee to acquire from the licensor other technologies or inputs he does not need or desire.

It would be interesting to clarify the reasons that the drafters of the commented text had to select the three mentioned examples. Previous versions of the document included a significantly longer list where restrictions on research and on use of personnel, price fixing, exclusive sales or representation agreements, tying agreements, export restrictions, and other practices were mentioned.[40] The list of practices negotiated by the UN Conference on a Code of Conduct on Transfer of Technology was even longer. It included:

i) grant-back provisions;
ii) challenges to validity;
iii) exclusive dealing;

---

[35] See, eg., the European Commission Decision of 15.6.2005, in *AstraZeneca*, COMP/A 37.507, paras 532 *et seq.*   [36] See, eg, Brault op. cit. (1995).

[37] See, eg, C Correa op. cit. (1998).   [38] See Chapter 9.

[39] See, eg, P Roffe, 'Control of anti-competitive practices in contractual licences under the TRIPS Agreement', in C Correa and A Yusuf, *Intellectual Property and International Trade. The TRIPS Agreement* (1998: London, Kluwer Law International), p 267.

[40] See the text of 22 November 1990, which was discussed at the Montreal Mid-Term Review of December 1990.

iv) restrictions on research;
v) restrictions on use of personnel;
vi) price-fixing;
vii) restrictions on adaptations;
viii) exclusive sales or representation agreements;
ix) tying arrangements;
x) export restrictions;
xi) patent-pooling or cross-licensing agreements and other arrangements;
xii) restrictions on publicity;
xiii) payments and other obligations after expiration of industrial property rights; and
xiv) restrictions after expiration of arrangements.[41]

One possible explanation for the choice of examples in Article 40.2 is that there may exist some consensus to consider the exemplified clauses, under certain conditions, as anti-competitive. One problem is, however, that Section 8 of the TRIPS Agreement applies to all types of intellectual property and certain practices which may be generally deemed as condemnable for some titles may not be equally viewed when related to other types of intellectual property.[42] In any case, an advantage of the provision as formulated is that any practice or condition relating to the licence of intellectual property rights could be subject to scrutiny and condemned, provided that the conditions stipulated in Article 40.2 are met.

Consultation system

40.3. Each Member shall enter, upon request, into consultations with any other Member which has cause to believe that an intellectual property right owner that is a national or domiciliary of the Member to which the request for consultations has been addressed is undertaking practices in violation of the requesting Member's laws and regulations on the subject matter of this Section, and which wishes to secure compliance with such legislation, without prejudice to any action under the law and to the full freedom of an ultimate decision of either Member. The Member addressed shall accord full and sympathetic consideration to, and shall afford adequate opportunity for, consultations with the requesting Member, and shall cooperate through supply of publicly available non-confidential information of relevance to the matter in question and of other information available to the Member, subject to domestic law and to the conclusion of mutually satisfactory agreements concerning the safeguarding of its confidentiality by the requesting Member.

Article 40.3 provides for a system of 'positive comity' regarding anti-competitive practices in licensing agreements. It applies in cases where a Member (Member A)

---

[41] See document UNCTAD TD/CODE TOT/47.
[42] For an analysis of competition law as applied to licenses of different rights in the context of the EC, see D Keeling, *Intellectual Property Rights in EU Law. Vol I, Free Movement and Competition Law* (2003; New York, Oxford University Press), pp 296–401.

considers that a national or domiciliary of another Member (Member B) is under-taking practices in violation of the former's laws and regulations on anti-competitive practices. In this situation, Member A may request for consultations with Member B and the latter 'shall accord full and sympathetic consideration to, and shall afford adequate opportunity' for such consultations. In addition Member B is obliged to cooperate 'through the supply of publicly available non-confidential information of relevance to the matter in question and of other information available to the Member, subject to domestic law and to the conclusion of mutually satisfactory agreements concerning the safeguarding of its confidentiality by the requesting Member' (Article 40.4).

In other words, Member B may be requested to supply publicly available as well as confidential information, but in the case of the latter its supply only refers to informa-tion which is 'available to the Member', which would exclude trade secrets except if in possession of the government (for instance, as a result of a submission for marketing approval of a product). The transfer of such information, in addition, is conditional upon national legislation of Member B and upon the establishment of confidentiality agreements with Member A. It may be expected that, under these conditions, the actual access to confidential information will be quite limited, if possible at all.

It is important to note that the consultation system set forth by Article 40.3 does not oblige in any manner Member B to initiate an investigation on its own, or in any way subject to control, a practice or condition that may be deemed anti-competitive by Member A. The system is triggered by the suspicion that a practice or condition violates Member A's 'laws and regulations on the subject matter of this Section', while the application of the system preserves 'the full freedom of an ultimate decision of either Member'. This provision rather requires Members to be available for consultations and to cooperate in a limited way.

The starting point for the application of this provision is, hence, the intention of Member A to secure compliance with its legislation on the matter. While in developed countries there is a long tradition and well-established enforcement procedures in the area of competition policy, most developing countries have, until recently, operated without a formal policy on this matter. Until 1990 only 16 developing countries had a formal competition policy, and although the number of countries that adopted legislation has greatly increased since then,[43] there are still many countries without specific legislation and, where such legislation exists, there is a need for a significant upgrading in enforcement capacity.[44] In particular,

---

[43] See A Singh, *Competition and Competition Policy in Emerging Markets: International and Developmental Dimensions*, G-24 Discussion Paper Series No 18 (2002 UNCTAD-Center for International Development Harvard University) available at <http://www.unctad.org/en/docs/gdsmdpbg2418_en.pdf>, last accessed on 25 November 2005, p 6.

[44] See, eg, T Serebrisky, *What Do We Know about Competition Agencies in Emerging and Transition Countries? Evidence on Workload, Personnel, Priority Sectors, and Training Needs*, World Bank Policy Research Working Paper 3221, February 2004, available at <info.worldbank.org/etools/docs/library/64578/comp-agencies.pdfwds.worldbank.org/external/default/WDSContentServer/IW3P/IB/2004/06/03/000009486_20040603154400/Rendered/PDF/wps3221COMPE TITION.pdf > , last accessed on 25 November 2005.

'developing country competition authorities, in general, do not have the resources or the experience to tackle international competition challenges'.[45]

Paradoxically, while the strengthening of intellectual property rights has taken place in developed countries in a framework of effective application of a competition policy, few developing countries have in place effective competition regimes for the control and remedy of abuses in the exercise of such rights. In the absence of such regimes, the expansion and strengthening of intellectual property rights required by the TRIPS Agreement may actually lead to anti-competitive behaviour to the detriment of competitors and consumers.

There is no evidence so far about the application of the consultation system provided for in Article 40.3.

> **40.4. A Member whose nationals or domiciliaries are subject to proceedings in another Member concerning alleged violation of that other Member's laws and regulations on the subject matter of this Section shall, upon request, be granted an opportunity for consultations by the other Member under the same conditions as those foreseen in paragraph 3.**

Consultations may also be requested by a Member whose nationals or domiciliaries are subject to proceedings in another Member concerning alleged violations of the latter's legislation on anti-competitive practices. In this case, the requesting Member 'shall be granted an opportunity for consultations' with the other Member under the same conditions as in the case of Article 40.3.

Article 40.4 represents the 'defensive' side of the consultation system established in this provision. It specifically allows Members to request consultation when their nationals or domiciliaries are subject to procedures in foreign countries, and mandates the Member where such procedures take place to be responsive to such request. As in the case of Article 40.3, consultations will be without prejudice to any action under the relevant national law and 'to the full freedom of an ultimate decision of either Member'; that is, judicial or administrative authorities will be free to decide in accordance with their own judgement of facts under the applicable law. There is no evidence on the effective application of Article 40.4 either.

Annex

Negotiating history[46]

In his 23 July 1990 report on the status of work in the TRIPS Negotiating Group, the Chairman (Lars E R Anell) presented two sets of proposals. In an Annex to the report, he

---

[45] P Mehta, 'Competition policy in developing countries: an Asia-Pacific perspective', Bulletin on Asia-Pacific Perspectives 2002/03, United Nations Economic Commission for Asia and the Pacific (UNESCAP), Bangkok, 2002, available at <http://www.unescap.org/pdd/publications/bulletin2002/ch7.pdf>, last accessed on 25 November 2005, p 183.

[46] For an analysis of the negotiating history, see UNCTAD-ICTSD op. cit. (2005), pp 214–66.

presented a composite text that was taken from various proposals by delegations to the Negotiating Group, indicating the source of each proposal by numerical reference to the source document.

Composite text of July 23 1990[47]

CONTROL OF ABUSIVE OR ANTI-COMPETITIVE PRACTICES IN CONTRACTUAL LICENCES

1. *National Legislation*

   lB PARTIES may specify in their national legislation practices in licensing contracts deemed to constitute an abuse of intellectual property rights or to have an adverse effect on competition in the relevant market, and adopt appropriate measures to prevent or control such practices. (See also point 6B of Part IX and point 6 of Section 4, points 5 and 6 of Section 5 and point 4.3 of Section 6 above.)

2. *Consultation and Co-operation*

   2B PARTIES agree that practices which restrain competition, limit access to the technology or to markets or foster monopolistic control, and which are engaged in by licensors, may have harmful effects on trade and transfer of technology among their countries. Accordingly, each PARTY agrees upon the request of any other PARTY to consult with respect to any such practices and to co-operate with other PARTIES with a view to ensuring that IPR owners, who are nationals or domiciliaries of its country, comply with the obligations prescribed in this respect by the national legislation of the PARTY granting them such rights.

Draft text transmitted to the Brussels Ministerial Conference (December 1990)

SECTION 8. CONTROL OF ABUSIVE OR ANTI-COMPETITIVE PRACTICES IN CONTRACTUAL LICENCES

Article 43

1. PARTIES agree that some licensing practices or conditions pertaining to intellectual property rights which restrain competition may have adverse effects on trade and may impede the transfer and dissemination of technology.

2B. PARTIES may specify in their national legislation licensing practices or conditions that may be deemed to constitute an abuse of intellectual property rights or to have an

---

[47] Chairman's Report to the GNG, Status of Work in the Negotiating Group, Negotiating Group on Trade-Related Aspects of Intellectual Property Rights, including Trade in Counterfeit Goods, MTN.GNG/NG11/W/76, 23 July 1990, presented by the Chairman of the TRIPS Negotiating Group (Lars E R Anell). Alternatives 'A' correspond to texts from developed countries and 'B' from developing countries.

adverse effect on competition in the relevant market, and may adopt appropriate measures to prevent or control such practices and conditions, including non-voluntary licensing in accordance with the provisions of Article 34 and the annulment of the contract or of those clauses of the contract deemed contrary to the laws and regulations governing competition and/or transfer of technology. The following practices and conditions may be subject to such measures where they are deemed to be abusive or anti-competitive: (i) grant-back provisions; (ii) challenges to validity; (iii) exclusive dealing; (iv) restrictions on research; (v) restrictions on use of personnel; (vi) price fixing; (vii) restrictions on adaptations; (viii) exclusive sales or representation agreements; (ix) tying arrangements; (x) export restrictions; (xi) patent pooling or cross-licensing agreements and other arrangements; (xii) restrictions on publicity; (xiii) payments and other obligations after expiration of industrial property rights; (xiv) restrictions after expiration of an arrangement.

3B. Each PARTY shall enter, upon request, into consultations with any other PARTY which has cause to believe that an intellectual property right owner that is a national or domiciliary of the PARTY to which the request for consultations has been addressed is undertaking practices in violation of the requesting PARTY's laws and regulations on the subject matter of this Section, and which wishes to secure compliance with such legislations, without prejudice to any action under the law and to the full freedom of an ultimate decision of either PARTY. The PARTY addressed shall accord full and sympathetic consideration to, and shall afford adequate opportunity for, consultations with the requesting PARTY, and shall co-operate through the supply of available information of relevance to the matter in question, subject to and dependent upon the assurances of confidentiality given by the requesting PARTY unless the party providing the information agrees to its disclosure or disclosure is compelled by law.

4. A PARTY whose nationals or domiciliaries are subject to proceedings in another PARTY concerning alleged violation of that other PARTY's laws and regulations on the subject matter of this Section shall, upon request, be granted an opportunity for consultations by the other PARTY under the same conditions as those foreseen in paragraph 3 above.

Chapter 13

ENFORCEMENT OF INTELLECTUAL PROPERTY RIGHTS[1]

Unlike pre-existing conventions on IPRs, the TRIPS Agreement contains a detailed set of provisions relating to the enforcement of such rights. The aim of Part III of the Agreement is to ensure that in addition to make available certain rights, Members adopt obligations to permit their effective exercise.[2] During the Tokyo Round attempts were initiated to deal with one of the outstanding problems regarding enforcement: the international trade in counterfeit goods. The US, in particular, later supported by the EC, was keen to introduce disciplines in GATT on this matter, an objective that was made clear at the beginning of the Uruguay Round[3] and later in the TRIPS Agreement.[4]

As noted in Chapter 1,[5] the drafters of the TRIPS Agreement recognized that differences in the legal means to enforce IPRs were enormous among countries, and that such differences could not be reasonably eliminated. The Preamble, hence, indicated that the negotiating parties recognized 'the need for new rules and disciplines concerning . . . (c) the provision of effective and appropriate means for the enforcement of trade-related intellectual property rights, taking into account differences in national legal systems'. The provision of Article 1.1[6] of the TRIPS Agreement becomes particularly important in the field of enforcement. Basically following the US[7] and EC[8] negotiating proposals and, in fact, without much controversy, TRIPS drafters agreed upon a large number of provisions that, rather than prescribing how to ensure enforcement, determine what the outcomes of the adopted measures should be. For this very reason, it is difficult or impossible to consider self-executing the enforcement provisions contained in Part III in

---

[1] This chapter is partially based on the contribution made by the author to UNCTAD-ICTSD, *Resource Book on TRIPS and Development* (2005: New York, Cambridge University Press), Part 4.

[2] See, eg, M Trebilcock and R Howse, *The Regulation of International Trade*, (1999: London and New York, Routledge, 2nd edn), pp 320–1.

[3] See the Punta del Este Declaration. See also B Hoekman and M Kostecki, *The Political Economy of the World Trading System, From GATT to WTO* (1997: Oxford University Press), p 151.

[4] The Preamble of the Agreement notes 'the need for a multilateral framework of principles, rules and disciplines dealing with international trade in counterfeit goods' (see Chapter 1).

[5] See p 8.   [6] See Chapter 2.

[7] See, eg, MTN.GNG/NG11/W/70 of 11 May 1990, Part 3.

[8] See, eg MTN.GNG/NG11/W/16 of 20 November 1987; MTN.GNG/NG11/W/31 of 30 May 1989.

the Agreement, even in countries where treaties are recognized direct effects.[9] In some countries, however, courts have admitted the direct application of some of such provisions in combination with domestic procedural rules.[10]

General obligations

41.1. Members shall ensure that enforcement procedures as specified in this Part are available under their law so as to permit effective action against any act of infringement of intellectual property rights covered by this Agreement, including expeditious remedies to prevent infringements and remedies which constitute a deterrent to further infringements. These procedures shall be applied in such a manner as to avoid the creation of barriers to legitimate trade and to provide for safeguards against their abuse.

Article 41 sets forth the general obligation regarding enforcement: to ensure that procedures as specified in this Part are available under the Member's national law 'so as to permit effective action against any act of infringement of intellectual property rights covered by this Agreement'.

Several aspects of this provision need careful attention.

First, Article 41 makes clear that the obligation imposed on Members is to make available enforcement procedures[11] to be determined under each domestic law. This is conceived as the right to take 'effective action against any act of infringement'. Of course the qualification of 'effective' (used also in other parts of the TRIPS Agreement)[12] leaves certain room for interpretation, but it conveys the meaning that the available legal actions should be instrumental to the pursued end. It is doubtful the extent to which the 'effectiveness' of enforcement measures could constitute the basis for a complaint under the DSU, in view of the fact that Members are free to determine the method to comply with the TRIPS obligations in accordance with Article 1.1 of the Agreement.[13] It is rather the absence of measures able to prevent or remedy infringement that may raise such complaints. Moreover, Members are only obliged to adopt the measures required in Part III and cannot, therefore, be required to implement other measures not provided for therein.[14]

[9] See, eg, J Dreier, 'TRIPs and the enforcement of intellectual property rights' in F Beier and G Schriker (eds), *From GATT to TRIPS—The Agreement on Trade-Related Aspects of Intellectual Property Rights* (1996: Munich, Max Planck Institute for Foreign and International Patent, Copyright and Competition Law pp 250–1.

[10] This was the case, for instance, with Article 50 of the TRIPS Agreement in Argentina. See, eg, J Kors (ed) *Patentes de invención. Diez años de jurisprudencia—Comentarios y fallos* (2005: Buenos Aires, La Ley-Colección CEIDIE).

[11] These procedures must be distinguished from those relating to the *acquisition* and *maintenance* of rights, which are dealt with in Part IV of the TRIPS Agreement (see below).

[12] See, eg, Article 27.3(b) (Chapter 14).

[13] The Preamble of the Agreement, as mentioned, also makes it clear that the provision of effective and appropriate means for the enforcement of trade-related intellectual property rights needs to take into account 'differences in national legal systems'. It should also be recalled that Members are not obliged to put in place a judicial system for the enforcement of intellectual property rights distinct from that for the enforcement of law in general (Article 41.5).   [14] See, eg, Dreier op. cit. (1996), p 260.

Second, enforcement measures[15] are broadly conceived as those that can be adopted 'against any act of infringement'[16] of IPRs. The central issue is, hence, infringement. What constitutes an act of infringement is determined by the substantive national laws, subject to the exceptions and defences provided thereunder.

Third, the obligation to provide enforcement measures applies to all 'intellectual property rights covered by this Agreement'; that is, to all rights specified in Part II thereof. Some provisions in Part III, however, are of general application, while others are specifically addressed to the protection of certain categories of IPRs (eg criminal sanctions relating to copyright and trademark infringement).[17]

An important issue is whether Members are obliged to apply the same measures with regard to rights not covered by the Agreement, such as the TRIPS-plus rights recognized in FTAs. The reply is probably negative, although, in practice, domestic laws are unlikely to differentiate procedures based on their coverage or not by the TRIPS Agreement. However, if the lack of effective enforcement measures were claimed with regard to rights not covered under the Agreement (for instance, technological protection measures regarding digited works), the matter could not be subject to a dispute settlement under the WTO rules.

Fourth, the enforcement procedures referred to in Article 41.1 include both *judicial* as well as *administrative* procedures. In fact, in some countries action against infringement, such as preliminary injunctions, can be granted by administrative authorities.

Finally, with the exception of measures referred to in Article 61, the enforcement procedures dealt with in Part III are of a *civil* nature and, therefore, they do not encompass punitive sanctions.

Article 41.1 requires the establishment of two types of remedies:

(a) **expeditious remedies to prevent infringements, and**
(b) **remedies which constitute a deterrent to further infringements.**

Although the obligation to provide 'expeditious remedies to prevent infringements' is stipulated in general terms in Article 41.1, the specific content of such obligation is developed in Article 50 (provisional measures) and Article 51 (border measures) of the Agreement. Members may not be required to go beyond what is required under these provisions.

The content of the obligation to provide 'remedies which constitute a deterrent to further infringements' is more difficult to understand since civil remedies are not normally intended to act as a deterrent of future infringement, but to compensate

---

[15] To 'enforce' means, in this context, to put in execution a particular law, writ, judgment, or the collection of a debt or fine (*Black's Law Dictionary*, 1990, 6th edn, p 528).

[16] Enforcement measures may aim at preventing or sanctioning infringement that has already occurred.

[17] Some measures are mandatory in certain circumstances (preliminary relief, injunctions, declaratory relief, damages, disposition or destruction of contraband, and criminal sanctions for wilful trademark counterfeiting and commercial copyright piracy) while others are optional (eg, recovery of the infringer's profit, attorneys' fees and costs, statutory damages, and *ex officio* border measures). See J Dratler, *Intellectual Property Law: Commercial, Creative, and Industrial Property* (1996: New York, Law Journal Seminars Press), para 1A–100.

for injury suffered by the right-holder.[18] Although in some jurisdictions, like the US, 'exemplary' or 'punitive' damages may be awarded in cases where wilful and malicious appropriation is proven,[19] the TRIPS Agreement (Article 45.1) only requires 'damages adequate to compensate for the injury', thereby excluding an obligation to enhance the plaintiff's damages. Hence, this obligation should be deemed to be complied with if a Member provides for provisional injunctions, compensation of damages, and seizure as mandated by the Agreement.[20]

The second sentence of Article 41.1 ('These procedures shall be applied in such a manner as to avoid the creation of barriers to legitimate trade and to provide for safeguards against their abuse') mandates the establishment of safeguards against the possibility of utilizing enforcement procedures to prevent legitimate competition and other legitimate acts.[21] The reference to 'barriers to legitimate trade' is found in the first paragraph of the Preamble to the TRIPS Agreement,[22] while the abuse of intellectual property rights is mentioned in Article 8.1 of the Agreement.[23] Article 48 specifies one of the measures that must be adopted in order to indemnify a party who has been affected by an abuse of enforcement procedures.

Cases of abuse of intellectual property rights may take place with regard to different categories of rights. Particular concerns have been raised by cases in the field of pharmaceuticals, which may impede legitimate competition and limit access to drugs. Based on wrongly granted patents, pharmaceutical companies often engage in strategic litigation to exclude competitors from the market.[24] In March 2003, for instance, the Federal Trade Commission found that a pharmaceutical company 'had deceived the US Patent and Trademark Office to obtain unwarranted patent protection'.[25] In Australia, specific language was added to the legislation implementing the FTA signed with the US allowing the imposition of penalties of up to 10 million Australian dollars on pharmaceutical patent-holders that are found to have filed frivolous suits to extend their patents and prevent generic copies of patented drugs from being marketed in Australia.[26]

---

[18] See C Heath, 'Comparative overview and the TRIPS enforcement procedures', in C Heath and L Petit (eds), *Patent Enforcement Worldwide. A Survey of 15 Countries* (2005: Portland, Hart Publishing), pp 11–12.

[19] See, eg, R Blair and T Cotter, *Intellectual Property. Economic and Legal Dimensions of Rights and Remedies* (2005: New York, Cambridge University Press), p 69.

[20] See below, Articles 44, 45, and 46.

[21] According to the panel report in *Canada–Pharmaceutical Products* (WT/DS114/R, 17 March 2000), as mentioned above, 'legitimate' must be defined in the way that it is often used in legal discourse—as a normative claim calling for protection of interests that are 'justifiable' in the sense that they are supported by relevant public policies or other social norms' (para 7.69).

[22] 'Desiring . . . to ensure that measures and procedures to enforce intellectual property rights do not themselves become barriers to legitimate trade; . . .'   [23] See Chapter 4 above.

[24] See, eg, Federal Trade Commission, '*Generic Drug Entry Prior to Patent Expiration*'. FTC Study, July 2002, <htpp://www.ftc.gov> (last accessed on 15 November 2003).

[25] Federal Trade Commission, 'FTC Charges Bristol-Myers Squibb with Pattern of Abusing Government Processes to Stifle Generic Drug Competition' (press release available at <http://www.ftc.gov/opa/2003/03/bms.htm>, last accessed in May 2006).

[26] Abuses may also take place in cases where patents over a gene that provides plants with resistance to a particular herbicide are invoked to impede the commercialization of a derivative of such

41.2. Procedures concerning the enforcement of intellectual property rights shall be fair and equitable. They shall not be unnecessarily complicated or costly, or entail unreasonable time-limits or unwarranted delays.

Article 41.2 introduces two general principles concerning enforcement procedures. Both are worded in general terms, leaving considerable room for differing interpretations. In case of a dispute, the burden of proof that established procedures do not correspond to these principles will be borne by the claimant.

The first principle requires the availability of enforcement procedures that are 'fair and equitable'. The concept of 'fair' procedures is further developed in Article 42. Obviously, since the objective of those procedures is to protect title-holders' interests, the main purpose of the provision in Article 41.2 is to indicate to Members that the legitimate interests of defendants should also be appropriately taken into account. Thus, it would be essential that the defendant be given an opportunity to be heard and that *inaudita parte* provisional measures be the exception rather than the rule.[27] It is also crucial that valuable assets of the defendant, such as trade secrets, be protected during the procedures, as provided for in Articles 34.3 and 43.

The second principle addresses aspects related to the efficiency of available procedures. Although they may be deemed as encompassed by the generality of the first sentence of Article 41.2, it adds concrete elements to be considered to assess whether enforcement procedures are fair and equitable.

It is very difficult to judge when a procedure is more complicated than necessary. The number of steps and requirements in an enforcement procedure will normally be determined by national or local legislation in accordance with the applicable law and practice. Members are free to determine the method of implementing its obligations,[28] and this freedom could not be limited by subjective considerations about the level of complication of the relevant procedures.

Similarly, it is difficult to establish when procedures are unnecessarily costly. The cost of patent infringement procedures is reportedly high in some jurisdictions, such as in the US, where the costs of a typical infringement suit are estimated to run to $1–3 million.[29] But much of this cost will depend on the party's decision, for instance, about the evidence to produce and how much to pay for attorneys' fees beyond what is determined by the court.

The existence of 'unreasonable time-limits' (for instance to substantiate evidence in civil proceedings) may be easier to establish than the two previous conditions, but still what is 'unreasonable' or not largely depends on subjective considerations.

Finally, legal procedures, including for the enforcement of intellectual property rights, often take a long time, even in developed countries.[30] To define what are

---

plants (where the protected gene cannot perform its function). See, eg, C Correa, 'La disputa sobre soja transgénica. Monsanto v Argentina', (2006) Le Monde Diplomatique/El Dipló, April, pp 4–5.

[27] See Article 50 below.   [28] See Article 1.1 in Chapter 4 above.

[29] A lawsuit with a value below US$1 million at risk would cost in the US an average of US$400,000. See Heath op. cit. (2005), p 12.

[30] It has been noted, for instance, that in France such procedures may take six to seven years in case the first instance decision is appealed, and up to ten years if the Supreme Court knows the case. See

'unwarranted delays' will also convey subjective appreciation. If a complaint were filed on this basis, it would be necessary to prove that the delay is attributable to the legal procedures as such, and not to the parties' conduct. In some cases—such as when strategic litigation aimed at harassing competitors takes place—the plaintiff may exploit all possible opportunities to delay a final decision, while in other cases it is the defendant who may do so.

In accordance with Article 62.4 of the TRIPS Agreement, Article 41.2 (as well as Article 41.3) applies to administrative revocation of intellectual property rights as well as to *inter partes* procedures such as opposition, revocation, and cancellation, when provided for under national laws.[31]

An important issue is whether determinations of non-compliance with Article 41.2 could be made on the basis of a particular case or only based on systemic, in-built features of the applicable enforcement procedures. The latter seems to be the rational approach, as isolated cases would not be sufficient to hold that the Member has failed to meet its obligations under that provision.

A complaint based on delays to comply with administrative procedures was decided by a panel in *European Communities—Measures affecting the approval and marketing of biotech products*. With respect to the application of Directives 90/ 220/EEC and 2001/18/EC by the EC, the panel found that 'the general *de facto* moratorium resulted in a failure to complete individual approval procedures without undue delay, and hence gave rise to an inconsistency with Article 8 and Annex C of the *SPS Agreement*'.[32] It also found that

> there was undue delay in the completion of the approval procedure with respect to 24 of the 27 relevant products. We therefore concluded that, in relation to the approval procedures concerning these 24 products, the European Communities has breached its obligations under Article 8 and Annex C of the *SPS Agreement.*[33]

The relevant concept in Annex C of the SPS Agreement is 'undue delay',[34] close to, albeit not identical to, 'unwarranted delays'[35] used in Article 41.2. Although in a different context, this case provides a precedent regarding non-compliance

---

Petit, 'The enforcement of patent rights in France' in Heath and Petit (eds) op. cit. (2005), p 142. Litigation is also a lengthy business in the US. According to one estimate, the duration of the 'average' patent suit in District Court is 31 months. See, eg, S Graham, and D Mowery, 'Intellectual Property in the US Software Industry', in WM Cohen and SA Merill (eds), *Patents in the Knowledge-based Economy*, (2003: Washington DC, Committee on Intellectual Property Rights in the Knowledge-Based Economy, National Research Council).

[31] These types of procedure are undertaken by the Patent and Trademark Offices in many jurisdictions, such as the by the European Patent Office and the US Patent and Trademark Office.

[32] WT/DS291/R, WT/DS292/R, WT/DS293/R, para 8.6.   [33] Idem, para 8.7.

[34] Article 1. 'Members shall ensure, with respect to any procedure to check and ensure the fulfilment of sanitary or phytosanitary measures, that: (a) such procedures are undertaken and completed without undue delay and in no less favourable manner for imported products than for like domestic products; . . .'.

[35] 'Undue' is 'excessive, disproportionate', while 'unwarranted' means 'unauthorized; unjustified', *Concise Oxford Dictionary* (1982: Oxford University Press, 7th edn), pp 1334 and 1348.

decided on the basis of a systematic delay in procedures directly attributable to acts of WTO Members.

41.3. Decisions on the merits of a case shall preferably be in writing and reasoned. They shall be made available at least to the parties to the proceeding without undue delay. Decisions on the merits of a case shall be based only on evidence in respect of which parties were offered the opportunity to be heard.

Article 41.3 contains several provisions regarding 'decisions on the merits of a case'. They only apply to judgments rendered after argument and investigation, and when it is determined which party is in the right, and not to preliminary, formal or merely procedural decisions, or to those taken by default or without trial.[36] In contrast to Article 63.1, Article 41.3 does not allude to *final* decisions, thereby suggesting that it applies both to final as well as to interlocutory decisions, if based on the merits of the case.

This Article first requires that such decisions on the merits of a case be 'preferably' made be in writing. The drafting indicates that this is an optional rather than a mandatory requirement.[37]

Second, decisions on the merits of a case must be 'reasoned'. Although it would have been logical to require that all decisions on the merits include the arguments by the authority rendering it, the adverb 'preferably' also seems to qualify the requirement of a reasoned decision. This would also be, hence, an optional requirement.

Third, Article 41.3 requires that decisions on the merits of a case be made available at least to the parties 'without undue delay'. As in the case of Article 41.2, there is considerable room to interpret when an 'undue delay' may exist.[38] The standard set out here is clearly lower than the one established in Article 50.4 ('without delay') with regard to provisional measures.[39]

Article 41.3 refers to 'at least to the parties' and, hence, it does not exclude that the decisions be informed to third parties or published. It does not mandate, however, the publication of such decisions.[40]

Finally, Article 41.3 prescribes that decisions on the merits of a case be based only on evidence in respect of which parties were offered the opportunity to be heard. The purpose of this provision is to require a proper adversarial procedure for all evidence submitted by the parties or from any other source.[41]

41.4. Parties to a proceeding shall have an opportunity for review by a judicial authority of final administrative decisions and, subject to jurisdictional provisions

---

[36] See *Black's Law Dictionary* (1991), p 588.

[37] The original US and EC proposals included the adverb 'regularly', but this might have entailed amendments in developed countries' laws which do not always apply that rule. See, eg, Dreier, op. cit. (1996), p 260.

[38] Note also that Articles 44.1 and 50.1(a) of the TRIPS Agreement require that action be taken 'immediately'. [39] See below pp 420–22.

[40] See below, Article 63.1, which requires publication of 'final judicial decisions and administrative rulings of general application'.

[41] See, eg, D Gervais, *The TRIPS Agreement. Drafting history and analysis* (2003: London; Sweet & Maxwell 2nd ed), p 198.

in a Member's law concerning the importance of a case, of at least the legal aspects of initial judicial decisions on the merits of a case. However, there shall be no obligation to provide an opportunity for review of acquittals in criminal cases.

Article 41.4 stipulates obligations regarding the review of:

• final administrative decisions; and
• initial judicial decisions on the merits of a case.[42]

With regard to final administrative decisions, the obligation is to provide for the review by 'a judicial authority'. This concept is more restrictive than the one used in Article 31(j) of the Agreement ('Other Use Without Authorization of the Right Holder') according to which 'any decision relating to the remuneration provided in respect of such use shall be subject to judicial review or other independent review by *a distinct higher authority* in that Member' (emphasis added). Article 41.4 clearly seems to exclude the intervention of administrative authorities, such as an appeal board of a patent office,[43] even if attributed quasi-judicial competence, because the notion of 'judicial' refers to a court of law.[44] In addition, Article 41.4 applies to *enforcement* procedures, while issues relating to the acquisition and maintenance of rights are dealt with in Article 62.5 of the Agreement.[45]

With regard to 'initial judicial decisions', Article 41.4 also mandates a judicial review but, based on 'jurisdictional provisions in a Member's law', it may be excluded in view of the importance of a case. This preserves a Member's right to prevent such decisions from being appealed in cases of minor economic importance, as provided for under many national laws.

Appeal in accordance with Article 41.4 must be conferred *at least* in relation to 'the legal aspects' of such decisions. This recognizes the fact that in many jurisdictions appeal courts do not consider factual aspects of the case but limit themselves to disputed legal aspects.

Finally, in criminal cases there shall be no obligation to provide an opportunity for review of an acquittal; that is, the legal and formal certification of the innocence of a person. There is no obligation either to provide for criminal sanctions under the TRIPS Agreement, except in some cases relating to copyright and trademark infringement.[46]

> **41.5.** It is understood that this Part does not create any obligation to put in place a judicial system for the enforcement of intellectual property rights distinct from that for the enforcement of law in general, nor does it affect the capacity of Members to enforce their law in general. Nothing in this Part creates any obligation with respect to the distribution of resources as between enforcement of intellectual property rights and the enforcement of law in general.

---

[42] See the commentary on Article 41.3 above regarding the concept of 'decision on the merits of a case'.   [43] For the opposite argument, see Heath op. cit. (2005), p 15.
[44] *Concise Oxford Dictionary* (1982: Oxford University Press, 7th edn), p 543.
[45] According to this provision, as examined below, final administrative decisions shall be subject in these cases to review 'by a judicial or quasi-judicial authority'.   [46] See below pp 448–50.

Article 41.5 makes it clear that Members are not obliged to establish a *special* court to deal with intellectual property issues, nor to allocate special funds to this area. This Article was introduced upon a proposal by the Indian delegation, and essentially reflects developing countries' concerns about the implications of Part III of the Agreement.[47] It was not part of the US and EC proposals that provided the basis for most of Part III of the Agreement.

A special jurisdiction to deal with intellectual property issues has been established in some countries, such as Thailand in 1999. It was previously introduced in 1982 in the US but only for appeals. The US Court of Appeal of the Federal Circuit has decisively influenced the evolution of the intellectual property law in that country since its creation. Although this was not the intent of the Congress, the new court 'significantly broadened and strengthened the rights of patent holders'[48] and, in particular, adopted a clear pro-patent stance. In the pre-Federal Circuit era only 35 per cent of challenged patents had been held valid by courts, against 67 per cent for the first ten years of the Federal Circuit.[49] Moreover, Landes and Posner found some evidence that the creation of the court 'increased the rate of growth of patent litigation'.[50] This case shows that, although a specialized jurisdiction may be important in order to address the complex issues involved in intellectual property cases, unintended consequences may derive from the establishment of special courts.[51]

Civil and administrative procedures and remedies

Fair and equitable procedures

42. Members shall make available to right holders[11] civil judicial procedures concerning the enforcement of any intellectual property right covered by this Agreement. Defendants shall have the right to written notice which is timely and contains sufficient detail, including the basis of the claims. Parties shall be allowed to be represented by independent legal counsel, and procedures shall not impose overly burdensome requirements concerning mandatory personal appearances. All parties to such procedures shall be duly entitled to substantiate their claims and to present all relevant evidence. The procedure shall provide a means

---

[47] See MTN.GNG/NG11/W/40, at 3, No 4(e).

[48] A Jaffe and J Lerner, *Innovation and Its Discontents: How Our Broken Patent System is Endangering Innovation and Progress, and What to Do About It* (2004: Princeton University Press), p 10. See also J Barton, 'Adapting the intellectual property system to new technologies', (1995), International Journal of Technology Management, vol. 10 No 2/3, p 163.

[49] W Landes and R Posner, *The Economic Structure of Intellectual Property Law* (2003: Cambridge, The Belknap Press of Harvard University Press), p 338.   [50] Idem, p 352.

[51] It is worth noting that in the Supreme Court decisions in *Merck KGaA v Integra Lifesciences Ltd, et al* of 13 June 2005, and in *Ebay Inc. et al v Mercexchange, LLC* Of 15 May 2006, the Court of Appeal of the Federal Circuit was overruled on critical high protection positions.

to identify and protect confidential information, unless this would be contrary to existing constitutional requirements.

¹¹ For the purpose of this Part, the term 'right holder' includes federations and associations having legal standing to assert such rights.

Article 42 requires Members to make available *civil judicial* procedures. Although this requirement does not seem to pose a significant problem to most Members, those with a strong tradition of administrative enforcement, such as China, may need to adapt their legislation. A literal interpretation of this provision would seem to rule out procedures not conducted by judicial courts. It would not seem to exclude, however, situations in which certain parts of the procedures are of an administrative nature (eg, the granting of provisional measures) provided that the possibility of appeal to judicial courts is not excluded.

Notably, Part III of the TRIPS Agreement does not refer to the 'owner'[52] of IPRs. This is the term used in Part II in relation to copyrights (Article 14.3), trademarks (eg, Article 16.1), industrial designs (Article 26.1) and patents (eg, Article 28.1). The option for the expression 'right-holder' may be due, on the one hand, to the fact that 'owner' is not suitable to the cases of geographical indications and undisclosed information; and, on the other, to the possibility for other parties (such as a licensee) to exercise such rights in enforcement procedures, when permitted by the applicable national law.

Footnote 11 specifies that the concept of 'right-holder includes federations and associations'. This definition is not only for the purposes of this Article but for the whole of Part III. Federations and associations encompass copyright collecting societies and other entities (such as producers' associations) that have recognized legal standing, according to national law, to file joint actions.

In addition to the basic obligation to make available civil procedures, Article 42 details several aspects of due processes of law, using wording that allows Members considerable flexibility to implement them. These elements are aimed at protecting the interests of both parties to the procedures, or specifically one of them. The 'fair and equitable procedures' should include the following:

(a) Defendants shall have the right to written notice which is timely and contains sufficient detail, including the basis of the claims. This obligation suggests that *inaudita parte* procedures (as allowed in Article 50 of the TRIPS Agreement) should be exceptional, as the rule is to allow the defendant to present his defences in due course.

(b) Parties shall be allowed to be represented by independent legal counsel. This will be, of course, facultative to the parties. The important point (especially for right-holders without domicile in the jurisdiction where litigation takes place)

---

[52] The concept of 'right-holder' is also used in the Agreement in relation to integrated circuits. Footnote 9 to Article 36 clarifies that 'the term "right holder" in this Section shall be understood as having the same meaning as the term "holder of the right" in the IPIC Treaty'. However, the concept of 'owner' is used with regard to copyrights, industrial designs, patents, and trademarks.

is that they may always act through legal representatives of their own choice. This does not exclude, however, requirements to make personal appearances, but this should not be 'overly burdensome'.

(c) All parties shall be duly entitled to substantiate their claims and to present all relevant evidence. The right to substantiate the claims is essential to a due process, at least for the plaintiff and defendant. National laws may extend this right to third parties joining the procedures.

(d) Finally, Article 42 establishes that the procedure shall provide a means 'to identify and protect confidential information', unless this would be contrary to existing constitutional requirements. The protection of such information is generally admitted in civil proceedings, but in some countries secrecy in civil judicial procedures may be prohibited as a matter of constitutional law. The reference to 'constitutional requirements' provides an indication that a mere legal requirement will not be sufficient to justify non-compliance with Article 42, if not of 'constitutional' nature. 'Existing' in the context of this provision should be interpreted as applicable at the time an issue concerning confidentiality is raised, since no other date is expressly referred to in this provision.

In *United States—Section 211 Omnibus Appropriations Act of 1998*,[53] the Appellate Body examined the concept of 'right holders'. It stated that

[P]ursuant to the first sentence of Article 42, civil judicial procedures must be made available to 'right holders' of intellectual property rights covered by the *TRIPS Agreement* so as to enable them to protect those rights against infringement. The United States seems to suggest that access to those rights may be limited to the *owner* of a trademark under United States law *(footnote omitted)*. The Panel defined the term 'right holders' as persons who have the legal capacity to assert rights *(footnote omitted)*. We agree with the Panel that the term 'right holders' as used in Article 42 is not limited to persons who have been established as owners of trademarks. Where the *TRIPS Agreement* confers rights exclusively on 'owners' of a right, it does so in express terms, such as in Article 16.1, which refers to the 'owner of a registered trademark'. By contrast, the term 'right holders' within the meaning of Article 42 also includes persons who claim to have legal standing to assert rights. This interpretation is also borne out by the fourth sentence of Article 42, which refers to 'parties'. Civil judicial procedures would not be fair and equitable if access to courts were not given to both complainants and defendants who purport to be owners of an intellectual property right.

The Appellate Body stressed the procedural nature of Article 42, in contrast to the substantive nature of the ownership in a defined category of trademarks imposed by Sections 211(a)(2) and (b) of the US statute (para 221). As a result, it ruled that an inconsistency with said Section did not amount to a violation of Article 42.[54]

---

[53] WT/DS176/AB/R, para 217.   [54] Idem, paras 221 and 226.

Evidence

43.1. The judicial authorities shall have the authority, where a party has presented reasonably available evidence sufficient to support its claims and has specified evidence relevant to substantiation of its claims which lies in the control of
the opposing party, to order that this evidence be produced by the opposing party,
subject in appropriate cases to conditions which ensure the protection of confidential information.

2. In cases in which a party to a proceeding voluntarily and without good reason
refuses access to, or otherwise does not provide necessary information within a
reasonable period, or significantly impedes a procedure relating to an enforcement
action, a Member may accord judicial authorities the authority to make preliminary and final determinations, affirmative or negative, on the basis of the information presented to them, including the complaint or the allegation presented by
the party adversely affected by the denial of access to information, subject to providing the parties an opportunity to be heard on the allegations or evidence.

In many cases of infringement of intellectual property rights, it is essential[55] to get
access to information or materials in possession of the other party to prove the
claims made. Although this will normally be of particular value for the plaintiff,
Article 43.1 applies to any of the *parties*. In some situations, the defendant may need
to get access to evidence in possession of his opponent to articulate his defence.

National procedures regarding production of evidence in possession of another
party significantly differ. In some cases, orders to that effect can only be issued for
the preservation of evidence where there is a strong case of infringement, while in
others (like the *saisie contrefaçon* applied in France) an order can be issued to determine whether infringement has occurred.[56] Article 43 follows the first approach,
although it would not rule out the second one as a 'more extensive protection' in
terms of Article 1.1 of the Agreement.[57] Members, in effect, are bound to provide
for the production of evidence under the control of the opposing party provided
that:

- a party has presented reasonably available evidence sufficient to support its
  claims; and
- said party has specified evidence relevant to substantiation of its claims which
  lies in the control of the opposing party.

Article 43.1, hence, imposes on the requesting party the initial burden to submit
'reasonably available' evidence, which should be enough to convince the judge that
an infringement has occurred, and also the burden to specify what is the evidence
to be presented by the other party. This requirement seems to exclude general
orders of inspection or seizure without a specific target, while in practice the judge
also has discretion to determine what the level of specification should be.

---

[55] See, eg, Dratler op. cit.(1997), para 1A-116.   [56] See Heat op. cit. (2005), p 16.
[57] See Chapter 2 above.

A further condition for the applicability of Article 43.1 is that the evidence to be submitted by the opposing party should lie in his control. This would exclude an obligation to present evidence that is in possession of third parties, such as suppliers or clients.

'Evidence' in the context of this provision should be deemed to include documentation or material objects in possession of the opposing party, such as possibly infringing products or machinery used to produce them. Since providing such evidence may interrupt the activities of the party or cause an economic loss, the orders referred to in Article 43.1 should be prudently granted in order to avoid abuses by the requesting party.

Article 43.1 does not specify at what stage of the procedures an order for the production of evidence by the opposing party may be granted. This will obviously depend on the regulations applicable at the national level. It is to be noted, however, that interim measures to preserve relevant evidence are provided for under Article 50.1 of the TRIPS Agreement, as examined below.[58]

Article 43.1 *in fine* sets out a limitation to orders to produce evidence, based on the protection of 'confidential information'. While such orders may be requested by some parties with the intent of obtaining confidential information from competitors, would-be infringers may argue confidentiality reasons in order to conceal relevant evidence. Again, that provision leaves the judicial authorities the task of determining the circumstances ('appropriate cases') in which this exception may apply.

Finally, Article 43.1, like Article 34.1 of the TRIPS Agreement[59] and many other provisions in Part III, does not set out a rule that could be directly invoked by private parties. It instead mandates Members to empower the judicial authorities to grant the orders referred to. Hence, a Member should be deemed to comply with Article 43.1 (and with other provisions framed in similar terms) when judges have the required competence (whether recognized explicitly or not), being understood that it will be a matter subject to judicial authorities' discretion whether such orders would be granted in particular cases or not.

Article 43.2 is of an optional nature and therefore, it does not contain minimum standards that could raise non-compliance complaints under the DSU. It rather provides an indication of what the negotiating parties deemed a desirable mode of dealing with the defendant's refusal to provide evidence requested in accordance with Article 43.1. Again here, the formulation used is what judicial authorities may have the authority to do. Given the optional nature of Article 43.2, Members may decide a different course of action in case of such refusal, or only partially follow the guidelines provided therein.

Article 43.2 alludes to three different situations where a party to a proceeding

- voluntarily and *without good reason* refuses access to necessary information within a reasonable period;

---

[58] See pp 433–5. [59] See Chapter 9 above.

- otherwise does not provide such information within a reasonable period; or
- impedes a procedure relating to an enforcement action.

The first two situations obviously seem to relate to requests made in accordance with Article 43.1, but Article 43.2 refers to 'information' and not to 'evidence', thereby excluding products, machinery, and other tools of production. The scope of the provision is also limited to information that is 'necessary' to make a determination and, by reference to Article 43.1, it should be interpreted that it only applies to information under the control of the requested party.

'Otherwise' in the second situation should be interpreted in relation to 'access' and not to 'good reason'. If not, this sentence would contradict the condition indicated above, since it would seem to empower the judge to adopt a determination even if the requested party had 'good reasons' not to provide access. Such an interpretation would put an excessive and unfair burden on the requested party.[60]

The third situation ('impedes a procedure relating to an enforcement action') is couched in much broader terms, since impediments to a procedure may be of different nature. It opens, in fact, a 'Pandora's box', since it would be up to the judicial authority to establish when a party has 'significantly' impeded an enforcement procedure. Obviously, the articulation of defences may not be deemed an impediment, if done in accordance with the applicable procedures.[61]

Article 43.2 does not authorize the making of a determination solely on the basis of the failure to provide the requested information, as the judicial authority is required to consider 'the information presented' to the authority, 'including' (but not only) 'the complaint or the allegation presented by the party adversely affected by the denial of access to information'. In addition, both parties, including the party required to produce evidence, must be given 'an opportunity to be heard on the allegations or evidence'.

Injunctions

44.1. The judicial authorities shall have the authority to order a party to desist from an infringement, inter alia to prevent the entry into the channels of commerce in their jurisdiction of imported goods that involve the infringement of an intellectual property right, immediately after customs clearance of such goods. Members are not obliged to accord such authority in respect of protected subject matter acquired or ordered by a person prior to knowing or having reasonable grounds to know that dealing in such subject matter would entail the infringement of an intellectual property right.

2. Notwithstanding the other provisions of this Part and provided that the provisions of Part II specifically addressing use by governments, or by third parties authorized by a government, without the authorization of the right holder are complied with, Members may limit the remedies available against such use to

---

[60] See UNCTAD-ICTSD op. cit. (2005), p 589.   [61] Ibidem.

payment of remuneration in accordance with subparagraph (h) of Article 31. In other cases, the remedies under this Part shall apply or, where these remedies are inconsistent with a Member's law, declaratory judgments and adequate compensation shall be available.

Both Article 44 and Article 50[62] of the TRIPS Agreement require the granting of injunctions; Article 44, however, deals with permanent injunctions, while Article 50 deals with *provisional* measures that may include *interim* injunctions. On the other hand, while Article 40 refers, *inter alia*, to an infringement after importation has taken place, Article 51 applies at the border; that is, before the release by the customs authorities of the infringing goods.[63]

The purpose of the measures to be adopted under Article 40 is to assure that a party desists from an infringement that was established according to the applicable procedures. Like other provisions in this Part, the 'judicial authorities shall have the authority' formulation leaves Members broad room to determine how that objective will be reached.

Article 44.1 mentions one of the possible objectives of an injunction, the prevention of entry into the channels of commerce of imported goods that involve the infringement of an intellectual property right, 'immediately after customs clearance of such goods'. This is only an illustration; the drafters of this provision probably wanted to emphasize that an injunction might need to be granted before the infringing goods enter into the commercial channels, without waiting until evidence could be provided that such was the case. Unlike Article 50 relating to border measures, Article 44 would be applicable to the infringement of any intellectual property right.

The granting of exceptions under Article 44.1 is not required in case of a *bona fide* acquirer; that is of a person who acquired or ordered a product 'prior to knowing or having reasonable grounds to know that dealing in such subject matter would entail the infringement of an intellectual property right'. The wording used ('Members are not obliged to accord such authority') suggests, however, that at least some negotiating parties[64] envisaged the possibility of extending, as a TRIPS-plus measure, the application of injunctions to such acquirers.[65] In Dratler's view, the exception operates like a 'sort of compulsory license by refusing an injunction and remitting the claimant to a damage remedy'.[66]

In a possibly groundbreaking decision in *Ebay Inc. et al v Mercexchange LLC* of 15 May 2006, the US Supreme Court stated that 'the decision whether to grant or deny injunctive relief rests within the equitable discretion of the district courts'.

---

[62] See pp 433–8 below.   [63] See below pp 438–41.

[64] The US and EC original proposals did not contain this limitation. The draft agreement as of 23 July 1990 read as follows: '1A. The judicial authorities shall have the authority to issue upon request an order that an infringement be refrained from or discontinued, irrespective of whatever the defendant has acted with intent or negligence' (W/76).

[65] Unless, for instance, they pay for the damages arising from the infringement.

[66] Dratler op. cit. (1997), para 1A-103.

This means that an infringement may not necessarily lead to an injunction, if the court is convinced, based on equity considerations, that it is not justified. Justice Kennedy, joined by Justices Stevens, Souter, and Breyer, elaborated that for some

firms, an injunction, and the potentially serious sanctions arising from its violation, can be employed as a bargaining tool to charge exorbitant fees to companies that seek to buy licences to practise the patent. When the patented invention is but a small component of the product the companies seek to produce and the threat of an injunction is employed simply for undue leverage in negotiations, legal damages may well be sufficient to compensate for the infringement and an injunction may not serve the public interest. In addition injunctive relief may have different consequences for the burgeoning number of patents over business methods, which were not of much economic and legal significance in earlier times. The potential vagueness and suspect validity of some of these patents may affect the calculus under the four-factor test.

The Court reversed in this case the Federal Circuit decision, which had been based on its 'general rule that courts will issue permanent injunctions against patent infringement absent exceptional circumstances'.[67] As noted by Dratler with regard to the *bona fide* acquirer, denying a permanent injunction despite the fact that an infringement has occurred, may be regarded as a *de facto* grant of a compulsory licence. Given, however, that Article 44.1 only mandates Members to give judicial authorities the power to grant injunctions, such authorities can exercise their discretion in deciding particular cases.

Despite the title of the provision ('Injunctions'), Article 44.2 goes beyond this issue and deals with remedies in cases of government use and compulsory licences where no infringement exists.

This provision—proposed by the US—closely follows the US legislation on patents and copyright.[68] The US law, in effect, limits the right of holders of patents and copyrights to seeking 'reasonable and entire compensation' from the US federal government where it has used their rights without authorization.[69] As examined elsewhere,[70] the US Federal government has made an extensive application of 'government use' and compulsory licensing[71] and it wanted to limit the remedies available where such uses were authorized.

---

[67] The petitioners operated popular Internet Web sites that allowed private sellers to list goods they wished to sell. The respondent sought to license its business method patent to the petitioners, but no agreement was reached. In the respondent's subsequent patent infringement suit, a jury found that its patent was valid, that the petitioners had infringed the patent, and that damages were appropriate (401 F 3d 1323, 1339). In other cases, however, the Court of Appeals of the Federal Circuit has denied permanent injunctions, for instance, when deemed overly broad, such as in the case of *IR v IXYS* regarding a patented semiconductor device (US Patent No 6,476,481). See, eg, <http://www.patentlyo.com/patent/2004/09/federal_circuit_1.html> (last accessed on 20 October 2006).

[68] See, eg, Dreier op. cit. (1996), p 262.   [69] See, eg, Dratler op. cit. (1997), para 1A-104.

[70] See, eg, J Reichman and C Hasenzahl, *Non-voluntary Licensing of Patented Inventions: Historical Perspective, Legal Framework under TRIPS, and an Overview of the Practice in Canada and the United States of America* (2002, Geneva, UNCTAD/ICTSD); C Correa, *Intellectual Property Rights and the Use of Compulsory Licenses: Options for Developing Countries* (1999: Geneva, South Centre).

[71] See above Chapter 9.

The basic rule in Article 44.2 is that in the case of government use or compulsory licence, Members may limit liabilities to a remuneration determined in accordance with subparagraph (h) of Article 31.[72] This only applies in case of the 'provisions of Part II specifically addressing use by governments, or by third parties authorized by a government', meaning that such limitation will only operate in the case of patents (Article 31) and layout-designs of integrated circuits (Article 37.2),[73] with the exclusion of other intellectual property rights.

Since the first sentence of Article 44.2 contains an optional provision, and given that the TRIPS Agreement sets forth minimum standards, it is implied that Members could subject government use and compulsory licensing to conditions of remuneration different than those stipulated for under Article 31(h) of the Agreement. For instance, under US law (28 USCS 1498), whenever an invention covered by a patent is used or manufactured by or for the US without consent of the patent owner the owner's sole remedy is an action against the US 'for the recovery of his reasonable and entire compensation. Reasonable and entire compensation shall include the owner's reasonable costs, including reasonable fees for expert witnesses and attorneys, in pursuing the action . . . '.

Another implication of the wording used in this provision ('provided that the provisions of Part II . . . are complied with') is that right-holders may request remedies other than the remuneration set forth in Article 31(h) if the conditions established by the TRIPS Agreement for authorizing government use or a compulsory licence have not been met. If that were the case the most likely scenario, however, would be the challenge by the right-holder of the act authorizing government use or granting a compulsory licence as such.

For other cases not covered under Articles 31 and 37.2, 'the remedies under this Part shall apply'. Unlike the first sentence of Article 44.2, the second sentence is mandatory. What the 'other cases' might be is unclear in the text, but may refer to compulsory licences with regard to copyright, which are provided for in the Annex to the Berne Convention and by many national laws under various circumstances, or with regard to industrial designs. Compulsory licences of trademarks are prohibited by the Agreement.[74]

Article 44.2 broadly refers to 'remedies under this Part' and not only to injunctions. In such 'other cases', however, where the remedies provided for in Part II 'are inconsistent with a Member's law, declaratory judgments and adequate compensation shall be available. This wording, unlike other provisions in Part III, does not refer to incompatibility with 'constitutional' rules, but just with 'a Member's law', giving Members significant latitude to determine which remedies are permissible and, hence, consistent under the Member's law.

Finally, Members have considerable room to determine when the compensation would be deemed 'adequate' under Article 44.2. The term 'compensation' may

---

[72] Idem.   [73] See Chapter 10 above.
[74] See Article 21 and its commentary above, pp 201–3.

allow different interpretations, ranging from indemnification for injury to consideration or price.[75] Thus, a reasonable royalty as would be payable under a freely negotiated contract could be deemed 'adequate' in this case, as well as an amount based on the recovery of costs. However, the possibility of enhancement for wilful and malicious conduct which, as mentioned above, is possible in some jurisdictions for the determination of damages would seem alien to the concept of 'compensation'.

Damages

45.1. The judicial authorities shall have the authority to order the infringer to pay the right holder damages adequate to compensate for the injury the right holder has suffered because of an infringement of that person's intellectual property right by an infringer who knowingly, or with reasonable grounds to know, engaged in infringing activity.

2. The judicial authorities shall also have the authority to order the infringer to pay the right holder expenses, which may include appropriate attorney's fees. In appropriate cases, Members may authorize the judicial authorities to order recovery of profits and/or payment of pre-established damages even where the infringer did not knowingly, or with reasonable grounds to know, engage in infringing activity.

The availability of damages and the amount of the award varies under national laws, often according to the type of intellectual property involved. Article 45 of the TRIPS Agreement imposes damages as a mandatory remedy. It requires the judicial authorities to have the power to order the infringer to pay the right-holder damages adequate to compensate for the injury the right-holder has suffered. Members may define when compensation is to be deemed 'adequate'. [76]

However, an infringer who did not know, or had no reasonable grounds to know, that he engaged in infringing activity is not required to pay damages, whatever the nature of his offence.[77] It is to be noted that there is only one provision in the Agreement that specifically mandates payment of a compensation by the *bona fide* acquirer: in the case of infringing layout-designs/topographics of integrated circuits, the *bona fide* acquirer is bound to pay the title-holder a sum equivalent to a reasonable royalty such as would be payable under a freely negotiated licence in respect of the protected layout-design (Article 37.1).[78]

Article 45.2 (first sentence) contains another 'the judicial authorities shall also have the authority' type of provision. It requires Members to empower the judges to order the infringer to pay the right-holder expenses, which *may* include 'appropriate'

---

[75] See *Black's Law Dictionary* (1990, 6th edn), p 194.

[76] 'Adequate' means 'sufficient, satisfactory (often with the implication of being barely so)', *Concise Oxford Dictionary* (1982: Oxford University Press, 7th edn), p 14.

[77] See, eg, Dratler op. cit. (1997), para 1A-108.   [78] See Chapter 10.

attorney's fees.[79] Members' obligations will be satisfied if judges are authorized to impose on the infringer the payment of expenses made in relation to the judicial action, but are not obliged to include attorney's fees, which is an exceptional measure in many jurisdictions.[80]

Lastly, Article 45.2 (second sentence) includes a further optional provision, according to which, in appropriate cases, Members *may* authorize the judicial authorities to order recovery of profits and/or payment of pre-established damages. Unlike Article 45.1, this provision specifically indicates that damages may be calculated so as to allow for the 'recovery of profits',[81] or be based on damages set by national laws ('pre-established damages'). This provision further indicates that this *may* apply even where the infringer did not knowingly, or with reasonable grounds to know, engage in infringing activity; that is, in respect of a *bona fide* acquirer or user of protected subject matter.[82]

Of course, Members are always allowed (but are not obliged) to provide for 'TRIPS-plus' measures in relation to damages,[83] but in doing so they do not need to comply necessarily with the conditions set forth in Article 45.2 (second sentence). Hence, a Member may provide for the recovery of profits or pre-established damages but limit these measures to culpable and negligent infringers only.

Other remedies

46. In order to create an effective deterrent to infringement, the judicial authorities shall have the authority to order that goods that they have found to be infringing be, without compensation of any sort, disposed of outside the channels of commerce in such a manner as to avoid any harm caused to the right holder, or, unless this would be contrary to existing constitutional requirements, destroyed. The judicial authorities shall also have the authority to order that materials and implements the predominant use of which has been in the creation of the infringing goods be, without compensation of any sort, disposed of outside the channels of commerce in such a manner as to minimize the risks of further infringements. In considering such requests, the need for proportionality between the seriousness of the infringement and the remedies ordered as well as the interests of third parties shall be taken into account. In regard to counterfeit trademark goods, the simple

[79] The facultative nature of this provision is in line with US law, under which it is discretionary to a US court to allow the recovery of costs and attorney's fees by the prevailing party. See, eg, W Herrington and G Thompson, *Intellectual Property Rights and United States International Trade Laws*, (2002: Oceana Publs Inc), pp 7–20.   [80] See, eg, Gervais op. cit. (2003), p 207.

[81] When the loss of profits is difficult to calculate, courts often admit compensation based on the amount of net profits made from infringement.

[82] The Draft of 23 July 1990 contained the following provision: '8A. The right holder shall be entitled to [obtain] [claim] from infringement [adequate] [full] compensation for injury he has suffered because of a [deliberate or negligent] infringement of his intellectual property right. The right holder shall also be entitled to claim remuneration for costs, including attorney fees, reasonably incurred in the proceedings. In appropriate cases, PARTIES may provide for recovery of profits and/or pre-established damages to be granted even where the infringer has not acted intentionally or negligently' (W/76).

[83] See Article 1 of the TRIPS Agreement, Chapter 2.

removal of the trademark unlawfully affixed shall not be sufficient, other than in exceptional cases, to permit release of the goods into the channels of commerce.

With the same approach used in most provisions in Part III, Article 46 obliges Members to give the judicial authorities additional powers 'to create an effective deterrent to infringement' where goods have been effectively found to be infringing. The measures that such authorities may have the power to adopt 'without compensation of any sort' to the infringer, include:

a) To remove from commercial circulation the infringing goods. Such a removal would not apply, however, if the commercialization would not cause harm to the right-holder (for instance, if distributed in local markets not supplied by the right-holder and leakage to markets of interest to him is unlikely to occur). With regard to counterfeit trademark goods, Article 46 establishes that the simple removal of the trademark[84] unlawfully affixed shall not be sufficient to permit release of the goods into commerce. The aim of this provision is to fight professional counterfeiting by preventing trademarks from being unlawfully fixed to the goods if released into commerce. However, simply removing the trademark may be possible 'in exceptional cases' that Article 46 does not define, thereby leaving Members freedom to determine when such cases may arise (eg cases of non-professional infringement).[85]

b) To destroy the infringing goods, unless this would be contrary to existing constitutional requirements. This is quite a strong sanction, since in the absence of requirements set forth in the constitution itself, destruction may be deemed mandatory and may lead to significant economic waste and be socially questionable, especially in developing countries. The infringing goods may be supplied to charities or to government (if not involved in commercial activities for the legitimate goods).[86] However, judicial authorities (who are given the authority but are not obliged to order this measure) can adopt less disruptive measures.

c) To dispose of outside the channels of commerce materials and implements used in the creation of the infringing goods. This measure would apply when the 'predominant' use of such materials and implements was to create infringing goods, and when disposition is necessary 'to minimize the risks of further infringements'.

Lastly, Article 46 subjects the adoption of these measures to a *proportionality test* under which the seriousness of the infringement and the remedies ordered, as well as the interests of third parties, need to be taken into account. This means that judicial authorities need to balance the interests at stake and, at their discretion, can refuse the granting of the measures described in the first and second sentences of

---

[84] It is interesting to note that the draft of 23 July 1990 (W/76) extended (though in a bracketed text) the same treatment to affixed geographical indications.   [85] See, eg, Gervais op. cit. (2003), p 209.
[86] These alternatives to destruction have been utilized, for instance, in the United States. See, eg, Dratler op. cit. (1997), para 1A-109.

Article 46. One of the considerations that such authorities can make relates to the effects of the mandated remedies on third parties, for instance, distributors who may have ordered and paid for the infringer merchandises without knowing that they were counterfeit goods.

Right of information

> **47. Members may provide that the judicial authorities shall have the authority, unless this would be out of proportion to the seriousness of the infringement, to order the infringer to inform the right holder of the identity of third persons involved in the production and distribution of the infringing goods or services and of their channels of distribution.**

The right to obtain information from the infringer is a 'may' provision; that is, Members are not obliged to stipulate it in national law. This provision only refers to orders by *judicial authorities*, and applies in *civil and in administrative procedures*.

The provision assumes that an infringement has been established: the obligation may be imposed on an 'infringer', and not generally on a 'defendant'. Moreover, the rule introduces a proportionality test; that is, this obligation would only apply in cases of serious infringements. Should a Member country choose to establish this obligation, the courts would have considerable leeway to determine when an infringement is sufficiently serious to justify this measure.

Since the infringer would be obliged to inform the right-holder and not directly the court, it may be assumed that the information is not indispensable for the court's decision, and that the judicial authorities should only order it upon request of the right-holder.

The content of the obligation is limited to providing information on:

a) the identity of third persons involved in the production and distribution of the infringing goods or services. The obligation to provide information about third parties is limited to their *identity*. The infringer would not be obliged to provide other information such as the type of business or commercial activities of such parties, methods, or technologies used, etc;

b) the channels of distribution of such third parties. The limits of the obligation to inform about 'channels of distribution' are more difficult to establish, since information about such channels may include data on persons, places of storage and sale, destination of infringing products, etc. This obligation does not seem to include upstream information about suppliers. Given the territoriality of IPRs, it would be reasonable to interpret that it only refers to distribution channels in the jurisdiction where infringement took place, but this point is unclear.

An obligation of the type established in Article 47 may be important to deal with professional infringers, so as to help the right-holder to locate and take action against the infringers' accomplices.[87]

---

[87] See, eg, Gervais op. cit. (2003), p 209.

Though Article 47 does not refer to the protection of confidential information, the general rule of Article 41 should apply.

Indemnification of the defendant

48. 1. **The judicial authorities shall have the authority to order a party at whose request measures were taken and who has abused enforcement procedures to provide to a party wrongfully enjoined or restrained adequate compensation for the injury suffered because of such abuse. The judicial authorities shall also have the authority to order the applicant to pay the defendant expenses, which may include appropriate attorney's fees.**

2. **In respect of the administration of any law pertaining to the protection or enforcement of intellectual property rights, Members shall only exempt both public authorities and officials from liability to appropriate remedial measures where actions are taken or intended in good faith in the course of the administration of that law.**

The risk of liability in enforcement procedures is a two-edged-sword.[88] Rightholders may knowingly and in bad faith use IPRs to block legitimate competition. In these cases, the defendant is likely to suffer an important economic injury, such as when a provisional measure forces him out of the market.

Article 48.1 addresses these issues in the typical 'the judicial authorities shall have the authority' format. It requires Members to empower judicial authorities to order a plaintiff who has 'abused' enforcement procedures to provide to a defendant 'wrongfully enjoined or restrained adequate compensation for the injury suffered because of such abuse'. This provision thus focuses on the *abuse* of enforcement procedures. The concept of abuse is also employed in several other provisions of the TRIPS Agreement (Articles 8.2, 40.2, 41.1, 50.3, 53.2, 63.1, and 67), thereby strongly indicating the Agreement's search for a balance between the protection of IPRs and the interests of third parties. Of course, when IPRs are abused not only the particular competitor whose activity has been restrained suffers, but also the general public unduly deprived of access to a competitive product or service.

An important interpretive issue is to determine when the exercise of enforcement proceedings may be deemed abusive. This would certainly be the case when the intention of the plaintiff has been to deliberately exclude an innocent competitor. But also in the absence of bad faith, abuse may take place when a serious departure from the reasonable use of enforcement proceedings is found.[89]

Article 48.1—which gives content to the general provisions contained in Article 8.2[90] and, more specifically, Article 41.1[91]—applies when a party has been 'wrongfully enjoined or restrained', for instance, due to the adoption of a preliminary

---

[88] See, eg, Dratler op. cit. (1997), para 1A-108.   [89] See, eg, Gervais op. cit. (2003), p 211.
[90] 'Appropriate measures, provided that they are consistent with the provisions of this Agreement, may be needed to prevent the abuse of intellectual property rights by right holders...'. See Chapter 4.   [91] See the analysis of this Article above, pp 410–12.

injunction. The plaintiff is required in these cases to pay an 'adequate compensation for the injury suffered'.[92]

Under a provision that mirrors Article 45.2,[93] the judicial authorities shall also have the authority to order the applicant to pay the defendant expenses, which *may* include 'appropriate attorney's fees'.

An important question arises as to whether Members may also provide for the compensation for the injury suffered by a defendant in an infringement suit, when he is determined to be innocent but an 'abuse' by the plaintiff cannot be established, for instance when in a controversial case the application of the doctrine of equivalents in patent litigation has led to a conclusion of non-infringement. In this case, if enjoined or restrained, the defendant may also have suffered an injury that the plaintiff should compensate. The Agreement does not prevent a Member from requiring the plaintiff to compensate the defendant in these cases. This interpretation is confirmed by Article 50.3, which specifically requires that judicial authorities shall have the authority to order the applicant to provide a security or equivalent assurance sufficient *to protect the defendant*, as well as to prevent abuse.[94] In fact, plaintiffs always have the option to initiate and pursue enforcement procedures without restraining the defendant's activities, and they should be liable if it is finally showed that their claim was wrong, even if not abusive.

Further, under Article 48.1 the judicial authorities shall also have the authority to order the applicant to pay the defendant expenses, which *may* include appropriate attorney's fees. This provision mandates a treatment to the defendant, who was the victim of abusive enforcement proceedings, equivalent to that conferred to the plaintiff under Article 45.1.

Article 48.2 establishes an obligation with regard to the *administration* of any law pertaining to the protection or enforcement of intellectual property rights. The purpose of the provision is to ensure that public authorities and officials are subject to liability where actions have been taken or intended in bad faith.

'Law' may be understood in the context of this provision, either in a formal sense, as legislation adopted by Congress, or in a material sense, as any regulation dealing with the enforcement of IPRs. To the extent that the provision refers to 'any' law, both federal and sub-federal legislation would be included. Further, no distinction is made between civil and criminal, or administrative and judicial procedures.

Article 48.2 prevents Members from exempting public authorities and officials from liability to appropriate remedial measures, except 'where actions are taken or intended in good faith in the course of the administration of that law'. Public authorities of any kind, whether judicial or administrative, and their officials are subject to this provision, which requires a judgment about the *intention* with which a measure has been adopted. Actions not conforming to the law, but adopted in good faith, may be exempted from the remedial measures mandated in this Article.

---

[92] See p 426 above the analysis on the concept of 'adequate compensation'.
[93] See pp 426–7 above.   [94] See p 436 below.

The Article leaves open to Members' a decision about the kind of 'remedial measures' that may be applied.[95] This provision applies whether actions were taken upon request by the interested party or *ex officio*, to the extent that such actions were made in the normal course of administration of enforcement-related laws. The burden of proof that actions were not taken or intended in good faith would rest with the party that alleges misconduct; in other words, *bona fide* would be presumed.

Though Article 48.2 does not differentiate with regard to the party that may claim remedial action, it is included under the title 'Indemnification of the Defendant'. This indicates that it is intended to protect the defendant from abuses committed with the intervention of public authorities, in logical connection to Article 48.1.

Administrative procedures

49. To the extent that any civil remedy can be ordered as a result of administrative procedures on the merits of a case, such procedures shall conform to principles equivalent in substance to those set forth in this Section.

Article 49 extends the application of the rules on procedures and civil remedies dealt with in Articles 41–48 to administrative procedures on the merits of the case. The rules applied, however, need not be identical but 'conform to principles equivalent in substance' to those contained in Section 2 of Part III. Conformity with the 'principles' and not with the 'provisions' is required, thereby suggesting that there is considerable room to adapt the provisions set forth in that Section to the characteristics (eg informalism) of administrative procedures. The determination of what the 'principles' are may certainly give rise to different opinions. Further, the equivalence required is 'in substance' and not in detail.

As noted above, administrative procedures are also subject to the general obligations set forth in Article 41.

In some countries, administrative enforcement procedures are of particular importance. In China, for instance, there is a 'dual-track' system of enforcement of IPRs, involving judicial or administrative authorities.[96] It has been estimated that around 90 per cent of all patent litigation in China has involved the administrative authorities.[97]

---

[95] In contrast, the draft of 23 July 1990 (W76) referred to 'compensation' only: 'PARTIES may provide for the possibility that such parties [may] [shall] be entitled to claim compensation from [authorities] [public officers] in appropriate cases, such as negligent or deliberate improper conduct. [they shall provide for such possibility in the case of administrative *ex officio* action.]').

[96] See, eg, L Xiaohai, 'Enforcement of intellectual property rights in the People's Republic of China', (2001), IIC, vol. 32, No 2, p 141.

[97] See, eg, M Murphy, 'Patent litigation in China. How does it work?', (2001), Patent World, June/July 2001, p 19.

Provisional measures

50. 1. The judicial authorities shall have the authority to order prompt and effective provisional measures:

    (a) to prevent an infringement of any intellectual property right from occurring, and in particular to prevent the entry into the channels of commerce in their jurisdiction of goods, including imported goods immediately after customs clearance;

    (b) to preserve relevant evidence in regard to the alleged infringement.

2. The judicial authorities shall have the authority to adopt provisional measures *inaudita altera parte* where appropriate, in particular where any delay is likely to cause irreparable harm to the right holder, or where there is a demonstrable risk of evidence being destroyed.

3. The judicial authorities shall have the authority to require the applicant to provide any reasonably available evidence in order to satisfy themselves with a sufficient degree of certainty that the applicant is the right holder and that the applicant's right is being infringed or that such infringement is imminent, and to order the applicant to provide a security or equivalent assurance sufficient to protect the defendant and to prevent abuse.

4. Where provisional measures have been adopted *inaudita altera parte*, the parties affected shall be given notice, without delay after the execution of the measures at the latest. A review, including a right to be heard, shall take place upon request of the defendant with a view to deciding, within a reasonable period after the notification of the measures, whether these measures shall be modified, revoked or confirmed.

5. The applicant may be required to supply other information necessary for the identification of the goods concerned by the authority that will execute the provisional measures.

6. Without prejudice to paragraph 4, provisional measures taken on the basis of paragraphs 1 and 2 shall, upon request by the defendant, be revoked or otherwise cease to have effect, if proceedings leading to a decision on the merits of the case are not initiated within a reasonable period, to be determined by the judicial authority ordering the measures where a Member's law so permits or, in the absence of such a determination, not to exceed 20 working days or 31 calendar days, whichever is the longer.

7. Where the provisional measures are revoked or where they lapse due to any act or omission by the applicant, or where it is subsequently found that there has been no infringement or threat of infringement of an intellectual property right, the judicial authorities shall have the authority to order the applicant, upon request of the defendant, to provide the defendant appropriate compensation for any injury caused by these measures.

8. To the extent that any provisional measure can be ordered as a result of administrative procedures, such procedures shall conform to principles equivalent in substance to those set forth in this Section.

Article 50 is the sole Article in Part 3 dealing with 'Provisional measures'. It contains important procedural rules to deal with infringements that are taking place that are imminent (Article 50.3).[98]

This Article sets forth the minimum requirements to be met by proceedings for provisional measures. Like other provisions in Part III, it establishes the obligation to empower judicial authorities (in this case, to grant provisional measures) and defines the results to be achieved rather than the conditions to do so. This leaves Members considerable leeway to implement the granting of provisional measures and, particularly, to determine the requirements to be imposed in accordance with each national legal system. Article 50 lacks the elements necessary to make it directly operative; however, as mentioned, it has been deemed self-executing by case law in some countries.[99]

The provisional measures, which should be 'prompt and effective', must be available to address two situations:

(a) to prevent an infringement of any intellectual property right from occurring[100] and, in particular, to prevent the entry into the channels of commerce in their jurisdiction of goods, including imported goods immediately *after* customs clearance.[101] This provision only applies to acts concerning commercialization *within* the jurisdiction of the Member,[102] and would not apply upon exportation of infringing goods;[103]

(b) to preserve relevant evidence with regard to the alleged infringement. The scope of the preliminary relief, according to this provision, embraces the preservation of any evidence relevant to establish the infringement, and not only of the infringing products. 'Anton Piller' orders have ordinarily been granted in common-law countries for this purpose.[104]

In many countries injunctions are difficult to obtain in intellectual property disputes, particularly those involving patent infringement, because in most cases damages are a sufficient remedy until the issues of infringement and (validity) are

---

[98] Note that Article 50.7 also refers to the 'threat' of infringement of an intellectual property right.

[99] See, eg, C Correa, 'Medidas cautelares en material de patentes de invención', (2002), Lexis Nexis Jurisprudencia Argentina, JA-2002-IV, No 8, pp 21–8.

[100] Provisional measures aiming at restraining a party from engaging in a particular act are generally known as 'preliminary' , 'interlocutory', or 'interim' injunctions. See, eg, *Managing Intellectual Property*, 'Interim relief. A worldwide survey', November 1997, pp 35–44.

[101] See Article 51 for measures to be adopted before customs clearance.

[102] The Brussels Convention on Jurisdiction in the Enforcement of Judgements in Civil and Commercial Matters, applicable within the European Community, allows a provisional measure to be requested in the jurisdiction of a State even in cases where the jurisdiction of another State is competent to take a decision on the merits of the case (Article 24). Cross-border injunctions have been granted by courts in the Netherlands and Germany (see, eg, *Managing Intellectual Property*, (1997), p 35.

[103] See, eg, Dreier op. cit. (1996), p 264.

[104] An 'Anton Piller order' may be adopted so as to require the defendant to permit the plaintiff's representatitives to enter the defendant's premises and remove infringing items or obtain other evidence (photocopies, photographs, etc) to be used to prove that an infringement has occurred.

settled at trial. Thus, in the US the judge would normally consider whether: there is a reasonable likelihood that the patent, if challenged by the defendant as being invalid, be declared valid; any delay in granting such measures will cause an irreparable harm to the patent-holder; the harm that may be caused to the title-holder exceeds the harm that the alleged infringer will suffer in case the measure was wrongly granted; there is a reasonable likelihood that the patent is infringed; and granting of the measure would be consistent with the public interest.[105] Preliminary injunctions have been characterized in the US as the exception rather than the rule, including in trademark cases; the granting of such injunctions is deemed an exercise of a very far-reaching power, never to be indulged in except in a case clearly demanding it.[106]

In Australia, a 'balance of convenience' must be in favour of granting the injunction; the court would also consider the age of the patent and whether the validity of the patent is an issue, and would generally refuse an injunction if the defendant undertakes to keep an account of profits and appears likely to be able to meet an award against a final trial.[107] The balance of convenience is also applied in the United Kingdom, among other countries.[108]

Similarly, in order to obtain interlocutory injunctions (*référés d'interdiction provisoires*) in France, the patent must not obviously be null and void and the infringement must appear serious; in Germany such measures are granted where infringement and validity are clearly beyond doubt, and normally in cases of literal infringement and not where questions of equivalence arise; in Mexico, injunctions in patent infringement hardly ever take place, and an official expert must determine whether the patent is likely to be used by the alleged infringer before a measure is granted; in the United Kingdom, it is also generally difficult to obtain an injunction because courts have taken the view that damages are quantifiable and would only proceed if damages are not an adequate remedy, taking the balance of convenience into account.[109]

Article 50.2 requires that the judicial authorities also have the authority to adopt provisional measures *inaudita altera parte*. This provision does not provide a general rule to establish when such measures are justified, but vaguely refers to its application 'where appropriate' and in two particular cases:

(a) where any delay is likely to cause irreparable harm to the right holder; or
(b) where there is a demonstrable risk of evidence being destroyed.

---

[105] See, eg, J Reichman and M Zinnani, 'Las medidas precautorias en el derecho estadounidense: el justo balance entre las partes', (2002), Lexis Nexis Jurisprudencia Argentina, JA 2002-IV, No 8, pp 15–21.

[106] See, eg, T McCarthy, *McCarthy on Trademarks and Unfair Competition*, (2002: West USA, Thomson), vol. 5, pp 30–59.

[107] See, eg, *Managing Intellectual Property* (1997), p 36.   [108] Idem, pp 37 and 43.

[109] Idem, pp 38, 39, 42, and 43.

In case (a) the critical element is the *delay as a cause* of an 'irreparable harm'.[110] The latter would exist if the right-holder were unlikely to obtain adequate compensation for damages (for instance, because the infringer had no permanent business activity in the country). The mere possibility of producing harm to the right-holder would not be sufficient to ignore the defendant's basic right to be heard before an injunction or other relief is granted.

In case (b) an *ex parte* provisional measure would proceed if the risk of evidence being destroyed is *demonstrable*. The applicant must duly substantiate his request.

It is up to Members to determine whether there are other cases in which *ex parte* provisional measures would be appropriate, but a prudent approach is advisable. In fact, in developed countries *ex parte* measures are only exceptionally granted. This is the case, for instance, in the US,[111] Germany, and France.[112] In Canada, patent infringement matters are not deemed to be of extreme urgency, and 'it is difficult to imagine the circumstances where a Canadian court would consider it appropriate to grant relief without notice where there was only an allegation of patent infringement'.[113]

Article 50.3 reflects the 'checks and balances' approach adopted in many provisions of Part III. The judicial authorities must have the authority to impose a number of requirements on the applicant of a provisional measure:

(a) to provide any reasonably available evidence in order to satisfy the authorities with a sufficient degree of certainty that the applicant (i) is the right-holder and (ii) that the applicant's right is being infringed or that such infringement is imminent;

(b) to provide a security or equivalent assurance 'sufficient to protect the defendant and to prevent abuse'. The amount of the security or other assurance is to be determined by the national authority. It must be sufficient not only to compensate the defendant for losses generated, but also to prevent the abusive use of provisional measures to interfere with legitimate competition.

The same balancing approach inspires Article 50.4, with regard to provisional measures adopted *ex parte*. The parties affected (that is, the alleged infringer, distributors, etc) shall be given notice, without delay after the execution of the measures *at the latest*. As drafted, this provision implies that notice may be given *before* the execution of the provisional measure. In addition, a review, including a right to be heard, shall take place upon request of the defendant with a view to deciding, within a reasonable period after the notification of the measures, whether these

---

[110] An example of this type of measure is the '*Mareva*' injunction allowed under common law to temporarily freeze defendant's assets (generally bank deposits) that are required to satisfy a judgment in order to prevent their dissipation or removal from the jurisdiction.

[111] See, eg, J Reichman and M Zinnani op. cit. (2002), p 19.

[112] See, eg, J Straus, 'Reversal of the burden of proof, the principle of "fair and equitable procedures" and preliminary injunctions under the TRIPS Agreement', The Journal of World Intellectual Property, (2000), vol. 3, No 6, pp 815–20.   [113] *Managing Intellectual Property* (1997), p 37.

measures shall be modified, revoked, or confirmed. This review may take place either before or after the execution of the measure, depending on the date of notification. If revoked, the compensation established in Article 50.7 would apply.

Article 50.5 contains a non-mandatory provision indicating that the applicant *may* be required to supply other information necessary for the identification of the goods concerned by the authority that will execute the provisional measures. This provision assumes that the authority that executes the measure may not be the (judicial) authority that ordered it, for instance, when the police or customs authorities intervene upon request of the latter.

Paragraphs 6 and 7 of Article 50 refer with certain detail to obligations that must be imposed on the applicant of provisional measures. They aim at establishing safeguards to protect the alleged infringer from misconduct or abuses.[114]

Article 50.6 protects the party affected by a provisional measure from actions that are not effectively pursued in courts by the applicant. It establishes the right of the affected party to request that the provisional measure be revoked or otherwise cease to have effect, if proceedings leading to a decision on the merits of the case are not initiated within a reasonable period. This period is to be determined by the judicial authority ordering the measures where a Member's law so permits. In the absence of such a determination, the period shall not exceed twenty working days or thirty-one calendar days, whichever is the longer. The judicial authority or the national law may certainly establish a shorter period for the applicant to initiate proceedings.

Article 50.7 requires Members to grant the judicial authorities the power to order the applicant, upon request of the defendant, to provide the defendant appropriate compensation for any injury caused by a provisional measure, in three cases:

(a) where the provisional measures are revoked. Revocation may take place on occasion of the review contemplated in Article 50.4.
(b) where such measures lapse due to any act or omission by the applicant; or
(c) where it is subsequently found that there has been no infringement or threat of infringement of an intellectual property right.

It is to be noted that this provision uses the term 'appropriate'[115] and not 'adequate' as in Articles 44.2 and 48.1, as examined above. It is unclear whether this difference was deliberate and intended to introduce a different standard.[116] In any case, the defendant should receive a compensation commensurate to 'any' injury caused, including lost benefits and expenses incurred.

Finally, Article 50.8 provides that to the extent that any provisional measure can be ordered as a result of administrative procedures, such procedures shall conform to 'principles equivalent in substance' to those set forth in other paragraphs

---

[114] See Article 41.1 above.
[115] 'Appropriate' is 'suitable or proper', *Concise Oxford Dictionary* (1982: Oxford University Press, 7th edn), p 53. [116] As argued, eg, by Gervais op. cit. (2003), p 205.

of Article 50. This provision makes it clear ('[T]o the extent that...') that Members[117] are not obliged to empower administrative authorities to grant provisional measures. It employs the same wording as in Article 49; that is, administrative procedures need not be identical to those applicable by judicial authorities, but respond to the same 'principles', in substance and not in detail.

Special requirements related to
border measures [12]

Suspension of release by customs authorities

51. Members shall, in conformity with the provisions set out below, adopt procedures[13] to enable a right holder, who has valid grounds for suspecting that the importation of counterfeit trademark or pirated copyright goods[14] may take place, to lodge an application in writing with competent authorities, administrative or judicial, for the suspension by the customs authorities of the release into free circulation of such goods. Members may enable such an application to be made in respect of goods which involve other infringements of intellectual property rights, provided that the requirements of this Section are met. Members may also provide for corresponding procedures concerning the suspension by the customs authorities of the release of infringing goods destined for exportation from their territories.

[12] Where a Member has dismantled substantially all controls over movement of goods across its border with another Member with which it forms part of a customs union, it shall not be required to apply the provisions of this Section at that border.
[13] It is understood that there shall be no obligation to apply such procedures to imports of goods put on the market in another country by or with the consent of the right holder, or to goods in transit.
[14] For the purposes of this Agreement:
  (a) 'counterfeit trademark goods' shall mean any goods, including packaging, bearing without authorization a trademark which is identical to the trademark validly registered in respect of such goods, or which cannot be distinguished in its essential aspects from such a trademark, and which thereby infringes the rights of the owner of the trademark in question under the law of the country of importation;
  (b) 'pirated copyright goods' shall mean any goods which are copies made without the consent of the right holder or person duly authorized by the right holder in the country of production and which are made directly or indirectly from an article where the making of that copy would have constituted an infringement of a copyright or a related right under the law of the country of importation.

Section IV introduces the first set of international rules on counterfeiting and copyright piracy, thereby materializing a major objective of the proponents of the

[117] Administrative authorities have the power to adopt provisional measures in some countries (eg Peru, Mexico, China) but in others they can only be conferred by judicial authorities.

TRIPS Agreement.[118] This Section has been largely modelled on the national laws[119] existing in developed countries at the time of the Uruguay Round negotiations. According to this Section, the customs authorities' intervention should take place after the merchandise has been transported into the territory of a Member, but *before* it is released for consumption.[120] The obligations established therein only apply with regard to the *importation* of counterfeit trademark or pirated copyright goods. Members *may* also provide for corresponding procedures for infringing goods destined for exportation, as provided for in some countries,[121] but this is a 'TRIPS-plus' requirement that Members are not obliged to implement.

Border measures are required because enforcement against infringement at the source of the imported goods has failed. An important feature of the procedures under Section IV is that they involve two separate steps. Customs authorities' intervention is required only with regard to the execution of a specific *provisional measure*, while it is up to the 'competent authorities, administrative or judicial' (Article 51) to *decide on the merits* of a particular case; that is, to determine, whether the goods at stake are or are not counterfeit trademark or pirated copyright goods.

According to Article 51, the application to suspend the release of goods must also be lodged with the 'competent authorities, administrative or judicial'. An 'administrative authority' in this context may be the customs authority itself, as established in some countries.[122] However, there is no obligation under Article 51 to empower such authority to directly adopt provisional measures, and in many countries this is an exclusive competence of the *judicial* authorities.

Members are obliged to adopt procedures as mandated in Article 51 *only* with regard to *counterfeit trademark* or *pirated copyright goods*, and not in respect of other types of infringement concerning trademarks (eg 'passing off',[123] improper use of a trademark) or copyright (eg substantial similarity, adaptation without the author's permission). This provision does not apply either to other types of intellectual property rights, such as patents.[124] The reason for this differentiation is

---

[118] The Preamble of the TRIPS Agreement recognizes 'the need for a multilateral framework of principles, rules and disciplines dealing with international trade in counterfeit goods'.

[119] For an analysis of national border regulations, see *Border Control of Intellectual Property Rights* (2002: London, Sweet & Maxwell).

[120] See, eg, Fabio Ponce Lopez, 'Observancia de los Derechos de la Propiedad Intelectual en Aduanas. Procedimientos, acciones y competencias (Parte III, Seccion 4 de los ADPIC)', Seminario de la OMPI para la Comunidad Andina, sobre la observancia de los derechos de la propiedad intelectual en frontera, Bogota, D C; 11 July 2002, p 2.

[121] See, eg, Article 246(c) of Decision 486 (Andean Community Common Regime on Industrial Property).   [122] Eg, Spain, Panama. See Ponce Lopez op. cit. (2002), p 9.

[123] 'Passing off' (also called sometimes 'palming off') takes place in cases where there is an (intentional) likelihood of confusion caused by the use of a similar trademark. See, eg, McCarthy op. cit. (2002), vol 4, pp 25–4 to 25–14.

[124] In some jurisdictions, border measures are applied to patents and other IPRs. For instance, in the US the International Trade Commission commonly issues broad injunctions or import restrictions

that infringement in the case of trademark counterfeiting and copyright piracy may be generally determined with certain ease, on the basis of the visual inspection of an imported good, since infringement will be apparent 'on its face'. This is not clearly the case where the infringement of a patent is claimed, since establishing it would normally require a thorough examination of often complex technical issues, including whether non-literal infringement exists.

In order to obtain the suspension of release, the right-holder must prove that he 'has valid grounds for suspecting' that infringing goods covered by Article 51 are being imported. He must show that there is *prima facie* an infringement. Unlike Article 50, however, this provision does not impose an 'irreparable harm' standard, despite that the measures at the border are adopted *inaudita altera parte*. Therefore, the likelihood of an infringement would be sufficient to trigger the procedures under Section 4.

It should be noted that Article 51 does not impose on customs authorities any obligation to inspect imported goods. In fact, such authorities routinely inspect a small fraction of such goods.[125] Moreover, there is no obligation to intervene *ex officio*. Article 51 requires a specific request by the right-holder for the customs authority to take action.

Footnote 12, quite logically, exempts Members that form part of a customs union from the application of Section 4, provided they have dismantled substantially all controls over the movement of goods across their border with other Members of the union.

Footnote 13 addresses the issue of parallel imports in the context of trademark and copyright protection. It indicates that the obligation to suspend the release of goods contained in Article 51 would not apply when the products have been put in commerce 'by or with the consent of the right holder'. Parallel trade in trademarked goods (often called 'grey market') is admitted in many countries. This is the case, for instance, in the US, where a Supreme Court decision of June 1989 allowed retailers to import trademarked foreign-made watches, cameras, perfumes, and other goods from foreign independent distributors.[126]

It could be argued that footnote 13 may also have interpretive value with regard to parallel trade in goods protected by other IPRs, particularly patents. If so, this

---

that prohibit unlicensed entry of products that infringe certain patents. For example, in the case of US Patent No 5,188,235, the ITC issued a general exclusion order prohibiting the unlicensed entry of plastic grocery bags that infringed a patent (see <http://patentlaw.typepad.com/patent/2004/08/itc_plastic_bag.html>, last accessed on 30 May 2006). See also Council Regulation (EC) No 1383/2003 of 22 July 2003 (Customs Regulation).

[125] See the commentary on Article 58 below.

[126] To get around the 1989 Supreme Court ruling, many manufacturers tried copyrighting the packaging on their goods. The Coalition to Protect the Integrity of American Trademarks (COPIAT) articulated this argument in the case of *Parfums Givenchy, Inc v Drug Emporium, Inc*, 38 F 3d 477 (9th Cir 1994), but in March 1998 the Supreme Court defeated this legal strategy. See P R Paradise, *Trademark Counterfeiting: Product Piracy and the Billion Dollar Threat to the US Economy*, (1999: Westport, Conn., Quorum Books), p 30.

would imply that parallel trade would not be legitimate when products are introduced in a foreign market *without the consent* of the right-holder, for instance, by a compulsory licence. However, the footnote clearly applies to certain cases of infringement of trademark and copyright only, and there is no solid basis to extend it into other fields in a manner that would limit the rights conferred to Members under Article 6 of the Agreement, as confirmed by the Doha Declaration on the TRIPS Agreement and Public Health.[127]

Footnote 13 also clarifies that it is not mandatory to apply border measures with regard to 'goods in transit'. Some countries, however, have extended those measures to such products.[128]

Footnote 14, finally, contains definitions for the purposes of the Agreement of 'counterfeit trademark goods' and of 'pirated copyright goods'. Reference to counterfeiting goods is made, in addition to Article 51, in the Preamble and in Articles 46, 59, 61, and 69, while pirated copyright goods or piracy are only referred to in Articles 61 and 69, as examined below. These definitions clarify that the possible existence of infringement is to be considered in accordance to the law of the country of importation. Trademark counterfeiting is not limited to the case of the unauthorized use of a trademark identical to the trademark validly registered in respect of such goods, but also includes cases where it 'cannot be distinguished in its essential aspects from such a trademark'. Copyright piracy, on the other hand, includes copies made 'directly or indirectly' from a copyrighted article, thereby including not only the first but subsequent copies of a protected work.

Application

52. Any right holder initiating the procedures under Article 51 shall be required to provide adequate evidence to satisfy the competent authorities that, under the laws of the country of importation, there is *prima facie* an infringement of the right holder's intellectual property right and to supply a sufficiently detailed description of the goods to make them readily recognizable by the customs authorities. The competent authorities shall inform the applicant within a reasonable period whether they have accepted the application and, where determined by the competent authorities, the period for which the customs authorities will take action.

---

[127] 'The effect of the provisions in the TRIPS Agreement that are relevant to the exhaustion of intellectual property rights is to leave each member free to establish its own regime for such exhaustion without challenge, subject to the MFN and national treatment provisions of Articles 3 and 4' (para. 5.d). See 'Doha Ministerial Declaration on the TRIPS Agreement and Public Health' (hereinafter 'the Doha Declaration'), WT/MIN(01)/DEC/W/2, 14 November 2001. See also Chapter 3.

[128] European Regulation 3295/94, for instance, applies to goods in 'external transit', that is, non-Community goods moving within the Community or exceptionally Community goods destined for export and for which custom procedures must be complied with.

A right-holder willing to obtain a border measure of the type established under Article 50 must comply with two basic requirements:[129]

(a) to provide 'adequate evidence' to satisfy the competent authorities that, under the laws of the country of importation, there is *prima facie* an infringement. This means that the evidence provided must satisfy the competent authorities that there is a likely infringement of IPRs;

(b) to supply a sufficiently detailed description of the goods to make them readily recognizable by the customs authorities. This provision only requires information for the customs authorities to identify the allegedly infringing goods, but their inspection to determine whether *prima facie* infringement exists or not can be made by a different authority, eg, by a court.

Finally, Article 52 requires the competent authorities to inform (whether in written form or not)[130] the applicant 'within a reasonable period' whether they have accepted the application and, where determined by the competent authorities, the period for which the customs authorities will take action. Only a 'reasonable period', to be determined by the Member's national law, is required. Notification need not be immediate or 'without delay' as provided for, for instance, under Article 50.4. The notification may include information about the period for which the customs authorities will detain the goods, where the competent authority has established such a period.[131]

Security or equivalent assurance

53. 1. The competent authorities shall have the authority to require an applicant to provide a security or equivalent assurance sufficient to protect the defendant and the competent authorities and to prevent abuse. Such security or equivalent assurance shall not unreasonably deter recourse to these procedures.

2. Where pursuant to an application under this Section the release of goods involving industrial designs, patents, layout-designs or undisclosed information into free circulation has been suspended by customs authorities on the basis of a decision other than by a judicial or other independent authority, and the period provided for in Article 55 has expired without the granting of provisional relief by the duly empowered authority, and provided that all other conditions for importation have been complied with, the owner, importer, or consignee of such goods shall be entitled to their release on the posting of a security in an amount sufficient to protect the right holder for any infringement. Payment of such security shall not prejudice any other remedy available to the right holder, it being understood that

---

[129] See also Article 53 with regard to securities or equivalent assurances.

[130] The requirement to inform in a written form applies, as discussed above, to decisions on the merits of the case (Article 41.3) and in respect of notices to the defendant (Article 42).

[131] The Draft of 23 July 1990 indicated in a bracketed text that was not finally adopted, the applicant's obligation to specify the length of the period for which the customs authorities would be requested to take action (W/76).

the security shall be released if the right holder fails to pursue the right of action within a reasonable period of time.

Article 53.2 only applies in relation to industrial designs, patents, layout-designs and undisclosed information, but not trademarks, copyright, and geographical indications. It is a 'slightly unusual provision',[132] since it regulates measures that Members are *not* obliged to order under Article 51, which, as examined above, is only mandatory with regard to counterfeit trademarks and pirated copyrights.

Article 53.1—drafted in the typical 'the competent authorities shall have the authority to' format—is intended to avoid abuses[133] by requiring the applicant of border measures to provide a security or equivalent assurance sufficient to protect the defendant and the competent authorities. The protection to be provided under this Article is for the defendant (though at this stage of the procedures there may be none) and the customs authorities as such, which may be liable in case they adopt measures that unjustifiably interfere with the legal activities of traders. The obligation to provide a security, thus, should act as a deterrent to anti-competitive practices.

Article 53.1, however, cautions that the security or equivalent assurance that is requested 'shall not unreasonably deter recourse to these procedures'; that is, it should not be of such an unreasonable amount that would inhibit interested parties to apply for border measures. This provision leaves significant latitude to Members to determine what 'unreasonable' means in this context.

Article 53.2 addresses the case in which the release of allegedly infringing goods into free circulation has been suspended by customs authorities on the basis of a decision *other than* by a judicial or other independent authority. This is, hence, a specific safeguard that applies when a court or an authority independent from the customs has not had an opportunity to consider the case and order the suspension.

This article applies where the period provided for in Article 55 has expired[134] without the granting of the provisional measure by the 'duly empowered authority' (which may be a court or another administrative authority independent from customs), and where all other conditions for importation (that is, the *normal* requirements imposed in the importing country) have been complied with.

Subject to these conditions, the owner, importer, or consignee of the allegedly infringing goods shall be entitled to their release on the posting of a security. No reference is made in this article to securing an 'adequate' or 'appropriate' compensation, as in other provisions of Part III, but simply to 'an amount sufficient to protect the right holder for any infringement'. Members are free to determine the criteria to determine such an amount. However, payment of the security shall not

---

[132] See Dreier op. cit. (1996), p 266, who notes that a similar provision was not in the original US and EC proposals, and that it was included because of the US fear that border measures could be abused in some developing countries as a device to obstruct the importation of US goods.

[133] The Draft of 23 July 1990 referred to 'avoid border enforcement procedures being abused by means of unjustified or frivolous applications' (W/76).

[134] See commentary on this Article below.

prejudice 'any other remedy available to the right holder'. The security shall be released if the right-holder fails to pursue the right of action within a 'reasonable' period of time, to be also determined by national law.

Notice of suspension

54. The importer and the applicant shall be promptly notified of the suspension of the release of goods according to Article 51.

Both the importer and the applicant must be notified if the suspension of the release of goods has been decided by the competent authority. This should be done 'promptly'. Though this may be interpreted as equivalent to 'without undue delay'[135] or 'immediately',[136] there is also here some latitude to determine the exact period. Of course, given the economic consequences that an unjustified suspension may entail, it would be to the benefit both of the applicant and of the importer (and also of the competent authority) that notice be given as soon as feasible.

Duration of suspension

55. If, within a period not exceeding 10 working days after the applicant has been served notice of the suspension, the customs authorities have not been informed that proceedings leading to a decision on the merits of the case have been initiated by a party other than the defendant, or that the duly empowered authority has taken provisional measures prolonging the suspension of the release of the goods, the goods shall be released, provided that all other conditions for importation or exportation have been complied with; in appropriate cases, this time-limit may be extended by another 10 working days. If proceedings leading to a decision on the merits of the case have been initiated, a review, including a right to be heard, shall take place upon request of the defendant with a view to deciding, within a reasonable period, whether these measures shall be modified, revoked or confirmed. Notwithstanding the above, where the suspension of the release of goods is carried out or continued in accordance with a provisional judicial measure, the provisions of paragraph 6 of Article 50 shall apply.

Article 55 explicitly applies to both imports and exports. Unlike other provisions commented on above, it contains a specific time period for action by the competent authority. Within a period not exceeding ten working days after the applicant has been of notified of the suspension, the allegedly infringing goods shall be released if the customs authorities have not been informed that:

(a) proceedings leading to a decision on the merits of the case have been initiated by a party other than the defendant; or
(b) the competent authority has taken provisional measures prolonging the suspension of the release of the goods.

---

[135] See Article 41.3.   [136] See Articles 44.1 and 50.1(c).

The condition under (a) requires that the applicant or another party initiated a case in order to obtain a decision on the merits of the case. If it is the defendant himself who has initiated such procedures, the release should be ordered. Article 55 seems to assume that the title-holder should request that a decision on the merits be taken by the same authority that adopted the provisional measure.

As in the case of Article 53.2, release is subject to compliance with 'all other conditions' for importation or exportation. In 'appropriate cases' (to be determined by Members' regulations), the ten-day period may be extended by another ten working days.

Article 55 specifies that if proceedings leading to a *decision on the merits of the case* have been initiated, a review, including a right to be heard, shall take place upon request of the defendant with a view to deciding, within a reasonable period, whether these measures shall be modified, revoked, or confirmed. It is to be noted that, unlike Article 50.4, the right to review is subject according to Article 55 to the initiation of proceedings on the merits of the case. However, where the suspension of the release of goods is carried out or continued in accordance with a provisional judicial measure, the provisions of paragraph 6 of Article 50 shall apply. As a result, a period not exceeding twenty working days or thirty-one calendar days, whichever is the longer, would apply. If a decision on the merits has been requested, the title-holder may also request that the provisional measure (that is, the suspension of release) be maintained until such decision is taken.

Indemnification of the importer and of the owner of the goods

56. Relevant authorities shall have the authority to order the applicant to pay the importer, the consignee and the owner of the goods appropriate compensation for any injury caused to them through the wrongful detention of goods or through the detention of goods released pursuant to Article 55.

Article 56 empowers the authorities that are competent according to the national law to order the applicant to pay the importer, the consignee, and the owner of the goods an 'appropriate' compensation if the suspension of the release of goods was 'wrongful' or where procedures to obtain a decision on the merits of the case was not initiated in accordance with Article 55.

The compensation must be sufficient to cover 'any injury caused', which may include lost benefits due to the detention or expenses incurred (eg attorneys' fees). Compensation is to be paid to the importer, the consignee, *and* the owner of the goods; that is, the applicant is liable to indemnify all those who may have suffered an economic loss because of the border measure.[137]

---

[137] There may also be other affected parties (eg carriers, distributors, retailers) who may potentially claim damages as well, but under general principles and rules of national law.

It is to be noted, finally, that the obligation to indemnify under this Article creates an objective liability, since it is not dependent on the bad faith or otherwise malicious intent of the applicant.

Right of inspection and information

> 57. Without prejudice to the protection of confidential information, Members shall provide the competent authorities the authority to give the right holder sufficient opportunity to have any goods detained by the customs authorities inspected in order to substantiate the right holder's claims. The competent authorities shall also have authority to give the importer an equivalent opportunity to have any such goods inspected. Where a positive determination has been made on the merits of a case, Members may provide the competent authorities the authority to inform the right holder of the names and addresses of the consignor, the importer and the consignee and of the quantity of the goods in question.

Article 57 provides (under the 'Members shall provide the competent authorities the authority' formulation) for two different kinds of rights in border procedures:

(a) the right of inspection: both the right-holder and the importer must be given 'sufficient opportunity' to have any goods detained inspected in order to substantiate the right-holder's claims or to articulate the defence, respectively;

(b) the right of information: Members *may* provide the competent authorities the authority to inform the right-holder of the names and addresses of the consignor, the importer, and the consignee and of the quantity of the goods in question. The obvious purpose of this provision (which is not mandatory anyway) is to allow the right-holder to act against all those that were possibly involved in the infringement; this is despite the fact that they may have acted in good faith and without having reasons to know that the goods were infringing. This right only arises (if established by the national law) where a *positive* determination has been made on the merits of a case.

Both the right of inspection and the right of information (if conferred) are subject to the protection of 'confidential information'.[138] Article 57 does not clarify in whose benefit this protection should be established, thereby suggesting that any party may invoke it and that the competent authorities must not confer such rights when a violation of such information may occur.

Ex officio action

> 58. Where Members require competent authorities to act upon their own initiative and to suspend the release of goods in respect of which they have acquired *prima facie* evidence that an intellectual property right is being infringed:
>
> (a) the competent authorities may at any time seek from the right holder any information that may assist them to exercise these powers;

---

[138] See the commentary on Article 42 above.

(b) the importer and the right holder shall be promptly notified of the suspension. Where the importer has lodged an appeal against the suspension with the competent authorities, the suspension shall be subject to the conditions, *mutatis mutandis*, set out at Article 55;

(c) Members shall only exempt both public authorities and officials from liability to appropriate remedial measures where actions are taken or intended in good faith.

The provisions in Articles 51–60 do not entail specific inspection obligations for customs authorities with regard to IPR-protected goods, nor to act *ex officio*. If they opt to do so, they must comply with the conditions set forth in Article 58. In general, customs authorities only inspect *ex officio* a small proportion of all trade, notably in order to verify the valuation of goods for the purpose of applying tariffs and other charges.[139]

Article 58 applies only 'where Members require competent authorities to act upon their own initiative and to suspend the release of goods in respect of which they have acquired *prima facie* evidence that an intellectual property right is being infringed'. This means that (a) said article is not binding in cases where national law does not provide for an *ex officio* intervention *and* for the power to suspend release; and (b) that establishing such a form of intervention is entirely left to Members' discretion.

Article 58(a) is formulated as a facultative provision, but a correct reading thereof would indicate that whenever the competent authorities seek information that may assist them to exercise these powers, the right-holders would be obliged to provide it. Failure to do so may obviously lead to a decision by the authorities not to take action in the particular case.

The obligation to notify the suspension equally applies with regard to the importer and the right-holder. Quite logically, Article 58(b) requires that the same conditions be applied to an appeal by the importer as established in Article 55.

Article 58(c), finally, does not contain conditions for *ex officio* measures but limits—like Article 48.2—Members' right to exempt public authorities and officials from liability to appropriate remedial measures to cases where actions were taken or intended in good faith in the course of the administration of that law.[140]

Remedies

59. Without prejudice to other rights of action open to the right holder and subject to the right of the defendant to seek review by a judicial authority, competent authorities shall have the authority to order the destruction or disposal of infringing goods in accordance with the principles set out in Article 46. In regard to counterfeit trademark goods, the authorities shall not allow the re-exportation of

---

[139] In the USA, for instance, customs examiners usually inspect about 5 per cent of the goods entering the country, looking for contraband, contaminated food products, diseased animals, and goods that are either illegal or pose a danger to the public. See, eg, Paradise op. cit. (1999), p 29.
[140] See Article 48.2 above.

the infringing goods in an unaltered state or subject them to a different customs procedure, other than in exceptional circumstances.

In the usual 'competent authorities shall have the authority to' format, this clause requires Members to empower the authorities (judicial or administrative) to order the destruction or disposal of infringing goods. This is subject to:

(a) the right of the defendant to seek review by a judicial authority;
(b) the 'principles' set out in Article 46, that is:

- without compensation of any sort;
- in order to avoid any harm caused to the right-holder;
- if not contrary to existing constitutional requirements.

In addition, counterfeit trademark goods cannot be re-exported in 'an unaltered state' but may be exported if somehow altered or subject to a different customs procedure, other than in exceptional circumstances. The Agreement is not explicit about the extent of the alteration, which is to be determined by national law. A reasonable standard would be an alteration that is sufficient to differentiate those products from those legitimately commercialized, for instance, by removing the infringing trademark.

De minimis imports

60. Members may exclude from the application of the above provisions small quantities of goods of a non-commercial nature contained in travelers' personal luggage or sent in small consignments.

'De minimis' clauses can be found in other components of the WTO system.[141] Article 60 is also a 'may' provision which reflects not only the difficulty that customs authorities face in controlling imports in small quantities, but also the fact that title-holders will not normally be interested in bearing the costs of enforcement procedures in such cases. The 'above provisions' refer to other provisions in Section 4.

Criminal procedures

61. Members shall provide for criminal procedures and penalties to be applied at least in cases of willful trademark counterfeiting or copyright piracy on a commercial scale. Remedies available shall include imprisonment and/or monetary fines sufficient to provide a deterrent, consistently with the level of penalties applied for crimes of a corresponding gravity. In appropriate cases, remedies available shall also include the seizure, forfeiture and destruction of the infringing

---

[141] See, eg, Article 5.8 of the Antidumping Agreement, Article 11.9 of the Agreement on Subsidies and Countervailing Measures.

goods and of any materials and implements the predominant use of which has been in the commission of the offence. Members may provide for criminal procedures and penalties to be applied in other cases of infringement of intellectual property rights, in particular where they are committed willfully and on a commercial scale.

Article 61 creates an obligation to provide for criminal procedures and penalties in cases of wilful trademark counterfeiting or copyright piracy on a commercial scale. Several aspects of this provision need to be highlighted.

First, though during the negotiations some delegations argued for a comprehensive application of criminal procedures and sanctions, this provision does not oblige Members to apply the same rule in other fields of intellectual property. Members are, however, free to do so, and many do in fact provide for such remedies and penalties in other areas, notably patents.

Second, criminal procedures and penalties are only required in relation to specific types of trademark and copyright infringement: trademark counterfeiting and copyright piracy, as defined in Article 51 of the Agreement. The provision, hence, does not cover other forms of violation, such as atypical uses of trademarks or reprography.

Third, Article 61 only covers 'wilful' infringement, thereby excluding acts done without knowing or having reasonable grounds to know that an infringement was taking place.

Lastly, infringement that cannot be deemed 'on a commercial scale' (eg isolated acts of infringement even if made for profit) is not subject to this provision.

The second and third sentences of Article 61 specify the content of criminal remedies, without going, however, into details. Penalties must include imprisonment *or* monetary fines, while Members may apply both measures and other criminal penalties if they wish. The standard to assess compliance with Article 61 is based on two elements: (a) remedies must be 'sufficient to provide a deterrent' to infringement; and (b) the *level* of penalties applied in these cases must be consistent with that applied for crimes of 'a corresponding gravity'. Members have considerable discretion to determine how to apply these standards and, particularly, to establish which are the crimes of comparable gravity in the national context.

In 'appropriate cases' (to be determined by the national law), remedies available shall also include the seizure, forfeiture, and destruction of the infringing goods and of any materials and implements the predominant use of which has been in the commission of the offence. Unlike Articles 46 and 59, which subject the destruction of goods to existing constitutional requirements, Article 61 does not contain this limitation. Though the difference may be justified by the criminal nature of the offence, it is also true that destruction of goods may represent a significant economic loss and be regarded as socially unacceptable.[142]

[142] In the case of conflict between a constitutional provision and the mandate in Article 61, an interesting case about the extent to which WTO rules limit national sovereignty may arise.

Article 61, last sentence, contains a 'may' provision emphasizing the Members' faculty to adopt a 'TRIPS-plus' approach, in particular, where infringement is committed wilfully and on a commercial scale. This sentence refers to other types of infringement in the field of trademark and copyright law, as well as to violations of other types of IPRs.

It must be noted that countries have had very different approaches with regard to the application of criminal penalties in cases of IPR infringement. In the US, for instance, criminal penalties and stiff civil remedies are available under federal law (and some state laws) for *intentionally* dealing in goods or services *knowingly* using a counterfeit mark.[143]

In many developing countries criminal penalties apply in cases of patent infringement as well. This may constitute an important deterrent for companies, especially small and medium enterprises, willing to operate around patented inventions. A criminal accusation carries out many negative effects (in terms of prestige, defence costs, restrictions to travel abroad, etc). Even if the defendants can prove themselves innocent, the risk of facing criminal actions may often be strong enough to dissuade a firm from activities that the title-holder may argue are infringing. Unlike the case of trademark counterfeiting or copyright piracy, a patent infringement cannot be established without an expert investigation, including determining whether there is 'equivalence' or not. This may explain why in countries that are deemed to confer a high level of patent protection, such as the US, there are no criminal penalties for patent infringement under federal law. In the US civil remedies are available: (1) an injunction against future infringement; and (2) compensatory damages (at least equal to a reasonable royalty), which may be trebled.[144]

Often, criminal sanctions are graduated according to the subject matter involved, the importance of the infringement, and whether subsequent offences take place. For instance, the US Copyright Act, as amended in 1992, stipulates that an infringement with regard to phonorecords becomes a felony depending on the number of infringing copies made or distributed and their retail value. The penalty may be up to five years' imprisonment, or a fine, or both, in case of reproduction or distribution of at least ten copies above a minimum retail value during six months. Imprisonment of up to ten years may apply in case of a second or subsequent infringement.[145]

---

[143] Federal criminal penalties include: (a) fines for individuals up to $2,000,000 ($5,000,000 for subsequent offences), or imprisonment not exceeding ten years (twenty years for subsequent offences), or both; and fines for corporations or partnership up to $5,000,000 ($15,000,000 for subsequent offences); and (b) destruction of Articles bearing the counterfeit mark. See Paradise op. cit. (1999), pp 8 and 18.

[144] See, eg, Paradise op. cit. (1999), p 14. The treble damages procedures for wilful infringement may deter those within a firm even from reading patents which may be relevant to their technologies.

[145] See, eg, Paradise op. cit. (1999), p 11.

Annex

Negotiating history[146]

In his 23 July 1990 report on the status of work in the TRIPS Negotiating Group, the Chairman (Lars E R Anell) presented two sets of proposals. In an Annex to the report, he presented a composite text that was taken from various proposals by delegations to the Negotiating Group, indicating the source of each proposal by numerical reference to the source document.

Composite text of July 23 1990[147]

ENFORCEMENT OF INTELLECTUAL PROPERTY RIGHTS
SECTION 1: GENERAL OBLIGATIONS

1. PARTIES shall ensure that effective [and appropriate] enforcement procedures are available under their national laws so as to enable action against any act of infringement of intellectual property rights covered by the agreement, including effective and expeditious remedies to stop (or prevent] infringements and remedies which constitute an effective deterrent to further infringements. In conformity with the provisions below, they shall provide such procedures [,internally and at the border,] by means of civil law, administrative law, or, where appropriate, criminal law, or a combination thereof. [Such procedures shall be provided consistently with each PARTY's legal and judicial systems and traditions and within the limits of its administrative resources and capabilities.] These procedures shall be applied in such a manner as to avoid the creation of barriers to legitimate trade and provide for safeguards against their abuse.

2. Procedures concerning the enforcement of intellectual proper rights shall be fair and equitable. They shall be [simple and expeditious] [not unnecessarily complicated, costly or time consuming, nor shall they be subject to unreasonable time-limits or unwarranted delays].

3A Decisions on the merits of a case shall [, as a general rule,] [preferably] be in writing and reasoned. They shall be made known at least to the parties to the dispute without undue delay. Decisions on the merits of a case shall only be based on such evidence in respect of which parties were offered the opportunity to be heard.

4A Parties to a dispute shall have an opportunity to appeal to a court of law against final administrative decisions [and [subject to jurisdictional provisions in national laws concerning the importance of a case, against the legal aspects of] all initial judicial decisions] on the merits of a case concerning the enforcement of an intellectual property right.

---

[146] For an analysis of the negotiating history, see UNCTAD-ICTSD op. cit. (2005), pp 214–66.
[147] Chairman's Report to the GNG, Status of Work in the Negotiating Group, Negotiating Group on Trade-Related Aspects of Intellectual Property Rights, including Trade in Counterfeit Goods, MTN.GNG/NG11/W/76, 23 July 1990, presented by the Chairman of the TRIPS Negotiating Group (Lars E R Anell). Alternatives 'A' correspond to texts from developed countries and 'B' from developing countries.

However, there shall be no obligation to provide an opportunity to appeal against acquittals in criminal cases.

4B Provision shall be made for appeal against initial judicial orders and for judicial review of administrative orders.

SECTION 2: CIVIL AND ADMINISTRATIVE PROCEDURES AND REMEDIES

5. *Fair and Equitable Procedures*

5A.1 PARTIES shall make available to right holders civil judicial procedures concerning the enforcement of any intellectual property right covered by this agreement.

5A.2 Defendants shall have the right to written notice which is timely and contains sufficient detail, including the basis of the claims.

5A.3 Parties shall be allowed to be represented by independent legal counsel, and procedures shall not impose overly burdensome requirements concerning personal appearances.

5A.4 All parties to such procedures shall be duly entitled to substantiate their claims and to present evidence.

5A.5 The procedure shall provide a means to identify and protect confidential information [without prejudice to the legitimate interests of any party to substantiate its claims].

5B There shall be prior notice given to parties to a legal proceeding and adequate opportunities for defence.

6. *Evidence of Proof*

6A.1 PARTIES shall provide courts with the authority, where a party has presented a (justifiable] [coherent] case and has identified evidence relevant to substantiation of its claim and which lies in the control of the opposing party, to order that this evidence be produced by the opposing party, subject to conditions which ensure the protection of confidential information. [For the purposes of this agreement, a justifiable case is one in which a party has presented to the court reasonably available evidence sufficient to [indicate that its claims are not without foundation] [support its claims]].

6A.2 In addition to the preceding procedure, PARTIES may also provide access to relevant evidence through, for example, measures to preserve evidence, use of search and seizure authority, by rule or by exercise of other judicial or administrative authority.

6A.3 In cases in which another PARTY refuses access to or impedes a party's compliance with a request to provide necessary information or a party to the proceeding refuses access to, or otherwise does not provide necessary information within a reasonable period, or significantly impedes a procedure relating to an enforcement action, [a PARTY may provide that] preliminary and final determinations, affirmative or negative, may be made on the basis of the complaint or the allegation presented by the party adversely affected by the denial of access to information and/or on other facts and evidence before the court, subject to providing the parties an opportunity to be heard on the allegations or evidence.

7. *Injunctions*

7A The judicial authorities shall have the authority to issue upon request an order that an infringement be refrained from or discontinued, irrespective of whether the defendant has acted with intent or negligence.

7B Injunctions must be available.

8. *Damages*

8A The right holder shall be entitled to [obtain] [claim] from the infringer [adequate] [full] compensation for the injury he has suffered because of a [deliberate or negligent] infringement of his intellectual property right. The right holder shall also be entitled to claim remuneration for costs, including attorney fees, reasonably incurred in the proceedings. In appropriate cases, PARTIES may provide for recovery of profits and/or pre-established damages to be granted even where the infringer has not acted intentionally or negligently.

8B Courts shall have the authority to award damages.

9. *Remedies against Governments*

9A Notwithstanding the other provisions of this Part, when a government is sued for infringement of an intellectual property right as a result of the use of that right by or for the government, PARTIES may limit remedies against the government to payment of [full] [adequate] compensation to the right holder.

10. *Other Remedies*

10A Where an intellectual property right has been found to be infringed, the court shall have the authority to order, upon request of the right holder, that the infringing goods, as well as materials and implements the predominant use of which has been in the creation of the infringing goods, be, without compensation of any sort, destroyed or disposed of outside the channels of commerce in such a manner as to minimise any harm caused to the right holder. In considering such a request, the need for proportionality between the seriousness of the infringement and the remedies ordered as well as the interests of third parties shall be taken into account. [In regard to counterfeit goods] [Other than in exceptional cases], the simple removal of the trade mark [or geographical indication] unlawfully affixed shall not be ordered.

11. *Right of Information*

11A (PARTIES may provide that,] unless this would be out of proportion to the seriousness of the infringement, the infringer may be ordered by a court to inform the right holder of the identity of third persons involved in the production and distribution of the infringing goods or services and of their channels of distribution.

12. *Indemnification of the Defendant*

12A.1 Parties wrongfully enjoined or restrained by any measures taken for the purpose of enforcing intellectual property rights shall be entitled to claim from the party at whose request the measures were taken adequate compensation for the injury suffered because of an abuse of enforcement procedures and to claim reimbursement for the costs, including attorney fees, reasonably incurred in the proceedings.

12A.2 PARTIES may provide for the possibility that such parties [may] [shall] be entitled to claim compensation from [authorities] [public officials] in appropriate cases, such as negligent or deliberate improper conduct. [They shall provide for such possibility in the case of administrative ex officio action.]

13. *Administrative Procedures*

13A Administrative procedures concerning the enforcement of intellectual property rights shall [conform to principles equivalent] [correspond in substance] to those set forth in this Section for application to judicial proceedings.

SECTION 3: PROVISIONAL MEASURES

14A.1.1 The judicial authorities shall have the authority to order, upon request, prompt and effective provisional measures:
  (i) to prevent an infringement of any intellectual property right from occurring or being continued, and in particular to prevent the goods from entering commercial channels;
  (ii) to preserve relevant evidence in regard to the alleged infringement.

14A.1.2 Where appropriate, provisional measures may be adopted inaudita altera parte, (in particular] where any delay is likely to cause irreparable harm to the right holder, or where there is a demonstrable risk of evidence being destroyed.

14A.2 The applicant shall be required to provide any reasonably available evidence so as to permit the court to establish with a sufficient degree of certainty that he is the right holder and that his right is being infringed or that such infringement is imminent [, and to provide a security or equivalent assurance sufficient (to protect the defendant and] to prevent abuse].

14A.3 Where provisional measures have been adopted inaudita altera parte, the parties affected shall be given notice, at the latest immediately after the execution of the measures. A review, including a right to be heard, shall take place upon request of the defendant with a view to deciding, within a reasonable period after the notification of the measures, whether these measures shall be modified, revoked or confirmed.

14A.4 Where provisional measures according to point 14A.1.1(i) are to be carried out by customs authorities, the applicant may be required to supply any other information necessary for the identification of the goods concerned.

14A.5 Without prejudice to point 14A.3, provisional measures taken on the basis of point 14.1 shall, upon request by the defendant, be revoked or otherwise cease to have effect, if proceedings leading to a decision on the merits of the case are not initiated within a reasonable period not exceeding [one month] [two weeks] after the notification of the provisional measures, unless determined otherwise by the court.

14A.6 Where the provisional measures are revoked or where they lapse due to any act or omission by the applicant, or where it is subsequently found that there has been no infringement or threat of infringement of an intellectual property right, the defendant shall be entitled to claim from the applicant adequate compensation for any injury caused [intentionally or negligently] by these measures, unless the parties reach an out-of-court settlement of the case.

14.7 Point 13 of this Part shall apply [accordingly] (*mutatis mutandis*) to provisional administrative procedures.

SECTION 4: SPECIAL REQUIREMENTS RELATED TO BORDER MEASURES[1]

15. *Suspension of Release by Customs Authorities*

15A Without prejudice to point 21 of this Part, PARTIES shall, in conformity with the provisions set out below, establish procedures according to which a right holder, who has valid grounds for suspecting that the importation of [goods which infringe his intellectual property right] [counterfeit trademark or pirated copyright goods] may take place, may lodge an application in writing with the competent authorities, administrative or judicial, for the suspension by the customs authorities of the release into free circulation of such goods. [This provision does not create an obligation to apply such procedures to parallel imports].

15B See point 8B of Part IX below.

15A.2 PARTIES may provide for corresponding procedures concerning the suspension by the customs authorities of the release of such goods destined for exportation from their territory.

16. *Application*

16A The application under point 15 must contain prima facie evidence of the alleged infringement and (evidence] that the applicant is the right holder. It must contain all pertinent information known or reasonably available to the applicant to enable the competent authority to act in knowledge of the facts at hand, and a sufficiently detailed description of the goods to make them readily recognisable by the customs authorities. [It must specify the length of period for which the customs authorities are requested to take action.] The applicant may also be required to supply any other information necessary for the identification of the goods concerned. The competent authorities shall inform the applicant within a reasonable period whether they have accepted the application and the period for which it will remain in force.

16B See point 9B(i) of Part IX.

17. *Security or Equivalent Assurance*

17A PARTIES shall seek to avoid border enforcement procedures being abused by means of unjustified or frivolous applications. For this purpose, they [may] (shall] require a right holder, who has lodged an application according to point 16 to provide a security or

---

[1] It will be made clear at an appropriate place in any agreement that, for the European Communities and for the purposes of this Section, the term 'border' is understood to mean the external border of the European Communities with third countries.

equivalent assurance. Such security or equivalent assurance shall not unreasonably deter recourse to these procedures.

17B See point 9B(ii) of Part IX.

18. *Duration of Suspension*

18A The importer and the applicant shall be promptly notified of the suspension of the release of goods according to point 15 above. If, within ten working days after the applicant has [been served with a notice of the] [received] notification of the suspension, the customs authorities have not been informed that the matter has been referred to the authority competent to take a decision on the merits of the case, or that the duly empowered authority has taken provisional measures, the goods shall be released, provided that all other conditions for importation or exportation have been complied with [and unless this would be contrary to provision of domestic law]. In exceptional cases, the above time-limit may be extended by another ten working days.

18B See points 8B (last sentence) and 9B(iii) of Part IX.

19. *Indemnification of the Importer and of the Owner of the Goods*

19A The importer and the owner of the goods shall be entitled to claim from the applicant adequate compensation for any injury caused [intentionally or negligently] to them through the wrongful detention of goods or through the detention of goods released pursuant to point 18 above.

20. *Right of Information and Inspection*

20A Without prejudice to the protection of confidential information, the competent authority shall be empowered to give the right holder sufficient opportunity to inspect any product detained by the customs authorities in order to substantiate his claims. [Unless this would be contrary to provisions of domestic law, the customs authorities shall inform the right-holder, upon request, of the names and addresses of the consignor, importer, consignee and of the quantity of the goods in question.]

21. *Ex Officio Action*

21A.1.1 PARTIES may provide that the customs authorities have the right, but not an obligation, to inform the right-holder or his representative, wherever they have reasons to suspect an imminent importation of products the release of which into free circulation would contravene intellectual property rights of that right-holder.

21A.1.2 The exercise of this right of information shall not imply any liability for the customs authorities.

21A.1.3 This right of information is without prejudice to the provisions at points 15 to 20, 22 and 23.

21A.2.1 PARTIES may require the competent authorities to act upon their own initiative and to suspend the release of goods in respect of which they have acquired [a sufficient degree of certainty] [prima facie evidence] that an intellectual property right is being infringed.

21A.2.2 In this case, the competent authorities may at any time seek from the right holder any information that may assist them to exercise these powers.

21A.2.3 The importer and the right holder shall be promptly notified of the suspension. Where the importer has lodged an appeal against the suspension with the competent authorities, the suspension shall be subject to the conditions, *mutatis mutandis*, set out at point 18 above.

21A.2.4 With regard to the importer's rights to claim compensation, the provisions at point 19 shall apply, *mutatis mutandis*.

22. *Remedies*

22A Without prejudice to the other rights of action open to the right holder, and subject to the right of the defendant to lodge an appeal to the judicial authorities, the competent authorities shall provide for the destruction or disposal of the infringing goods in accordance with the principles set out at point 10 above. [Other than in exceptional circumstances] [With respect to counterfeit goods], the authorities shall not allow the re-exportation of the infringing goods in an unaltered state or subject them to a different customs procedure.

22B See point 10B of Part IX below.

23. *De Minimis Imports*

23A PARTIES may exclude from the application of the above provisions small quantities of goods of a non-commercial nature contained in travellers' personal luggage or sent in small consignments.

SECTION 5: CRIMINAL PROCEDURES

24. PARTIES shall provide for criminal procedures and penalties to be applied in cases of wilful [trademark counterfeiting and copyright piracy on a commercial scale] [infringements of trademarks and copyright on a commercial scale] [infringements on a commercial scale of intellectual property rights concerned by this agreement]. Remedies available shall include imprisonment and monetary fines sufficient to provide an effective deterrent and in appropriate cases the seizure, forfeiture and destruction of the infringing goods and of any device [the predominant use of which has been] [used] in the commission of the offence. PARTIES may provide for criminal procedures and penalties to be applied in cases of infringement of any other intellectual property right, in particular where it is committed wilfully and on a commercial scale.

PART IX: TRADE IN COUNTERFEIT AND PIRATED GOODS

1. *Preamble*

1B.1 Desirous of providing for adequate procedures and remedies to discourage international trade in counterfeit and pirated goods while ensuring an unimpeded flow of trade in legitimate goods;

1B.2 Deeming it highly desirable to ensure competition in international trade and to prevent arrangements which may restrain such competition;

1B.3 Recognizing the need to take into consideration the public policy objectives underlying national systems for the protection of intellectual property, including developmental and technological objectives;

1B.4 Recognizing also the special needs of the least developed countries in respect of maximum flexibility in the application of this Agreement in order to enable them to create a sound and viable technological base.

2. *Objective*

2B With respect to intellectual property and international trade, PARTIES agree on the following objectives:
  (i) To clarify GATT provisions related to the effects of the enforcement of intellectual property rights on international trade, in particular articles IX and XX(d), and to provide for adequate procedures and remedies to discourage international trade in counterfeit and pirated goods.
 (ii) To ensure that such procedures and remedies do not themselves become barriers to legitimate trade and are not applied in a discriminatory manner to imported goods.
(iii) To ensure free flow of goods and prevent arrangements, effected by private or public commercial enterprises, which may result in the division of markets or otherwise restrain competition, thus having harmful effects on international trade.

SECTION 2: GUIDING PRINCIPLES AND NORMS

3. *Trade in Counterfeit and Pirated Goods*

3B.1 PARTIES undertake to discourage trade in counterfeit and pirated goods and to combat such trade without inhibiting the free flow of legitimate trade. For this purpose, PARTIES shall exchange information and promote cooperation between customs authorities with respect to trade in counterfeit and pirated goods. They shall also adopt in their respective national legislation the necessary measures, procedures and remedies in this respect.

3B.2 For the purposes of this Agreement, trade in counterfeit goods means trade in goods which infringe a trademark validly registered in respect of such goods in the importing country, while trade in pirated goods means trade in goods which constitute a slavish copy of a work protected by copyright under the legislation of the country of importation.

4. *Safeguard against Creation of Trade Impediments in the Application of Measures and Procedures to Enforce Intellectual Property Rights*

4B In the application of national measures and procedures to enforce intellectual property rights, PARTIES undertake to avoid the creation of impediments or distortions to international trade, and to refrain from applying their national legislation in a discriminatory manner to imports from the territories of other PARTIES. For this purpose, they shall observe the principles of national treatment and MFN enshrined in the GATT.

5. *Non-recourse to Unilateral Measures*

5B PARTIES shall refrain, in relation to each other, from threatening or having recourse to unilaterally decided economic measures of any kind aimed at ensuring the enforcement of intellectual property rights.

6. *Control of Anti-competitive and Trade-distorting Practices*

6B PARTIES shall co-operate with each other to ensure the free flow of goods and prevent that intellectual property rights are used, through arrangements among enterprises, to create restrictions or distortions to international trade or to engage in anti-competitive practices having adverse effects on their trade. For this purpose, they undertake to exchange information and to agree upon the request of any other PARTY to consult with respect to any such practices and to take such measures in their territory as may be deemed appropriate with a view to eliminating the adverse effects of such practices.

7. *Transparency*

7B Laws, regulations, judicial decisions and administrative rulings pertaining to the application of the principles and norms prescribed in points 2 to 5 shall be made publicly available in the official language of the Party adopting such texts and, shall be provided, upon request, to any other Party.

SECTION 3: BORDER MEASURES RELATED TO COUNTERFEIT OR PIRATED GOODS

8. *Suspension of Customs Clearance*

8B PARTTES shall adopt the necessary measures and procedures, whether judicial or administrative, to enable intellectual property right holders, who may have valid grounds for suspecting that imported goods infringe their trademark or constitute a slavish copy of a work protected by copyright in accordance with the national legislation of the importing country, to obtain the suspension by the customs authorities of clearance from customs of such goods. Such suspension shall be for a limited period of time pending a determination by the competent authorities whether the goods are infringing.

8A (See point 15A of Part IV above).

9. *Safeguards against Obstacles to Legitimate Trade*

9B (i) Persons initiating the procedure for the suspension of clearance from customs shall be required to provide adequate documentary evidence to satisfy the competent authorities that prima facie there is an infringement of their right to protection in accordance with the relevant laws of the country of importation.

(ii) Such persons shall also be required to provide security by bond or deposit of money in an amount sufficient to indemnify the authorities or to hold the importer harmless from loss or damage resulting from the action undertaken.

(iii) The importers of such goods or other persons affected by the procedure shall be informed promptly of actions taken and shall be entitled to a judicial review of any final decision taken by an administrative authority.

9A (See points 16A, 17A and 18A of Part IV above).

10. *Disposal of Infringing Goods*

10B Where it is finally determined that the goods are infringing in accordance with the relevant laws of the importing country, the competent authorities shall provide for the forfeiture, destruction or disposal of the goods in a manner not prejudicial to the interests of the right holder.

10A (See point 22 of Part IV above).

Draft text transmitted to the Brussels Ministerial Conference (December 1990)

PART III: ENFORCEMENT OF INTELLECTUAL PROPERTY RIGHTS

SECTION 1: GENERAL OBLIGATIONS

Article 44

1. PARTIES shall ensure that enforcement procedures as specified in this Part are available under their national laws so as to permit effective action against any act of infringement of intellectual property rights covered by this Agreement, including expeditious remedies to prevent infringements and remedies which constitute a deterrent to further 'infringements'. These procedures shall be applied in such a manner as to avoid the creation of barriers to legitimate trade and to provide for safeguards against their abuse.

2. Procedures concerning the enforcement of intellectual property rights shall be fair and equitable. They shall not be unnecessarily complicated or costly, or entail unreasonable time-limits or unwarranted delays.

3. Decisions on the merits of a case shall preferably be in writing and reasoned. They shall be made available at least to the parties to the dispute without undue delay. Decisions on the merits of a case shall be based only on evidence in respect of which parties were offered the opportunity to be heard.

4. Parties to a dispute shall have an opportunity for review by a judicial authority of final administrative decisions and, subject to jurisdictional provisions in national laws concerning the importance of a case, of at least the legal aspects of initial judicial decisions on the merits of a case. However, there shall be no obligation to provide an opportunity for review of acquittals in criminal cases.

5. It is understood that this Part does not create any obligation to put in place a judicial system for the enforcement of intellectual property rights distinct from that for the enforcement of laws in general, nor does it affect the capacity of PARTIES to enforce their laws in general.

SECTION 2: CIVIL AND ADMINISTRATIVE
PROCEDURES AND REMEDIES

Article 45
Fair and Equitable Procedures

PARTIES shall make available to right holders civil judicial procedures concerning the enforcement of any intellectual property right covered by this agreement. Defendants shall have the right to written notice which is timely and contains sufficient detail, including the basis of the claims. Parties shall be allowed to be represented by independent legal counsel, and procedures shall not impose overly burdensome requirements concerning mandatory personal appearances. All parties to such procedures shall be duly entitled to substantiate their claims and to present all relevant evidence. The procedure shall provide a means to identify and protect confidential information, unless this would be contrary to existing constitutional requirements.

Article 46
Evidence of Proof

1. The judicial authorities shall have the authority, where a party has presented reasonably available evidence sufficient to support its claims and has specified evidence relevant to substantiation of its claims which lies in the control of the opposing party, to order that this evidence be produced by the opposing party, subject in appropriate cases to conditions which ensure the protection of confidential information.

2. In cases in which a party to a proceeding voluntarily and without good reason refuses access to, or otherwise does not provide necessary information within a reasonable period, or significantly impedes a procedure relating to an enforcement action, a PARTY may accord judicial authorities the authority to make preliminary and final determinations, affirmative or negative, on the basis of the information presented to them, including the complaint or the allegation presented by the party adversely affected by the denial of access to information, subject to providing the parties an opportunity to be heard on the allegations or evidence.

Article 47
Injunctions

The judicial authorities shall have the authority to order a party to desist from an infringement, inter alia to prevent the entry into the channels of commerce in their jurisdiction of imported goods that involve the infringement of an intellectual property right, immediately after customs clearance of such goods. PARTIES are not obliged to accord such authority in respect of protected subject matter acquired or ordered by a person prior to knowing or having reasonable grounds to know that dealing in such subject matter would entail the infringement of an intellectual property right.

2. Notwithstanding the other provisions of this Part and provided that the provisions of Part II specifically addressing use by governments, or by third parties authorised by a government, without the authorisation of the right holder are complied with, PARTIES may limit the remedies available against such use to payment of remuneration in

accordance with sub-paragraph (h) of Article 34 above. In other cases, the remedies under this Part shall apply or, where these remedies are inconsistent with national law, declaratory judgments and adequate compensation shall be available.

Article 48
Damages

1. The judicial authorities shall have the authority to order the infringer to pay the right holder damages adequate to compensate for the injury the right holder has suffered because of an infringement of his intellectual property right by an infringer who knew or had reasonable grounds to know that he was engaged in infringing activity.

2. The judicial authorities shall also have the authority to order the infringer to pay the right holder expenses, which may include appropriate attorney's fees. In appropriate cases, PARTIES may authorise the judicial authorities to order recovery of profits and/or payment of pre-established damages even where the infringer did not know or had no reasonable grounds to know that he was engaged in infringing activity.

Article 49
Other Remedies

In order to create an effective deterrent to infringement, the judicial authorities shall have the authority to order that goods that they have found to be infringing be, without compensation of any sort, disposed of outside the channels of commerce in such a manner as to avoid any harm caused to the right holder, or, unless this would be contrary to existing constitutional requirements, destroyed. The judicial authorities shall also have the authority to order that materials and implements the predominant use of which has been in the creation of the infringing goods be, without compensation of any sort, disposed of outside the channels of commerce in such a manner as to minimise the risks of further infringements. In considering such requests, the need for proportionality between the seriousness of the infringement and the remedies ordered as well as the interests of third parties shall be taken into account. In regard to counterfeit goods, the simple removal of the trademark unlawfully affixed shall not be sufficient, other than in exceptional cases, to permit release of the goods into the channels of commerce.

Article 50
Right of Information

PARTIES may provide that the judicial authorities shall have the authority, unless this would be out of proportion to the seriousness of the infringement, to order the infringer to inform the right holder of the identity of third persons involved in the production and distribution of the infringing goods or services and of their channels of distribution.

Article 51
Indemnification of the Defendant

1. The judicial authorities shall have the authority to order a party at whose request measures were taken and who has abused enforcement procedures to provide to a party wrongfully

enjoined or restrained adequate compensation for the injury suffered because of such abuse. The judicial authorities shall also have the authority to order the applicant to pay the defendant expenses, which may include appropriate attorney's fees.

2. In respect of the administration of any law pertaining to the protection or enforcement of intellectual property rights, PARTIES shall not exempt public authorities or officials from liability, except for actions taken or intended in good faith in the course of the administration of such laws.

Article 52
Administrative Procedures

To the extent that any civil remedy can be ordered as a result of administrative procedures on the merits of a case, such procedures shall conform to principles equivalent in substance to those set forth in this Section.

SECTION 3: PROVISIONAL MEASURES

Article 53

1. The judicial authorities shall have the authority to order prompt and effective provisional measures:
(a) to prevent an infringement of any intellectual property right [from occurring], and in particular to prevent the entry into the channels of commerce in their jurisdiction of goods, including imported goods immediately after customs clearance;
(b) to preserve relevant evidence in regard to the alleged infringement.

2. The judicial authorities shall have the authority to adopt provisional measures *inaudita altera parte* where appropriate, in particular where any delay is likely to cause irreparable harm to the right holder, or where there is a demonstrable risk of evidence being destroyed.

3. The judicial authorities shall have the authority to require the applicant to provide any reasonably available evidence in order to satisfy themselves with a sufficient degree of certainty that the applicant is the right holder and that his right is being infringed or that such infringement is imminent, and to order the applicant to provide a security or equivalent assurance sufficient to protect the defendant and to prevent abuse.

4. Where provisional measures have been adopted *inaudita altera parte*, the parties affected shall be given notice, without delay after the execution of the measures at the latest. A review, including a right to be heard, shall take place upon request of the defendant with a view to deciding, within a reasonable period after the notification of the measures, whether these measures shall be modified, revoked or confirmed.

5. The applicant may be required to supply other information necessary for the identification of the goods concerned by the authority that will execute the provisional measures.

6. Without prejudice to paragraph 4 above, provisional measures taken on the basis of paragraphs 1 and 2 above shall, upon request by the defendant, be revoked or otherwise cease to have effect, if proceedings leading to a decision on the merits of the case are not initiated within a reasonable period, to be determined by the judicial authority ordering

the measures where national law so permits or, in the absence of such a determination, not to exceed 20 working days or 31 calendar days, whichever is the longer.

7. Where the provisional measures are revoked or where they lapse due to any act or omission by the applicant, or where it is subsequently found that there has been no infringement or threat of infringement of an intellectual property right, the judicial authorities shall have the authority to order the applicant, upon request of the defendant, to provide the defendant appropriate compensation for any injury caused by these measures.

8. To the extent that any provisional measure can be ordered as a result of administrative procedures, such procedures shall conform to principles equivalent in substance to those set forth in this Section.

SECTION 4: SPECIAL REQUIREMENTS RELATED TO BORDER MEASURES

Article 54
Suspension of Release by Customs Authorities

PARTIES shall, in conformity with the provisions set out below, adopt procedures to enable a right holder, who has valid grounds for suspecting that the importation of counterfeit trademark or pirated copyright goods may take place, to lodge an application in writing with competent authorities, administrative or judicial, for the suspension by the customs authorities of the release into free circulation of such goods. PARTIES may enable such an application to be made in respect of goods which involve other infringements of intellectual property rights, provided that the requirements of this Section are met. PARTIES may also provide for corresponding procedures concerning the suspension by the customs authorities of the release of infringing goods destined for exportation from their territories.

Article 55
Application

Any right holder initiating the procedures under Article 54 above shall be required to provide adequate evidence to satisfy the competent authorities that, under the laws of the country of importation, there is prima facie an infringement of his intellectual property right and 'Where a PARTY has dismantled substantially all controls over movement of goods across its border with another PARTY with which it forms part of a customs union, it shall not be required to apply the provisions of this Section at that border.

2 It is understood that there shall be no obligation to apply such procedures to imports of goods put on the market in another country by or with the-consent of the right holder, or to goods in transit.

3 For the purposes of this Agreement:-

Counterfeit trademark goods shall mean any goods, including packaging, bearing without authorisation a trademark which is identical to the trademark validly registered in respect of such goods, or which cannot be distinguished in its essential aspects from such a trademark, and which thereby infringes the rights of the owner of the trademark in question under the law of the country of importation.

Pirated copyright goods shall mean any goods which are copies made without the consent of the-right holder or person duly authorised by him in the country of production and which are made directly or indirectly from an article where the making of that copy constitutes an infringement of a copyright or a related right under the law of the country of importation. The competent authorities shall inform the applicant within a reasonable period whether they have accepted the application and, where determined by the competent authorities, the period for which the customs authorities will take action.

Article 56
Security or Equivalent Assurance

The competent authorities shall have the authority to require an applicant to provide a security or equivalent assurance sufficient to protect the defendant and the competent authorities and to prevent abuse. Such security or equivalent assurance shall not unreasonably deter recourse to these procedures.

Article 57
Notice of Suspension

The importer and the applicant shall be promptly notified of the suspension of the release of goods according to Article 54 above.

Article 58
Duration of Suspension

If, within a period not exceeding ten working days after the applicant has been served notice of the suspension, the customs authorities have not been informed that proceedings leading to a decision on the merits of the case have been initiated by a party other than the defendant, or that the duly empowered authority has taken provisional measures prolonging the suspension of the release of the goods, the goods shall be released, provided that all other conditions for importation or exportation have been complied with; in appropriate cases, this time-limit may be extended by another ten working days. Notwithstanding the above, where the suspension of the release of goods is carried out or continued in accordance with a provisional judicial measure, the provisions of Article 53.6 above shall apply.

Article 59
Indemnification of the Importer and of the Owner of the Goods

Relevant authorities shall have the authority to order the applicant to pay the importer, the consignee and the owner of the goods appropriate compensation for any injury caused to them through the wrongful detention of goods or through the detention of goods released pursuant to Article 58 above.

Article 60
Right of Inspection and Information

Without prejudice to the protection of confidential information, PARTIES shall provide the competent authorities the authority to give the right holder sufficient opportunity to have any product detained by the customs authorities inspected in order to substantiate his claims. The competent authorities shall also have authority to give the importer an equivalent opportunity to have any such product inspected. Where a positive determination has been made on the merits of a case, PARTIES may provide the competent authorities the authority to inform the right holder of the names and addresses of the consignor, the importer and the consignee and of the quantity of the goods in question.

Article 61
Ex Officio Action

Where PARTIES require competent authorities to act upon their own initiative and to suspend the release of goods in respect of which they have acquired prima facie evidence that an intellectual property right is being infringed:

(a) the competent authorities may at any time seek from the right holder any information that may assist them to exercise these powers;

(b) the importer and the right holder shall be promptly notified of the suspension. Where the importer has lodged an appeal against the suspension with the competent authorities, the suspension shall be subject to the conditions, *mutatis mutandis*, set out at Article 58 above;

(c) public authorities or officials shall not be exempted by PARTIES from liability, except for actions taken or intended in good faith.

Article 62
Remedies

Without prejudice to other rights of action open to the right holder and subject to the right of the defendant to seek review by a judicial authority, competent authorities shall have the authority to order the destruction or disposal of infringing goods in accordance with the principles set out in Article 49 above. In regard to counterfeit goods, the authorities shall not allow the re-exportation of the infringing goods in an unaltered state or subject them to a different customs procedure, other than in exceptional circumstances.

Article 63
De Minimis Imports

PARTIES may exclude from the application of the above provisions small quantities of goods of a non-commercial nature contained in travellers' personal luggage or sent in small consignments.

SECTION 5: CRIMINAL PROCEDURES

Article 64

PARTIES shall provide for criminal procedures and penalties to be applied at least in cases of wilful trademark counterfeiting or copyright piracy on a commercial scale. Remedies available shall include imprisonment and/or monetary fines sufficient to provide a deterrent, consistently with the level of penalties applied for crimes of a corresponding gravity. In appropriate cases, remedies available shall also include the seizure, forfeiture and destruction of the infringing goods and of any materials and implements the predominant use of which has been in the commission of the offence. PARTIES must provide for criminal procedures and penalties to be applied in other cases of infringement of intellectual property rights, in particular where they are committed wilfully and on a commercial scale.

Chapter 14

ACQUISITION AND MAINTENANCE OF INTELLECTUAL PROPERTY RIGHTS, DISPUTE PREVENTION AND SETTLEMENT, TRANSITIONAL AND INSTITUTIONAL ARRANGEMENTS, AND FINAL PROVISIONS

Acquisition and maintenance of IPRs

62.1. Members may require, as a condition of the acquisition or maintenance of the intellectual property rights provided for under Sections 2 through 6 of Part II, compliance with reasonable procedures and formalities. Such procedures and formalities shall be consistent with the provisions of this Agreement.

Different aspects relating to the procedures for the acquisition and maintenance of intellectual property rights are regulated in Article 62 of the TRIPS Agreement. Its main purpose is to ensure that the application of national legislation on this matter does not unjustifiably impair the access to and exercise of such rights.

Article 62.1 reaffirms the Members' right to provide for the 'compliance with reasonable procedures and formalities' to acquire or maintain intellectual property rights. This provision applies to intellectual property rights provided for under Sections 2–6 of Part II of the TRIPS Agreement; that is, it is limited to trademarks, industrial designs, geographical indications, patents, and layout-designs of integrated circuits. Copyrights—consistently with Article 5.2 of the Berne Convention—cannot be subject to such formalities. The same applies to 'undisclosed information' given, in this case, to the very nature of the protected subject matter which is not subject to registration.

What is 'reasonable' for the purposes of this Article will have to be determined in the context of the applicable national law, depending on the rights involved and the nature and objectives of the procedures and formalities.

The second sentence in Article 62.1 clarifies that '[S]uch procedures and formalities shall be consistent with the provisions of this Agreement'. This obviously applies to the categories of intellectual property rights dealt with in Sections 2–6 of Part II of the Agreement. Several provisions in Part II refer to conditions for the acquisition of rights, such as Article 15.3, which stipulates that '[M]embers may make registrability depend on use. However, actual use of a trademark shall not be a condition for filing an application for registration.'[1] Other provisions specifically refer to the maintenance of rights. Thus, Article 19.2 specifies that '[W]hen subject to the control of its owner, use of a trademark by another person shall be recognized as use of the trademark for the purpose of maintaining the registration'.[2]

> **62.2. Where the acquisition of an intellectual property right is subject to the right being granted or registered, Members shall ensure that the procedures for grant or registration, subject to compliance with the substantive conditions for acquisition of the right, permit the granting or registration of the right within a reasonable period of time so as to avoid unwarranted curtailment of the period of protection.**

In many countries, the examination of trademark and, particularly, patent applications are subject to a considerable delay, mainly due to the limitation of resources available to national offices to handle such applications.

Article 62.2 establishes a very general rule, the application of which may, however, give rise to claims under the dispute settlement mechanism. The procedures concerning the acquisition of rights should permit, in accordance with this provision, 'the granting or registration of the right within a reasonable period of time so as to avoid unwarranted curtailment of the period of protection' (Article 62.2).

Of course, there is significant latitude to establish what 'reasonable' is in this context. One possible indicator of what a 'reasonable period' is, may be the standard set by the US government in free trade agreements (FTAs) signed since 2000 with a number of developed and developing countries.[3] Thus, the FTA with Dominican Republic and the Central American countries (DR-CAFTA) as well as the FTA with Chile stipulate that an 'unreasonable delay' in patent examination shall be understood as a delay of more than five years from filing or three years after request for examination. In the case of FTAs signed by the USA with developed countries (Australia and Singapore) these terms are four and two years, respectively.

What can be deemed 'reasonable' for the purposes of Article 62.2 will depend on the level of development and the resources a particular Member can devote to the procedures involved in the acquisition of intellectual property rights. Members have no obligation to allocate specific resources for the management and enforcement of such rights.[4] Understandably, developing countries have other more urgent priorities and may not devote resources as substantial as those allocated in rich countries, such as in the US, where the Patent and Trademark office spends more

---

[1] See pp 180–2 above.   [2] See pp 196–9 above.

[3] United States–Jordan free trade agreement (2001); United States–Chile free trade agreement, signed at Miami 6 June 2003; entered into force 1 January 2004 (Chile FTA). United States–Singapore free trade agreement, signed at Washington 6 May 2003; entered into force 1 Jan 2004 (Singapore FTA). United States–Morocco free trade agreement, signed at Washington 15 June 2004 (Morocco FTA); entered into force on 1 July 2005. United States–Dominican Republic–Central America free trade agreement, signed at Washington 28 May 2004 and 5 Aug 2004. Parties: Costa Rica, Dominican Republic, El Salvador, Guatemala, Honduras, Nicaragua, and the United States (CAFTA). United States–Bahrain free trade agreement, signed at Washington 14 Sept 2004. (Bahrain FTA).

[4] See commentary on Article 41.5 above.

than $1 billion annually. It is also to be noted that problems with patent examination do not only exist in developing countries. In Japan, for instance, the average pendency until the *first* action by the patent office was approximately 26 months in 2004, and the number of applications awaiting examination was approximately 500,000.[5]

The purpose of Article 62.2 is 'to avoid unwarranted curtailment of the period of protection'. Some countries have adopted measures—not required by the TRIPS Agreement—that address this issue. They allow, for instance, the applicant to take some measures against infringement before the grant of a patent (after the publication of the application or its notification to a third party),[6] or to be compensated for third parties' acts that took place before such grant and that would have infringed the patent.

In addition, some countries allow for an extension of the patent term to compensate for unreasonable delays in the examination procedures. For instance, in accordance with US law Title 35, Part II, Chapter 14, Section 154, (b)(1)(B), there is a 'guarantee of no more than 3-year application pendency':

> Subject to the limitations under paragraph (2), if the issue of an original patent is delayed due to the failure of the United States Patent and Trademark Office to issue a patent within 3 years after the actual filing date of the application in the United States, not including—
>
> (i) any time consumed by continued examination of the application requested by the applicant under section 132(b);
>
> (ii) any time consumed by a proceeding under section 135(a), any time consumed by the imposition of an order under section 181, or any time consumed by appellate review by the Board of Patent Appeals and Interferences or by a Federal court; or
>
> (iii) any delay in the processing of the application by the United States Patent and Trademark Office requested by the applicant except as permitted by paragraph (3)(C), the term of the patent shall be extended 1 day for each day after the end of that 3-year period until the patent is issued.

However, in accordance of sub-paragraph (C) (i) of the same provision,

> The period of adjustment of the term of a patent under paragraph (1) shall be reduced by a period equal to the period of time during which the applicant failed to engage in reasonable efforts to conclude prosecution of the application.

The extension of the patent term due to delays in the patent examination process has also been incorporated into the US FTAs referred to.[7] For instance, the DR-CAFTA provides in Article 15.6(a) that

---

[5] Bill to Patent Law Amendment Reducing Patent Pendency, April 2004, Japan Patent Office Ministry of Economy, Trade and Industry, available at <http://www.jpo.go.jp/torikumi_e/hiroba_e/hourei_e/amendment2004.htm> (last accessed on 20 October 2006).

[6] See, eg, F Pollaud-Dulian, *Droit de la Propriéte Industrielle* (1999: Paris, Montchrestien), p 187.

[7] The US and EU law, as well as the US FTAs, also provide for the extension of the patent term to compensate for unreasonable delays in the procedures for the marketing approval of medicines. See, eg, C Correa, 'Implications of bilateral free trade agreements on access to medicines', (2006) Bulletin of the World Health Organization, vol. 84, No 5, May.

Each Party, at the request of the patent owner, shall adjust the term of a patent to compensate for unreasonable delays that occur in granting the patent. For purposes of this paragraph, an unreasonable delay shall at least include a delay in the issuance of the patent of more than five years from the date of filing of the application in the territory of the Party, or three years after a request for examination of the application has been made, whichever is later, provided that periods attributable to actions of the patent applicant need not be included in the determination of such delays.[8]

The possibility of a patent term extension creates uncertainty for competitors and, when effective, has obvious consequences for the public, as it delays the introduction of competing products with the ensuing loss of consumer welfare. Certainly, the best solution would not seem to provide for such an extension, but to improve the capacity of national agencies to undertake the examination procedures. The interest of both applicants and concerned authorities would have been best served by more concrete provisions in the TRIPS Agreement for assistance to developing countries in this regard.[9]

62.3. Article 4 of the Paris Convention (1967) shall apply *mutatis mutandis* to service marks.

Article 4 of the Paris Convention establishes a 'priority right', according to which

Any person who has duly filed an application for a patent, or for the registration of a utility model, or of an industrial design, or of a trademark, in one of the countries of the Union, or his successor in title, shall enjoy, for the purpose of filing in the other countries, a right of priority during the periods hereinafter fixed (Article 4(1)).

The priority period for trademarks is six months counted from the date of the first regular filing in a country of the Paris Union.

Article 62.3 only makes sure that trademarks for goods and for services are put on the same footing, consistently with Section 2, Part II of the TRIPS Agreement[10] both substantively and with regard to procedures concerning their acquisition on the basis of a claimed priority.

62.4. Procedures concerning the acquisition or maintenance of intellectual property rights and, where a Member's law provides for such procedures, administrative revocation and *inter partes* procedures such as opposition, revocation and cancellation, shall be governed by the general principles set out in paragraphs 2 and 3 of Article 41.

Article 62.4 extends the provisions contained in paragraphs 2 and 3 of Article 41 of the TRIPS Agreement relating to civil judicial procedures, to administrative revocation and to *inter partes* procedures of an administrative nature. Paragraph 2 contains a general provision concerning the fairness, cost and time of procedures,

---

[8] Available at <http://www.ustr.gov/assets/Trade_Agreements/Bilateral/CAFTA/CAFTA-DR_Final_Texts/asset_upload_file934_3935.pdf> (last accessed on 25 November 2006).
[9] See below Article 67.　　[10] See commentary on Article 41.5 above.

while paragraph 3 stipulates some conditions regarding the decisions taken as a result of such procedures.[11]

The administration is in some situations cases entitled to revoke an intellectual property rights ex officio or upon request of an interested party, for instance, when a title has been granted to a person who had no right to apply for it. The TRIPS Agreement also obliges Members to cancel existing intellectual property rights in some circumstances.[12]

Inter partes procedures may be conducted under the authority of an administrative body for various reasons, including opposition to the grant of intellectual property rights, revocation or cancellation thereof. For instance, in the US such procedures are conducted to establish inventorship, when there is controversy about who first made a claimed invention.

Article 62.4 refers, in particular, to *inter partes* procedures of opposition, revocation and cancellation. This provision conveys an implicit recognition of the legitimacy under the TRIPS Agreement of such procedures. In particular, it suggests that both pre-grant and post-grant opposition procedures—with the intervention as a party of the opposing person—are compatible with the Agreement.[13]

> 62.5. Final administrative decisions in any of the procedures referred to under paragraph 4 shall be subject to review by a judicial or quasi-judicial authority. However, there shall be no obligation to provide an opportunity for such review of decisions in cases of unsuccessful opposition or administrative revocation, provided that the grounds for such procedures can be the subject of invalidation procedures.

Final decisions in the procedures referred to in Article 62.4 need to be subject to the possibility of review by a judicial or 'quasi-judicial authority'. The latter concept is likely to be unclear in many legal systems. It would have been preferable to refer to a 'distinct higher authority', as under Article 31(i) of the TRIPS Agreement.[14] This provision logically aims at protecting the applicants or rightsholders against arbitrary or otherwise questionable decisions taken by an administrative authority.

---

[11] See pp 410–17 above.

[12] For instance, in accordance with Article 22.3 of the Agreement a Member 'shall, *ex officio* if its legislation so permits or at the request of an interested party, refuse or invalidate the registration of a trademark which contains or consists of a geographical indication with respect to goods not originating in the territory indicated, if use of the indication in the trademark for such goods in that Member is of such a nature as to mislead the public as to the true place of origin'. See pp 230–1 above.

[13] Some recent FTAs signed by the USA have excluded the possibility of providing for pre-grant opposition procedures. For instance, Article 16.7.4 of the US–Singapore FTA stipulates that '[E]ach Party shall provide that a patent may only be revoked on grounds that would have justified a refusal to grant the patent, or that pertain to the insufficiency of or unauthorized amendments to the patent specification, non-disclosure or misrepresentation of prescribed, material particulars, fraud, and misrepresentation. Where such proceedings include opposition proceedings, a Party may not make such proceedings available prior to the grant of the patent' (available at <http://www.ustr.gov/assets/ Trade_Agreements/Bilateral/Singapore_FTA/Final_Texts/asset_upload_file708_4036.pdf> (last accessed on 27 May 2006).   [14] See Chapter 9 above.

In accordance with the second sentence of the commented provision, the review of a final decision may be excluded, however, in cases of 'unsuccessful opposition or administrative revocation' except where the review is requested on grounds of 'invalidation procedures'.[15] This sentence—contrary to the purpose of the first sentence of this Article—allows Members to limit the review of decisions when an opposition or request for revocation has been dismissed by an administrative authority. However, the wording used ('there shall be no obligation to provide . . .') makes clear that Members have the option to provide for such a review, even in cases where the invalidation of procedures is not the ground for requesting review. Providing for such review may, in fact, ensure that procedures are 'fair and equitable' as generally provided for enforcement measures in Article 41.2 of the Agreement.[16]

Dispute prevention and settlement

Articles 63 and 64 contain rules aimed at preventing and settling disputes concerning the implementation of the TRIPS Agreement.

> **63.1. Laws and regulations, and final judicial decisions and administrative rulings of general application, made effective by a Member pertaining to the subject matter of this Agreement (the availability, scope, acquisition, enforcement and prevention of the abuse of intellectual property rights) shall be published, or where such publication is not practicable made publicly available, in a national language, in such a manner as to enable governments and right holders to become acquainted with them. Agreements concerning the subject matter of this Agreement which are in force between the government or a governmental agency of a Member and the government or a governmental agency of another Member shall also be published.**

Prevention of disputes is basically sought under the TRIPS Agreement through the rules on 'transparency' contained in Article 63. This Article includes three types of obligation.

First, Members must ensure the publication 'in a national language' of laws and regulations, final judicial decisions, and administrative rulings of a general application, as well as agreements concerning IPRs entered into between governments or governmental agencies of Member countries. If publication is not practicable, Members must otherwise make publicly available such instruments and decisions.

The transparency obligation, as contained in Article X of the GATT 1947, has been one of the pillars of the multilateral trade system put in operation by that

---

[15] Here again it would have been clearer to use the expression of Article 31(i), which refers to 'the legal validity of any decision'.　　　　　[16] See pp 413–5 above.

agreement.[17] The purpose of this obligation in the context of the TRIPS Agreement is similar and quite obvious. However, Article 63.1 expressly states that its end is 'to enable governments and right holders to become acquainted with' the specified measures and decisions.

It is important to note that the transparency obligation does not require Members to effectively publish all specified measures and decisions. Where 'publication is not practicable', a Member will comply with that obligation if it makes them 'publicly available'. The key interpretive issue is here when publication may be deemed not to be 'practicable'. This may happen, for instance, with regard to final judicial decisions, as in many countries they are not systematically published and courts or the governments do not have the means to do so. If right-holders or governments can obtain final decisions from the courts or other offices, compliance with the provision will be ensured anyway.

On the other hand, publication, if made, may be on paper or in electronic format, including through a web page. Publication may also be made through public or private publishers.

The transparency obligation in Article 63.1 covers:

- laws;
- regulations;
- final judicial decisions;
- administrative rulings of general application; and
- bilateral intergovernmental or inter-agency agreements.

There are no significant interpretive issues relating to laws and regulations. Clearly, the drafting suggests that 'regulations' refer to something other than 'laws' (although that concept may encompass the latter in certain contexts), namely measures adopted by the administration to implement a law.

One issue that may deserve interpretation arises, instead, with regard to the qualification of 'final' judicial decisions, since it might be difficult to establish in some cases whether a decision definitely precludes the consideration of the issue on which a decision has been taken.[18]

---

[17] Article X of the GATT: '1. Laws, regulations, judicial decisions and administrative rulings of general application, made effective by any contracting party, pertaining to the classification or the valuation of products for customs purposes, or to rates of duty, taxes or other charges, or to requirements, restrictions or prohibitions on imports or exports or on the transfer of payments therefor, or affecting their sale, distribution, transportation, insurance, warehousing inspection, exhibition, processing, mixing or other use, shall be published promptly in such a manner as to enable governments and traders to become acquainted with them. Agreements affecting international trade policy which are in force between the government or a governmental agency of any contracting party and the government or governmental agency of any other contracting party shall also be published. The provisions of this paragraph shall not require any contracting party to disclose confidential information which would impede law enforcement or otherwise be contrary to the public interest or would prejudice the legitimate commercial interests of particular enterprises, public or private.'

[18] See UNCTAD-ICTSD, *Resource Book on TRIPS and Development* (2005: New York, Cambridge University Press), p 642.

Another issue of interest is when an administrative ruling may be deemed 'of general application', since rulings address particular situations ex post, as opposed to the case of administrative regulations that set the rules for future behaviour by the addressed parties. A ruling that may be applied to similar cases is not a ruling 'of general application'. For instance, the refusal to grant a certain category of claims as contained in a particular patent application could arguably be the basis for the refusal of other applications containing the same category of claims, but it will still be a ruling of individual application.

A possible interpretation may be based on GATT jurisprudence. A ruling 'of general application' may be considered a measure adopted to settle a particular situation but applicable to an unidentified number of other parties. In a case relating to the interpretation of Article X.1 of GATT, the panel held[19] the following:

We note that Article X:1 of GATT 1994, which also uses the language 'of general application', includes 'administrative rulings' in its scope. The mere fact that the restraint at issue was an administrative order does not prevent us from concluding that the restraint was a measure of general application. Nor does the fact that it was a country-specific measure exclude the possibility of it being a measure of general application. If, for instance, the restraint was addressed to a specific company or applied to a specific shipment, it would not have qualified as a measure of general application. However, to the extent that the restraint affects an unidentified number of economic operators, including domestic and foreign producers, we find it to be a measure of general application.[20]

The interpretation of Article 63.1 was addressed in *India–Patent Protection for Pharmaceutical and Agricultural Chemical Products*,[21] where the Panel ruled that India had not published the adopted regulation for receiving patent applications under the 'mail-box'[22] established by Article 70.8 of the TRIPS Agreement in a manner consistent with Article 63.1.[23] The dispute related to an instruction given to the patent office to admit applications under the 'mail box' and eventually grant 'exclusive marketing rights' in accordance with Article 70.9 of the TRIPS Agreement,[24] after a transitional measure adopted for the same purpose had lapsed. The existence of that instruction had been made public through a written answer from

---

[19] See also UNCTAD-ICTSD op. cit. (2005), p 642.

[20] See *United States–Restrictions on Imports of Cotton and Man-made Fibre Underwear*, Report of the Panel of 8 November 1996, WTO document WT/DS24/R, at para p 7.65. The Appellate Body confirmed this interpretation:

'The Panel found that the safeguard restraint measure imposed by the United States is "a measure of general application" within the contemplation of Article X:2. We agree with this finding. While the restraint measure was addressed to particular, ie named, exporting Members, including Appellant Costa Rica, as contemplated by Article 6.4, ATC, we note that the measure did not try to become specific as to the individual persons or entities engaged in exporting the specified textile or clothing items to the importing Member and hence affected by the proposed restraint' (Report of the Appellate Body of 10 February 1997, WTO document WT/DS24/AB/R, p 19).

[21] WT/DS50/R (Report by the Panel).		[22] See pp 514–15 below.

[23] This finding, however, was reversed by the Appellate Body on procedural grounds as the terms of reference of the complaint submitted by the United States did not include a reference to Article 63. See WT/DS50/AB/R (Report of the Appellate Body), paras 85–96.		[24] See pp 514–15 below.

the government to a question made by a member of the Indian Parliament. The panel held that any mechanism for the implementation of the 'mail box' provision would constitute a measure of 'general application' under Article 63.1.[25]

Article 63.1 clarifies that only the measures and decisions specified therein that are 'made effective by a Member' are subject to the transparency obligation. This means that it does not apply to draft measures or to measures that have not entered into force yet. This limitation is consistent with the sovereign right of Members to decide how to implement its obligations under the TRIPS Agreement.[26]

The transparency obligation only applies with regard to measures 'pertaining to the subject matter of this Agreement (the availability, scope, acquisition, enforcement and prevention of the abuse of intellectual property rights)'. Interestingly, the Agreement does not contain specific provisions to prevent the abuse of intellectual property rights.[27] A possible interpretation to this reference is the intention of some of the negotiating parties of ensuring transparency about measures that may limit the exercise of such rights, such as laws dealing with anti-competitive practices. However, it would be reasonable to understand this provision as only requiring transparency with regard to measures that specifically address the abusive acquisition or exercise of intellectual property rights.

In addition, the Agreement does not cover all areas of intellectual property, such as utility models. Hence, there would be no obligation to publish or make available laws and regulations, decisions, and international agreements relating to non-covered subject matter.

The obligation regarding publication also encompasses 'agreements concerning the subject matter of this Agreement'. However, only agreements 'which are in force' and which have been established between Members or their agencies are subject to this obligation. Hence, it does not apply to agreements in force between a Member or its agencies and a non-Member or its agencies, and it only seems to apply to bilateral agreements.[28] This is a somehow surprising limitation since, as examined,[29] the most-favoured nation (MFN) clause applies both in cases where advantages are granted to Members as well as to non-Members. The transparency obligation, as defined, would not permit Members to monitor whether the application of the MFN clause could be triggered by agreements with non-Members. Nothing however, prevents a Member from publishing or otherwise making available such agreements. Moreover, given the ease with which information circulates today, international agreements with non-Members are unlikely to remain inaccessible to other Members.

---

[25] See WT/DS50/R, para 7.48.

[26] However, in the process of accession to the WTO, some countries have accepted expanded transparency obligations. Chinese Taipei, for instance, made a commitment to circulate legislation to WTO Members for comment with specified time limits.

[27] Some enforcement provisions in the Part III do have, however, that objective. See pp 410–12 above.

[28] The provision refers to agreements between 'a Member' and 'another Member', in the singular. See also below the commentary on para 3 of Article 63.   [29] See Chapter 2 above.

Interestingly, the provision not only covers agreements between the governments as such, but also those established between Members' governmental agencies. This is probably aimed at capturing agreements that may be entered into, for instance, between patent offices for harmonizing criteria of examination or otherwise improve and speed up the process of patent examination.

Finally, it is to be noted that Members are bound to publish or make available measures and decisions, as examined above, 'in a national language', thereby allowing Members with more than one official language to choose in which language that obligation will be complied with.

> 63.2. Members shall notify the laws and regulations referred to in paragraph 1 to the Council for TRIPS in order to assist that Council in its review of the operation of this Agreement. The Council shall attempt to minimize the burden on Members in carrying out this obligation and may decide to waive the obligation to notify such laws and regulations directly to the Council if consultations with WIPO on the establishment of a common register containing these laws and regulations are successful. The Council shall also consider in this connection any action required regarding notifications pursuant to the obligations under this Agreement stemming from the provisions of Article 6ter of the Paris Convention (1967).

Members are bound to notify the Council of TRIPS of laws and regulations pertaining to the subject matter of the Agreement in order to assist the Council for TRIPS 'in its review of the operation of this Agreement'. Clearly, the scope of this obligation is narrower than that of Article 63.1, as only 'laws and regulations' are to be notified. The same caveat mentioned with regard to Article 63.1 applies here as to the limitation of the obligation to the areas of intellectual property actually covered by the Agreement.

Final judicial decisions (as well as administrative rulings of general application) need not be notified. It would have been extremely cumbersome for Members to notify such decisions. However, some imbalance is generated by this limitation between common-law and continental-law countries, since case law plays a key role in determining the legal regime in the former.

The purpose of the notification under Article 63.2 is to 'assist' the Council for TRIPS 'in its review of the operation of this Agreement'. This Article is, hence, linked to Articles 68 and 71.1 of the TRIPS Agreement, which provide for different types of review by the Council.[30]

Article 63.2 mandates the Council for TRIPS, in soft language, to 'attempt to minimize the burden of Members in carrying out this obligation' and authorizes it to waive the notification obligation if negotiations with WIPO to establish a common register are successful. Such negotiations led, in fact, to the adoption of an agreement between WTO and WIPO and to the establishment of a register[31]

---

[30] See pp 504–6 and 517–19 below.

[31] See Agreement Between the World Intellectual Property Organization and the World Trade Organization (available at <http://www.wto.org/english/tratop_e/trips_e/wtowip_e.htm>, last accessed on 25 May 2006).

under which WTO may request free-of-charge copies of laws and regulations notified to the WIPO secretariat.

The Council for TRIPS shall also consider any action required regarding notifications on State emblems, official signs, and hallmarks indicating control of warranty, that Members may desire to protect in accordance with Article 6*ter* of the Paris Convention.[32] Although elliptical, this provision seems to indicate that Members may notify such emblems, official signs, and hallmarks to the Council for TRIPS while, in accordance with the Paris Convention, the members of the Union were bound to communicate them 'reciprocally, through the intermediary of the International Bureau'.[33]

A violation to Article 63.2 was found in the already mentioned report by a WTO panel in *India–Patent Protection for Pharmaceutical and Agricultural Chemical Products*,[34] since it was found that India had failed to notify the Council for TRIPS measures intended to implement paras 8 and 9 of Article 70 of the TRIPS Agreement.[35] The panel's ruling was also reversed, however, by the Appellate Body on procedural grounds.

> **3. Each Member shall be prepared to supply, in response to a written request from another Member, information of the sort referred to in paragraph 1. A Member, having reason to believe that a specific judicial decision or administrative ruling or bilateral agreement in the area of intellectual property rights affects its rights under this Agreement, may also request in writing to be given access to or be informed in sufficient detail of such specific judicial decisions or administrative rulings or bilateral agreements.**

Members are also bound, under the transparency obligation, to supply, in response to a written request from another Member, information on the laws, regulations, decisions, and agreements referred to in Article 63.1. This obligation supplements that contained in para 1 of the same Article. The second sentence of this paragraph poses an important interpretive question. It neither refers to 'final' judicial decisions nor specifies that administrative decisions to be informed upon request are those of 'general application'. In addition, it generally alludes to any 'bilateral agreement in the area of intellectual property rights'. As drafted, it is much broader than the publication obligation of para 1, as examined above, since it might be deemed to create an obligation to supply any decision, whether final or not, any administrative ruling including those of individual application, bilateral

---

[32] This Article protects against the use as trademarks or elements of trademarks, without authorization from the competent authorities, of such emblems, signs, and hallmarks.

[33] Article 63*ter* (3)(a) provides that 'the countries of the Union agree to communicate reciprocally, through the intermediary of the International Bureau, the list of State emblems, and official signs and hallmarks indicating control and warranty, which they desire, or may hereafter desire, to place wholly or within certain limits under the protection of this Article, and all subsequent modifications of such list. Each country of the Union shall in due course make available to the public the lists so communicated. Nevertheless such communication is not obligatory in respect of flags of States.'

[34] WT/DS50/R. [35] See pp 514–17 below.

treaties with members and non-members regarding, in addition, any intellectual property right, whether covered or not by the Agreement.

An expansive reading of the second sentence may lead to an excessive burden on Members and to some intrusion into their judicial and administrative activities. It is to be noted that the right to request information arises when a Member has reason to believe that a measure or decision 'affects its rights under this Agreement'. This means that the existence of a measure or decision affecting a particular right-holder would not be sufficient basis for a valid request under this paragraph; there should be the possibility of a concrete violation of the Agreement affecting the requesting Member's rights under the Agreement.

Obviously, requests of information under Article 63.3 should be addressed to a Member through normal official channels, and not directly to its courts or agencies, such as the patent and trademark office.

> **4. Nothing in paragraphs 1, 2 and 3 shall require Members to disclose confidential information which would impede law enforcement or otherwise be contrary to the public interest or would prejudice the legitimate commercial interests of particular enterprises, public or private.**

Article 63.4 closely follows the wording of Article X of the GATT. It provides that nothing in Article 63 shall require the disclosure of 'confidential information'. Requested Members may, hence, refuse to disclose information of this kind. Article 63.4, however, limits the scope of the concept of 'confidential information'. Unlike other provisions in the Agreement that refer to parties' confidential information' (such as Article 40.3[36]), Article 63.4 only deems viable a refusal to provide such information when the supply thereof:

- would impede law enforcement;
- be otherwise contrary to the public interest; or
- would prejudice the legitimate commercial interests of particular enterprises, public or private.

The first situation may arise, for instance, where the requested Member is conducting an investigation that may be frustrated by the leak of information.

The concept of 'public interest' is only used twice in the TRIPS Agreement: in Article 8.1 and in this provision. The determination of cases where supplying information may be 'contrary to the public interest' obviously corresponds to the requested Member, who would enjoy a broad margin to make its own judgement on the matter. Although such determination might be challenged by another Member, it will be hard for a panel or the Appellate Body to intrude into a Member's determination of what its public interest is.

Access to information may also be refused when it 'would prejudice the legitimate commercial interests of particular enterprises, public or private'. This provision

---

[36] See pp 404–6 above.

seems to limit the protection of 'undisclosed information' provided for in Article 39 of the TRIPS Agreement,[37] because it would only be possible for a Member to refuse disclosure on the grounds that such prejudice will occur. As a matter of fact, it might be presumed that any disclosure of confidential information prejudices 'the legitimate commercial interests' of a company, as the very basis of the protection of such information is its commercial value.[38]

It is also of note that the only confidential information that may be refused in accordance with Article 63.4 is that belonging to 'enterprises'. No reference is made to personal or government information. Despite this gap, a Member may certainly consider that it is against the 'public interest' to disclose information affecting privacy or the performance of governmental functions.

Dispute settlement

64.1. The provisions of Articles XXII and XXIII of GATT 1994 as elaborated and applied by the Dispute Settlement Understanding shall apply to consultations and the settlement of disputes under this Agreement except as otherwise specifically provided herein.

Dispute settlement on TRIPS matters is governed by Articles XXII and XXIII of GATT 1994 and, in particular, by the Dispute Settlement Understanding (DSU) adopted as one of the outcomes of the Uruguay Round.

The Agreement Establishing the WTO introduced significant changes to the dispute settlement mechanism as operated under the GATT. The Dispute Settlement Body (DSB) is composed of all WTO Members. There is a definite time frame for the various steps and stages leading to a ruling. Thus, panel reports must be adopted, in principle, within nine months. Panel reports may be appealed before the Appellate Body, a permanent organ of the WTO. A very important element in the new system is the semi-automaticity derived from the 'negative consensus rule' for the adoption of panel reports. The disagreement of the party which is not favoured may not block in any case the decision by the DSB.[39]

Trade retaliations, where authorized, should take place, in principle, in the same sector in which the dispute occurs. If retaliation in that sector is deemed ineffective or impracticable, however, it can take place in a different sector. The adoption of the DSU excludes, as a matter of principle, the application of unilateral measures against a Member which is considered by another Member as noncomplying with the TRIPS Agreement. The new system goes further than the

---

[37] See pp 369–73 above.   [38] See commentary on Article 39.2.
[39] See, eg, M Tebilcock and R Howse, *The Regulation of International Trade* (1999: London, Routledge, 2nd edn), pp 51–94.

previous one under GATT in restraining such measures.[40] However, a panel found that Sections 301 to 310 of that US Trade Act were not inconsistent with WTO rules.[41]

It is important to note that a complaining Member does not need to produce evidence that a TRIPS-inconsistent domestic measure nullifies or impairs benefits conferred by the Agreement to that Member. It has no need to prove either that such an inconsistent measure has generated quantifiable damages. To the extent that an inconsistency with the TRIPS standards can be shown, there is automatically a *prima facie* presumption that such nullification or impairment has occurred. Although, in theory, that presumption could be rebutted by the complained Member,

in the history of GATT/WTO dispute settlement, there has not been one single case where the respondent could successfully rebut the presumption of impairment by denying an adverse impact of its measure on other Parties/Members. In other words, despite the language employed in Article 3:8 DSU, the presumption established by the violation of a WTO rule is practically not rebuttable, it is in fact an *irrefutable* presumption. Consequently, the only way for the respondent to win the case is to convince the panel or the Appellate Body that there is no violation in the first place; either by addressing the asserted violation as such, or by providing evidence that the violation is justified under an exception clause.[42]

Complaints relating to the TRIPS Agreement were filed in 25 cases, the majority of which (64 per cent) by the US (see Table 14.1). It is also to be noted that in an arbitration decision[43] Ecuador was authorized to suspend its obligations under the TRIPS Agreement as retaliation against the EC for maintaining measures found inconsistent in an adverse ruling.[44]

As indicated in Table 14. 1, seven of the cases involving the TRIPS Agreement have led to the establishment of a panel. Only two of them (concerning, in fact, the same matter) involved a developing country.[45] They dealt with issues relating

---

[40] See, eg, Industrial Structure Council (1994), 1994 Report on Unfair Trade Policies by major trading partners, *Trade Policies and WTO*, Tokyo. The letter by the US Federal Government (15 December 1993) sending the Trade Agreements resulting from the Uruguay Round for approval by the Congress stated, in this regard, that action under Section 301 of the Trade Act of 1974 will be legitimized 'at the end of the dispute settlement process' under the Dispute Settlement Understanding.

[41] *United States–Section 301–310 of the Trade Act of 1974*, Report of the WTO Panel, WT/DS152/R (2000).

[42] UNCTAD-ICTSD op. cit. (2005), p 666.

[43] Decision by the Arbitrators, *European Communities–Regime for the Importation, Sale and Distribution of Bananas–Recourse to Arbitration by the European Communities under Article 22.6 of the DSU*, WT/DS27/ARB/ECU, 24 March 2000.

[44] See *European Economic Community–Regime for the Importation, Sale and Distribution of Bananas*, WT/DS27/AB/R (1997).

[45] Rulings made under the WTO dispute settlement mechanism are only applicable to the parties to the dispute. The EC and its Member States were not a party in the case initially brought by the USA against India and, hence, were bound to initiate separate proceedings under the DSU.

Table 14.1: Dispute Settlement Understanding Involving the TRIPS Agreement

Case No. DS/* (IP/D/*)	Title	Date of Request for Consultations	Complainant	Respondent	Status
28(1)	*Japan–Measures Concerning Sound Recordings*	9 February 1996	US	Japan	Mutually Agreed Solution
36(2)	*Pakistan–Patent Protection for Pharmaceutical and Agricultural Chemical Products*	30 April 1996	US	Pakistan	Mutually Agreed Solution
37(3)	*Portugal–Patent Protection Under the Industrial Property Act*	30 April 1996	US	Portugal	Mutually Agreed Solution
42(4)	*Japan–Measures Concerning Sound Recordings*	28 May 1996	EC	Japan	Mutually Agreed Solution
50(5)	*India–Patent Protection for Pharmaceutical and Agricultural Chemical Products*	2 July 1996	US	India	AB Report Adopted
59(6)	*Indonesia–Certain Measures Affecting the Automobile Industry*	8 October 1996	US	Indonesia	Panel Report Adopted
79(7)	*India–Patent Protection for Pharmaceutical and Agricultural Chemical Products*	28 April 1997	EC	India	Panel Report Adopted
82(8)	*Ireland–Measures Affecting the Grant of Copyright and Neighbouring Rights*	14 May 1997	US	Ireland	Mutually Agreed Solution
83(9)	*Denmark–Measures Affecting the Enforcement of Intellectual Property Rights*	14 May 1997	US	Denmark	Mutually Agreed Solution
86(10)	*Sweden–Measures Affecting the Enforcement of Intellectual Property Rights*	28 May 1997	US	Sweden	Mutually Agreed Solution

Table 14.1 (*cont.*)

Case No. DS/* (IP/D/*)	Title	Date of Request for Consultations	Complainant	Respondent	Status
114(11)	*Canada–Patent Protection of Pharmaceutical Products*	19 December 1997	EC	Canada	Panel Report Adopted
115(12)	*EC–Measures Affecting the Grant of Copyright and Neighbouring Rights*	6 January 1998	US	EC	Mutually Agreed Solution
124(13)	*EC–Enforcement of Intellectual Property Rights for Motion Pictures and Television Programs*	30 April 1998	US	EC	Mutually Agreed Solution
125(14)	*Greece–Enforcement of Intellectual Property Rights for Motion Pictures and Television Programs*	4 May 1998	US	Greece	Mutually Agreed Solution
153(15)	*European Communities–Patent Protection for Pharmaceutical and Agricultural Chemical Products*	2 December 1998	Canada	EC	No Panel or Settlement
160(16)	*US–Section 110(5) of US Copyright Act*	26 January 1999	EC	US	Panel Report Adopted
170(17)	*Canada–Term of Patent Protection*	6 May 1999	US	Canada	AB Report Adopted
171(18)	*Argentina–Patent Protection for Pharmaceuticals and Test Data Protection for Agricultural Chemicals*	6 May 1999	US	Argentina	Mutually Agreed Solution
174(19)	*EC–Protection of Trademarks and Geographical Indications for Agricultural Products and Foodstuffs*	1 June 1999	US	EC	Panel Report Adopted

Table 14.1 (*cont.*)

Case No. DS/* (IP/D/*)	Title	Date of Request for Consultations	Complainant	Respondent	Status
176(20)	*US–Section 211 Omnibus Appropriations Act of 1998*	8 July 1999	EC	US	AB Report Adopted
186(21)	*US–Section 337 of the Tariff Act of 1930 and Amendments thereto*	12 January 2000	EC	US	No Panel or Settlement
196(22)	*Argentina–Certain Measures on the Protection of Patents and Test Data*	30 May 2000	US	Argentina	Mutually Agreed Solution
199(23)	*Brazil–Measures Affecting Patent Protection*	30 May 2000	US	Brazil	Mutually Agreed Solution
224(24)	*US–US Patents Code*	31 January 2001	Brazil	US	No Panel or Settlement
290(25)	*EC–Protection of Trademarks and Geographical Indications for Agricultural Products and Foodstuffs*	17 April 2003	Australia	EC	Panel Report Adopted

Source: M Gad, 'TRIPS dispute settlement and developing country interests', in C Correa and A Yusuf, *Intellectual Property and International Trade. The TRIPS Agreement* (forthcoming: London, Kluwer Law International, 2nd edn).

to the implementation of Article 70.8 (the 'mailbox' provision) by India.[46] The third case, brought by the US against Canada with respect to the extension of the term of patents granted before the entry into force of the Agreement (Article 70.2), found Canada to be in violation of the Agreement.[47] There were two other cases between developed countries, in which the issues of exceptions to patent rights (brought by the EC and their Member States against Canada[48]) and

---

[46] See *India–Patent Protection for Pharmaceutical and Agricultural Chemical Products*, WT/DS50/AB/R (1998), and *India–Patent Protection for Pharmaceutical and Agricultural Chemical Products*, WT/DS79/R (1998).

[47] See *Canada–Term of Patent Protection*, WT/DS170/AB/R (2000).

[48] See *Canada–Patent Protection for Pharmaceutical Products*, WT/DS114/R (2000).

copyright (brought by the EC and their Member States against the US[49]) were considered. Another case, brought by the EC and their Member States against the US,[50] involved the protection of trademarks and tradenames. Finally, the US complained against the EC and its Member States regarding geographical indications.[51]

The rulings in these cases have confirmed the applicability of the method of interpretation codified in Articles 31 and 32 of the Vienna Convention to TRIPS-related disputes. The panels' or Appellate Body's reports contain general considerations that are relevant for the interpretation[52] and implementation of the TRIPS Agreement.[53]

In *India–Patent Protection for Pharmaceutical and Agricultural Chemical Products*,[54] the AB dismissed the expansive interpretation of the panel (which had held that 'legitimate expectations' of the US had been frustrated) and confirmed that the TRIPS Agreement, like any other WTO agreement, should be literally interpreted. The panel stated:

We must bear in mind that the TRIPS Agreement, the entire text of which was newly negotiated in the Uruguay Round and occupies a relatively self-contained, sui generis, status in the WTO Agreement, nevertheless is an integral part of the WTO system, which itself builds upon the experience of nearly half a century under the GATT 1947 [. . .] Indeed, in light of the fact that the TRIPS Agreement was negotiated as a part of the overall balance of concessions in the Uruguay Round, it would be inappropriate not to apply the same principles in interpreting the TRIPS Agreement as those applicable to the interpretation of other parts of the WTO Agreement.[55]

---

[49] See *United States–Section 110(5) of the US Copyright Act*, WT/DS160/R (2000).

[50] *United States–Section 211 Omnibus Appropriations Act of 1998*, WT/DS176/AB/R (2002).

[51] *European Communities–Protection of Trademarks and Geographical Indications for Agricultural Products and Foodstuffs* (WT/DS174/R) of 15 March 2005.

[52] It is to be recalled that in accordance with Article 3.2 of the DSU, the dispute settlement mechanism should 'preserve the rights and obligations of Members under the covered agreements', and that that role of the panels and the AB is only 'to clarify the existing provisions of those agreements in accordance with customary rules of interpretation of public international law'. Authoritative interpretations of the WTO agreements can only be issued by the WTO Members themselves. Article IX.2 of the Agreement Establishing the WTO provides: 'The Ministerial Conference and the General Council shall have the exclusive authority to adopt interpretations of this Agreement and of the Multilateral Trade Agreements. In the case of an interpretation of a Multilateral Trade Agreement in Annex 1, they shall exercise their authority on the basis of a recommendation by the Council overseeing the functioning of that Agreement. The decision to adopt an interpretation shall be taken by a three–fourths majority of the Members. This paragraph shall not be used in a manner that would undermine the amendment provisions in Article X.'

[53] See, eg, O Cattaneo, 'The Interpretation of the TRIPS Agreement: Considerations for the WTO Panels and Appellate Body', (2000), Journal of World Intellectual Property, September, vol. 3, No 5, pp 627–81; C Correa, 'The TRIPS Agreement from the perspective of developing countries', in P Macrory, A Appleton, and M Plummer (eds), *The World Trade Organization: Legal, Economic and Political Analysis* (2005: New York, Springer); UNCTAD-ICTSD op. cit. (2005), pp 690–704.   [54] WT/DS50/R, 5 September 1997.

[55] WT/DS50/R, 5 September 1997, para 7.19.

The AB considered that[56]

The Panel misapplies Article 31 of the Vienna Convention. The Panel misunderstands the concept of legitimate expectations in the context of the customary rules of interpretation of public international law. The legitimate expectations of the parties to a treaty are reflected in the language of the treaty itself. The duty of a treaty interpreter is to examine the words of the treaty to determine the intentions of the parties. This should be done in accordance with the principles of treaty interpretation set out in Article 31 of the Vienna Convention. But these principles of interpretation neither require nor condone the imputation into a treaty of words that are not there or the importation into a treaty of concepts that were not intended.[57]

In the same case, as discussed in Chapter 2, the extent to which a panel or the AB may interpret national law in order to establish its consistency with the TRIPS Agreement was considered. The AB emphasized that such interpretation is necessary but solely to determine compliance with the established obligations.[58]

In *Canada–Patent Protection for Pharmaceutical Products*, the panel elaborated on the context for the interpretation of the TRIPS Agreement in accordance with Article 31, para 2, of the Vienna Convention. It concluded that such context did not include only the text and Preamble of the TRIPS Agreement itself but, it also included, inter alia, the provisions of the other international instruments on intellectual property incorporated into the TRIPS Agreement.[59] The panel held the following:

In the framework of the TRIPS Agreement, which incorporates certain provisions of the major pre-existing international instruments on intellectual property, the context to which the Panel may have recourse for the purposes of interpretation of specific TRIPS provisions [...] is not restricted to the text, Preamble and Annexes to the TRIPS Agreement itself, but also includes the provisions of the other international instruments on intellectual property incorporated into the TRIPS Agreement, as well as any agreement between the parties relating to these Agreements within the meaning of Article 31:2 of the Vienna Convention on the Law of Treaties. Thus [...] Article 9:2 of the Berne Convention for the Protection of Literary and Artistic Works [...] is an important contextual element for the interpretation of Article 30 of the TRIPS Agreement.[60]

Most importantly, in the same case the panel applied Article 7 and Article 8.1 of the Agreement[61] to develop its interpretation of Article 30 of the Agreement. The panel stated that

Article 30's very existence amounts to a recognition that the definition of patent rights contained in Article 28 would need certain adjustments. On the other hand, the three limiting

---

[56] The panel had concluded in the same case that '[S]ince the TRIPS Agreement is one of the Multilateral Trade Agreements, we must be guided by the jurisprudence established under GATT 1947 in interpreting the provisions of the TRIPS Agreement unless there is a contrary provision . . .'. See WT/DS50/R, para 7.19.   [57] WT/DS50/AB/R, 19 December 1997, para 45.
[58] Idem, para 66.   [59] See Chapter 2 above.   [60] WT/DS114/R, para 7.14.
[61] See Chapter 3 above.

Acquisition and maintenance of IPRs

conditions attached to Article 30 testify strongly that the negotiators of the Agreement did not intend Article 30 to bring about what would be equivalent to a renegotiation of the basic balance of the Agreement. Obviously, the exact scope of Article 30's authority will depend on the specific meaning given to its limiting conditions. The words of those conditions must be examined with particular care on this point. Both the goals and the limitations stated in Articles 7 and 8.1 must obviously be borne in mind when doing so as well as those of other provisions of the TRIPS Agreement which indicate its object and purposes.[62]

Despite the clear reference to Articles 7 and 8.1, as discussed in Chapter 4, the panel introduced a subjective conception of the 'policy' of patent laws, relying on its understanding of the intent and practical effect of those laws rather than on the referenced provisions of the Agreement.[63]

It is important to bear in mind in this regard that para 5(a) of the 'Doha Declaration on the TRIPS Agreement and Public Health[64] established that:

In applying the customary rules of interpretation of public international law, each provision of the TRIPS Agreement shall be read in the light of the object and purpose of the Agreement as expressed, in particular, in its objectives and principles.

Some of the TRIPS-related rulings referred to the negotiating history of the TRIPS Agreement and of the incorporated conventions, and used elements of such history to confirm the interpretation given to particular provisions. In *India–Patent Protection for Pharmaceutical and Agricultural Chemical Products*, for example, the panel used the negotiating history of the TRIPS Agreement to confirm its interpretation of Article 70.8:

The findings above can be confirmed by the negotiating history of the TRIPS Agreement. We note that in the negotiation of the TRIPS Agreement the question of patent protection for pharmaceutical and agricultural chemicals products was a key issue, which was negotiated as part of a complex of related issues concerning the scope of the protection to be accorded to patents and some related rights and the timing of the economic impact of such protection. A critical part of the deal struck was that developing countries that did not provide product patent protection for pharmaceutical and agricultural chemicals were permitted to delay the introduction thereof for a period of ten years from the entry into force of the WTO Agreement. However, if they chose to do so, they were required to put in place a means by which patent applications for such inventions could be filed so as to allow the preservation of their novelty and priority for the purposes of determining their eligibility for protection by a patent after the expiry of the transitional period. In addition, they were required to provide also for exclusive marketing rights in respect of the products in question

---

62 WT/DS114/R, para 7.26.
63 See R Howse, 'The Canadian Medicine Panel: A Dangerous Precedent in Dangerous Times', *Bridges: Between Trade and Sustainable Development* (2000), Year 4, No 3. See also S Williams, 'Developing TRIPS Jurisprudence—The First Six Years and Beyond', (2001), 4(2) Journal of World Intellectual Property, p 191.
64 'Doha Ministerial Declaration on the TRIPS Agreement and Public Health', WT/MIN(01)/DEC/W/2, 14 November 2001.

if those products obtained marketing approval during the transitional period, subject to a number of conditions.[65]

In *United States–Section 110(5) of the US Copyright Act*, the panel supported its interpretation by reference to the negotiating history of the Berne Convention that has become part of the TRIPS Agreement.[66] Further, in *United States–Section 211 Omnibus Appropriations Act of 1998*, the panel relied on the preparatory work of the Paris Convention (1967). The EC argued that such an invocation was erroneous under Article 32 of the Vienna Convention, since none of the conditions for the application of that rule were present in this case and the history of the Paris Convention failed to provide a clear indication of the intentions of the negotiators. The Appellate Body, however, confirmed its own interpretation of Article 6*quinquies*B of the Convention relying on the negotiating history of the Paris Convention.[67]

Another important interpretive issue, as discussed in Chapter 2, is the extent to which WTO bodies may apply an evolutionary interpretation to the TRIPS Agreement, as such an approach may lead to an expansive interpretation of the obligations actually assumed by Members. In *Canada–Patent Protection for Pharmaceutical Products*, the panel examined the status of the legislation *at the time of the negotiation* of the Agreement to determine the concept of 'legitimate interest' as contained in Article 30. This approach was consistent with the general principle of treaty interpretation requiring that the meaning of the terms of a treaty be considered at the time of its signature.[68]

However, in *United States–Section 110(5) of the US Copyright Act*, the panel considered that the WIPO Copyright Treaty of 1996 should be viewed as 'relevant to seek contextual guidance . . . when developing interpretations that avoid conflicts within the overall multilateral copyright framework . . .'.[69] Although the panel cautioned that the statement concerning Article 10 of that Treaty did not fall under the Vienna Convention rules on a subsequent treaty on the same matter or subsequent practice,[70] the recourse to a post-TRIPS treaty to interpret obligations under the TRIPS Agreement represents a risky and troubling approach[71] as

---

[65] WT/DS50/R, para 7.40. The panel also stated: 'The observation above can be confirmed by the drafting history of the TRIPS Agreement. Exclusive marketing rights were a *quid pro quo* for the delay of the availability of product patents for pharmaceutical and agricultural chemical products until 1 January 2005, based on a careful balancing of obligations between interested parties during the Uruguay Round negotiations'. Idem para 7.72.

[66] See WT/DS160/R (2000) above note 24, para 6.18. The panel held that the 'minor exceptions' doctrine—not formally incorporated either in Berne or in the TRIPS Agreement—was part of the 'Berne *acquis*' (paras 6.60–6.66).

[67] See WT/DS176/AB/R (2002) above note 25, paras 145–6.

[68] WT/DS114/R above note 23, para 7.82. See also I Brownlie, *Principles of Public International Law* (1998: Oxford University Press), p 627.

[69] WT/DS160/R (2000) para 6.70.   [70] See a discussion of this case in Chapter 5.

[71] According to Sara Williams, this was one of the panel's 'most adventurous remarks' and 'an aberration from the Panel's otherwise constructionist approach', above note 64, p 203.

it may lead to the creation of TRIPS-plus obligations via interpretations, in clear contradiction to the already quoted Article 3.2 of the DSU.

> **64.2. Subparagraphs 1(b) and 1(c) of Article XXIII of GATT 1994 shall not apply to the settlement of disputes under this Agreement for a period of five years from the date of entry into force of the WTO Agreement.**

The TRIPS Agreement provided for an interim period of five years during which 'non-violation' complaints, as contemplated in Article XXIII.1(b) and (c) of GATT 1994, would not apply to the settlement of disputes.

'Non-violation' complaints may be articulated under the GATT when a Member adopts measures that do not violate its obligations but lead, de facto, to the nullification or impairment of benefits accruing to the complaining Member (Article XXIII.1(b) GATT). Such complaints, if accepted, may result in the withdrawal of concessions by that Member; however, the complained against Member that adopted them is not required to remove or amend the measures at stake.[72] In addition, Article XXIII.1(c) of GATT refers to what have been called 'situation' complaints, which may arise when certain situations (and not particular measures) frustrate legitimate commercial expectations.

The introduction of non-violation and situation complaints in the context of the TRIPS Agreement was approved, subject to the moratorium contained in Article 64.2, at a very late stage of TRIPS negotiations, after considerable resistance by developing countries.[73] This resistance has continued thereafter and, in fact, with the exception of the USA and Switzerland, WTO Members seem largely opposed to make such complaints applicable to TRIPS matters. There are good reasons for this position. The TRIPS Agreement represents a significant intrusion of WTO rules 'beyond the borders', as it sets out minimum standards that largely affect domestic activities and transactions, and not only international trade. Admitting non-violation complaints would only expand further the possibility of intrusion regarding non-intellectual-property measures. The legal measures required to implement TRIPS are of a nature very different from the measures that may be applied in the context of trade in goods and services,[74] as they are contained in laws and regulations that may be scrutinized to determine whether the required level of protection has been conferred or not. Members cannot legitimately expect more regarding the availability and enforcement of intellectual property rights than what is specifically demanded by the TRIPS Agreement. If upheld, non-violation complaints could extraordinarily reduce the room for Members to adopt public policies, clearly to an extent unforeseen by the parties that negotiated the TRIPS Agreement.

If, for instance, a Member established price controls applicable to patented products, would it be possible to argue that such control impairs the benefits

---

[72] See Article 26 of the DSU.   [73] See eg, UNCTAD-ICTSD op. cit. (2005), p 663.
[74] Non-violation complaints are also applicable in accordance with Article XXIII.3 of GATTS.

normally accruing to patent owners and that, hence, a non-violation complaint could be validly filed? Price controls do not affect the availability or exercise of any of the exclusive rights granted by a patent in conformity with Article 28.1 of the TRIPS Agreement.[75] Patents, like other intellectual property rights, only confer negative rights; they do not create positive rights nor, in particular, can they give rise to expectations about any particular level of commercial benefit. A Member has no limitation whatsoever to determine conditions for the commercialization of patented products, including to prohibit their circulation for sanitary or other reasons, as necessary.[76] The AB was perfectly right, hence, to reject, in *India–Patent Protection for Pharmaceutical and Agricultural Chemical Products*,[77] the theory that there are 'legitimate expectations' of the parties beyond what is reflected in the language of the TRIPS Agreement itself.[78]

Admitting non-violation complaints might, finally, open the door for threatening weak WTO Members with complaints aimed at inducing changes in public policies in a multiplicity of fields, and could embark the WTO dispute settlement bodies in ruling on measures that are within the policy space reserved by Members when adopting the TRIPS Agreement.

> **64.3. During the time period referred to in paragraph 2, the Council for TRIPS shall examine the scope and modalities for complaints of the type provided for under subparagraphs 1(b) and 1(c) of Article XXIII of GATT 1994 made pursuant to this Agreement, and submit its recommendations to the Ministerial Conference for approval. Any decision of the Ministerial Conference to approve such recommendations or to extend the period in paragraph 2 shall be made only by consensus, and approved recommendations shall be effective for all Members without further formal acceptance process.**

During the period provided for in para 2, the Council for TRIPS was due to examine the scope and modalities for complaints of the type mentioned therein. The Council for TRIPS started to consider the issue,[79] as mandated, but deep differences arose among Members. The recommendations have not been elaborated and submitted yet, despite the fact that the moratorium ended on 1 January 2005. The period to examine the scope of modalities referred to was extended by the WTO Ministerial Conference held in Doha in 2001 until the Fifth Conference, which took place in Cancun in 2003. The negotiations at this Conference collapsed and no decision on the matter was taken.

---

[75] See Chapter 9 above.

[76] If such prohibition were deemed, for instance, to be an unjustified technical barrier to trade, the affected Member might have recourse to a claim under the TBT Agreement, but not under the TRIPS Agreement.   [77] WT/DS50/AB/R, 19 December 1997.

[78] Idem, para 45.

[79] See, eg, Note by the WTO Secretariat, Non-Violation Complaints and the TRIPS Agreement, IP/C/W/124 of 28 January 1999; Summary Note by the WTO Secretariat, Non-Violation Complaints and Situation Complaints, IP/C/W/349 of 29 June 2002; United States of America, Non-Violation Nullification or Impairment under the TRIPS Agreement, JOB (99)/4439 of 26 July 1999.

As reported by the WTO Secretariat,

[I]n May 2003, the TRIPS Council chairperson listed four possibilities for a recommendation: (1) banning non-violation complaints in TRIPS completely, (2) allowing the complaints to be handled under the WTO's dispute settlement rules as applies to goods and services cases, (3) allowing non-violation complaints but subject to special 'modalities' (ie ways of dealing with them), and (4) extending the moratorium. In response, most members favoured banning non-violation complaints completely (option 1), or extending the moratorium (option 4).[80]

The Ministerial Conference of Hong Kong, finally, took note 'of the work done by the Council for Trade-Related Aspects of Intellectual Property Rights pursuant to paragraph 11.1 of the Doha Decision on Implementation-Related Issues and Concerns and paragraph 1.h of the Decision adopted by the General Council on 1 August 2004, and direct it to continue its examination of the scope and modalities for complaints of the types provided for under subparagraphs 1(b) and 1(c) of Article XXIII of GATT 1994 and make recommendations to our next Session. It is agreed that, in the meantime, Members will not initiate such complaints under the TRIPS Agreement'.[81]

Article 64.3 is an incomplete rule, as it does not indicate what the legal status of non-violation and situation complaints would be if there were no agreement at the Council of TRIPS on the scope and modalities for their application, or if the Council's recommendations were not approved by the Ministerial Conference by consensus. At the same time, said Article requires that extensions be adopted by consensus, but does not determine the consequences of the inability to reach them.

The effect of the lack of action by the Council of TRIPS and the Ministerial Conference is to maintain the status quo. Non-violation and situation complaints have not become applicable in the TRIPS context. The very imperfect provision contained in Article 64.3 does not provide a basis for their automatic application, absent a determination of the referred to scope and modalities. As concluded after a thorough analysis of the subject,

the concept of non-violation is extraneous to intellectual property rights. As a matter of policy, it might therefore be suggested that the incorporation of such concept into an agreement on intellectual property rights would constitute an exceptional move and should have to be agreed upon in express terms. The mere lapse of a delay should not represent a sufficient basis for such a fundamental change in the area of IPRs.[82]

---

[80] WTO Secretariat, TRIPS: 'Non-Violation' Complaints (Article 64.2), Background and the current situation, available at <http://www.wto.org/english/tratop_e/trips_e/nonviolation_background_e.htm> (last accessed on 8 February 2006).

[81] Paragraph 45, Ministerial Declaration, WT/MIN(05)/DEC, 22 December 2005, available at <http://www.wto.org/english/thewto_e/minist_e/min05_e/final_text_e.htm> (last accessed on 26 May 2006).

[82] UNCTAD-ICTSD op. cit. (2005), p 675. See also F Abbott, *Non-Violation Nullification or Impairment Causes of Action under the TRIPS Agreement and the Fifth Ministerial Conference: A Warning and Reminder*, Quaker United Nations Office, Occasional Paper 11, Geneva, July 2003, available at <http://www.quno.org> (last accessed on 26 May 2006).

Transitional arrangements

65.1. Subject to the provisions of paragraphs 2, 3 and 4, no Member shall be obliged to apply the provisions of this Agreement before the expiry of a general period of one year following the date of entry into force of the WTO Agreement.

All WTO Members could avail themselves of one year after the date of entry into force of the WTO Agreement (1 January 1995) to comply with the obligations relating to intellectual property protection. The reason for this is quite obvious: most or all Members, including developed country Members, needed to introduce changes into their legislation in order to comply with the standards set out by the TRIPS Agreement, especially with those contained in Part II. For instance, the US[83] changed the term of patent protection from seventeen years counted from the date of grant to twenty years from the filing date in order to align with Article 33 of the Agreement.[84]

The application of para 1 of Article 65 is subject, however, to the provisions of paras 2, 3, and 4 of the same Article, which allow for additional transitional periods, as examined below.

As the wording of Article 65.1 clearly suggests, the allowed transitional period was automatic. Hence, no Member could file a complaint regarding TRIPS matters before the expiration of that period whether or not a Member that could benefit therefrom had declared its intention to delay the implementation of the Agreement.

65.2. A developing country Member is entitled to delay for a further period of four years the date of application, as defined in paragraph 1, of the provisions of this Agreement other than Articles 3, 4 and 5.

Developing countries[85] were provided an additional period of four years (that is, until 1 January 2000) to implement their obligations under the TRIPS Agreement, except for obligations concerning national treatment (Article 3),[86] the most-favoured-nation clause (Article 4),[87] and the application of procedures provided in multilateral agreements concluded under the auspices of WIPO relating to the acquisition or maintenance of intellectual property rights (Article 5).[88] These provisions became immediately applicable after the expiry of the aforementioned one-year period contained in Article 65.1 (that is, 1 January 1996) thereby ensuring right-holders from any Member a level playing field in developing countries with respect to domestic right holders and those from other Members.

Like the period established in Article 65.1, the 'additional' period contained in Article 65.2 was of an automatic nature in the sense that no declaration or other act

---

[83] See the Uruguay Round Agreements Act, 1994.   [84] See pp 434–44 above.

[85] There are no WTO definitions of 'developed' or 'developing' countries. Developing countries in the WTO are designated on the basis of self-selection, although this is not necessarily automatically accepted in all WTO bodies.   [86] See Chapter 2 above.

[87] Idem.   [88] Idem.

was required in order to enjoy it. In some developing countries, foreign companies attempted to convince local courts that the transitional period was not applicable in the absence of a specific reservation or declaration.[89] In addition, the US continued to apply its Special 301 during that period to threaten the application of trade retaliations against countries that did not provide certain standards of protection, and suspended in some cases concessions under the System of Generalized Preferences (SGP).[90] However, no complaint against a developing country was initiated under the DSU regarding TRIPS matters before 1 January 2000.

In addition to Articles 3, 4, and 5 of the TRIPS Agreement, the transitional period of Article 65.2 did not apply to the provisions dealing with dispute settlement (Article 64),[91] the 'mail-box' (Article 70.8), and exclusive marketing rights (Article 70.9),[92] as well as with regard to other procedural provisions. In *India–Patent Protection for Pharmaceutical and Agricultural Chemical Products*,[93] the panel rejected the Indian argument that it was not obliged to apply the transparency obligation, as contained in Article 63 of the Agreement.[94] The panel argued that the TRIPS procedural provisions had been understood by the TRIPS Council as applying either as of 1 January 1995 or from the time the corresponding substantive obligation had to be respected in accordance with the transitional arrangements in Part VI. It noted that Article 64 was applicable as of the entry into force of the Agreement's obligations.[95] It also held that since the obligation in Article 70.8 was applicable as of 1 January 1995, Article 63 was also applicable since that date.[96]

Article 65.2 should be read in conjunction with paras 8 and 9 of Article 70, as the latter introduce obligations regarding patent protection for pharmaceutical and agricultural chemical products.[97]

> **65.3. Any other Member which is in the process of transformation from a centrally-planned into a market, free-enterprise economy and which is undertaking structural reform of its intellectual property system and facing special problems in the preparation and implementation of intellectual property laws and regulations, may also benefit from a period of delay as foreseen in paragraph 2.**

Article 65.3 extends the same treatment conferred to developing countries to the so-called 'economies in transition', that is, Members 'in the process of transformation from a centrally-planned into a market, free-enterprise economy'.

---

[89] See, the jurisprudence of of the Supreme Court of Argentina—which dismissed the referred to argument—in J Kors (Coord.), *Patentes de invención. Diez años de jurisprudencia-Comentarios y fallos* (2005: Buenos Aires, La Ley-CEIDIE); see also *EI du Pont de Nemours and Co v INPI*, Third Jurisdiction No 2004/0053855-05, where a Brazilian court held that the transitional period of Article 65.2 was enjoyable automatically and that 'only the intention of rejecting the benefit of the transitional period shall be formalized'.

[90] For instance, 50 per cent of Argentina's trade preferences under the US SGP were cancelled by the USTR in 1997, on grounds of non-compliance with international standards of protection regarding test data.   [91] See pp 516–17 below.

[92] See pp 516–17 below.   [93] See WT/DS50/R.   [94] See p 477 above.

[95] See WT/DS50/R, paras 7.46 and 7.47.   [96] Ibidem.   [97] See pp 514–17 below.

Those Members were also bound, however, to comply with national treatment, MFN obligations, and those emerging from WIPO treaties referred to in Article 5 of the Agreement, as of 1 January 1996.

Unlike Article 65.2, Article 65.3 makes the applicability of the additional transitional period to economies in transition conditional upon two circumstances. The Member in question should be

- undertaking a structural reform of its intellectual property system; and
- facing special problems in the preparation and implementation of intellectual property laws and regulations.

Despite these conditions, the applicability of the transitional period was automatic, as in the case of Article 65.2; that is, there was no need to make a declaration to enjoy it. In fact, 'the establishment of an IP system that is tailored to free market requirements would appear to provide a strong *prima facie* case of 'special problems' in countries moving away from centralized planned economies.[98]

> 65.4. To the extent that a developing country Member is obliged by this Agreement to extend product patent protection to areas of technology not so protectable in its territory on the general date of application of this Agreement for that Member, as defined in paragraph 2, it may delay the application of the provisions on product patents of Section 5 of Part II to such areas of technology for an additional period of five years.

In addition to the general transitional period contained in Article 65.2, a further period of five years (until 1 January 2005) was contemplated for developing country Members[99] which were bound to introduce product patent protection in areas of technology not so protected in their territory on the general date of application of the Agreement for that country. This provision could benefit developing countries that, for instance, only granted process patent protection or no protection at all in pharmaceuticals. Possible beneficiaries of this provision, however, were only those countries that 'on the general date of application of this Agreement for that Member, as defined in paragraph 2' did not confer patent protection in respect of certain products. The date referred to is 1 January 2000.

Although at the beginning of the Uruguay Round more than fifty countries did not grant patent protection for pharmaceutical products,[100] only a few (eg, India, Egypt) had not introduced such protection by the time the TRIPS Agreement was enforceable in accordance with Article 65.2.

For instance, by 1 January 2000, the majority of Latin American countries that had historically excluded product pharmaceutical patents had already introduced them. They relinquished, hence, the right to postpone such introduction until 1 January 2005. The only exceptions in the region were Uruguay (which granted

[98] UNCTAD-ICTSD op. cit. (2005), p 714.
[99] This additional period did not apply to economies in transition.
[100] See UNCTAD, *The TRIPS Agreement and Developing Countries* (1996: Geneva), p 30.

such patents as of 2002) and Paraguay (as of 2003). The reasons for relinquishing the transitional period of Article 65.4 varied from country to country, but the pressures exerted by the US industry and government are possibly prominent among them, as illustrated by the Argentine case.[101]

Article 65. 4 gave no chance to a developing country Member that had changed its legislation to recognize product patents before 1 January 2000, to suppress such protection and reinstate it after the expiry of the period stipulated in Article 65.4.

The additional transitional period granted by Article 65.4 was of particular importance in the pharmaceutical sector as it, for instance, permitted India to develop a vibrant industry that became a major provider of low-priced medicines and pharmaceutical active ingredients. The end of that period raised concerns regarding the future supply of medicines to developing countries, and was one of the key considerations that led to the adoption of para 6 of the Doha Declaration on the TRIPS Agreement and Public Health.[102]

It is worth noting, finally, that as the transitional periods provided for in Article 65 stipulate a definite term, countries acceding to the WTO after their expiry would not be able to avail themselves thereof for implementing their obligations under the TRIPS Agreement. In fact, acceding countries have been required to either implement such obligations immediately or even before the process of accession is completed.

> **65.5. A Member availing itself of a transitional period under paragraphs 1, 2, 3 or 4 shall ensure that any changes in its laws, regulations and practice made during that period do not result in a lesser degree of consistency with the provisions of this Agreement.**

The 'freezing-clause' contained in Article 65.5 prevented changes that would result in 'a lesser degree of consistency with the provisions of this Agreement' during the transitional periods provided for in paras 1–4 of the same Article. This provision is inapplicable after the expiry of the transitional periods as it clearly indicates that it covers changes 'made during that period'. It was also inapplicable to countries that did not avail themselves of the transitional periods.

---

[101] On 30 March 1995 the Argentine Congress enacted a new Patent Law (No 24.48). While the law included an eight-year transition period for pharmaceutical patent protection, the US Pharmaceutical Research Manufacturers Association (PhRMA) and the Office of the United States Representative (USTR) exerted pressures to shorten the transitional period and lobbied for the introduction of retroactive ('*pipeline*') protection for products patented in other countries but not marketed in Argentina. As a result, the Executive Power vetoed sixteen Articles of Law 24.481 and issued Decree No. 621/95 which essentially substituted the law, re-established revalidation patents and provided for pipeline protection. In the context of a serious institutional conflict between the Executive Power and the Congress, the latter overturned the Decree and passed Law 24.572 in October 1995, which only accepted the veto to half of the Articles questioned by the Executive Power. However, it shortened the transitional period from eight to five years (without any pipeline protection). Finally, on 20 March 1996, the Executive Power issued a new regulation (Decree No 260/96) in line with the patent law (as amended). See, eg, F Sequelra, *Patent Protection for Pharmaceutical Products: the Argentinean Experience*, (1999), Dissertation, University of Warwick.   [102] See Chapter 9 above.

This Article refers not only to laws and regulations but also to 'practice', a concept also used with a similar meaning in Article 1.1 ('legal system and practice') of the Agreement. 'Practice' may be deemed to exist[103] when administrative or judicial decisions present a recognizable pattern. Hence, isolated decisions eventually showing a 'lesser degree of consistency with the provisions of this Agreement' would have not been sufficient to consider that a violation of Article 65.5 had occurred.

It has sometimes been argued that Article 65.5 prevented developing country Members from introducing any changes that would diminish the level of protection of intellectual property rights. However, an absolute 'rolling back' proscription was neither intended nor derives from the wording of Article 65.5. This article only prevented a developing country Member from reducing its level of protection below the minimum standards provided for by the Agreement, but not to introduce changes that would preserve the consistency of the law, regulations, and practice with the Agreement. Since Members are only obliged to comply with such minimum standards, it would have been irrational to impose on Members under a transitional period the obligation to keep levels of protection above such standards. For instance, if a Member provided for twenty-five years of patent protection counted from the filing date, the Member could have perfectly reduced it to twenty years, as this was the minimum required by Article 33 of the Agreement.[104]

Transitional period for least-developed countries

66.1. In view of the special needs and requirements of least-developed country Members, their economic, financial and administrative constraints, and their need for flexibility to create a viable technological base, such Members shall not be required to apply the provisions of this Agreement, other than Articles 3, 4 and 5, for a period of 10 years from the date of application as defined under paragraph 1 of Article 65. The Council for TRIPS shall, upon duly motivated request by a least-developed country Member, accord extensions of this period.

Least-developed countries[105] were not required to apply the TRIPS Agreement's provisions—other than Articles 3, 4, and 5—for a period of ten years from the general date of entry into force of the WTO Agreement (that is, 1 January 2006). Extensions to this period can be agreed upon by the Council of TRIPS 'upon duly motivated request'.

The wording of this provision suggests that in order to develop a 'viable technological base' LDCs need a flexible intellectual property system, that is, less protection than that required under the Agreement. This is in contrast to the main

---

[103] 'To practise' means to 'perform habitually, apply in action', *Concise Oxford Dictionary* (1982: Oxford University Press, 7th edn), p 805.   [104] See pp 343–4 above.

[105] There are currently 32 Least Developed Country (LDC) Members in the WTO. Eight additional LDCs are in the process of accession (Bhutan, Cape Verde, Ethiopia, Laos, Samoa, Sudan, Vanuatu, and Yemen). Equatorial Guinea and Sao Tome & Principe are WTO Observers.

argument of the proponents of the TRIPS Agreement, in the sense that more intellectual property protection would almost automatically lead to more innovation, and is rather in tune with developing countries' demand for more flexibility and policy space to develop their own technological capacities.

The Doha Declaration on TRIPS and Public Health stated in para 7 that

> ... We also agree that the least-developed country members will not be obliged, with respect to pharmaceutical products, to implement or apply Sections 5 and 7 of Part II of the TRIPS Agreement or to enforce rights provided for under these Sections until 1 January 2016, without prejudice to the right of least-developed country members to seek other extensions of the transition periods as provided for in Article 66.1 of the TRIPS Agreement. We instruct the Council for TRIPS to take the necessary action to give effect to this pursuant to Article 66.1 of the TRIPS Agreement.

Given the problems created by patents for access to medicines, and the gravity of the public health problems in developing countries and LDCs,[106] said Declaration permitted LDCs to opt for an extension of the transitional period provided for under Article 66.1 in relation to pharmaceutical patents. Paragraph 7 contains a 'duly motivated request'[107] in the sense of Article 66.1 of the TRIPS Agreement. The Declaration explicitly preserved the right of LDCs to request extensions for other matters (not related to pharmaceutical patents) in accordance with Article 66.1's procedure,[108] without diminishing either their right to request further extensions for pharmaceutical patents after 2016.

Although the extension was agreed upon with regard to 'pharmaceutical products', the protection conferred to a patented process encompasses, according to Article 28.1(b) of the TRIPS Agreement, the protection of the products directly obtained with such process. Hence, the extension of the transitional period also applies to process patents. Likewise, the extension would apply to cases involving uses or indications of a pharmaceutical product, since claims in these cases refer to a product (although protection only extends to its utilization and not to the product as such).

The extension of the transitional period agreed upon in the Declaration referred to also applies in relation to Section 7 (undisclosed information) of Part II of the TRIPS Agreement.

An important practical aspect is to determine which are the LDCs that can effectively benefit from para 7 of the Doha Declaration. Out of thirty African LDCs,[109] only two (Eritrea and Angola) do not seem to grant patents for

---

[106] See para 1 of the Delaration.

[107] Though para 7 does not amend Article 66.1 of the Agreement, it is innovative with regard to the procedure applicable for the extension of the transitional period for LDCs.

[108] In fact, it would have seemed more logical to extend the transitional period for all fields of technology since, unless individual extensions are accorded, LDCs would be required anyway to bear the costs of granting patents in other sectors.

[109] Twelve out of the thirty African LDCs are members of the African Intellectual Property Organization (OAPI) and eight of the African Industrial Property Organization (ARIPO).

pharmaceuticals.[110] Can an LDC that provides patent protection roll-back and nullify such protection? Since paragraph 7 exempts LDCs from enforcement, such countries may decide not to enforce granted patents and thereby allow competition in the respective product market. It might also be possible to change the law and derogate patent protection until the expiry of the transitional period. All this will be perfectly compatible with WTO rules and could raise no complaints from other Members. However, patent owners might rely on the national law and eventually put forward constitutional arguments in order to preserve their rights under granted patents.[111]

In implementing para 7 of the Doha Declaration, the Council for TRIPS adopted on 27 June 2001 a decision on the 'Extension of the Transition Period under Article 66.1 of the TRIPS Agreement for Least-Developed Country Members for Certain Obligations with Respect to Pharmaceutical Products'[112] (see Box 14.1).

Another crucial point raised by para 7 of the Doha Declaration was whether LDCs would be obliged to grant exclusive marketing rights (EMRs) under Article 70.9[113] during the extended transitional period. Paragraph 7 did not explicitly

---

Box 14.1: Extension of the transition period under Article 66.1 of the TRIPS Agreement for least-developed country Members for certain obligations with respect to pharmaceutical products

The Council for Trade-Related Aspects of Intellectual Property Rights (the 'Council for TRIPS'),

Having regard to paragraph 1 of Article 66 of the TRIPS Agreement;

Having regard to the instruction of the Ministerial Conference to the Council for TRIPS contained in paragraph 7 of the Declaration on the TRIPS Agreement and Public Health (WT/MIN(01)/DEC/2) (the 'Declaration');

Considering that paragraph 7 of the Declaration constitutes a duly motivated request by the least-developed country Members for an extension of the period under paragraph 1 of Article 66 of the TRIPS Agreement;

Decides as follows:

1. Least-developed country Members will not be obliged, with respect to pharmaceutical products, to implement or apply Sections 5 and 7 of Part II of the TRIPS Agreement or to enforce rights provided for under these Sections until 1 January 2016.

2. This decision is made without prejudice to the right of least-developed country Members to seek other extensions of the period provided for in paragraph 1 of Article 66 of the TRIPS Agreement.

---

[110] The majority of non-African LDCs also seem to confer patent protection for pharmaceutical products, due to the application of their 'ex-metropolis' legislation (personal communication from WIPO Secretariat).   [111] See, eg, UNCTAD-ICTSD op. cit. (2005), p 721.
[112] IP/C/25, 1 July 2002, available at <http://www.wto.org/english/tratop_e/trips_e/art66_1_e.htm> (last accessed on 26 May 2006).   [113] See pp 516–17 below.

exclude the application of that provision. If LDCs were bound to grant EMRs,[114] the concession made by the Doha Declaration to LDCs would have been of very limited practical value, since access to generic pharmaceutical products could have been effectively blocked for at least five years under EMRs.[115]

The General Council adopted on 8 July 2002 a Decision on 'Least-Developed Country Members—Obligations Under Article 70.9 of the TRIPS Agreement with Respect to Pharmaceutical Products'[116] (see Box 14.2), which clarified that LDCs, were exempted from Article 70.9; that is, from the granting of EMRs.

Box 14.2: Least-developed country Members—obligations under Article 70.9 of the TRIPS Agreement with respect to pharmaceutical products

---

Having regard to paragraphs 1, 3 and 4 of Article IX of the Marrakesh Agreement Establishing the World Trade Organization (the 'WTO Agreement');

Conducting the functions of the Ministerial Conference in the interval between meetings pursuant to paragraph 2 of Article IV of the WTO Agreement;

Noting the decision of the Council for TRIPS on the Extension of the Transition Period under Article 66.1 of the TRIPS Agreement for Least-Developed Country Members for Certain Obligations with respect to Pharmaceutical Products (IP/C/25) (the 'Decision'), adopted by the Council for TRIPS at its meeting of 25–27 June 2002 pursuant to the instructions of the Ministerial Conference contained in paragraph 7 of the Declaration on the TRIPS Agreement and Public Health (WT/MIN(01)/DEC/2) (the 'Declaration');

Considering that obligations under paragraph 9 of Article 70 of the TRIPS Agreement, where applicable, should not prevent attainment of the objectives of paragraph 7 of the Declaration;

Noting that, in light of the foregoing, exceptional circumstances exist justifying a waiver from paragraph 9 of Article 70 of the TRIPS Agreement with respect to pharmaceutical products in respect of least-developed country Members;

Decides as follows:

1. The obligations of least-developed country Members under paragraph 9 of Article 70 of the TRIPS Agreement shall be waived with respect to pharmaceutical products until 1 January 2016.

2. This waiver shall be reviewed by the Ministerial Conference not later than one year after it is granted, and thereafter annually until the waiver terminates, in accordance with the provisions of paragraph 4 of Article IX of the WTO Agreement.

---

[114] Article 70.8 makes it clear that its application (and that of Article 70.9 which provides for EMRs) proceeds 'notwithstanding the provisions of Part IV' which includes Article 66.1.

[115] It has been suggested that para 7 of the Doha Declaration could be interpreted as also relieving LDC Members from the 'mailbox' obligation contained in Article 70.8 of the Agreement. See UNCTAD-ICTSD op. cit. (2005), p 719.

[116] WT/L/478, 12 July 2002, available at <http://www.wto.org/english/tratop_e/trips_e/art70_9_e.htm> (last accessed on 26 May 2006).

While the two Decisions mentioned effectively extended the transitional period for LDCs with regard to Sections 5 and 7 of the TRIPS Agreement, they only referred, as mentioned, to pharmaceutical products. LDCs were bound to apply all other provisions of the Agreement as of 1 January 2006. Shortly before this deadline, LDCs jointly requested an extension of that period to the Council for TRIPS. The Council for TRIPS agreed on 29 November 2005 to extend the transitional period until 1 July 2013, or until such a date on which they cease to be a least-developed country Member, whichever date is earlier (see Box 14.3). The Decision established a 'freezing clause' similar to that contained in Article 65.5,[117] which was not applicable to LDCs.

Box 14.3: Extension of the transition period under Article 66.1 for least-developed country Members

Decision of the Council for TRIPS of 29 November 2005

The Council for Trade-Related Aspects of Intellectual Property Rights (the 'Council for TRIPS'),

Having regard to paragraph 1 of Article 66 of the TRIPS Agreement (the 'Agreement');

Recalling that, unless extended, the transition period granted to least-developed country Members under Article 66.1 of the Agreement will expire on 1 January 2006;

Having regard to the request from least-developed country Members of the World Trade Organization (the 'WTO'), dated 13 October 2005, for an extension of their transition period under Article 66.1 of the Agreement contained in document IP/C/W/457;

Recognizing the special needs and requirements of least-developed country Members, the economic, financial and administrative constraints that they continue to face, and their need for flexibility to create a viable technological base;

Recognizing the continuing needs of least-developed country Members for technical and financial cooperation so as to enable them to realize the cultural, social, technological and other developmental objectives of intellectual property protection;

Decides as follows:

I

Extension of the transition period under Article 66.1 of the Agreement for least-developed country Members

1. Least-developed country Members shall not be required to apply the provisions of the Agreement, other than Articles 3, 4 and 5, until 1 July 2013, or until such a date on which they cease to be a least-developed country Member, whichever date is earlier.

---

[117] See pp 494–5 above.

II

Enhanced technical cooperation for least-developed country Members

2. With a view to facilitating targeted technical and financial cooperation pro-grammes, all the least-developed country Members will provide to the Council for TRIPS, preferably by 1 January 2008, as much information as possible on their individual priority needs for technical and financial cooperation in order to assist them taking steps necessary to implement the TRIPS Agreement.

3. Developed country Members shall provide technical and financial cooperation in favor of least-developed country Members in accordance with Article 67 of the Agreement in order to effectively address the needs identified in accordance with paragraph 2.

4. In order to assist least-developed country Members to draw up the information to be presented in accordance with paragraph 2, and with a view to making technical assistance and capacity building as effective and operational as possible, the WTO shall seek to enhance its cooperation with the World Intellectual Property Organization and with other relevant international organizations.

III

General provisions

5. Least-developed country Members will ensure that any changes in their laws, regu-lations and practice made during the additional transitional period do not result in a lesser degree of consistency with the provisions of the TRIPS Agreement.

6. This Decision is without prejudice to the Decision of the Council for TRIPS of 27 June 2002 on 'Extension of the Transition Period under Article 66.1 of the TRIPS Agreement for Least Developed Country Members for Certain Obligations with respect to Pharmaceutical Products' (IP/C/25), and to the right of least-developed country Members to seek further extensions of the period provided for in paragraph 1 of Article 66 of the Agreement.

While the authority of the Council for TRIPS to impose a 'freezing' clause as provided for in para 5 of this Decision is questionable, it was correct to indicate that this extension is without prejudice to the extension of the transitional period with respect to pharmaceutical products, as conferred under IP/C/25, and to the right of LDCs to seek further extensions of the period provided for in para 1 of Article 66 of the Agreement.

Technology transfer to LDCs

66.2. Developed country Members shall provide incentives to enterprises and institutions in their territories for the purpose of promoting and encouraging technology transfer to least-developed country Members in order to enable them to create a sound and viable technological base.

According to Article 66.2, developed Member countries are obliged to provide incentives under their legislation to enterprises and institutions in their territories for the purpose of promoting and encouraging the transfer of technology to LDCs 'in order to enable them to create a sound and viable technological base'. It has been unclear how this obligation was to be implemented, given the generality of the text and the lack of criteria to assess the efficacy of the measures to be adopted.

At its meeting of September 1998, the Council for TRIPS agreed to put on the agenda the question of the review of the implementation of Article 66.2 and to circulate a questionnaire on the matter in an informal document of the Council. On 19 February 2003, the Council adopted a Decision on the Implementation of Article 66.2 of the TRIPS Agreement, which establishes mechanisms for 'ensuring the monitoring and full implementation of the obligations in Article 66.2', including the obligation to 'submit annually reports on actions taken or planned in pursuance of their commitments' under said Article and their review by the Council at its end-of-year meeting each year. The reports on the implementation of Article 66.2 shall, subject to the protection of business confidential information, provide, inter alia, the following information:

(a) an overview of the incentives regime put in place to fulfil the obligations of Article 66.2, including any specific legislative, policy, and regulatory framework;

(b) identification of the type of incentive and the government agency or other entity making it available;

(c) eligible enterprises and other institutions in the territory of the Member providing the incentives; and

(d) any information available on the functioning in practice of these incentives, such as:
   - statistical and/or other information on the use of the incentives in question by the eligible enterprises and institutions;
   - the type of technology that has been transferred by these enterprises and institutions, and the terms on which it has been transferred;
   - the mode of technology transfer;
   - the least-developed countries to which these enterprises and institutions have transferred technology, and the extent to which the incentives are specific to least-developed countries; and
   - any additional information available that would help assess the effects of the measures in promoting and encouraging technology transfer to least-developed country Members in order to enable them to create a sound and viable technological base.

The issue of transfer of technology to LDCs was also addressed in para 7 of the Doha Declaration on the TRIPS Agreement and Public Health, which reaffirmed

the commitment of developed-country Members to provide incentives to their enterprises and institutions to promote and encourage technology transfer to least-developed country Members pursuant to Article 66.2.

Though the wording in para 7 is broad, its inclusion in the Doha Declaration indicates that effective incentives should be granted in developed countries in order to specifically foster the transfer to LDCs of health-related technologies, including pharmaceutical technologies. An interesting aspect of the Declaration is that it refers to 'commitments of developed-country Members', thereby confirming that Article 66.2 does not contain a mere 'best efforts' obligation.

The Decision of 19 February 2003 and the Doha Declaration are steps forward for the implementation of Article 66.2, but concrete measures to facilitate access to technologies by LDCs are still inexistent or insufficient. Given that Article 66.2 belongs to a treaty specifically dealing with technologies protected under intellectual property rights, a logical interpretation is that developed countries are obliged to transfer IPR-protected technologies, and not only those that are already in the public domain.

Future negotiations on Article 66.2 may aim at further specifying the obligations of developed countries under Article 66.2, for instance, in respect of the transfer of environmentally sound technologies and other 'horizontal' technologies that may contribute to developing a solid and viable technological base. LDCs may also aim at proposing the review of other WTO agreements, such as the Agreement on Subsidies and Countervailing Measures, in a manner that facilitates compliance with Article 66.2.

> **67. In order to facilitate the implementation of this Agreement, developed country Members shall provide, on request and on mutually agreed terms and conditions, technical and financial cooperation in favour of developing and least-developed country Members. Such cooperation shall include assistance in the preparation of laws and regulations on the protection and enforcement of intellectual property rights as well as on the prevention of their abuse, and shall include support regarding the establishment or reinforcement of domestic offices and agencies relevant to these matters, including the training of personnel.**

The commitment by developed country Members to provide technical and financial cooperation to developing and least-developed country Members 'to facilitate the implementation' of the TRIPS Agreement, is general and subject in any case to 'mutually agreed terms'. This means that although there is a duty imposed on developed countries to provide technical and financial cooperation, its supply will depend, in the last instance, on the willingness of developed countries and the resources they decide to allocate for that purpose.

While the purpose of the technical cooperation is generally defined as facilitating 'the implementation of this Agreement', Article 67 indicates some of the components to be included:

- assistance in the preparation of laws and regulations on the protection and enforcement of intellectual property rights as well as on the prevention of their abuse; and

- support regarding the establishment or reinforcement of domestic offices and agencies relevant to these matters, including the training of personnel.

Paragraph 3 of the Decision of the Council for TRIPS of 29 November 2005[118] indicates that developed country Members shall provide technical and financial cooperation in favour of LDCs in accordance with Article 67 of the Agreement 'in order to effectively address the needs identified in accordance with paragraph 2' of the same Decision. This Decision, however, should not be read as making the supply of cooperation under Article 67 conditional upon receiving the information as stipulated in para 2 of the same Decision, since that would add a conditionality not present in the TRIPS Agreement.

The Decision of the Council for TRIPS of 29 November 2005 (see Box 14.3) also contains a section on adopted 'Enhanced technical cooperation for least-developed country Members' which requires LDCs to provide 'as much information as possible on their individual priority needs for technical and financial cooperation in order to assist them taking steps necessary to implement the TRIPS Agreement' (para 2). It also stipulates that in order to assist LDCs to draw up the information to be presented, and 'with a view to making technical assistance and capacity building as effective and operational as possible', the WTO shall seek to enhance its cooperation with WIPO and with other relevant international organizations.

Some developed country governments have traditionally provided technical assistance in the field of intellectual property, mainly through training. The European Patent Office has also been active in this regard. A significant part of international technical assistance in intellectual property is supplied, however, through international organizations, notably WIPO and the WTO. The WHO has also given such assistance in matters related to intellectual property and public health.

There has been considerable debate about the content and modalities of technical assistance.[119] The 'Agenda for Development' submitted to the WIPO General Assembly by Argentina and Brazil, and supported by other developing countries, specifically highlighted the need to ensure that WIPO, as 'the main multilateral provider of technical assistance in the field of intellectual property', provides technical cooperation that

should contribute to ensuring that the social costs of IP protection are kept at a minimum. WIPO's legislative assistance should ensure that national laws on intellectual property are tailored to meet each country's level of development and are fully responsive to the specific needs and problems of individual societies. It also must be directed towards

---

[118] See Box 14.3.

[119] See, eg, Commission on Intellectual Property (CIPR), *Integrating Intellectual Property Rights and Development Policy*, 2002, available at <www.iprcommission.org> (last accessed on 26 May 2006); T Pengelly, *Technical Assistance for the Formulation and Implementation of Intellectual Property Policy in Developing Countries and Transition Economies* (2005: Geneva, ICTSD); M Kostecki, 'What Technical Assistance to Redress the Balance in Favour of Developing Nations?', available at <www.iprsonline.org/unctadictsd/docs/Kostecki%20%20Final.pdf> (last accessed on 26 May 2006).

assisting developing countries to make full use of the flexibilities in existing intellectual property agreements, in particular to promote important public policy objectives.[120]

One particular problem affecting the provision of technical assistance in the area of intellectual property is the existence of a number of types of bias. Kostecki has identified the following types of bias: (i) technical assistance is used as a promotional tool by the organizations which fund and/or deliver those programmes to encourage a wider acceptance or better implementation of the IP treaties that they administer (*provider bias*); (ii) technical assistance consultants who are IP experts tend to favour stricter protection of IP rights (*expert bias*); (iii) IP-related know-how and do-how conveyed in technical assistance programmes is focused on developed country experience and concerns (*contents bias*); (iv) most IP technical assistance programmes ignore or underestimate the theory of development stages in the field of intellectual property (*ideological bias*); and (v) most IP technical assistance programmes overemphasize the message that lower standards of IP protection would limit rather than attract FDI (*FDI bias*).[121]

Institutional arrangements and final provisions

Council for TRIPS

68. The Council for TRIPS shall monitor the operation of this Agreement and, in particular, Members' compliance with their obligations hereunder, and shall afford Members the opportunity of consulting on matters relating to the trade-related aspects of intellectual property rights. It shall carry out such other responsibilities as assigned to it by the Members, and it shall, in particular, provide any assistance requested by them in the context of dispute settlement procedures. In carrying out its functions, the Council for TRIPS may consult with and seek information from any source it deems appropriate. In consultation with WIPO, the Council shall seek to establish, within one year of its first meeting, appropriate arrangements for cooperation with bodies of that Organization.

A Council to specifically deal with TRIPS matters is established by Article 68. The functions attributed to the Council are those specified in this Article, plus 'any other responsibilities assigned to it by the Members'. This means that Members may instruct the Council to undertake tasks not referred to in Article 68. An example was the instruction given to the Council by Ministers in para 6 of the Doha Declaration on the TRIPS Agreement and Public Health.[122]

---

[120] See WIPO document WO/GA/31/11, Annex, p 5.

[121] See ICTSD Meeting Report ICTSD Dialogue on Technical Cooperation for IP Policy in Developing Countries Geneva, 11–12 July 2005, p 2, available at <http://www.iprsonline.org/ictsd/docs/2005-07-11_Summary.pdf> (last accessed on 28 May 2006).

[122] See Chapter 9 above.

The Council for TRIPS performs, in particular, the following functions:

(a) to monitor the operation of the TRIPS Agreement and, in particular, Members' compliance with their obligations thereunder;[123]
(b) to provide Members the opportunity of consulting on matters relating to the trade-related aspects of intellectual property rights;
(c) to provide any assistance requested by Members in the context of dispute settlement procedures.

In addition, the Council was mandated to conduct consultations with WIPO and seek to establish, 'within one year of its first meeting, appropriate arrangements for cooperation with bodies of that Organization'. This agreement was promptly established.[124] It entered into force on 1 January 1996. It provides the following:

• WIPO shall make available to WTO Members and nationals as well as to the WTO Secretariat and the Council for TRIPS, laws and regulations contained in the WIPO database and provide to the same parties access to computerized databases of the International Bureau containing laws and regulations.

• a mechanism for notifications relating to Article 6*ter* of the Paris Convention;

• supply of technical assistance to developing countries and LDCs which are members of WIPO or WTO.

In addition to the specific mandate described in Article 68, the Council has been entrusted particular functions in different provisions of the TRIPS Agreement, notably:

• notification of exceptions provided for in the Agreement (Articles 1.3, 3.1, 4(d), and 63.2) for which specific guidelines have been issued;[125]
• reviewing the application of the provisions on geographical indications (Article 24.2);
• undertaking negotiations for the establishment of a multilateral system of notification and registration of geographical indications for wines (Article 23.4);[126]
• extending, upon motivated request by LDC Members, the transitional period stipulated for these countries (Article 66.1);
• reviewing the implementation of the TRIPS Agreement at two-year intervals and making proposals for its amendment (Article 71).

---

[123] See below commentary on Article 71.1 regarding the reviews to be undertaken by the Council for TRIPS.   [124] See <http://www.wto.org/english/tratop_e/trips_e/wtowip_e.htm>.
[125] See *Technical Cooperation Handbook on Notification Requirements*, WTO document WT/TC/NOTIF/TRIPS/1, which is available in the documents on-line section of the WTO website <http://www.wto.org>. See also the WTO's IP gateway page at <http://www.wto.org/english/tratop_e/trips_e/trips_e.htm> ('Notifications under the TRIPS Agreement') (last accessed on 26 May 2006).
[126] It is to be noted that in para 18 of the Doha Ministerial Declaration (WT/MIN(01)/DEC/1 of 20 November 2001), Members agreed to negotiate such multilateral system on wines *and spirits* (not mentioned in Article 23.4) by the Fifth Session of the Ministerial Conference.

In carrying out its functions, the Council for TRIPS may consult with and seek information from any source it deems appropriate. Decisions are taken by consensus, and may be referred to the General Council in cases of disagreement.

The Council for TRIPS holds regular sessions and has met in 'special sessions'[127] for negotiations on a multilateral system for notifying and registering geographical indications for wines and spirits. It has also held special sessions on TRIPS and public health in 2001, which eventually led to the adoption of the Doha Declaration on the matter.[128]

International cooperation

> 69. Members agree to cooperate with each other with a view to eliminating international trade in goods infringing intellectual property rights. For this purpose, they shall establish and notify contact points in their administrations and be ready to exchange information on trade in infringing goods. They shall, in particular, promote the exchange of information and cooperation between customs authorities with regard to trade in counterfeit trademark goods and pirated copyright goods.

Members agreed in Article 69 to cooperate with a view to 'eliminating international trade in goods infringing intellectual property rights', through exchange of information and the designation of 'contact points' in their administrations. Particular emphasis is given to cooperation and exchange of information between customs with respect to counterfeit trademark and pirated copyright goods.

This provision essentially reflects the interests of developed country Members in enhancing the enforcement of intellectual property rights as they relate to 'international trade'. The objective set ('eliminating' trade in infringing goods) is quite ambitious. This provision arguably covers trans-border trade only and not that taking place within the jurisdiction of a Member. The foreseen cooperation, hence, would focus on exports, imports, and goods in transit. Notably, this provision does not contemplate any cooperation in order to prevent the abuse of intellectual property rights that create barriers to international trade, despite that this is an objective stated in other provisions of the Agreement.[129]

Protection of existing subject matter

> 70.1. This Agreement does not give rise to obligations in respect of acts which occurred before the date of application of the Agreement for the Member in question.

One important and controversial issue during TRIPS negotiations was the eventual recognition of patent rights and other intellectual property rights on a

---

[127] Annual reports of the TRIPS Council to the General Council and minutes of the meetings of the TRIPS Council (documents 'IP/C/M/*') are available on the WTO web page <http://www.wto.org> (last accessed on 26 May 2006).   [128] See Chapter 9 above.

[129] See, eg Articles 63.1 and 67 above.

retroactive basis. The Agreement adopted a negative stand on such a recognition thereby dismissing 'pipeline'-type solutions as promoted by the US for patents.[130]

Article 70.1 made clear that the Agreement only gave rise to obligations for the future, and not in respect of acts which occurred before the date of application of the Agreement in a Member. This was a key component of the political deal that paved the way for the adoption of the Agreement in the Uruguay Round. The 'date of application of the Agreement for the Member in question' refers to the date on which the Agreement became enforceable in a Member, that is, 1 January 1996 for developed countries, and 1 January 2000 for developing countries and economies in transition. That date will be 1 January 2013 for LDCs.[131] Patent applications relating to pharmaceutical and agrochemical products filed in Members that enjoyed the additional transitional period of Article 65.4 were subject to paras 8 and 9 of Article 70.

A key interpretive issue is what 'acts' means in the context of Article 70.1. There are two possible meanings: 'acts' by private parties and by governments. Since the provision does not make any distinction, it is reasonable to consider that both are covered.[132] As a result, acts done by private parties, for instance, use of a trademark or an invention that was not protected in the Member country cannot give rise to any liability. In the case of 'acts' by governments, for instance, the refusal of a patent application on an invention not eligible for protection, there will be no obligation to review such decision.

In *Canada–Term of Patent Protection*, Canada argued that government acts granting patents for seventeen years (counted from the date of grant) were also covered under the non-retroactivity clause of Article 70.1. However, this argument was dismissed. The AB held that[133]

Article 28 of the Vienna Convention covers not only any 'act', but also any 'fact' or 'situation which ceased to exist'. Article 28 establishes that, in the absence of a contrary intention, treaty provisions do not apply to 'any situation which ceased to exist' before the treaty's entry into force for a party to the treaty. Logically, it seems to us that Article 28 also necessarily implies that, absent a contrary intention, treaty obligations do apply to any 'situation' which has not ceased to exist—that is, to any situation that arose in the past, but continues to exist under the new treaty. Indeed, the very use of the word 'situation' suggests something that subsists and continues over time; it would, therefore, include 'subject matter existing and which is protected', such as Old Act patents at issue in this dispute, even though those

---

[130] Under this proposal, countries which introduced patent protection for pharmaceuticals as a result of the TRIPS obligations would have to extend it not only to inventions covered in new applications made after the introduction of such protection, but also to any invention covered in patent applications made prior to that date, provided that the invention had not been commercialized. This approach was incorporated, for instance, by the Mexican Industrial Property Law as revised in June 1991, by the patent law of China (only for applications filed after 1986) and by Brazil (1996).

[131] See pp 499–500 above.

[132] See WT/DS170/AB/R (2000), para 54.   [133] Idem.

patents, and the rights conferred by those patents, arose from 'acts which occurred' before the date of application of the TRIPS Agreement for Canada (paragraph 72).

We note that Article 28 of the Vienna Convention is not applicable if 'a different intention appears from the treaty or is otherwise established'. We see no such 'different intention' in Article 70. Despite some differences in wording and structure from Article 28, we do not see Article 70.1 as in any way establishing 'a different intention' within the meaning of Article 28 of the Vienna Convention (paragraph 74).

In summary, the AB interpreted that situations derived from acts prior to the date of application of the Agreement for the Member in question may be subject to TRIPS disciplines. There must be, however, some limits to this doctrine. For instance, if a compulsory licence was granted before the date of application of the Agreement for the Member in question, there will be no obligation to adapt the conditions thereof to those established by Article 31 of the TRIPS Agreement.[134]

> **70.2. Except as otherwise provided for in this Agreement, this Agreement gives rise to obligations in respect of all subject matter existing at the date of application of this Agreement for the Member in question, and which is protected in that Member on the said date, or which meets or comes subsequently to meet the criteria for protection under the terms of this Agreement. In respect of this paragraph and paragraphs 3 and 4, copyright obligations with respect to existing works shall be solely determined under Article 18 of the Berne Convention (1971), and obligations with respect to the rights of producers of phonograms and performers in existing phonograms shall be determined solely under Article 18 of the Berne Convention (1971) as made applicable under paragraph 6 of Article 14 of this Agreement.**

In accordance with Article 70.2, the Agreement will give rise to obligations in respect of all subject matter existing at the date of application of the Agreement for a Member, to the extent that such a subject matter was protected on said date or subsequently came to meet the criteria for protection. Subject matter that was in the public domain (for instance, an invention that had lost novelty due to the publication of the patent application in a foreign country) was not protected subject matter and could not subsequently come to meet the criteria for protection. The determinant factor to establish whether a certain subject matter 'was protected' was what the applicable domestic legislation provided for before the date referred to, and not what that legislation should have provided for, had the Agreement been enforceable at that time.

Situations in which subject matter 'meets or comes subsequently to meet the criteria for protection under the terms of this Agreement' alludes to cases where acts or facts necessary for acquiring protection take place after the date of application of the Agreement for the Member in question. Examples would be the reduction to practice of an invention (as required by US law)[135] or the conclusion of the procedures for the registration of a trademark.

---

[134] See further on this issue Article 70.6 below.
[135] See UNCTAD-ICTSD op. cit. (2005), p 759.

The 'date of application of this Agreement for the Member in question' is the same mentioned in Article 70.1; that is, it depends on the applicable transitional period according to the respective Member's category as developed or developing country, economy in transition, or LDC.

Article 70.2 further clarifies that with respect to copyright and related rights solely Article 18 of the Berne Convention shall be applicable.[136] The reference to the Berne Convention implies that only works that had fallen into the public domain at the date of the application of the Agreement for the Member either in the country of origin or in the country of protection need to be protected under the Agreement. It has been argued that works (and phonograms) that were not protected before that date because they failed to meet formalities or other requirements imposed by national legislation would, however, fall under the protection conferred under the TRIPS Agreement.[137] This interpretation, which would create protection for works that had never been protected, does not seem to be authorized by a literal interpretation of Article 18(1) and (2) of the Berne Convention, which is premised on the pre-existence of copyright protection in the relevant works.

The same solution will be applicable to the rights of phonogram producers and performers 'in existing phonograms', as Article 70.2 also refers to Article 18 of the Berne Convention in their regard.

Some countries needed to change their national legislation in order to restore rights in foreign works and phonograms, as a result of the application of Article 70 of the TRIPS Agreement. Thus, Section 514 of the US Uruguay Round Agreement Act (URAA) restored full copyright protection to all foreign works which had been exploited in the US without authorization in the past because of failure to comply with US formalities.[138] Copyrights in eligible foreign works were restored automatically from the 'date of restoration'. Since restoration was automatic, the owner of the restored copyright did not have to register his work, and

---

[136] Article 18 of the Berne Convention stipulates that protection can not be claimed when a work has fallen in the public domain because of expiry of the term of protection in the country of origin or where the protection is claimed.

[137] P Katzenberger, 'TRIPS and copyright law', in *From GATT to TRIPS–The Agreement on Trade-Related Aspects of Intellectual Property Rights*, F. Beier and G. Schricker (eds) (1996: Munich, IIC Studies Max Planck Institute for Foreign and International Patent, Copyright and Competition Law), p 81.

[138] Section 514 of the URAA restored copyright protection in certain foreign works still under protection in a source country but in the public domain in the United States. It also granted protection to sound recordings fixed prior to 15 February 1972. To qualify for restoration, a work must be an original work of authorship that is protected under subsection (a), is not in the public domain in the source country through expiration of the term of protection, and is in the public domain in the United States because of noncompliance with formalities, lack of subject matter protection in the case of a sound recording fixed before 15 February 1972, or lack of national eligibility. A further requirement to qualify is that, at the time the work was created, at least one author or right holder (in the case of a sound recording) must have been a national or domiciliary of an eligible country; and if the work is published, it must not have been published in the United States within 30 days of first publication in the eligible country.

the exploitation of many public domain movies, shows, and musical pieces became illegal.[139] A group of artists, however, filed a complaint in September 2001 challenging Congress's ability to reclassify materials as copyrighted once they have passed into the public domain.[140]

As mentioned above, Article 14.6[141] of the TRIPS Agreement provides for the retroactive protection in respect of the right of performers and producers of phonograms with the possible exceptions and under the conditions provided for in Article 18 of the Berne Convention.[142] As a result, the Agreement recognizes the rights conferred in para 1–3 of Article 14 in respect of producers of phonograms and performers in existing phonograms for which the fifty-year terms of protection had not expired at the date of application of the TRIPS Agreement for the Member in question.

The application of Article 14.6 of the TRIPS Agreement gave rise to the first dispute under the Agreement as early as February 1996 (see Table 14.1 above). Although Japan extended the term of protection with regard to phonograms from twenty to fifty years, it only recognized such protection as of 1971. As the result of consultations with the US, Japan amended its copyright law and retroactively provided protection from 1946 onwards.

> **70.3. There shall be no obligation to restore protection to subject matter which on the date of application of this Agreement for the Member in question has fallen into the public domain.**

Consistently with para 1 of Article 70, para 3 thereof does not oblige restoration of protection to subject matter which on the date of application of the Agreement for the Member in question had fallen into the public domain. The date referred to here is the same as in paras 1 and 2 of this Article.

This is the only provision in the whole TRIPS Agreement that refers to the concept of 'public domain'. This concept has traditionally been defined as consisting in the pool of information not subject to intellectual property rights;[143] that is, information that can be freely used without authorization by or payment to third parties.[144]

Information in the public domain is:

(i) information for which IPR protection has expired;
(ii) information that was eligible for protection but which lost it because of a failure to comply with certain requirements;

---

[139] See <http://www.cyberlaw.stanford.edu/packets/vol_1_no_12/002081.shtml> (last accessed on 21 May 2005).

[140] See *Golan v Ashcroft*, No. CIV.A.01-B-1854, 2004 WL 615569, (D Colo 15 Mar 2004).

[141] See pp 167–8 above.

[142] WIPO, *Implications of the TRIPS Agreement on Treaties Administered by WIPO* (1997: Geneva), WO/GA/XV/1, p 31.

[143] See, eg, W Van Caenegem, 'The Public Domain: Scientia Nullius', (2002) European Intellectual Property Review, 24(6), p 324.

[144] Exceptionally, in some countries the reproduction of artistic works that have fallen into the public domain is subject to payment to the State ('*domaine public payant*').

(iii) information that is outside the scope of intellectual property law because it is not eligible for protection according to the law.

It has been noted that 'information is not in the public domain by its public good nature or even by its governmental origin but as the result of a network of formal and informal social agreements, explicit or implicit but entrenched in common law and in the culture of a society'.[145] The scope of the public domain can, hence, be more or less broad, depending on the modalities and scope of appropriation determined by the States' law.

The basic premise for the application of Article 70.3 is that protection of some subject matter existed, since protection cannot be *restored* if such protection did not exist and elapse, for whatever reason, before the date referred to.

It should be noted that this is an optional provision ('[T]here shall be no obligation . . . '); that is, a Member might opt to restore the protection of subject matter that has fallen into the public domain, without being obliged to do it.

> **70.4. In respect of any acts in respect of specific objects embodying protected subject matter which become infringing under the terms of legislation in conformity with this Agreement, and which were commenced, or in respect of which a significant investment was made, before the date of acceptance of the WTO Agreement by that Member, any Member may provide for a limitation of the remedies available to the right holder as to the continued performance of such acts after the date of application of this Agreement for that Member. In such cases the Member shall, however, at least provide for the payment of equitable remuneration.**

Article 70.4 confirms the application of the Agreement for the future. It extends a special treatment to acts that became infringing but that were commenced or in respect of which a significant investment was made before the acceptance of the Agreement by a Member. This provision refers to 'acts' that become infringing, and not to subject matter that becomes protected as in Article 70.2. Possible hypotheses, hence, include cases in which the scope of protection has been expanded under the TRIPS Agreement with regard to already protected subject matter, for instance, by incorporating exclusive rights that were not provided for before the TRIPS-consistent legislation was adopted.

The date on which this obligation is triggered is different from that established in paras 1–3 of Article 70 and in any other article of the TRIPS Agreement. The 'date of acceptance of the WTO Agreement' would be prior to the dates of applicability of the TRIPS Agreement in conformity with Article 65, as it refers to the WTO Agreement itself.[146]

---

[145] C Forero-Pineda, 'Scientific Research, Information Flows, and the Impact of Database Protection on Developing Countries', in J Esanu and P Uhlir (eds), *Open Access and the Public Domain in Digital Data and Information for Science, Proceedings of an international symposium* (2004: Washington, DC, The National Academies Press), p 40.

[146] The 'acceptance' of the WTO Agreement is 1 January 1995 for countries that were already GATT Contracting Parties. It will be different for subsequently acceding countries, depending on the date in which the respective accession agreements enter into force.

Consistently with para 1 of Article 70, para 4 only applies to acts made after the date of acceptance of the WTO Agreement by the Member; that is, it has no retroactive effects. In fact, the aim of this provision is to mitigate the effects of the introduction of a broader protection, by limiting the remedies available to the right-holder.

Members may choose what remedies they will provide. As a minimum, they must provide for the payment of an 'equitable remuneration' to the title-holder.[147] They may exclude or limit the applicability of other remedies (eg ban to use or sale of a protected product). What a 'significant investment' and an 'equitable remuneration' are, is a matter left to the interpretation of local authorities, subject in any case to judicial review.[148]

The expression 'equitable remuneration' is also used in Article 14.4 of the TRIPS Agreement[149] while in Article 31(h)[150] reference is made to 'adequate remuneration'. It is difficult to establish a clear difference between these concepts from a practical point of view, since in both cases Members have considerable leeway to determine what is 'equitable' or 'adequate' under the circumstances of a particular case.

> 70.5. A Member is not obliged to apply the provisions of Article 11 and of paragraph 4 of Article 14 with respect to originals or copies purchased prior to the date of application of this Agreement for that Member.

Article 70.5 also provides for an optional rule. In the case of computer programs, cinematographic works and phonograms, rental rights may not apply with respect to originals or copies purchased prior to the date of application of the Agreement to the respective Member.[151] This seems a logical solution, since the acquirer of such originals or copies was not subject to the additional rights created by Articles 11 and 14.4.

> 70.6. Members shall not be required to apply Article 31, or the requirement in paragraph 1 of Article 27 that patent rights shall be enjoyable without discrimination as to the field of technology, to use without the authorization of the right holder where authorization for such use was granted by the government before the date this Agreement became known.

Compulsory licences granted by a government before the date on which the Agreement 'became known' need not observe the prescriptions of Article 31.[152] The same applies to provisions discriminating about the field of technology and which would be regarded as inconsistent with Article 27.1.[153]

---

[147] This interpretation was confirmed in the settlement agreement reached between the US and Argentina which, *inter alia*, included a complaint regarding this matter. See WT/DS171/3, WT/DS196/4, IP/D/18/Add.1, IP/D/22/Add.1, p 7.

[148] See above, Article 41.4 of the TRIPS Agreement.   [149] See pp 311–24 above.

[150] See pp 322–3 above.

[151] This date is also dependent on the expiry of the transitional periods for different categories of Members.   [152] See pp 311–24 above.

[153] See pp 271–87 above.

The main purpose of this provision was to anticipate the applicability of Articles 27.1 and 31 to compulsory licences eventually granted before the date of application of the Agreement for the Member. This provision was most probably aimed at addressing the particular situation of the Canadian patent law and its compulsory licensing system. The date when the 'Agreement became known' could only be the date on which the Final Uruguay Round Act was signed in Marrakesh: 15 April 1994. Hence, if this provision was effectively aimed at Canada, the additional time of application gained was one year, seven-and-a-half months (the general date of application of the Agreement for Canada was 1 January 2006).

> 70.7. In the case of intellectual property rights for which protection is conditional upon registration, applications for protection which are pending on the date of application of this Agreement for the Member in question shall be permitted to be amended to claim any enhanced protection provided under the provisions of this Agreement. Such amendments shall not include new matter.

A first interpretive issue posed by this Article is its scope of application. Which are the 'intellectual property rights for which protection is conditional upon registration'? Copyrights and undisclosed information are excluded, while trademarks and geographical indications are included. Doubtful is the case of patents since the term 'registration' is not ordinarily associated with the field of patents.[154] Whether industrial designs and layout-designs of integrated circuits are covered or not would depend on the applicable national law.

In accordance with Article 70.7, if there was an application pending at the time the Agreement becomes enforceable in a Member (ie, 1 January 2000 for developing countries) it will be possible to amend the application to claim 'any enhanced protection under the provisions of this Agreement'. There are not many situations in which the applicant may 'claim' an enhanced protection, since the rights (for instance, those granted by a trademark) are generally conferred *ex lege* and are not dependent on the terms of the application. This provision may be understood, however, in the sense that the applicant may benefit from such enhanced protection even though his application was made before the date of application of the Agreement.

However, the applicability of this paragraph is further narrowed by the last sentence, according to which 'such amendments shall not include new matter'. It is reasonable to interpret 'new' in this context in relation to the matter claimed when the application was filed. If this provision were deemed applicable to patents, hence, a process claim could not be transformed into a product claim, as it would include new matter.

An expansive interpretation of Article 70.7 was given by the US in the complaint submitted against Argentina in 2000. The US held that Argentina placed 'impermissible limitations on certain transitional patents so as to limit the exclusive rights conferred by these patents, and to deny the opportunity for patentees to

---

[154] See, eg, UNCTAD-ICTSD op. cit. (2005), p 765.

amend pending applications in order to claim certain enhanced protection provided by the TRIPS Agreement'.[155] Argentina rejected this argument; it was finally agreed that Argentina 'will fulfill its WTO obligations on this matter through its legal system and practices, including decisions of the Supreme Court of Justice.[156]

Pharmaceutical and agrochemical products

70.8. Where a Member does not make available as of the date of entry into force of the WTO Agreement patent protection for pharmaceutical and agricultural chemical products commensurate with its obligations under Article 27, that Member shall:

(a) notwithstanding the provisions of Part VI, provide as from the date of entry into force of the WTO Agreement a means by which applications for patents for such inventions can be filed;

(b) apply to these applications, as of the date of application of this Agreement, the criteria for patentability as laid down in this Agreement as if those criteria were being applied on the date of filing in that Member or, where priority is available and claimed, the priority date of the application; and

(c) provide patent protection in accordance with this Agreement as from the grant of the patent and for the remainder of the patent term, counted from the filing date in accordance with Article 33 of this Agreement, for those of these applications that meet the criteria for protection referred to in subparagraph (b).

The relevance of patent protection in pharmaceutical and agrochemical products has reflected itself in two specific transitional provisions, which establish rights that are not granted to title-holders in other areas of technology.

There is no definition of what constitute 'pharmaceutical and agricultural chemical products'. The former may be deemed as products with a therapeutic use; that is, suitable for the prevention or treatment of a disease, while the latter would be limited to chemical substances of use in agriculture, such as pesticides and herbicides.

Applications relating to pharmaceutical and agricultural chemical products had to be received in a Member, according to Article 70.8, since the date of entry into force of the WTO Agreement (ie, 1 January 1995). For this purpose, Members were

---

[155] See WT/DS196/1 IP/D/22, 6 June 2000, *Argentina–Certain measures on the protection of patents and test data: Request for Consultations by the United States.* The aim of this part of the complaint was to allow that patent applications made under the pre-TRIPS law in Argentina for *processes* could be converted into applications regarding the *products* themselves.

[156] See WT/DS171/3, WT/DS196/4, IP/D/18/Add.1, IP/D/22/Add.1 20 June 2002, para 8(b). In reversing decisions of the lower courts, the Argentine Supreme Court considered that Article 70.7 of the TRIPS Agreement did not provide a basis for the conversion of process into product patent applications. See 'Pfizer Inc. c/ Instituto Nacional de la Propiedad Industrial s/ denegatoria de patente, decision of 21 May 2002, available at <http://www.inpi.gov.ar/pdf/Pfizer.pdf> (last accessed on 28 May 2006).

required to provide 'a means by which applications for patents for such inventions can be filed'. This means is what has been named 'mail-box'. As mentioned above,[157] the application of the 'mail-box' provision was considered in two cases brought against India, which confirmed the need for a Member to receive patent applications for pharmaceuticals and agrochemical products as of that date.

Patents are to be granted, in accordance with Article 70.8, only after the Agreement entered into force in the Member in question at the expiry of the applicable transitional periods, as allowed by Article 65.[158] The time lag between application and granting could thus be significant—up to ten years for Members availing themselves of the transitional period permitted by Article 65.4.

Article 70.8 preserved, nevertheless, the novelty of the invention through a legal fiction based on the assessment of novelty (and other criteria for patentability) on the date of the filing of the application in that Member, or of the priority date, if applicable. The reference to the priority date obviously alludes to the 'priority right' provided for in the Paris Convention (Article 4). It indicates that applications could be validly made under the 'mail-box' provision when the first application in a member of the Paris Union or WTO had taken place on or after 1 January 1994.

One interesting issue is whether Members could initiate the examination of the applications in the mail-box before the end of the applicable transitional period. Dratler Jr addressed this issue and convincingly explained that

[T]he words 'as of the date of application of this Agreement' require some interpretation. They cannot be construed as fixing the time for applying the three substantive criteria for patentability—novelty, inventive step, and capability of industrial application. If so interpreted, they would contradict the clear meaning of the rest of the clause. Therefore, they must be interpreted as applying not to the substantive requirements for examination, but to the actual time for examination. In other words, they appear *to preclude any Member from examining patent applications of this kind early, before that Member is required to grant such patents* under the transition rules, in order to cut off exclusive marketing rights under Article 70:9 (emphasis added).[159]

In fact, Members that applied transitional periods only started the examination of mail-box applications at the expiry of such periods.[160] In India, for instance, it commenced after 1 January 2005.

---

[157] See pp 479–88 above.   [158] See pp 491–5 above.

[159] J Dratler, *Intellectual Property Law, Commercial, Creative, and Industrial Property* (1999: New York, Law Journals Seminars Press), para 1A.06[9].

[160] In Morocco and Tunisia, more than 800 'mail-box' applications were made between 1995 and 2005. The provisional term allowed by Article 65.4 was also applied in Egypt, where around 3,000 applications were received in that period. See O Mellouk, 'Struggling to balance free trade with access to medicines in the post-TRIPS era throughout the Arab World', paper submitted to the Regional Arab Dialogue on Intellectual Property Rights, Innovation and Sustainable Development, UNCTAD-ICTSD, Alexandria, 26–28 June 2005, available at <http://www.iprsonline.org/unctadictsd/docs/Mellouk_ArabRD_Health.pdf> (last accessed on 28 May 2006). In India, around 9,000 applications have been reported as submitted to the mail-box.

The patents granted on the basis of mail-box applications will last for the remainder of the patent term, counted from the filing date.

> 70.9. Where a product is the subject of a patent application in a Member in accordance with paragraph 8(a), exclusive marketing rights shall be granted, notwithstanding the provisions of Part VI, for a period of five years after obtaining marketing approval in that Member or until a product patent is granted or rejected in that Member, whichever period is shorter, provided that, subsequent to the entry into force of the WTO Agreement, a patent application has been filed and a patent granted for that product in another Member and marketing approval obtained in such other Member.

Notwithstanding that the transitional periods granted under Article 65 extend the possibility of non-patentability for pharmaceutical and agricultural chemical products in developing countries for a total term of up to ten years after the entry into force of the WTO Agreement (ie, 1 January 2005), the practical effects of this transition are limited by Article 70.9. It establishes the right to obtain 'exclusive marketing rights' (EMRs) for those products before a patent can be obtained.[161] Such rights can be claimed if the following conditions are met:

a) a patent application has been filed in a Member after the entry into force of the Agreement;

b) a patent application has been filed in another Member after the entry into force of the Agreement and a patent has been granted;

c) marketing approval for the protected product has been obtained in said other Member;

d) marketing approval has been obtained in the Member mentioned in (a) above.

Whenever these conditions are fulfilled, the Member must grant 'exclusive marketing rights' for five years after obtaining market approval in that Member. Those rights will be terminated, however, if (a) the corresponding patent is finally granted; or (b) the patent application is rejected in that Member.

The Agreement is silent about the conditions under which a patent is to be granted in another Member in order to be used as a basis for asserting EMRs. Some countries grant patents without substantive examination. Granting EMRs on the basis of a patent that may have been rejected if subject to examination, could obviously lead to abuses of this provision.[162]

Article 70.9 is also silent about the content and scope of the 'exclusive marketing rights'. Given that exclusivity is only predicated with regard to 'marketing', acts of importation, production, use, or experimentation, as well as of exportation

---

[161] The notion of 'exclusive marketing rights' seems to have been derived from the European Council Decision of 19 December 1991 on the grant of a 'Supplementary Protection Certificate' to expired pharmaceutical patents.

[162] In Argentina, for instance, an EMR was applied for and obtained on the basis of a patent granted in Luxembourg, where no substantive examination exists.

that do not lead to 'marketing' in the jurisdiction of the Member granting the EMRs, are not banned. The same applies to acts related to procedures for the marketing approval of a competitive product.

In addition, the right-holder of EMRs could not be in a better position than a patentee: the abuse of a dominant position, public health needs, or other justified reasons may be sufficient ground to grant compulsory licences (or to revoke the right in cases of abuses).

Obviously, EMRs could only be granted while the transitional periods were in force in a particular Member.[163]

Review and amendment

71.1. The Council for TRIPS shall review the implementation of this Agreement after the expiration of the transitional period referred to in paragraph 2 of Article 65. The Council shall, having regard to the experience gained in its implementation, review it two years after that date, and at identical intervals thereafter. The Council may also undertake reviews in the light of any relevant new developments which might warrant modification or amendment of this Agreement.

Article 71.1 refers to three types of 'review':

(a) Review of implementation
In accordance with the first sentence of this Article, the Council for TRIPS was mandated to start reviews on the implementation of the Agreement as of 1 January 2000. Reviews actually started, however, in July 1996 with an examination of the legislation of developed country Members in the area of copyright and related rights.

The purpose of the review of 'implementation', which is mandatory, is to ensure due compliance with the Agreement by all Members. As examined above,[164] this review will be enabled by the notification of laws and regulations to the Council pursuant to Article 63.2 of the Agreement.

The procedures for these reviews provide for written questions and replies prior to the review meeting, with follow-up questions and replies during the course of the meeting. At subsequent meetings of the Council, an opportunity is given to follow up points emerging from the review session which delegations consider have not been adequately addressed.[165] Obviously, the question-and-answer process does not generate any commitment to adopt the opinions of other

---

[163] Some EMRs were granted during the transitional periods, for instance, in Argentina and India. In the case of Brazil, EMRs were granted in one case in favour of Aventis, in 2004, based on patent application PI 9508789-3 of 7 June 1995. This was a flawed application of Article 70.9 of the TRIPS Agreement, as Brazil was not applying any transitional period.   [164] See pp 476–7.
[165] See <http://www.wto.org/english/tratop_e/trips_e/intel8_e.htm> (last accessed on 26 May 2006).

Acquisition and maintenance of IPRs

Members and, in particular, to amend aspects of laws and regulations that might be questioned. It may be useful, however, to identify areas of disagreement and eventually seek amicable solutions to divergent views.

(b) Biannual review based on experience gained

In addition to the implementation reviews referred to, the Council is also mandated to undertake, as of 1 January 2002, and at intervals of two years thereafter, a 'review'. Although the wording is ambiguous, this provision does seem to refer to the review of the Agreement as such, since it is to be based on 'the experience gained in its implementation'. Such review might lead to proposals for amendments of the Agreement that should be dealt with by the Ministerial Conference. So far, only one amendment to the Agreement has been proposed and approved.[166]

(c) Review based on new developments

Reviews can also be made not just on gained experience, but 'in the light of any relevant new development which might warrant modification or amendment of this Agreement'. The provision does not refer to the nature of the 'developments'. They may directly relate to intellectual property rights (eg new forms of protection) but also to technological, economic, or social circumstances. The first amendment to the Agreement was based, in fact, on the recognition of the grave public health problems affecting developing countries and LDCs.[167]

> 71.2. Amendments merely serving the purpose of adjusting to higher levels of protection of intellectual property rights achieved, and in force, in other multilateral agreements and accepted under those agreements by all Members of the WTO may be referred to the Ministerial Conference for action in accordance with paragraph 6 of Article X of the WTO Agreement on the basis of a consensus proposal from the Council for TRIPS.

An exceptional procedure for amendments is established in Article 71.2. Its aim would be to 'merely' serve the purpose of 'adjusting to higher levels of protection of intellectual property rights'.

This provision reflects the philosophy that underpinned the adoption of the TRIPS Agreement, which has been regarded in some business circles as the bottom line or first step towards higher levels of protection. This is evidenced by the adoption of the WIPO treaties in 1996 and, in particular, by the negotiation of FTAs by the US and the EU, particularly with developing countries.[168]

The mere adjustment allowed in Article 71.2 is subject, however, to strict conditions.

First, it should refer to 'higher levels of protection', suggesting that it could not encompass new matters or modalities of intellectual property rights not covered under the Agreement.

---

[166] Consisting of the incorporation of a new Article 31*bis*. See pp 324–5 above.
[167] See above the Doha Declaration on the TRIPS Agreement and Public Health.
[168] See p 25 above.

Second, such higher levels of protection should be actually *in force* on the basis of other multilateral agreements. Agreements that have not entered into force would not provide a sufficient ground.

Third, the agreements should be multilateral and accepted by *all* Members of the WTO. This would be an exceptional situation, since international agreements on intellectual property outside the WTO (with the exception of the Paris and Berne Conventions) have a more limited membership.

Naturally, a proposal for action by the Ministerial Conference in accordance with para 6 of Article X of the WTO Agreement could only be submitted on the basis of a consensus achieved in the Council for TRIPS.

Reservations

72. Reservations may not be entered in respect of any of the provisions of this Agreement without the consent of the other Members.

The legal regime of reservations has been codified in Articles 19–23 of the Vienna Convention. However, the issue of reservation in international treaties is of extreme complexity.[169]

The TRIPS Agreement has followed a very simple approach: it does not admit reservations, unless they have the consent of the other Members. The Agreement is, thus, a closed package that Member countries must implement without the possibility of excluding the application of particular provisions. However, as examined above,[170] Members can resort to a number of exceptions provided for under the intellectual property conventions incorporated into the Agreement. Waivers can also be adapted in accordance with WTO rules, as illustrated by the already examined Decision of 30 August 2003, which waived compliance with paras (g) and (h) of Article 31 of the TRIPS Agreement.

Security exceptions

73. Nothing in this Agreement shall be construed:

(a) to require a Member to furnish any information the disclosure of which it considers contrary to its essential security interests; or

(b) to prevent a Member from taking any action which it considers necessary for the protection of its essential security interests;

    (i) relating to fissionable materials or the materials from which they are derived;

    (ii) relating to the traffic in arms, ammunition and implements of war and to such traffic in other goods and materials as is carried on directly or indirectly for the purpose of supplying a military establishment;

    (iii) taken in time of war or other emergency in international relations; or

---

[169] See, eg, A Aust, *Modern Treaty Law and Practice* (2000: Cambridge University Press), p 100.
[170] See pp 59–60.

(c) **to prevent a Member from taking any action in pursuance of its obligations under the United Nations Charter for the maintenance of international peace and security.**

Article 73 permits a Member not to provide information, or to take action deemed necessary for the protection of 'essential security interests' in particular cases. Neither can the Agreement be construed as preventing Members from taking action in pursuance of a Member's obligations under the UN Charter for the maintenance of international peace and security.

The wording of this provision echoes Article XXI of GATT and Article XIV *bis* of GATS. The jurisprudence developed in relation to Article XXI of GATT may, hence, be relevant for the interpretation of Article 73 of the TRIPS Agreement. While the exception contained therein leaves great latitude to Members in the determination of security reasons, such determination is not exempted from scrutiny. It might be subject to review under the DSU, like other measures that may be deemed inconsistent with the Agreement. In particular, a security exception may not be successfully invoked to exclusively protect commercial interests.[171] However, a health crisis or a natural disaster may justify the invocation of such an exception.

Annex

Negotiating history

In his 23 July 1990 report on the status of work in the TRIPS Negotiating Group, the Chairman (Lars E R Anell) presented two sets of proposals. In an Annex to the report, he presented a composite text that was taken from various proposals by delegations to the Negotiating Group, indicating the source of each proposal by numerical reference to the source document.

Composite text of July 23 1990[172]

ACQUISITION OF INTELLECTUAL PROPERTY RIGHTS AND RELATED INTER-PARTES PROCEDURES

1A Where the acquisition of an intellectual property right covered by this Annex is subject to the intellectual property right being granted or registered, PARTIES shall provide for

---

[171] See, eg, UNCTAD-ICTSD op. cit. (2005), p 804.

[172] Chairman's Report to the GNG, Status of Work in the Negotiating Group, Negotiating Group on Trade-Related Aspects of Intellectual Property Rights, including Trade in Counterfeit Goods, MTN.GNG/NG11/W/76, 23 July 1990, presented by the Chairman of the TRIPS Negotiating Group (Lars E R Anell). Alternatives 'A' correspond to texts from developed countries and 'B' from developing countries.

procedures which permit, subject to the substantive conditions for acquiring the intellectual property right being fulfilled, the granting or registration of the right [within a reasonable period of time so as to avoid that the period of protection is unduly curtailed] [and] [at reasonable cost] [at a cost commensurate with the service rendered].

2A Procedures concerning the acquisition or renewal of such intellectual property rights shall be governed by the general principles set out in Part IV at points 3 and 5.

3A Where the national law provides for opposition, revocation, cancellation or similar inter-partes procedures, they shall be [at reasonable cost] expeditious, effective, fair and equitable. [(Such procedures shall give all parties concerned an opportunity to present their views and provide for rulings to be made on the basis of equitable and clear criteria.]

4A Final administrative decisions concerning the acquisition of an intellectual property right or any other matter subject to an inter-partes procedure referred to at point 3 above (other than pre-grant opposition procedures], shall be subject to the right of appeal in a court of law or quasi-judicial body.

DISPUTE PREVENTION AND SETTLEMENT

1. *Transparency (68, 70, 71, 73, 74)*

1.1.1 [National (73)] (Publication) laws, regulations, judicial decisions and administrative rulings [of general application (68, 70, 74)] [of a precedential value (73)], [and all international agreements and decisions of international bodies (73)] [made effective by any PARTY, (70, 74)] pertaining to [the availability, scope, acquisition and enforcement of (68)] [the protection of (74)] intellectual property [rights (68, 74)] [laws (73)] (68, 70, 73, 74)] [the application of the principles and norms prescribed at points 9 and 11 of Part I and point 2A.1 of Part IV above (71)] shall be:

– published promptly by PARTIES. (73)

– [published, or where such publication is not practicable, (74)] made [publicly (74)] available [promptly (74)] in such a manner as to enable governments [of the PARTIES (74)] and [traders (68)] [other interested parties (74)] to become acquainted with them. (68, 74)

– shall be subject to the provisions of Article X of the General Agreement. (70)

– made publicly available in the official language of the PARTY adopting such texts and, shall be provided, upon request, to any other PARTY. (71)

1.1.2 Agreements concerning the protection of intellectual property rights which are in force between the government or governmental agency of any PARTY and the government or a governmental agency of any other PARTY to the Agreement shall also be published or made publicly available. The provision of this paragraph shall not require PARTIES to disclose confidential information which would impede law enforcement or otherwise be contrary to the public interest or would prejudice the legitimate commercial interests of particular enterprises, public or private. (74) (Notification)

1.2A PARTIES shall notify the laws and regulations referred to above to the Committee on Trade Related Intellectual Property Rights in order to assist the Committee in its review of the operation of this Annex. The Committee shall enter into consultations with the World Intellectual Property Organisation in order to agree, if possible, on the establishment of a common register containing these laws and regulations. If these consultations are successful, the Committee may decide to waive the obligation to notify such laws and regulations directly to the Committee. (68)

1.2B. 1 The Committee established under point 1B of Part VIII below shall ensure, in co-operation with the World Intellectual Property Organization and other international organizations, as appropriate, access to all international agreements, decisions of international bodies, national laws, regulations, judicial decisions and administrative rulings of a precedential value, related to the intellectual property laws of the PARTIES. (73)

1.2B. 2 PARTIES shall promptly notify all international agreements, national laws and regulations, judicial decisions and administrative rulings of a precedential value relying upon an exception of the principles of National Treatment and Most-Favoured Nation Treatment through the Committee to the other PARTIES. (73)

1.2C PARTIES shall inform the TRIPS Committee, established under point 1C of Part VIII below, of any changes in their national laws and regulations concerning the protection of intellectual property rights (and any changes in their administration). PARTIES engaged in a special arrangement as stipulated in point 8B.2C.2 of Part II above shall inform the TRIPS Committee of the conclusion of such a special arrangement together with an outline of its contents. (74) (Information on Request)

1.3A A PARTY, having reason to believe that a specific judicial decision, administrative ruling or bilateral agreement in the area of intellectual property rights affects its rights under this Annex, may request in writing to be given access to or be informed in sufficient detail of such specific judicial decisions and administrative rulings or bilateral agreement. (68)

1.3B PARTIES shall, upon request from other PARTIES, provide information as promptly and as comprehensively as possible concerning application and administration of their national laws and regulations related to the protection of intellectual property rights. PARTIES shall notify the TRIPS Committee of the request and the Provision of such information and shall provide the same information, when requested by other PARTIES, to the TRIPS Committee. (74)

1.3C PARTIES shall ensure that an enquiry point exists which is able to answer all reasonable enquiries from other PARTIES and persons and legal entities thereof regarding the PARTY's laws, regulations, and requirements for protection and enforcement of intellectual property rights. (73)

2. *Prior Consultation (68), Dispute Prevention (73)*

2A PARTIES shall make reasonable efforts within the framework of their constitutional systems to inform and, upon request, to consult with the other PARTIES on possible changes in their intellectual property right laws and regulations, and in the administration of such laws and regulations relevant to the operation of this Annex. (68) Whenever laws, regulations and practices relevant to, and affecting, the protection and enforcement of intellectual property rights are under review or intended to be introduced by a PARTY to this Agreement, such PARTY shall

– publish, in an official GATT language, a notice in a publication at an early appropriate stage that it proposes to introduce, amend or abolish legislation or regulation; (73)

– promptly provide, upon request, draft legislation and draft regulations, including explanatory materials, to such PARTIES; (73)

– allow, without discrimination, reasonable time of no less than [X] months for other - PARTIES to submit comments in writing on the basis of the General Agreement; (73)

– consult with interested PARTIES, upon request, on the basis of comments submitted. (73)

2B.2 None of these obligations is meant to limit the sovereignty of PARTIES to legislate, regulate and adjudicate in conformity with international obligations. (73)

3. *Dispute Settlement (68, 71, 73); Consultation. Dispute Settlement (74)*

3A Contracting parties agree that in the area of trade related intellectual property rights covered by this Annex they shall, in relation to each other, abide by the dispute settlement rules and procedures of the General Agreement, and the recommendations, rulings and decisions of the CONTRACTING PARTIES, and not have recourse in relation to other contracting parties to unilaterally decided economic measures of any kind. Furthermore, they undertake to modify and administer their domestic legislation and related procedures in a manner ensuring the conformity of all measures taken thereunder with the above commitment. (68)

(i) Disputes arising under this PART shall be settled on the basis of Article XXII and Article XXIII and in accordance with the consolidated instrument [name]. (73)

(ii) Non-compliance with obligations under this PART shall be deemed to cause nullification and impairment of advantages and benefits accruing under the General Agreement on Tariffs and Trade. (73)

(iii) PARTIES shall refrain from taking any measure against another PARTY other than those provided for under the rules on dispute settlement within the General Agreement on Tariffs and Trade. (73)

3C A PARTY shall not suspend, or threaten to suspend, its obligations under the Agreement without abiding by the procedures for settlement of disputes set out in this section. (74)

3D.1 Consultations (71)

(a) Where a dispute arises concerning the interpretation or implementation of any provisions of this Agreement, a PARTY may bring the matter to the attention of another PARTY and request the latter to enter into consultations with it. (71)

(b) The PARTY so requested shall provide promptly an adequate opportunity for the requested consultations. (71)

(c) PARTIES engaged in consultations shall attempt to reach, within a reasonable period of time, a mutually satisfactory solution to the dispute. (71)

Other Means of Settlement (71)

3.D.2 If a mutually satisfactory solution is not reached within a reasonable period of time through the consultations referred to at point 3D.1, PARTIES to the dispute may agree to resort to other means designed to lead to an amicable settlement of their dispute, such as good offices, conciliation, mediation and arbitration. (71)

3D.3 Non-Recourse to Unilateral Measures (71)

PARTIES shall refrain, in relation to each other, from threatening or having recourse to unilaterally decided measures of any kind aimed at ensuring the enforcement of intellectual property rights. (71)
(See also point 11 of Part II above).

PART VII: TRANSITIONAL ARRANGEMENTS

1. *Transitional Period (68); Transitional Arrangements for Developing Countries and Technical Cooperation (73); Transitional Arrangements (74)*

1A PARTIES shall take all necessary steps to ensure the conformity of their laws, regulations and practice with the provisions of this Annex within a period of not more than [-] years following its entry into force. The Committee on Trade Related Intellectual Property Rights may decide, upon duly motivated request, that developing countries which face special problems in the preparation and implementation of intellectual property laws, dispose of an additional period not exceeding [-] years, with the exception of points 6, 7 and 8 of PART II, in respect of which this additional period shall not apply. Furthermore, the Committee may, upon duly motivated request, extend this additional period by a further period not exceeding [-] years in respect of least developed countries. (68)

1B.1 Developing Countries (73)

(i) With a view to achieve full and successful adjustment and compliance with levels of protection and enforcement set forth in Parts III and IV above, and provided that existing levels of protection and enforcement are not reduced, developing PARTIES may not apply such standards for a period of a total of [X] years beginning with the date of acceptance or accession of such PARTY, but not later than the year [Z]. (73)

(ii) Delay in implementation of obligations under Parts III and IV above may be extended upon duly motivated request for a further period not exceeding [X] years by the Committee established under point 1B of Part VIII below. Such decision shall take into account the level of technological and commercial development of the requesting PARTY. (73)

(iii) Non-application of levels of protection set forth in Parts III and IV above after final expiration of the transitional period agreed shall entitle other PARTIES, without prejudice to other rights under the General Agreement, to suspend the application points 7 and 8 of Part II above and grant protection of intellectual property rights on the basis of reciprocity. (73)

1B.Z Least-Developed Countries (73)

(i) With a view to achieve full and successful adjustment and compliance with levels of protection and enforcement set forth in Parts III and IV above, least developed PARTIES are not expected to apply such standards for a period of a total of [X+Y] years. (73).

(ii) Delay of implementation of obligations may be further extended upon request by the Committee established under point 1B of Part VIII below. (73)

2. *Technical Assistance (68); Technical Cooperation (73); International Cooperation. Technical Assistance (74)*

2A Developed PARTIES shall, if requested, advise developing PARTIES on the preparation and implementation of domestic legislation on the protection and enforcement of intellectual property rights covered by this Annex as well as the prevention of their abuse, and shall grant them technical assistance on mutually agreed terms and conditions, regarding the establishment of domestic offices and agencies relevant to the implementation of their intellectual property legislation, including the training of officials employed in their respective governments. (68) ZB PARTIES to this Agreement shall provide for technical co-operation to developing and least developed PARTIES upon coordination by the Committee established under point 1B of Part VIII below in collaboration with the World Intellectual Property Organization, and other international organizations, as appropriate. Upon request, such co-operation includes support and advice as to training of personnel, the introduction, amendment and implementation of national laws, regulations and practices, and assistance by the Committee for settlement of disputes.

PART VIII: INSTITUTIONAL ARRANGEMENTS: FINAL PROVISIONS

Committee on Trade-Related Intellectual Property Rights (68); The Committee on Trade-Related Aspects of Intellectual Property Law (73); The TRIPS Committee (74)

1A PARTIES shall establish a Committee on Trade Related Intellectual Property Rights composed of representatives from each PARTY. The Committee shall elect its own chairman, establish its own rules of procedures and shall meet not less than once a year and otherwise upon request of any PARTY. The Committee shall monitor the operation of this Annex and, in particular, PARTIES' compliance with their obligations hereunder, and shall afford PARTIES the opportunity of consulting on matters relating to trade related intellectual property rights. It shall carry out such other responsibilities as assigned to it by the CONTRACTING PARTIES, and it shall, in particular, provide any assistance requested by them in the context of procedures under Articles XXII and XXIII of the General Agreement. In carrying out its functions, the Committee may consult with and seek information from any source they deem appropriate. (68)

1B (i) All PARTIES shall be represented in the Committee on Trade-Related Aspects of Intellectual Property Rights (hereinafter the Committee). It shall elect its Chairman annually and meet as necessary, but not less than once a year. It shall carry out its responsibilities as assigned to it under this PART or by the PARTIES. It may establish working groups. (73)

(ii) The Committee shall monitor the implementation and operation of this PART, taking into account the objectives thereof. It shall examine periodical country reports prepared by the GATT Secretariat on laws, regulations, practices and international agreements related to, and affecting, the protection of intellectual property rights. It shall make recommendations, as appropriate, to the PARTIES concerned. (73)

(iii) The Committee shall periodically agree upon a schedule of country reports. It shall adopt a work programme and coordinate activities of PARTIES in the field of technical cooperation. (73)

(iv) The Committee shall annually report to the CONTRACTING PARTIES. It may submit recommendations. (73)

(v) The Committee is entitled to elaborate and adopt guidelines for the interpretation, in particular of PARTS III and IV above. It shall take into account relevant findings of adopted panel reports. (73)

1C The TRIPS Committee composed of representatives of the PARTIES shall be established. The TRIPS Committee shall carry out functions under this Agreement or otherwise assigned to it by the PARTIES. (74) Joint Expert Gron (68), Joint Group of Experts (73)

2A In order to promote cooperation between the Committee on Trade Related Intellectual Property Rights and bodies under the World Intellectual Property Organisation, the latter shall be invited by the Committee to serve together with the GATT Secretariat as Secretariat for a joint Expert Group which shall consist of representatives of the CONTRACTING PARTIES and of the Member States of the Paris and Berne Unions. The Expert Group shall, when requested to do so by the Committee, advise the Committee on technical matters under consideration. (68)

2B In order to promote co-operation between the Committee and bodies under the World Intellectual Property Organization, the Committee may establish, as appropriate, Joint Groups of Experts consisting of representatives of the PARTIES and of the Member States of the Unions created by the Paris Convention (1967) and the Berne Convention (1971) respectively. Upon request of the Committee, the Joint Groups of Experts shall give advice on technical matters under consideration. (73)

Other Conventions (68)

PARTIES shall, within a period of [-] years, adhere to the Paris Convention (1967), and the Berne Convention (1971). They shall also give careful consideration to adhering to other international conventions on intellectual property with a view to strengthening the international framework for the protection of intellectual property rights and furthering the development of legitimate trade. (68)

4. *International Cooperation (68)*

PARTIES agree to co-operate with each other with a view to eliminating international trade in goods infringing intellectual property rights. For this purpose they shall establish and notify contact points in their national administrations, and shall be ready to exchange information on trade in infringing goods. They shall, in particular, promote the exchange of information and co-operation between customs authorities with regard to trade in counterfeit goods. (68)

(See also point 1.1 of Part IX below)

5. *Relationship to Other Parts of the General Agreement on Tariffs and Trade (73)*

Other provisions of the General Agreement shall apply to the extent that this PART does not provide for more specific rights, obligations and exceptions thereof. (73)

(See also point 5 of PART II)

6. *Provisional Application (73)*

Pending the entry into force in accordance with Article XXX:l, this PART shall be applied provisionally. It shall become effective between PARTIES upon acceptance at (date). For each other contracting party, it shall apply provisionally with the thirtieth day following the date of accession. (73)

7. *Review and Amendment (68); Amendments (73)*

7A PARTIES shall review the implementation of this Annex after the expiration of the transitional period referred to at point 1 of Part VII above. They shall, having regard to the experience gained in its implementation, review it [-] years after that date, and at identical intervals thereafter. The PARTIES shall also undertake reviews in the light of any relevant new developments which might warrant modification or amendment of this annex. (68)

7B (i) Amendments to this PART shall take effect in accordance with the provisions on entry into force and on provisional application. (73)

(ii) Amendments merely serving the purpose to adjust to higher levels of protection of intellectual property rights achieved, and in force, in other multilateral agreements and accepted by all PARTIES may be adopted by the Committee. (73)

8. *Withdrawal (73)*

Pending the entry into force, withdrawal from this PART shall be effected in accordance with the Protocol of Provisional Application of the General Agreement on Tariffs and Trade or the respective Protocol of Accession of contracting parties to the General Agreement on Tariffs and Trade. (73)

Draft text transmitted to the Brussels Ministerial Conference (December 1990)

Part IV: Acquisition and Maintenance of Intellectual Property Rights and Related Inter-Partes Procedures

Article 65

1. PARTIES may require, as a condition of the acquisition or maintenance of the intellectual property rights provided for under Sections 2–6 of Part II of this Agreement, compliance with reasonable procedures and formalities. Such procedures and formalities shall be consistent with the provisions of this Agreement.

2. Where the acquisition of an intellectual property right is subject to the right being granted or registered, PARTIES shall ensure that the procedures for grant or registration, subject to compliance with the substantive conditions for acquisition of the right, permit the granting or registration of the right within a reasonable period of time so as to avoid unwarranted curtailment of the period of protection.

3. Article 4 of the Paris Convention (1967) shall apply *mutatis mutandis* to service marks.

4. Procedures concerning the acquisition or maintenance of intellectual property rights and, where the national law provides for such procedures, opposition, revocation, cancellation or similar inter partes procedures, shall be governed by the general principles set out in paragraphs 2 and 3 of Article 44.

5. Final administrative decisions in any of the procedures referred to under paragraph 4 above shall be subject to review by a judicial or quasi-judicial authority. However, there shall be no obligation to provide an opportunity for such review of decisions in cases of unsuccessful opposition or administrative revocation, provided that the grounds for such procedures can be the subject of invalidation procedures.

PART V: DISPUTE PREVENTION AND SETTLEMENT

Article 66
Transparency

1. Laws and regulations, and final judicial decisions and administrative rulings of general application, made effective by any PARTY pertaining to the subject matter of this Agreement (the availability, scope, acquisition, enforcement and prevention of the abuse of intellectual property rights) shall be published, or where such publication is not practicable made publicly available, in a national language, in such a manner as to enable governments and right holders to become acquainted with them. Agreements concerning the subject matter of this Agreement which are in force between the government or a governmental agency of any PARTY and the government or a governmental agency of any other PARTY shall also be published.

2. PARTIES shall notify the laws and regulations referred to in paragraph 1 above to the Committee established under Part VII below in order to assist that Committee in its review of the operation of this Agreement. The Committee shall attempt to minimise the burden on PARTIES in carrying out this obligation and may decide to waive the obligation to notify such laws and regulations directly to the Committee if consultations with the World Intellectual Property Organisation on the establishment of a common register containing these laws and regulations are successful. The Committee shall also consider in this connection any action required regarding notifications pursuant to the obligations under this Agreement stemming from the provisions of Article 6*ter* of the Paris Convention (1967).

3. Each PARTY shall be prepared to supply, in response to a written request from another PARTY, information of the sort referred to in paragraph 1 above. A PARTY, having reason to believe that a specific judicial decision or administrative ruling or bilateral agreement in the area of intellectual property rights affects its rights under this Agreement, may also request in writing to be given access to or be informed in sufficient detail of such specific judicial decisions or administrative rulings or bilateral agreements.

4. Nothing in paragraphs 1 to 3 above shall require PARTIES to disclose confidential information which would impede law enforcement or otherwise be contrary to the public interest or would prejudice the legitimate commercial interests of particular enterprises, public or private.

Article 67
Dispute Settlement

PARTIES shall not have recourse in relation to other PARTIES to unilaterally decided economic measures of any kind. Furthermore, they undertake to modify and administer their domestic legislation and related procedures in a manner ensuring the conformity of all measures taken thereunder with the above commitment.

PART VI: TRANSITIONAL ARRANGEMENTS

Article 68
Transitional Arrangements

1. Subject to the provisions of paragraphs 2 and 3 below, PARTIES shall not be obliged to apply the provisions of this Agreement before the expiry. of a period of [...] years following the date of entry into force of this Agreement for that PARTY.

2. Any developing country PARTY may delay for a period of [...] years the date of application, as defined under paragraph 1 above, of the provisions of this Agreement, other than Articles 3, 4 and 5 [, insofar as compliance with those provisions requires the amendment of domestic laws, regulations or practice].

3. Any other PARTY which is undertaking structural reform of its intellectual property system and faces special problems in the preparation and implementation of intellectual property laws, may also benefit from a period of delay as foreseen in paragraph 2 above.

4. Any PARTY availing itself of a transitional period under paragraphs 1, 2 or 3 shall ensure that any changes in its domestic laws, regulations and practice made during that period do not result in a lesser degree of consistency with the provisions of this Agreement.

5. Any PARTY availing itself of a transitional period in accordance with paragraph 2 or 3 above shall provide, on accession, a schedule setting out its timetable for application of the provisions of this Agreement. [This timetable shall be without commitment.] [The Committee established under Part VII below may authorise, upon duly motivated request, departures, consistent with provisions of paragraph 2 or 3 above, from the timetable.]

Article 69
Least-Developed Countries

1. In view of their special needs and requirements, their economic, financial and administrative constraints, and their need for flexibility to create a viable technological base, least-developed country PARTIES shall not be required to apply the provisions of this Agreement, other than Articles 3, 4 [and 5, insofar as compliance with those provisions requires the amendment of domestic laws, regulations or practices for a period of [...] years from the date of application as defined under paragraph 1 of Article 68 above. The Committee shall, upon duly motivated request by a least-developed country PARTY, accord extensions of this period.] The requirement of paragraph 5 of Article 68 above shall not apply to least-developed country PARTIES.

2. Developed country PARTIES shall provide incentives to enterprises and institutions in their territories for the purpose of promoting and encouraging technology transfer to least-developed country PARTIES in order to enable them to create a sound and viable techno-logical base.

Article 70
Technical Cooperation

In order to facilitate the implementation of this Agreement, developed country PARTIES shall provide, on request and on mutually agreed terms and conditions, technical and financial cooperation in favour of developing and least-developed country PARTIES. Such cooperation shall include assistance in the preparation of domestic legislation on the pro-tection and enforcement of intellectual property rights as well as on the prevention of their abuse, and shall include support regarding the establishment or reinforcement of domestic offices and agencies relevant to these matters, including the training of personnel.

PART VII: INSTITUTIONAL ARRANGEMENTS: FINAL PROVISIONS

Article 71
Committee on Trade Related Intellectual Property Rights

PARTIES shall establish a Committee on Trade Related Intellectual Property Rights com-posed of representatives from each PARTY. The Committee shall elect its own chairperson, establish its own rules of procedure and shall meet not less than once a year and otherwise upon request of any PARTY. The Committee shall monitor the operation of this agreement and, in particular, PARTIES' compliance with their obligations hereunder, and shall afford PARTIES the opportunity of consulting on matters relating to trade related intellectual property rights. It shall carry out such other responsibilities as assigned to it by the PAR-TIES, and it shall, in particular, provide any assistance requested by them in the context of dispute settlement procedures. In carrying out its functions, the Committee may consult with and seek information from any source they deem appropriate. In consultation with the World Intellectual Property Organization, the Committee shall seek to establish, within one year of its first meeting, appropriate arrangements for co-operation with bodies of that Organization.

Article 72
International Cooperation

PARTIES agree to co-operate with each other with a view to eliminating international trade in goods infringing intellectual property rights. For this purpose, they shall establish and notify contact points in their national administrations and be ready to exchange infor-mation on trade in infringing goods. They shall, in particular, promote the exchange of information and co-operation between customs authorities with regard to trade in coun-terfeit goods.

Article 73
Protection of Existing Intellectual Property

1. PARTIES shall apply the provisions of Articles 3, 4 and 5 of Part I, of Sections 2, 3, 7 and 8 of Part II, of Part III and of Part IV to subject matter under protection in a PARTY

on the date of application of the provisions of this Agreement for that PARTY as defined in Part VI above.

2. PARTIES are not obliged to apply the provisions of Sections 1, 4, 5 and 6 of Part II to subject matter under protection in a PARTY on the date of application of the provisions of this Agreement for that PARTY, subject to the provisions of Article[s] 15 [and 16.6]. Subject matter in respect of which the procedures for the acquisition of rights have been initiated as of that date for which, however, the intellectual property title has not yet been granted shall [not] benefit from the provisions of this Agreement. Nothing in this Agreement shall affect other subject matter covered by these Sections which is already in existence and not under protection in a PARTY on the date of application of the provisions of this Agreement for that PARTY, subject to the provisions of Article[s] 15 [and 16.6].

3. The application of Articles 2 and 6 of this Agreement to existing intellectual property shall be governed by paragraphs 1 and 2 of this Article, as appropriate to the intellectual property right in question.

Article 74s
Review and Amendment

1. PARTIES shall review the implementation of this Agreement after the expiration of the transitional period referred to in paragraph 2 of Article 68 above. They shall, having regard to the experience gained in its implementation, review it [] years after that date, and at identical intervals thereafter. The PARTIES may undertake reviews in the light of any relevant new developments which might warrant modification or amendment of this Agreement.

2. Amendments merely serving the purpose of adjusting to higher levels of protection of intellectual property rights achieved, and in force, in other multilateral agreements and accepted by all PARTIES may be adopted by the Committee.

[Article 75
Reservations

A PARTY may only enter reservations in respect of any of the provisions of this Agreement at the time of entry into force of this Agreement for that PARTY and with the consent of the other PARTIES.]

APPENDIX 1

Agreement on Trade-Related Aspects of Intellectual Property Rights

PART I: GENERAL PROVISIONS AND BASIC PRINCIPLES

PART II: STANDARDS CONCERNING THE AVAILABILITY, SCOPE AND USE OF INTELLECTUAL PROPERTY RIGHTS
1. Copyright and Related Rights
2. Trademarks
3. Geographical Indications
4. Industrial Designs
5. Patents
6. Layout-Designs (Topographies) of Integrated Circuits
7. Protection of Undisclosed Information
8. Control of Anti-Competitive Practices in Contractual Licences

PART III: ENFORCEMENT OF INTELLECTUAL PROPERTY RIGHTS
1. General Obligations
2. Civil and Administrative Procedures and Remedies
3. Provisional Measures
4. Special Requirements Related to Border Measures
5. Criminal Procedures

PART IV: ACQUISITION AND MAINTENANCE OF INTELLECTUAL PROPERTY RIGHTS AND RELATED *INTER-PARTES* PROCEDURES

PART V: DISPUTE PREVENTION AND SETTLEMENT

PART VI: TRANSITIONAL ARRANGEMENTS

PART VII: INSTITUTIONAL ARRANGEMENTS; FINAL PROVISIONS

Agreement on Trade-Related Aspects
of Intellectual Property Rights

Members,

Desiring to reduce distortions and impediments to international trade, and taking into account the need to promote effective and adequate protection of intellectual property rights, and to ensure that measures and procedures to enforce intellectual property rights do not themselves become barriers to legitimate trade;

Recognizing, to this end, the need for new rules and disciplines concerning:

(a) the applicability of the basic principles of GATT 1994 and of relevant international intellectual property agreements or conventions;

(b) the provision of adequate standards and principles concerning the availability, scope and use of trade-related intellectual property rights;

(c) the provision of effective and appropriate means for the enforcement of trade-related intellectual property rights, taking into account differences in national legal systems;

(d) the provision of effective and expeditious procedures for the multilateral prevention and settlement of disputes between governments; and

(e) transitional arrangements aiming at the fullest participation in the results of the negotiations;

Recognizing the need for a multilateral framework of principles, rules and disciplines dealing with international trade in counterfeit goods;

Recognizing that intellectual property rights are private rights;

Recognizing the underlying public policy objectives of national systems for the protection of intellectual property, including developmental and technological objectives;

Recognizing also the special needs of the least-developed country Members in respect of maximum flexibility in the domestic implementation of laws and regulations in order to enable them to create a sound and viable technological base;

Emphasizing the importance of reducing tensions by reaching strengthened commitments to resolve disputes on trade-related intellectual property issues through multilateral procedures;

Desiring to establish a mutually supportive relationship between the WTO and the World Intellectual Property Organization (referred to in this Agreement as "WIPO") as well as other relevant international organizations;

Hereby agree as follows:

Part I: General Provisions and Basic Principles

Article 1
Nature and Scope of Obligations

1. Members shall give effect to the provisions of this Agreement. Members may, but shall not be obliged to, implement in their law more extensive protection than is required by this Agreement, provided that such protection does not contravene the provisions of this Agreement. Members shall be free to determine the appropriate method of implementing the provisions of this Agreement within their own legal system and practice.

2. For the purposes of this Agreement, the term "intellectual property" refers to all categories of intellectual property that are the subject of Sections 1 through 7 of Part II.

3. Members shall accord the treatment provided for in this Agreement to the nationals of other Members.[1] In respect of the relevant intellectual property right, the nationals of other Members shall be understood as those natural or legal persons that would meet the criteria for eligibility for protection provided for in the Paris Convention (1967), the Berne Convention (1971), the Rome Convention and the Treaty on Intellectual Property in Respect of Integrated Circuits, were all Members of the WTO members of those conventions.[2] Any Member availing itself of the possibilities provided in paragraph 3 of Article 5 or paragraph 2 of Article 6 of the Rome Convention shall make a notification as foreseen in those provisions to the Council for Trade-Related Aspects of Intellectual Property Rights (the "Council for TRIPS").

Article 2
Intellectual Property Conventions

1. In respect of Parts II, III and IV of this Agreement, Members shall comply with Articles 1 through 12, and Article 19, of the Paris Convention (1967).

2. Nothing in Parts I to IV of this Agreement shall derogate from existing obligations that Members may have to each other under the Paris Convention, the Berne Convention, the Rome Convention and the Treaty on Intellectual Property in Respect of Integrated Circuits.

Article 3
National Treatment

1. Each Member shall accord to the nationals of other Members treatment no less favourable than that it accords to its own nationals with regard to the protection[3] of intellectual property, subject to the exceptions already provided in, respectively, the Paris Convention (1967), the Berne Convention (1971), the Rome Convention or the Treaty on Intellectual Property in Respect of Integrated Circuits. In respect of performers, producers of phonograms and broadcasting organizations, this obligation only applies in respect of the rights provided under this Agreement. Any Member availing itself of the possibilities provided in Article 6 of the Berne Convention (1971) or paragraph 1(b) of

---

[1] When "nationals" are referred to in this Agreement, they shall be deemed, in the case of a separate customs territory Member of the WTO, to mean persons, natural or legal, who are domiciled or who have a real and effective industrial or commercial establishment in that customs territory.

[2] In this Agreement, "Paris Convention" refers to the Paris Convention for the Protection of Industrial Property; "Paris Convention (1967)" refers to the Stockholm Act of this Convention of 14 July 1967. "Berne Convention" refers to the Berne Convention for the Protection of Literary and Artistic Works; "Berne Convention (1971)" refers to the Paris Act of this Convention of 24 July 1971. "Rome Convention" refers to the International Convention for the Protection of Performers, Producers of Phonograms and Broadcasting Organizations, adopted at Rome on 26 October 1961. "Treaty on Intellectual Property in Respect of Integrated Circuits" (IPIC Treaty) refers to the Treaty on Intellectual Property in Respect of Integrated Circuits, adopted at Washington on 26 May 1989. "WTO Agreement" refers to the Agreement Establishing the WTO.

[3] For the purposes of Articles 3 and 4, "protection" shall include matters affecting the availability, acquisition, scope, maintenance and enforcement of intellectual property rights as well as those matters affecting the use of intellectual property rights specifically addressed in this Agreement.

Article 16 of the Rome Convention shall make a notification as foreseen in those provisions to the Council for TRIPS.

2. Members may avail themselves of the exceptions permitted under paragraph 1 in relation to judicial and administrative procedures, including the designation of an address for service or the appointment of an agent within the jurisdiction of a Member, only where such exceptions are necessary to secure compliance with laws and regulations which are not inconsistent with the provisions of this Agreement and where such practices are not applied in a manner which would constitute a disguised restriction on trade.

Article 4
Most-Favoured-Nation Treatment

With regard to the protection of intellectual property, any advantage, favour, privilege or immunity granted by a Member to the nationals of any other country shall be accorded immediately and unconditionally to the nationals of all other Members. Exempted from this obligation are any advantage, favour, privilege or immunity accorded by a Member:

(a) deriving from international agreements on judicial assistance or law enforcement of a general nature and not particularly confined to the protection of intellectual property;

(b) granted in accordance with the provisions of the Berne Convention (1971) or the Rome Convention authorizing that the treatment accorded be a function not of national treatment but of the treatment accorded in another country;

(c) in respect of the rights of performers, producers of phonograms and broadcasting organizations not provided under this Agreement;

(d) deriving from international agreements related to the protection of intellectual property which entered into force prior to the entry into force of the WTO Agreement, provided that such agreements are notified to the Council for TRIPS and do not constitute an arbitrary or unjustifiable discrimination against nationals of other Members.

Article 5
Multilateral Agreements on Acquisition or Maintenance of Protection

The obligations under Articles 3 and 4 do not apply to procedures provided in multilateral agreements concluded under the auspices of WIPO relating to the acquisition or maintenance of intellectual property rights.

Article 6
Exhaustion

For the purposes of dispute settlement under this Agreement, subject to the provisions of Articles 3 and 4 nothing in this Agreement shall be used to address the issue of the exhaustion of intellectual property rights.

Article 7
Objectives

The protection and enforcement of intellectual property rights should contribute to the promotion of technological innovation and to the transfer and dissemination of technology, to the mutual advantage of producers and users of technological knowledge and in a manner conducive to social and economic welfare, and to a balance of rights and obligations.

Article 8
Principles

1. Members may, in formulating or amending their laws and regulations, adopt measures necessary to protect public health and nutrition, and to promote the public interest in sectors of vital importance to their socio-economic and technological development, provided that such measures are consistent with the provisions of this Agreement.

2. Appropriate measures, provided that they are consistent with the provisions of this Agreement, may be needed to prevent the abuse of intellectual property rights by right holders or the resort to practices which unreasonably restrain trade or adversely affect the international transfer of technology.

PART II: STANDARDS CONCERNING THE AVAILABILITY, SCOPE AND USE OF INTELLECTUAL PROPERTY RIGHTS

SECTION I: COPYRIGHT AND RELATED RIGHTS

Article 9
Relation to the Berne Convention

1. Members shall comply with Articles 1 through 21 of the Berne Convention (1971) and the Appendix thereto. However, Members shall not have rights or obligations under this Agreement in respect of the rights conferred under Article 6*bis* of that Convention or of the rights derived therefrom.

2. Copyright protection shall extend to expressions and not to ideas, procedures, methods of operation or mathematical concepts as such.

Article 10
Computer Programs and Compilations of Data

1. Computer programs, whether in source or object code, shall be protected as literary works under the Berne Convention (1971).

2. Compilations of data or other material, whether in machine readable or other form, which by reason of the selection or arrangement of their contents constitute intellectual creations shall be protected as such. Such protection, which shall not extend to the data or material itself, shall be without prejudice to any copyright subsisting in the data or material itself.

Article 11
Rental Rights

In respect of at least computer programs and cinematographic works, a Member shall provide authors and their successors in title the right to authorize or to prohibit the commercial rental to the public of originals or copies of their copyright works. A Member shall be excepted from this obligation in respect of cinematographic works unless such rental has led to widespread copying of such works which is materially impairing the exclusive right of reproduction conferred in that Member on authors and their successors in title. In respect of computer programs, this obligation does not apply to rentals where the program itself is not the essential object of the rental.

Article 12
Term of Protection

Whenever the term of protection of a work, other than a photographic work or a work of applied art, is calculated on a basis other than the life of a natural person, such term shall be no less than 50 years from the end of the calendar year of authorized publication, or, failing such authorized publication within 50 years from the making of the work, 50 years from the end of the calendar year of making.

Article 13
Limitations and Exceptions

Members shall confine limitations or exceptions to exclusive rights to certain special cases which do not conflict with a normal exploitation of the work and do not unreasonably prejudice the legitimate interests of the right holder.

Article 14
Protection of Performers, Producers of Phonograms (Sound Recordings)
and Broadcasting Organizations

1. In respect of a fixation of their performance on a phonogram, performers shall have the possibility of preventing the following acts when undertaken without their authorization: the fixation of their unfixed performance and the reproduction of such fixation. Performers shall also have the possibility of preventing the following acts when undertaken without their authorization: the broadcasting by wireless means and the communication to the public of their live performance.
2. Producers of phonograms shall enjoy the right to authorize or prohibit the direct or indirect reproduction of their phonograms.
3. Broadcasting organizations shall have the right to prohibit the following acts when undertaken without their authorization: the fixation, the reproduction of fixations, and the rebroadcasting by wireless means of broadcasts, as well as the communication to the public of television broadcasts of the same. Where Members do not grant such rights to broadcasting organizations, they shall provide owners of copyright in the subject matter of broadcasts with the possibility of preventing the above acts, subject to the provisions of the Berne Convention (1971).
4. The provisions of Article 11 in respect of computer programs shall apply *mutatis mutandis* to producers of phonograms and any other right holders in phonograms as determined in a Member's law. If on 15 April 1994 a Member has in force a system of equitable remuneration of right holders in respect of the rental of phonograms, it may maintain such system provided that the commercial rental of phonograms is not giving rise to the material impairment of the exclusive rights of reproduction of right holders.
5. The term of the protection available under this Agreement to performers and producers of phonograms shall last at least until the end of a period of 50 years computed from the end of the calendar year in which the fixation was made or the performance took place.

The term of protection granted pursuant to paragraph 3 shall last for at least 20 years from the end of the calendar year in which the broadcast took place.

6. Any Member may, in relation to the rights conferred under paragraphs 1, 2 and 3, provide for conditions, limitations, exceptions and reservations to the extent permitted by the Rome Convention. However, the provisions of Article 18 of the Berne Convention (1971) shall also apply, *mutatis mutandis*, to the rights of performers and producers of phonograms in phonograms.

SECTION 2: TRADEMARKS

Article 15
Protectable Subject Matter

1. Any sign, or any combination of signs, capable of distinguishing the goods or services of one undertaking from those of other undertakings, shall be capable of constituting a trademark. Such signs, in particular words including personal names, letters, numerals, figurative elements and combinations of colours as well as any combination of such signs, shall be eligible for registration as trademarks. Where signs are not inherently capable of distinguishing the relevant goods or services, Members may make registrability depend on distinctiveness acquired through use. Members may require, as a condition of registration, that signs be visually perceptible.

2. Paragraph 1 shall not be understood to prevent a Member from denying registration of a trademark on other grounds, provided that they do not derogate from the provisions of the Paris Convention (1967).

3. Members may make registrability depend on use. However, actual use of a trademark shall not be a condition for filing an application for registration. An application shall not be refused solely on the ground that intended use has not taken place before the expiry of a period of three years from the date of application.

4. The nature of the goods or services to which a trademark is to be applied shall in no case form an obstacle to registration of the trademark.

5. Members shall publish each trademark either before it is registered or promptly after it is registered and shall afford a reasonable opportunity for petitions to cancel the registration. In addition, Members may afford an opportunity for the registration of a trademark to be opposed.

Article 16
Rights Conferred

1. The owner of a registered trademark shall have the exclusive right to prevent all third parties not having the ownerís consent from using in the course of trade identical or similar signs for goods or services which are identical or similar to those in respect of which the trademark is registered where such use would result in a likelihood of confusion. In case of the use of an identical sign for identical goods or services, a likelihood of confusion shall be presumed. The rights described above shall not prejudice any existing prior rights, nor shall they affect the possibility of Members making rights available on the basis of use.

2. Article 6*bis* of the Paris Convention (1967) shall apply, *mutatis mutandis*, to services. In determining whether a trademark is well-known, Members shall take account of the knowledge of the trademark in the relevant sector of the public, including knowledge in the Member concerned which has been obtained as a result of the promotion of the trademark.
3. Article 6*bis* of the Paris Convention (1967) shall apply, *mutatis mutandis*, to goods or services which are not similar to those in respect of which a trademark is registered, provided that use of that trademark in relation to those goods or services would indicate a connection between those goods or services and the owner of the registered trademark and provided that the interests of the owner of the registered trademark are likely to be damaged by such use.

Article 17
Exceptions

Members may provide limited exceptions to the rights conferred by a trademark, such as fair use of descriptive terms, provided that such exceptions take account of the legitimate interests of the owner of the trademark and of third parties.

Article 18
Term of Protection

Initial registration, and each renewal of registration, of a trademark shall be for a term of no less than seven years. The registration of a trademark shall be renewable indefinitely.

Article 19
Requirement of Use

1. If use is required to maintain a registration, the registration may be cancelled only after an uninterrupted period of at least three years of non-use, unless valid reasons based on the existence of obstacles to such use are shown by the trademark owner. Circumstances arising independently of the will of the owner of the trademark which constitute an obstacle to the use of the trademark, such as import restrictions on or other government requirements for goods or services protected by the trademark, shall be recognized as valid reasons for non-use.
2. When subject to the control of its owner, use of a trademark by another person shall be recognized as use of the trademark for the purpose of maintaining the registration.

Article 20
Other Requirements

The use of a trademark in the course of trade shall not be unjustifiably encumbered by special requirements, such as use with another trademark, use in a special form or use in a manner detrimental to its capability to distinguish the goods or services of one undertaking from those of other undertakings. This will not preclude a requirement prescribing the use of the trademark identifying the undertaking producing the goods or services along with, but without linking it to, the trademark distinguishing the specific goods or services in question of that undertaking.

Article 21
Licensing and Assignment

Members may determine conditions on the licensing and assignment of trademarks, it being understood that the compulsory licensing of trademarks shall not be permitted and that the owner of a registered trademark shall have the right to assign the trademark with or without the transfer of the business to which the trademark belongs.

SECTION 3: GEOGRAPHICAL INDICATIONS

Article 22
Protection of Geographical Indications

1. Geographical indications are, for the purposes of this Agreement, indications which identify a good as originating in the territory of a Member, or a region or locality in that territory, where a given quality, reputation or other characteristic of the good is essentially attributable to its geographical origin.
2. In respect of geographical indications, Members shall provide the legal means for interested parties to prevent:

(a) the use of any means in the designation or presentation of a good that indicates or suggests that the good in question originates in a geographical area other than the true place of origin in a manner which misleads the public as to the geographical origin of the good;

(b) any use which constitutes an act of unfair competition within the meaning of Article 10*bis* of the Paris Convention (1967).

3. A Member shall, *ex officio* if its legislation so permits or at the request of an interested party, refuse or invalidate the registration of a trademark which contains or consists of a geographical indication with respect to goods not originating in the territory indicated, if use of the indication in the trademark for such goods in that Member is of such a nature as to mislead the public as to the true place of origin.
4. The protection under paragraphs 1, 2 and 3 shall be applicable against a geographical indication which, although literally true as to the territory, region or locality in which the goods originate, falsely represents to the public that the goods originate in another territory.

Article 23
Additional Protection for Geographical Indications for
Wines and Spirits

1. Each Member shall provide the legal means for interested parties to prevent use of a geographical indication identifying wines for wines not originating in the place indicated by the geographical indication in question or identifying spirits for spirits not originating in the place indicated by the geographical indication in question, even where the true origin of the goods is indicated or the geographical indication is used in translation or accompanied by expressions such as "kind", "type", "style", "imitation" or the like.[4]

---

[4] Notwithstanding the first sentence of Article 42, Members may, with respect to these obligations, instead provide for enforcement by administrative action.

2. The registration of a trademark for wines which contains or consists of a geographical indication identifying wines or for spirits which contains or consists of a geographical indication identifying spirits shall be refused or invalidated, *ex officio* if a Member's legislation so permits or at the request of an interested party, with respect to such wines or spirits not having this origin.

3. In the case of homonymous geographical indications for wines, protection shall be accorded to each indication, subject to the provisions of paragraph 4 of Article 22. Each Member shall determine the practical conditions under which the homonymous indications in question will be differentiated from each other, taking into account the need to ensure equitable treatment of the producers concerned and that consumers are not misled.

4. In order to facilitate the protection of geographical indications for wines, negotiations shall be undertaken in the Council for TRIPS concerning the establishment of a multilateral system of notification and registration of geographical indications for wines eligible for protection in those Members participating in the system.

Article 24
International Negotiations; Exceptions

1. Members agree to enter into negotiations aimed at increasing the protection of individual geographical indications under Article 23. The provisions of paragraphs 4 through 8 below shall not be used by a Member to refuse to conduct negotiations or to conclude bilateral or multilateral agreements. In the context of such negotiations, Members shall be willing to consider the continued applicability of these provisions to individual geographical indications whose use was the subject of such negotiations.

2. The Council for TRIPS shall keep under review the application of the provisions of this Section;the first such review shall take place within two years of the entry into force of the WTO Agreement. Any matter affecting the compliance with the obligations under these provisions may be drawn to the attention of the Council, which, at the request of a Member, shall consult with any Member or Members in respect of such matter in respect of which it has not been possible to find a satisfactory solution through bilateral or plurilateral consultations between the Members concerned. The Council shall take such action as may be agreed to facilitate the operation and further the objectives of this Section.

3. In implementing this Section, a Member shall not diminish the protection of geographical indications that existed in that Member immediately prior to the date of entry into force of the WTO Agreement.

4. Nothing in this Section shall require a Member to prevent continued and similar use of a particular geographical indication of another Member identifying wines or spirits in connection with goods or services by any of its nationals or domiciliaries who have used that geographical indication in a continuous manner with regard to the same or related goods or services in the territory of that Member either (a) for at least 10 years preceding 15 April 1994 or (b) in good faith preceding that date.

5. Where a trademark has been applied for or registered in good faith, or where rights to a trademark have been acquired through use in good faith either:

(a) before the date of application of these provisions in that Member as defined in Part VI; or

(b) before the geographical indication is protected in its country of origin;

measures adopted to implement this Section shall not prejudice eligibility for or the validity of the registration of a trademark, or the right to use a trademark, on the basis that such a trademark is identical with, or similar to, a geographical indication.

6. Nothing in this Section shall require a Member to apply its provisions in respect of a geographical indication of any other Member with respect to goods or services for which the relevant indication is identical with the term customary in common language as the common name for such goods or services in the territory of that Member. Nothing in this Section shall require a Member to apply its provisions in respect of a geographical indication of any other Member with respect to products of the vine for which the relevant indication is identical with the customary name of a grape variety existing in the territory of that Member as of the date of entry into force of the WTO Agreement.

7. A Member may provide that any request made under this Section in connection with the use or registration of a trademark must be presented within five years after the adverse use of the protected indication has become generally known in that Member or after the date of registration of the trademark in that Member provided that the trademark has been published by that date, if such date is earlier than the date on which the adverse use became generally known in that Member, provided that the geographical indication is not used or registered in bad faith.

8. The provisions of this Section shall in no way prejudice the right of any person to use, in the course of trade, that personís name or the name of that personís predecessor in business, except where such name is used in such a manner as to mislead the public.

9. There shall be no obligation under this Agreement to protect geographical indications which are not or cease to be protected in their country of origin, or which have fallen into disuse in that country.

SECTION 4: INDUSTRIAL DESIGNS

Article 25
Requirements for Protection

1. Members shall provide for the protection of independently created industrial designs that are new or original. Members may provide that designs are not new or original if they do not significantly differ from known designs or combinations of known design features. Members may provide that such protection shall not extend to designs dictated essentially by technical or functional considerations.

2. Each Member shall ensure that requirements for securing protection for textile designs, in particular in regard to any cost, examination or publication, do not unreasonably impair the opportunity to seek and obtain such protection. Members shall be free to meet this obligation through industrial design law or through copyright law.

Article 26
Protection

1. The owner of a protected industrial design shall have the right to prevent third parties not having the ownerís consent from making, selling or importing articles bearing or

embodying a design which is a copy, or substantially a copy, of the protected design, when such acts are undertaken for commercial purposes.

2. Members may provide limited exceptions to the protection of industrial designs, provided that such exceptions do not unreasonably conflict with the normal exploitation of protected industrial designs and do not unreasonably prejudice the legitimate interests of the owner of the protected design, taking account of the legitimate interests of third parties.

3. The duration of protection available shall amount to at least 10 years.

SECTION 5:PATENTS

Article 27
Patentable Subject Matter

1. Subject to the provisions of paragraphs 2 and 3, patents shall be available for any inventions, whether products or processes, in all fields of technology, provided that they are new, involve an inventive step and are capable of industrial application.[5] Subject to paragraph 4 of Article 65, paragraph 8 of Article 70 and paragraph 3 of this Article, patents shall be available and patent rights enjoyable without discrimination as to the place of invention, the field of technology and whether products are imported or locally produced.

2. Members may exclude from patentability inventions, the prevention within their territory of the commercial exploitation of which is necessary to protect *ordre public* or morality, including to protect human, animal or plant life or health or to avoid serious prejudice to the environment, provided that such exclusion is not made merely because the exploitation is prohibited by their law.

3. Members may also exclude from patentability:

(a) diagnostic, therapeutic and surgical methods for the treatment of humans or animals;

(b) plants and animals other than micro-organisms, and essentially biological processes for the production of plants or animals other than non-biological and microbiological processes. However,Members shall provide for the protection of plant varieties either by patents or by an effective *sui generis* system or by any combination thereof. The provisions of this subparagraph shall be reviewed four years after the date of entry into force of the WTO Agreement.

Article 28
Rights Conferred

1. A patent shall confer on its owner the following exclusive rights:

(a) where the subject matter of a patent is a product, to prevent third parties not having the owneri̇s consent from the acts of: making, using, offering for sale, selling, or importing[6] for these purposes that product;

---

[5] For the purposes of this Article, the terms "inventive step" and "capable of industrial application" may be deemed by a Member to be synonymous with the terms "non-obvious" and "useful" respectively.

[6] This right, like all other rights conferred under this Agreement in respect of the use, sale, importation or other distribution of goods, is subject to the provisions of Article 6.

(b) where the subject matter of a patent is a process, to prevent third parties not having the owneris consent from the act of using the process, and from the acts of: using, offering for sale, selling, or importing for these purposes at least the product obtained directly by that process.

2. Patent owners shall also have the right to assign, or transfer by succession, the patent and to conclude licensing contracts.

Article 29
Conditions on Patent Applicants

1. Members shall require that an applicant for a patent shall disclose the invention in a manner sufficiently clear and complete for the invention to be carried out by a person skilled in the art and may require the applicant to indicate the best mode for carrying out the invention known to the inventor at the filing date or, where priority is claimed, at the priority date of the application.
2. Members may require an applicant for a patent to provide information concerning the applicantís corresponding foreign applications and grants.

Article 30
Exceptions to Rights Conferred

Members may provide limited exceptions to the exclusive rights conferred by a patent, provided that such exceptions do not unreasonably conflict with a normal exploitation of the patent and do not unreasonably prejudice the legitimate interests of the patent owner, taking account of the legitimate interests of third parties.

Article 31
Other Use Without Authorization of the Right Holder

Where the law of a Member allows for other use[7] of the subject matter of a patent without the authorization of the right holder, including use by the government or third parties authorized by the government, the following provisions shall be respected:

(a) authorization of such use shall be considered on its individual merits;
(b) such use may only be permitted if, prior to such use, the proposed user has made efforts to obtain authorization from the right holder on reasonable commercial terms and conditions and that such efforts have not been successful within a reasonable period of time. This requirement may be waived by a Member in the case of a national emergency or other circumstances of extreme urgency or in cases of public non-commercial use. In situations of national emergency or other circumstances of extreme urgency, the right holder shall, nevertheless, be notified as soon as reasonably practicable. In the case of public non-commercial use, where the government or contractor, without making a patent search, knows or has demonstrable grounds to know that a valid patent is or will be used by or for the government, the right holder shall be informed promptly;
(c) the scope and duration of such use shall be limited to the purpose for which it was authorized, and in the case of semi-conductor technology shall only be for public

---

[7] "Other use" refers to use other than that allowed under Article 30.

non-commercial use or to remedy a practice determined after judicial or administrative process to be anti-competitive;

(d) such use shall be non-exclusive;

(e) such use shall be non-assignable, except with that part of the enterprise or goodwill which enjoys such use;

(f) any such use shall be authorized predominantly for the supply of the domestic market of the Member authorizing such use;

(g) authorization for such use shall be liable, subject to adequate protection of the legitimate interests of the persons so authorized, to be terminated if and when the circumstances which led to it cease to exist and are unlikely to recur. The competent authority shall have the authority to review, upon motivated request, the continued existence of these circumstances;

(h) the right holder shall be paid adequate remuneration in the circumstances of each case, taking into account the economic value of the authorization;

(i) the legal validity of any decision relating to the authorization of such use shall be subject to judicial review or other independent review by a distinct higher authority in that Member;

(j) any decision relating to the remuneration provided in respect of such use shall be subject to judicial review or other independent review by a distinct higher authority in that Member;

(k) Members are not obliged to apply the conditions set forth in subparagraphs (b) and (f) where such use is permitted to remedy a practice determined after judicial or administrative process to be anti-competitive. The need to correct anti-competitive practices may be taken into account in determining the amount of remuneration in such cases. Competent authorities shall have the authority to refuse termination of authorization if and when the conditions which led to such authorization are likely to recur;

(l) where such use is authorized to permit the exploitation of a patent ("the second patent") which cannot be exploited without infringing another patent ("the first patent"), the following additional conditions shall apply:

   (i) the invention claimed in the second patent shall involve an important technical advance of considerable economic significance in relation to the invention claimed in the first patent;

   (ii) the owner of the first patent shall be entitled to a cross-licence on reasonable terms to use the invention claimed in the second patent; and

   (iii) the use authorized in respect of the first patent shall be non-assignable except with the assignment of the second patent.

Article 32
Revocation/Forfeiture

An opportunity for judicial review of any decision to revoke or forfeit a patent shall be available.

Article 33
Term of Protection

The term of protection available shall not end before the expiration of a period of twenty years counted from the filing date.[8]

---

[8] It is understood that those Members which do not have a system of original grant may provide that the term of protection shall be computed from the filing date in the system of original grant.

Article 34
Process Patents:Burden of Proof

1. For the purposes of civil proceedings in respect of the infringement of the rights of the owner referred to in paragraph 1(b) of Article 28, if the subject matter of a patent is a process for obtaining a product, the judicial authorities shall have the authority to order the defendant to prove that the process to obtain an identical product is different from the patented process. Therefore, Members shall provide, in at least one of the following circumstances, that any identical product when produced without the consent of the patent owner shall, in the absence of proof to the contrary, be deemed to have been obtained by the patented process:

(a) if the product obtained by the patented process is new;

(b) if there is a substantial likelihood that the identical product was made by the process and the owner of the patent has been unable through reasonable efforts to determine the process actually used.

2. Any Member shall be free to provide that the burden of proof indicated in paragraph 1 shall be on the alleged infringer only if the condition referred to in subparagraph (a) is fulfilled or only if the condition referred to in subparagraph (b) is fulfilled.

3. In the adduction of proof to the contrary, the legitimate interests of defendants in protecting their manufacturing and business secrets shall be taken into account.

SECTION 6: LAYOUT-DESIGNS (TOPOGRAPHIES) OF INTEGRATED CIRCUITS

Article 35
Relation to the IPIC Treaty

Members agree to provide protection to the layout-designs (topographies) of integrated circuits (referred to in this Agreement as "layout-designs") in accordance with Articles 2 through 7 (other than paragraph 3 of Article 6), Article 12 and paragraph 3 of Article 16 of the Treaty on Intellectual Property in Respect of Integrated Circuits and, in addition, to comply with the following provisions.

Article 36
Scope of the Protection

Subject to the provisions of paragraph 1 of Article 37, Members shall consider unlawful the following acts if performed without the authorization of the right holder:[9] importing, selling, or otherwise distributing for commercial purposes a protected layout-design, an integrated circuit in which a protected layout-design is incorporated, or an article incorporating such an integrated circuit only in so far as it continues to contain an unlawfully reproduced layout-design.

Article 37
Acts Not Requiring the Authorization of the Right Holder

1. Notwithstanding Article 36, no Member shall consider unlawful the performance of any of the acts referred to in that Article in respect of an integrated circuit incorporating an

---

[9] The term "right holder" in this Section shall be understood as having the same meaning as the term "holder of the right" in the IPIC Treaty.

unlawfully reproduced layout-design or any article incorporating such an integrated circuit where the person performing or ordering such acts did not know and had no reasonable ground to know, when acquiring the integrated circuit or article incorporating such an integrated circuit, that it incorporated an unlawfully reproduced layout-design. Members shall provide that, after the time that such person has received sufficient notice that the layout-design was unlawfully reproduced, that person may perform any of the acts with respect to the stock on hand or ordered before such time, but shall be liable to pay to the right holder a sum equivalent to a reasonable royalty such as would be payable under a freely negotiated licence in respect of such a layout-design.

2. The conditions set out in subparagraphs (a) through (k) of Article 31 shall apply *mutatis mutandis* in the event of any non-voluntary licensing of a layout-design or of its use by or for the government without the authorization of the right holder.

Article 38
Term of Protection

1. In Members requiring registration as a condition of protection, the term of protection of layout-designs shall not end before the expiration of a period of 10 years counted from the date of filing an application for registration or from the first commercial exploitation wherever in the world it occurs.

2. In Members not requiring registration as a condition for protection, layout-designs shall be protected for a term of no less than 10 years from the date of the first commercial exploitation wherever in the world it occurs.

3. Notwithstanding paragraphs 1 and 2, a Member may provide that protection shall lapse 15 years after the creation of the layout-design.

SECTION 7: PROTECTION OF UNDISCLOSED INFORMATION

Article 39

1. In the course of ensuring effective protection against unfair competition as provided in Article 10*bis* of the Paris Convention (1967), Members shall protect undisclosed information in accordance with paragraph 2 and data submitted to governments or governmental agencies in accordance with paragraph 3.

2. Natural and legal persons shall have the possibility of preventing information lawfully within their control from being disclosed to, acquired by, or used by others without their consent in a manner contrary to honest commercial practices[10] so long as such information:

(a) is secret in the sense that it is not, as a body or in the precise configuration and assembly of its components, generally known among or readily accessible to persons within the circles that normally deal with the kind of information in question;

(b) has commercial value because it is secret; and

---

[10] For the purpose of this provision, "a manner contrary to honest commercial practices" shall mean at least practices such as breach of contract, breach of confidence and inducement to breach, and includes the acquisition of undisclosed information by third parties who knew, or were grossly negligent in failing to know, that such practices were involved in the acquisition.

(c) has been subject to reasonable steps under the circumstances, by the person lawfully in control of the information, to keep it secret.

3. Members, when requiring, as a condition of approving the marketing of pharmaceutical or of agricultural chemical products which utilize new chemical entities, the submission of undisclosed test or other data, the origination of which involves a considerable effort, shall protect such data against unfair commercial use. In addition, Members shall protect such data against disclosure, except where necessary to protect the public, or unless steps are taken to ensure that the data are protected against unfair commercial use.

SECTION 8: CONTROL OF ANTI-COMPETITIVE PRACTICES IN CONTRACTUAL LICENCES

Article 40

1. Members agree that some licensing practices or conditions pertaining to intellectual property rights which restrain competition may have adverse effects on trade and may impede the transfer and dissemination of technology.
2. Nothing in this Agreement shall prevent Members from specifying in their legislation licensing practices or conditions that may in particular cases constitute an abuse of intellectual property rights having an adverse effect on competition in the relevant market. As provided above, a Member may adopt, consistently with the other provisions of this Agreement, appropriate measures to prevent or control such practices, which may include for example exclusive grantback conditions, conditions preventing challenges to validity and coercive package licensing, in the light of the relevant laws and regulations of that Member.
3. Each Member shall enter, upon request, into consultations with any other Member which has cause to believe that an intellectual property right owner that is a national or domiciliary of the Member to which the request for consultations has been addressed is undertaking practices in violation of the requesting Member's laws and regulations on the subject matter of this Section, and which wishes to secure compliance with such legislation, without prejudice to any action under the law and to the full freedom of an ultimate decision of either Member. The Member addressed shall accord full and sympathetic consideration to, and shall afford adequate opportunity for, consultations with the requesting Member, and shall cooperate through supply of publicly available non-confidential information of relevance to the matter in question and of other information available to the Member, subject to domestic law and to the conclusion of mutually satisfactory agreements concerning the safeguarding of its confidentiality by the requesting Member.
4. A Member whose nationals or domiciliaries are subject to proceedings in another Member concerning alleged violation of that other Member's laws and regulations on the subject matter of this Section shall, upon request, be granted an opportunity for consultations by the other Member under the same conditions as those foreseen in paragraph 3.

PART III: ENFORCEMENT OF INTELLECTUAL PROPERTY RIGHTS

SECTION 1: GENERAL OBLIGATIONS

Article 41

1. Members shall ensure that enforcement procedures as specified in this Part are available under their law so as to permit effective action against any act of infringement of intellectual property rights covered by this Agreement, including expeditious remedies to prevent infringements and remedies which constitute a deterrent to further infringements. These procedures shall be applied in such a manner as to avoid the creation of barriers to legitimate trade and to provide for safeguards against their abuse.

2. Procedures concerning the enforcement of intellectual property rights shall be fair and equitable. They shall not be unnecessarily complicated or costly, or entail unreasonable time-limits or unwarranted delays.

3. Decisions on the merits of a case shall preferably be in writing and reasoned. They shall be made available at least to the parties to the proceeding without undue delay. Decisions on the merits of a case shall be based only on evidence in respect of which parties were offered the opportunity to be heard.

4. Parties to a proceeding shall have an opportunity for review by a judicial authority of final administrative decisions and, subject to jurisdictional provisions in a Member's law concerning the importance of a case, of at least the legal aspects of initial judicial decisions on the merits of a case. However, there shall be no obligation to provide an opportunity for review of acquittals in criminal cases.

5. It is understood that this Part does not create any obligation to put in place a judicial system for the enforcement of intellectual property rights distinct from that for the enforcement of law in general, nor does it affect the capacity of Members to enforce their law in general. Nothing in this Part creates any obligation with respect to the distribution of resources as between enforcement of intellectual property rights and the enforcement of law in general.

SECTION 2: CIVIL AND ADMINISTRATIVE PROCEDURES AND REMEDIES

Article 42
Fair and Equitable Procedures

Members shall make available to right holders[11] civil judicial procedures concerning the enforcement of any intellectual property right covered by this Agreement. Defendants shall have the right to written notice which is timely and contains sufficient detail, including the basis of the claims. Parties shall be allowed to be represented by independent legal counsel, and procedures shall not impose overly burdensome requirements concerning mandatory personal appearances. All parties to such procedures shall be duly entitled to substantiate their claims and to present all relevant evidence. The procedure shall provide a

---

[11] For the purpose of this Part, the term "right holder" includes federations and associations having legal standing to assert such rights.

means to identify and protect confidential information, unless this would be contrary to existing constitutional requirements.

Article 43
Evidence

1. The judicial authorities shall have the authority, where a party has presented reasonably available evidence sufficient to support its claims and has specified evidence relevant to substantiation of its claims which lies in the control of the opposing party, to order that this evidence be produced by the opposing party, subject in appropriate cases to conditions which ensure the protection of confidential information.

2. In cases in which a party to a proceeding voluntarily and without good reason refuses access to, or otherwise does not provide necessary information within a reasonable period, or significantly impedes a procedure relating to an enforcement action, a Member may accord judicial authorities the authority to make preliminary and final determinations, affirmative or negative, on the basis of the information presented to them, including the complaint or the allegation presented by the party adversely affected by the denial of access to information, subject to providing the parties an opportunity to be heard on the allegations or evidence.

Article 44
Injunctions

1. The judicial authorities shall have the authority to order a party to desist from an infringement, inter alia to prevent the entry into the channels of commerce in their jurisdiction of imported goods that involve the infringement of an intellectual property right, immediately after customs clearance of such goods. Members are not obliged to accord such authority in respect of protected subject matter acquired or ordered by a person prior to knowing or having reasonable grounds to know that dealing in such subject matter would entail the infringement of an intellectual property right.

2. Notwithstanding the other provisions of this Part and provided that the provisions of Part II specifically addressing use by governments, or by third parties authorized by a government, without the authorization of the right holder are complied with, Members may limit the remedies available against such use to payment of remuneration in accordance with subparagraph (h) of Article 31. In other cases, the remedies under this Part shall apply or, where these remedies are inconsistent with a Member's law, declaratory judgments and adequate compensation shall be available.

Article 45
Damages

1. The judicial authorities shall have the authority to order the infringer to pay the right holder damages adequate to compensate for the injury the right holder has suffered because of an infringement of that person's intellectual property right by an infringer who knowingly, or with reasonable grounds to know, engaged in infringing activity.

2. The judicial authorities shall also have the authority to order the infringer to pay the right holder expenses, which may include appropriate attorney's fees. In appropriate cases, Members may authorize the judicial authorities to order recovery of profits and/or

payment of pre-established damages even where the infringer did not knowingly, or with reasonable grounds to know, engage in infringing activity.

Article 46
Other Remedies

In order to create an effective deterrent to infringement, the judicial authorities shall have the authority to order that goods that they have found to be infringing be, without compensation of any sort, disposed of outside the channels of commerce in such a manner as to avoid any harm caused to the right holder, or, unless this would be contrary to existing constitutional requirements, destroyed. The judicial authorities shall also have the authority to order that materials and implements the predominant use of which has been in the creation of the infringing goods be, without compensation of any sort, disposed of outside the channels of commerce in such a manner as to minimize the risks of further infringements. In considering such requests, the need for proportionality between the seriousness of the infringement and the remedies ordered as well as the interests of third parties shall be taken into account. In regard to counterfeit trademark goods, the simple removal of the trademark unlawfully affixed shall not be sufficient, other than in exceptional cases, to permit release of the goods into the channels of commerce.

Article 47
Right of Information

Members may provide that the judicial authorities shall have the authority, unless this would be out of proportion to the seriousness of the infringement, to order the infringer to inform the right holder of the identity of third persons involved in the production and distribution of the infringing goods or services and of their channels of distribution.

Article 48
Indemnification of the Defendant

1. The judicial authorities shall have the authority to order a party at whose request measures were taken and who has abused enforcement procedures to provide to a party wrongfully enjoined or restrained adequate compensation for the injury suffered because of such abuse. The judicial authorities shall also have the authority to order the applicant to pay the defendant expenses, which may include appropriate attorney's fees.
2. In respect of the administration of any law pertaining to the protection or enforcement of intellectual property rights, Members shall only exempt both public authorities and officials from liability to appropriate remedial measures where actions are taken or intended in good faith in the course of the administration of that law.

Article 49
Administrative Procedures

To the extent that any civil remedy can be ordered as a result of administrative procedures on the merits of a case, such procedures shall conform to principles equivalent in substance to those set forth in this Section.

SECTION 3: PROVISIONAL MEASURES

Article 50

1. The judicial authorities shall have the authority to order prompt and effective provisional measures:

(a) to prevent an infringement of any intellectual property right from occurring, and in particular to prevent the entry into the channels of commerce in their jurisdiction of goods, including imported goods immediately after customs clearance;

(b) to preserve relevant evidence in regard to the alleged infringement.

2. The judicial authorities shall have the authority to adopt provisional measures inaudita altera parte where appropriate, in particular where any delay is likely to cause irreparable harm to the right holder, or where there is a demonstrable risk of evidence being destroyed.

3. The judicial authorities shall have the authority to require the applicant to provide any reasonably available evidence in order to satisfy themselves with a sufficient degree of certainty that the applicant is the right holder and that the applicantís right is being infringed or that such infringement is imminent, and to order the applicant to provide a security or equivalent assurance sufficient to protect the defendant and to prevent abuse.

4. Where provisional measures have been adopted inaudita altera parte, the parties affected shall be given notice, without delay after the execution of the measures at the latest. A review, including a right to be heard, shall take place upon request of the defendant with a view to deciding, within a reasonable period after the notification of the measures, whether these measures shall be modified, revoked or confirmed.

5. The applicant may be required to supply other information necessary for the identification of the goods concerned by the authority that will execute the provisional measures.

6. Without prejudice to paragraph 4, provisional measures taken on the basis of paragraphs 1 and 2 shall, upon request by the defendant, be revoked or otherwise cease to have effect, if proceedings leading to a decision on the merits of the case are not initiated within a reasonable period, to be determined by the judicial authority ordering the measures where a Member's law so permits or, in the absence of such a determination, not to exceed 20 working days or 31 calendar days, whichever is the longer.

7. Where the provisional measures are revoked or where they lapse due to any act or omission by the applicant, or where it is subsequently found that there has been no infringement or threat of infringement of an intellectual property right, the judicial authorities shall have the authority to order the applicant, upon request of the defendant, to provide the defendant appropriate compensation for any injury caused by these measures.

8. To the extent that any provisional measure can be ordered as a result of administrative procedures, such procedures shall conform to principles equivalent in substance to those set forth in this Section.

SECTION 4: SPECIAL REQUIREMENTS RELATED TO BORDER MEASURES[12]

Article 51
Suspension of Release by Customs Authorities

Members shall, in conformity with the provisions set out below, adopt procedures[13] to enable a right holder, who has valid grounds for suspecting that the importation of counterfeit trademark or pirated copyright goods[14] may take place, to lodge an application in writing with competent authorities, administrative or judicial, for the suspension by the customs authorities of the release into free circulation of such goods. Members may enable such an application to be made in respect of goods which involve other infringements of intellectual property rights, provided that the requirements of this Section are met. Members may also provide for corresponding procedures concerning the suspension by the customs authorities of the release of infringing goods destined for exportation from their territories.

Article 52
Application

Any right holder initiating the procedures under Article 51 shall be required to provide adequate evidence to satisfy the competent authorities that, under the laws of the country of importation, there is *prima facie* an infringement of the right holderís intellectual property right and to supply a sufficiently detailed description of the goods to make them readily recognizable by the customs authorities. The competent authorities shall inform the applicant within a reasonable period whether they have accepted the application and, where determined by the competent authorities, the period for which the customs authorities will take action.

Article 53
Security or Equivalent Assurance

1. The competent authorities shall have the authority to require an applicant to provide a security or equivalent assurance sufficient to protect the defendant and the competent authorities and to prevent abuse. Such security or equivalent assurance shall not unreasonably deter recourse to these procedures.

---

[12] Where a Member has dismantled substantially all controls over movement of goods across its border with another Member with which it forms part of a customs union, it shall not be required to apply the provisions of this Section at that border.

[13] It is understood that there shall be no obligation to apply such procedures to imports of goods put on the market in another country by or with the consent of the right holder, or to goods in transit.

[14] For the purposes of this Agreement:

(a) "counterfeit trademark goods" shall mean any goods, including packaging, bearing without authorization a trademark which is identical to the trademark validly registered in respect of such goods, or which cannot be distinguished in its essential aspects from such a trademark, and which thereby infringes the rights of the owner of the trademark in question under the law of the country of importation;

(b) "pirated copyright goods" shall mean any goods which are copies made without the consent of the right holder or person duly authorized by the right holder in the country of production and which are made directly or indirectly from an article where the making of that copy would have constituted an infringement of a copyright or a related right under the law of the country of importation.

2. Where pursuant to an application under this Section the release of goods involving industrial designs, patents, layout-designs or undisclosed information into free circulation has been suspended by customs authorities on the basis of a decision other than by a judicial or other independent authority, and the period provided for in Article 55 has expired without the granting of provisional relief by the duly empowered authority, and provided that all other conditions for importation have been complied with, the owner, importer, or consignee of such goods shall be entitled to their release on the posting of a security in an amount sufficient to protect the right holder for any infringement. Payment of such security shall not prejudice any other remedy available to the right holder, it being understood that the security shall be released if the right holder fails to pursue the right of action within a reasonable period of time.

Article 54
Notice of Suspension

The importer and the applicant shall be promptly notified of the suspension of the release of goods according to Article 51.

Article 55
Duration of Suspension

If, within a period not exceeding 10 working days after the applicant has been served notice of the suspension, the customs authorities have not been informed that proceedings leading to a decision on the merits of the case have been initiated by a party other than the defendant, or that the duly empowered authority has taken provisional measures prolonging the suspension of the release of the goods, the goods shall be released, provided that all other conditions for importation or exportation have been complied with;in appropriate cases, this time-limit may be extended by another 10 working days. If proceedings leading to a decision on the merits of the case have been initiated, a review, including a right to be heard, shall take place upon request of the defendant with a view to deciding, within a reasonable period, whether these measures shall be modified, revoked or confirmed. Notwithstanding the above, where the suspension of the release of goods is carried out or continued in accordance with a provisional judicial measure, the provisions of paragraph 6 of Article 50 shall apply.

Article 56
*Indemnification of the Importer
and of the Owner of the Goods*

Relevant authorities shall have the authority to order the applicant to pay the importer, the consignee and the owner of the goods appropriate compensation for any injury caused to them through the wrongful detention of goods or through the detention of goods released pursuant to Article 55.

Article 57
Right of Inspection and Information

Without prejudice to the protection of confidential information, Members shall provide the competent authorities the authority to give the right holder sufficient opportunity to have any goods detained by the customs authorities inspected in order to substantiate the right holderís claims. The competent authorities shall also have authority to give the importer an equivalent opportunity to have any such goods inspected. Where a positive determination has been made on the merits of a case, Members may provide the competent authorities the authority to inform the right holder of the names and addresses of the consignor, the importer and the consignee and of the quantity of the goods in question.

Article 58
Ex officio Action

Where Members require competent authorities to act upon their own initiative and to suspend the release of goods in respect of which they have acquired *prima facie* evidence that an intellectual property right is being infringed:

(a) the competent authorities may at any time seek from the right holder any information that may assist them to exercise these powers;

(b) the importer and the right holder shall be promptly notified of the suspension. Where the importer has lodged an appeal against the suspension with the competent authorities, the suspension shall be subject to the conditions, *mutatis mutandis*, set out at Article 55;

(c) Members shall only exempt both public authorities and officials from liability to appropriate remedial measures where actions are taken or intended in good faith.

Article 59
Remedies

Without prejudice to other rights of action open to the right holder and subject to the right of the defendant to seek review by a judicial authority, competent authorities shall have the authority to order the destruction or disposal of infringing goods in accordance with the principles set out in Article 46. In regard to counterfeit trademark goods, the authorities shall not allow the re-exportation of the infringing goods in an unaltered state or subject them to a different customs procedure, other than in exceptional circumstances.

Article 60
De Minimis Imports

Members may exclude from the application of the above provisions small quantities of goods of a non-commercial nature contained in travellers' personal luggage or sent in small consignments.

SECTION 5: CRIMINAL PROCEDURES

Article 61

Members shall provide for criminal procedures and penalties to be applied at least in cases of wilful trademark counterfeiting or copyright piracy on a commercial scale. Remedies available shall include imprisonment and/or monetary fines sufficient to provide a deterrent, consistently with the level of penalties applied for crimes of a corresponding gravity. In appropriate cases, remedies available shall also include the seizure, forfeiture and destruction of the infringing goods and of any materials and implements the predominant use of which has been in the commission of the offence. Members may provide for criminal procedures and penalties to be applied in other cases of infringement of intellectual property rights, in particular where they are committed wilfully and on a commercial scale.

PART IV: ACQUISITION AND MAINTENANCE OF INTELLECTUAL PROPERTY RIGHTS AND RELATED *INTER-PARTES* PROCEDURES

Article 62

1. Members may require, as a condition of the acquisition or maintenance of the intellectual property rights provided for under Sections 2 through 6 of Part II, compliance with reasonable procedures and formalities. Such procedures and formalities shall be consistent with the provisions of this Agreement.
2. Where the acquisition of an intellectual property right is subject to the right being granted or registered, Members shall ensure that the procedures for grant or registration, subject to compliance with the substantive conditions for acquisition of the right, permit the granting or registration of the right within a reasonable period of time so as to avoid unwarranted curtailment of the period of protection.
3. Article 4 of the Paris Convention (1967) shall apply *mutatis mutandis* to service marks.
4. Procedures concerning the acquisition or maintenance of intellectual property rights and, where a Member's law provides for such procedures, administrative revocation and inter partes procedures such as opposition, revocation and cancellation, shall be governed by the general principles set out in paragraphs 2 and 3 of Article 41.
5. Final administrative decisions in any of the procedures referred to under paragraph 4 shall be subject to review by a judicial or quasi-judicial authority. However, there shall be no obligation to provide an opportunity for such review of decisions in cases of unsuccessful opposition or administrative revocation, provided that the grounds for such procedures can be the subject of invalidation procedures.

PART V: DISPUTE PREVENTION AND SETTLEMENT

Article 63
Transparency

1. Laws and regulations, and final judicial decisions and administrative rulings of general application, made effective by a Member pertaining to the subject matter of this Agreement (the availability, scope, acquisition, enforcement and prevention of the abuse of intellectual property rights) shall be published, or where such publication is not practicable made publicly available, in a national language, in such a manner as to enable governments and right holders to become acquainted with them. Agreements concerning the subject matter of this Agreement which are in force between the government or a governmental agency of a Member and the government or a governmental agency of another Member shall also be published.
2. Members shall notify the laws and regulations referred to in paragraph 1 to the Council for TRIPS in order to assist that Council in its review of the operation of this Agreement.

The Council shall attempt to minimize the burden on Members in carrying out this obligation and may decide to waive the obligation to notify such laws and regulations directly to the Council if consultations with WIPO on the establishment of a common register containing these laws and regulations are successful. The Council shall also consider in this connection any action required regarding notifications pursuant to the obligations under this Agreement stemming from the provisions of Article 6*ter* of the Paris Convention (1967).

3. Each Member shall be prepared to supply, in response to a written request from another Member, information of the sort referred to in paragraph 1. A Member, having reason to believe that a specific judicial decision or administrative ruling or bilateral agreement in the area of intellectual property rights affects its rights under this Agreement, may also request in writing to be given access to or be informed in sufficient detail of such specific judicial decisions or administrative rulings or bilateral agreements.

4. Nothing in paragraphs 1, 2 and 3 shall require Members to disclose confidential information which would impede law enforcement or otherwise be contrary to the public interest or would prejudice the legitimate commercial interests of particular enterprises, public or private.

Article 64
Dispute Settlement

1. The provisions of Articles XXII and XXIII of GATT 1994 as elaborated and applied by the Dispute Settlement Understanding shall apply to consultations and the settlement of disputes under this Agreement except as otherwise specifically provided herein.

2. Subparagraphs 1(b) and 1(c) of Article XXIII of GATT 1994 shall not apply to the settlement of disputes under this Agreement for a period of five years from the date of entry into force of the WTO Agreement.

3. During the time period referred to in paragraph 2, the Council for TRIPS shall examine the scope and modalities for complaints of the type provided for under subparagraphs 1(b) and 1(c) of Article XXIII of GATT 1994 made pursuant to this Agreement, and submit its recommendations to the Ministerial Conference for approval. Any decision of the Ministerial Conference to approve such recommendations or to extend the period in paragraph 2 shall be made only by consensus, and approved recommendations shall be effective for all Members without further formal acceptance process.

PART VI: TRANSITIONAL ARRANGEMENTS

Article 65
Transitional Arrangements

1. Subject to the provisions of paragraphs 2, 3 and 4, no Member shall be obliged to apply the provisions of this Agreement before the expiry of a general period of one year following the date of entry into force of the WTO Agreement.

2. A developing country Member is entitled to delay for a further period of four years the date of application, as defined in paragraph 1, of the provisions of this Agreement other than Articles 3, 4 and 5.

3. Any other Member which is in the process of transformation from a centrally-planned into a market, free-enterprise economy and which is undertaking structural reform of its intellectual property system and facing special problems in the preparation and implementation of intellectual property laws and regulations, may also benefit from a period of delay as foreseen in paragraph 2.

4. To the extent that a developing country Member is obliged by this Agreement to extend product patent protection to areas of technology not so protectable in its territory on the general date of application of this Agreement for that Member, as defined in paragraph 2, it may delay the application of the provisions on product patents of Section 5 of Part II to such areas of technology for an additional period of five years.

5. A Member availing itself of a transitional period under paragraphs 1, 2, 3 or 4 shall ensure that any changes in its laws, regulations and practice made during that period do not result in a lesser degree of consistency with the provisions of this Agreement.

Article 66
Least-Developed Country Members

1. In view of the special needs and requirements of least-developed country Members, their economic, financial and administrative constraints, and their need for flexibility to create a viable technological base, such Members shall not be required to apply the provisions of this Agreement, other than Articles 3, 4 and 5, for a period of 10 years from the date of application as defined under paragraph 1 of Article 65. The Council for TRIPS shall, upon duly motivated request by a least-developed country Member, accord extensions of this period.

2. Developed country Members shall provide incentives to enterprises and institutions in their territories for the purpose of promoting and encouraging technology transfer to least-developed country Members in order to enable them to create a sound and viable technological base.

Article 67
Technical Cooperation

In order to facilitate the implementation of this Agreement, developed country Members shall provide, on request and on mutually agreed terms and conditions, technical and financial cooperation in favour of developing and least-developed country Members. Such cooperation shall include assistance in the preparation of laws and regulations on the protection and enforcement of intellectual property rights as well as on the prevention of their abuse, and shall include support regarding the establishment or reinforcement of domestic offices and agencies relevant to these matters, including the training of personnel.

PART VII: INSTITUTIONAL ARRANGEMENTS; FINAL PROVISIONS

Article 68
Council for Trade-Related Aspects of Intellectual Property Rights

The Council for TRIPS shall monitor the operation of this Agreement and, in particular, Members' compliance with their obligations hereunder, and shall afford Members the opportunity of consulting on matters relating to the trade-related aspects of intellectual property rights. It shall carry out such other responsibilities as assigned to it by the Members, and it shall, in particular, provide any assistance requested by them in the context of dispute settlement procedures. In carrying out its functions, the Council for TRIPS may consult with and seek information from any source it deems appropriate. In consultation with WIPO, the Council shall seek to establish, within one year of its first meeting, appropriate arrangements for cooperation with bodies of that Organization.

Article 69
International Cooperation

Members agree to cooperate with each other with a view to eliminating international trade in goods infringing intellectual property rights. For this purpose, they shall establish and notify contact points in their administrations and be ready to exchange information on trade in infringing goods. They shall, in particular, promote the exchange of information and cooperation between customs authorities with regard to trade in counterfeit trademark goods and pirated copyright goods.

Article 70
Protection of Existing Subject Matter

1. This Agreement does not give rise to obligations in respect of acts which occurred before the date of application of the Agreement for the Member in question.

2. Except as otherwise provided for in this Agreement, this Agreement gives rise to obligations in respect of all subject matter existing at the date of application of this Agreement for the Member in question, and which is protected in that Member on the said date, or which meets or comes subsequently to meet the criteria for protection under the terms of this Agreement. In respect of this paragraph and paragraphs 3 and 4, copyright obligations with respect to existing works shall be solely determined under Article 18 of the Berne Convention (1971), and obligations with respect to the rights of producers of phonograms and performers in existing phonograms shall be determined solely under Article 18 of the Berne Convention (1971) as made applicable under paragraph 6 of Article 14 of this Agreement.

3. There shall be no obligation to restore protection to subject matter which on the date of application of this Agreement for the Member in question has fallen into the public domain.

4. In respect of any acts in respect of specific objects embodying protected subject matter which become infringing under the terms of legislation in conformity with this Agreement, and which were commenced, or in respect of which a significant investment was made, before the date of acceptance of the WTO Agreement by that Member, any Member may provide for a limitation of the remedies available to the right holder as to the continued performance of such acts after the date of application of this Agreement for that Member. In such cases the Member shall, however, at least provide for the payment of equitable remuneration.

5. A Member is not obliged to apply the provisions of Article 11 and of paragraph 4 of Article 14 with respect to originals or copies purchased prior to the date of application of this Agreement for that Member.

6. Members shall not be required to apply Article 31, or the requirement in paragraph 1 of Article 27 that patent rights shall be enjoyable without discrimination as to the field

of technology, to use without the authorization of the right holder where authorization for such use was granted by the government before the date this Agreement became known.

7. In the case of intellectual property rights for which protection is conditional upon registration, applications for protection which are pending on the date of application of this Agreement for the Member in question shall be permitted to be amended to claim any enhanced protection provided under the provisions of this Agreement. Such amendments shall not include new matter.

8. Where a Member does not make available as of the date of entry into force of the WTO Agreement patent protection for pharmaceutical and agricultural chemical products commensurate with its obligations under Article 27, that Member shall:

(a) notwithstanding the provisions of Part VI, provide as from the date of entry into force of the WTO Agreement a means by which applications for patents for such inventions can be filed;

(b) apply to these applications, as of the date of application of this Agreement, the criteria for patentability as laid down in this Agreement as if those criteria were being applied on the date of filing in that Member or, where priority is available and claimed, the priority date of the application; and

(c) provide patent protection in accordance with this Agreement as from the grant of the patent and for the remainder of the patent term, counted from the filing date in accordance with Article 33 of this Agreement, for those of these applications that meet the criteria for protection referred to in subparagraph (b).

9. Where a product is the subject of a patent application in a Member in accordance with paragraph 8(a), exclusive marketing rights shall be granted, notwithstanding the provisions of Part VI, for a period of five years after obtaining marketing approval in that Member or until a product patent is granted or rejected in that Member, whichever period is shorter, provided that, subsequent to the entry into force of the WTO Agreement, a patent application has been filed and a patent granted for that product in another Member and marketing approval obtained in such other Member.

Article 71
Review and Amendment

1. The Council for TRIPS shall review the implementation of this Agreement after the expiration of the transitional period referred to in paragraph 2 of Article 65. The Council shall, having regard to the experience gained in its implementation, review it two years after that date, and at identical intervals thereafter. The Council may also undertake reviews in the light of any relevant new developments which might warrant modification or amendment of this Agreement.

2. Amendments merely serving the purpose of adjusting to higher levels of protection of intellectual property rights achieved, and in force, in other multilateral agreements and accepted under those agreements by all Members of the WTO may be referred to the Ministerial Conference for action in accordance with paragraph 6 of Article X of the WTO Agreement on the basis of a consensus proposal from the Council for TRIPS.

Article 72
Reservations

Reservations may not be entered in respect of any of the provisions of this Agreement without the consent of the other Members.

Article 73
Security Exceptions

Nothing in this Agreement shall be construed:

(a) to require a Member to furnish any information the disclosure of which it considers contrary to its essential security interests;or

(b) to prevent a Member from taking any action which it considers necessary for the protection of its essential security interests;

    (i)   relating to fissionable materials or the materials from which they are derived;

    (ii) relating to the traffic in arms, ammunition and implements of war and to such traffic in other goods and materials as is carried on directly or indirectly for the purpose of supplying a military establishment;

    (iii) taken in time of war or other emergency in international relations; or

(c) to prevent a Member from taking any action in pursuance of its obligations under the United Nations Charter for the maintenance of international peace and security.

APPENDIX 2

Declaration on the TRIPS Agreement and Public Health

WT/MIN(01)/DEC/2

Adopted on 14 November 2001

1. We recognize the gravity of the public health problems afflicting many developing and least-developed countries, especially those resulting from HIV/AIDS, tuberculosis, malaria and other epidemics.

2. We stress the need for the WTO Agreement on Trade-Related Aspects of Intellectual Property Rights (TRIPS Agreement) to be part of the wider national and international action to address these problems.

3. We recognize that intellectual property protection is important for the development of new medicines. We also recognize the concerns about its effects on prices.

4. We agree that the TRIPS Agreement does not and should not prevent members from taking measures to protect public health. Accordingly, while reiterating our commitment to the TRIPS Agreement, we affirm that the Agreement can and should be interpreted and implemented in a manner supportive of WTO members' right to protect public health and, in particular, to promote access to medicines for all.

In this connection, we reaffirm the right of WTO members to use, to the full, the provisions in the TRIPS Agreement, which provide flexibility for this purpose.

5. Accordingly and in the light of paragraph 4 above, while maintaining our commitments in the TRIPS Agreement, we recognize that these flexibilities include:

a. In applying the customary rules of interpretation of public international law, each provision of the TRIPS Agreement shall be read in the light of the object and purpose of the Agreement as expressed, in particular, in its objectives and principles.

b. Each member has the right to grant compulsory licences and the freedom to determine the grounds upon which such licences are granted.

c. Each member has the right to determine what constitutes a national emergency or other circumstances of extreme urgency, it being understood that public health crises, including those relating to HIV/AIDS, tuberculosis, malaria and other epidemics, can represent a national emergency or other circumstances of extreme urgency.

d. The effect of the provisions in the TRIPS Agreement that are relevant to the exhaustion of intellectual property rights is to leave each member free to establish its own regime for such exhaustion without challenge, subject to the MFN and national treatment provisions of Articles 3 and 4.

6. We recognize that WTO members with insufficient or no manufacturing capacities in the pharmaceutical sector could face difficulties in making effective use of compulsory licensing under the TRIPS Agreement. We instruct the Council for TRIPS to find an expeditious solution to this problem and to report to the General Council before the end of 2002.

7. We reaffirm the commitment of developed-country members to provide incentives to their enterprises and institutions to promote and encourage technology transfer to least-developed country members pursuant to Article 66.2. We also agree that the least-developed country members will not be obliged, with respect to pharmaceutical products, to implement or apply Sections 5 and 7 of Part II of the TRIPS Agreement or to enforce rights provided for under these Sections until 1 January 2016, without prejudice to the right of least-developed country members to seek other extensions of the transition periods as provided for in Article 66.1 of the TRIPS Agreement. We instruct the Council for TRIPS to take the necessary action to give effect to this pursuant to Article 66.1 of the TRIPS Agreement.

Index